Psychological Management
of Individual Performance

WILEY HANDBOOKS IN THE PSYCHOLOGY
OF MANAGEMENT IN ORGANIZATIONS

Series Editor **Peter Herriot**

Psychological Management of Individual Performance
Edited by Sabine Sonnentag

Further titles in preparation

Psychological Management
of Individual Performance

Edited by

Sabine Sonnentag

Technical University of Braunschweig, Germany

JOHN WILEY & SONS, LTD

Other Wiley Editorial Offices

John Wiley & Sons, Inc., 605 Third Avenue,
New York, NY 10158-0012, USA

WILEY-VCH Verlag GmbH, Pappelallee 3,
D-69469 Weinheim, Germany

John Wiley & Sons Australia, Ltd., 33 Park Road, Milton,
Queensland 4064, Australia

John Wiley & Sons (Asia) Pte, Ltd., 2 Clementi Loop #02-01,
Jin Xing Distripark, Singapore 129809

John Wiley & Sons (Canada), Ltd., 22 Worcester Road,
Rexdale, Ontario M9W 1L1, Canada

British Library Cataloguing in Publication Data

A catalogue record for this book is available from the British Library

ISBN 0-471-87726-3

Typeset in 10/12pt Times from the authors' disks by TechBooks, New Delhi, India
Printed and bound in Great Britain by Antony Rowe Ltd, Chippenham, Wiltshire
This book is printed on acid-free paper responsibly manufactured from sustainable forestry,
in which at least two trees are planted for each one used for paper production.

Contents

About the Editor

Professor Dr Sabine Sonnentag, Institute of Psychology, Technical University of Braunschweig, Spielmannstrasse 19, D-38092 Braunschweig, Germany.

Sabine Sonnentag is a Professor of Work and Organizational Psychology at the Technical University of Braunschweig, Germany. She studied psychology at the Free University Berlin and received her Ph.D. from the Technical University of Braunschweig. Subsequently she worked at the University of Giessen the University of Amsterdam and the University of Konstanz.

One of her major research areas refers to expertise and excellent performance at work. In several studies in the fields of software design and engineering she examined how high and moderate performers differ with respect to problem solving and communication processes. Her other research interests include learning at work, teamwork and individual well-being, and recovery and unwinding processes. Currently, she serves as an Associate Editor of the *Journal of Occupational and Organizational Psychology*. She is a member of the Editorial Boards of *Applied Psychology: An International Review* and the *European Journal of Work and Organizational Psychology*.

About the Contributors

Prof. Dr Jen Algera, Department of Technology and Work, Faculty of Technology Management, Eindhoven University of Technology, P.O. Box 513, NL-5600 MB Eindhoven, The Netherlands.

Jen A. Algera is a part-time Professor of Personnel Management at Eindhoven University of Technology, the Netherlands. In addition, he is managing director of HRAdviesNed, a HRM consultancy group. In both jobs he focuses his research and consultancy on performance management at the individual level, the group level, as well as the organization level.

Dr Wieby Altink, SHL Nederland B.V., Arthur van Schendelstraat 612, postbus 1047, NL-3500BA Utrecht, The Netherlands.

Wieby Altink is program manager consultant at SHL Nederland BV. She is responsible for the innovation of consultancy services (assessment, development and HR advice) as well as all client projects that integrate consultancy, training, and product (instrument) activities. She studied work and Organizational psychology and worked as an assistant professor and an associate professor with the Department of Work and Organizational Psychology at the "Vrije Universiteit van Amsterdam".

In addition, she performed the job of business unit manager with the SHL organization; together with approximately 20 colleagues she supplied consultancy, training, and products to many client organizations in the Netherlands and in an international context. Her current interests are: "How can people and organisations develop themselves together in their work, tasks and goals?"

Dr James G. Clawson, Darden Graduate School of Business Administration, University of Virginia, Box 6550, Charlottesville, Virginia, VA 22906, U.S.A.

James G. Clawson is a Professor of Business Administration at the Darden Graduate School of Business Administration at the University of Virginia. He has authored *Level Three Leadership*, and co-authored '*Self Assessment and Career Development* and *An MBA's Guide to Self Assessment and Career Development*. His research interests include leadership, mentoring, and career management. He has written dozens of articles and hundreds of cases and consulted with a variety of Fortune 100 firms on these issues.

Dr Rendel D. de Jong, Utrecht University, Faculteit Sociale Wetenschappen, Heidelberglaan, 13584 CS, Utrecht, The Netherlands.

Rendel de Jong teaches Psychology of Work and Health and Personnel Psychology at Utrecht University, Department of Social and Organizational Psychology. His research interests include leadership, personality, team functioning, mental health, and performance. As a consultant, Rendel de Jong is engaged in coaching and counseling managers and management teams.

Prof. Dr Jürgen Deller, Department of Business Psychology, University of Applied Sciences, Wilschenbrucher Weg 84A, D-21335 Lueneburg, Germany.

Jürgen Deller started his career 1979 with Commerzbank AG as an apprentice, and later as investment adviser. In 1982–1983 he studied economics, history, and political science at Judson College, Elgin, Illinois, followed by studies of economics and psychology at Kiel University; he submitted his Master's thesis in Psychology on Situational Interviews in 1991, and completed his Ph.D. on Intercultural Aptitude Testing at the University of the Armed Forces Hamburg in 1998. In 1991 he joined the corporate headquarters of Daimler-Benz group, Stuttgart, as international management trainee, later HR manager, and worked with DaimlerChrysler Services (debis) AG, Berlin, from 1996 to 1999 as senior manager in the HR board member's office and as head of Corporate Leadership Development IT Services. Since 2000 he has been a Professor of Organizational Psychology in the Department of business psychology at the University of Applied Sciences in Lueneburg, and since September 2000 the department head. He has written many articles on personnel selection, management development, international HR management and business ethics.

Gesa Drewes, Dieter Strametz & Partner, Villa im Park, D-65835 Liederbach, Germany.

Gesa Drewes is a consultant and project manager with Dieter Strametz & Partner (DSP), a human resources consultancy in Frankfurt, Germany. She received a degree in Psychology from the Justus-Liebig University in Giessen, Germany. At DSP she is responsible for projects in the areas of training, organizational development, as well as personnel selection. Her work focuses on issues such as performance appraisal management, assessment centers, customer satisfaction, communication and leadership skills and behavior.

Neil E. Fassina, Joseph L. Rotman School of Management, University of Toronto, 105 St. George St.,Toronto, Ontario, Canada M5S 3E6.

Neil Fassina received his B.Sc. in Psychology from the University of Calgary. He is currently a doctoral student of organizational behavior and human resource management at the University of Toronto. A student member of the Canadian and American Psychological Associations, Society for Industrial and Organizational Psychology, Center for the Advancement of Research Methodology and Analysis, and the Academy of Management, and his primary research focus is on the application of social cognitive theory, justice theory, and goal setting to organizational issues.

Prof. Dr Clive Fletcher, Department of Psychology, Goldsmiths' College, University of London, New Cross, London SE 14 6NW, UK.

Clive Fletcher is professor of psychology at Goldsmiths' College, University of London. He is a Fellow of the British Psychological Society and a former chairman of its occupational psychology section. After completing his Ph.D., he worked for more than six years in the Behavioural Sciences Research Division of the Civil Service Department, then moved back into an academic position. He has authored well over one hundred publications and conference papers, nearly all of which have focused on assessment centers, psychometrics, the selection interview, performance appraisal, and performance management. His current research interests include candidate perspectives in assessment situations, self-assessment and self-awareness, and multi-source feedback. In his role as a consultant, he has advised many major organizations in both public and private sectors.

Prof. Dr Michael Frese, Department of Psychology, University of Giessen, Otto-Behaghel-Strasse 10 D-35394 Giessen, Germany.

Michael Frese is professor and chair of the Unit Work and Organizational Psychology at the University of Giessen. He is also adjunct professor at the University of Pennsylvania and part-time professor at the University of Amsterdam.

Michael Frese is the president elect of the International Association of Applied Psychology and is internationally well known; he was the editor of *Applied Psychology: An International Review* for six years and serves on several editorial boards. He has written and edited about 20 books and more than 200 journal and book articles. Michael Frese has lectured extensively and is also an adviser and lecturer to the management of many companies in various European countries. He has worked, and is still working, in the areas of entrepreneurship, errors and mistakes at work, motivation (particularly self-starting motivation as in the example of initiative), training, stress at work, human–computer interaction, occupational socialization, and performance.

Betti Hamilton, Management Department, School of Business Administration, University of Miami, 414D Jenkins Building, Coral Gables, FL 33124-9145, U.S.A.

Betti Hamilton is a third-year doctoral student at the University of Miami, Coral Gables, Florida. She received her masters in business administration from the Department of Management at Wright State University in 1993. Her research interests include mentorship, leadership, and team management. She is a member of the Academy of Management, Southern Management Association, and the American Psychological Association (APA) Division 14 (the Society of Industrial and Organizational Psychology). She has presented papers at the Academy of Management and Southern Management annual meetings. She has served on the New Doctoral Student Consortium Committee, the Academy Placement Committee, and is a Graduate Student Senate Representative. Ms. Hamilton has taught Organizational Behavior courses at undergraduate level. She has also served as teaching assistant for master's level courses at the University of Miami.

Prof. Dr Beryl Hesketh, Faculty of Science, The University of Sydney, Carslaw Building F07, NSW 2006, Australia.

Beryl Hesketh completed her Ph.D. at Massey University in New Zealand, and has taught I/O Psychology at several universities in New Zealand and Australia, having introduced graduate programs at the University of New South Wales and at Macquarie University. In 1995 she chaired the Inaugural Australian Industrial and Organizational Psychology Conference, and received the Elton Mayo Award in 1997 for her contributions to I/O research and training in Australia and internationally. She has published widely in the areas of career decision making, selection and training, with a current project on developing adaptive expertise in fire fighters. She is Dean of the Faculty of Science at the University of Sydney.

Dr David A. Hofmann, Department of Management, Eli Broad School of Management, Michigan State University, East Lansing, Michigan 48824-1122, U.S.A.

David A. Hofmann is an associate professor of management at Michigan State University. He received his B.A. degree from Furman University (1986) in Business Administration, his M.S. degree from the University of Central Florida (1988) in Industrial/Organizational Psychology, and his Ph.D. from the Pennsylvania State University (1992) in Industrial/Organizational Psychology. His primary research interests include how individual, group/team, leadership, and organizational factors relate to safety problems, the interpretation of accident causes, and the occurrence of accidents as well as perceptions of commitment and accountability for both safety and quality performance. Other interests include multi-level modeling, organizational surveys and assessment methodologies, and organizational change. In 1992 he was awarded the Yoder–Henemen Personnel Research Award from the Society of Human Resource Management.

Dr Karolina Ivancic, Faculty of Science, The University of Sydney, Carslaw Building F07, NSW 2006, Australia.

Karolina Ivancic completed her Ph.D. at the University of New South Wales where she investigated whether exposure to errors during training promoted the transfer of cognitive skills. She has since been involved in designing a training manual and video for the field supervisors of post-graduate students. Her most recent research project involved examining the effects of exposure to errors on driver skill and self-confidence using a driving simulator undertaken while employed by the University of Sydney as a post-doctoral research officer. Karolina Ivancic died in 2001.

Prof. Dr Susan E. Jackson, 94 Rockafeller Road, Room 216, School of Management and Labor Relations, Rutgers University, Piscataway, NJ 08854-8054, U.S.A.

Susan E. Jackson is professor of human resource management in the School of Management and Labor Relations at Rutgers University, where she serves as graduate director for the Doctoral Program in Industrial Relations and Human Resources. She received her B.A. in Psychology and Sociology from the University of Minnesota, and her M.A. and Ph.D. in Organizational Psychology from the University of California, Berkeley. Her primary area of expertise is the strategic management of human resources; special interests include managing team effectiveness, workforce diversity, and knowledge management. She has authored or co-authored over 100 articles on these and related topics. Her books include *Managing Human Resources: A Partnership Perspective* (with Randall S. Schuler), *Strategic Human Resource Management* (with Randall S. Schuler), *Creating Tomorrow's Organizations: A Handbook for Future Research in Organizational Behavior* (with Cary L. Cooper), and *Diversity in Work Teams: Research Paradigms for a Changing Workplace* (with M. N. Ruderman). An active member of the International Association of Applied Psychology, the Society for Industrial and Organizational Psychology, and the Academy of Management, she currently serves on the editorial boards of *Applied Psychology: An International Review*; *Journal of Applied Psychology; Journal of Occupational and Organizational Psychology; Organizational Dynamics;* and *Human Resource Management Journal.*

Prof. Dr Ruth Kanfer, School of Psychology, 274 5th St., MC 0170, Georgia Institute of Technology, Atlanta, GA 30332-0170, U.S.A.

Ruth Kanfer is a professor of psychology at the Georgia Institute of Technology in Atlanta, Georgia, U.S.A. She has written extensively on work motivation/self-regulatory processes in adult skill training, job search, and job performance. Dr. Kanfer has served on the editorial boards of several scientific journals, including *Journal of Applied Psychology; Applied Psychology: An International Review; Organizational Behavior and Human Decision Processes; Human Performance,* and *Basic and Applied Social Psychology.* She is a Fellow of the American Psychological

Association, the American Psychological Society, and the Society of Industrial and Organizational Psychology, and served as chair of the Organizational Behavior Division of the Academy of Management in 1999–2000.

Tracy M. Kantrowitz, School of Psychology, 274 5th St., MC 0170, Georgia Institute of Technology, Atlanta, GA 30332-0170, U.S.A.

Tracy M. Kantrowitz is a graduate student in the industrial/organizational psychology program at Georgia Institute of Technology, Atlanta, Georgia, U.S.A. Her research interests include personality and motivational influences on job search behavior and employment outcomes, and the role of general cognitive ability, personality traits, and motivational processes in work behavior and job performance.

Dr P.A.M. Kleingeld, Department of Technology and Work, Faculty of Technology Management, Eindhoven University of Technology, P.O. Box 513, NL-5600 MB Eindhoven, The Netherlands.

Ad Kleingeld has a Ph.D. in Industrial Engineering and Management Science. He currently holds a research position at the faculty of Technology Management of Eindhoven University of Technology, the Netherlands. His Ph.D. research compared participatory design and implementation of a performance measurement and feedback system to non-participatory implementation with respect to improvement of employee performance and attitudes toward the system. His current research focuses on tools for supporting problem solving and task strategy development of individuals and groups and on the design of reward systems which fit with existing task and goal interdependencies.

Prof. Dr Martin Kleinmann, University of Marburg, Department of Psychology, Work- and Organizational Psychology, Gutenbergstrasse 18, 35032 Marburg, Germany.

Martin Kleinmann studied psychology and computer science at the University of Kiel and the University of Konstanz, Germany (1981–1987), Henkel KgaA: Personnel affairs (1988–1989), a Ph.D. in Psychology from the University of Kiel (1991), and scientific assistant at the University of Kiel (1991–1997). Since 1997, he has been a full professor for industrial and organizational psychology at the University of Marburg, Germany.

Prof. Dr Gary Latham, Joseph L. Rotman School of Management, University of Toronto, 105 St. George St., Toronto, Ontario, Canada M5S 3E6.

Gary P. Latham is the Secretary of State Professor of Organizational Effectiveness in the Faculty of Management at the University of Toronto. He has been awarded Fellow status by both the American and Canadian Psychological Associations, the American Psychological Society, and the Academy of Management. In 1996, he was made a Fellow of the Royal Society of Canada. He is the past president of the Canadian Psychological Association. Dr. Latham's contributions to the field of human resources has been in the areas of performance management, selection and training and development. He is the co-developer of the Behavioral Observation Scales (with K. Wexley) and the Situational Interview (with L. M. Saari, E. D. Pursell, and M. Campion).

Prof. Dr Edwin A. Locke, Robert H. Smith School of Business, University of Maryland, 3331 Van Munching Hall, College Park, MD 20742, U.S.A.

Edwin Locke is Dean's Professor of Leadership and Motivation at the R.H. Smith School of Business at the University of Maryland, College Park. He received his Ph.D. in Industrial Psychology from Cornell University in 1964. He has published over 210 chapters and articles in professional journals. He is the author or editor of nine books, including *A Theory of Goal Setting and Task Performance* (Prentice Hall, 1990, with G. Latham), and *The Prime Movers: Traits of the Great Wealth Creators* (AMACOM, 2000). Dr. Locke has been elected a Fellow of the American Psychological Association, of the American Psychological Society, and of the Academy of Management. He received the Distinguished Scientific Contribution Award of the Society for Industrial and Organizational Psychology, and the Career Contribution Award from the Academy of Management (Human Resource Division). He is a member of the Board of Advisers of the Ayn Rand Institute.

Dr Daniela Lohaus, CMG Industrie GmbH, Kölner Straße 6, D-65760 Eschborn, Germany.

Daniela Lohaus, has been marketing manager with Hoechst AG (1988–1990), studied Psychology and Business Administration, gained on M.Sc. in Occupational Psychology from the University of Nottingham (1993) and Ph.D. in Psychology from the University of Marburg (1998), and, since 1999, is the human resources manager for personnel development and recruitment with PASS Consulting Group. She was a lecturer at the University of Marburg (1996–1999) and at the University of Applied Sciences in Frankfurt since 1999.

Dr Douglas S. Newburg, Thoracic Surgery Department, Medical School, University of Virginia, Charlottesville, Virginia, 22908–0395, U.S.A.

Doug Newburg is the associate director of education for the General Surgery Department at the University of Virginia Medical Center. He has a doctorate in sports psychology and works as a performance counselor for high-level performers. Doug Newburg's experience in Final Four level NCAA basketball and his interest in healthy life styles led him to the research presented in the chapter written for this volume. He currently works at the medical center and manages his own firm, giving seminars and workshops on the resonance principle. He has written *Resonance: Desire Over Fear* and co-authored several articles on this topic.

Dr Frederik L. Oswald, Michigan State University, 129 Psychology Research Bldg, East Lansing, MI 48824-1117, U.S.A.

Fred Oswald received his Ph.D. degree (1999) in psychology from the University of Minnesota and is currently an assistant professor in industrial/organizational psychology at Michigan State University. His general research interests and current projects are both psychological and statistical/methodological in nature: personnel selection; theory, modeling, and measurement of job performance; differential prediction and adverse impact, particularly by racial and gender subgroups; measurement and analysis of ability, personality, and vocational interests; web-based testing in employment and research settings; meta-analysis and mixed-effects models; and profile-matching and profile-clustering techniques.

Dr Sharon K. Parker, Australian Graduate School of Management, UNSW Sydney, NSW 2052, Australia.

Sharon K. Parker is a faculty member at the Australian Graduate School of Management, The University of New South Wales, in Sydney, Australia. She was previously at the Institute of Work Psychology, the University of Sheffield, U.K. Her current research interests concern how work design and related practices affect the development of flexible role orientations, proactivity, role breadth self-efficacy, and perspective-taking among employees. Other research interests include stress, safety, performance, and equal opportunities. She has published on these topics in tier one journals such as the *Journal of Applied Psychology* and *Academy of Management Journal*. She recently co-authored a book published by Sage on work design called *Job and Work Design: Organizing Work To Promote Well-being and Effectiveness*.

Narda Quigley, 218C Van Munching Hall, University of Maryland, Department of Organizational Behavior College Park, MD 20472, U.S.A.

Narda Quigley is a doctoral student in Management and Organization at the Robert H. Smith School of Business at the University of Maryland. As an undergraduate, she double-majored in Economics and International Relations at the University of Pennsylania. In her doctoral program, she is majoring in Organizational Behavior and minoring in Human Resources Management. Her research interests include organizational culture, the effects of incentives on knowledge-sharing, and the effects of personality and individual differences on workplace outcomes.

Prof. Dr Sabine Remdisch, University of Applied Sciences, Department of Business Psychology, Wilschenbrucher Weg 69, D-21335 Lueneburg, Germany.

Sabine Remdisch is professor of business psychology at the University of Applied Sciences in Lueneburg, Germany. She received her doctorate in Work and Organizational Psychology from the University of Giessen in 1998. From 1996 to 1998 she was guest researcher at the University of Amsterdam. Her research has focused on teamwork in the production area, team performance measurement, team development, and the aspect of leadership.

Her professional career began in 1994 at General Motors (Opel Germany). There she has focused on Human Resource Management and evaluation studies and worked as an organizational consultant in that field. Areas of her present work are competency management and feedback processes.

Bernd Runde, Work and Organizational Psychology, University of Osnabrück, Seminarstraße 20, D-49076 Osnabrück, Germany.

Bernd Runde works at the Department of Work and Organizational Psychology at the University of Osnabrueck and is currently completing his Ph.D. thesis on social competencies. He studied psychology in Osnabrueck and Goettingen and the main foci of his work are social competencies (diagnosis and training), change management (realization of an international project on relevant effective and ineffective features of change projects), employee surveys, and follow-up change projects.

Mariëlle L. Rutten, M.A., GITP Consultants, Berg en Dalseweg 127, NL-6522 BE Nijmegen, The Netherlands.

M.L. (Mariëlle) Rutten studied cultural and religious psychology at the University of Nijmegen in the Netherlands. After her graduation, she spent a year doing research at Eindhoven University of Technology. She is currently working as a consultant for GITP International B.V., a consultancy firm specializing in Human Resource Management.

Prof. Dr Terri A. Scandura, Management Department, School of Business Administration, University of Miami, 414D Jenkins Building, Coral Gables, FL 33124-9145, U.S.A.

Terri Scandura (Ph.D., University of Cincinnati) is a professor of management and psychology at the University of Miami, Florida. Her interests include leadership, mentorship, and research methods and she has published in the *Journal of Applied Psychology*, the *Academy of Management Journal*, the *Journal of Management*, the *Journal of Vocational Behavior*, the *Journal of International Business Studies*, and many others. She is a member of the American Psychological Association and the Academy of Management. She is a Southern Management Association fellow and Program-Chair Elect. She serves on editorial boards for the *Academy of Management Journal*, the *Journal of Management*, *Leadership Quarterly*, *Group and Organization Management* and the *Journal of Vocational Behavior*. Dr Scandura has been a visiting scholar in Japan, the United Kingdom, Australia, Hong Kong, and China. She has taught organizational behavior and leadership at undergraduate and MBA levels, and Organizational Behavior and Research Methods at doctoral level.

Ulrich S. Schoop, Department of Psychology, University of Trier, D-54286 Trier, Germany.

Ulrich S. Schoop is a student of psychology and philosophy at the University of Trier, Germany, where he received his undergraduate degree in psychology (1997). He has studied abroad in Poona, India (College for Development Studies and Activities), and particpated in student exchange with the I/O psychology program at the University of Minnesota, U.S.A. He currently works as a research assistant for Prof. Dr L. Montada and has gained extensive practical experience in consulting, personnel selection, and personnel development for managers. His actual research topics of interest include: practical intelligence of managers, diagnostics, and conflict management.

Prof. Dr Randall S. Schuler, 94 Rockafeller Road, Room 216, School of Management and Labor Relations, Rutgers University, Piscataway, NJ 088548054, U.S.A.

Randall S. Schuler is a Professor of Human Resource Strategy and Director of the Center for Global Strategic Human Resource Management in the Department of Human Resource Management. His interests are global human resource management, strategic human resource management, the human resource management function in organizations, and the interface of business strategy and human resource tasks. He has authored or edited over 40 books including *Strategic Human Resource Management: A Reader, International Human Resource Management* (3rd edn.), *Managing Human Resources: A Partnership Perspective* (7th edn.), *Cases in Managing Organizations and People* (6th edn.), *La gestion de los Recursos Humanos, Managing Human Resources* (6th edn.), *La gestion des Ressources Humaines au seuil de l'an 2000, Internationales Personalmanagement*, and *Managing Job Stress*. In addition, he has contributed over 40 chapters to reading books and has published over 100 articles in professional journals and academic proceedings. Presently, he is on the editorial boards of *Organizational Dynamics, Journal of World Business, Journal of Occupational and Organizational Psychology, Human Resource Planning, Human Resource Management, The International Journal of Human Resource Management, Asia Pacific Journal of Human Resources, Journal of Occupational Behavior, Journal of International Management*,

Journal of International Management Reviews, and *Journal of Market-Focused Management*. He is a Fellow of the American Psychological Association and the Society for Industrial/Organizational Psychology, a past editor of the *Journal of World Business* and a past co-editor of the *Journal of Operations Management*.

Dr Oliver Strohm, Institute for Work Research and Organizational Consultancy, Obere Zäune 14, CH-8001 Zurich, Switzerland.

Oliver Strohm, studied in psychology at the University of Konstanz, Germany and received his Ph.D. in Work and Organizational Psychology at the University of Berne, Switzerland (1995). He worked as a Research Assistant at the Institute of Work Psychology at the Swiss Federal Institute of Technology in Zurich, Switzerland, and was head of the department "Enterprise Strategies and Concepts" of the CIM-Center of the region of Zurich. He was the Coordinator of a Quality and Change Program at the Swiss Federal Institute of Technology in Zurich. Since 1998 Oliver Strohm has been a partner and CEO of the Institute for Work Research and Organizational Consultancy in Zurich. His current activities include research in the field of Change Management and Micro-politics in Change Processes, as well as consulting activities for diverse companies of different sizes and branches in the field of organizational and leadership development and human resource management.

Dr Paul E. Tesluk, University of Maryland, U.S.A, Robert H. Smith School of Business, Department of Management & Organization, 3346 Van Munching Hall, University of Maryland, College Park, MD 20742-1815, U.S.A.

Paul Tesluk is an Assistant Professor in Management and Organization in the Robert H. Smith School of Business at the University of Maryland. Previously, he was an Assistant Professor at Tulane University. He received his Ph.D. in Industrial/Organizational Psychology from Penn State University. His research interests include the design and implementation of high-involvement workplace systems, work team performance, and work experience and managerial development. His work has been published in such journals as *Personnel Psychology*, *Academy of Management Journal*, and *Journal of Applied Psychology*. He has received awards for his research on team effectiveness (S. Rains Wallace Dissertation Award) and work experience (William A. Owens Scholarly Achievement Award) from the Society for Industrial/Organizational Psychology.

Prof. Dr Henk Thierry, University of Tilburg, Dept. of Human Resource Science, P.O. Box 90153, 5000 LE Tilburg, The Netherlands.

Henk Thierry studied Psychology at the Free University in Amsterdam. In 1971 he was appointed as Associate Professor, since late 1975 as Full Professor in Work and Organizational Psychology at the University of Amsterdam. In 1993 he got a new chair in Human Resource Science at Tilburg University. Since 2000 he is Professor in Work and Organizational Psychology at that University. In 1972–1973 he worked at the Institute for Social Research of the University of Michigan, Ann Arbor. In 1982–1983 he was engaged as research fellow at the Netherlands Institute for Advanced Studies in Social and Behavioral Sciences (NIAS) in Wassenaar. In 1989 he taught a spring term at the Graduate School of Business Administration of the University of Washington, Seattle. He has lectured at Universities in many other countries.

His research domain covers pay and compensation at work, work time arrangements and be-havioral effects, work motivation, and strategic Human Resource Management. Recently, he co-authored (with Pieter J.D. Drenth and Charles J. De Wolff) the second edition of the *Handbook of Work and Organizational Psychology* (Psychology Press, 1998). He is engaged in cross-national research on meanings of pay, performance measurement (Pritchard), and leadership and organi-zation culture (House). He is member of various editorial boards, e.g. associate editor of *Applied Psychology: An International Review*.

Nick Turner, The Institute of Work Psychology, The University of Sheffield, Mushroom Lane, Sheffield S10 2TN, U.K.

Nick Turner is a Ph.D. student at the Institute of Work Psychology, The University of Sheffield, U.K. He studied previously at Queen's University, Canada, and WHU-Koblenz, Germany. As a member of Sharon Parker's UK research team, Nick is investigating how changes in work design affect employee safety. In addition, he is learning how to teach, and is collaborating on projects to do with 'positive' organizational psychology; the links between organizational practices, company safety performance, and financial performance; the concept of safety role breadth; and relationships between moral development, perspective-taking, and transformational leadership

Prof. Dr Jaap J. van Muijen, LTP, Jozef Israelskade 46, NL-1072 SB Amsterdam, The Netherlands.

Jaap van Muijen is senior consultant and member of the board at LTP (a middle-large consultancy firm in the Netherlands) and Lecturer at the Institute for Business Education, Castle Zeist. He is an active researcher and consultant in the fields of organizational culture, leadership, commitment and motivation, team development, group performance, and, Human Resource Management. He is a member of the international research group FOCUS. This group consists of researchers from twelve countries and the research topic concerns the influence of national context on organizational culture and management. He received his Ph.D. at the Vrije Universiteit Amsterdam in 1994. He published several articles and books about organizational culture, leadership, Human Resource Management and psychological contract.

Dr Harrie F. J.M. van Tuijl, Department of Technology and Work, Faculty of Technology Management, Eindhoven University of Technology, P.O. Box 513, NL-5600 MB Eindhoven, The Netherlands.

Harrie van Tuijl has a Ph.D. in experimental psychology from Nijmegen University, The Netherlands. He is an Associate professor in personnel management at Eindhoven University of Technology, Faculty of Technology Management, Department of Technology and Work. During the past decade he has been involved in a number of applied research projects, both in profit and in not for profit organizations, on the design and implementation of feedback and goal setting systems, based on the ProMES method. Implementing such productivity enhancement systems often requires a long term involvement of the researcher in the organization concerned, because support has to be given in, among others, the areas of training and reward systems.

His main research interests are: productivity enhancement, organizational learning, group problem solving strategies, self managing teams, self-regulation, consistency between control systems. He has published several articles and book chapters on these topics.

Helma Verhagen, Fuji Photo Film B.V., Oudenstaart 1, P.O. box 90156, NL-5000 LJ Tilburg, The Netherlands.

Helma Verhagen is senior staff officer Human Development within the department for personnel and environmental affairs at Fuji Photo Film b.v. in Tilburg (The Netherlands). In this function she is responsible for activities and policy on the area of management development and communication. Before this she was senior consultant at the management consultancy firm SHL in the Netherlands, specializing in assessment and development projects within organizations. She studied Work and Organizational Psychology at the Katholieke Universiteit Brabant (KUB) and graduated in Personnel Psychology.

Brigitte Winkler, A47 Consulting, Corporate Development and Management Diagnostic, Agnesstrasse 47, D-80798 München, Germany.

Brigitte Winkler is an international consultant for organizational development and management diagnostic in Munich, Germany. She studied psychology at the Technical University of Berlin and at the Ludwig-Maximilians-Universität in Munich and subsequently worked at HypoVereinsbank in various Human Resources Management positions in Germany and the United Kingdom. In 1998 she was promoted to Director of Human Resources Development, with responsibility for Management Diagnostic and Management Development for the bank in Germany and its branches and subsidiaries abroad. In this senior management function she was actively involved in the merger between Hypo-Bank and Vereinsbank and was responsible for designing and implementing new procedures and tools for the selection and development of managers. At the end of 1999, together with two business partners, she set up her own consultancy firm-A47 consulting, corporate development and management diagnostic in Munich.

One of her main fields of interest is the practical application of theory. She teaches students of Psychology how to apply this in a professional setting and regularly teaches industrial and organizational psychology at the Justus von Liebig University of Giessen, at the Ludwig-Maximilians-Universität in Munich and at the Technical University in Munich. She is a certified supervisor and has post-graduate qualifications in organisational development and behaviour therapy. Since 1993 she has been a member of the Academy of Management.

Series Preface

Peter Herriot
The Empower Group

The dictionary definition of 'handbook' runs as follows:

- A book of instruction or guidance, as for an occupation; a manual
- A guidebook for travellers
- A reference book in a particular field
- A scholarly book on a particular subject, often consisting of separate essays or articles.

These definitions are placed in the historical order of their appearance in the language. So the earliest use of a handbook was as a set of instructions which members of particular occupations kept at hand in order to be able to refer to them when they were uncertain of how to tackle a problem at work. The most recent definition, by way of contrast, refers to a scholarly book consisting of separate essays or articles.

It is the modest ambition of the Wiley Handbooks in the Psychology of Management in Organizations to reverse the course of (linguistic) history! We want to get back to the idea of handbooks as resources to which members of occupations can refer in order to get help in addressing the problems they face. The occupational members primarily involved here are work and organizational psychologists, human resource managers and professionals, and organizational managers in general. And the problems they face are those that force themselves with ever greater urgency upon public and private sector organizations alike: issues such as how to manage employees' performance effectively; how to facilitate learning in organizations; how to benefit from a diversity of employees; and how to manage organizational change so that staff are engaged and supported.

Now the claim to provide something useful for professionals, rather than a set of scholarly articles, is a bold one. What is required if such a claim is to be justified? First, practising professionals need a clear theoretical basis from which to analyse the issues they face, and upon which to base their solutions. Practice without underpinning theory is merely applying what has worked in some situations to other ones without knowing why, and hoping they will work there too. This is blind empiricism.

Theory without practice, on the other hand, is mere indulgence. It is indulgent because theories in applied science can never be properly tested except by application, that is, their attempted use in solving problems in the real world. A handbook in the original sense of the word will therefore contain elements of practice as well as statements of theory. The Wiley Handbooks in the Psychology of Management in Organizations seek to demonstrate by descriptions of case studies, methods of intervention, and instruments of assessment, how theory may be applied in practice to address real organizational issues.

It is clear that Work and Organizational Psychology is a core discipline for addressing such issues as those listed above, for they all depend for their solution upon an understanding of individuals' behaviour at work, and of the likely effects of various organisational interventions upon the stakeholders involved. These latter include employees, customers, shareholders, suppliers, and the wider community (2).

The success criterion for these handbooks, then, is a simple one: Will professionals find them useful in their practice? If they also help in the development of apprentice professionals-for example, by being used on training courses-then so much the better. The field of Work and Organisational Psychology is currently at risk from a failure to integrate theory and practice (3). Theory and research often seem to practitioners to address issues of interest only to academics; and practice appears to academics to lack careful empirical, let alone theoretical, underpinning. These handbooks will help to bridge this divide, and thereby justify the title of 'Handbook'.

What is clear is that if we psychologists fail to impact upon the urgent issues which currently crowd in upon organisations, then those who claim to address them better or faster will gain power and influence. This will happen even if their solutions offer little longer-term benefit to clients. The Wiley Handbooks in the Psychology of Management in Organisations provide a resource to help professionals serve their clients more effectively.

This first handbook first in the series is edited by Sabine Sonnentag, and addresses a pressing management issue. When commercial competitiveness or government funding depend upon continuous improvements in efficiency and productivity, how can Work and Organisational Psychology help manage employees' performance so as to achieve them? The international contributors tackle such knotty problems as how to maximise individuals' capabilities by designing work in appropriate ways; how best to assess and review performance; how to utilise training and mentoring to enhance performance; how to design reward systems which lead to improved performance; how to persuade everyone in an organisation that performance is a fundamentally important issue; and how to help employees to better manage their own performance. These are the key questions in the field; and academics and practitioners have collaborated to provide a contemporary, stimulating, and above all useful set of answers.

REFERENCES

1.   *The Random House Dictionary of the English Language* (2nd edn.) (1987). New York: Random House.
2.   Hodgkinson, G. P., & Herriot, P. (2002) The role of psychologists in enhancing organisational effectiveness. In I. Robertson, M. Callinan, & D. Bartram (Eds.), *The Role of Individual Performance in Organisational Effectiveness*. Chichester: Wiley.
3.   Anderson, N., Herriot, P., & Hodgkinson, G. P. (2001) The practitioner–researcher divide in Industrial, Work, and Organisational (IWO) Psychology: Where are we now, and where do we go from here? *Journal of Occupational and Organisational Psychology* (in press).

Preface

Individual performance is one of the key variables that work and organizational psychologists want to explain and predict in their research. Similarly, many intervention techniques and programs implemented within organizations aim at the improvement of individual performance. Unfortunately, topics and interventions that are relevant for individual performance are often scattered in various domains and discussed in isolation. This volume aims at an overview of issues relevant for individual performance in today's work organizations and summarizes psychological knowledge about individual performance at work. The book presents both research findings and practical applications within organizations and covers topics such as performance concepts and predictors for work performance, performance assessment methods, interventions for enhancing performance, and approaches for ensuring performance in a wider organizational context.

To compete in a global economy, organizations continue to undergo fundamental changes. We are witnessing developments toward learning organizations characterized by constant change processes and high degrees of flexibility. As illustrated by many of the chapters in this volume, these developments have implications for the management of individual performance. For example, broader role definitions emerging from these recent developments cause changes in what is meant by 'good performance'. The prediction of an individual's future performance in a job he or she has never done before becomes a major challenge. To help individuals to cope with the changing work requirements, it becomes increasingly important that organizations invest in training and comprehensive approaches to human resource management.

This volumes aims at a close link between academic research and practical implementation. Therefore, it follows a specific design: with the exception of the first chapter, which discusses performance concepts and theory, two chapters are devoted to each topic. In this 'dyadic' design, one chapter adopts the more academic perspective, while the other addresses the topic from a practitioner's point of view. More specifically, the authors of the academic chapters clarify concepts, describe models and theories; they summarize evidence from empirical research, develop and refine models on individual performance also suggest directions for future research. The authors who focus on the practitioner's perspective describe how today's organizations address the performance issue; present concepts and programs pursued in organizations, illustrate approaches in case studies, report from implementation experiences in organizations, and give guidelines on how to put specific approaches into practice. Although, the two perspectives often complement each other, the readers may occasionally detect some friction or even contradictory statements, which clearly shows that there is a need for an intensification of the debate between 'the academics' and 'the practitioners'. I hope, therefore, that this volume provides valuable input for this debate.

The volume comprises four parts. Each part addresses specific questions that academics and practitioners will face when dealing with individual performance at work.

Part I refers to such questions as "What do we mean by performance?" and "What are the factors contributing to good individual performance?". Chapters in Part I focus on performance concepts and theory, and discuss major predictors of performance, particularly person predictors and workplace predictors. The academic chapter by Sabine Sonnentag and Michael Frese offers an introduction into contemporary performance research. It presents core performance concepts, distinguishes three major research perspectives on performance (namely an individual differences perspective, a situational perspective, and a performance regulation perspective) and discusses how recent developments in organizations may affect performance concepts and performance-related research.

In their academic chapter on person predictors of performance, Ruth Kanfer and Tracy Kantrowitz provide a review on ability and non-ability predictors of performance. The authors summarize empirical evidence from research which shows that both general cognitive ability and personality variables—particularly conscientiousness and extraversion—contribute to the prediction of job performance. They evaluate progress and problems of this research area and discuss prospects for future research. Particularly, they argue that more theoretical work is highly needed in order to improve our understanding of the relationship between the examined predictor variables and job performance. Jürgen Deller, Fred Oswald, and Ulrich Schoop discuss person predictors of performance from a practitioner's perspective. They adopt a broader view and describe the selection procedure for a management development program of a large information service division. In their chapter, they illustrate the use of a personality questionnaire within a broader, multi-method selection and development procedure.

Sharon Parker and Nick Turner present an academic view on the importance of work design for individual performance. They summarize past research findings and propose a model on the linkages between work design and individual performance. They describe various mechanisms by which work design may affect performance and argue that both individual-level and organization-level factors might have a moderating effect on the work design–performance relationship. Oliver Strohm turns to the practical side of work design and describes job design principles based on the sociotechnical systems approach and action theory. He argues that the job (re-)design *process* is crucial for the success of any job design intervention. In two case studies, Oliver Strohm illustrates how to redesign jobs and how to conduct the change process.

Part II of this volume is devoted to the question: "How can we measure performance?" It presents perspectives on how to assess individual performance within a performance appraisal procedure and how to assess potential in order to predict future performance. Clive Fletcher approaches performance appraisal from an academic perspective and focuses on the role of motivation, personality, and interpersonal relationships in appraisal—issues that have been neglected in past performance appraisal research. Specifically, he examines how the appraiser, the appraisee, and their relationship impact the appraisal process interaction and ultimately the appraisal outcome. Gesa Drewes and Bernd Runde offer practical advice of how to design performance appraisal procedures within organizations. They discuss the various goals of performance appraisal systems, describe appraisal methods, and give suggestions on how to implement a performance appraisal system within an organization. They pay particular attention to 360-degree feedback and highlight specific success factors for both the 360-degree feedback approach and performance appraisal systems in general.

Besides the assessment of past and present performance, organizations are highly interested in measuring performance potential and in predicting future performance. Daniela Lohaus and Martin Kleinmann's chapter deals with the assessment of performance potential from an academic perspective, putting great emphasis on conceptual and methodological issues. Additionally, they provide an overview of potential analysis methods and particularly focus on assessment centers. Wieby Altink and Helma Verhagen approach the issues of potential assessment from a more practice-oriented perspective. They link their description of what constitutes 'potential' to a broader discussion of recent and future developments in work and organizational contexts. They present methods of how to measure potential and give an overview of approaches that aim at the development of potential. They illustrate the implementation of potential assessment and development with a case study of a large production company.

Part III centers around the crucial question. "How can we improve performance?" Contributors to this part suggest answers in five areas: goal setting and feedback interventions; training; mentoring; pay and reward systems; and a broader human research management. For many years goal-setting theory has been one of the most powerful approaches for improving performance. In their academic chapter Gary Latham, Edwin Locke, and Neil Fassina examine whether the 'High Performance Cycle' developed earlier by Locke and Latham is "standing the test of time". Their review of recent empirical research on goal setting shows substantial support for the 'High Performance Cycle'. Moreover, this chapter demonstrates how goal-setting research has made progress during the last decade. Jen Algera, Ad Kleingeld, and Harrie van Tuijl discuss how goal setting and feedback intervention can be put into practice. Basically, they argue that long-term implementation of goal setting in organizational practice creates specific difficulties that are often overlooked in goal-setting research. By referring to case experiences they develop specific guidelines on how to introduce goal setting and feedback interventions in organizations and how to make them a sustained success.

In their academic chapter on training, Beryl Hesketh and Karolina Ivancic address the question of how to design training interventions that meet organizations' need for a highly skilled, expert-like workforce. By drawing on literature from expertise research, and cognitive and organizational psychology, they describe (transfer of) training needs analysis, training design principles, training methods, and organizational issues which impact training as well as evaluation issues. Brigitte Winkler approaches the training process from a practitioner's perspective and describes the core steps within the development and implementation of training programs. She presents detailed examples from an introductory-level leadership training within a large organization and provides specific guidelines for putting training programs into practice.

Terri Scandura and Betti Hamilton, as well as Jim Clawson and Douglas Newburg, focus on mentoring and its relationship to individual performance. In their academic chapter, Terri Scandura and Betti Hamilton provide a review of the empirical literature on mentoring and describe the benefits that mentoring can have for the protegé, the mentor, and the organization. They suggest that mentoring has a positive effect on various performance indicators, including learning and innovation. Jim Clawson and Douglas Newburg continue on the practical side of mentoring, specifically describing how to design a mentoring program and commenting on some typical problems that one might confront when putting such a program into practice. They describe a specific non-traditional approach to mentoring which was successfully implemented in the surgery department of a university medical center.

In his academic chapter, Henk Thierry adresses the question whether and how pay and rewards systems enhance individual performance. He gives an extensive overview of various theoretical approaches and subsequently summarizes empirical evidence from older and more recent studies. His review of the literature shows that some—but not all—types of pay-for-performance implementations have a positive effect on individual performance. Harrie van Tuijl, Ad Kleingeld, Jen Algera, and Mariëlle Rutten present two case studies on performance improvement through pay and reward systems. Specifically, they provide a detailed description of the Productivity Measurement and Enhancement System (ProMES). On the basis of two case studies, they illustrate how this system works in organizational practice. They demonstrate how to design and implement such a system and how to overcome its potential pitfalls.

In addition to the chapters that are devoted to specific topics and approaches of performance enhancement, an academic and a practice chapter on Human Resource Management (HRM) offer a more detailed picture. More specifically these chapters point out why and how organizations should aim toward integrating the various specific performance enhancement approaches. Susan Jackson and Randall Schuler suggest 'a strategic perspective' for managing individual performance and, in their academic chapter, specify the conditions HRM systems must meet in order to ensure high individual and organizational performance. They argue that a HRM system must not only address the concerns of multiple stakeholder, but it must also (a) be linked to the organization's business strategy, (b) be designed as an integrated and coherent system, and (c) be continuously monitored, evaluated, and revised. In her practice chapter, Sabine Remdisch provides a case description of a modern HRM system and its relevance for performance. She presents a large automobile manufacturer's principles for HRM in a learning organization. She describes the role of the HRM department, discusses specific HRM products and services, and suggests some guidelines on how to overcome barriers on the way to becoming a learning organization.

Part IV broadens the view and provides answers to the question: "What contextual factors affect performance?" Specifically, contributors address issues such as individual well-being and organizational culture. In her academic chapter, Sabine Sonnentag links research on individual performance to research on work-related well-being. She discusses if and how well-being and performance are empirically related and argues, particularly, that self-regulation might account for such a relationship. She suggests some research questions to be addressed in the future. Rendel de Jong addresses the practical side of the well-being–performance interface. He presents an overview of individual-level and organization-level approaches to stress management and their impact on individual well-being and performance. In a short case description Rendel de Jong provides an example of how to implement an individually tailored stress management intervention which aims at the improvement of both well-being and performance.

The academic chapter by Paul Tesluk, David Hofmann, and Narda Quigley deals with the linkage between organizational culture and individual outcomes. The authors develop a framework in which they integrate macro-level and micro-level organizational research. They describe the mechanisms through which organizational culture is linked to individual performance and organizational effectiveness. Additionally, they describe specific patterns of cultural dimensions which are related to high performance. Jaap van Muijen approaches organizational culture from a practitioner's point of view. He describes a merger situation from his experience as a consultant and discusses how this merger affected organizational culture. He points out how an organization may work toward a change in culture and how it may improve performance through this culture change. More specifically, he explains that the choice for a specific organizational culture has implications for the approaches through which high individual performance is achieved.

Sabine Sonnentag

PART I

Performance: Concept, Theory, and Predictors

CHAPTER 1

Performance Concepts and Performance Theory

Sabine Sonnentag
Technical University of Braunschweig, Braunschweig, Germany, and
Michael Frese
University of Giessen, Giessen, Germany

SUMMARY

This chapter gives an overview of research on individual performance. Individual performance is highly important for an organization as a whole and for the individuals working in it. Performance comprises both a behavioral and an outcome aspect. It is a multi-dimensional and dynamic concept. This chapter presents three perspectives on performance: an individual differences perspective with a focus on individual characteristics as sources for variation in performance; a situational perspective with a focus on situational aspects as facilitators and impediments for performance; and a performance regulation perspective with a focus on the performance process. The chapter describes how current changes in the nature of work such as the focus on continuous learning and proactivity, increase in team work, improved technology, and trends toward globalization have an impact on the performance concept and future performance research.

Psychological Management of Individual Performance. Edited by Sabine Sonnentag.
© 2002 John Wiley & Sons, Ltd.

INTRODUCTION

Individual performance is a core concept within work and organizational psychology. During the past 10 or 15 years, researchers have made progress in clarifying and extending the performance concept (Campbell, 1990). Moreover, advances have been made in specifying major predictors and processes associated with individual performance. With the ongoing changes that we are witnessing within organizations today, the performance concepts and performance requirements are undergoing changes as well (Ilgen & Pulakos, 1999).

In this chapter, we summarize the major lines within performance-related research. With this overview we want to contribute to an integration of the scattered field of performance-related research. First, we briefly discuss the relevance of individual performance both for individuals and organizations. We provide a definition of performance and describe its multi-dimensional and dynamic nature. Subsequently, we present three different perspectives on performance: the individual differences perspective, the situational perspective, and the performance regulation perspective. Finally, we summarize current trends in the nature of work and discuss how these trends may affect the performance concept as well as broader performance research and management.

RELEVANCE OF INDIVIDUAL PERFORMANCE

Organizations need highly performing individuals in order to meet their goals, to deliver the products and services they specialized in, and finally to achieve competitive advantage. Performance is also important for the individual. Accomplishing tasks and performing at a high level can be a source of satisfaction, with feelings of mastery and pride. Low performance and not achieving the goals might be experienced as dissatisfying or even as a personal failure. Moreover, performance—if it is recognized by others within the organization—is often rewarded by financial and other benefits. Performance is a major—although not the only—prerequisite for future career development and success in the labor market. Although there might be exceptions, high performers get promoted more easily within an organization and generally have better career opportunities than low performers (VanScotter, Motowidlo, & Cross, 2000).

The high relevance of individual performance is also reflected in work and organizational psychological research. To get a clearer picture about the importance of individual performance in empirical research we conducted a literature search in the twelve of the major work and organizational psychology journals.[1] These journals cover a broad range of individual, group-level and organizational-level phenomena. Based on this literature search we located a total number of 146 meta-analyses within the past 20 years. Among these meta-analyses, about a half (54.8%) addressed individual performance as a core construct.[2] In the majority of these meta-analyses, individual performance was the dependent variable or outcome measure (72.5%). In about 6% of those meta-analyses that included individual performance measures, individual performance was the independent or predictor variable. Twenty-one per cent of the meta-analyses addressed performance appraisal and performance measurement issues.

The widespread use of individual performance measures in single studies and meta-analyses shows that individual performance is a key variable in work and organizational psychology. Interestingly, individual performance is mainly treated as a dependent variable—which makes perfect sense from a practical point of view: individual performance is something organizations want to enhance and optimize.

DEFINITION OF PERFORMANCE

Despite the great relevance of individual performance and the widespread use of job performance as an outcome measure in empirical research, relatively little effort has been spent on clarifying the performance concept. Still, in 1990, Campbell described the literature on the structure and content of performance "a virtual desert" (p. 704). However, during the past 10 to 15 years, one can witness an increasing interest in developing a definition of performance and specifying the performance concept.

Authors agree that when conceptualizing performance one has to differentiate between an action (i.e., behavioral) aspect and an outcome aspect of performance (Campbell, 1990; Campbell, McCloy, Oppler, & Sager, 1993; Kanfer, 1990; Roe, 1999). The behavioral aspect refers to what an individual does in the work situation. It encompasses behaviors such as assembling parts of a car engine, selling personal computers, teaching basic reading skills to elementary school children, or performing heart surgery. Not every behavior is subsumed under the performance concept, but only behavior which is relevant for the organizational goals: "Performance is what the organization hires one to do, and do well" (Campbell et al., 1993, p. 40). Thus, performance is not defined by the action itself but by judgemental and evaluative processes (cf. Ilgen & Schneider, 1991; Motowidlo, Borman, & Schmit, 1997). Moreover, only actions which can be scaled, i.e., measured, are considered to constitute performance (Campbell et al., 1993).

The outcome aspect refers to the consequence or result of the individual's behavior. The above described behaviors may result in outcomes such as numbers of engines assembled, sales figures, pupils' reading proficiency, or number of successful heart operations. In many situations, the behavioral and outcome aspects are related empirically, but they do not overlap completely. Outcome aspects of performance depend also on factors other than the individual's behavior. For example, imagine a teacher who delivers a perfect reading lesson (behavioral aspect of performance), but one or two of his pupils nevertheless do not improve their reading skills because of their intellectual deficits (outcome aspect of performance). Or imagine a sales employee in the telecommunication business who shows only mediocre performance in the direct interaction with potential clients (behavioral aspect of performance), but nevertheless achieves high sales figure for mobile phones (outcome aspect of performance) because of a general high demand for mobile phone equipment.

In practice, it might be difficult to describe the action aspect of performance without any reference to the outcome aspect. Because not any action but only actions relevant for organizational goals constitute performance, one needs criteria for evaluating the degree to which an individual's performance meets the organizational goals. It is difficult to imagine how to conceptualize such criteria without simultaneously considering the outcome aspect of performance at the same time. Thus, the emphasis on performance being an action does not really solve all the problems.

Moreover, despite the general agreement that the behavioral and the outcome aspect of performance have to be differentiated, authors do not completely agree about which of these two aspects should be labelled 'performance'. In the remainder of this chapter we follow the suggestion of Campbell et al. (1993) and refer to the behavioral aspect when we speak about performance.

PERFORMANCE AS A MULTI-DIMENSIONAL CONCEPT

Performance is a multi-dimensional concept. On the most basic level, Borman and Motowidlo (1993) distinguish between task and contextual performance. Task performance refers to an individual's proficiency with which he or she performs activities which contribute to the organization's 'technical core'. This contribution can be both direct (e.g., in the case of production workers), or indirect (e.g., in the case of managers or staff personnel). Contextual performance refers to activities which do not contribute to the technical core but which support the organizational, social, and psychological environment in which organizational goals are pursued. Contextual performance includes not only behaviors such as helping coworkers or being a reliable member of the organization, but also making suggestions about how to improve work procedures.

Three basic assumptions are associated with the differentiation between task and contextual performance (Borman & Motowidlo, 1997; Motowidlo & Schmit, 1999): (1) Activities relevant for task performance vary between jobs whereas contextual performance activities are relatively similar across jobs; (2) task performance is related to ability, whereas contextual performance is related to personality and motivation; (3) task performance is more prescribed and constitutes in-role behavior, whereas contextual performance is more discretionary and extra-role.

TASK PERFORMANCE

Task performance in itself is multi-dimensional. For example, among the eight performance components proposed by Campbell (1990), there are five factors which refer to task performance (cf. Campbell, Gasser, & Oswald, 1996; Motowidlo & Schmit, 1999): (1) job-specific task proficiency, (2) non-job-specific task proficiency, (3) written and oral communication proficiency, (4) supervision—in the case of a supervisory or leadership position—and partly (5) management/administration. Each of these factors comprises a number of subfactors which may vary between different jobs. For example, the management/administration factor comprises subdimensions such as (1) planning and organizing, (2) guiding, directing, and motivating subordinates and providing feedback, (3) training, coaching, and developing subordinates, (4) communicating effectively and keeping others informed (Borman & Brush, 1993).

In recent years, researchers paid attention to specific aspects of task performance. For example, innovation and customer-oriented behavior become increasingly important as organizations put greater emphasis on customer service (Anderson & King, 1993; Bowen & Waldman, 1999).

CONTEXTUAL PERFORMANCE

Researchers have developed a number of contextual performance concepts. On a very general level, one can differentiate between two types of contextual performance:

behaviors which aim primarily at the smooth functioning of the organization as it is at the present moment, and proactive behaviors which aim at changing and improving work procedures and organizational processes. The 'stabilizing' contextual performance behaviors include organizational citizenship behavior with its five components altruism, conscientiousness, civic virtue, courtesy, and sportsmanship (Organ, 1988), some aspects of organizational spontaneity (e.g., helping coworkers, protecting the organization, George & Brief, 1992) and of prosocial organizational behavior (Brief & Motowidlo, 1986). The more pro-active behaviors include personal initiative (Frese, Fay, Hilburger, Leng, & Tag, 1997; Frese, Garst, & Fay, 2000; Frese, Kring, Soose, & Zempel, 1996), voice (Van Dyne & LePine, 1998), taking charge (Morrison & Phelps, 1999). Thus, contextual performance is not a single set of uniform behaviors, but is in itself a multidimensional concept (Van Dyne & LePine, 1998).

RELATIONSHIP BETWEEN TASK AND CONTEXTUAL PERFORMANCE

Task and contextual performance can be easily distinguished at the conceptual level. There is also increasing evidence that these two concepts can also be separated empirically (e.g., Morrison & Phelps, 1999; Motowidlo & Van Scotter, 1994; Van Scotter & Motowidlo, 1996; Williams & Anderson, 1991). Additionally, task performance and contextual performance factors such as job dedication and interpersonal facilitation contribute uniquely to overall performance in managerial jobs (Conway, 1999).

Moreover, contextual performance is predicted by other individual variables than is task performance. Abilities and skills tend to predict task performance while personality and related factors tend to predict contextual performance (Borman & Motowidlo, 1997; Hattrup, O'Connell, & Wingate, 1998; Motowidlo & Van Scotter, 1994). However, specific aspects of contextual performance such as personal initiative have been shown to be predicted both by ability and motivational factors (Fay & Frese, 2001).

PERFORMANCE AS A DYNAMIC CONCEPT

Individual performance is not stable over time. Variability in an individual's performance over time reflects (1) learning processes and other long-term changes and (2) temporary changes in performance.

Individual performance changes as a result of learning. Studies showed that performance initially increases with increasing time spent in a specific job and later reaches a plateau (Avolio, Waldman, & McDaniel, 1990; McDaniel, Schmidt, & Hunter, 1988; Quiñones, Ford, & Teachout, 1995). Moreover, the processes underlying performance change over time. During early phases of skill acquisition, performance relies largely on 'controlled processing', the availability of declarative knowledge and the optimal allocation of limited attentional resources, whereas later in the skill acquisition process, performance largely relies on automatic processing, procedural knowledge, and psychomotor abilities (Ackerman, 1988; Kanfer & Ackerman, 1989).

To identify the processes underlying changes of job performance, Murphy (1989) differentiated between a transition and a maintenance stage. The transition stage occurs when individuals are new in a job and when the tasks are novel. The maintenance stage occurs when the knowledge and skills needed to perform the job are learned and when task accomplishment becomes automatic. For performing during the transition phase, cognitive ability is highly relevant. During the maintenance stage, cognitive ability becomes less important and other dispositional factors (motivation, interests, values) increase in relevance.

Performance changes over time are not invariable across individuals. There is increasing empirical evidence that individuals differ with respect to patterns of intra-individual change (Hofmann, Jacobs, & Gerras, 1992; Ployhard & Hakel, 1998; Zickar & Slaughter, 1999). These findings indicate that there is no uniform pattern of performance development over time.

Additionally, there is short-term variability in performance which is due to changes in an individual's psycho-physiological state, including processing capacity across time (Kahneman, 1973). These changes may be caused by long working hours, disturbances of the circadian rhythm, or exposure to stress and may result in fatigue or in a decrease in activity. However, these states do not necessarily result in a performance decrease. Individuals are, for example, able to compensate for fatigue, be it by switching to different strategies or by increasing effort (Hockey, 1997; Van der Linden, Sonnentag, Frese, & Van Dyck, 2001; Sperandio, 1971).

PERSPECTIVES ON PERFORMANCE

Researchers have adopted various perspectives for studying performance. On the most general level one can differentiate between three different perspectives: (1) an individual differences perspective which searches for individual characteristics (e.g., general mental ability, personality) as sources for variation in performance, (2) a situational perspective which focuses on situational aspects as facilitators and impediments for performance, and (3) a performance regulation perspective which describes the performance process. These perspectives are not mutually exclusive but approach the performance phenomenon from different angles which complement one another.

In this section, we will present these three perspectives and the core questions to be addressed by each perspective in detail. We will summarize the major theoretical approaches and findings from empirical research and will describe the practical implications associated with these perspectives. Table 1.1 presents an overview of these three perspectives.

There is a large body of research which showed that motivation is essential for performance. Motivational constructs related to performance can be partly subsumed under the individual differences perspectives (e.g., need for achievement), partly under the situational perspectives (e.g., extrinsic rewards), and partly under the performance regulation perspective (e.g., goal setting). We will refer to some of the most relevant motivational approaches within each perspective. However, a thorough review of the motivational literature is beyond the scope of this chapter. Interested readers may refer to Ambrose and Kulik (1999) and Kanfer (1992) for overviews.

INDIVIDUAL DIFFERENCES PERSPECTIVE

The individual differences perspective focuses on performance differences between individuals and seeks to identify the underlying factors. The core question to be answered by this perspective is: Which individuals perform best? The basic idea is that differences in

TABLE 1.1 Overview of perspectives on performance

	Individual differences perspective	Situational perspective	Performance regulation perspective
Core question	Which individuals perform best?	In which situations do individuals perform best?	How does the performance process look like? What is happening when someone is 'performing'?
Core assumptions and findings	Cognitive ability Motivation and Personality Professional experience	Job characteristics Role stressors Situational constraints	Action process factors Adequate hierarchical level
Practical implications for performance improvement	Training Personnel selection Exposure to specific experiences	Job design	Goal setting Feedback interventions Behavior modification Improvement of action process Training Job design

performance between individuals can be explained by individual differences in abilities, personality and/or motivation.

Campbell (1990) proposed a general model of individual differences in performance which became very influential (cf. also Campbell et al., 1993). In his model, Campbell differentiates performance components (e.g., job-specific task proficiency), determinants of job performance components and predictors of these determinants. Campbell describes the performance components as a function of three determinants (1) declarative knowledge, (2) procedural knowledge and skills, and (3) motivation. Declarative knowledge includes knowledge about facts, principles, goals, and the self. It is assumed to be a function of a person's abilities, personality, interests, education, training, experience, and aptitude-treatment interactions. Procedural knowledge and skills include cognitive and psychomotor skills, physical skill, self-management skill, and interpersonal skill. Predictors of procedural knowledge and skills are again abilities, personality, interests, education, training, experience, and aptitude-treatment interactions—and additionally practice. Motivation comprises choice to perform, level of effort, and persistence of effort. Campbell does not make specific assumptions about the predictors of motivation. He assumes that there are interactions between the three types of performance determinants, but does not specify them in detail (cf. Campbell et al., 1996). In his model, Campbell (1990) largely neglects situational variables as predictors of performance (cf. Hesketh & Neal, 1999, for a discussion of this issue). Campbell et al. (1996) summarized studies that identified job knowledge and job skills—as measured by work sample tests—as predictors of individual performance. Moreover, ability and experience were predictors of job knowledge and job skills, but had no direct effect on job performance. Campbell et al. interpret these findings as support for their model with declarative knowledge, procedural knowledge, and motivation acting as the only direct determinants of performance.

Motowidlo et al. (1997) built on the work of Campbell et al. They agree that cognitive ability variables have an effect on task knowledge, task skills, and task habits. However, personality variables are assumed to have an effect on contextual knowledge, contextual skill, contextual habits and, additionally, task habits. Task knowledge, task skills, and task habits in turn are seen as predictors of task performance; contextual knowledge, contextual skill, and contextual habits are regarded as predictors of contextual performance. This implies that task performance is predominantly a function of cognitive ability and contextual performance is predominantly a function of personality. However, according to this model cognitive ability has a minor effect on contextual performance—mediated by contextual knowledge—and personality has a minor effect on task performance—mediated by task habits. Motowidlo and Van Scotter (1994) largely supported this model.

There is a large body of research which addresses individual performance within the individual differences perspective. Empirical studies in this area are not always explicitly linked to the models proposed by Campbell (1990) or Motowidlo et al. (1997). Nevertheless, virtually all studies on individual predictors of job performance can be subsumed under the individual differences perspective. More specifically, this research addresses cognitive ability, personality, motivational factors, and experience as predictors of job performance.

Meta-analytic evidence speaks for a strong relationship between cognitive ability and job performance. Individuals with high cognitive abilities perform better than individuals with low cognitive abilities across a broad range of different jobs (Bobko, Roth, & Potosky, 1999; Hunter & Hunter, 1984; Schmidt & Hunter, 1998). Most authors assume an underlying mechanism of cognitive ability helping to acquire job knowledge and job skills which in turn have a positive impact on job performance (Schmidt, Hunter, Outerbride, & Goff, 1988; Schmidt, Hunter, & Outerbridge, 1986).

Researchers also addressed the question whether personality accounts for performance differences across individuals. Meta-analyses showed that the general relationships between personality factors and job performance are relatively small; the strongest relationships emerged for neuroticism/emotional stability and conscientiousness (Barrick & Mount, 1991; Tett, Jackson, & Rothstein, 1991). However, the relevance of specific personality factors for performance varies between different jobs (cf. Vinchur, Schippmann, Switzer, & Roth, 1998) (for a more detailed discussion on personality and job performance, cf. Kanfer & Kantrowitz in this volume).

Individual differences in motivation may be caused by differences in motivational traits and differences in motivational skills (Kanfer & Heggestad, 1997). Motivational traits are closely related to personality constructs, but they are more narrow and more relevant for motivational processes, i.e., the intensity and persistence of an action. Kanfer and Heggestad (1997) described achievement and anxiety as two basic work-relevant motivational traits. Vinchur et al.'s meta-analysis provides evidence for the need for achievement to be related to job performance (Vinchur et al., 1998). Motivational skills refer to self-regulatory strategies pursued during goal striving. In contrast to motivational traits, motivational skills are assumed to be more domain-specific and influenced by situational factors as well as learning and training experiences. Motivational skills comprise emotional control and motivation control (Kanfer & Heggestad, 1997; Kuhl, 1985).

Self-efficacy—the belief that one can execute an action well—is another construct in the motivational domain which is highly relevant for performance (Bandura, 1997; Stajkovic & Luthans, 1998). More specifically, self-efficacy has been shown to be related both to task performance, such as business success in small business owners (Baum, Locke, & Smith, in press), as well as to contextual performance, such as personal initiative

(Speier & Frese, 1997) and developing ideas and suggestions within an organizational suggestion system (Frese, Teng, & Wijnen, 1999). Additionally, self-efficacy has been of particular importance in the learning process. For example, in a careful process analysis, Mitchell, Hopper, Daniels, and George-Falvy (1994) have looked at the effects of self-efficacy on learning. In the beginning of the learning process, self-efficacy is a better predictor of performance than goals, while this relationship is reversed at a later stage.

Moreover, professional experience shows a positive, although small relationship with job performance (Quiñones et al., 1995). Additionally, there are interactions between predictors from several areas. For example, high achievement motivation was found to enhance the effects of high cognitive ability (O'Reilly & Chatman, 1994).

Some practical implications follow from this individual differences perspective. Above all, the individual differences perspective suggests a focus on personnel selection. For ensuring high individual performance, organizations need to select individuals on the basis of their abilities, experiences, and personality. The individual differences perspective also suggests that training programs should be implemented which aim at improving individual prerequisites for high performance. More specifically, training should address knowledge and skills relevant for task accomplishment. Furthermore, exposing individuals to specific experiences such as traineeships and mentoring programs are assumed to have a beneficial effect on individuals' job performance.

SITUATIONAL PERSPECTIVE

The situational perspective refers to factors in the individuals' environment which stimulate and support or hinder performance. The core question to be answered is: In which situations do individuals perform best? The situational perspective encompasses approaches which focus on workplace factors but also specific motivational approaches which follow for example from expectancy theory (Vroom, 1964) or approaches which aim at improving performance by reward systems or by establishing perceptions of equity and fairness (Adams, 1963; Greenberg, 1990). Most of the existing leadership research can be subsumed under this perspective. Because of space constraints, we will concentrate on workplace factors as major situational predictors of individual performance. Interested readers may refer to Folger and Cropanzano (1998), Lawler (2000) and Van Eerde and Thierry (1996) for specific motivational approaches, or to Yukl (1998) for research within the leadership domain.

With respect to workplace factors and their relationship to individual performance two major approaches can be differentiated: (1) those that focus on situational factors which enhance and facilitate performance and (2) those that attend to situational factors which impede performance.

A prominent approach within the first category is the job characteristics model (Hackman & Oldham, 1976). In this model, Hackman and Oldham assumed that job characteristics (i.e., skill variety, task identity, task significance, autonomy, feedback) have an effect on critical psychological states (i.e., experienced meaningfulness, experienced responsibility for work outcomes, knowledge of the results of the work activities) which in turn have an effect on personal and work outcomes, including job performance. Additionally, they expected an interaction effect with employee growth need strength. In essense, the job characteristics model is a motivational model on job performance (for an alternative interpretation, cf. Wall & Jackson, 1995). Meta-analytic findings suggest that there is a small, but positive relationship between job characteristics and job performance (Fried, 1991; Fried & Ferris, 1987). Guzzo, Jette, and Katzell (1985) also reported positive effects of work redesign interventions on performance. The cross-sectional nature of many studies does not allow for a causal interpretation. For example, it might be that individuals who show high performance get the better jobs. However, intervention studies showed that job design suggested by a job characteristics model has a positive effect on performance (Griffin, 1991; Wall & Clegg, 1981).

Sociotechnical systems theory (Trist & Bamforth, 1951) also falls in this first category of job design approaches which specify workplace factors that enhance performance. Basically, sociotechnical systems theory describes work systems as composed of social and technical subsystems and suggests that performance improvement can only follow from the joint optimization of both subsystems. In more detail, sociotechnical systems theory suggests a number of job design principles such as the compatibility between the design process and its objectives, a minimal specification of tasks, methods, and task allocations, and the control of problems and unforeseen events as near as to their origins as possible (for a fuller description cf. Cherns, 1976; Clegg, 2000).

As Parker and Turner (this volume) pointed out, sociotechnical systems theory is more concerned with group performance than with individual performance. However, one can assume that work situations designed on the basis of this approach have also positive effects on individual performance.

Approaches in the second category focus on factors that have a detrimental effect on performance. Within role theory (Kahn, Wolfe, Quinn, Snoek, & Rosenthal, 1964), role ambiguity and role conflict are conceptualized as stressors that impede performance. However, empirical support for the assumed negative effects of role ambiguity and role conflict is weak (Jackson & Schuler, 1985). In a recent meta-analysis Tubbs and Collins (2000) found a negative relationship between role ambiguity and performance in professional, technical, and managerial jobs. Additionally, they found a negative relationship between role ambiguity and self-ratings of performance. However, the 90% credibility interval of all other effect sizes included zero. Similarly, neither Jackson and Schuler (1985) nor Tubbs and Collins (2000) found a significant relationship between role conflict and job performance.

Situational constraints include stressors such as lack of necessary information, problems with machines and supplies as well as stressors within the work environment. Situational constraints are assumed to impair job performance directly. For example, when a machine breaks down one cannot continue to accomplish the task and therefore performance will suffer immediately. Moreover, situational constraints, as other stressors, can have an indirect effect on performance by requiring additional regulation capacity (Greiner & Leitner, 1989). Additional regulation capacity over and above the one needed for accomplishing the task is required for dealing with the constraints. Because human regulatory capacity is limited, less capacity is available for accomplishing the task and, as a consequence, performance decreases. However, empirical support for the assumed detrimental effect of situational constraints and other stressors on performance is mixed (Jex, 1998). Recently, Fay and Sonnentag (2002) have shown that stressors can even have a positive effect on personal initiative, i.e., one aspect of contextual performance.

These findings suggest that within a situational perspective, the performance-enhancing factors (e.g., control at work, meaningful tasks) play a more important role than stressors. Framed differently, the lack of positive features in the work situation such as control at work threatens performance more than the presence of some stressors (cf. Karasek & Theorell, 1990, for a related argument). In terms of practical implications, the situational perspective suggests that individual performance can be improved by job design interventions. For example, empirical job design studies have shown that performance increases when employees are given more control over the work process (Wall, Corbett, Martin, Clegg, & Jackson, 1990; Wall, Jackson, & Davids, 1992).

PERFORMANCE REGULATION PERSPECTIVE

The performance regulation perspective takes a different look at individual performance and is less interested in person or situational predictors of performance. Rather, this perspective focuses on the performance process itself and conceptualizes it as an action process. It addresses as its core questions: 'How does the performance process look like?' and "What is happening when someone is 'performing'?" Typical examples for the performance regulation perspective include the expert research approach within cognitive psychology (Ericsson & Lehmann, 1996) and the action theory approach of performance (Frese & Sonnentag, 2000; Frese & Zapf, 1994; Hacker, 1973; Hacker, 1998). Most of these approaches focus on regulatory forces within the individual.

Research on expertise and excellence has a long tradition within cognitive psychology (Ericsson & Smith, 1991) and is increasingly referred to within work and organizational psychology (Sonnentag, 2000). It is one of the main goals of expertise research to identify what distinguishes individuals at different performance levels (Ericsson & Smith, 1991). More specifically, expertise research focuses on process characteristics of the task accomplishment process. It aims at a description of the differences between high and moderate performers while working on a task. Crucial findings within this field are that high performers differ from moderate performers in the way they approach their tasks and how they arrive at solutions (for an overview, cf. Sonnentag, 2000). For example, during problem comprehension, high performers focus on abstract and general information, they proceed from general to specific information, and apply a 'relational strategy' in which they combine and integrate various aspects of the task and the solution process (Isenberg, 1986; Koubek & Salvendy, 1991; Shaft & Vessey, 1998). Moreover, high performers focus more on long-range goals and show more planning in complex and ill-structured tasks, but not in well-structured tasks (Leithwood & Steinbach, 1995; Sujan, Weitz, & Kumar, 1994).

The action theory approach (Frese & Zapf, 1994) describes the performance process—as any other action—from both a process and a structural point of view. The process point of view focuses on the sequential aspects of an action, while the structural point of view refers to its hierarchical organization.

From the process point of view, goal development, information search, planning, execution of the action and its monitoring, and feedback processing can be distinguished (Frese & Zapf, 1994; Hacker, 1998). Performance depends on high goals, a good mental model, detailed planning, and good feedback processes. Frese and Sonnentag (2000) derived propositions about the relationship between these various action process phases and performance. For example, with respect to information search they hypothesized that processing of action-relevant, important—but parsimonious—and realistic information is crucial for high performance. A study in the domain of software design showed that excellent and moderate performers differed with respect to problem comprehension, planning, feedback processing, and task focus (Sonnentag, 1998).

Roe (1999) suggested a very broad approach to performance regulation, in which he incorporated the action theory approach as one of five perspectives. The other four components of performance regulation are: energetic regulation, emotional regulation, vitality regulation, and self-image regulation. Roe assumes that all these five types of regulation are involved in performance regulation.

The process regulation perspective is closely linked to specific performance improvement interventions. The most prominent interventions are goal setting (Locke & Latham, 1990) and feedback interventions (Ilgen, Fisher, & Taylor, 1979). The basic idea of goal setting as a performance improvement intervention is that setting specific and difficult goals results in better performance than no or 'do-your-best' goals (Locke & Latham, 1990). Goal-setting theory assumes that goals affect performance via four mediating mechanisms: effort, persistence, direction, and task strategies. The benefits of goal setting on performance have been shown in virtually hundreds of empirical studies (Locke & Latham, 1990; Latham, Locke, & Fassina, this volume). Meta-analyses showed that goal setting belongs to one of the most powerful work-related intervention programs (e.g., Guzzo et al., 1985). The performance regulation perspective suggests that an improvement of the action process itself improves performance. For example, individual should be encouraged to set long-range goals and to engage in appropriate planning, feedback seeking, and feedback processing. This perspective assumes that training interventions can be useful in achieving such changes. Additionally, job design interventions can help to improve the action process (Wall & Jackson, 1995).

There is a long tradition within psychology which assumes that feedback has a positive effect on performance (for a critical evaluation, cf. Kluger & DeNisi, 1996). Indeed, there is broad evidence that feedback enhances performance if the feedback is task-related. Feedback which refers primarily to self-related processes, however has no or at least a detrimental effect on performance—even if it is 'positive' feedback (Kluger & DeNisi, 1996). Moreover, a combination of a goal-setting intervention with a feedback intervention results in better performance than a goal-setting intervention alone (Neubert, 1998). A specific intervention approach which draws on the benefits of goal setting and feedback is the Productivity Measurement and Enhancement System (ProMES; Pritchard, Jones, Roth, Stuebing, & Ekeberg, 1989). ProMES suggests a procedure of how organizational units can improve their productivity by identifying their products, developing indicators, establishing contingencies, and finally putting the system together as a feedback system (for details see Van Tuijl et al., this volume).

A rather different approach to performance regulation is the behavior modification perspective. Based on reinforcement theory (Luthans & Kreitner, 1975) this approach is not primarily interested in the processes within the individual which regulate performance but in regulative interventions from outside the individual, particularly positive reinforcement. Such reinforcements can comprise financial interventions, non-financial interventions such as performance feedback, social rewards such as attention and recognition, or a combination of all these types of reinforcements. Meta-analytic findings suggest that such behavior modification interventions have a positive effect on task performance, both in the manufacturing and in the service sector (Stajkovic & Luthans, 1997).

Relationships Among the Various Perspectives

The three perspectives represent different approaches to the performance phenomenon and our description stresses the differences between these perspectives. However, researchers often combine two or more approaches when explaining performance. For example, there are combinations between the individual differences and the situational perspective (e.g., Barrick & Mount, 1993; Colarelli, Dean, & Konstans, 1987). In essence, the job characteristic model assumes that a combination of situational factors (i.e., job characteristics) and individual differences factors (i.e., growth need strength) is crucial for individual performance (Hackman & Oldham, 1976). Similarly, Waldman (1994) suggested a model of performance in which he integrated the individual differences perspective with the situational perspective. He assumes that both person factors (i.e., individual difference variables) and system factors (i.e., situational variables) have an effect on job performance. In addition, he assumes that system factors moderate the effects of the person factors.

Mitchell (1997) proposed a model on job performance in which he explicitly combined the individual differences and situational perspective. He postulated that both 'individual inputs' (i.e., individual difference variables) and 'job context' (i.e., situational variables) have a direct effect on motivated behavior by providing necessary skills in the case of individual inputs, and by enabling vs. limiting behavior in the case of the job context. Motivated behavior in turn affects performance. Mitchell assumes that individual differences and job context additionally affect motivated behavior via motivational processes such as arousal, attention, direction, intensity, and persistence.

Despite these efforts, a comprehensive model which integrates all the various performance perspectives is still missing. Particularly, it is largely unclear how individual and situational variables come into play within the performance process. We suggest that it would be particularly helpful to develop a model which combines the individual differences and situational perspective with the performance regulation perspective. Such a model should specify how cognitive ability and motivational factors—probably in interaction with situational variables—translate into the performance process, i.e., how they effect the setting of goals, problem comprehension, planning and feedback processing, as well as the 'choice' of the appropriate hierarchical level of action regulation.

PERFORMANCE IN A CHANGING WORLD OF WORK

At present, organizations and work as a whole are undergoing dramatic changes (Cooper & Jackson, 1997; Howard, 1995) which have implications for conceptualizing and understanding performance (Ilgen & Pulakos, 1999). In this section we focus on five major trends: the importance of continuous learning, the relevance of proactivity, increase in teamwork, globalization, and technology. With the description of these trends we illustrate possible and necessary avenues for future research on individual performance.

Continuous Learning

Because of technological innovations and changes in organizational structures and processes, individual work requirements are quickly changing. As a consequence, continuous learning and competence development become increasingly important. Individuals need to be willing and able to engage in continuous learning processes in order to accomplish their present and future tasks successfully. This development has implications for our theorizing on performance. Campbell (1999), Hesketh and Neal (1999) and London and Mone (1999) proposed to incorporate learning into the performance concept. Similarly, Pulakos, Arad, Donovan, and Plamondon (2000) recently suggested 'adaptive performance' as a new performance concept in which 'learning' constitutes a major performance dimension.

This development is a profound departure from past conceptualizations in which learning was seen as a prerequisite for performance, i.e., learning mattered mostly with respect to future performance in which the newly acquired skills or knowledge were needed. Now, learning itself is seen as part of the performance concept, which should be measured and rewarded as a performance component (London & Smither, 1999).

One might question whether it makes sense to include learning into the core of the performance concept. For example, one might argue that what ultimately counts for an organization is the individuals' performance and not their learning—although learning might help to perform well. This line of reasoning stresses that learning is a highly relevant predictor of performance but is not performance itself.

Nevertheless, even if we do not want to go so far as to conceptualize learning as part of performance, permanently changing work requirements and associated demands for learning have an effect on our theorizing about performance. Research on skill acquisition has shown that the predictors of performance differ across the various phases of skill acquisition (Ackerman, 1988; Murphy, 1989). When learning becomes a continuous necessity, the duration and occurrence of the traditional skill acquisition versus maintenance stage changes. Then, skill acquisition is no longer a single event which is completed before the maintenance stage starts. Rather, individuals will go back and forth between the skill acquisition and the maintenance phase. This implies that ability (i.e., general mental ability) becomes increasingly important because it is needed during the skill acquisition phase (Murphy, 1989).

PROACTIVITY

In today's work environments proactivity becomes increasingly important. To perform well it is no longer sufficient to comply with prescribed job requirements but to go beyond what is formally requested (Frese, 1997; Parker, Wall, & Jackson, 1997). This development has consequences for conceptualizing performance and for specifying performance predictors. With respect to the performance concept, proactive behaviors such as personal initiative become an essential part of contextual performance (Frese et al., 1996, 1997). Moreover, personal initiative has been shown to be related to company performance, particularly in entrepreneurial businesses (Koop, De Reu, & Frese, 2000). One can assume that the relevance of personal initiative and similar behaviors (cf. Morrison & Phelps, 1999) increases further when environmental and global changes become even more dynamic.

In addition, this development implies that proactivity might become an important predictor of task performance. For example, research has shown that a proactive personality is related to job performance in real estate agents (Crant, 1995). Other variables such as role breadth self-efficacy plays a similar role (Parker, 1998).

WORKING IN TEAMS

Organizations are increasingly implementing teamwork and other group work arrangements (Ilgen, 1999; West, Borrill, & Unsworth, 1998). Therefore, one might argue that organizations become more interested in team performance than in individual performance. However, because teams are composed of individuals, team processes and team performance cannot be completely understood and improved without taking individual performance into account. From the perspective of individual performance, three interrelated aspects are important here. First, which individual difference variables predict individual performance within a teamwork setting? Second, which aspects of individual performance are relevant for team performance? Third, how does individual performance translate into team performance?

As an answer to the first question, researchers have suggested that task-related skills and knowledge are not sufficient when accomplishing tasks in a team-work setting. Additionally, interpersonal and self-management skills and knowledge are regarded to be essential for performing well in a team-work setting (Stevens & Campion, 1994). With respect to the second question, individual task performance is necessary for high team performance. Moreover, for a team to accomplish its often interrelated tasks, this will not be sufficient. One can assume that specific facets of contextual performance, particularly helping and altruistic behavior, are highly relevant here. For example, Podsakoff, Ahearne, and MacKenzie (1997) have shown that helping was positively related to both quantity and quality aspects of group performance in a production setting.

The third question of how individual performance translates into team performance refers to the discussion on multiple levels within organizational research (Kozlowski & Klein, 2000; Rousseau, 1985). The question might sound trivial and the answer straightforward when the tasks to be accomplished are additive and team performance is just the sum of team members' individual performance, e.g., when all team members assemble a product independently from one another—however, then one might question whether this group is a team at all. In many teamwork settings in which tasks are disjunctive and in which members are mutually dependent on one another, the combination of individual performances into team performance is much more complex (Sonnentag, 1999).

GLOBALIZATION

'Globalization' has become a catchword when describing today's business world. Globalization comprises two major developments: first, production and services are produced for a global market and they compete world wide; second, companies' workforces become increasingly global, i.e., 'culturally diverse'. With respect to the delivery of global products and services, the consequences of globalizations are most obvious within direct employee–customer interactions. What is regarded as good individual performance in these interactions varies largely between different cultures. When companies ignore these differences and implement globally the identical selection, training, and performance evaluation procedures, they might miss those feature and behaviors which are perceived as the most appropriate in a specific culture, i.e., those which constitute high individual performance.

Also the fact that many companies employ a globally composed workforce is linked to issues of individual performance. For example, individuals in culturally diverse teams and expatriates are faced with very specific requirements. Individual performance in these set-tings is predicted by a complex set of specific variables (Ones & Viswesvaran, 1997). This specific set of variable, however, might be less predictive for individual performance in mono-cultural settings. Moreover, performance appraisal issues differ largely across cul-tures (Cox & Tung, 1997). Thus, globally operating companies are faced with great chal-lenges when trying to implement an identical performance appraisal system world wide.

TECHNOLOGY

Technology, particularly computer and information systems, play an important role in most work processes. In many jobs, individual work behavior, thus performance, is very closely linked to the use of technology-based systems. For example, it is nearly impos-sible to imagine the work of a CNC machine operator without reference to the CNC machine. This development has implications for conceptualizing and measuring perfor-mance. As Hesketh and Neal (1999) have pointed out, the widespread use of technology in work processes threatens traditional views of performance in which performance is conceptualized as behavior which is completely under the control of the individual (Campbell, 1990). Practically, it becomes very difficult to separate the technology's and the individual's contribution to individual performance. Hesketh and Neal introduced a person by technology ($P \times T$) interaction perspective on performance and suggested that the way an individual uses the technology is an important performance component. Moreover, with the increased implementation of well-designed user interfaces of techni-cally highly sophisticated devices, the relevance of specific skills and knowledge needed in previous work systems decreases while other skills and knowledge become more important in the performance process (for a broader debate, cf. Wall & Davids, 1992).

CONCLUSION

In this chapter we described individual performance as an individual's measurable be-havior which is relevant for organizational goals. We characterized performance as multi-dimensional and dynamic in nature. We proposed three major perspectives within performance-related research, namely an individual differences perspective, a situational perspective, and a performance regulation perspective. Each of these perspectives is asso-ciated with specific performance enhancement interventions. Our review of the literature suggests that an integration of the three different perspectives on performance is needed. Particularly, linking the individual differences and the situational perspective to the per-formance relation perspective seems to be promising. Such an integration is necessary for understanding *why* specific individual characteristics and situational factors result in high individual performance.

Our analysis of meta-analyses on individual performance showed that most of the previous research conceptualized individual performance as the dependent variable. This makes perfect sense when aiming at the explaination of performance and developing practical interventions. At the same time, this finding implies that individual performance was only seldom conceptualized as the independent variable. Here, clearly more research is needed which addresses the possible consequences of high versus low individual performance.

The ongoing changes in the today's organizations have implications for our conceptualizations and research endeavors on performance. More specifically, future performance-related research must pay more attention to learning and proactivity issues. Further theory development is needed with respect to the interface between individual and team level performance. This comprises questions such as the translation of individual into team level performance and the role of team process variables in enhancing individual performance. Globalization of work processes and the increased use of complex technological systems suggest that individual performance cannot be fully understood without reference to the context in which it is accomplished.

NOTES

1. We scanned the volumes published between 1980 and 1999 of the following journals: *Academy of Management Journal*; *Academy of Management Review*; *Administrative Science Quarterly*; *Applied Psychology: An International Review*; *Human Performance*; *Journal of Applied Psychology*; *Journal of Management*; *Journal of Occupational (and Organizational) Psychology*; *Journal of Organizational Behavior*; *Journal of Vocational Behavior*; *Organizational Behavior and Human Performance/Organizational Behavior and Human Decision Processes*; *Personnel Psychology*.
2. One might argue that this figure is an overestimation of the acutal use of individual performance measures and concepts in meta-analyses because two of the journals are particularly devoted to performance issues (*Human Performance, Organizational Behavior and Human Performance/Organizational Behavior and Human Decision Processes*). However, when excluding these two journals from our analysis, the overall picture remains the same: 51.5% of all meta-analyses published in the remaining ten journals refer to individual performance as a core concept.

REFERENCES

Ackerman, P. L. (1988). Determinants of individual differences during skill acquisition: Cognitive abilities and information processing. *Journal of Experimental Psychology: General*, **117**, 288–318.

Adams, J. S. (1963). Towards an understanding of inequity. *Journal of Abnormal and Social Psychology*, **67**, 422–436.

Ambrose, M. L., & Kulik, C. T. (1999). Old friends, new faces: Motivation research in the 1990s. *Journal of Management*, **25**, 231–292.

Anderson, N., & King, N. (1993). Innovation in organizations. In C. L. Cooper & I. T. Robertson (Eds.), *International review of industrial and organizational psychology* (pp. 1–34). Chichester: Wiley.

Avolio, B. J., Waldman, D. A., & McDaniel, M. A. (1990). Age and work performance in non-managerial jobs: The effects of experience and occupational type. *Academy of Management Journal*, **33**, 407–422.

Bandura, A. (1997). *Self-efficacy: The exercise of control*: Freeman.

Barrick, M. R., & Mount, M. K. (1991). The Big Five personality dimensions and job performance: A meta-analysis. *Personnel Psychology*, **44**, 1–26.

Barrick, M. R., & Mount, M. K. (1993). Autonomy as a moderator of the relationships between the Big Five personality dimensions and job performance. *Journal of Applied Psychology*, **78**, 111–118.

Baum, J. R., Locke, E. A., & Smith, K. G. (in press). A multi-dimensional model of venture growth. *Academy of Management Journal*.

Bobko, P., Roth, P. L., & Potosky, D. (1999). Derivation and implications of a meta-analytic matrix incorporating cognitive ability, alternative predictors, and job performance. *Personnel Psychology*, **52**, 561–589.

Borman, W. C., & Brush, D. H. (1993). More progress toward a taxonomy of managerial performance requirements. *Human Performance*, **6**, 1–21.

Borman, W. C., & Motowidlo, S. J. (1993). Expanding the criterion domain to include elements of contextual performance. In N. Schmitt & W. Borman (Eds.), *Personnel selection in organizations* (pp. 71–98). New York: Jossey-Bass.

Borman, W. C., & Motowidlo, S. J. (1997). Task performance and contextual performance: The meaning for personnel selection research. *Human Performance*, **10**, 99–109.

Bowen, D. E., & Waldman, D. A. (1999). Customer-driven employee performance. In D. R. Ilgen & E. D. Pulakos (Eds.), *The changing nature of performance: Implications for staffing, motivation, and development* (pp. 154–191). San Francisco: Jossey-Bass.

Brief, A. P., & Motowidlo, S. J. (1986). Prosocial organizational behavior. *Academy of Management Review*, **11**, 710–725.

Campbell, J. P. (1990). Modeling the performance prediction problem in industrial and organizational psychology. In M. D. Dunnette & L. M. Hough (Eds.), *Handbook of industrial and organizational psychology* (Vol. 1, pp. 687–732). Palo Alto: Consulting Psychologists Press.

Campbell, J. P. (1999). The definition and measurement of performance in the new age. In D. R. Ilgen & E. D. Pulakos (Eds.), *The changing nature of performance. Implications for staffing, motivation, and development* (pp. 399–429). San Francisco: Jossey-Bass.

Campbell, J. P., Gasser, M. B., & Oswald, F. L. (1996). The substantive nature of job performance variability. In K. R. Murphy (Ed.), *Individual differences and behavior in organizations* (pp. 258–299). San Francisco: Jossey-Bass.

Campbell, J. P., McCloy, R. A., Oppler, S. H., & Sager, C. E. (1993). A theory of performance. In E. Schmitt, W. C. Borman, & Associates (Eds.), *Personnel selection in organizations* (pp. 35–70). San Francisco: Jossey-Bass.

Cherns, A. (1976). The principles of sociotechnical design. *Human Relations*, **29**, 783–792.

Clegg, C. (2000). Sociotechnical principles for system design. *Applied Ergonomics*, **31**, 463–477.

Colarelli, S. M., Dean, R. A., & Konstans, C. (1987). Comparative effects of personal and situational influences on job outcomes of new professionals. *Journal of Applied Psychology*, **72**, 558–566.

Conway, J. M. (1999). Distinguishing contextual performance from task performance for managerial jobs. *Journal of Applied Psychology*, **84**, 3–13.

Cooper, C. L., & Jackson, S. E. (Eds.) (1997). *Creating tomorrow's organizations. A handbook for future research in organizational behavior*. Chichester: Wiley.

Cox, T. J., & Tung, R. L. (1997). The multicultural organization revisited. In C. L. Cooper & S. E. Jackson (Eds.), *Creating tomorrow's organizations. A handbook for future research in organizational behavior* (pp. 7–28). Chichester: Wiley.

Crant, J. M. (1995). The Proactive Personality Scale and objective job performance among real estate agents. *Journal of Applied Psychology*, **80**, 532–537.

Ericsson, K. A., & Lehmann, A. C. (1996). Expert and exceptional performance: Evidence of maximal adaptation to task constraints. *Annual Review of Psychology*, **47**, 273–305.

Ericsson, K. A., & Smith, J. (1991). Prospects and limits of the empirical study of expertise: An introduction. In K. A. Ericsson & J. Smith (Eds.), *Toward a general theory of expertise: Prospects and limits* (pp. 1–38). Cambridge: Cambridge University Press.

Fay, D., & Frese, M. (2001). The concepts of personal initiative (PI): An overview of validity studies. *Human Performance*, **14**, 97–124.

Fay, D., & Sonnentag, S. (2002). Rethinking the effects of stressors: A longitudinal study on personal initiative. *Journal of Occupational Health Psychology*, 7.

Folger, R., & Cropanzano, R. (1998). *Organizational justice and human resource management*. Thousand Oaks: Sage.

Frese, M. (1997). Dynamic self-reliance: An important concept for work in the twenty-first century. In C. L. Cooper & S. E. Jackson (Eds.), *Creating tomorrow's organizations: A handbook for future research in organizational behavior* (pp. 399–416). Chichester: Wiley.

Frese, M., Fay, D., Hilburger, T., Leng, K., & Tag, A. (1997). The concept of personal initiative: Operationalization, reliability and validity in two German samples. *Journal of Occupational and Organizational Psychology*, **70**, 139–161.

Frese, M., Garst, H., & Fay, D. (2000). Control and complexity in work and the development of personal initiative (PI): A four-wave longitudinal structural equation model of occupational socialization. *University of Giessen: Manuscript submitted for publication.*

Frese, M., Kring, W., Soose, A., & Zempel, J. (1996). Personal initiative at work: Differences between East and West Germany. *Academy of Management Journal,* **39**, 37–63.

Frese, M., & Sonnentag, S. (2000). High performance: An action theory approach. *Working paper. University of Giessen and University of Konstanz.*

Frese, M., Teng, E., & Wijnen, C. J. D. (1999). Helping to improve suggestion systems: Predictors of making suggestions in companies. *Journal of Organizational Behavior,* **20**, 1139–1155.

Frese, M., & Zapf, D. (1994). Action as the core of work psychology: A german approach. In H. C. Triandis, M. D. Dunnette, & L. M. Hough (Eds.), *Handbook of industrial and organizational psychology* (2nd edn., Vol. 4, pp. 271–340). Palo Alto, CA: Consulting Psychologists Press.

Fried, Y. (1991). Meta-analytic comparison of the Job Diagnostic Survey and Job Characteristics inventory as correlates of work satisfaction and performance. *Journal of Applied Psychology,* **76**, 690–697.

Fried, Y., & Ferris, G. R. (1987). The validity of the job characteristics model: A review and meta-analysis. *Personnel Psychology,* **40**, 287–322.

George, J. M., & Brief, A. P. (1992). Feeling good–doing good: A conceptual analysis of the mood at work–organizational spontaneity relationship. *Psychological Bulletin,* **112**, 310–329.

Greenberg, J. (1990). Organizational justice: Yesterday, today, and tomorrow. *Journal of Management,* **16**, 399–432.

Greiner, B. A., & Leitner, K. (1989). Assessment of job stress: The RHIA-instrument. In K. Landau & W. Rohmert (Eds.), *Recent developments in work analysis* (pp. 53–66). London: Taylor & Francis.

Griffin, R. W. (1991). Effects of work redesign on employee perceptions, attitudes and behaviors: A long-term investigation. *Academy of Management Journal,* **34**, 425–435.

Guzzo, R. A., Jette, R. D., & Katzell, R. A. (1985). The effects of psychologically based intervention programs on worker productivity: A meta-analysis. *Personnel Psychology,* **38**, 275–291.

Hacker, W. (1973). *Allgemeine Arbeits- und Ingenieurpsychologie: Psychische Struktur und Regulation von Arbeitstätigkeiten.* Berlin: VEB Deutscher Verlag der Wissenschaften.

Hacker, W. (1998). *Allgemeine Arbeitspsychologie: Psychische Regulation von Arbeitstätigkeiten.* Bern: Huber.

Hackman, J. R., & Oldham, G. R. (1976). Motivation through the design of work: Test of a theory. *Organizational Behavior and Human Performance,* **16**, 250–279.

Hattrup, K., O'Connell, M. S., & Wingate, P. H. (1998). Prediction of multidimensional criteria: Distinguishing task and contextual performance. *Human Performance,* **11**, 305–319.

Hesketh, B., & Neal, A. (1999). Technology and performance. In D. R. Ilgen & E. D. Pulakos (Eds.), *The changing nature of performance. Implications for staffing, motivation, and development* (pp. 21–55). San Francisco, CA: Jossey-Bass.

Hockey, G. R. J. (1997). Compensatory control in the regulation of human performance under stress and high workload: A cognitive-energetical framework. *Biological Psychology,* **45**, 73–93.

Hofmann, D. A., Jacobs, R., & Gerras, S. J. (1992). Mapping individual performance over time. *Journal of Applied Psychology,* **77**, 185–195.

Howard, A. (Ed.) (1995). *The changing nature of work.* San Francisco, CA: Jossey-Bass.

Hunter, J. E., & Hunter, R. F. (1984). Validity and utility of alternative predictors of job performance. *Psychological Bulletin,* **96**, 72–98.

Ilgen, D. R. (1999). Teams embedded in organizations: Some implications. *American Psychologist,* **54**, 129–139.

Ilgen, D. R., Fisher, C. D., & Taylor, M. S. (1979). Consequences of individual feedback on behavior in organizations. *Journal of Applied Psychology,* **64**, 349–371.

Ilgen, D. R., & Pulakos, E. D. (Eds.) (1999). *The changing nature of performance: Implications for staffing, motivation, and development.* San Francisco: Jossey-Bass.

Ilgen, D. R., & Schneider, J. (1991). Performance measurement: A multi-discipline view. In C. L. Cooper & I. T. Robertson (Eds.), *International review of industrial and organizational psychology* (Vol. 6, pp. 71–108). Chichester: Wiley.

Isenberg, D. J. (1986). Thinking and managing: A verbal protocol analysis of managerial problem solving. *Academy of Management Journal*, **29**, 775–788.

Jackson, S. E., & Schuler, R. S. (1985). A meta-analysis and conceptual critique of research on role ambiguity and role conflict in work settings. *Organizational Behavior and Human Performance*, **33**, 1–21.

Jex, S. M. (1998). *Stress and job performance: Theory, research, and implications for managerial practice*. Thousand Oaks, CA: Sage.

Kahn, R. L., Wolfe, D. M., Quinn, R. P., Snoek, J. D., & Rosenthal, R. A. (1964). *Organizational stress: Studies in role conflict and ambiguity*. New York: Wiley.

Kahneman, D. (1973). *Attention and effort*. Englewood Cliffs, NJ: Prentice-Hall.

Kanfer, R. (1990). Motivation theory and industrial and organizational psychology. In M. D. Dunnette & L. M. Hough (Eds.), *Handbook of industrial and organizational psychology* (2nd edn., Vol. 1, pp. 75–170). Palo Alto, CA: Consulting Psychologists Press.

Kanfer, R. (1992). Work motivation: New directions in theory and research. In C. L. Cooper & I. T. Robertson (Eds.), *International review of industrial and organizational psychology* (Vol. 7, pp. 1–53). Chichester: Wiley.

Kanfer, R., & Ackerman, P. L. (1989). Motivation and cognitive abilities: An integrative/aptitude-treatment interaction approach to skill acquisition. *Journal of Applied Psychology*, **74**, 657–690.

Kanfer, R., & Heggestad, E. D. (1997). Motivational traits and skills: A person-centred approach to work motivation. In L. L. Cummings & B. M. Staw (Eds.), *Research in organizational behavior* (Vol. 19, pp. 1–56). Greenwich, CT: JAI Press.

Karasek, R., & Theorell, T. (1990). *Healthy work: Stress, productivity and the reconstruction of working life*. New York: Basic Books.

Kluger, A. N., & DeNisi, A. S. (1996). The effects of feedback interventions on performance: A historical review, a meta-analysis, and a preliminary feedback intervention theory. *Psychological Bulletin*, **119**, 254–284.

Koop, S., De Reu, T., & Frese, M. (2000). Sociodemographic factors, entrepreneural orientation, personal initiative, and environmental problems in Uganda. In M. Frese (Ed.), *Success and failure of microbusiness owners in Africa: A psychological approach* (pp. 55–76). Westport, CT: Quorum.

Koubek, R. J., & Salvendy, G. (1991). Cognitive performance of super-experts on computer program modification tasks. *Ergonomics*, **34**, 1095–1112.

Kozlowski, S. W. J., & Klein, K. J. (2000). A multilevel approach to theory and research in organizations. Contextual, temporal, and emergent processes. In K. J. Klein & S. W. J. Kozlowski (Eds.), *Multilevel theory, research, and methods in organizations. Foundations, extensions, and new directions* (pp. 3–90). San Francisco: Jossey-Bass.

Kuhl, J. (1985). Volitional mediators of cognition-behavior consistency: Self-regulatory processes and action vs. state orientation. In J. Kuhl & J. Beckmann (Eds.), *Action control: From cognition to behavior* (pp. 101–128). New York: Springer.

Lawler, E. E. I. (2000). *Rewarding excellence: Pay strategies for the new economy*. San Francisco, CA: Jossey-Bass.

Leithwood, K., & Steinbach, R. (1995). *Expert problem solving: Evidence from school and district leaders*. Albany, NY: State University of New York Press.

Locke, E. A., & Latham, G. O. (1990). *A theory of goal setting and task performance*. Englewood Cliffs, NJ: Prentice Hall.

London, M., & Mone, E. M. (1999). Continuous learning. In D. R. Ilgen & E. D. Pulakos (Eds.), *The changing nature of performance. Implications for staffing, motivation, and development* (pp. 119–153). San Francisco, CA: Jossey-Bass.

London, M., & Smither, J. W. (1999). Career-related continuous learning. In G. R. Ferris (Ed.), *Research in personnel and human resources management* (pp. 81–121). Stamford, CT: JAI Press.

Luthans, F., & Kreitner, R. (1975). *Organizational behavior modification*. Glenview, IL: Scott.

McDaniel, M. A., Schmidt, F. L., & Hunter, J. E. (1988). Job experience correlates of job performance. *Journal of Applied Psychology*, **73**, 327–330.

Mitchell, T. R. (1997). Matching motivational strategies with organizational contexts. In L. L. Cummings & B. M. Staw (Eds.), *Research in organizational behavior* (Vol. 19, pp. 57–149). Greenwich, CT: JAI.

Mitchell, T. R., Hopper, H., Daniels, D., & George-Falvy, J. (1994). Predicting self-efficacy and performance during skill acquisition. *Journal of Applied Psychology*, **79**, 506–517.

Morrison, E. W., & Phelps, C. C. (1999). Taking charge at work: Extrarole efforts to initiate workplace change. *Academy of Management Journal*, **42**, 403–419.

Motowidlo, S. J., Borman, W. C., & Schmit, M. J. (1997). A theory of individual differences in task and contextual performance. *Human Performance*, **10**, 71–83.

Motowidlo, S. J., & Schmit, M. J. (1999). Performance assessment in unique jobs. In D. R. Ilgen & E. D. Pulakos (Eds.), *The changing nature of job performance: Implications for staffing, motivation, and development* (pp. 56–86). San Francisco, CA: Jossey-Bass.

Motowidlo, S. J., & Van Scotter, J. R. (1994). Evidence that task performance should be distinguished from contextual performance. *Journal of Applied Psychology*, **79**, 475–480.

Murphy, K. R. (1989). Is the relationship between cognitive ability and job performance stable over time? *Human Performance*, **2**, 183–200.

Neubert, M. J. (1998). The value of feedback and goal setting over goal setting alone and potential moderators of this effect: A meta-analysis. *Human Performance*, **11**, 321–335.

Ones, D. S., & Viswesvaran, C. (1997). Personality determinants in the prediction of aspects of expatriate job success. In Z. Aycan (Ed.), *New approaches to employee management. Vol. 4: Expatriate management: Theory and research* (pp. 63–92). Greenwich, CT: JAI Press.

O'Reilly, C. A., & Chatman, J. A. (1994). Working smarter and harder: A longitudinal study of managerial success. *Administrative Sciene Quarterly*, **39**, 603–627.

Organ, D. W. (1988). *Organizational citizenship behavior: The good soldier syndrome*. Lexington, MA: Lexington.

Parker, S. K. (1998). Enhancing role breadth self-efficacy: The roles of job enrichment and other organizational interventions. *Journal of Applied Psychology*, **83**, 835–852.

Parker, S. K., Wall, T. D., & Jackson, P. R. (1997). "That's not my job": Developing flexible employee work orientations. *Academy of Management Journal*, **40**, 899–929.

Ployhard, R. E., & Hakel, M. D. (1998). The substantive nature of performance variability: Predicting interindividual differences in intraindividual performance. *Personnel Psychology*, **51**, 859–901.

Podsakoff, P. M., Ahearne, M., & MacKenzie, S. B. (1997). Organizational citizenship behavior and the quantity and quality of work group performance. *Journal of Applied Psychology*, **82**, 262–270.

Pritchard, R. D., Jones, S. D., Roth, P. L., Stuebing, K. K., & Ekeberg, S. E. (1989). The evaluation of an integrated approach to measuring organizational productivity. *Personnel Psychology*, **42**, 69–115.

Pulakos, E. D., Arad, S., Donovan, M. A., & Plamondon, K. E. (2000). Adaptability in the workplace: Development of a taxonomy of adaptive performance. *Journal of Applied Psychology*, **85**, 612–624.

Quiñones, M. A., Ford, J. K., & Teachout, M. S. (1995). The relationship between work experience and job performance: A conceptual and meta-analytic review. *Personnel Psychology*, **48**, 887–910.

Roe, R. A. (1999). Work performance: A multiple regulation perspective. In C. L. Cooper & I. T. Robertson (Eds.), *International review of industrial and organizational psychology* (Vol. 14, pp. 231–335). Chichester: Wiley.

Rousseau, D. M. (1985). Issues of level in organizational research: Multi-level and cross-level perspectives. In L. L. Cummings & B. Staw (Eds.), *Research in organizational behavior* (Vol. 7, pp. 1–37). Greenwich, CT: JAI Press.

Schmidt, F. L., & Hunter, J. E. (1998). The validity and utility of selection methods in personnel psychology: Practical and theoretical implications of 85 years of research findings. *Psychological Bulletin*, **124**, 262–274.

Schmidt, F. L., Hunter, J. E., Outerbride, A. N., & Goff, S. (1988). Joint relation of experience and ability with job performance: Test of three hypotheses. *Journal of Applied Psychology*, **73**, 46–57.

Schmidt, F. L., Hunter, J. E., & Outerbridge, A. N. (1986). Impact of job experience and ability on job knowledge, work sample performance, and supervisory ratings of job performance. *Journal of Applied Psychology*, **71**, 432–439.

Shaft, T. M., & Vessey, I. (1998). The relevance of application domain knowledge: Characterizing the computer program comprehension process. *Journal of Management Information Systems*, **15**, 51–78.

Sonnentag, S. (1998). Expertise in professional software design: A process study. *Journal of Applied Psychology*, **83**, 703–715.

Sonnentag, S. (1999). *Why star-performers enhance team performance: A theoretical model*. Paper presented at the Ninth European Congress of Work and Organizational Psychology, 12–15 May 1999, Espoo-Helsinki, Finland.

Sonnentag, S. (2000). Expertise at work: Experience and excellent performance. In C. L. Cooper & I. T. Robertson (Eds.), *International review of industrial and organizational psychology* (pp. 223–264). Chichester: Wiley.

Speier, C., & Frese, M. (1997). Self-efficacy as a mediator between ressources at work and personal initiative: A longitudinal field study in East Germany. *Human Performance*, **10**, 171–192.

Sperandio, J. C. (1971). Variation of operator's strategies and regulating effects on workload. *Ergonomics*, **14**, 571–577.

Stajkovic, A. D., & Luthans, F. (1997). A meta-analysis of the effects of organizational behavior modification on task performance. *Academy of Management Journal*, **40**, 1122–1149.

Stajkovic, A. D., & Luthans, F. (1998). Self-efficacy and work-related performance: A meta-analysis. *Psychological Bulletin*, **124**, 240–261.

Stevens, M. J., & Campion, M. A. (1994). The knowledge, skill, and ability requirements for teamwork: Implications for human resource management. *Journal of Management*, **20**, 503–530.

Sujan, H., Weitz, B. A., & Kumar, N. (1994). Learning orientation, working smart, and effective selling. *Journal of Marketing*, **58**, 39–52.

Tett, R. P., Jackson, D. N., & Rothstein, M. (1991). Personality measures as predictors of job performance: A meta-analytic review. *Personnel Psychology*, **44**, 703–742.

Trist, E. L., & Bamforth, K. W. (1951). Some social and psychological consequences of the long-wall method of coal-getting. *Human Relations*, **4**, 3–38.

Tubbs, T. C., & Collins, J. M. (2000). Jackson and Schuler (1985) revisited: a meta-analysis of the relationships between role ambiguity, role conflict, and job performance. *Journal of Management*, **26**, 155–169.

Van der Linden, D., Sonnentag, S., Frese, M., & Van Dyck, C. (2001). Exploration strategies, performance, and error consequences when learning a complex computer task. *Behaviour and Information Technology*, **20**, 189–198.

Van Dyne, L., & LePine, J. A. (1998). Helping and voice extra-role behaviors: Evidence of construct and predictive validity. *Academy of Management Journal*, **41**, 108–119.

Van Eerde, W., & Thierry, H. (1996). Vroom's expectancy models and work-related criteria: A meta-analysis. *Journal of Applied Psychology*, **81**, 575–586.

Van Scotter, J., Motowidlo, S. J., & Cross, T. C. (2000). Effects of task performance and contextual performance on systemic rewards. *Journal of Applied Psychology*, **85**, 526–535.

Van Scotter, J. R., & Motowidlo, S. J. (1996). Interpersonal facilitation and job dedication as seperate facets of contextual performance. *Journal of Applied Psychology*, **81**, 525–531.

Vinchur, A. J., Schippmann, J. S., Switzer, F. S., & Roth, P. L. (1998). A meta-analytic review of predictors of job performance for salespeople. *Journal of Applied Psychology*, **83**, 586–597.

Vroom, V. H. (1964). *Work and motivation*. New York: Wiley.

Waldman, D. A. (1994). Contributions of total quality management to the theory of work performance. *Academy of Management Review*, **19**, 510–536.

Wall, T. D., & Clegg, C. W. (1981). A longitudinal field study of group work redesign. *Journal of Occupational Behavior*, **2**, 31–49.

Wall, T. D., Corbett, M., Martin, R., Clegg, C. W., & Jackson, P. R. (1990). Advanced manufacturing technology, work design, and performance: A change study. *Journal of Applied Psychology*, **75**, 691–697.

Wall, T. D., & Davids, K. (1992). Shopfloor work organization and advanced manufacturing technology. In C. L. Cooper & I. R. Robertson (Eds.), *International review of industrial and organizational psychology* (pp. 363–398). Chichester: Wiley.

Wall, T. D., & Jackson, P. R. (1995). New manufacturing initiatives and shopfloor job design. In A. Howard (Ed.), *The changing nature of work* (pp. 139–174). San Francisco, CA: Jossey-Bass.

Wall, T. D., Jackson, P. R., & Davids, K. (1992). Operator work design and robotics system performance: A serendipitous field study. *Journal of Applied Psychology*, **77**, 353–362.

West, M. A., Borrill, C. S., & Unsworth, K. L. (1998). Team effectiveness in organizations. In C. L. Cooper & I. T. Robertson (Eds.), *International review of industrial and organizational psychology* (Vol. 13, pp. 1–48). Chichester: Wiley.

Williams, L. J., & Anderson, S. E. (1991). Job satisfaction and organizational commitment as predictors of organizational citizinship and in-role behaviors. *Journal of Management*, **17**, 601–617.

Yukl, G. A. (1998). *Leadership in organizations* (4th edn.). Upper Saddle River, NJ: Prentice Hall.

Zickar, M. J., & Slaughter, J. E. (1999). Examining creative performance over time using hierarchical linear modeling: An illustration using film directors. *Human Performance*, **12**, 211–230.

CHAPTER 2

Ability and Non-ability Predictors of Job Performance

Ruth Kanfer and **Tracy M. Kantrowitz**
Georgia Institute of Technology, Atlanta, USA

SUMMARY

This chapter reviews recent advances in theory and research on general cognitive ability and non-ability predictors of job performance. New theoretical developments delineating how intelligence and ability relate to performance are described. Results of meta-analytic findings on general cognitive ability, personality, and biodata/interview relations to job performance are reviewed, followed by a review of research examining the incremental predictive validity of non-ability measures over ability predictors for work behavior and job performance. The meta-analytic findings provide compelling evidence for the predictive validity of general cognitive ability for job performance and, to a lesser extent, evidence for the predictive validity of some personality traits for job performance. We discuss abiding issues related to construct mismatch, non-linear relations between the predictor and criterion, and bidirectionality. Future research directions that focus on the "how and why" for observed trait–job performance relationships are recommended.

INTRODUCTION

The prediction of job performance involves the application of psychological theory from basic domains of psychology (e.g., intelligence, personality, motivation, emotion) to knowledge about job conditions and requirements. In conducting research on the predictive validity of various ability and non-ability factors, industrial/organizational (I/O) psychologists seek to answer two fundamental questions: (1) What role do person factors play in determining job performance? (2) How may theories and tests be used to improve predictions of person–job fit? Answers to these questions have theoretical implications for the development of theories of work behavior and job performance, as well as practical implications for the development of effective personnel selection, training, and placement systems in organizational settings.

The purpose of this chapter is to review significant advances in theory and research on general cognitive ability (also referred to in the literature as intelligence or general mental ability) and non-ability predictors of individual differences in job performance over the past 15 years. A comprehensive, historical account of progress in the cognitive and non-ability domains is beyond the scope of the present chapter (for historical reviews, see, e.g., Kanfer, Ackerman, Murtha, & Goff, 1995; Murphy, 1996) in this chapter we focus on recent developments in order to provide a more complete account of the progress and research trends that have occurred in the field since the mid-1980s.

Prior to the mid-1980s, studies of ability and non-ability predictors of job performance proceeded largely independently. In the ability domain, theoretical and empirical advances in the construction of tests of intelligence (e.g., Binet & Simon, 1905) provided the foundation for a substantial number of studies demonstrating the validity of general intelligence tests for predicting applicant selection and occupational success (cf. Viteles, 1930). In addition, researchers (e.g., Kelly, 1928; Thomson, 1916) refined a second "group factors" approach. This approach utilized specialized aptitude batteries to test group factors (e.g., spatial, verbal ability) shown to be job related, culminating in the kinds of multiple-aptitude batteries used by the US Army Air Forces during World War II (Flanagan, 1948). Although evidence demonstrating the validity of these two approaches in predicting job performance mounted through the mid-1980s, concerns about the lack of evidence demonstrating the broad validity of general intelligence tests for predicting job performance precluded their widespread use in civilian settings.

In contrast, in the non-ability domain the absence of a broad organizing framework for non-cognitive constructs led to disparate research programs on the role of non-ability factors. During the early part of the twentieth century, personality tests were frequently used to identify and reject maladjusted individuals (Ellis & Conrad, 1948). However, reviews of the empirical literature investigating the predictive validity of personality measures were pessimistic and suggested a general failure to achieve consensus on the validity of such measures for predicting job performance (e.g., Crutchfield, Woodworth, & Albrecht, 1958; Guion & Gottier, 1965).

During the past 15 years, however, a number of studies have been conducted using validity generalization methods (e.g., meta-analysis, Hunter, Schmidt, & Jackson, 1982). In these studies, researchers aggregate prior empirical findings to determine the estimated true-score relations between ability and performance after correcting for statistical artifacts (e.g., predictor unreliability, sampling error). Results of meta-analytic studies show non-trivial relations between general cognitive ability and job performance, and have led to widespread agreement in the field regarding the validity of general cognitive ability for the efficient prediction of performance. As a result, research interest in the ability domain has shifted away from documentation of the predictive validity of general ability for job performance in favor of theory and research exploring the relations between abilities, job knowledge, and performance.

At the same time, the application of advances in the structure of personality provided the necessary organizational framework for coordinating seemingly disparate research on the predictive validity of various personality and motivation variables. Coupled with the use of meta-analytic methods for estimating true-score relations between personality dimensions and job performance, industrial/organizational (I/O) researchers have now begun to accumulate substantial evidence for the predictive validity of particular non-ability traits for job performance.

In addition to shifts taking place in both the ability and non-ability domains, I/O researchers have shown increasing interest in further delineating performance criteria. Spurred by advances in job analysis and increasing recognition of the fundamental changes taking place in both the nature of work and the US workforce, research on the criterion side has increasingly focused on identifying the informal, social, and interpersonal elements that contribute to overall job performance. The broadening of performance criteria to include relational dimensions suggests an expanding role for theory and research on non-ability predictors of performance.

This chapter is organized into five sections. In the first section we review contemporary theoretical and empirical developments pertaining to general cognitive ability and knowledge predictors of job performance. In the second section, we describe progress in the personality/non-ability trait domain. In the third section, we survey recent studies investigating non-ability predictors of performance derived from alternative predictor measures (e.g., biodata, interviews). In the fourth section, we consider recent integrative work investigating ability and non-ability person predictors of job performance. In particular, we focus on studies that examine the incremental predictive validity of non-ability predictors over ability predictors for work behavior and job performance. In the fifth and final section we summarize progress over the past 15 years, identify potential limitations and problems in current research, and present recommendations for future research.

GENERAL COGNITIVE ABILITY AND JOB KNOWLEDGE

There is little disagreement that human cognitive abilities serve as a major determinant of variability in job performance (e.g., Hunter, 1983; Murphy & Shiarella, 1997; Wagner, 1997). As noted by Kanfer et al. (1995), the widespread use of ability tests for personnel selection and placement in industry can be traced in large part to the use of theoretically derived ability tests developed for selection and classification of US military personnel during World Wars I and II. However, based partly on the WWII success of tailored ability batteries for predicting success in specific tasks (e.g., pilot, navigator, gunman, etc.), and organizational concerns about the lack of scientific evidence for the criterion-related validity of broad intelligence measures (e.g., Kelly, 1928; Thomson, 1916) to job performance, post-war industries tended to reduce industry use of general ability tests in applicant selection in favor of differentiated abilities tests (e.g., tests of verbal abilities, memory, fluency).

TABLE 2.1   Meta-analytic results for cognitive ability–performance relations

		Cognitive ability		
Reference		k	N	r
Dunnette (1972)[a]	Performance	—	—	.45
Pearlman et al. (1980)[abc]	Proficiency	194	17539	.52
	Training	65	32157	.71
Schmidt et al. (1980)[bcd]	Proficiency	42	1299	.73
	Training	9	1635	.91
Callender and Osburn (1981)[cd]	Performance	37	3219	.32
	Training	14	1694	.54
Schmidt et al. (1981)[bd]	Performance	16	1486	.26
Hunter (1982)[a]	Ratings	10	—	.48
Vineberg and Joyner (1982)[a]	Ratings	11		.28
Hunter and Hunter (1984)[bcde]	Proficiency	—	—	.45
	Training	—	—	.54
Schmitt et al. (1984)[e]	Performance	53	40230	.25
Schmitt et al. (1997)	Performance	—	—	.29
Vinchur et al. (1998)[cd]	Ratings	25	1770	.31
Bobko et al. (1999)	Performance	—	41553	.30
Colquitt et al. (in press)[bce]	Skill acquisition	17	6713	.38

Notes: k = number of correlations; N = number of individuals across k samples; r = estimated true-score relation.
[a]Reanalyzed and reported in Hunter and Hunter (1984).
[b]Estimated true-score relation corrected for predictor unreliability.
[c]Estimated true-score relation corrected for criterion unreliability.
[d]Estimated true-score relation corrected for range restriction.
[e]Estimated true-score relation corrected for sampling error.

Nonetheless, many I/O researchers continued to regard measures of general cognitive ability as efficient predictors of job performance and occupational success. During the late 1970s and 1980s, the introduction of the validity generalization approach to I/O psychology research by Schmidt, Hunter and their colleagues (e.g., Hunter et al., 1982) provided a method by which researchers could aggregate results across studies to estimate true-score relations. These meta-analytic studies of ability–performance relations provided empirical evidence indicating the predictive validity of general cognitive ability measures for job performance across a wide range of jobs.

Our review of the literature yielded 13 meta-analytic studies on cognitive ability–performance relations published over the past two decades. Table 2.1 presents a summary of the results of these meta-analytic studies on ability–performance relations, organized by study and further by criterion type (overall performance, supervisor ratings, proficiency, training, skill acquisition). (Values reported in Table 2.1 represent estimated true-score relations, with values corrected for predictor unreliability, criterion unreliability, range restriction, and sampling error as noted).[1] The magnitude of obtained estimated true-score relations is hypothesized to vary by criterion type. That is, while overall performance and supervisor ratings represents multidimensional outcomes defined generally as observable behavior relevant to organizational goals (Campbell, McCloy, Oppler, & Sager, 1995), job proficiency is generally more narrowly defined as a task-relevant outcome (e.g., Schmidt, Gast-Rosenberg, & Hunter, 1980). Training success and skill acquisition criteria represent level of performance attainment brought about by changes in behavior (Ackerman, 1988; Pearlman, Schmidt, & Hunter, 1980).

Eight meta-analytic studies examined ability–job performance relations (Bobko, Roth, & Potosky, 1999; Callender & Osburn, 1981; Dunnette, 1972; Schmidt, Hunter, & Caplan, 1981; Schmitt, Gooding, Noe, & Kirsch, 1984; Schmitt, Rogers, Chan, Sheppard, & Jennings, 1997; Vinchur, Schippmann, Switzer, & Roth, 1998; Vineberg & Joyner, 1982), four meta-analytic studies investigated ability relations to both job performance and training outcome criteria (Callender & Osburn, 1981; Hunter & Hunter, 1984; Pearlman et al., 1980; Schmidt et al., 1980), and one study examined ability relations to skill acquisition (Colquitt, LePine, & Noe, 2000). As shown in Table 2.1, results of each meta-analytic study shows a positive relationship between individual differences in general cognitive ability and work-related outcome criteria.

Further examination of results shown in Table 2.1 suggests that that the size of validity coefficients obtained varies as a function of the criterion used. Validity coefficients also vary as a function of the corrections that are made. In general, with the exception of findings obtained by Colquitt et al. (2000; $r = .38$), validities tend to be highest for prediction of training criteria (ranging from .54 to .91), followed by job proficiency ratings (.52 and .73), followed by overall job performance/supervisory ratings (ranging from .25 to .32). The higher predictive validities for training measures compared to overall, multi-dimensional job performance measures suggests that individual differences in general cognitive ability may account for more variance in performance when performance is defined in terms of skill acquisition or job proficiency (see, e.g., Ackerman, 1994, for a discussion of this issue).

The accumulated meta-analytic findings indicate that individual differences in general cognitive ability can be expected to account for variance in performance across a wide range of jobs. From a scientific perspective, however, the size of the estimated true-score correlations (ranging from .25 to .91) suggests that the overall meta-analytic findings tell only part of the story. That is, the variability of predictive validities for ability on performance criteria suggests that ability influences on performance may be moderated by unspecified factors (such as task demands) and may accrue through multiple pathways.

During the past decade, several new streams of research have emerged that more precisely delineate the scientific basis for observed ability–performance relationships. Below, we discuss three of these recent research streams: (1) theory and research investigating ability–performance relations as a function of task demands, (2) studies investigating ability, job knowledge, and job performance relations, and (3) theory and research conceptualizing adult intelligence in terms of process and knowledge, rather than in terms of a general ability factor.

The first contemporary line of inquiry addresses the notion that job demands may moderate the strength of the relationship between general cognitive ability and performance (Gottfredson, 1986). Building upon an integration of cognitive, information processing theory and ability theory, Ackerman (1988), for example, proposed that in tasks characterized largely by consistent information processing components, general ability and broad content abilities should be most strongly associated with the initial, novel stage of task performance (such as during training) and less associated with performance in intermediate and late stages of task performance (such as after substantial job tenure). As such, for jobs with predominantly consistent task requirements, general ability should be most highly related to individual differences in performance during the initial stage of task practice or performance, but decline in predictive validity for performance during later stages of practice and experience.

In contrast, tasks that involve inconsistent information processing components are expected to show little substantial change in ability–performance relations across phases of skill development. That is, for (inconsistent) tasks in which stimulus–response associations change (precluding the proceduralization of task components) individual differences in general cognitive ability are predicted to remain strongly associated with performance throughout phases of skill acquisition. Empirical evidence to support these predictions is provided by Ackerman and his colleagues (Ackerman & Kanfer, 1993; Ackerman, Kanfer, & Goff, 1995) in the context of air traffic controller training. Similarly, Ree and Earles (1992) summarized research evidence indicating the pervasive efficacy of general ability in predicting initial job performance in nearly every occupational domain. However, Ree and Earles (1992) suggest that individual differences in general cognitive ability predicts job performance regardless of job/task requirements. To the extent that individuals may proceduralize large components of job performance, and to the extent that job performance ratings assess job proficiency (rather than judgments involving contextual or adaptive job requirements), Ackerman's theory implies that the development of job expertise moderates the cognitive ability–performance relation.

A second stream of relevant research has focused on individual differences in job knowledge as the proximal ability-related determinant of job performance. In particular, Hunter (1983) proposed that general cognitive ability should be related to performance in two ways: (1) through the extent to which the job calls for general mental activities, such as planning, memory, and reasoning, and (2) through the extent to which an individual masters the requisite job knowledge. Hunter (1983) further defined requisite job knowledge along two dimensions: (1) knowledge of technical information about objects and concepts required to do the job, and (2) knowledge of processes and judgmental criteria required for efficient action on the job.

Relevant to this hypothesis, we identified two reanalyses utilizing validity generalization procedures (Dunnette, 1972; Hunter, 1982, as reported in Hunter & Hunter, 1984) to investigate the relationship between individual differences in job knowledge and performance criteria. Results obtained in both studies found large-sized estimated true-score relations between job knowledge and job performance ($r = .51$) and performance ratings ($r = .48$).

In a meta-analytic-derived path model using military and non-military samples, Hunter (1983) found that the estimated true-score correlation between job knowledge and job performance was .67. Results obtained in the path model further indicated that general ability exerts a direct effect on job knowledge, which in turn influences job performance. Interestingly, Hunter (1983) also noted that supervisory ratings of performance were better predicted by individual differences in job knowledge than by general cognitive ability.

Further evidence to support Hunter's emphasis on job knowledge as a mediator of ability–job performance relations is provided in a cross-sectional study by Schmidt, Hunter, and Outerbridge (1986) investigating the impact of job experience, ability, and job knowledge on performance. Schmidt et al. (1986) found that job knowledge was the strongest predictor of job performance ($r = .74$), with both ability and job experience influencing job performance primarily through job knowledge. In a second related study, Schmidt, Hunter, Outerbridge, and Goff (1988) examined the relative influence of experience and ability on job performance. Results obtained provided support for the validity of ability as a predictor of job knowledge, which in turn exerted a direct influence on job performance.

A third stream of research derives from recent work by Ackerman and his colleagues (Ackerman, 2000; Beier & Ackerman, 2001; Rolfhus & Ackerman, 1999). Ackerman proposed a conceptualization of adult intelligence that appears to take account of the distinctive influences of cognitive ability and knowledge on action. Ackerman's PPIK theory (see Ackerman, 1996, for a complete description) recasts adult intelligence as an investment function of Process, Personality, and Interests, which lead to individual differences in Knowledge. In contrast to research conceptualizing individual differences in general intelligence as a unitary factor (Spearman's g), Ackerman draws upon and extends previous theory and research by Cattell and Horn (e.g., Cattell, 1963; Horn & Cattell, 1966) that distinguishes between two dimensions; namely fluid (Gf) and crystallized (Gc) intelligence. In the Cattell formulation, Gf is reflected in individual differences in intelligence-as-process, or general cognitive ability. In contrast, Gc is reflected in individual differences in intelligence-as-knowledge, as acquired through experiential and educational means. Although Ackerman's theory is designed for broad applications in educational and vocational contexts, the theory has implications for prediction of job performance as well. Specifically, individual differences in intelligence-as-process are proposed to exert a direct effect on performance (depending on the task) as well as an indirect effect on performance through individual differences in the accumulation of knowledge. Individual differences in intelligence-as-knowledge can be expected to influence performance through the experiential and educational amassing of domain-relevant knowledge (e.g., knowledge of computer technology should be a strong predictor of performance for computer programmers and technicians). Consistent with Hunter's (1983) notion of an ability–knowledge–performance pathway, as well as empirical findings obtained by Schmidt, Hunter and colleagues (Hunter, 1983; Schmidt et al., 1986; Schmidt et al., 1988), Ackerman's theory provides a broad theoretical foundation for the observed findings, suggests that greater attention be paid to developing individual difference measures of knowledge, and provides a potential integration of ability and non-ability predictors of performance.

In summary, meta-analytic findings reported over the past two decades provide compelling evidence for the predictive validity of general cognitive ability for job performance, and the use of such measures in a wide range of selection contexts. Recent theory and research has been directed toward understanding the sources of variability underlying observed ability–performance relations. Consistent with findings by Ackerman and others (e.g., Ackerman, 1988; Fleishman, 1972), the direct influence of general cognitive ability on performance appears related to task demands. General ability–performance relations tend to be highest in jobs and tasks that demand sustained attentional effort, such as in skill acquisition or complex jobs such as air traffic control. In contrast, when tasks can be highly proceduralized with practice, as is characteristic of less complex jobs such as assembly work, general cognitive ability–performance proficiency relations may be weaker, particularly among skilled employees.

In addition to direct influences of general cognitive ability on job performance, several studies suggest that ability also influences job performance indirectly through its effects on job knowledge, particularly in tasks that involve skilled performances. For example, among assembly workers, individual differences in machine knowledge may exert a stronger influence on performance proficiency than individual differences in general cognitive ability. For purposes of personnel selection, the indirect influence of abilities on knowledge suggests that criterion-related validities of general cognitive ability and job knowledge will depend both on the nature of the task and the performance to be predicted. In inconsistent tasks, ability is likely to play a substantial role in the prediction of job performance regardless of job knowledge. However, in consistent tasks, job knowledge may play a larger role in predicting performance compared to ability, particularly when prediction is focused on performance proficiency.

Another consideration pertains to the extent to which meta-analytic findings generalize to contemporary work environments where emphasis is placed on ancillary or contextual performance dimensions (e.g., organizational citizenship, team performance, theft, absenteeism). In the manufacturing and industrial sectors, job performance typically refers to observable behaviors and outputs, such as number of bolts assembled or shoes made. In the product development and service sectors, however, a substantial aspect of performance involves interpersonal skills and tasks. To the extent that individual differences in cognitive abilities have been shown to be weakly or unrelated to several non-cognitive traits involving interpersonal tendencies (Ackerman & Heggestad, 1997), individual differences in general cognitive ability may show weaker relations to measures of job performance that incorporate such dimensions. In the next section, we address these issues in our consideration of research on personality and other non-ability predictors of job performance.

PERSONALITY/NON-ABILITY TRAITS

The story of contemporary developments in the personality–performance domain stands in stark contrast to developments in the ability–performance domain. As noted in previous reviews by Kanfer et al. (1995) and Murphy (1996), the use of personality tests for purposes of personnel selection waxed and waned for much of the twentieth century. Unlike research in the ability domain, no grand theories of personality guided empirical research on the predictive validity of trait measures for job performance (with the exception, perhaps, of the McClelland, Atkinson, Clark, and Lowell (1953) formulation of need for achievement); studies of personality–performance relations were often only loosely related to personality theory and there was little coordination of findings investigating similar trait constructs. In short, theory and research on non-ability prediction of job performance was in the scholarly doldrums, and reviews of the predictive validity of personality tests for job performance remained generally pessimistic (e.g., Guion & Gottier, 1965; Schmitt et al., 1984).

Beginning in the early 1980s, however, interest in personality trait prediction of work behavior and performance burgeoned (e.g., Weiss & Adler, 1984). Similar to the history of ability research more than half a century earlier, the major forces underlying the renewal of interest in trait research were new theoretical developments in a basic domain of psychology (personality) and the development of valid trait measures for normal adults. In particular, the rising popularity of the Five Factor Model (FFM) of personality (Goldberg, 1990), the development of multidimensional personality inventories designed to assess these factors, and the fading of the situationism debate in social psychology (in which person factors were proposed to exert less influence on behavior than situational influences, see Mischel, 1969) set the stage for significant progress in re-evaluation of the predictive validity of personality traits for job performance. As a result of work over the past two decades, recent reviews of non-ability predictors of work performance have been generally positive and optimistic (e.g., Barrick & Mount, 1991; Hough & Schneider, 1996; Kanfer et al., 1995).

The changing outlook with respect to the predictive validity of non-ability measures for job performance stems largely from recent meta-analytic studies that organize non-cognitive predictors according to the Five Factor Model (FFM) of personality. In the FFM, the structure of personality is described in terms of distinct five individual difference factors; emotional stability (also known as neuroticism), extroversion, openness to experience, agreeableness, and conscientiousness. According to the FFM, individuals high in *neuroticism* report tendencies and behaviors related to negative affectivity as reflected in self-reports of anxiety, subjective distress, and dissatisfaction. *Extroversion* refers to tendencies and behaviors related to positive affectivity, as reflected in self-reports of enthusiasm, happiness, vigor, and social responsiveness. *Openness to experience* describes individuals who are imaginative, sensitive, empathic, inquisitive and tolerant. Individuals high on the *agreeableness* dimension are typically characterized as kind, likable, cooperative, helpful, and considerate. *Conscientiousness* refers to tendencies or behaviors related to dependability, conformity, and perseverance.

Barrick and Mount (1991) provided one of the earliest and most widely recognized meta-analytic studies on personality–job performance relations. However, a perusal of the literature indicates that, since 1991, there have been at least 11 meta-analytic studies of personality–performance and personality–training outcome relations (Barrick & Mount, 1991; Barrick, Judge, & Mount, 2000; Bobko et al., 1999; Colquitt et al., 2000; Mount & Barrick, 1995; Mount, Barrick, & Stewart, 1998; Organ & Ryan, 1995; Salgado, 1997; 1998; Schmitt et al., 1997; Tett, Jackson, & Rothstein, 1991; Vinchur et al., 1998). In each of these meta-analytic studies, the FFM (or similar alternative conceptualizations, see Hough, Eaton, Dunnette, Kamp, & McCloy, 1990) is used to organize the predictor space. Similar to meta-analyses of general cognitive ability–performance relations, a variety of methods have been used to organize the criterion space, including overall performance, ratings, proficiency, and training. Table 2.2 summarizes the results of meta-analytic personality–job performance and personality–training outcome results appearing in the literature between 1990 and 2000.

Several aspects of the findings shown in Table 2.2 warrant comment. Specifically, we note that:

(1) Individual differences in personality, organized around the FFM, show several significant relations to job performance. In particular, the strongest, most pervasive estimated true-score relation between personality and overall job performance across occupational groups is found for conscientiousness (validities ranging from .12 to .31), followed by extroversion (validities ranging from .09 to .16), and emotional stability (.08 to .22). Meta-analytic findings for openness to experience indicate relatively small validities for job performance (ranging from −.03 to .27 for openness to experience and from −.01 to .33 for agreeableness). Recently, however, Barrick et al. (2000) have reported substantially stronger predictive validity ($r = .13$) for agreeableness in jobs that require high levels of social interaction. Taken together, these findings suggest that individuals who report higher levels of conscientiousness, higher levels of extroversion, and lower levels of emotional distress are likely to show higher levels of job performance.

TABLE 2.2 Meta-analytic results for personality–performance relations

Study		Neuroticism			Extroversion			Openness			Agreeableness			Conscientiousness		
		k	N	r	k	N	r	k	N	r	k	N	r	k	N	r
Hough et al. (1990)	Training	44	—	-.16	47	—	.08	7	—	.14	5	—	.10	26	—	.11
	Proficiency	146	—	-.13	175	—	.04	32	—	.01	48	—	-.01	102	—	.13
Barrick and Mount (1991)[bcde]	Performance	135	20562	-.08	139	21974	.13	91	15939	.04	125	19685	.07	141	22653	.22
	Proficiency	87	11635	-.07	89	12396	.10	55	9454	-.03	80	11526	.06	92	12893	.23
	Training	19	3283	-.07	17	3101	.26	14	2700	.25	19	3685	.10	17	3585	.23
	Ratings	95	12739	-.09	93	12943	.14	62	10639	.04	83	12467	.09	94	14059	.26
Tett et al. (1991)[bce]	Performance	10	900	-.22	15	2302	.16	10	1304	.27	4	280	.33	7	450	.18
Organ and Ryan (1995)[bce]	OCB-altruism	6	1201	-.06	7	1021	.15	—	—	—	6	916	.13	11	2172	.22
	OCB-compliance	5	847	-.12	6	934	.07	—	—	—	6	916	.11	10	1818	.30
Mount and Barrick (1995)	Proficiency	—	—	—	—	—	—	—	—	—	—	—	—	172	31275	.31
	Training	—	—	—	—	—	—	—	—	—	—	—	—	21	4106	.30
Salgado (1997)[bcd]	Proficiency	32	3877	-.19	30	3806	.12	18	2722	.09	26	3466	.02	24	3295	.25
	Training	6	470	-.27	4	383	.03	4	477	.26	5	415	.31	3	324	.39
	Ratings	22	2799	-.18	22	2799	.14	11	1629	.02	19	2574	-.02	18	2241	.26
Schmitt et al. (1997)	Performance	—	—	—	—	—	—	—	—	—	—	—	—	—	—	.12
Mount et al. (1998)[bcde]	Performance	11	1586	-.18	10	1507	.14	10	1507	.17	11	1586	.21	11	1586	.26
	Ratings	10	1491	-.19	9	1412	.14	9	1412	.10	10	1491	.27	10	1491	.20
Salgado (1998)[bcd]	Performance	49	6383	-.14	45	6098	.09	28	4385	.05	37	5174	.01	35	4985	.12
Vinchur et al. (1998)[cd]	Ratings	24	3134	-.10	27	3112	.18	8	804	.11	23	2342	.06	19	2186	.21
	Performance	—	—	—	—	—	—	—	—	—	—	—	—	—	—	.18
Bobko et al. (1999)	Performance	—	—	—	—	—	—	—	—	—	—	—	—	—	36229	.27
Barrick et al. (2000)	Performance	—	—	-.13	—	—	.15	—	—	.07	—	—	.13	—	—	—
	Training	—	—	-.09	—	—	.28	—	—	.33	—	—	.14	—	—	—
Colquitt et al. (in press)[bce]	Proficiency	1	106	.12	—	—	—	—	—	—	—	—	—	6	839	.27
	Skill acquisition	4	368	-.15	—	—	—	—	—	—	—	—	—	—	—	-.05

Notes: k = number of correlations; N = number of individuals across k samples; r = estimated true-score relation.

[a] Reanalyzed and reported in Hunter and Hunter (1984).
[b] Estimated true-score relation corrected for predictor unreliability.
[c] Estimated true-score relation corrected for criterion unreliability.
[d] Estimated true-score relation corrected for range restriction.
[e] Estimated true-score relation corrected for sampling error.

(2) Similar to meta-analytic findings with respect to personality-performance relations, meta-analytic findings for personality-training outcome relations show small-to-moderate-sized predictive validities for conscientiousness (ranging from −.05 to .39). In addition, however, emotional stability, extroversion and openness to experience show generally higher validities for training outcomes (ranging from .07 to .27 for emotional stability; ranging from .03 to .28 for extroversion; ranging from .14 to .33 for openness to experience) compared to job performance. This pattern of findings is consistent with educational and training research indicating the important influence of social adjustment, emotional control, and intellectual curiosity for effective learning (see, e.g., Kanfer, 1991).

(3) The influence of personality factors on job performance is moderated by the type of performance criterion employed. Organ and Ryan (1995), for example, found that extroversion was negatively related to organizational citizenship behaviors (a form of contextual performance). Similarly, Mount et al. (1998) found that emotional stability was more strongly associated with team performance measures than overall job proficiency measures.

(4) Validities for personality predictors of performance are generally lower than validities obtained for ability predictors of overall job performance. For example, whereas Hunter and Hunter (1984) obtained a validity of $r = .45$ for ability–performance relations, the highest validity correlation coefficient obtained by Barrick and Mount (1991) was .23 (for the relationship between conscientiousness and job performance).

In summary, the results obtained using meta-analytic methods provide compelling new evidence for the potential predictive validity of some non-ability traits for job performance and training outcomes. Specifically, the meta-analytic findings suggest that individual differences in conscientiousness and extroversion are positively related to job performance in a wide variety of jobs. Although validities for the relationship between emotional stability and performance are smaller, the pattern of findings obtained to date further suggests that individuals who are more anxious are less likely to perform well in training and job contexts.

ALTERNATIVE NON-ABILITY MEASURES

During the past 15 years, I/O researchers have focused increasing attention on the predictive validity of commonly used selection tools such as interviews and biodata (background data). These tools purportedly assess non-ability predictors of performance, though the structure and content of such measures vary greatly. Although early reviews of the predictive validity of these alternative non-ability predictors were often negative (e.g., Thayer, 1977), recent meta-analytic findings suggest that such measures may provide useful information for predicting job performance. In this section, we briefly review recent meta-analytic evidence for the predictive validities of these other person predictors of performance.

INTERVIEWS

There have been several narrative reviews and meta-analyses on the predictive validity of selection interviews during the past two decades (Bobko et al., 1999; Cortina,

Goldstein, Payne, Davison, & Gilliland, 2000; Huffcutt & Arthur, 1994; Hunter & Hunter, 1984; McDaniel, Whetzel, Schmidt, & Maurer, 1994; Reilly & Chao, 1982; Wiesner & Cronshaw, 1988; Wright, Lichtenfels, & Pursell, 1989). Results of meta-analytic studies indicate estimated true-score validities for interviews ranging from .06 (Cortina et al., 2000) to .37 (Huffcutt & Arthur, 1994; McDaniel et al., 1994). Findings by Cortina et al. (2000) further indicate that the predictive validities for interviews tends to be higher using structured interviews ($r = .27$) compared to unstructured interviews ($r = .06$). But the reasons for the observed relationship between interview scores and job performance remain relatively poorly understood. Schneider and Schmitt (1986) suggested that interviews may be particularly useful for predicting individual differences in personality traits (e.g., conscientiousness). Moreover, it is important to make sure that the variance captured by these procedures is not the same as that captured by general ability and personality traits. That is, to move the field forward, these tests must provide *incremental* predictive validity, when considered along with extant general ability and personality variables.

BIODATA

Biodata, or background measures, contain items that are typically selected on the basis of their conceptual and empirical relation to the job under consideration. In addition to potential assessment of cognitive abilities and personality traits, biodata items may assess values, attitudes, skills, work style, and previous work experiences (see, e.g., Mumford & Stokes, 1991, Mumford & Whetzel, 1997 for reviews). Biodata items may include, for example, questions about job behaviors (e.g., how many days per week do you typically stay late to finish a work assignment?), questions about reactions in particular situations (e.g., how often have you asked coworkers to help you complete a difficult assignment?), or items assessing work attitudes (e.g., how important has it been for you to consistently produce a high quantity of work?).

Over the past 15 years, the predictive validity of biodata measures has been examined in several empirical and meta-analytic studies (Bobko et al., 1999; Schmitt et al., 1997; Vinchur et al., 1998). Results of the meta-analytic studies indicate estimated true-score and predictive validities for overall job performance ranging from .24 to .52 (Schmitt et al., 1997; Vinchur et al., 1998). Similar to interview measures, a number of researchers have noted that the predictive validity of biodata measures may be due in part to the extent to which these measures capture variance associated with individual differences in cognitive abilities and personality dimensions (Mount, Witt, & Barrick, 2000). However, the inclusion of biodata items aimed at other non-ability factors, such as interests, values, and attitudes, suggests that biodata predictors may assess unique and valid aspects of the predictor space not captured in ability or personality measures.

INCREMENTAL PREDICTIVE VALIDITY

A central question for those interested in the predictive validity of biodata and interview measures pertains to the extent to which these measures provide incremental validity, beyond that of general cognitive ability and personality traits, for training and job performance. In this section we discuss these relationships and results of recent studies investigating the incremental predictive validity of personality variables and alternative, non-ability predictor measures beyond that provided by measures of general cognitive ability.

As discussed by Kanfer et al. (1995), the question of whether a measure provides incremental predictive validity over another measure depends critically upon the extent to which the two measures exhibit shared variance. For example, if the association between general cognitive ability and personality is zero, then an association between personality and job performance can be expected to result in incremental predictive validity. However, if the two constructs are associated, then the demonstration of incremental predictive validity will depend upon the extent to which their non-shared variance in the personality measure relates to the criterion.

Evidence on the relationship between general cognitive ability and personality relations is provided by Ackerman and Heggestad (1997) in a recent large-scale meta-analytic review of ability–personality relations. They found that agreeableness was unrelated to general cognitive ability ($r = .01$) and that conscientiousness and extroversion were only weakly related to general cognitive ability ($r = .02$ and $.08$, respectively). In contrast, openness to experience was positively related to general cognitive ability ($r = .33$), and neuroticism (operationalized as test anxiety) was negatively related to general cognitive ability ($r = -.33$).

From an incremental predictive validity perspective, the Ackerman and Heggestad (1997) findings suggest that personality measures assessing openness to experience, intellectual curiosity, and neuroticism (that shares variance with general cognitive ability) may be less likely to show incremental predictive validity beyond that of cognitive ability measures. In contrast, the weaker associations between general cognitive ability and the FFM dimensions of conscientiousness, agreeableness, and extroversion suggest greater potential for these dimensions to provide incremental predictive validity for job performance.

Several studies provide empirical evidence for the joint or incremental validity of personality traits for job performance beyond that of general cognitive ability (e.g., Mount et al., 2000; Neuman & Wright, 1999; Salgado, 1998). Although the variables and methods used in each study preclude direct comparison of results, the findings obtained across studies suggest that select FFM dimensions, and in particular the conscientiousness dimension, provide incremental predictive validity for job performance (beyond that of general cognitive ability). Salgado (1998), for example, found that conscientiousness and neuroticism, when examined separately, contributed a similar amount of incremental predictive validity to job performance (11% for conscientiousness and 10% for neuroticism) beyond that accounted for by general cognitive ability. In an empirical examination of skills, ability, and personality determinants of team performance, Neuman and Wright (1999) found that conscientiousness and agreeableness together contributed an additional 8% to variance accounted for in peer ratings, beyond that of cognitive ability and skills. In an empirical study of person predictors of clerical job performance, Mount et al. (2000) found that the FFM personality dimensions (taken together) contributed between 5 and 13% to variance accounted for in clerical job performance, beyond that accounted for by tenure and general cognitive ability.

Two recent studies have also examined the incremental predictive validity of interviews and biodata predictors beyond that of general cognitive ability and personality (Cortina et al., 2000; Mount et al., 2000). Results obtained by Cortina et al. (2000) indicated that structured interviews provide incremental predictive validity of about 17% variance accounted for, beyond that provided by general mental ability and personality. Cortina et al. (2000) suggested that structured interviews may tap individual differences in job knowledge or job experiences. Similarly, Mount et al. (2000), found that their biodata scale contributed between 2 and 9% additional variance in measures of clerical job performance, beyond that of tenure, general mental ability, and personality.

PROGRESS, PROBLEMS, AND PROSPECTS FOR FUTURE RESEARCH

PROGRESS

Over the past 15 years, research on person prediction of individual differences in performance has enjoyed a period of sustained growth. The application of validity generalization methods to the ability domain provides abundant evidence for the potential validity of general cognitive ability in the prediction of job performance across a range of occupations and criterion measures. The demonstration of the predictive validity of general mental ability tests for performance across a wide range of jobs provides useful information for practitioners. However, new research investigating the person–task conditions that may mediate general cognitive ability–performance relations has important implications for practitioners considering the value of cognitive ability tests for predicting different aspects of job performance. In an era of increasing workforce diversity, investigations of the pathways by which individual differences in cognitive abilities influence job performance offers substantial promise for better prediction of job expertise and promise for the prediction of job performance among older workers. For example, consistent with Hunter (1983) and Ackerman (1996), the emphasis on job knowledge as a mediator of ability–performance relations suggests why older, more experienced workers in knowledge work may outperform younger workers with higher levels of general cognitive ability, and why younger workers may outperform more senior workers in the acquisition of novel job skills.

In the non-ability domain, the application of the FFM has provided I/O researchers with a common framework for organizing personality trait constructs and measures into meaningful factors and evaluating the predictive validity of each factor for job performance. Results in this area provide converging evidence for the validity of conscientiousness as a non-ability trait that predicts job performance across a wide range of jobs and performance criteria. At the same time, conceptual developments on the criterion side, delineating the social and contextual aspects of job performance that may come into play in supervisory judgments of performance, have served to clarify the conditions under which some personality traits may predict relevant job performance.

The increasingly coordinated mapping of non-ability (FFM) personality predictor and criterion constructs suggests that the FFM personality constructs may add unique variance to the prediction of job performance. To date, meta-analytic and incremental predictive validity evidence most strongly supports the contribution of conscientiousness as a predictor of job performance. These results are consistent with the long-standing assumption that dependability, reliability, and an orientation to perform well are critical components of effective performance in most jobs. In contrast, agreeableness, extroversion, openness to experience, and neuroticism represent traits that may be more important in some jobs or situations than others. Agreeableness and extroversion, for example, reflect individual differences in social functioning that may be more important in jobs involving substantial social interaction (e.g., sales) than in jobs that do not demand much social interaction (e.g., writing). Barrick et al. (2000), for instance, show the unique predictive validity of agreeableness for teamwork performance ratings, and extroversion for sales/service performance ratings. However, recent studies (e.g., Ackerman & Rolfhus, 1999; Rolfhus & Ackerman, 1999) also provide evidence to suggest a negative relationship between extroversion and intelligence.

Although research evidence does not support the notion that openness to experience makes a substantial contribution to prediction of variance in job performance, meta-analytic research on personality–training outcome relations suggests that openness to experience does provide strong predictive validity in learning/training environments. In these environments, where skill acquisition typically involves volitional effort and intrinsic motivation, an individual's propensity for new learning is positively related to training outcomes.

Findings with respect to the predictive validity of neuroticism for job performance are more problematic. Although emotional stability, conceptualized in terms of general emotional adjustment, has long been regarded as an important factor upon which to rule out applicants for stressful or dangerous jobs, results obtained in meta-analytic studies suggest only weak predictive validity for job performance using non-clinical personality measures. Further consideration is needed regarding how individual differences in emotional adjustment, anxiety, or emotional regulation may influence work behavior and job performance.

The success of research in the ability and personality domains has encouraged I/O researchers to reconsider the validity of alternative predictors, such as biodata and interviews. Although these measures are commonly used, and recent meta-analyses suggest that such measures may capture important variance in the job performance criterion, very little is known about the predictor space assessed by such measures. Incremental predictive validity studies suggest that biodata and structured interviews assess valid variance in the criterion, beyond that of general cognitive ability and broad personality tests. Further research to investigate the unique aspects of the predictor domain tapped by alternative measures, and how these aspects relate to job performance represents the next important step in this area.

PROBLEMS

Despite the formidable progress in person prediction of job performance over the past 15 years, a number of theoretical and empirical issues remain. These issues are discussed next.

The first problem pertains to construct mismatch, or the extent to which ability and non-ability predictor tests correspond to criterion measures of job performance. Cronbach (1949) was among the first to suggest that ability and non-ability measures differ in terms of their construction and purpose for prediction. In particular, ability measures, interviews and test-based training outcome measures, are designed to provide measures of maximal performance, that is, an assessment of what an individual can do under conditions of maximal effort. In contrast, non-ability personality measures and measures of job performance generally provide assessment of an individual's typical dispositional tendencies and performance, respectively; that is, what an individual does under representative conditions.

As such, meta-analytic findings on general cognitive ability–performance relations must be interpreted in terms of a mismatch between the predictor (a test of "maximal" performance) and the criterion (a measure of "typical" performance). Predictive validities in these studies thus represent estimated true-score relations between what an individual is capable of under maximal effort conditions and what an individual does under typical job conditions, and so may under- or overestimate the influence of general mental ability for job performance.

In a step that moves toward addressing this problem, Ackerman (1994) suggested that the psychometric premise that intelligence is best associated with maximal performance is incomplete. He argued that measures of intelligence often contain both typical and maximal properties, and that such measures may be integrated with non-ability measures using an intelligence perspective that distinguishes between maximal and typical measures of ability in terms of intelligence as process (maximal) and intelligence as knowledge (typical). Though such a perspective has yet to gain widespread attention in the I/O research literature, the trend toward integrated assessment of person factors suggests that this issue will receive increasing attention in the future. In the I/O domain, personality measures appear to provide significant incremental validity when the criterion of interest involves job behaviors other than technical performance (e.g., interpersonal skills, employee dependability). As such, it appears reasonable to expect that the integrated use of ability (maximal) and personality (typical) measures will be most helpful when the criterion includes consideration of an individual's typical behaviors in the broader work context as well as performance of designated tasks.

Meta-analyses of personality–job performance relations avoid the typical–maximal form of construct mismatch, but are vulnerable to two other forms of construct mismatch. First, as noted by Wittmann and Suess (1999), a mismatch may occur in terms of the breadth of the predictor and criterion spaces. In personality–performance research, for example, a broad measure of conscientiousness may be used to predict a narrow measure of technical job performance. Such forms of mismatch lead to predictive validities that may under- or overestimate relations among the underlying trait and performance constructs. Second, as noted by Murtha, Kanfer, and Ackerman (1996), dimensions of personality may not be consistent across environments. For example, individuals who are conscientious in home environments may be considerably less so in work environments. Personality measures designed to assess cross-situational personality traits may provide poor prediction of such behaviors in a particular environment, such as work.

A second concern pertains to the field's heavy reliance on the meta-analytic framework for extending knowledge about person–performance relations. Standard meta-analytic methods assume linearity between the predictor and criterion. In personality–job performance relations, the assumption of linearity may be inappropriate when the underlying function between the personality dimension and the performance criteria are non-linear (cf. Eysenck, 1995; Snow, 1989). In the workplace, for example, extroverted tendencies might cause individuals to spend too much or too little time talking with coworkers, contributing to lower levels of job performance compared to individuals who show moderate extroversion tendencies.

A related issue in the personality–performance domain pertains to the potential bidirectionality of personality constructs. As Tett et al. (1999) noted, personality (and other non-ability measures) differ from ability measures in their potential for bidirectionality.

Among ability measures, there is little concern with the assumption of a positive linear relation between ability score and performance throughout the range of scores. Higher levels of cognitive ability, for example, are regarded as more desirable for job performance regardless of job demands. In contrast, higher levels of extroversion may be desirable for jobs involving social interaction and team leadership, but may not be desirable for jobs that require intense concentration on solitary tasks.

Tett et al. (1999) argued that meta-analytic procedures used to assess the validities of personality–performance relations assume linear relations between personality constructs and performance throughout the range of responses, and so may cause a distortion in findings. To address this problem, Tett et al. (1999) proposed an extension of meta-analytic procedures. Applying the proposed procedures to the data set examined in their previous meta-analysis, they found that validities for several of the personality–performance relations to be higher than previously reported. Although the effectiveness of Tett et al.'s (1999) proposed methods for extending standard meta-analysis is a technical question that requires further evaluation, it is clear that I/O researchers will need to pay greater attention to issues of non-linearity and bidirectionality in future research.

Meta-analytic studies of ability–performance and personality–performance relations build upon advances in basic psychology domains, most notably intelligence and personality. Meta-analyses of ability–performance relations during the past 15 years have relied on long-standing conceptions of intelligence positing a unitary general factor (Spearman, 1904). This conceptualization enables aggregation of studies using often diverse measures of intelligence or cognitive ability. As such, observed relationships between ability and performance are interpreted in terms of the influence of general mental ability on job performance. However, conceptualizations of intelligence that distinguish between individual differences in crystallized and fluid intelligence (e.g., Cattell, 1963) suggest that further attention be paid to how such conceptions of intelligence may affect the generalizability of conclusions based on meta-analyses assuming a unitary conception of general intelligence, especially when the prediction of performance moves beyond entry-level jobs and young adults.

In the personality–performance domain, the FFM provided the first comprehensive organizing framework useful for meta-analytic investigations. Although the FFM has proved useful, a number of I/O researchers have raised troubling concerns about the adequacy of FFM and criterion constructs for the current "world of work". Non-ability constructs traditionally considered important determinants of performance, such as motivation, interests, and values, are not easily fitted within the FFM. As a consequence, research aimed at investigating new constructs, such as personal initiative (Frese, Fay, Hilburger, Leng, & Tag, 1997), proactive personality (Seibert, Crant, & Kraimer, 1999), and motivational traits and skills (Kanfer & Heggestad, 1997) tend to receive less attention in I/O meta-analytic research employing the FFM taxonomy.

Similarly, the reliance on archival data, in which job performance is often undifferentiated with respect to the aspects of the criterion domain tapped by the performance measure, is also problematic. Recent advances in the criterion domain, distinguishing between job performance with respect to technical (Campbell et al., 1995), contextual (Motowidlo & Van Scotter, 1994), and adaptive (Pulakos, Arad, Donovan, & Plamandon, 2000) dimensions have not been adequately addressed in meta-analytic research. For research to evaluate the role of person constructs not readily captured within the FFM framework (e.g., personal initiative), studies must also contain performance measures that assess corresponding aspects of the criterion domain (e.g., entrepreneurial behaviors). To date, evidence for the general predictive validity of ability and non-ability measures is often provided by assessing predictor–performance relations across occupational groupings that confound status, job conditions, prior experience and skills, and task requirements (e.g., professionals, managers, sales). In the contemporary workplace, such occupational groupings may be less useful than groupings based on job environments (e.g., Holland & Gottfredson, 1992) or an analysis of job demands. In the USA, for example, Schneider, Ackerman, and Kanfer (1996) suggested that the growth of service sector jobs has placed increasing emphasis on an individual's "people skills" (cf. Schneider et al., 1996). How to map such ill-defined job skill requirements to the person predictor domain is not obvious. Recent work by Mount et al. (1998), for example, shows differential validity of select personality traits for teamwork and dyadic service interactions. Future research to investigate the possible differential validities of particular ability and non-ability traits as a function of the type of "people skills", "work styles", "learning styles", or "self-management skills" required in present-day jobs is likely to be particularly informative.

Another issue in the personality–job performance domain pertains to the current scarcity of data addressing the question of "how and why" broad individual differences in non-ability traits influence job performance. For example, meta-analytic findings provide convergent evidence for the positive influence of conscientiousness on job performance. But relatively little is known about why individuals who are higher in conscientiousness are better employees beyond the notion that good traits go together (Thorndike, 1940; Ackerman & Humphreys, 1990). Kanfer et al. (1995) posited that "distal" traits such as conscientiousness influence job performance through more proximal self-regulatory processes. Although Mount and Barrick (1995) provide empirical evidence to support this view, additional research is needed to "unpack" the observed predictor–criterion relations. That is, what aspects of conscientiousness (e.g., achievement orientation, dependability, reliability, tolerance for authority) are most important? Further, how do these trait tendencies operate on dimensions of performance? For example, it may be that conscientiousness exerts a differential influence on different performance dimensions, such that higher levels of conscientiousness exert a positive effect on work attendance and compliance with organizational policies, but little effect on dimensions of performance involving intellectual tasks such as abstraction, reasoning, or innovation (cf. non-significant relations between conscientiousness and cognitive ability, Ackerman & Heggestad, 1997). Research into these issues helps to further refine the nomological network of constructs linking person and job performance constructs.

A final concern pertains to the emerging literature investigating the joint and incremental predictive validities of ability, personality, and other personnel selection tools such as biodata and interviews. To date, although recent investigations by Mount et al. (2000) and Cortina et al. (2000) show the independent predictive validity and potential value of biodata and structured interview instruments, little is known about the unique elements of the predictor space that such measures appear to assess. Cortina et al. (2000), for example, suggested that structured interviews may tap job knowledge and/or individual differences in job task experiences.

In a related vein, apparent inconsistencies in the accumulated meta-analytic findings have not been fully explored. Ackerman (2000), for example, found that individual differences in extroversion were negatively related to measures of fluid and crystallized intelligence. However, findings by several researchers (e.g., Barrick & Mount, 1991) indicate a positive relationship between extroversion and job performance. If general cognitive ability is positively related to job knowledge (as suggested by Schmidt et al., 1986) and job performance, and extroversion is positively related to job performance, then what is the relationship between extroversion and job knowledge? If a negative relationship between extroversion and job knowledge is obtained, there may be an interaction or asymmetric trade-off function between intellect and sociability factors in the prediction of job performance. Persons high in both general cognitive ability and extroversion, for example, might develop less job knowledge compared to persons high in general cognitive ability but low in extroversion. To the extent that the development of job knowledge contributes significantly to job performance, such as in training contexts, higher levels of extroversion may dampen the positive influence of general ability on performance.

PROSPECTS

In their review of recent person predictor research, Mount and Barrick (1998) note: ". . . there are now two dispositional predictors in our field whose validity generalizes: general mental ability and conscientiousness. Thus, no matter what job you are selecting for, if you want employees who will turn out to be good performers, you should hire those who work smarter and work harder" (p. 856). We concur that over the past two decades, I/O psychologists have provided critical empirical evidence to support longstanding assumptions about the broad validity of general mental ability and non-ability traits for prediction of job performance. As such, it can be argued that with these issues largely settled, contemporary research efforts need only tie up loose ends.

We disagree, and suggest that such a conclusion represents what the physicist Feynman (1985) describes as "cargo cult science", a term based on Feynman's observation of the failure of a group of island natives in the Pacific Ocean to reinstate cargo shipments of supplies to their island after the end of WWII despite their extensive efforts to refurbish and staff the abandoned landing strip. As Feynman (1985) noted, the islanders simply did not recognize that the reason the cargo planes did not return to the island was a function of the war's end, and had nothing to do with the precision with which the islanders recreated the landing environment.

As described by Feynman (1985), cargo cult science is characterized by slavish adherence to scientific procedures in the absence of theoretical understanding and the development of alternative explanations for observed effects. According to Feynman (1985), such approaches ultimately fail in terms of advancing scientific knowledge or understanding. Meta-analytic findings over the past 15 years have produced provocative results. But to avoid the consequences of cargo cult science, we suggest that future research will need to focus greater attention on answering fundamental questions about the relationships among predictor and criterion constructs, and providing alternative explanations for variability in predictor–performance relations.

ACKNOWLEDGEMENT

This research was supported in part by a grant to the first author from the National Institute of Aging (AG16648-1).

NOTE

1. It is often overlooked, but critical to note that these reported values are, in essence, never actually observed in the real-world. Rather, they represent an ideal that can only be approximated, such as the speed of an object on a frictionless inclined plane.

REFERENCES

Ackerman, P. L. (1988). Determinants of individual differences during skill acquisition: Cognitive abilities and information processing. *Journal of Experimental Psychology: General*, **117**, 288–318.

Ackerman, P. L. (1994). Intelligence, attention, and learning: Maximal and typical performance. In D. K. Detterman (Ed.), *Current topics in human intelligence: Vol. 4: Theories of intelligence* (pp. 1–27). Norwood, NJ: Ablex.

Ackerman, P. L. (1996). A theory of adult intellectual development: Process, personality, interests, and knowledge. *Intelligence*, **22**, 229–259.

Ackerman, P. L. (2000). Domain-specific knowledge as the "dark matter" of adult intelligence: Gf/Gc, personality, and interest correlates. *Journal of Gerontology: Psychological Sciences*, **55B**, 69–84.

Ackerman, P. L., & Heggestad, E. D. (1997). Intelligence, personality, and interests: Evidence for overlapping traits. *Psychological Bulletin*, **121**, 219–245.

Ackerman, P. L., & Humphreys, L. G. (1990). Individual differences in industrial and organizational psychology. In M. D. Dunnette & L. M. Hough (Eds.), *Handbook of industrial and organizational psychology* (2nd edn., Vol. 1, pp. 223–282). Palo Alto, CA: Consulting Psychologists Press.

Ackerman, P. L., & Kanfer, R. (1993). Integrating laboratory and field study for improving selection: Development of a battery for predicting air traffic controller success. *Journal of Applied Psychology*, **78**, 413–432.

Ackerman, P. L., Kanfer, R., & Goff, M. (1995). Cognitive and noncognitive determinants and consequences of complex skill acquisition. *Journal of Experimental Psychology: Applied*, **1**, 270–304.

Ackerman, P. L., & Rolfhus, E. L. (1999). The locus of adult intelligence: Knowledge, abilities, and nonability traits. *Psychology and Aging*, **14**, 314–330.

Barrick, M. R., Judge, T. A., & Mount, M. K. (2000). *Personality and work*. Master tutorial presented at the annual meeting of the Society for Industrial and Organizational Psychology. New Orleans, LA.

Barrick, M. R., & Mount, M. K. (1991). The big five personality dimensions and job performance: A meta-analysis. *Personnel Psychology*, **44**, 1–26.

Beier, M. E., & Ackerman, P. L. (2001). Current events knowledge in adults: An investigation of age, intelligence, and non-ability determinants. *Psychology & Aging*, **16**, 615–628.

Binet, A., & Simon, T. (1905). Methods nouvelles pour le diagnostique du niveau intellectuel des anormaux [New methods for the diagnosis of the intellectual levels of subnormals] (E. S. Kite, Trans.). In J. J. Jenkins & D. G. Paterson (Reprint Eds.), *Studies in individual differences: The search for intelligence* (pp. 96–111). New York: Appleton-Century-Crofts. (Reprinted in 1961.)

Bobko, P., Roth, P. L., & Potosky, D. (1999). Derivation and implications of a meta-analytic matrix incorporating cognitive ability, alternative predictors, and job performance. *Personnel Psychology*, **52**, 561–589.

Callender, J. C., & Osburn, H. G. (1981). Testing the constancy of validity with computer-generated sampling distributions of the multiplicative model variance estimate: Results for petroleum industry validation research. *Journal of Applied Psychology*, **66**, 274–281.

Campbell, J. P., McCloy, R. A., Oppler, S. H., & Sager, C. E. (1995). A theory of performance. In N. Schmitt & W. Borman (Eds.), *Personnel selection in organizations*. San Francisco: Jossey-Bass.

Cattell, R. B. (1963). Theory of fluid and crystallized intelligence. *Journal of Educational Psychology*, **54**, 1–22.

Colquitt, J. A., LePine, J. A., & Noe, R. A. (2000). Toward an integrative theory of training motivation: A meta-analytic path analysis of 20 years of research. *Journal of Applied Psychology*, **85**, 670–707.

Cortina, J. M., Goldstein, N. B., Payne, S. C., Davison, H. K., & Gilliland, S. W. (2000). The incremental validity of interview scores over and above cognitive ability and conscientiousness scores. *Personnel Psychology*, **53**, 325–351.

Cronbach, L. J. (1949). *Essential of psychological testing* (1st edn.). New York: Harper.

Crutchfield, R. S., Woodworth, D. G., & Albrecht, R. E. (1958). Perceptual performance and the effective person. *Personnel Laboratories Report*. USAF Wright Air Development Center Technical Note.

Dunnette, M. D. (1972). *Validity study results for jobs relevant to the petroleum refining industry*. Washington, DC: American Petroleum Industry.

Ellis, A., & Conrad, H. S. (1948). The validity of personality inventories in military practice. *Psychological Bulletin*, **45**, 385–426.

Eysenck, H. J. (1995). Meta-analysis—does it make sense? *American Psychologist*, **50**, 110–111.

Feynman, R. P. (1985). *Surely you're joking, Mr. Feynman: Adventures of a curious character*. New York: W.W. Norton Inc.

Flanagan, J. C. (Ed.) (1948). *Army Air Forces Aviation Psychology Program research reports: 1. The Aviation Psychology Program in the Army Air Forces*. Washington, DC: Government Printing Office.

Fleishman, E. A. (1972). On the relation between abilities, learning, and human performance. *American Psychologist*, **27**, 1017–1032.

Frese, M., Fay, D., Hilburger, T., Leng, K., & Tag, A. (1997). The concept of personal initiative: Operationalization, reliability, and validity in two German samples. *Journal of Occupational and Organizational Psychology*, **70**, 139–161.

Goldberg, L. R. (1990). An alternative "description of personality": The Big-Five factor structure. *Journal of Personality and Social Psychology*, **59**, 1216–1229.

Gottfredson, L. S. (1986). Why g matters: The complexity of everyday life. *Intelligence*, **24**, 79–132.

Guion, R. M., & Gottier, R. F. (1965). Validity of personality measures in personnel selection. *Personnel Psychology*, **18**, 135–164.

Holland, J. L., & Gottfredson, G. D. (1992). Studies of the hexagonal model: An evaluation of the perils of stalking the perfect hexagon. *Journal of Vocational Behavior*, **40**, 158–170.

Horn, J. L., & Cattell, R. B. (1966). Refinement and test of the theory of fluid and crystallized general intelligences. *Journal of Educational Psychology*, **57**, 253–270.

Hough, L. M., Eaton, N. K., Dunnette, M. D., Kamp, J. D., & McCloy, R. A. (1990). Criterion-related validities of personality constructs and the effect of response distortion on those validities. *Journal of Applied Psychology*, **75**, 581–595.

Hough, L. M., & Schneider, R. J. (1996). Personality traits, taxonomies, and applications to organizations. In K. R. Murphy (Ed.), *Individual differences and behavior in organizations* (pp. 31–88). San Francisco: Jossey-Bass.

Huffcutt, A. I., & Arthur, W. A. (1994). Hunter and Hunter (1984) revisited: Interview validity for entry-level jobs. *Journal of Applied Psychology*, **79**, 184–190.

Hunter, J. E. (1982). *The validity of content valid tests and the basis for ranking*. Paper presented at the International Personnel Management Association Conference, Minneapolis, MN.

Hunter, J. E. (1983). A causal analysis of cognitive ability, job knowledge, job performance, and supervisor ratings. In F. Landy, S. Zedeck, & J. Cleveland (Eds.), *Performance measurement and theory*. London: Erlbaum.

Hunter, J. E., & Hunter, R. F. (1984). Validity and utility of alternative predictors of job performance. *Psychological Bulletin*, **96**, 72–98.

Hunter, J. E., Schmidt, F. L., & Jackson, G. B. (1982). *Meta-analysis: Cumulating research findings across studies.* Beverly Hills: Sage.

Kanfer, R. (1991). Motivation theory and industrial and organizational psychology. In M. D. Dunnette & L. M. Hough (Eds.), *Handbook of industrial and organizational psychology* (pp.75–170). Palo Alto, CA: Consulting Psychologists Press, Inc.

Kanfer, R., Ackerman, P. L., Murtha, T., & Goff, M. (1995). Personality and intelligence in industrial and organizational psychology. In D. H. Saklofske & M. Zeidner (Eds.), *International handbook of personality and intelligence* (pp. 577–602). New York: Plenum.

Kanfer, R., & Heggestad, E. (1997). Motivational traits and skills: A person-centered approach to work motivation. In L. L. Cummings & B. M. Staw (Eds.), *Research in organizational behavior* (Vol. 19, pp. 1–57). Greenwich, CT: JAI Press.

Kelly, T. L. (1928). *Crossroads in the mind of man: A study of differentiable mental abilities.* Stanford, CA: Stanford University Press.

McDaniel, M. A., Whetzel, D. L., Schmidt, F. L., & Maurer, S. D. (1994). The validity of employment interviews: A comprehensive review and meta-analysis. *Journal of Applied Psychology*, **79**, 599–616.

McClelland, D. C., Atkinson, J. W., Clark, R. A., & Lowell, E. L. (1953). *The achievement motive.* New York: Appleton-Century-Crofts.

Mischel, W. (1969). Continuity and change in personality. *American Psychologist*, **24**, 1012–1018.

Motowidlo, S. J., & Van Scotter, J. R. (1994). Evidence that task performance should be distinguished from contextual performance. *Journal of Applied Psychology*, **79**, 475–480.

Mount, M. K., & Barrick, M. R. (1995). The Big Five personality dimensions: Implications for research and practice in human resource management. In L. L. Cummings & B. M. Staw (Eds.), *Research in organizational behavior* (Vol. 13, pp. 153–2000). Greenwich, CT: JAI Press.

Mount, M. K., & Barrick, M. R. (1998). Five reasons why the "Big Five" article has been frequently cited. *Personnel Psychology*, **51**, 849–857.

Mount, M. K., Barrick, M. R., & Stewart, G. L. (1998). Five-factor model of personality and performance in jobs involving interpersonal interactions. *Human Performance*, **11**, 145–165.

Mount, M. K., Witt, L. A., & Barrick, M. R. (2000). Incremental validity of empirically keyed biodata scales over GMA and the five factor personality constructs. *Personnel Psychology*, **53**, 299–323.

Mumford, M. D., & Stokes, G. S. (1991). Developmental determinants of individual action: Theory and practice in applying background measures. In M. D. Dunnette & L. M. Hough (Eds.), *Handbook of industrial and organizational psychology* (pp. 61–138). Palo Alto: Consulting Psychologists Press.

Mumford, M. D., & Whetzel, D. L. (1997). Background data. In D. L. Whetzel & G. R. Wheaton (Eds.), *Applied measurement methods in industrial psychology* (pp. 207–239). Palo Alto • • •.

Murphy, K. R. (1996). Individual differences and behavior in organizations: Much more than *g*. In K. R. Murphy (Ed.), *Individual differences and behavior in organizations* (pp. 3–30). San Francisco: Jossey-Bass.

Murphy, K. R., & Shiarella, A. H. (1997). Implications of the multidimensional nature of job performance for the validity of selection tests: Multivariate frameworks for studying test validity. *Personnel Psychology*, **50**, 823–854.

Murtha, T. C., Kanfer, R., & Ackerman, P. L. (1996). Toward an interactionist taxonomy of personality and situations: An integrative situational–dispositional representation of personality traits. *Journal of Personality and Social Psychology*, **79**, 193–207.

Neuman, G. A., & Wright, J. (1999). Team effectiveness: Beyond skills and cognitive ability. *Journal of Applied Psychology*, **84**, 376–389.

Organ, D. W., & Ryan, K. (1995). A meta-analytic review of attitudinal and dispositional predictors of organizational citizenship behavior. *Personnel Psychology*, **48**, 775–802.

Pearlman, K., Schmidt, F. L., & Hunter, J. E. (1980). Validity generalization results for tests used to predict training success and job proficiency in clerical occupations. *Journal of Applied Psychology*, **65**, 373–406.

Pulakos, E. D., Arad, S., Donovan, S., & Plamandon, K. E. (2000). Adaptability in the workplace: Development of a taxonomy of adaptive performance. *Journal of Applied Psychology*, **85**, 612–624.

Ree, M. J., & Earles, J. A. (1992). Intelligence is the best predictor of job performance. *Current Directions in Psychological Science*, **1**, 86–88.

Reilly, R. R., & Chao, G. T. (1982). Validity and fairness of some alternative employee selection procedures. *Personnel Psychology*, **35**, 1–62.

Rolfhus, E. L., & Ackerman, P. L. (1999). Assessing individual differences in knowledge: Knowledge, intelligence, and related traits. *Journal of Educational Psychology*, **91**, 511–526.

Salgado, J. F. (1997). The five factor model of personality and job performance in the European community. *Journal of Applied Psychology*, **82**, 30–43.

Salgado, J. F. (1998). Big five personality dimensions and job performance in army and civil occupations: A European perspective. *Human Performance*, **11**, 271–288.

Schmidt, F. L., Gast-Rosenberg, I., & Hunter, J. E. (1980). Validity generalization results for computer programmers. *Journal of Applied Psychology*, **65**, 643–661.

Schmidt, F. L., Hunter, J. E., & Caplan, J. R. (1981). Validity generalization results for two job groups in the petroleum industry. *Journal of Applied Psychology*, **66**, 261–273.

Schmidt, F. L., Hunter, J. E., & Outerbridge, A. N. (1986). Impact of job experience and ability on job knowledge, work sample performance, and supervisory ratings of job performance. *Journal of Applied Psychology*, **71**, 432–439.

Schmidt, F. L., Hunter, J. E., Outerbridge, A. N., & Goff, S. (1988). Joint relation of experience and ability with job performance: Test of three hypotheses. *Journal of Applied Psychology*, **73**, 46–57.

Schmitt, N., Gooding, R. Z., Noe, R. A., & Kirsch, M. (1984). Metaanalyses of validity studies published between 1964 and 1982 and the investigation of study characteristics. *Personnel Psychology*, **37**, 407–422.

Schmitt, N., Rogers, W., Chan, D., Sheppard, L., & Jennings, D. (1997). Adverse impact and predictive efficiency of various predictor combinations. *Journal of Applied Psychology*, **82**, 719–730.

Schneider, R. J., Ackerman, P. L., & Kanfer, R. (1996). To "act wisely in human relations:" Exploring the dimensions of social competence. *Personality and Individual Differences*, **21**, 469–481.

Schneider, B., & Schmitt, N. (1986). Staffing organizations (2nd edn.). Glenview, IL: Scott, Foresman.

Seibert, S. E., Crant, J. M., & Kraimer, M. L. (1999). Proactive personality and career success. *Journal of Applied Psychology*, **84**, 416–427.

Snow, R. E. (1989). Aptitude-treatment interaction as a framework for research on individual differences in learning. In P. L. Ackerman, R. J. Sternberg, & R. Glaser (Eds.), *Learning and individual differences. Advances in theory and research* (pp. 13–59). New York: W. H. Freeman.

Spearman, C. (1904). 'General intelligence', objectively determined and measured. *American Journal of Psychology*, **15**, 201–293.

Tett, R. P., Jackson, D. N., & Rothstein, M. (1991). Personality measures as predictors of job performance: A meta-analytic review. *Personnel Psychology*, **44**, 703–742.

Tett, R. P., Jackson, D. N., Rothstein, M., & Reddon, J. R. (1999). Meta-analysis of bidirectional relations in personality-job performance research. *Human Performance*, **12**, 1–29.

Thayer, P. W. (1977). Somethings old, somethings new. *Personnel Psychology*, **30**, 513–524.

Thomson, G. H. (1916). A hierarchy without a general factor. *British Journal of Psychology*, **8**, 271–281.

Thorndike, E. L. (1940). "Constancy" of the IQ. *Psychological Bulletin*, **37**, 167–186.

Vinchur, A. J., Schippmann, J. S., Switzer, F. S., & Roth, P. L. (1998). A meta-analytic review of predictors of job performance for salespeople. *Journal of Applied Psychology*, **83**, 586–597.

Vineberg, R., & Joyner, J. N. (1982). *Prediction of job performance: Review of military studies*. Alexandria, VA: Human Resources Research Organization.

Viteles, M. S. (1930). Psychology in industry. *Psychological Bulletin*, **27**, 567–635.

Wagner, R. K. (1997). Intelligence, training, and employment. *American Psychologist*, **52**, 1059–1069.

Weiss, H. M., & Adler, S. (1984). Personality and organizational behavior. In B. M. Staw & L. L. Cummings (Eds.), *Research in Organizational Behavior*, **6**, 1–50.

Wiesner, W. H., & Cronshaw, S. F. (1988). A meta-analytic investigation of the impact of interview format and degree of structure on the validity of the employment interview. *Journal of Occupational and Organizational Psychology*, **61**, 275–290.

Wittmann, W. W., & Suess, H. M. (1999). Investigating the paths between working memory, intelligence, knowledge, and complex problem-solving performances via Brunswik symmetry. In P. L. Ackerman, P. C. Kyllonen, & R. Roberts (Eds.), *Learning and individual differences: Process, trait, and content determinants*. Washington, DC: American Psychological Association.

Wright, P. M., Lichtenfels, P. A., & Pursell, E. D. (1989). The structured interview: Additional studies and a meta-analysis. *Journal of Occupational and Organizational Psychology*, **62**, 191–199.

debis Career Development Center: Personality Scales within a Process-Oriented Development Instrument for Management High Potentials

Jürgen Deller
University of Applied Sciences Lüneburg, Germany
Frederick L. Oswald
Michigan State University, East Lansing, MI, USA, and
Ulrich S. Schoop
University of Trier, Germany

Psychological Management of Individual Performance. Edited by Sabine Sonnentag.
© 2002 John Wiley & Sons, Ltd.

Summary

The nature of today's work and workplace is dynamic, complex, and increasingly global and diverse in nature. As a result, business enterprises have become acutely aware of the importance for developing and securing a new generation of qualified high-potential managers. The potential of an organization's own employees and high-level personnel has been of greater focus in management development, if only because of tight labor market pressures that require businesses to develop and retain talent in order to remain competitive. A central task of the human resources department of DaimlerChrysler Services, the service division of the DaimlerChrysler group, is to operate a successful system of professional development and support—and to evaluate, give feedback on, and revise the system on a continuous basis. This chapter introduces the career development process for senior managers. On this basis, the role of personality scales within a process-oriented development instrument for senior management is discussed.

INTRODUCTION

The nature of today's work and workplace is dynamic, complex, and increasingly global and diverse in nature (Kehoe, 2000; Ilgen & Pulakos, 1999). As a result, business enterprises have become acutely aware of the importance for developing and securing a new generation of qualified high-potential managers. The potential of an organization's own employees and high-level personnel has been of greater focus in management development, if only because of tight labor market pressures that require businesses to develop and retain talent within the organization in order to remain competitive. Potential is of critical importance for both individual and organizational performance. From the individual perspective, potential is one of the key enablers of performance. Potential can be seen as a career prerequisite. For its realization, potential needs the individual's willingness to perform. Performance based on potential lays an important foundation for the future individual development in an organization, since the diagnosis and the realization of an individual's potential is a necessary basis for subsequent development activities.

From the organizational perspective, individual potential is a necessary basis for the realization of the organization's strategic development goals. Thus developing individual potential on different hierarchical levels plays a key role in the future company development. The organizational decision for individual development activities is made based on potential and usually performance diagnoses. Organizations can assess potential using different procedures. Critical aspects in potential assessment include the assessment orientation on fairness and equality in order to assure a sound basis for development decisions. Organizations should evaluate the utility of such procedures and communicate the results in the language understood in business: dollars, not correlation coefficients.

In the context of contemporary business phrases such as 'global competition', 'faster innovation cycles', 'flat hierarchies', and 'higher flexibility', the deliberate strategy of internally developing and promoting those with potential management success has many advantages. Particularly in the service sector, organizations are interested in retaining outstanding employees who, ideally, will be able to advance their career by managing complex tasks and the resources required to complete them. Professional human resource managers are essential in addressing this challenging goal, because they are uniquely qualified to develop a system of effective developmental tools, learning plans, and career instruments. It is also essential to integrate the organization's vision of developing and promoting employees and high-level personnel into the organization's formal guidelines and policies and—perhaps most importantly—into the existing organizational culture.

DaimlerChrysler Services (debis) AG, the service division of the DaimlerChrysler group, has long striven to meet the challenge of supporting its large base of employees and managers in order to achieve its business goals. A central task of their human resources (HR) department is to develop and implement a successful system of professional development and support—*and* to evaluate, give feedback on, and revise the system on a continuous basis. This requires the HR department to cooperate in projects with debis members from both central and decentralized business units to realize a viable management development system that incorporates and satisfies the concerns of all parties.

It is obvious that technical knowledge, skill, and ability are fundamental prerequisites for managerial success. Today's economy is more service-oriented and more team- and teamwork-oriented, however; social knowledge and social competence are therefore more critical and more widely recognized as success factors for high-level personnel (Campbell, Gasser, & Oswald, 1996; Motowidlo, Borman, & Schmit, 1997; Schneider, 2000). Communication skills, as well as cooperative or teamwork skills, are in high demand, particularly in future-oriented teams and workgroups. In the service sector, such skills are at least as essential as the specialized knowledge required to perform the job effectively; for instance, a vital key to success is communicating with the consumer or client in order to build interpersonal relationships with mutual trust. Furthermore, managers must exercise independent and responsible thinking and behavior within a social context, and such behavior may be inspired more by personality and social skills than by one's technical knowledge or skill. In fact, for managers, social skills may be thought of—at least in part—as an essential vehicle for communicating technical knowledge and skill. Technical or specialized careers should have promotion tracks within them; career advancement should not necessarily move into a general management position, leaving technical expertise and experience behind. Special career tracks for project managers should be established—tracks that are distinct from line managers but with comparable benefits. This suggestion is of special relevance in Germany, where individuals and organizations consider general management as the typical and desirable career advance. Careful and purposeful promotion of high-potential leaders from within their respective specialties guides them toward new job requirements and tasks that best fit their particular capabilities and personalities. Employees at debis are asked to seek new development possibilities tailored to their individual needs, keeping in mind the objective of career succession into some type of higher-level managerial position. In turn, a central aspect of every manager's job is employee career development. Employees not only receive direct managerial support; they also receive broader support from the HR department of debis, which takes over a coordinating and consulting function.

THE COMPANY AND ITS MANAGEMENT DEVELOPMENT PROGRAM

The Berlin-based DaimlerChrysler Services (debis) AG was first established in 1990 as Daimler Benz InterServices (debis) AG, the service sector of today's DaimlerChrysler group that consists of two major service divisions: the debis Financial Services and debis Information Technology (IT) Services divisions. The Financial Services company is mainly focused on product-related financing, and the IT Services company deals with a wide-ranging array of IT services, including IT consulting, adjusting standard software, and operating and maintaining computing centers and networks. The IT company has been growing at a faster rate than the field of IT as a whole; therefore the company appears to offer some relative advantages that have spurred its growth. Thus, the revenue of the IT Services branch alone increased by approximately 31% to 2.9 billion Euro in 1999 (debis's overall revenue stood at 13 billion euros), a trend that continues at present. debis IT Services employs approximately 20,000 employees. In light of its rapid growth and the sheer numbers in its workforce, debis decentralizes its business activities by maintaining small independent divisions and companies. The development process that we will present was implemented in debis IT Services as a pilot test; the process of implementing debis Financial Services divisions in the NAFTA region has just begun.

The Department for Corporate Leadership Development, a corporate function within debis AG, has developed a general process for the professional management development of all of the organization's members, regardless of their present career stage in the organization. Individual departments stay in close contact and cooperation with the more decentralized HR senior managers and HR developers. Compared with past managerial development structures, this new structure represents a clear improvement for the employees and the company. Steps of the process—and measures for assessing the quality of those steps—incorporate all areas within the organization, from marketing and recruiting up to their top executive program. The debis Career Development Center is devoted to a holistic concept of management development (MD), focusing on the entire career development and career progression process, from line management up through senior management (cf. Deller & Schoop, 2000).

We use the debis Career Development Center's MD system as an example of a process-oriented system for the modern service sector business. It represents a new and important part of debis's system for promoting up-and-coming managers, and in general serves as one example that points out some of the issues raised when creating an MD system. The debis selection system begins long before the assessment center, which serves as a realistic job preview for employees who begin undertaking responsible leadership positions just before receiving department manager appointments. For debis as a whole, the system's aim is to create an effective, structured process that diagnoses employees' career progress and career potential, with the intended long-term effect of developing and retaining high-potential managers.

REQUIREMENTS FOR THE NEW MANAGEMENT DEVELOPMENT SYSTEM

Many criteria allow for a multi-faceted, detailed evaluation of an MD system: (1) gauging the extent of management and organizational acceptance (e.g., whether the system adopts a practice/applied orientation); (2) the economy of the system (e.g., whether the time, labor, and money expended are worth the return on investment); and (3) its criterion-related validity across different criteria, samples, and organizational settings of interest. It is a continuous challenge to develop criteria along these three axes while incorporating scientific accuracy and theoretical appropriateness alongside business-related requirements and constraints. Another challenge is how in the assessment process, statements about concerning managerial potential are predictive or forward-looking in nature. Such statements envision some sort of static future (i.e., statements control for situational factors external to the individual, or situation × individual factors), yet statements about managerial potential ideally reflect the debis Career Development Center's process-orientation philosophy—a philosophy that, appropriately, mirrors the constant changes typical of everyday life in business management. Future interest in the study and understanding of the "employee-in-organization" interaction—the fact that managerial potential is to some extent a product of not just the person, but the person *and* the situation—will generate more accurate and useful predictions about the managerial potential of employees.

In addition to the commitment to a process orientation, it is critical for the organization to define management development clearly, and to ensure that the MD procedure is in concord with this definition. Communicating concrete, goal-oriented development options based explicitly on scores from the diagnostic managerial potential measures is of utmost importance. MD processes at debis are enacted organization-wide and consider the overall business context, reflecting aspects particularly relevant to the service sector. Last but not least, it is especially important that results are easily communicated, comprehensible, and done in a standardized manner across the many decentralized departments of debis.

In the context of the debis corporate culture, employees must (a) clearly understand the MD process being implemented, (b) perceive the MD process, and their part in that process, as fair, and (c) recognize the connection between the ideas behind the process and the implementation of those ideas, where the engagement in and reinforcement for MD-related behaviors are clearly outlined. The debis Career Development Center process reflects and operationalizes the management development culture of debis.

THE INTEGRATION OF THE DIFFERENT INTEREST GROUPS AND THE ROLE OF UNDERSTANDING

Including different interest groups in the MD definition phase was a meaningful and intentional action during the construction of the debis Career Development Center. The superordinate emphasis on the participants' career development marked a fundamental shift from previous MD approaches; previously, individual interest groups focused on how participants fit their own particular concerns. A drive for clarity in defining the process cycle and evaluation criteria—and communicating this information to participants—presumably increased acceptance and motivation for participation. The company work council was integrated in the decision-making processes, both in communicating assessment center (AC) information and in observing AC activities.

The specific interests of managers is essential in this process, because different decentralized management committees make development decisions within their areas of responsibility. Managers' AC observations were connected with managers' experiences of day-to-day work; thus, the ideas and implementation behind the AC was understood and refined within the larger context of the organization. Management determines and resolves any disagreements regarding statements about potential managers' performance in the AC. Personnel management understands itself in this context as an advisory partner, whose major task lies in the development and supply of HR methods having an increase in value both diagnostically for the employee and economically for the organization. At the same time, personnel management ensures a professional process. This understanding reflects a current trend in the role of the personnel department, where the HR department is more active during MD processes, especially when deciding to advance individuals into high-level positions of leadership and responsibility. The challenge of debis is to transform the purely administrative function of personnel management into more strategic and steering functions that clearly require the ideas and feedback of other areas of management.

THE DEBIS CAREER DEVELOPMENT CENTER

The following section concerns itself in more detail with the background and the current conditions of the debis Career Development Center. First, we explicate different goals that are pursued with this development instrument, describing concepts and guidelines, and specifying the key steps in the process of overseeing the Development Center. The last section details the singular elements and outstanding features of the instrument as they relate to the role of the external adviser.

OBJECTIVES FOR THE DEBIS CAREER DEVELOPMENT CENTER

The debis Career Development Center (dCDC) is a mandatory component of management development with debis. The following goals are pursued:

- First of all, the dCDC should guarantee the first-class quality of management potentials as an important factor in successfully surviving and surpassing the competition. Consequently, for debis, the importance of the HR department in the context of overall strategic management plans is growing.
- It is of outstanding importance for debis to embed MD diagnostic tools into the management development processes of individual divisions. It is important for debis to inform—and be informed by—the decisions of the decentralized business units. Primarily, the decentralized business units that appoint participants for the dCDC are responsible for the final decision about a participant's managerial potential.
- The contents of these assessment tools are oriented at business-specific aspects. That is, the tools are not theory-driven just for theory's sake. The dCDC supports and supplements available information about an employee's managerial potential, particularly in connection with the DaimlerChrysler evaluation instrument COMPASS (Competence Planning and Appraisal System). The dCDC is a crucial part within the personnel decision-making processes and forms the basis for concrete MD measures. Therefore, it constitutes an important part of the diagnostic expertise of HR assessment at debis.
- During the continued application of the MD process, standards and quality will constantly seek improvement in connecting MD with the dual goals of personal development and organizational value-added change. The development orientation of the process makes it possible to identify potentials for promotion at an earlier phase than if the process were not in place, which allows potentials more time on managerial development activities.

The debis Career Development Center has a couple of additional major goals:

- debis aims to have the dCDC obtain a beneficial training effect while also meeting the company's benchmarks for quality assurance and comparable evaluation standards across the company's divisions.
- debis seeks to intensify the employees' management development, because developing the individual employee is the epicenter of the total MD process. In the context of the debis Career Development Center, statements about employees are related to their general managerial potential and not to any single concrete job position, although, as mentioned previously, future refinements of the dCDC may take an "employee-in-organization" approach, taking different general job families into account when making predictions about an individual's managerial potential.

The results of the debis CDC offer the following information for superiors making judgments about managerial potential:

- a differentiated and broad diagnosis of the development profile of those with managerial potential and of those in need of developing such potential; the development profile concerns both the technical side and the leadership-potential side of management;
- data concerning the time limits for filling managerial positions in the organization; and
- individual strengths and areas for further learning and skills training; this information is used to design individual development plans.

FOUNDATIONS OF THE DEBIS CAREER DEVELOPMENT CENTER

In analyzing individuals' managerial potential, the debis Career Development Center ties its informational features with a developmental focus. The dCDC is based on the following foundations:

- The development of managerial potential is steered by a process geared toward producing and organizing managerial development portfolios for individuals within each of the different units of the decentralized divisions of debis.
- Management development integrates the pre-selection, the assessment instrument, and the development portfolios into a system having standardized criteria at both the selection and process steps.
- Development portfolios are created for all management potentials that may qualify for a department manager position. Potentials are classified after the earliest possible appointment period, differentiating different types of potentials (see Figure 3.1) and different development perspectives from the COMPASS procedure.
- Management committees are responsible for the key decisions about pre-selection, classifying individuals into development portfolios, and the final appointments for department managers. The HR department experts focus on ensuring high quality during the process.
- Only those potentials who underwent evaluation in the COMPASS procedure take part in the dCDC process. These individuals were deemed capable, in the near future, to take over executive functions at the next level of their career progression.
- Admission and classification into high-potential development portfolios are conditions for internal promotion as the department manager or for comparable career promotions.

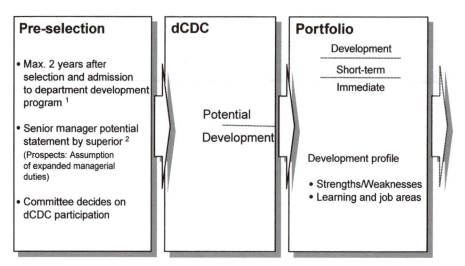

1. Exceptions only with committee approval and individual diagnosis.
2. Members of candidate's staff may submit statements to HR manager. HR manager collects potential statements from superiors. If inconsistencies appear, HR manager initiates individual diagnosis.

FIGURE 3.1   Pre-selection, dCDC and the portfolios are the constituents of an integrated development process

The debis Career Development Center and the development portfolios differentiate three groups of potentials (as shown in Figure 3.2) with a special development perspectives: the "long-term potential" classification applies to those who can fill the department manager position after undergoing further development steps and more unique diagnostics for examining potential. These individuals will be re-classified by future committee decision. Those classified as "short-term potential" can fill the position after completing a short concrete development project and following reconsideration by a general committee. "Immediate potentials" can fill the position after the Development Center and by committee decision.

The three core components of the internal development of managers are the pre-selection process, the dCDC, and the development portfolio. Potentials enter the pre-selection procedure no later than two years after their entrance into the division promotion system—for example, in the context of internship programs. The first assessment in the pre-selection process that takes place is related to the individual's general potential for a managerial position. The immediate superior—who consults with peer managers as well as the higher-level supervisor—makes this assessment. In addition to that procedure, employees are encouraged to apply for the dCDC program themselves, contacting their personnel manager and obtaining superiors' statements about managerial potential. When different sources disagree about potential, the personnel manager initiates a single assessment procedure carried out by the personnel department or by high-level personnel. The management committee always makes the final decision about participation in the dCDC (see Figure 3.3). Identifying managerial potential goes hand in hand with developing promotion possibilities. In summary, classifying individuals into one of the three aforementioned potential groups (long-term, short-term, immediate potential) is based on past achievement, statements about managerial potential, and on assessment

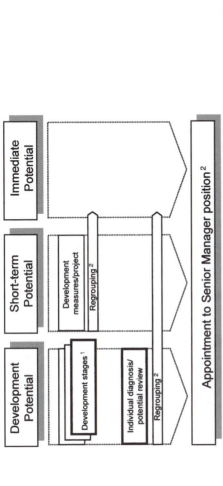

Development Potential | **Short-term Potential** | **Immediate Potential**

Development stages [1]

Individual diagnosis/ potential review

Development measures/project

Regrouping [2]

Regrouping [2]

Appointment to Senior Manager position [2]

- **"Development potentials"** may be appointed by committee decision after a further development station and individual diagnosis.

- **"Short-term potentials"** may be appointed by committee decision after further development in task and regrouping.

- **"Immediate potentials"** may be appointed by committee decision following dCDC.

1. For example, horizontal rotation. 2. By committee decision.

FIGURE 3.2 dCDC and the portfolios differentiate between three potential groups with corresponding development prospects

• Individual development is managed by decentralized management committees in the debis business units.

• Unit committee approval is required for participation in dCDC.

• Admitting a high-potential candidate to the Portfolio commits the candidate to participation in the dCDC process.

• dCDC outcomes are used as the yardstick in Portfolio grouping.

• Committee approval is required to further develop a dCDC recommendation.

• Admission to and grouping in the Portfolio is required before an internal Senior Manager appointment [1] or comparable career move can be made.

1. Temporary appointments are not foreseen; conceivably, future Leadership members may act as deputy Senior Managers on a temporary basis without being officially appointed.

FIGURE 3.3 Guidelines for pre-selection, dCDC outcomes and development

center results. Employees' classifications are entered in the HR database and become part of their personal development portfolio. The development portfolio contains concrete individual strengths, development needs, and critical learning areas. After reviewing the portfolio, the direct superior and the personnel manager agree upon development measures assigned to each employee. The respective management committee confirms the final agreement on development measures.

NECESSARY PROCESS STEPS FOR QUALITY ASSURANCE

Specifying the steps in the process for pre-selecting and classifying participants serves to standardize the execution of the process, even given differences across the decentralized departments of debis. Personnel managers and the management committee cooperate closely in this system. The management committee, together with the personnel manager, establishes the current open positions for department manager and designates potential participants for dCDC. The personnel manager asks the superiors to designate potentials based upon the existing statements about managerial potential, and then sets a meeting with those potentials. The personnel manager then provides the dCDC with information about what they will require for training; and the manager informs the responsible co-ordinating departments about job requirements for the subsequent year. A provisional development portfolio database contains names of designated potentials, and in the case of potentials with insufficient data, discussions between different supervisors about the potentials' status take place. Beyond this, personnel managers agree upon the potentials participating (or not participating) in the seminar, and they discuss the potentials' port-folios in the management committee. The select group of participants assigned to the dCDC seminar follows the rule of thumb: N = number of open positions for department managers + 30%.

If possible, the personnel manager participates in assessment center feedback. Within four weeks after the seminar, participants and the responsible superiors engage in a management development conversation. Based on that, they find an agreement over concrete development measures for the employee and the employee's superior. The management committee is then informed about how the personnel managers classified participants. They also get information about the seminar results, the development portfolio and the planned development plans for each participant. This committee then decides on the appointment of 'immediate potential' and the re-classification of 'short-term potentials' and 'long-term potentials.' If necessary, the committee recommends further development programs or projects for the promotion of the potentials.

THE ROLE OF PERSONALITY SCALES IN THE DEVELOPMENT AND PROGRESS TOWARD A SENIOR MANAGEMENT POSITION

THE BACKGROUND FOR USING PSYCHOLOGICAL TESTS

In recent years, personality tests have made substantial progress in psychometric quality (statistical rigor) and face validity (test-taker attitudes and acceptance of tests). Simultaneously, the use of personality testing in personnel selection is growing (Robertson & Kinder, 1993). Barrick and Mount (1993) note in their meta-analysis that, in studies, some of the scales used to measure personality (e.g., MMPI clinical scales) were not designed to predict job performance in normal populations; therefore they might not be expected to show good validity for job-related criteria. Some of the recent instruments for normal personality are more predictive. They are based on research findings such as the "big five" personality factors, others are self-report personality inventories focused on occupationally relevant (as opposed to clinically relevant) factors, such as the Occupational Personality Questionnaire (OPQ) (Saville, Holdsworth, Nyfield, Cramp, & Mabey, 1984).

Personality constructs as well as General Mental Ability (GMA) tests have been shown to be valid predictors of job performance in numerous settings and for a wide range of criterion types (Mount, Witt, & Barrick, 2000). During the 1990s research has shown quite consistently that at least some personality measures are valid predictors of performance (e.g., Barrick & Mount, 1991; Salgado, 1997; Tett, Jackson, & Rothstein, 1991). According to Mount et al. (2000), validities of personality constructs have been shown to differ depending on the nature of the job and the type of criteria, but each has been shown to be a valid predictor when linked to appropriate criteria.

Different authors discuss the applicability of personality scales in selection as well as in development (e.g., Hossiep, Paschen, & Mühlhaus, 2000; Paschen & Hossiep, 1999). The dCDC process applies psychological tests assessing personality and cognitive ability or GMA. Support for the use of psychological tests supplementing the MD system is the finding that the criterion-related validity of leadership or managerial potential (in an assessment center) provides useful information, and we know that multiple information sources provide a better picture about one's future leadership functions (Sarges, 2000). By using dCDC, a rich broad picture or perspective of a person emerges from a "diagnostic triad" (Deller, 2000):

- objective information (e.g., professional history, education);
- external observations and ratings (e.g., observation of behavior, interview impressions);
- self-image of the participants (e.g., self-description during the interview or in a questionnaire).

Therefore, the personality questionnaire adds additional information to the diagnostic information relevant to the self-image learned about in the assessment center. It is the combination of the three elements—self-image, outside image and objective information—that leads to a comprehensive understanding of the candidate. Omitting parts of this diagnostic triad restricts this broad perspective. For that reason, using psychological tests should be only one kind of approach in assessment contexts.

Finally, note that tests of verbal and numerical intelligence are designed to understand the maximum performance of the individual at hand, because the tests reflect ability under time pressure, a condition that places test-takers under motivation levels that may be higher than is typical on the job (DuBois, Sackett, Zedeck, & Fogli, 1993; Sackett, Zedeck, & Fogli, 1988).

Besides the fundamental consideration of self-image, what lines of reasoning for using personality tests have been especially convincing? The aspects shown in Figure 3.4 are salient.

THE OCCUPATIONAL PERSONALITY QUESTIONNAIRE AND ITS ANALYSIS

The core element in helping to recognize and understand the participant's self-image—besides the aspects covered by the interview—is the Occupational Personality Questionnaire (OPQ) (Saville et al., 1984; Saville & Holdsworth, 1990). This questionnaire was

---

- Good personality tests yield psychometrically reliable and valid information about a person's traits (i.e., consistencies in behavior over time and across situations). Traits are shown to have implications for job performance (e.g., conscientiousness, extraversion, autonomy; Barrick & Mount, 1993).

- Individual results can be examined with respect to reference-group norms (e.g., a "professional and managerial" group).

- As tests are being applied to specific organizations and groups within organizations, more refined normative data can be established.

- Tests are relatively easy to administer and are even available in computer-based versions.

FIGURE 3.4   Advantages of Personality Tests

TABLE 3.1 Internal consistency reliability for the Occupational Personality Questionnaire ($N = 146$) (Saville, Cramp, & Henley, 1995)

Scale	Alpha	Scale	Alpha
Relationships with people		*Thinking style* (contd.)	
Persuasive	.76	Conceptual	.77
Controlling	.86	Innovative	.84
Independent	.74	Forward planning	.75
Outgoing	.81	Detail conscious	.81
Affiliative	.86	Conscientious	.76
Socially confident	.80		
Modest	.68	*Feelings and emotions*	
Democratic	.78	Relaxed	.80
Caring	.75	Worrying	.73
		Tough minded	.80
Thinking style		Emotional control	.85
Practical	.79	Optimistic	.86
Data rational	.84	Critical	.79
Artistic	.88	Active	.83
Behavioural	.83	Competitive	.72
Traditional	.80	Achieving	.68
Change orientated	.76	Decisive	.76

developed during the early 1980s and was supported by organizations in the private and public sectors. The development of the OPQ progressed via literature surveys, critical incident techniques and repertory grid analysis. The theoretical basis is similar to that of other trait-based measures of personality. It proposes that cross-situational, stable differences in temperament and disposition, which play a role in determining behavior, can be identified and measured with the help of self-report questionnaires (cf. Robertson & Kinder, 1993).

The OPQ attempts to measure psychological traits of particular relevance to the normal working population. As such, it may be particularly appropriate for attempting to predict job-relevant behavior. The questionnaire is widely used and has been translated into some 15 different languages for use around the world (Saville, Sik, Nyfield, Hackston, & MacIver, 1996). Several versions of the questionnaire have been developed. Normative data, factor analyses, reliability coefficients, validity coefficients, and construct validation evidence are available (Saville & Holdsworth, 1990).

As depicted in Table 3.1, this personality questionnaire consists of 30 different scales. They can be analyzed at the scale level or aggregates of scales. Each scale is related to one of the three general areas "relationships with people", "thinking styles", or "feelings and emotions". Internal consistency reliability coefficients (i.e., Cronbach's alpha) are calculated to ensure the stability of rank-ordering individuals on the measures. The reliability of the measurement for the scales is good, as Table 3.1 (Saville, Cramp, & Henley, 1995) shows.

The research of Robertson and Kinder (1993) has revealed criterion-related validity for single OPQ personality scales (not corrected for unreliability or range restriction) of up to .32 with the highest values for criteria such as creativity, analysis, and judgment. Their results showed that personality variables added unique criterion-related information beyond that provided by measures of ability alone. The construct validity of the scales (i.e., a check on the existence of theoretically predicted correlations with alternative measures) is acceptable (Robertson & Kinder, 1993; Saville & Holdsworth, 1990). In general, the OPQ scales display high internal consistency and there is good convergent and discriminant validity at the item level, with each item loading on its own scale higher than it does on any other scale (Robertson & Kinder, 1993).

In the first step using the OPQ in the dCDC assessment center, the OPQ is related to dCDC criteria. This analysis comprises references to strengths and weaknesses of the participant's personality. The OPQ offers further options for analysis, where one may compare the results of specific norms from samples consisting of reference groups in different organizations. Also, different OPQ scales measure personality aspects contributing to a higher criterion-related validity than using the overall dCDC assessment center result alone. Scales measuring conscientiousness or integrity have the potential to add incremental validity to the correlation of measures of intelligence with job performance, and the overall correlation of these personality measures is higher than the correlation of an assessment center result (without any tests included) with an overall job performance criterion (Schmidt & Hunter, 2000).

The following analysis options are offered by the Occupational Personality Questionnaire:

- analysis on the scale level (e.g., persuasive, innovative, competitive)
- analysis of team type styles (e.g., coordinator, shaper, completer)
- analysis of leadership styles (e.g., directive, participative, negotiatory)
- analysis of subordinate styles (e.g., receptive, self-reliant, informative)
- analysis of selling styles (e.g., enthusiast, perseverer, business winner).

Behavioral descriptions for each analysis option are available to participants in a personal written report obtained after test completion.

Altogether, this personality test results in well-suited information reflecting the participants' personal and professional development goals. Moreover, comparing one's self-image with one's outside image is informative to participants, and differences between self- and outside image can be relevant for the assessor's diagnostic judgments about the participant.

The extent that a participant's self-image is realistic and communicated by the evaluation is a diagnostic element in and of itself. These differences enable the assessors to better understand the participant's "subjective reality" (cf. Sarges, 1995, p. 486). They also are excellent starting points for personnel development and coaching.

CONCRETE EXPERIENCE USING PERSONALITY SCALES IN A DEVELOPMENT ASSESSMENT CENTER

What kind of concrete experiences have we made applying personality scales in the debis Career Development Center? We present a brief outline here.

In the first assessment centers, candidates did not receive explicit feedback on their personality test results alone. Rather, they received feedback only on the overall result of the debis Career Development Center across all different elements. This was done to underline that all diagnostic elements of the assessment center were of equal importance. Results from all the different assessment center elements contributed to the overall result.

All specific elements were discussed with participants, but even this specific information contrasts with the desire of many participants to obtain very specific results about their scores on their personality test.

For this reason, the feedback strategy was altered such that after the assessment center every participant received a personal narrative report of the OPQ results. This report also showed results of a norm group against which to qualify individual results. The norm group will eventually be the group of all former and actual dCDC participants; because the program had just started, however, a group of "professional and managerial" employees provided by the consultant company was used as the norm group. The narrative report did not address any personnel development aspects, and, even more important, this narrative report stood alone and was not integrated with the diagnostic information collected from other perspectives in the remaining parts of the AC and development needs identified therein. So this concept was turned down again, especially since the integration of personality test results into the overall result was not apparent to the participants. Also the participant's subjective reflection of receiving only partial information may lead to attributing greater importance of this self-image perspective, neglecting other elements of the diagnostic triad.

All this again led to a further development in modification: the personality test results are fully and explicitly integrated in the feedback process of the debis Career Development Center. All the pieces of the puzzle of a person's career development are verbalized. Consequently, given this information reflecting a broad understanding of the employee, the employee is led into fruitful discussions about further opportunities for development and career advancement.

CURRENT CHALLENGES AND DISCUSSION

The answers to the following questions are of importance for an evaluation of the success of the debis Career Development Center: How does the past result look like with reference to acceptance, validity and success? Are modifications of the procedure necessary? Were the postulated goals achieved? To what extent were the success criteria fulfilled? Are there effects visible in the organizational culture and politics? If yes, what do they look like? How far did the integration of the different interest groups succeed?

A positive summary about the present project's status can be made in the sense that the experiences with the previous model led to some substantial modifications in the construction of this development system which have resulted in positive effects. The goals and requirements in terms of the procedure are defined clearly and serve as a strong basis for building the debis Career Development Center. The shifting from traditional selection procedures to a more development-oriented organization offers clear advantages from the employee's point of view, and can also prove to be very meaningful from a business perspective in the long term. The process and development/diagnosis components—despite all methodical difficulties—form an integral and critical aspect of the debis Career Development Center. The roles for participants, management, and the personnel department are formulated clearly, thereby allowing for direct implementation and change when needed, as well as highlighting to all parties the many advantages conferred to the organization.

The next step in the continuing development process of the debis Career Development Center will be its validation. Validation efforts will recognize and include different perspectives, such as the assessors, participants, work council, members of the board of management, and HR managers. It is also important to validate a shorter (more time- and cost-efficient) version of the diagnostic instrument. Can the same quality of results be achieved with less time investment?

The assessment center needs to be closely integrated with viable development plans, lest we regress toward individuals receiving only brief behavioral recommendations and vague agreements about the future training they will receive. Structured examples for development plans are necessary to make the consequences and subsequent steps after participation in the assessment center clearer and more understandable, and to communicate more clearly development plans internally as well.

Future work on the debis managerial potential system should address a further question: How can the individual development portfolios provided in this complex procedure be more standardized, and therefore more interpretable and meaningful? One possible modification is to refine the dimensionality of the general 'managerial potential' concept, for example, by incorporating some aspects of achievement. Thus individual development portfolios can be more sensitively and sensibly used across different contexts. However, greater multi-dimensionality may increase certain problems and biases; in the present example, we would have to ensure that observers and evaluating supervisors could reliably and accurately differentiate achievement and potential.

Whether even to implement an assessment center procedure at all is a decision point worth discussing. Many alternatives are in the repertoire of today's management development systems: 360° feedback, management appraisals, management reviews, or competency reviews are a few of those applied procedures. Traditional assessment centers have been criticized as reflecting the assessment methods more stably than the underlying psychological constructs they are intended to tap (Sackett & Dreher, 1982; Sackett & Harris, 1988). However, assessment centers differ greatly across organizations and many ACs have shown criterion-related validity levels that are in line with other predictors of managerial performance (Gaugler, Rosenthal, Thornton, & Bentson, 1987). In the particular case of the debis Career Development Center, the targeted group is young employees prior to their promotion in managerial positions—a relevant sample where development-oriented assessment center is demonstrated to be a good realistic instrument for detecting managerial potential.

After this initial development of the process for the German-based information technology division of debis, the entire process will now be expanded to the group's financial services companies, which are located predominantly in the USA. The process will be comparable internationally, and the expansion of the process will lead to new perspectives on the adequacy of the dCDC process within different business and country cultures. Critical aspects in transferring the system across cultures exist: using a new language (English instead of German); accepting different assessment center elements that are culture-bound; accepting the personality scales used (a parallel version of the European OPQ); and planning assessment centers that include native and non-native English speakers.

Altogether, it can be said that the debis Career Development Center is a promising system for the internal promotion of debis employees showing managerial potential.

REFERENCES

Barrick, M. R., & Mount, M. K. (1991). The Big Five personality dimensions and job performance: A meta-analysis. *Personnel Psychology, 44*, 1–26.

Barrick, M. R., & Mount, M. K. (1993). Autonomy as a moderator of the relationships between the Big Five personality dimensions and job performance. *Journal of Applied Psychology, 78*, 111–118.

Campbell, J. P., Gasser, M. B., & Oswald, F. L. (1996). The substantive nature of job performance variability. In K. R. Murphy (Ed.), *Individual differences and behavior in organizations* (pp. 258–299). San Francisco: Jossey-Bass.

Deller, J. (2000, May). *debis Career Development Center—Persönlichkeitsskalen im Rahmen des Entwicklungsprozesses zum Abteilungsleiter*. Vortrag auf dem 3. Deutschen IIR Assessment Center-Kongress, Offenbach/Germany.

Deller, J., & Schoop, U. (2000). Personalentwicklung als Business Partner: Das debis Career Development Center als ein prozeßorientiertes Entwicklungsinstrument für Nachwuchsführungskräfte. In M. Kleinmann & B. Strauß (Eds.), *Potentialfeststellung und Personalentwicklung* (2., überarb. und erw. Aufl., pp. 271–285). Göttingen: Verlag für Angewandte Psychologie.

DuBois, C. L., Sackett, P. R., Zedeck, S., & Fogli, L. (1993). Further exploration of typical and maximum performance criteria: Definitional issues, prediction, and White–Black differences. *Journal of Applied Psychology, 78*, 205–211.

Gaugler, B. B., Rosenthal, D. B., Thornton, G. C., & Bentson, C. (1987). Meta-analysis of assessment center validity. *Journal of Applied Psychology, 72*, 493–511.

Hossiep, R., Paschen, M., & Mühlhaus, O. (2000). *Persönlichkeitstests im Personalmanagement*. Göttingen: Verlag für Angewandte Psychologie.

Ilgen, D. R., & Pulakos, E. D. (Eds.) (1999). *The changing nature of performance: Implications for staffing, motivation, and development*. San Francisco: Jossey-Bass.

Kehoe, J. F. (Ed.) (2000). *Managing selection in changing organization: Human resource strategies*. San Francisco: Jossey-Bass.

Motowidlo, S. J., Borman, W. C., & Schmit, M. J. (1997). A theory of individual differences in task and contextual performance. *Human Performance, 10*, 71–83.

Mount, M. K., Witt, L. A., & Barrick, M. R. (2000). Incremental validity of empirically keyed biodata scales over GMA and the Five Factor personality constructs. *Personnel Psychology, 53*, 299–323.

Paschen, M., & Hossiep, R. (1999). Psychologische Fragebogen als Bestandteil der AC-Methode. In W. Jochmann (Ed.), *Innovationen im Assessment-Center* (pp. 129–155). Stuttgart: Schäffer-Poeschel.

Robertson, I. T., & Kinder, A. (1993). Personality and job competences: The criterion-related validity of some personality variables. *Journal of Occupational and Organizational Psychology, 66*, 225–244.

Sackett, P. R., & Dreher, G. F. (1982). Constructs and assessment center dimensions: Some troubling empirical findings. *Journal of Applied Psychology, 67*, 401–410.

Sackett, P. R., & Harris, M. M. (1988). A further examination of the constructs underlying assessment center ratings. *Journal of Business and Psychology, 3*, 214–229.

Sackett, P. R., Zedeck, S., & Fogli, L. (1988). Relations between measures of typical and maximum job performance. *Journal of Applied Psychology, 73*, 482–486.

Salgado, J. F. (1997). The five factor model of personality and job performance in the European Community. *Journal of Applied Psychology, 82*, 30–43.

Sarges, W. (1995). Interviews. In W. Sarges (Ed.), *Management-Diagnostik* (2. Aufl., pp. 475–489). Göttingen: Hogrefe.

Sarges, W. (2000). Einleitende Überlegungen. In R. Hossiep, M. Paschen, & O. Mühlhaus (Eds.), *Persönlichkeitstests im Personalmanagement* (S. XV–XIX). Göttingen: Verlag für Angewandte Psychologie.

Schmidt, F. L., & Hunter, J. E. (2000). Messbare Personmerkmale: Stabilität, Variabilität und Validität zur Vorhersage zukünftiger Berufsleistung und berufsbezogenen Lernens.

In M. Kleinmann & B. Strauß (Eds.), *Potentialfeststellung und Personalentwicklung* (2., überarb. und erw. Aufl., pp. 15–43). Göttingen: Verlag für Angewandte Psychologie.

Saville, P., Cramp, L., & Henley, S. (1995). *OPQ course handbook*. Esher: Saville & Holdsworth.

Saville, P., & Holdsworth, R. (1990). *Occupational Personality Questionnaire manual*. Esher: Saville & Holdsworth.

Saville, P., Holdsworth, R., Nyfield, G., Cramp, L., & Mabey, W. (1984). *The Occupational Personality Questionnaires (OPQ)*. London: Saville & Holdsworth.

Saville, P., Sik, G., Nyfield, G., Hackston, J., & MacIver, R. (1996). A demonstration of the validity of the Occupational Personality Questionnaire (OPQ) in the measurement of job competencies across time in separate organisations. *Applied Psychology: An International Review*, **45**, 243–262.

Schneider, R. J. (1992). *An individual-differences approach to understanding and predicting social competence*. Unpublished doctoral dissertation. University of Minnesota, Minneapolis.

Tett, R. P., Jackson, D. N., & Rothstein, M. (1991). Personality measures as predictors of job performance: A meta-analytic review. *Personnel Psychology*, **44**, 703–742.

CHAPTER 4

Work Design and Individual Work Performance: Research Findings and an Agenda for Future Inquiry

Sharon K. Parker
The University of New South Wales, Sydney, Australia, and
Nick Turner
University of Sheffield, Sheffield, UK

SUMMARY

All of the major work design theories propose that autonomous forms of work design will enhance individual job performance. However, empirical evidence for this proposition is mixed. In part, the inconsistent results reflect methodological weaknesses of many studies in the area. Recent rigorous studies have shown positive links between enriched work and individual job performance, suggesting that a more convincing pattern of findings might be obtained with methodologically improved designs. However, the confused picture of results is also likely to reflect the rather limited approach taken to investigating this topic. Consequently, we propose a model for future research with three key features. First, our model proposes that enriched work design influences individual work performance via three key categories of psychological mechanisms: motivation, knowledge and skill, and opportunity. Second, we propose that the link between work design and performance is moderated by various individual and organizational contingencies. Third, the model proposes an expanded criterion which recognizes that an employee's performance can extend beyond the execution of specified tasks to include contextual, proactive and adaptive behaviours. Considering these three features together, we believe that the conceptual framework will promote a more precise understanding of how work design affects individual work performance.

Psychological Management of Individual Performance. Edited by Sabine Sonnentag.

INTRODUCTION

Work design continues to be in vogue. For the past three decades or so, empowerment, self-managing teams, high-performance work teams and other such work design practices have been much espoused within organizations (Mohrman & Cohen, 1995; Parker & Wall, 1998). Empowered teams, for example, are suggested to have the potential to enhance flexibility, improve service to customers, and facilitate faster lead times, such that, "when all of the pieces of the empowerment puzzle fit tightly together, teams will be ready to work at full power" (Kirkman & Rosen, 2000, p. 65). With claims like this, it is not surprising that recent company interest in work design derives not so much from a desire to improve employee well-being or morale, but from a belief that certain types of work design will achieve competitive advantage. Despite this, remarkably little systematic research attention has been paid to how job performance is actually affected by work design.

The purpose of this chapter is to outline and integrate research on the relationship between work design and individual job performance. In the first section, we focus on the concept of individual job performance. We then describe work design and the major theoretical perspectives that have emerged on this topic. Next, we look at the intersection between these two research areas, summarizing empirical studies that have investigated how work design affects performance. Finally, we propose a research agenda by outlining a model to guide future inquiry and some important methodological considerations in investigating how, when, and why work design relates to individual job performance.

INDIVIDUAL WORK PERFORMANCE

Although performance can be conceptualized and measured at broader levels (i.e., group, organization, industry), our focus in this chapter is on individual job performance. In line with Campbell, McCloy, Oppler, and Sager (1993), individual job performance refers to behaviours enacted by an employee that are aimed at meeting organizational goals. The concept is distinguishable from other terms often used as synonyms, such as effectiveness (i.e., the resulting usefulness or value of the performance to the organization) and productivity (i.e., the cost of achieving a certain level of effectiveness). Individual job performance is also distinct from group and organizational performance, although studies have shown that particular types of individual performance can contribute to the performance outcomes of units of analysis beyond the individual, including work groups (Podsakoff, Ahearne, & MacKenzie, 1997) and organizations (Ostroff, 1992).

Accumulating research on individual job performance (see Sonnentag & Frese, this volume, for further details) suggests that it is multi-faceted. Although multiple dimensions have been identified (e.g., Campbell et al., 1993), two broad aspects that have been distinguished are contextual performance and task performance (Borman & Motowidlo, 1993). Contextual performance refers to activities that support the organizational, social, and psychological context within which the job is performed, such as helping others and being on time, whereas task performance relates to the core technical activities carried out by individuals within their jobs. Studies show that both task and contextual aspects independently contribute to ratings of overall job performance (e.g., Motowidlo & Van Scotter, 1994).

More recently, discretionary behaviors over and above contextual performance have also been suggested. Several researchers (e.g., Morrison & Phelps, 1999; Parker, 1998) have argued that proactive behaviors, such as using initiative and introducing change, represent aspects that are not encapsulated by the more passive concept of contextual performance. Similarly, Pulakos, Arad, Donovan, and Plamondon (2000) have developed a model of adaptive performance with eight specific dimensions, such as solving problems creatively and learning new work approaches. How these dimensions of adaptive and proactive performance relate to each other, and to task and contextual performance, has not been investigated. The broad point is that contextual, proactive, and adaptive performance all encompass aspects over and above technical proficiency. We consider all of these aspects to be part of individual performance and, to reflect this broader emphasis, so we use the term individual *work* performance rather than individual job performance.

As well as defining performance and its dimensions, research on this topic has established knowledge, skill, and motivation as key determinants of work performance (Campbell et al., 1993). Blumberg and Pringle (1982) proposed as a further determinant of performance the degree of opportunity in the job, that is, the chance to apply knowledge, skills, and motivation. Since then, and related to the notion of opportunity, Neal and Griffin (1999) proposed technology as a factor that can affect performance independently of knowledge, skill, and motivation.

In addition to these more proximal determinants of performance (namely knowledge, skill, motivation, and opportunity/technology), many individual and organizational antecedents have also been investigated (see Sonnentag & Frese, this volume). Our focus in this chapter is on work design as an antecedent to task and contextual performance. In particular, we propose that work design affects performance via the mechanisms of knowledge, skill, motivation and opportunity. First, however, we look at work design theories and identify what has already been proposed in terms of a link between performance and work design.

WORK DESIGN

The topic of work design concerns the content and organization of employees' day-to-day physical, mental, and interpersonal job tasks, such as the way tasks are grouped together and how the tasks are supervised. Work design research is concerned with those work characteristics that affect not only employees (e.g., their attitudes, motivation, behavior, cognitions, well-being, performance) but also their organizations (e.g., absence, productivity, turnover). A key work design characteristic is the degree of autonomy that employees have over their work tasks, including when tasks are performed, by which methods, where, and by whom. Additional characteristics of work design include, for example, the variety of tasks, the feedback employees receive from their tasks, the extent to which employees have the opportunity to learn, and the cognitive and emotional demands present in the job (see Parker & Wall, 1998).

JOB SIMPLIFICATION AND WORK REDESIGN

Importantly, the content and arrangement of work tasks often reflect choices, albeit not necessarily conscious or deliberate ones, made by managers, designers, engineers, and even employees. More often than not, jobs are designed on the basis of long-standing assumptions about the need to control employees' activities. These 'taken for granted' assumptions about the way to design work largely derive from ideas developed in late 1800s and early 1900s, such as the concept of scientific management proposed by Frederick Taylor (Taylor, 1911). A key concept of Taylorism is that of job simplification, or the breaking down of jobs into narrow tasks and the removal of employees' decision-making responsibilities in an attempt to enhance efficiency and control. Ideas such as job simplification have been very persistent, and pervade the design of work in many modern organizations.

There are, however, alternative work design choices available to managers and job designers. Largely as a result of accumulating evidence that job simplification was dissatisfying for employees, and even jeopardized their mental health, recommendations were put forward to 'redesign' work. An early recommendation for work redesign was job rotation (i.e., increasing job variety by having employees move from one task to another), and another was job enlargement (i.e., increasing job variety by expanding the job to include additional tasks). However, to replace the employee discretion and autonomy that job simplification had removed, job enrichment and autonomous work groups were proposed to enrich individual jobs and groups of jobs, respectively. The work design practices of job enrichment and autonomous work groups are closely related to the major theories of work design, which we now consider.

Major Theories of Work Design and their Implications for Job Performance

An early theory of work design was Herzberg, Mausner, and Snyderman's (1959) *Two Factor Theory*, which proposed different determinants of job satisfaction and job dissatisfaction. Although important in stimulating research and promoting the practice of job enrichment, the Two Factor Theory has not stood the test of time (see Parker & Wall, 1998). More important and popular today is the *Job Characteristics Model* (JCM; Hackman & Oldham, 1976), which proposes five core job characteristics as important for the motivation and performance of employees: skill variety, task identity (completing a whole piece of work), task significance (a job with meaning and impact on others), autonomy, and job feedback. These job characteristics are proposed to lead to positive outcomes (e.g., higher work satisfaction, internal work motivation, work performance, lower absenteeism and turnover) via three critical psychological states (experienced meaningfulness, experienced responsibility, and knowledge of results). The model was held to be particularly applicable to individuals high in growth need strength, that is, individuals who attach a high degree of importance to challenge and personal development. On the whole, the broad propositions of the Job Characteristics Model concerning a link between work characteristics and outcomes such as job satisfaction have been supported (Parker & Wall, 1998), and growth need strength has been shown to moderate the relationship between job characteristics and outcomes such as job satisfaction (e.g., Gerhart, 1987) and activated mood states (Saavedra & Kwun, 2000). However, other predictions, such as the mediating role of the critical psychological states, have not been consistently upheld (Oldham, 1996).

In terms of employee performance, the primary mechanism proposed by the Job Characteristics Model is motivation. Thus, it is assumed that people work harder because they are doing meaningful jobs that satisfy their need for growth. At the same time, because they expect that working hard will lead to doing a good job (Bandura, 1982), higher-order needs are being fulfilled. One issue with the Job Characteristics Model, however, is that it posits work performance as part of a set of outcomes including job satisfaction and internal work motivation, with the implication that these outcomes should be positively interrelated. Yet reviews of studies testing these relationships challenge this assumption. For example, a review of the literature by Iaffaldano and Muchinsky (1985) showed that the best estimate of the true correlation between job satisfaction and performance was .17 (see also Podsakoff & Williams, 1986, on this topic). The low correlation, combined with inconsistent evidence that the core job characteristics promote performance, does not provide categorical support for the Job Characteristics Model. However, it might be that the basic principles are correct, but that insufficient attention has been given to contingency factors that influence the point at which work design affects employee performance. We return to this issue of contingencies later.

Another key work design theory is the *sociotechnical systems* (STS) *approach*. In contrast to the Job Characteristics Model, which is largely about the design of individual jobs, the sociotechnical systems approach has implications for the design of groups of jobs, specifically the design of autonomous work groups. Sociotechnical systems theory is a broad theory developed at the Tavistock Institute of Human Relations in London during the 1950s (e.g., Trist & Bamforth, 1951). One of the core propositions of this theory is that the social and technical subsystems in organizations should be designed in parallel with joint optimization of the two. Key principles of socio-technical systems theory (Cherns, 1976) relevant to work design include that methods of working should be minimally specified (i.e., method control); that variances in the work processes (e.g., breakdowns) should be handled at source by the employees rather than controlled by supervisors or specialists; and that roles should be multi-functional and multi-skilled. At the group level, these principles result in the design of autonomous work groups (also called 'self-managing teams', 'self-directed work groups', or other such terms) in which multi-skilled team members decide on their own methods of working and manage as many as possible of the day-to-day problems they encounter, with access to and authority over the resources needed to get the tasks done.

The sociotechnical systems approach certainly assumes performance gains of auto-nomous work groups, such as the flexibility gains resulting from multi-skilling or the efficiency gains resulting from teams responding to problems at the source rather than waiting for specialists. However, in terms of individual performance, the implications of sociotechnical systems theory are unclear. Relating socio-technical design to individual performance is antithetical to the systems approach underlying socio-technical theory, which necessarily considers the interaction of components beyond the individual level of analysis, and thus factors outside of any one person's control (Clegg, 2000). Not surprisingly, studies that have looked at sociotechnical systems work designs in relation to performance (e.g., Cohen, Ledford, & Spreitzer, 1996) have often focused on out-comes such as productivity or perceived effectiveness, both of which are broader than individual performance.

As well as the Job Characteristics Model and sociotechnical systems theory described so far, other theoretical perspectives also inform work design research (Parker & Wall, 1998). One that is particularly informative is *action theory*, a broad theory with a Ger-man origin (Hacker, Skell, & Straub, 1968; see Frese & Zapf, 1994, for an overview in

English). At its core is the idea that work is goal directed and action oriented. The action process involves a goal that motivates or 'pulls' the action. Thus actions proceed from a goal to a plan, to the execution, and to getting feedback. An action, however, is also regulated by cognition with the regulation taking place at different levels, from largely unconscious processing to ready-made action programs, to conscious problem solving and to a meta-cognitive level. In terms of the specific topic of work design and job performance, this emphasis on cognitive processes is an important contribution of action theory. Whereas the Job Characteristics Model emphasizes motivation, action theory points to more cognitive explanations for the performance-enhancing effects of work design.

A related consideration to understanding both the cognitive and motivational mechanisms of work design is *psychological empowerment theory* (Spreitzer, 1995; Thomas & Veldhouse, 1990). Contemporary research in this area has made a distinction between situational empowerment or empowerment practices (e.g., self-managing teams, participative management) and the cognitive motivational states (or 'assessments') that result from these practices. The latter include: impact, competence, meaningfulness, and choice. Similar to Hackman and Oldham's (1976) notion of knowledge of results, the impact cognition describes employees' awareness that they are "making a difference" (Thomas & Veldhouse, 1990, p. 672) by having the intended effect on the work environment. Competence is similar to Bandura's (1982) notion of self-efficacy, and represents the degree of confidence employees have in their own work-related skills. Meaningfulness is analogous to Hackman and Oldham's (1976) experienced meaningfulness, and is described by Thomas and Veldhouse (1990) as an individual's "intrinsic caring" (p. 672) about a work goal or project. Finally, choice captures the degree to which employees feel that their actions are self-determined, and therefore overlaps with the work characteristic of autonomy.

Although some of the dimensions of psychological empowerment are similar to previous conceptualizations (notably the JCM's psychological states), the approach adds value by exploring the motivational dimensions of interpersonal and organizational factors such as leadership (Spreitzer, De Janasz, & Quinn, 1999) and relationships with coworkers (Liden, Wayne, & Sparrowe, 2000). From the work design and performance perspective, this approach also contributes to theory by highlighting the cognitive-motivational state of self-efficacy as a potential mediator between job content and outcomes, and illustrates further the influence of contextual factors on the psychology of work design.

In summary, all of the major theories of work design propose that work enrichment will lead to enhanced performance, although the theories vary in the extent to which they focus more on individual work performance than on aggregate outcomes, and in their emphasis on particular mechanisms (motivational, cognitive or other) as explanations for why performance is enhanced.

WORK DESIGN AND INDIVIDUAL WORK PERFORMANCE: EMPIRICAL STUDIES

As described earlier, practitioners often assume that work enrichment will enhance performance, and such an assumption is entirely consistent with theoretical predictions. But what is the empirical evidence? On the whole, reviews of the literature show that much stronger and more consistent effects of work design have been obtained for attitudinal outcomes such as job satisfaction and internal work motivation than for job performance (see Griffin, Welsh, & Morehead, 1981; Fried & Ferris, 1987; Kelly, 1992; Kopelman, 1985). For example, based on their review of the link between perceived task characteristics and employee performance, Griffin et al. (1981) concluded that the link between performance and task perceptions is inconsistent. Some studies show no significant relationship between task perceptions and performance (e.g., Hackman & Oldham, 1976), while other studies have shown significant relationships (e.g., Griffin, 1982). In a later review, Stone (1986) found that job scope (i.e., a job with high levels of core work characteristics) was positively correlated to job performance in 11 field studies, but had a negative correlation in three laboratory studies. At about the same time, Fried and Ferris (1987) found a correlation of .23 between job scope and performance (see also Berlinger, Glick, & Rodgers, 1988).

One important point worth making is that many of the studies included in the above reviews and meta-analyses have methodological weaknesses. For example, the Fried and Ferris (1987) review focused mostly on laboratory studies that typically use students carrying out tasks of limited duration. Laboratory studies offer control and measurement advantages, but lack external validity (e.g., they typically ignore the economic exchange aspect of work; Kelly, 1992). Not surprisingly, comparisons of laboratory and field studies on work design show different results (Stone, 1986; Berlinger et al., 1988). Another problem is the dominance of cross-sectional field studies in work design research. These studies have the advantage of external validity, but do not allow conclusions to be made about the direction of causality. In many cases, the studies focus on naturally occurring variations in job content rather than change, yet an employee who has experienced work redesign is likely to react differently to the same job carried out by someone recruited into the post.

A methodological improvement is the longitudinal field survey or field experiment in which the effects of work redesign are tracked over time. Such studies offer advantages, although they often lack control groups which means that one cannot be certain whether work design or some other change caused the outcomes. Ideally, longitudinal field experiments involve comparing the effects of an intervention group (i.e., people who experience work design) against a control group (i.e., people who do not experience work design). Although providing a high level of methodological rigour, one problem with the longitudinal field experiments is that they have mostly been conducted over relatively short periods. An exception is the study by Griffin (1991) which investigated the effects of work redesign (e.g., increased skill variety and job autonomy) on the attitudes, perceptions, and performance of 526 bank tellers over a two-year time period. Job satisfaction and organizational commitment improved in the first six months, but then declined to initial levels. In contrast, performance (assessed via supervisory ratings) did not increase in the first six months after the work redesign but significantly improved after 24 and 48 months. This study therefore not only established a link between work redesign and performance, but it demonstrated the value of looking at patterns of change over extended periods. Had only a six-month study been conducted, for example, the conclusion would have been that the work redesign did not enhance performance.

In an effort to overcome the problems associated with weaker studies, Kelly (1992) reviewed 31 methodologically rigorous studies concerned with the link between performance or productivity and job perceptions, job satisfaction, or job motivation. Kelly selected field experiments (e.g., Griffin, 1991; Wall, Kemp, Jackson, & Clegg, 1986) using pre-test and post-test measurement, control and experimental groups, or both. Kelly found support for a link between job perception, intrinsic motivation, and work performance in only three out of the nine studies that contained data on all three variables. Productivity increases were larger with improvements in intrinsic motivation than without, but because the number of studies in each category was small, the difference was not statistically significant. Productivity gains were also higher when employees perceived an improvement in job content than when they did not, although again the difference was not significant. There was no general link between perceptions of improved job content and better job performance. Consistent with earlier reviews, and consistent with literature on participative decision making (e.g., Miller & Monge, 1986), Kelly (1992) concluded that the results for job satisfaction are more consistent with theoretical predictions than the results for job performance. Kelly proposed a 'twin-track' model of job redesign in which job satisfaction is suggested to be strongly influenced by perceptions of job content, whereas performance outcomes occur via other mechanisms, such as improved efficiency that arises from changing work methods, work intensification, changed expectancies (i.e., employees perceiving closer links between effort, performance, and valued rewards), and enhanced motivation because of the improved goal setting that often occurs at the same time as work redesign.

Since Kelly's (1992) review, there have been only a handful of methodologically rigorous studies that have examined the impact between work design and performance. Wall, Corbett, Martin, Clegg, and Jackson (1990) carried out an early study on machine operators making printed circuit boards. The study investigated the performance effects of training operators to diagnose the errors causing the downtime, and providing the workers with the discretion to correct (and prevent) these faults. There was a reduction in overall downtime after the intervention, supporting the idea that work redesign can enhance performance. In a follow-up study, Jackson and Wall (1991) focused on the mechanisms involved in the link between operator control and reduced machine downtime. One mechanism is that downtime is reduced because operators can respond more quickly than the specialists, who typically need to be called out. Another potential mechanism is that, over time, operators learn to anticipate and prevent faults from happening, which in turn leads to reduced downtime. Results supported the latter interpretation. Overall, there was an initial decrease in downtime of 20%, followed by a larger delayed decrease of 70%. The decreased amount of downtime remained at the same level between the intervention and a one-year follow-up, yet no change was found in the downtime per incident. This pattern of results suggested that operators had learnt to prevent the faults from occurring.

A later study (Wall, Jackson, & Davids, 1992) investigated the effects of introducing a new payment system linked to system performance, which resulted in operators taking greater responsibility for fixing machine faults. Even though there was no formal work redesign, evidence for initial gains in system performance pointed to quick response, with lagged gains attributable to operators actively anticipating and preventing faults (Wall et al., 1992). Continuing on a similar theme, Leach, Jackson, and Wall (2000) investigated the performance effects of giving the cutting and packaging operators greater feedback about their performance. Feedback was enhanced through regular discussion of faults with engineers and managers, and via the public display of information on system performance. The number of call-outs to specialists was reduced, with a complementary increase in machine utilization, lasting at least 40 weeks after the intervention. The researchers attributed these system improvements to an increase in operator knowledge and felt production responsibility, rather than intrinsic motivation, which did not change throughout the study period. Most recently, Leach, Wall, and Jackson (2000) demonstrated in the same empowerment intervention context that increases in self-efficacy and job knowledge occurred to a greater extent among novices than among expert employees.

A similar pattern of results is found in the broader psychological empowerment literature. Recent research suggests that certain elements of psychological empowerment such as competence (Spreitzer, Kizilos, & Nason, 1997), self-efficacy (Stajkovic & Luthans, 1998), and impact (Spreitzer et al., 1997) are positively associated with higher performance. However, the relationship between job content, psychological empowerment, and performance is less clear cut. Although Liden et al. (2000) also found that competence was related to higher individual performance, their hypothesis that the job characteristics–performance relationship was mediated by empowerment did not hold. Rather, they found that high-quality relationships between coworkers complemented the role of competence as a determinant of enhanced individual performance. From a work design and performance perspective, results like this indicate that joint consideration of the social and technical dimensions of work is needed before considering the extent to which work design alone contributes to performance.

In summary, there is evidence to suggest that work design can result in enhanced job performance, although the picture remains far from clear. Interestingly, the clearest results come from the more rigorous studies outlined above, which suggest that methodological inadequacies of recent study might contribute to this confusion. The inconsistent findings probably also reflect the fact that the link between work design and performance is both indirect and contingent, as findings from the recent psychological empowerment literature suggest. We expand these latter arguments below.

DEVELOPING THE RESEARCH AGENDA AND A PROPOSED MODEL

We propose that there are three important ways of helping to unscramble the relationship between work design and individual job performance: identifying why work design affects performance outcomes (i.e., considering mechanisms); investigating individual and organizational contingencies that mitigate or strengthen the link between work design and performance (i.e., considering moderators); and expanding the criterion of individual work performance. We address each of these in turn, and then make methodological suggestions to help to progress research along these avenues.

MECHANISMS BY WHICH WORK DESIGN AFFECTS PERFORMANCE

Work design is proposed to affect performance via particular mechanisms, and it is essential to specify and test these mechanisms if we are to better our understanding on this topic. As Kelly (1992, p. 154) claimed: "any evaluation of a job re-design theory must . . . seek to establish whether any observed improvements have actually been produced by these mechanisms, rather than by other factors not specified by theory."

To date, various mechanisms by which work design might affect performance have been proposed. However, as we have pointed out, little effort has been made to link these mechanisms systematically to the known determinants of job performance, such as knowledge/skill, motivation, and opportunity (Blumberg & Pringle, 1982). In this section, we describe known and potential psychological mechanisms underpinning the link between work design and performance according to these three categories of performance determinants. There are also non-psychological mechanisms that can explain the link between work design and productivity (e.g., efficiency gains, cost savings due to fewer supervisors, work intensification; Kelly, 1992), but psychological mechanisms are our focus here.

Motivation

The primary mechanism suggested by the JCM to explain why work design can enhance performance is that of motivated effort, or 'working harder' (e.g., Campion & McClelland, 1993; Wall & Martin, 1987). Need satisfaction and expectancy-based motivational explanations are, respectively, that people work better because they are doing a meaningful job that satisfies their need for growth, and because they expect that working hard will lead to good performance which in turn leads to higher-order needs being fulfilled. There are various similar motivational explanations, for example:

• performance is enhanced because people in enriched jobs are less motivated to behave in dysfunctional ways (e.g., avoiding boring tasks; Berlinger et al., 1988);
• job satisfaction is enhanced because employees in enriched jobs feel they are making better use of their skills (Cordery, Sevastos, & Parker, 1992);
• work redesign often encompasses the establishment of motivating goals (Kelly, 1992); and
• work redesign results in closer links between effort, good performance, and valued rewards (Kelly, 1992).

All of these motivational explanations suggest that work redesign leads to greater motivated effort, which in turn enhances individual work performance.

Another potential motivational mechanism underpinning the link between work design and performance is proactive motivation (Parker, 2000). This involves not just a willingness to put in more effort, but also a willingness to apply one's effort in proactive and flexible ways. In this vein, Porter and Lawler (1968) suggested that an individual's abilities and traits (i.e., capacity) set the upper limits for performance, while a person's role perception (i.e., his definition of successful performance of the job) determines whether the effort is turned into good performance. If the role perception is inappropriate, this could result in inappropriate performance (e.g., a police officer who sees her job as filling jail cells will have many false arrests). Proactive motivation is about having, among other things, a flexible role orientation in which the employees recognize the need to be flexible and self-starting to perform their job effectively (Parker, Wall, & Jackson, 1997).

Recent evidence suggests that work redesign can enhance proactive motivation, effectively reversing the 'learned helplessness' that has been suggested to arise from long-term exposure to job simplification (e.g., Karasek & Theorell, 1990). Parker et al. (1997) showed that when job autonomy was increased, employees developed a flexible and proactive role orientation. Employees moved away from a narrow 'that's not my job' mentality to an orientation in which they felt responsible for broader problems and recognized the importance of being proactive. Another study demonstrated how job autonomy, as well as improved communication quality, was associated with greater 'role breadth self-efficacy' (Parker, 1998). Employees perceived themselves to be more capable of carrying out a range of proactive, interpersonal and integrative tasks beyond prescribed technical requirements (e.g., designing improved procedures, presenting information to management, and meeting with customers or suppliers). Studies by Frese and colleagues have also shown that enhanced job complexity is associated with the display of more personal initiative (Frese, Kring, Soose, & Zempel, 1996), and that this association can be partly attributed to the development of greater work-related self-efficacy (Speier & Frese, 1997). Collectively, these studies demonstrate that work design has the potential to do more than simply motivate employees to put in greater effort; it can facilitate the development of more proactive motivational mind-sets and behaviours that are likely to be particular important in today's dynamic and flexible organizations.

The development of proactive motivation could also be indicative of a deeper-level change, or a change in motivating dispositions. It has been argued that work design can change people's temperament, especially over the long term (Frese, 1982; Volpert, 1975). In action theory, for example, "the human is seen as an active rather that a passive being who changes the world through work actions and thereby changes him or herself" (Frese & Zapf, 1994, p. 86). Considering personality development as an outcome of work design relates to the view that human development is a continuous process extending throughout the life span (e.g., Baltes & Schaie, 1973), and the view that personality and the environment interact to bring about change in both elements (Endler & Magnusson, 1976).

Proposing that work design can affect stable personality traits is a rather contentious proposition, and might indeed contradict the very definition of personality for some. To date, there is no evidence that work design affects any of the well-established 'Big Five' personality dimensions. However, it is plausible to expect that work design might affect some more specific individual aspects traditionally considered to be relatively stable, such as growth need strength, need for achievement, and self-esteem (Parker & Wall, 1998). For example, if an employee is in a simplified job for many years, the person is likely to adapt his/her aspirations for growth to the situation. Similarly, over time, an employee placed in a work group might find his/her preference for interdependent working changing, depending on the nature of the tasks and rewards (Wageman, 1995). Redesigning employees' work therefore might result in those employees developing higher growth needs or need for belonging (Baumeister & Leary, 1995). There is some evidence, albeit fairly scarce, that supports the notion of changing dispositions. Frese (1982) cited studies showing that simplified jobs can lead to a sense of resignation, apathy, and a reduced level of aspiration. Brousseau (1983) also found links between job scope and changes in active orientation. More recently, Wageman (1995) has shown that individual differences in preference for autonomy come into congruence over time based on the tasks and rewards faced by employees in work groups. Similarly, as we described above, there is evidence that passive motivational states, which could be quite stable, can be reversed via the introduction of work redesign (Parker, 1998; Parker et al., 1997).

The idea that work design can affect employee personality implies spillover effects of work design into people's non-working lives (Parker & Wall, 1998). Frese and Zapf (1994) suggested that complex work environments facilitate the development of long-range goals that could then transfer to non-work activities. Related to these arguments, some studies have shown that employees in challenging jobs are most active in leisure and other activities outside of work (e.g., Goiten & Seashore, 1980). Crouter (1984) showed that participation at work increased women's desire for participation in decision-making within the home. These studies are consistent with the idea that work design might, in some individuals, affect aspects that have traditionally been considered quite stable. Work design might thus have more profound and long-lasting motivational effects than we have assumed until now.

Acquisition and development of knowledge and skill

The notion that work design promotes skill acquisition and development is a reasonably long-standing one. By increasing job variety, for example, individuals learn a broader array of skills that can be flexibly deployed. The idea that enriched work design can have cognitive implications has also been around for some time. For example, based on action theory, Frese and Zapf (1994) argued that job autonomy leads to a process of "intellectual penetration" (p. 43) from which employees develop a deeper understanding of the task and its requirements. They suggested: "people who have control can do better because they can choose adequate strategies to deal with the situation. They can plan ahead, they are more flexible in case something goes wrong" (p. 77). This resonates with the set of work design-performance studies by Wall and colleagues reviewed earlier, which show that work design can result in employees developing more in-depth and anticipatory knowledge about their work tasks which, in turn, enhances performance.

As well as developing more in-depth knowledge about a particular machine or task, it is also likely that work design facilitates the development of broader and more integrated knowledge and perspectives about the entire work system and its context, such as the requirements of customers, the reasons for supply problems, and how departments coordinate their activities (Parker et al., 1997). Lawler (1992, p. 85), for example, reasoned that enhancing autonomy promotes improvements in performance "because employees have a broader perspective on the work process and as a result can catch errors and make corrections that might have gone undetected in more traditional work designs in which employees lacked the knowledge to recognize them". Consistent with these arguments, Parker and Axtell (2001) showed that job autonomy was associated with greater integrated understanding (e.g., understanding about other departments, customers, etc.), which was in turn associated with employees being more able to adopt the perspective of their internal suppliers.

Finally, it is also possible that work design can, over the long term, affect cognitive development. In a set of studies investigating this idea, Kohn and Schooler (1978, 1982) showed that self-directed work leads to an increase in intellectual flexibility (i.e., an individual's ability to deal with complex cognitive problems). Schleicher (1973, cited in Frese & Zapf, 1994) also reported an association between work design and intelligence. Thus, as well as changing the content of what people know, work design can potentially lead to changes in the way people structure and organize their knowledge. Put another way, work design might lead to employees becoming more 'expert-like' in the way they think; for example, the way that knowledge is interrelated, the way they perceive and represent problems, and the problem-solving strategies they use. Consistent with this idea, Leach et al. (2000) found that the enhanced feedback associated with work redesign resulted in novice operators developing greater cognitive complexity (i.e., more differentiated cognitive structures) about their machinery.

Opportunity

In relation to individual performance, Blumberg and Pringle (1982) argued that motivation, knowledge, and skills are insufficient on their own, and that individuals also need an opportunity to apply their knowledge, skill, and motivation. Opportunity can be constrained by demarcations, tight supervision, technology, electronic performance monitoring (which is essentially a combination of technology and tight supervision), and other such features of the work environment and culture. Work enrichment can reduce or remove these constraints, as suggested by the 'quick response' mechanism (Wall et al., 1992). This term describes the situation in which employees have the opportunity, via enhanced autonomy, to solve problems more quickly using their pre-existing knowledge rather than having to wait for a supervisor or specialist. The more variances and uncertainties there are to deal with, such as where there is advanced manufacturing technology, the more important the quick response mechanism is likely to be (Walton & Susman, 1987).

We propose work design can also affect opportunity in another longer-term way: role expansion. The idea is that work design can result in employees' expanding their jobs—or stretching the boundary of their jobs to include additional tasks and responsibilities—thereby continually developing opportunity for applying their knowledge, skill, and motivation. Other terms that have been used to express the concept of role expansion include emergent roles (Ilgen & Hollenbeck, 1991), task revision (Staw & Boettger, 1990), job crafting (Wrzesniewski & Dutton, 2001), and role innovation (Van Maanen & Schein, 1979). One possibility is that the process of role expansion might occur through the mediating processes of knowledge, skill, and motivation. For example, enriched work could lead to increased proactive motivation, such as greater role breadth self-efficacy, which in turn leads individuals to take on more emergent task elements and craft a broader role.

MODERATORS OF THE WORK DESIGN AND PERFORMANCE RELATIONSHIP

The inconsistencies in research findings regarding the link between work design and performance could be because work designs promote performance for some individuals, or in some situations, but not in all cases. We now turn to explore this idea of individual and organizational contingencies affecting work design–performance links.

Individual contingencies

The primary individual factor considered in relation to work design is growth need strength (GNS). Meta-analytic reviews by Fried and Ferris (1987) and Spector (1985) concluded that GNS moderated the relationship between work characteristics and performance. However, Loher, Noe, Moeller, & Fitzgerald (1985) in their meta-analysis found that GNS did not moderate the relationship between work characteristics and performance. Since then, Oldham (1996) speculated that this inconsistency might have arisen because the different reviews relied on different interpretations of GNS (e.g., Spector, 1985, included need for achievement and need for autonomy as proxies for GNS). A further explanation of the inconsistencies is that GNS is important in some circumstances but not necessarily in others. For example, if work enrichment is expected to enhance performance primarily via enhancing knowledge, then the GNS of employees might be of minimal consequence.

A whole range of other individual variables has also been considered as moderators (Wall & Martin, 1987), including the need for autonomy, Protestant Work Ethic, role stress, extrinsic satisfaction, and job longevity. However, as with the research on GNS, the outcomes of these studies have been rather inconsistent. Kemp and Cook (1983) proposed that, rather than trying to find moderators that are replicable across situations, we should aim to "specify the conditions under which moderators are important" (p. 896). Parker and Wall (1998) suggested several individual-difference variables that could be important moderators of work design that have been neglected, including self-efficacy, tolerance of role ambiguity, change orientation, proactive personality, and preference for group working. For example, because job redesign usually involves looser and more emergent job descriptions, it could be hypothesized that individuals who cannot tolerate ambiguity (i.e., who prefer more tightly prescribed jobs) will experience fewer benefits of work enrichment. Related to this idea, Parker and Sprigg (1999) found that employees with a more proactive personality responded more favourably to 'active' jobs (i.e., jobs with high autonomy and high demands) than employees with a more passive personality. Whether proactive personality moderates the work design–performance relationship is unknown. Demographic variables such as age, gender, ethnicity, as well as other forms of diversity, could also moderate the effect of work design on outcomes (Parker & Wall, 1998).

Organizational contingencies

In the same way that one would expect individuals to respond differently to work design, it is pretty clear that the effects of work design will vary depending on the context. Adopting this approach, Cummings and Blumberg (1987) proposed three organizational factors that influence the choice and effects of work design over and above individual factors: technical interdependence, technical uncertainty, and environmental uncertainty.

Technical interdependence concerns the degree of required cooperation to make a product or service. In situations where interdependence is low, such as the job of a personal secretary, Cummings and Blumberg (1987) recommended individual job redesigns such as job enrichment. However, if technical interdependence is high, and employees need to cooperate and share information to get their job done, work should be designed at the group level so that members can coordinate interrelated tasks. The implication is that a mismatch between the form of work design and the degree of interdependence will lead to underperformance. The premise that group forms of work design, or team working, are most appropriate when there is interdependence between tasks is widely accepted within the team effectiveness literature (e.g., Wageman, 1995; Liden, Wayne, & Bradway, 1997). However, this does not mean that organizations necessarily act in accordance with the premise. In the content of a wire-making company, Sprigg, Jackson, and Parker (2000) reported that team working was successful within the wire rope-making area where employees could cooperate to make a wire rope, but it was not successful in the wire-drawing area because there was little need or opportunity for employees to cooperate. Statistical analyses showed that it was the lack of interdependence in the wire rope-making area that explained the differential outcomes.

Cummings and Blumberg (1987) also suggested the importance of technical uncertainty, or the amount of information processing and decision-making required when executing the task, and environmental uncertainty, or the extent to which the environment is unpredictable and dynamic. Others have also identified the importance of the degree of uncertainty (also referred to as 'operational uncertainty' and 'process uncertainty') in the work environment in shaping work design decisions (e.g., Wall & Jackson, 1995; Wall, Cordery, & Clegg, in press.) The idea is that, the greater the degree of uncertainty, the more important an enriched work design. A highly uncertain situation means there are many decisions to be made and many information-processing requirements, hence control cannot be achieved through direct supervision or the routinization of rules and procedures (Ouchi, 1977). In these cases, it is argued that decision-making rights should be devolved to the lowest level possible. These work design-related arguments parallel those introduced in the organizational theory literature over 40 years ago. Burns and Stalker (1961) observed that mechanistic structures worked best in stable and predictable situations, whereas organic structures with decentralized decision making were most suited to uncertain and dynamic environments.

The implication from the above is that job redesign involving enhanced autonomy is most likely to lead to performance gains where uncertainty is high. The study by Wall et al. (1990), described earlier, provided some support for this suggestion. In addition to showing a linking between increased operator job autonomy and performance, they found that the gains were greatest for highly uncertain machines that were used to insert more delicate components. There was little gain in performance for low production uncertainty machines. A study in a quite different context (i.e., autonomous group working within water treatment plants), showed the same pattern of most performance improvement in areas with high production uncertainty (Cordery, Wright, Morrison, & Wall, in press).

One explanation for these findings is that it is in uncertain contexts where the proposed knowledge-based mechanism underpinning the link between work design and performance applies (Wall & Jackson, 1995; Parker & Wall, 1998). When uncertainty is low, this essentially means that problems are relatively predictable and the 'one best way' of solving them can be identified and specified. However, in highly uncertain settings, problems are less predictable and it is not necessarily clear how to solve them. In other words, there are higher information-processing requirements. In such a situation, autonomy will allow employees to use existing knowledge and acquire new knowledge. This same argument can also be applied to some of the other proposed mechanisms. For example, it is in highly uncertain situations that employee proactivity and cognitive complexity is most likely to be critical for individuals' effective performance (Parker, 2000). Nevertheless, although contextual performance might be more important under complex and uncertain condition, situational constraints such as tight deadlines or safety-critical situations might force employees to focus on task-related behaviours instead (Griffin, Neal, & Neale, 2000).

One proviso that does not appear among existing evidence about work design, uncertainty, and performance is consideration of the relative maturity of the work design structure. It is conceivable that the performance of employees involved in less well-developed work design initiatives might suffer under conditions of high uncertainty, especially if employees are not given adequate support. Employees who are only just adapting to increases in autonomy might benefit from more stable technological conditions under which to develop on-the-job knowledge, participate in formal training, and gain confidence in their expanded core tasks. In high variance conditions, if employees are to be successful in utilizing control to enhance performance, they are likely to need a great deal of support and coaching in the early stages of the redesign. It is important to investigate the effect of the implementation stage of the work redesign on the link between work design, uncertainty, and performance.

In addition to interdependence and uncertainty, there are other organizational factors that are likely to affect whether job redesign leads to enhanced performance. Some of these factors pertain to the process of introducing work redesign, such as the extent to which employees participate in the work redesign, the consideration given to various stakeholders (e.g., supervisors, unions, middle managers), and the degree of leader support for the change initiative. For example, if there is insufficient support from senior management for the work redesign, the so-called work redesign will have little or no impact on job content and therefore will not affect outcomes (such as in the case of 'pseudo-empowerment'). Although there is not a great deal of research investigating the process of work design, one of the clearest messages to emerge on this topic is the importance of involving people who will be affected by the work redesign in its planning and implementation (Davis & Wacker, 1987; Parker & Wall, 1998). A participative change process can lead to greater acceptance and ownership of the work redesign and a higher quality end solution (e.g., the work redesign is carried through for a reasonable trial period). It is also consistent with the sociotechnical principle of compatibility; that is, if the objectives of work redesign are to create a system capable of adapting to change and using the creative capacities of people, then the design process should reflect this (Cherns, 1976). There is some, albeit not much, evidence of the importance of participation in work redesign (Seeborg, 1978; Parker, Myers, & Wall, 1995). Generally, while there is a vast literature on organizational change and how it should be managed, the attention given to work redesign processes has been rather limited and researchers have urged greater attention to this issue (e.g., Oldham, 1996).

Work redesign is typically considered a multi-system intervention in which changes to multiple systems (control, human resources, technological, information systems) need to be made in parallel with changes to work organization for it to be effective (e.g., Oldham & Hackman, 1980; Parker & Wall, 1998). The delicacy with which parts of a system interrelate is an organizational reality that is often conveniently ignored by work design research reports. As such, a set of contingency factors vital to getting a more complete understanding of work redesign is the extent to which supporting changes are made, such as providing employees with adequate training, designing appropriate reward systems, ensuring necessary performance feedback systems, and providing adequate staffing levels. If these wider systemic changes do not occur, this can inhibit the extent of real change in job content or affect the degree to which enriched job content leads to performance outcomes. As an example of the latter, if employees are given greater autonomy to make decisions but they are not given adequate training to make informed decisions, then the work redesign is likely to be ineffective and could even have detrimental consequences for performance. Furthermore, if multiple elements of the larger system interfere with one another (e.g., providing training for staff in the absence of sufficient staff to cover employees attending that training), then the redesign becomes counter-productive and employee resistance to further changes might result. Although the potential moderating influence of these factors on the work design–performance link is highly plausible, they have rarely been categorized or systematically investigated in the work design literature.

EXPANDING THE CRITERION OF INDIVIDUAL WORK PERFORMANCE

Inconsistent results from studies investigating the link between work design and performance might also have arisen because different indicators of performance have been used in different studies. To provide a fair test of the link between work design and performance, there is a need to expand the criterion domain, not only by extending the time frame over which a particular performance criterion is assessed (some performance effects are likely to be evident in the longer term), but also in terms of broadening what is considered as performance. For example, when examining the effects of work design on performance, there has been a tendency to focus on production-related indicators such as the amount produced, machine use, or cost savings. However, as Dunphy and Bryant (1996) pointed out, work redesigns can add value in ways that are not typically assessed, such as by making gradual improvements to work processes, by enhancing quality, and by responsiveness to customers. Some of these performance effects are likely to be evident in the longer term, we encourage future work design researches to capture potential change over varying lengths of time.

In terms of individual work performance, consistent with advances in the performance literature, it is important to consider how work design affects not just task performance (e.g., amount produced) but also contextual performance (e.g., helping and cooperating with colleagues), proactive behaviors, and adaptive performance. These types of discretionary behaviors are increasingly seen as critical in today's flexible organizations where, for example, employees need to be willing to work flexibly, think for themselves, make suggestions, and carry out an emergent and changing work role (e.g., Frese et al., 1996; Parker, 2000; Pulakos et al., 2000). We also suggest considering workplace safety as another dimension of individual work performance. Safety is increasingly being recognized as a performance outcome (e.g., Griffin & Neal, 2000; Wood, Barling, Lasaosa, Turner, & Parker, 2000), and initial evidence suggests that work design characteristics such as job autonomy can affect safety (e.g., Shannon, Mayr, & Haines, 1997).

Expanding the criterion of individual work performance opens up the possibility that work design might have different effects depending on the type of performance outcome investigated, as well as the possibility that these effects might occur via different mechanisms. For example, the motivational mechanism proposed to underpin the link between work design and performance might apply most strongly to contextual performance, as suggested by Neal and Griffin (1999), whereas a cognitive mechanism might apply most strongly to task performance. Expanding the criterion domain also highlights additional mechanisms by which work design might affect performance, such as the possibility that work design enhances proactive motivation which in turn leads employees to be more proactive and innovative.

SUMMARY OF RESEARCH AGENDA AND A MODEL TO GUIDE FURTHER INQUIRY

Based on the above discussion, Figure 4.1 shows a suggested model linking enriched work design and individual work performance. This model draws on, and aims to integrate, existing models of work performance (e.g., Blumberg & Pringle, 1982; Campbell et al., 1993; Neal & Griffin, 1999) as well as existing models of work design (e.g., Wall & Jackson, 1995; Parker & Wall, 1998).

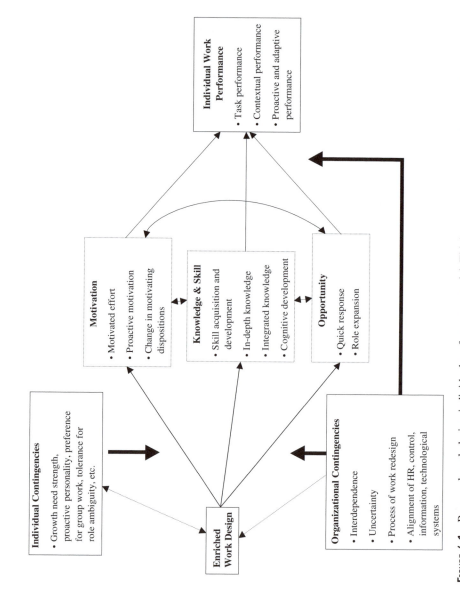

FIGURE 4.1 Proposed work design-individual performance model. Thick arrows represent moderating influences.

There are five key features of model. First, the outcome variable is described as *individual work performance* rather than individual job performance to signify that an employee's performance can extend beyond the execution of specified tasks in a job description to include contextual, proactive, and adaptive behaviors that support the wider work environment. Second, the model proposes that enriched work design influences individual work performance via three key categories of *psychological mechanisms*: *motivation* (motivated effort, proactive motivation, change in motivating dispositions), *knowledge and skill* (skill acquisition and development, in-depth knowledge, integrated knowledge, and cognitive development), and *opportunity* (quick response, job crafting/ role revision). Although it is likely that there are stronger links between some of these mechanisms and the different types of work performance as proposed by Neal and Griffin (1999), these more specific suggestions are not depicted in this initial version of the model. The mechanisms are also suggested to influence each other. For example, if a person acquires greater knowledge about customers, then that is likely to enhance his/her proactive motivation. Likewise, the greater the opportunity arising from enriched work design, the more learning and knowledge development that is likely to occur; and the more learning and development that occurs, the more roles might be expanded.

Third, we propose that the link between work design and performance is moderated by *individual* and *organizational contingencies*. We suggest that individual contingencies will primarily influence the links between enriched work design and performance determinants (i.e., knowledge/skill, motivation, and opportunity). For example, if an individual has a low tolerance for role ambiguity, enriched work design might have less impact on his/her motivation than if he/she had tolerance for role ambiguity. Similarly, a proactive individual might take advantage of the opportunities offered by work redesign to a greater extent than a more passive individual. It is possible that individual contingencies will also moderate the relationship between mediators and performance, although we see these moderating influences as likely to be weaker than those affecting links between enriched work design and performance determinants. The model also shows the proposed moderating influence of organizational and contextual variables on the links between work design and the performance determinants (e.g., enriched work design accompanied by poor training is less likely to promote knowledge development than if adequate training is in place), as well as the links between the performance determinants and individual work performance (e.g., proactive motivation is more likely to be important for effective performance in highly uncertain situations than in less uncertain environments).

Fourth, the double-arrow dotted path from enriched work design to individual contingencies depicts, first, that enriched work design might affect the development of relatively stable individual variables (e.g., growth need strength, proactive personality, cognitive development) which in turn act as moderators; and, second, that individual differences might enhance or inhibit the degree to which work is enriched. For example, employees with a proactive personality are more likely to actively influence the work environment to enhance their job autonomy.

Fifth, the arrow from organizational contingencies to enriched work design depicts that enriched work design is potentially more possible and feasible in some situations compared to others (e.g., higher levels of uncertainty create more scope for enrichment; some forms of technology such as assembly lines inhibit the potential for enriching jobs).

METHODOLOGICAL SUGGESTIONS FOR FURTHER RESEARCH

Work design research has often been criticized on methodological grounds (e.g., Parker & Wall, 1998). Some key issues include the use of perceptual measures of work characteristics rather than objective measures, and the prevalence of problematic research designs (e.g., laboratory studies using students, cross-sectional field studies). These criticisms also apply to this more specific topic of work design and individual performance, although we pointed to some studies that have moved the area forward through their rigorous designs and their use of organizational samples, such as the longitudinal study by Griffin (1991) and the studies in the last decade by Wall and colleagues in Sheffield. Ideally, of course, we need not just longitudinal designs, but designs that allow assessment of long-term, as well as short-term, effects of work design on performance. Some of the more learning-based and developmental changes we proposed are only likely to occur in the long term, and thus might be invisible to cross-sectional studies.

A notorious difficulty for this research is the assessment of performance. One approach is to use supervisor or peer ratings of employees' behaviours (e.g., Griffin, 1991) or gather performance appraisal data. However, although better than self-ratings, biases can occur in these ratings, such as observational biases that arise because supervisors cannot observe the individual at all times, or actor–observer biases such as when actors attribute good performance to their own behaviour and observers attribute good performance to external factors. Another issue is that expectations for performance can increase over time, making it difficult to establish whether changes in actual behaviour have occurred. Using more objective indicators of performance (e.g., amount produced, machine utilization, customer satisfaction) overcomes some of the problems associated with performance ratings, especially in combination with rigorous research designs. Nevertheless, measures of objective job performance are typically influenced by more than individual performance, and many of these factors are beyond the control of the employee (e.g., quality of raw materials, timeliness of supplies, technology). In addition, these measures are often rather narrow and short term, reflecting the status quo rather than performance requirements for the future.

It is clear there is no one best measure of individual job performance, which highlights the value of obtaining multiple sources of data (e.g., appraisals, objective performance data, archival safety data) and attempting to triangulate the findings. Developments in other fields, such as new methods of assessing customer satisfaction (e.g., the use of mystery shoppers) could usefully be exploited. Likewise, developments in statistical techniques (e.g., hierarchical linear modeling procedures) allow the teasing out of effects at different levels—individual, group, and organizational—which will help researchers to disaggregate the effects of work design on individual work performance from broader consequences. This endeavor will also be helped by the increasing use of information technologies to collect information on employees' work performance (e.g., Horton, Buck, Waterson, & Clegg, 2000).

A final methodological point concerns the independent variable; that is, when evaluating work redesigns, it is often hard to isolate the effects of a change in job content from other changes implemented simultaneously (e.g., improved communication, changed reward systems, increased training). Even with the Sheffield field studies, which are rigorous in many other respects, we cannot be sure that the positive performance effects arose solely because of changes in job content. In all likelihood, as we have proposed, work design requires changes in supporting systems to be effective. However, to date, we have not been particularly effective at systematically documenting or analyzing these complementary and supporting changes that often occur in parallel with changes in work content.

CONCLUSION

We started the chapter by describing how work design initiatives are currently very popular, at least nominally, because it is believed there will be dramatic performance benefits. Our analysis suggests that there is no clear cut or definitive case that work enrichment enhances performance. However, there is sufficient evidence to suggest that work enrichment promotes better performance in some cases, and for some individuals. Indeed, given that most organizations are becoming more dynamic and uncertain as a result of technological and market forces, and that uncertainty appears to be a conducive context for work design-related performance benefits, it is likely that the role of work design as a driver of performance will become more salient. Some of the ways enriched work design can promote performance include that it increases employee motivation to work harder and to be more proactive, promotes the acquisition and development of knowledge and skills, and provides the opportunity for employees to apply existing knowledge, skill, and motivation. Moving the area forward now requires both more detailed theory and more systematic rigorous empirical work. To this end, we have proposed a model to guide future inquiry that has an expanded performance criterion and that specifies mechanisms by which work design might affect performance and some contingency factors that might mitigate or enhance this relationship.

ACKNOWLEDGEMENT

We would like to thank Julian Barling, Mark Griffin, Toby Wall, and Helen Williams for constructive feedback on earlier drafts of this chapter. We also wish to acknowledge the financial support of the Australian AGSM Centre for Corporate Change, the UK Health and Safety Executive, and the Social Sciences and Humanities Research Council of Canada.

REFERENCES

Baltes, P. B., & Schaie, K. W. (1973). *Lifespan developmental psychology: Personality and socialization*. New York: Academic Press.

Bandura, A. (1982). Self-efficacy mechanism in human agency. *American Psychologist*, **37**, 122–147.

Baumeister, R. F., & Leary, M. R. (1995). The need to belong: Desire for interpersonal attachments as a fundamental human motivation. *Psychological Bulletin*, **117**, 497–529.

Berlinger, L. R., Glick, W. H., & Rodgers, R. C. (1988). Job enrichment and performance improvements. In J. P. Campbell & R. J. Campbell (Eds.), *Productivity in organizations*. San Francisco: Jossey-Bass.

Blumberg, M., & Pringle, C. (1982). The missing opportunity in organisational research. *Academy of Management Review*, **7**, 360–369.

Borman, W. C., & Motowidlo, S. J. (1993). Expanding the criteria domain to include elements of contextual performance. In N. Schmitt & W. C. Borman (Eds.), *Personnel selection in organizations* (pp. 71–98). San Francisco: Jossey-Bass.

Brousseau, K. R. (1983). Toward a dynamic model of job–person relationships: Findings, research questions, and implications for work system design. *Academy of Management Review*, **8**, 33–45.

Burns, T., & Stalker, G. M. (1961). *The management of innovation*. London: Tavistock.

Campbell, J. P., McCloy, R. A., Oppler, S. H., & Sager, C. E. (1993). A theory of performance. In N. Schmitt, W. C. Borman, & Associates (Eds.), *Personnel selection in organizations* (pp. 35–70). San Francisco: Jossey-Bass.

Campion, M. A., & McClelland, C. L. (1993). Follow-up and extension of the inter-disciplinary costs and benefits of enlarged jobs. *Journal of Applied Psychology*, **78**, 339–351.

Cherns, A. B. (1976). The principles of socio-technical design. *Human Relations*, **29**, 783–792.

Clegg, C. W. (2000). Sociotechnical principles for system design. *Applied Ergonomics*, **31**, 463–477.

Cohen, S. G., Ledford, Jr., G. E., & Spreitzer, G. M. (1996). A predictive model of self-managing work team effectiveness. *Human Relations*, **49**, 643–676.

Cordery, J. L., Sevastos, P. P., & Parker, S. K. (1992, July). *Job design, skill utilization, and psychological well-being at work: Preliminary test of a model*. Paper presented at XXV International Congress of Psychology, Brussels.

Cordery, J. L., Wright, B. M., Morrison, D., & Wall, T. D. (in press). Production uncertainty as a moderator of the effectiveness of self-managing work team interventions: A field study. *Academy of Management Journal*.

Crouter, A. C. (1984). Participative work as an influence on human development. *Journal of Applied Developmental Psychology*, **5**, 71–90.

Cummings, T. G., & Blumberg, M. (1987). Advanced manufacturing technology and work design. In T. D. Wall, C. W. Clegg, & N. J. Kemp (Eds.), *The human side of advanced manufacturing technology* (pp. 37–60). Chichester: Wiley.

Davis, L. E., & Wacker, G. J. (1987). Job design. In G. Salvendy (Ed.), *Handbook of human factors* (pp. 431–445). New York: Wiley.

Dunphy, D., & Bryant, B. (1996). Teams: Panaceas or prescriptions for improved performance. *Human Relations*, **49**, 677–699.

Endler, N. S., & Magnusson, D. (1976). *Interactional psychology and personality*. Washington, DC: Hemisphere.

Frese, M. (1982). Occupational socialisation and psychological development: An under emphasised perspective in industrial psychology. *Journal of Occupational Psychology*, **55**, 209–224.

Frese, M., Kring, W., Soose, A., & Zempel, J. (1996). Personal initiative at work: Differences between East and West Germany. *Academy of Management Journal*, **39**, 37–63.

Frese, M., & Zapf, D. (1994). Action as the core of work psychology: A German approach. In H. C. Triandis, M. D. Dunnette, & J. M. Hough (Eds.), *Handbook of industrial and organisational psychology*, Vol. 4 (2nd edn., pp. 271–340). Palo Alto, CA: Consulting Psychologists Press.

Fried, Y., & Ferris, G. R. (1987). The validity of the job characteristics model: A review and meta-analysis. *Personnel Psychology*, **40**, 287–322.

Gerhart, B. (1987). How important are dispositional factors as deterimants of job satisfaction? Implications for job design and other personnel programs. *Journal of Applied Psychology*, **72**, 366–373.

Goiten, B., & Seashore, S. (1980). *Worker participation: A national survey report*. Ann Arbor, MI: Survey Research Center, University of Michigan.

Griffin, M. A., & Neal, A. (2000). Perceptions of safety at work: A framework for linking safety climate to safety performance, knowledge, and motivation. *Journal of Occupational Health Psychology*, **5**, 347–358.

Griffin, M. A., Neal, A., & Neale, M. (2000). The contribution of task performance and contextual performance to effectiveness: Investigating the role of situational constraints. *Applied Psychology: An International Review*, **49**, 517–533.

Griffin, R. W. (1982). Perceived task characteristics and employee productivity and satisfaction. *Human Relations*, **35**, 927–938.

Griffin, R. W. (1991). Effects of work redesign on employee perceptions, attitudes and behaviours: A long-term investigation. *Academy of Management Journal*, **34**, 425–435.

Griffin, R. W., Welsh, M. A., & Morehead, G. (1981). Perceived task characteristics and employee performance: A literature review. *Academy of Management Review*, **6**, 655–664.

Hacker, W., Skell, W., & Straub, W. (1968). *Arbeitspsychologie und wissenschaftlich-techische revolution*. Berlin: Deutscher Verlag der Wissenschaften.

Hackman, J. R., & Oldham, G. (1976). Motivation through the design of work: Test of a theory. *Organizational Behavior and Human Performance*, **16**, 250–279.

Herzberg, F., Mausner, B., & Snyderman, B. (1959). *The motivation to work*. New York: Wiley.

Horton, R. P., Buck, T., Waterson, P. E., & Clegg, C. W. (2000). Explaining intranet use with the Technology Acceptance Model. *Journal of Information Technology*, **16**, 237–249.

Iaffaldano, M. T., & Muchinsky, P. M. (1985). Job satisfaction and job performance: A meta-analysis. *Psychological Bulletin*, **97**, 251–273.

Ilgen, D. R., & Hollenbeck, J. R. (1991). The structure of work: Job design and roles. In M. D. Dunnette & L. M. Hough (Eds.), *Handbook of industrial and organizational psychology* (2nd edn., pp. 165–207). Palo Alto, CA: Consulting Psychologists.

Jackson, P. R., & Wall, T. D. (1991). How does operator control enhance performance of advanced manufacturing technology? *Ergonomics*, **34**, 1301–1311.

Karasek, R. A., & Theorell, T. (1990). *Healthy work: Stress, productivity, and the reconstruction of working life*. New York: Basic Books.

Kelly, J. E. (1992). Does job re-design theory explain job re-design outcomes? *Human Relations*, **45**, 753–774.

Kemp, N. J., & Cook, J. D. (1983). Job longevity and growth need strength as joint moderators of the task design–job satisfaction relationship. *Human Relations*, **36**, 883–898.

Kirkman, B. L., & Rosen, B. (2000). Powering up teams. *Organizational Dynamics*, **23**, 48–66.

Kohn, M. L., & Schooler, C. (1978). The reciprocal effects of the substantive complexity of work on intellectual complexity: A longitudinal assessment. *American Journal of Sociology*, **48**, 24–52.

Kohn, M. L., & Schooler, C. (1982). Job conditions and personality: A longitudinal assessment of their reciprocal effects. *American Journal of Sociology*, **87**, 1257–1286.

Kopelman, R. E. (1985). Job redesign and productivity: A review of the evidence. *National Productivity Review*, **4**, 237–255.

Lawler, E. E. (1992). *The ultimate advantage: Creating the high involvement organization*. San Francisco: Jossey-Bass.

Leach, D. J., Jackson, P. R., & Wall, T. D. (2001). Realising the potential of empowerment: The impact of a feedback intervention on the performance of complex technology. Ergonomics, **44**, 870–886.

Leach, D. J., Wall, T. D., & Jackson, P. R. (2001). Operator empowerment and the performance of complex technology: Development of a measure of job knowledge and examination of mechanisms. *Manuscript submitted for publication*.

Liden, R. C., Wayne, S. J., & Bradway, L. K. (1997). Task interdependence as a moderator of the relation between group control and performance. *Human Relations*, **50**, 169–181.

Liden, R. C., Wayne, S. J., & Sparrowe, R. T. (2000). An examination of the mediating role of psychological empowerment on the relations between job, interpersonal relationships, and work outcomes. *Journal of Applied Psychology*, **85**, 407–416.

Loher, B. T., Noe, R. A., Moeller, N. L., & Fitzgerald, M. P. (1985). A meta-analysis of the relation of job characteristics to job satisfaction. *Journal of Applied Psychology*, **70**, 280–289.

Miller, K. I., & Monge, P. R. (1986). Participation, satisfaction and productivity: A meta-analytic review. *Academy of Management Journal*, **29**, 727–753.

Mohrman, S. A., & Cohen, S. G. (1995). When people get out of the box: New relationships, new systems. In A. Howard (Ed.), *The changing nature of work* (pp. 365–410). San Francisco: Jossey-Bass.

Morrison, E. W., & Phelps, C. C. (1999). Taking charge at work: Extra-role efforts to initiate workplace change. *Academy of Management Journal*, **42**, 403–419.

Motowidlo, S. J., & Van Scotter, J. R. (1994). Evidence that task performance should be distinguished from contextual performance. *Journal of Applied Psychology*, **79**, 475–480.

Neal, A., & Griffin, M. A. (1999). Developing a theory of performance for human resource management. *Asia Pacific Journal of Human Resources*, **37**, 44–60.

Oldham, G. R., & Hackman, J. R. (1980). Work design in the organisational context. In B. Staw & L. L. Cummings (Eds.), *Research in organizational behavior*, Vol. 2. Greenwich, CT: JAI Press.

Oldham, G. (1976). Job characteristics and internal motivation: The moderating effect of interpersonal and individual variables. *Human Relations*, **29**, 559–569.

Oldham, G. R. (1996). Job Design. In C. L. Cooper & I. T. Robertson (Eds.), *International review of industrial and organizational psychology*, Vol. 11 (pp. 33–60). Wiley.

Ostroff, C. (1992). The relationship between satisfaction, attitudes, and performance: An organization level analysis. *Journal of Applied Psychology*, **77**, 963–974.

Ouchi, W. G. (1977). The relationship between organisational structure and organisational control. *Administrative Science Quarterly*, **22**, 95–113.

Parker, S. K. (1998). Role breadth self-efficacy: Relationship with work enrichment and other organizational practices. *Journal of Applied Psychology*, **83**, 835–852.

Parker, S. K. (2000). From passive to proactive motivation: The importance of flexible role orientations and role breadth self-efficacy. *Applied Psychology: An International Review*, **49**, 447–469.

Parker, S. K., & Axtell, C. M. (2001). Seeing another point of view: Antecedents and outcomes of employee perspective taking. *Academy of Management Journal.*

Parker, S. K., & Sprigg, C. A. (1999). Minimizing strain and maximizing learning: The role of job demands, job control, and proactive personality. *Journal of Applied Psychology*, **84**, 925–993.

Parker, S. K., Myers, C., & Wall, T. D. (1995). The effects of a manufacturing initiative on employee jobs and strain. In S. A. Robertson (Ed.), *Contemporary Ergonomics 1995* (pp. 37–42). London: Taylor & Francis.

Parker, S. K., & Wall, T. D. (1998). *Job and work design: Organizing work to promote well-being and effectiveness.* London: Sage.

Parker, S. K., Wall, T. D., & Jackson, P. R. (1997). "That's not my job": Developing flexible employee work orientations. *Academy of Management Journal*, **40**, 899–929.

Podsakoff, P. M., & Williams, J. J. (1986). The relationship between job performance and job satisfaction. In E. A. Locke (Ed.), *Generalizing from laboratory to field settings*. Lexington, MA: Lexington Books.

Podsakoff, P. M., Ahearne, M., & MacKenzie, S. B. (1997). Organizational citizenship behavior and the quality and quantity of work group performance. *Journal of Applied Psychology*, **82**, 262–270.

Porter, L. W., & Lawler, E. E. (1968). *Managerial attitudes and performance*. Homewood, IL: Irwin.

Pulakos, E. D., Arad, S., Donovan, M. A., & Plamondon, K. E. (2000). Adaptability in the workplace: Development of a taxonomy of adaptive performance. *Journal of Applied Psychology*, **85**, 612–624.

Saavedra, R., & Kwun, S. K. (2000). Affective states in job characteristic theory. *Journal of Organizational Behavior*, **21**, 131–146.

Schleicher, R. (1973). Intelligenzleistungen: Erwachsener in Abhängigkeit vom Niveau beruflicher Tätigkeit. *Probleme und Ergebnisse der Psychologie*, **44**, 24–25.

Seeborg, I. (1978). The influence of employee participation in job redesign. *Journal of Applied Behavioural Science*, **14**, 87–98.

Shannon, H. S., Mayr, J., & Haines, T. (1997). Overview of the relationship between organizational and workplace factors and injury rates. *Safety Science*, **26**, 201–217.

Spector, P. E. (1985). Higher-order need strength as a moderator of the job scope–employee outcome relationship: A meta-analysis. *Journal of Occupational Psychology*, **58**, 119–127.

Speier, C., & Frese, M. (1997). Generalized self-efficacy as a mediator and moderator between control and complexity at work and personal initiative: A longitudinal study in East Germany. *Human Performance*, **10**, 171–192.

Spreitzer, G. M. (1995). Psychological empowerment in the workplace: Dimensions, measurement, and validation. *Academy of Management Journal*, **38**, 1442–1465.

Spreitzer, G. M., De Janasz, S. C., & Quinn, R. E. (1999). Empowered to lead: The role of psychological empowerment in leadership. *Journal of Organizational Behavior*, **20**, 511–526.

Spreitzer, G. M., Kizilos, M. A., & Nason, S. W. (1997). A dimensional analysis of the relationship between psychological empowerment and effectiveness, satisfaction, and strain. *Journal of Management*, **23**, 679–704.

Sprigg, C. A., Jackson, P. R., & Parker, S. K. (2000). Production team-working: The importance of interdependence for employee strain and satisfaction. *Human Relations*, **53**, 1519–1543.

Stajkovic, A. D., & Luthans, F. (1998). Self-efficacy and work-related performance: A meta-analysis. *Psychological Bulletin*, **2**, 240–261.

Staw, B., & Boettger, R. (1990). Task revision: A neglected form of work performance. *Academy of Management Journal*, **33**, 534–559.

Stone, E. F. (1986). Job scope–job satisfaction and job scope–job performance relationships. In E. A. Locke (Ed.), *Generalizing from laboratory to field settings*. Lexington, MA: Lexington Books.

Taylor, F. W. (1911). *The principles of scientific management*. New York: Harper.

Thomas, K. W., & Veldhouse, B. A. (1990). Cognitive elements of empowerment: An "interpretive" model of intrinsic task motivation. *Academy of Management Review*, **15**, 666–681.

Trist, E. L., & Bamforth, K. W. (1951). Some social and psychological consequences of the long-wall method of coal-getting. *Human Relations*, **4**, 3.38.

Van Maanen, J., & Schein, E. H. (1979). Toward a theory of organisational socialisation. *Research in Organisational Behaviour*, **1**, 203–264.

Volpert, W. (1975). Die Lohnarbeitswissenschaft und die Psychologie der Arbeitstätigkeit. In P. Brobkurth & W. Volpert (Eds.), *Lohnarbeitspsychologie*. Frankfurt am Main: Fischer.

Wageman, R. (1995). Interdependence and group effectiveness. *Administrative Science Quarterly*, **40**, 145–180.

Wall, T. D., & Martin, R. (1987). Job and work design. In C. L. Cooper & I. T. Robertson (Eds.), *International review of industrial and organisational psychology* (pp. 61–91). Chichester: Wiley.

Wall, T. D., & Jackson, P. R. (1995). New manufacturing initiatives and shopfloor work design. In A. Howard (Ed.), *The changing nature of work* (pp. 139–174). San Francisco: Jossey-Bass.

Wall, T. D., Cordery, J., & Clegg, C. W. (in press). Empowerment, performance, and operational uncertainty: A theoretical integration. *Applied Psychology: An International Review*.

Wall, T. D., Jackson, P. R., & Davids, K. (1992). Operator work design and robotics system performance: A serendipitous field study. *Journal of Applied Psychology*, **77**, 353–362.

Wall, T. D., Kemp, N. J., Jackson, P. R., & Clegg, C. W. (1986). An outcome evaluation of autonomous work groups: A long-term field experiment. *Academy of Management Journal*, **29**, 280–304.

Wall, T. D., Corbett, M. J., Martin, R., Clegg, C. W., & Jackson, P. R. (1990). Advanced manufacturing technology, work design and performance: A change study. *Journal of Applied Psychology*, **75**, 691–697.

Walton, R. E., & Susman, G. E. (1987, March–April). People policies for the new machines. *Harvard Business Review*, 98–106.

Wood, S. J., Barling, J., Lasaosa, A., Turner, N., & Parker, S. K. (2000). Organizational practices and safety performance. *Manuscript in preparation*. University of Sheffield, UK.

Wrzesniewski, A., & Dutton, J. E. (2001). Crafting a job: Revisioning employees as active crafters of their work. *Academy of Management Review*, **26**, 179–201.

Organizational Design and Organizational Development as a Precondition for Good Job Design and High Job Performance

Oliver Strohm

Institute for Work Research and Organizational Consultancy, Zurich, Switzerland

SUMMARY

This chapter describes concepts and criteria for an integral design of work tasks, work systems, and work structures as crucial preconditions for individual job performance. Concepts and criteria for a participative and sustainable change management are also presented. These concepts and criteria are derived from the sociotechnical systems approach and the action regulation theory. Two case studies illustrate the application of these approaches. With regard to the positive and restrictive experiences which have been made in the two case studies, general conclusions for the design and development of work tasks, work systems, and work structures facilitating high job performance are derived.

Psychological Management of Individual Performance. Edited by Sabine Sonnentag.
© 2002 John Wiley & Sons, Ltd.

INTRODUCTION

Globalization, intensification of competition, and technological advancements—to mention just a few of the current challenges to businesses—demand that companies develop innovative organizational design forms that in particular foster a high degree of utilization and development of employee qualifications (see Pfeffer, 1998). A look at the recent literature on management and change concepts that seek to provide optimal solutions to these challenges reveals an enormous body of new vocabulary and terms. The extent to which the new terminology and catchwords accentuate—or ignore—human aspects and human needs varies widely.

The chapter presents and discusses design concepts grounded in work and organizational psychology that are conceived to provide both humane and economic business design and development. Practical applications of the concepts are reported in detail within the framework of two case studies. These practical implications are derived from a sociotechnical systems approach and the action regulation theory.

INTEGRAL DESIGN CONCEPTS

Various findings show that the effectiveness and efficiency of an enterprise, as well as the quality of job design and resulting job performance at the individual level, are determined by the degree of sociotechnical optimization of work tasks, work systems, and work structures (see Emery, 1959; Trist, 1981; Ulich, 1989). Sociotechnical optimization aims toward the joint optimization of the utilization and development of the employees' qualifications, the implementation of advanced technology, and the design of the work organization (people–technology–organization-approach; see Figure 5.1). Sociotechnically optimized enterprises are characterized by decentralization at the level of the enterprise, functional integration at the level of organizational units, work in self-regulated groups, and qualified work at the level of individual work tasks. Therefore, it is necessary to have well-founded design criteria on the level of order processing, work systems, work groups, and individual work tasks.

Criteria for the design of order processing, work systems, work groups, and individual work tasks that are in line with the sociotechnical systems approach (see Strohm & Ulich, 1998) and action regulation theory (see Volpert, 1989; Hacker, 1994) are shown in Figure 5.2. Box 5.1 illustrates the definition of the criteria in detail. For the effective design on the group level and on the individual level, criteria can be derived from the action regulation theory. The design has to aim toward the creation of complete tasks, which means that they require processes of goal-setting, planning, performing, controlling and feedback.

This also means that a sociotechnically optimized design of work systems is a necessary prerequisite for the design of tasks that are complete and challenging both in content and socially—as crucial aspects of a humane job design—at the group as well as the individual level.

The implementation and use of IT solutions, as significant determining factors in technical–organizational convergence, have a major impact upon the degree of autonomy to fulfill tasks and upon the degree of flexibility, both with regard to time and place, in performing work. In this connection, concepts such as telecommuting and non-territorial office structures are of great interest.

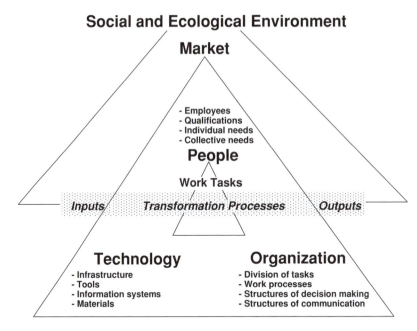

FIGURE 5.1   The people–technology–organization–approach

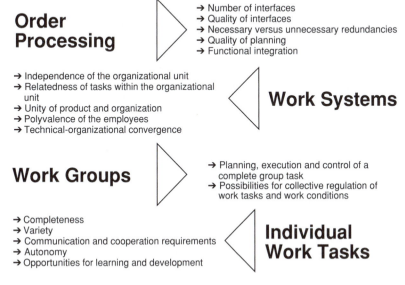

FIGURE 5.2   Criteria for design of order processing, work systems, work groups and individual work tasks

Box 5.1 Definition of criteria for the design of order processing, work systems, work groups, individual work tasks (see Ulich, 1989; Strohm & Ulich, 1998)

Criteria for the design of order processing

(1) *Number of interfaces*
The number of internal and external interfaces within the total order processing.

(2) *Quality of interfaces*
The degree to which the information and partial results, which are exchanged at the interfaces, fulfill defined quality standards.

(3) *Necessary and unnecessary redundancies*
The degree to which redundancies within the order processing are necessary and planned or unnecessary and therefore a waste of resources.

(4) *Quality of planning*
The degree to which order processing is planned realistically, carefully, and with sufficient degrees of freedom for the regulation of fluctuations and disturbances.

(5) *Functional integration*
The degree to which order processing is characterized by self-contained partial processes.

Criteria for the design of work systems

(1) *Independence of the organizational unit*
This criterion concerns the degree to which an organizational unit performs whole tasks, so that it is in a position to register fluctuations and disturbances where they arise and to counter-balance them itself.

(2) *Relatedness of tasks within the organizational unit*
This criterion examines the various part tasks within an organizational unit as to their relatedness in terms of content.

(3) *Unity of product and organization*
Using this criterion, the degree to which resulting products and outputs can be assigned to the organizational unit in terms of both quality and quantity is assessed.

(4) *Polyvalence of the employees*
This criterion examines the extent to which employees within an organizational unit are qualified to fulfill or perform various part tasks so that they lend mutual support to one another and save flexibility within the organizational unit.

(5) *Technical-organizational convergence*
This criterion assesses the degree to which there is an optimal fit between technological requirements and conditions and organizational requirements and conditions.

Criteria for the design of work groups

(1) *Task-related self-regulation*
This criterion concerns the extent to which a work group performs collectively and independently task-related processes of goal setting, planning, performing and controlling.

(2) *Self-regulation concerning working conditions*
This aspect relates to the extent to which a work group independently and collectively decides, for example, about their working time, further qualification, internal leadership and investments.

Criteria for the design of individual work task

(1) *Completeness*
This criterion assesses the extent to which individual tasks imply elements of planning, performing, and controlling as well as the possibility of matching the results of one's work with the requirements.

(2) *Variety*
This criterion relates to the extent to which the performance of individual tasks makes demands on different bodily functions and sense organs.

(3) *Communication and cooperation requirements*
This criterion refers to the extent to which coping with one's work requires collaboration and cooperation.

(4) *Autonomy*
This criterion assesses the extent to which individual tasks include clearly defined possibilities of disposition and decision making.

(5) *Opportunities for learning and development*
This aspect concerns the difficulty and complexity of a task, and therefore requires the use and further development of one's qualifications or even the acquisition of new qualifications.

Figure 5.3 shows a summary of the factors influencing individual job performance. In this context, we start from the premise that what the individual may do, can do, and wants to do—as significant predictors of high job performance—depend largely on the design of the organization and the task, the company's measures for personnel development, and individual career and development paths within the enterprise (see Hall, 1995). It is important to emphasize that the development of the organization and the development of individual prerequisites of performance have to be linked by distinct vertical and horizontal career paths. This is an expression of the close—and in company practice frequently lacking—relationship between organization design and development on one hand and human resource management on the other.

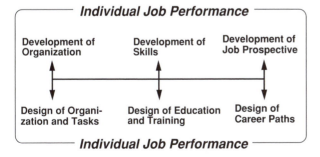

FIGURE 5.3   Significant factors influencing individual job performance

PERFORMANCE-ORIENTED JOB DESIGN AND THE DESIGN OF ORGANIZATIONAL DEVELOPMENT

There is much more knowledge available on how work and jobs should be designed than on how the design processes should be managed in order to attain these work and job solutions. Therefore, high-quality change management and continuous improvement processes are crucial to developing and establishing good job design.

Figure 5.4 shows a logical procedure and the interdependence of different design steps within fundamental change processes. With regard to effectiveness, efficiency, and humane working conditions, it is vital to overcome traditional, functionally oriented work organization and leadership structures. Therefore, in sustainable change processes it is often necessary—as we have discussed—to define work systems with complete work tasks and processes, which are based on a well-founded strategy.

This focus on tasks is a precondition for the design of order processing, work systems, work groups, and work tasks that are in line with the criteria described above.

In such processes, an equal importance should be assigned to humane and economic goals. This can be reinforced by principles of change that have a solid basis and foster confidence between management and employees. Examples of well-founded and important principles for change processes include the following:

- Changes should be made on the basis of sound evaluation of the strengths and weaknesses of the organization. This evaluation should be based on the outlined levels of the design of order processing, work systems, work groups and the individual works tasks.
- Changes should be made that meet the criteria of a humane, effective, and efficient design of organization and jobs. Sustainable change processes should be well balanced concerning goals of the employees and goals of the company.
- Changes should be oriented toward well-founded criteria for the design of order processing, work systems, work groups and the individual works tasks.
- Changes should proceed while informing and involving employees at all levels.

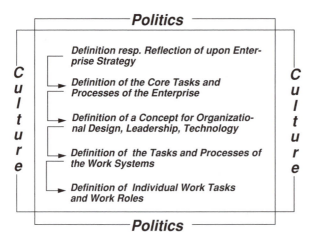

FIGURE 5.4   Logical procedure in complex change processes

- Changes should include examination and adaptation of job conditions (such as work hours, salary).
- Changes should occur in combination with effective training measures.
- Changes should establish effective job prospective and career paths for the employees.

Management and employees should reach agreement on such principles early in the change process. Management should be able to guarantee its obligation to apply the principles to the entire change process (see Schein, 1980).

Criteria for the quality of the change process itself can be defined from different perspectives. From the perspective of employees, there are various criteria of decisive importance:

- faith in the real results of change
- readiness for change
- ownership of the change process
- appropriate pace of change
- visible improvements during the change process
- belief in personal benefits through the change.

There are subjective and objective indications for these criteria. The important aspect is the way in which the employees' attitudes, concrete behavior, and personal commitment evolve during the process of change with regard to the criteria described (Argyris & Schön, 1978).

In sum, the transition from a traditional work and organizational design to an innovative design founded in work and organizational psychology requires professional change processes and change management that are based on thorough reflection upon the organizational and management structures, work processes, and individual work activities. Only these will fulfill the prerequisites for a new design that will support sustainable performance increases at the individual level and, in consequence, at the level of the entire enterprise. In addition, however, it is crucial to ensure that such processes are not dictated from above by experts; rather, the goal of employee-oriented and performance-fostering work design can be achieved through an employee-oriented design and change process.

The following case studies illustrate the possibilities for such change processes and the resulting effects.

CASE STUDY I

ORGANIZATION DEVELOPMENT IN A COMPANY IN THE MACHINE-BUILDING INDUSTRY

The pre-change situation

To improve its own position on the world market, a medium-sized company in the machine-building industry with 160 employees undertook a fundamental and proactive change project. We supported this project as consultants. The most important human-oriented and enterprise-oriented goals of the change are shown in Table 5.1.

The company had been organized according to classic principles (see Figure 5.5). This had led to familiar problem areas, such as department-restricted thinking, diffusion of responsibility, long cycle times, limited delivery reliability, and qualitative under-challenging of various groups of employees.

TABLE 5.1   Important human-oriented and enterprise-oriented goals of the project

Human-oriented goals	Enterprise-oriented goals
Increase in responsibility	Improvement in customer orientation
Job enrichment	Higher accuracy of delivery time
Training and employee development	Reduction of total cycle time
Improvement in collaboration	Increase in competitiveness
Continued employment	Increase in transparency

The change process

The most important steps and milestones of the project are shown in Table 5.2. In summary, the most important milestones of this project were: (1) the preparation of the management; (2) the analysis and evaluation of the status-quo; (3) the conceptual work in the areas of organization and leadership, salary-system and lay-out design; (4) the qualification of the group speakers and the employees; (5) the implementation based on pilot projects and starting workshops; and (6) the evaluation of the new working and organizational structures. The whole process from the beginning to the complete implementation took two years. Part of the reason lies in the participative character of the change process, which involved employees from different hierarchical levels and departments.

This procedure led to a fundamental redesign of the whole company, with completely newly defined work systems. Service, as well as research and engineering, standardization, and quality management, were defined as strategically important new work systems. The departments of disposition, work preparation and purchasing were abolished and transferred to an integrated department of material planning (see Figure 5.5).

The newly defined work systems are far-reaching, in line with the criteria outlined in Figure 5.2. One hierarchical level was eliminated and the work groups are now organized according to the principle of self-directed groups. Therefore, among other things, they choose their group speaker autonomously. The layout was also changed extensively. The work groups were spatially integrated and the work group material planning was spatially transferred into the production.

The implementation workshops were of great importance within the operational change process, and all employees of the various work systems participated in these workshops. The most important topics of the workshops were:

- common specification of the tasks and work processes, respectively of the inputs, the transformation processes, and the outputs of the work system
- agreements concerning internal work organization
- determination of the actual and target figures of polyvalence
- development of a training scheme for mutual training on the job
- agreements concerning internal leadership, coordination, and common secondary tasks
- agreements upon rules of collaboration and team work
- improving openness to questions of social competence within work groups
- agreements upon crucial features of performance of the work system.

Evaluation of the change process

A first evaluation of the new work, organizational, and management structures was carried out by document analysis, individual interviews, group interviews, and written survey and contained objective and subjective data material.

TABLE 5.2   Important steps and milestones of the project

Time	Steps
11.1994	Agreement between management and the consultants about the start of, and collaboration on, the project.
2.1995	Workshop with the managers on the subjects of (1) sociotechnical systems design, (2) approaches for an integrated analysis and evaluation of the company, (3) first definition of project goals, as well as (4) forming the project team.
3.1995	Further definition of goals and principles for the project. Agreements with the works council. Planning the strategy.
4/5.1995	Analysis and evaluation of the company with a multi-level approach considering people, technology, and the organization. Presentation of the results of the company evaluation to management, project team, and to the employees in a company meeting. Establishing the project organization.
From 6.1995	Start of conceptual work concerning variants of organizational design and leadership. Introduction of measurements concerning training and education as well as principles of self-control in the manufacturing department.
From 9.1995	Start of conceptual work on a new salary system.
3.1996	Workshops with management and a general company meeting to inform all staff and to discuss the new work structures in terms of organizational design and leadership and the modified salary system. Selection of four internal coaches to support the implementation processes.
From 4.1996	Start of the conceptual work on a new layout.
5.1996	Implementation workshops dealing with three work systems on different topics. Training workshops with prospective group speakers of the work systems on topics such as problem solving in work groups, conflicts in work groups, dealing with difficult group members.
6/7.1996	Start with the three work systems to gain pilot experience. Election of group speakers in the work systems. Workshop with the enlarged management on the topic of new requirements concerning leadership.
8.1996	Written survey of the employees on the leadership behavior of the enlarged management.
From 9.1996	Further startup workshops and training workshops with all work systems and group speakers. Further election of group speakers for the work systems.
11.1996	Additional workshop with the enlarged management. Presentation of the results of the evaluation of leadership behavior of the enlarged management.
From 1.1997	Implementation of the new enterprise concept in the whole company. Implementation of bonus components of the modified salary system.
6.1997	First evaluation of the new enterprise concept in a workshop with the enlarged management and the group speakers of the work systems.
3.1998	Systematic evaluation of the new enterprise concept with a multi-level approach. Derivation of further change processes and strategies.

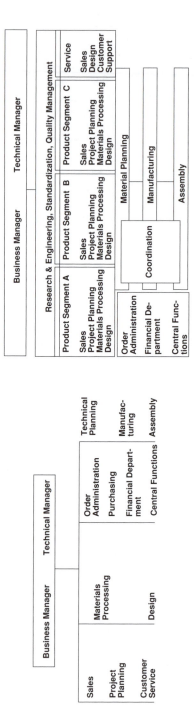

FIGURE 5.5 The old and new enterprise concepts of the company

The evaluation identified a number of improvements, but also revealed areas that required further development.

Table 5.3 shows examples of how the newly designed organizational units were rated by us according to some of the criteria outlined in Figure 5.2. The evaluation revealed that there were increases in the independence of the organizational units, in the interconnectedness of tasks, in the unity of product and organization, and in the possibilities for self-regulation within the organizational units. The degree of polyvalence remained the same or was even somewhat worse. This can be explained by the fact that the new design had also led to a new composition of personnel in the organizational units. This tended to increase the heterogeneity of qualifications in the organizational units. Moreover, the evaluation revealed that the "on the job" qualification measures that had been agreed upon had not been realized, or implemented, due to time constraints.

TABLE 5.3 Changes in the design of the organizational units

Criteria	Change
Independence of the organizational units	↗
Relatedness of tasks within the organizational units	↗
Unity of product and organization within the organizational units	↗
Polyvalence of the employees within the organizational units	↘ ↕
Possibilities for self-regulation within the organizational units	↗

Figure 5.6 shows employees' perceptions of various dimensions of the new work situation. On the whole, the employees rate their experience as positive. However, employees also perceive an increase in the workload and in work demands.

In view of the way employees perceived the changes, it is not surprising that the great majority of employees stated that they would not want to return to the old form of work and organization.

As to economic aspects, the company's situation also showed improvement towards the goals connected with the change process. Some noteworthy examples of improvement included:

• improvement of accuracy of delivery time in the service business from 48% to 87% in one year
• considerable reduction of cycle time
• increase of turnover by coping with an increased amount of orders—parallel to the change process
• higher productivity
• higher transparency of the processes
• continuous improvements in the quality of processes and results.

In relation to these effects, we should not neglect to take into account that, in addition to the work design measures outlined, a variable component in the salary system for achievement of workgroup- and order-processing-related goals was also introduced. It has to be assumed, that the measures of work design, which above all led to a more direct and improved cooperation and collaboration, as well as to performance-based components of the salary system, resulted in the outlined improvements of the overall performance of the company.

One major problem still remaining is the behavior of some members of the enlarged management. Strong claims to power are leading to forms of micropolitics that place difficult constraints on the employees in various work systems (see Buchanan & Badham, 1998).

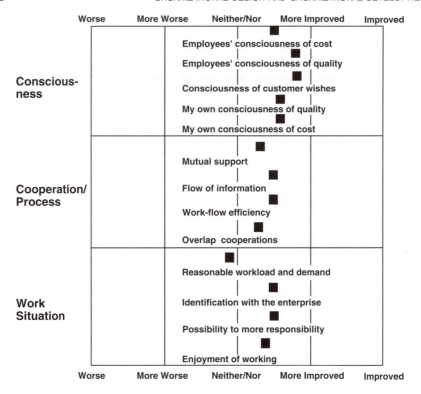

FIGURE 5.6 Employees' perceptions of the changes ($N = 106$)

This problem was also voiced within the framework of the evaluation. Employees rated the behavior of management with regard to fostering continuing implementation of the change process as less than positive and exemplary. Since 1998, the machine-building firm has continued a steady company development on its own. As a part of that process, one person from Human Resource Management, as an internal change agent, continues to monitor the implementation of formal aspects, such as the selection and training of group speakers, and to initiate internal evaluations and assessments.

CASE STUDY II

ORGANIZATIONAL DEVELOPMENT IN A HUMAN RESOURCE MANAGEMENT DEPARTMENT

The pre-change situation

In the administrative, operations, and service units of a large educational and research institute, a program of change was undertaken in order to gain a sustainable increase in effectiveness, quality, and efficiency.

In this connection, the institute initiated a program of organizational development in the human resources department. A study of prevailing conditions revealed the following problems in the work situation of the 20 employees in the department:

- procedures mainly administrative; intensive paperwork
- multiple, poorly defined interfaces

- high degree of managerial density
- high degree of division of labor
- simultaneous lack of qualitative challenge and quantitative overload
- social conflicts.

As a result, a number of employees in the unit were very dissatisfied with their work situation and demanded changes. They hoped to see the development of expanded human resources as well as enhancement of the content of their tasks and roles.

The change process

With this as a mandate, the change process comprised the following milestones in the period from 1996 to 1998:

- workshop for the purposes of reflection upon and sensitization to the problems leading to a formulation of the target areas for change
- analysis and evaluation of the unit with a multi-level-approach under consideration of people, technology, and organization
- precise formulation of goals, definition of action approaches and definition of organization of the project
- development of a service portfolio defining future services and quality standards of the unit; derivation of required personnel to support such services
- development of an effective concept for organization and management of the unit
- step-by-step implementation of the innovations and measures.

The project set goals for improvements at the level of employee, department, and the institute as a whole.

Prior to the restructuring, the department had been divided into a total of four personnel areas, each having a human resource manager, a secretary, and an assistant secretary. There were also various specialized functions. The new concept of organization and management set up units for the administration of personnel, the counseling of personnel, and a newly created unit for personnel and organizational development. This resulted in a conclusive separation of administration from actual personnel and organizational work (see Figure 5.7). The management structure established co-management at the uppermost level.

Personnel administration is organized as a self-regulating team. The team speaker, selected by the team, takes on internal coordination functions and represents the team externally. Weekly team meetings serve work-related agreements and planning.

Cooperation between personnel administration and personnel counseling is achieved in a matrix-oriented form with designated contact persons. The functions of area secretary and assistant secretary have been eliminated. Employees in personnel administration have been upgraded to personnel specialists. This process of increasing qualifications occurred to a large extent mutually and "on the job". The new organizational concept also contains a career concept that allows for career paths to personnel specialist, personnel manager assistant, personnel manager, personnel developer, and organization developer.

Implementation of the new orientation and the new organization and management concept comprised, among others, the following steps:

- recruitment and introduction of new employees
- level-appropriate qualification measures, for example in the areas of Human Resource Management, IT, communication skills, and client-centered and service-oriented behavior
- design of and move to new office spaces
- new design of the personnel department's outreach using flyers and intranet.

Evaluation of the change process

About a year after implementing the new work organization, the personnel administration and personnel counseling units were evaluated. This first evaluation was also carried out

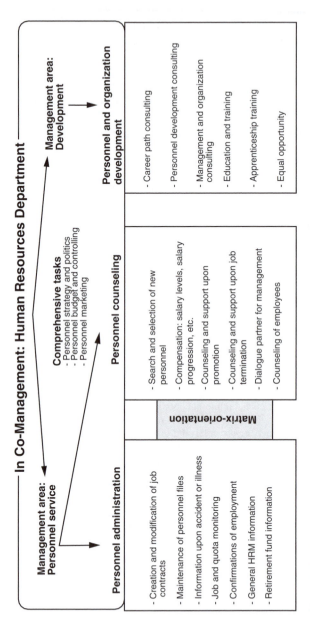

FIGURE 5.7 The new organization and management concept of the personnel department

by document analysis, individual interviews, group interviews, and written survey. This evaluation produced the following results:

• Human resources work is based on thorough reflection and its services have been enlarged.
• Human resources work is professional and has a more proactive/counseling character.
• Various "clients" of the personnel department rate the changes as positive.
• The levels of competence and work satisfaction of the employees have increased.
• Collaboration and cooperation within the department have improved significantly.

Figure 5.8, which confirms these generally valid statements, shows the effects of the change process as reported by the employees. As can be seen, the employees report definite improvement of the situation in the department with regard to service, organization, management, and work content.

The evaluation also revealed, however, that various problems and areas for improvement persist in the department:

• Various "clients" criticize the changes and the enlarged services or see them as superfluous.
• Matrix-oriented cooperation between personnel administration and personnel counseling is not optimal in the case of certain employees.
• The newly designed human resources work is strategically not sufficiently anchored within the organization.
• Various interfaces to the "client" and within the department require further specification.
• The various management roles and tasks require further clarification and development.
• Error quotas in personnel administration remain still too high and should be reduced.

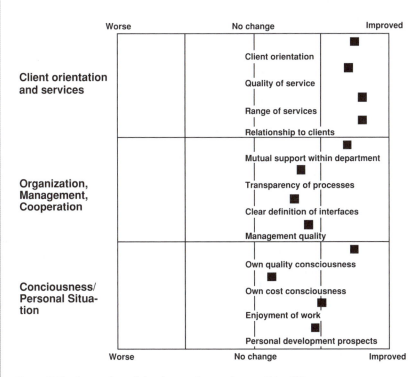

FIGURE 5.8   Perception of the changes by employees ($N = 17$)

With regard to the last problem area listed above, it is important to take into account that the extensive changes in the department, the training of new employees, and the further training of existing employees all led initially to constraints on performance and quality. This resulted in critical evaluations by some "clients". That fundamental restructuring frequently results in an initial period of reduced performance is a well-known phenomenon that was not sufficiently anticipated and communicated in this case. These deficits of quality could be balanced after a while and were transformed into goal-oriented improvements.

Accordingly, when the results of the evaluation were presented, additional measures were discussed that could contribute to a higher degree of professionalism.

In the time since, the department has undergone some further change. The fact that the newly defined personnel work did not find the necessary acceptance with the highest level of management in the organization led to a change in management. A new head now manages the department. With this, an additional hierarchical level was introduced. Otherwise, the organization concept as outlined, and the expanded work roles of staff members, were retained. When a new IT system was implemented, the area of payroll administration was also integrated into the department. This further increased the functional integration—independence, task relatedness, and unity—of product and organization. However, as a result of the changes in management, some employees have since left the department or the institute.

CONCLUSIONS

The experience gained in the course of the above and similar cases of change processes shows that the forms of organization design and development selected are significant predictors of individual and company performance levels. In such processes, it is crucial that issues such as strategic goals and the organization, management and, in particular, the design of individual work activity and work roles be worked through progressively and together with the employees. In summary, some of the most important findings on the design of such processes are the following:

- Value-oriented change concepts that are well-founded in theory and practice support integrated redesigns.
- Integrated approaches require interdisciplinary thinking and acting.
- Effective and sustainable changes require fundamental considerations.
- The success of changes is widely determined by professionalism and consistency on the part of management.
- Externally, change processes must necessarily involve, in balanced form, both valuing and empathy on the one hand, and confrontation and irritation on the other.

On principle, these processes require an image that relies on the employee's potential and willingness to achieve. These important prerequisites have to be combined with the idea of an organization that meets the outlined criteria, fulfills the objectives, and allows scope for individual autonomous decision making. Furthermore, these processes demand a certain time constraint, which must not only be realistic but be based on the principle that a sustainable dynamism and stability of performance—together with performance-oriented action—needs to be monitored continuously and professionally to ensure that implementation of the redesign provides the expected results from both technology and staff.

REFERENCES

Argyris, Ch., & Schön, D. A. (1978). *Organizational learning: A theory of active perspective.* London/Amsterdam/Don Mills, Ontario/Sydney.

Buchanan, D., & Badham, R. (1998*). Winning the turf game: Power, politics, and organizational change.* London: Paul Chapman Publishing.

Emery, F. E. (1959). *Characteristics of sociotechnical systems.* London: Tavistock, document no. 527.

Hacker, W. (1994). Action regulation theory and occupational psychology. Review of German empirical research since 1987. *The German Journal of Psychology*, **18**, 91–120.

Hall, B. P. (1995). *Values shift. A guide to personal and organizational transformation.* Rockport: Twin Light.

Pfeffer, J. (1998). *The human equation: Building profits by putting people first.* Boston: Harvard Business School Press.

Schein, E. H. (1980). *Organizational psychology.* Englewood Cliffs, NJ.

Strohm, O., & Ulich, E. (1998). Integral analysis and evaluation of enterprises. A multilevel approach in terms of people, technology and organization. *Human Factors and Ergonomics in Manufacturing*, **8**, 233–250.

Trist, E. L. (1981). *The evolution of sociotechnical systems. Issues in the quality of working life.* Occasional Paper No. 2. Toronto: Ontario Quality of Working Life Centre.

Ulich, E. (1989). Humanization of work—concepts and cases. In J. Fallon, H. P. Pfister, & J. Brebner (Eds.), *Advances in industrial and organizational psychology* (pp. 133–143). Amsterdam: North Holland.

Volpert, W. (1989). Work and personality development from the viewpoint of the action regulation theory. In H. Leymann & H. Kornbluh (Eds.), *Socialization and learning at work. A new approach to the learning process in the workplace and society* (pp. 215–232). Aldershot: Avebury.

Part II

Assessing Performance

CHAPTER 6

Appraisal: An Individual Psychological Perspective

Clive Fletcher

Goldsmiths' College, London, UK

SUMMARY

With the radical changes that have taken place in organisations in recent years, performance appraisal (PA) systems have increasingly changed to reflect wider business needs and priorities. However, the success of such systems remains strongly dependent on the behaviour and dispositions of those participating in the appraisal process. This chapter offers a psychological analysis of the role of motivation, personality, and interpersonal relationships in PA. It examines variables impacting on the appraisers' behaviour (including organisational politics and conflict avoidance), on appraisees' behaviour (including need for achievement, goal orientation, self-awareness, self-efficacy, self-esteem, locus of control, and feedback attitudes) and on the relationship between the two parties. It is argued that research on such variables and how they influence the handling of appraisal interviews will be more effective in enhancing PA effectiveness than will further work on systems perspectives or the continued search for the "perfect" rating scale.

Psychological Management of Individual Performance. Edited by Sabine Sonnentag.

INTRODUCTION

Performance Appraisal (PA) is a generic term covering a variety of processes whereby an individual's work performance is assessed, usually by that person's line manager, and discussed with a view to solving problems, improving performance and developing the individual appraised. It has a long and perhaps not very distinguished history in organisational life. Despite the fact that it is all too often seen as problematic or ineffective in some respects, it not only persists as a feature of large organisations but has actually increased in its range of application. For example, in the UK during the 1990s it was systematically introduced into elements of the public sector which had not used it before, while in the private sector it was applied to a greater spread of levels and staff groups in organisations (Fletcher, 1997a). Also, new aspects of appraisal, such as multi-source feedback (so-called 360 degree feedback) have become popular; Antonioni (1996, p. 24) observed that "without question, 360 degree appraisals are taking hold in American business".

However, to gain an understanding of where PA is today, it is helpful to look briefly at how it has evolved. Its origins can be traced back as far as the First World War, but to appreciate contemporary perspectives it is not necessary to go back beyond the 1950s and 1960s. In the 1950s, personality-based appraisal systems were quite common. These were associated with a belief in the importance of feedback as an aid to learning and as a motivating mechanism. Then McGregor's (1957) famous article, in which he took an "uneasy look" at PA, expressed criticism of personality-based ratings and identified them as a principal reason for the tendency of managers to avoid doing appraisals if possible. This line of thought was taken up by other writers in the field and, with the additional influence of the concept of Management By Objectives (MBO), appraisal practice in the 1960s shifted to a greater emphasis on goal-setting and the assessment of performance-related abilities (and, much more recently, competencies) rather than personality. In the decade that followed, PA practices were influenced by equal opportunities legislation. In line with this, the practice of having report forms as confidential documents not available for scrutiny by the person appraised largely died out. The late 1980s, and the whole of the 1990s, saw organisations undergo a process of rapid and successive change. The nature of these changes—downsizing, delayering, etc.—had implications for the way that PA was applied (Fletcher, 1997b). For example, with fewer management levels and greater autonomy for individual managers, the traditional practice of having the line manager as the appraiser sometimes became difficult to apply—because of both the number of potential appraisees and the limited contact their immediate boss might have with them. Along with these changes, many companies introduced performance management systems in an attempt to improve performance and manage human resources in a more integrated and consistent manner (Williams, 1998). Almost inevitably, PA became a central mechanism in this more holistic approach. Thus, the aims, context and processes of PA have increasingly reflected the wider business needs and priorities of the organisations operating it, as well as legal requirements.

This shift has been noted in numerous radical critiques and analyses of appraisal. These have portrayed appraisal as a management control process that tries to ensure that subordinates act in accordance with organisational goals, and have tended to dismiss any pretence of appraisal being a process that has any benefit for the person appraised (e.g. Newton & Findlay, 1996; Townley, 1999). The approach of many of these writers is influenced by Foucault (1981) and the result is a representation of PA as simply a mechanism for, and expression of, management power and manipulation. There is indeed some danger that in closely lining-up PA with business planning and organisational mission statements, attention to individual psychological needs is reduced. However, as will be seen in the main sections of this chapter, this kind of radical analysis reflects a rather monothematic and overly-simple account. The reality of appraisal is that it acts as a meeting point for a very diverse range of motives and actions of the organisation, the appraisers and those appraised. No matter what the organisation's aims might be, little is likely to be achieved without considering the roles and attitudes of the people who have to make appraisal work—the managers and their subordinates. As the research reviewed below indicates, failure to do so makes PA less effective as a vehicle for motivating performance improvement.

Many of the practical and process aspects of PA are dealt with in the chapter by Drewes and Runde in this volume. The present chapter, however, is concerned with an academic perspective on PA, and specifically with a psychological analysis of the role of motivation, personality and interpersonal relationships in appraisal. First, though, it is important to present a brief overview of research on PA.

RESEARCH ON PERFORMANCE APPRAISAL

PA is one of the more heavily researched topics in work psychology. However, much of this effort has been directed first to studies of different types of rating scale and how they should be used, and then—more recently—to seeking to understand the cognitive processes underlying the assessments made by managers of their staff (e.g. DeNisi, 1997). There are many excellent reviews of this literature (e.g. Landy & Farr, 1980; Austin & Villanova, 1992; Arvey & Murphy, 1998). The vast majority of this particular research stream has emanated from the USA, perhaps to some extent driven by the impact of Equal Opportunities legislation there. It is difficult to find an equivalent stream of work in Europe, but—as will be suggested below—this may be no great loss. The other dominant research theme has been that stemming from organisational justice theory (Greenberg, 1986; Korsgaard & Roberson, 1995). In relation to PA, this breaks down into the concepts of Distributive Justice, which deals with the perceived fairness of assessment and reward, and Procedural Justice, which deals with the perceived fairness of the process whereby those assessment and reward decisions are arrived at (Greenberg, 1986). In particular, a great deal of attention has been paid to subordinate participation level or "voice" in the appraisal process; the general observation being that higher levels of participation are more likely to lead to positive perceptions of procedurally-just appraisal (Cawley, Keeping, & Levy, 1998).

There have been many insights generated by these streams of work, and they have helped illuminate such questions as the effectiveness of various methods of training raters (Woehr & Huffcutt, 1994). That said, the practical value of the research emphasis on rating methods and the cognitive processes involved in using them has to be questioned. Apart from anything else, after so much research over so many years, one might expect the quality of assessment in appraisal by now to be well-nigh perfect. The reality is that there is little or no evidence to suggest that appraisal ratings typically found in organisations have significantly improved in terms of their "accuracy" or other psychometric properties.

The majority of organisations still report being dissatisfied with their appraisal systems (Fletcher, 1997a) for a variety of reasons. The explanation for this lack of impact of what has often been research of high technical quality is perhaps to be found in some of the underpinning assumptions. Hogan (1987) suggests that much of the work has treated appraisers as faulty but motivationally neutral elements of the appraisal process and has concentrated on improving these faults with improved rating scale formats and training. Other writers, too, have identified this implicit picture of the appraiser (e.g. Longenecker & Ludwig, 1990; Tziner, Latham, Price, & Haccoun, 1996) and criticised it for failing to take account of the dynamic, motivational context in which appraisal takes place. In other words, the assessments made and other aspects of what goes on in an appraisal process have relatively little to do with issues of "accuracy" per se.

Even the organisational justice research has its limitations. While certainly grounded in the realities of organisational life, it provides a somewhat broad-brush approach to understanding what goes on in appraisal. The meta-analysis reported by Cawley, Keeping and Levy (1998) makes the useful distinction between instrumental participation— which is participation for the purpose of influencing an end result—and value-expressive participation—participation for the sake of having one's voice heard. They found that the latter had a stronger relationship with reaction criteria than did the former. Participation is without doubt important in a number of ways in appraisal, including at the outset in developing the scheme (Silverman & Wexley, 1984), and it feeds in to perceptions of procedural justice. But it has been found that candidates' views of procedural justice in a selection context changed adversely when a rejection decision was communicated (Cunningham-Snell, Anderson, Fletcher, & Gibb, 1998). It can be argued, therefore, that procedural justice perceptions are themselves subject to the influence of deeper psychological reactions. In addition, they are likely to be impacted by individual and cultural differences (see below).

Perhaps, rather surprisingly, one key element of the appraisal process has been relatively neglected by research in recent years, and that is the appraisal interview (AI) itself. Most PA systems require the line manager to hold an interview with the person appraised to discuss the assessment made, be it against objectives or on competency dimensions or both. Although there are numerous "how to" books giving advice on the handling of the AI, little of the content could claim a strong research base as this does not seem to exist. Yet as Kikoski and Litterer (1983, p. 33) point out, the AI is the point of delivery of PA, and in their view is "the Achilles' heel of the entire process". Some of the earlier writers and researchers in the field did look very specifically at what went on in the AI (e.g. Maier, 1958; Meyer, Kay, & French, 1965; Kay, Meyer, & French, 1965; Rothaus, Morton, & Hanson, 1965; Burke & Wilcox, 1969; Burke, Weitzel, & Weir, 1978; Greller, 1975; Nemeroff & Wexley, 1979) but this has been a less popular focus for investigation since. Given that this is the face-to-face interaction element in the PA process, and much is likely to depend on it, the paucity of work done—in marked contrast to the selection interview—is regrettable. The methodological difficulties in studying the AI directly may be partly to blame. However, organisational psychologists preferring to stay within their comfort zone of measurement issues is possibly a (less excusable) factor.

The remainder of the present chapter will seek to address some of the imbalances in the academic literature by examining PA in terms of the psychological orientations of the appraiser and the appraisee, rather than from an organisational, procedural or psychometric standpoint. It will outline some of the main psychological variables that appear to be important in the appraisal process, and in particular in the appraisal interview, and look at what research evidence is available to help us to understand their impact on the outcomes of appraisal. Specifically, the proposal will be advanced that, to a large extent, the effectiveness of appraisal is determined by the make-up and attitudes of the appraiser and the appraisee, and by the quality of relationship that exists between them.

PSYCHOLOGICAL VARIABLES IMPACTING ON APPRAISAL

The formal purposes of appraisal vary to some extent from one organisation to another, and across time. For example, in periods of economic recession or when a company runs into economic problems, it is not untypical to find that developmental aspects of appraisal are de-emphasised and the focus is very strongly on performance improvement and achieving short-term results. One of the most frequent criticisms of PA generally is that it has too many objectives, and not all of them are very consistent with each other (Fletcher & Williams, 1992). But it is the view of those objectives taken by the appraiser and the appraisee that will shape the appraisal and what results from it, and their views are in turn influenced by their own motives, attitudes, and dispositions (Dulewicz & Fletcher, 1989). Figure 6.1 presents a simple model for viewing this relationship.

The organisation's needs and priorities are reflected in the stated purposes of the PA system, and in the documentation and any training that is associated with it. While this acts as a backdrop for the appraisal process, the interaction (principally in the AI) will be determined more by the orientation of the appraiser and appraisee. The appraiser's orientation is likely to be influenced by a variety of factors, including organisational pressures and politics, and personality attributes. The appraisee's orientation is likely to be influenced by perceived levels of competence and personality factors—particularly those relevant to seeking and using feedback. The third element that influences the appraisal interaction is the existing relationship between the manager and the individual appraised, which is impacted by the characteristics of both parties.

These three elements will now be examined in more detail and the relevant research evidence described.

THE APPRAISER

The attitude of managers towards carrying out PA seems to be ambivalent at best. It is frequently observed that they avoid carrying out appraisals. In one UK survey (Industrial Society, 1997) less than two-thirds of organisations reported a better than 67% appraisal completion rate—and this is one of the more favourable findings! Various studies have found that appraisers either see no consequences for them of conducting appraisals or just negative consequences (Napier & Latham, 1986). Why does this rather bleak situation arise? Various writers have offered analyses of PA from the point of view of the appraiser. Cleveland and Murphy (1992) suggest that the appraiser's goals are:

(1) projecting a favourable image of the work unit they lead so as to reflect well on them personally
(2) procuring access to organisational resources and rewards
(3) presenting themselves as a caring boss
(4) avoiding conflict with subordinates and the negative consequences of that
(5) avoiding disapproval from peers.

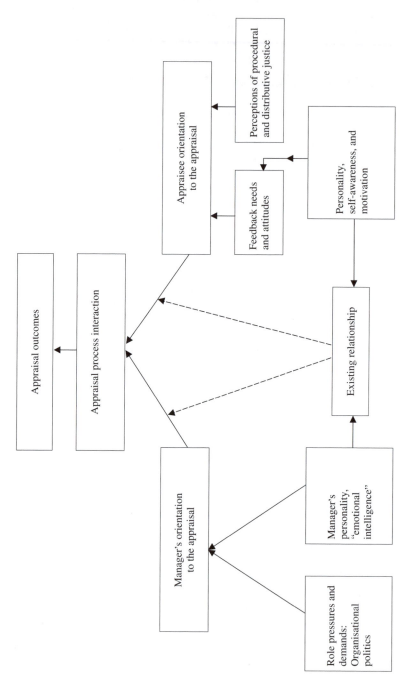

FIGURE 6.1 What influences the appraisal interaction?

Some of these goals support one another, such as (3) and (4), though managing those and still achieving (1) and (5) is less straightforward. The appraisers may present a picture of all their staff being good performers, but this has to be consistent with other information about the performance of the unit and also has to be done in such a way as not to alienate peers. The latter may react adversely if one of their colleagues presents their unit as being unrealistically high in performance, not least because this might have implications for the way any money available for performance-related pay is shared out.

Longenecker and his colleagues have specifically focused on the politics of appraisal in a number of studies and articles (Longenecker, Gioia, & Sims, Jr., 1987; Longenecker & Gioia, 1988; Longenecker, Liverpool, & Wilson, 1988; Longenecker, 1989; Gioia & Longenecker, 1994). Among other things, this research identified the following reasons why managers inflated their ratings of subordinates:

- believing that accurate ratings would have a damaging effect on subordinate motivation and performance
- desire to improve the subordinate's chances of getting a pay rise
- a wish to avoid others outside the department seeing evidence of internal problems and conflicts
- preventing a permanent written record of poor performance coming into being which might have longer-term implications for the subordinate
- need to protect subordinates whose performance had suffered from the effects of personal problems
- wanting to reward subordinates who had put in a lot of effort even if the end result was not so good
- avoiding confrontation and potential conflict with "difficult" subordinates
- aiming to promote out of the department subordinates who were disliked or problem performers.

Though less frequently reported, some reasons for deliberately manipulating performance assessments in a downward direction were also uncovered:

- scaring people into performing better
- punishing difficult or non-compliant subordinates
- encouraging unwanted subordinates to leave
- minimising the merit pay award(s)
- complying with organisational restrictions on the number of higher ratings given.

The general observation from this research is that managers frequently allow their appraisal of staff to be influenced by non-performance issues. Gioia and Longenecker (1994) found that the higher an individual rose in an organisation, the more political the appraisal process becomes.

One the themes picked out both by Cleveland and Murphy and by Longenecker is the avoidance of conflict. This has been addressed many other times in the literature under the guise of the effects of criticism or negative feedback on performance. Meyer et al. (1965) were among the first to report the tendency for more than a small amount of criticism in the appraisal interview to lead to lower motivation and achievement; although this has not always been replicated, the reluctance of appraisers to give unfavourable feedback has often been noted (Fletcher, 1994). The appraisal is usually an annual activity, and many managers seem to be unwilling to risk the quality of their relationships with their staff for the rest of the year by tackling performance weaknesses in the AI. Perhaps this is one of the reasons why Harris, Smith and Champagne (1995) found that ratings given for administrative reasons were more lenient than those given solely for research purposes. Similarly, in the context of multi-source feedback, ratings given as an input to appraisal are more positive than those given simply as part of an individual development exercise (McEvoy & Buller, 1987; Pollack & Pollack, 1996).

The extent to which managers are susceptible to these other influences on their assessment of subordinates, their willingness to convey such assessments, and the manner in which they do it are likely to be determined by various factors. These may include their confidence in their own position, their relationship with the subordinate (dealt with below), their attributional style and their personality. Greater confidence and sense of security in one's own position should facilitate greater openness and honesty with others, but a lack of security may increase the temptation to indulge in manipulative strategies. However, the latter may also to some degree reflect personality; Tziner et al. (1996) found a correlation of .33 between Machiavellianism and a questionnaire measure of political considerations in PA. Several other personality characteristics that seem relevant here come under the general heading of the popular notion of emotional intelligence, including, empathy, self-awareness, sensitivity to others, integrity, and emotional resilience (Higgs & Dulewicz, 1999; Salovey & Mayer, 1990). Although at the time of writing no research has looked at the relationship between "EQ" and appraisal, it holds some promise as a line of enquiry. The influence of attributional style on appraisal has been examined over some years (e.g. Knowlton & Mitchell, 1980) and has been shown to be susceptible to such factors as gender bias in appraisers. It will be discussed further below.

THE APPRAISEE

Interestingly, more has been said about the reactions and attitudes of the person appraised than about the appraising manager. Kikoski and Litterer (1983, p. 35) paint a rather lurid picture of the emotional turmoil that an AI can be for the appraisee: "guilt, fear, pleasure, regret and hope are only some of the emotions which are at work here. More than this, one's past performance is on display, one's future may be on the table in a sort of 'public self disclosure'—one of the most powerful yet rarely-used personal interactions."

They suggest that self-disclosure makes people more vulnerable. The theme of emotional vulnerability is one which surfaces in numerous studies. For example, Kay et al. (1965) found that criticism in the AI was threatening to the appraisee and led to a poorer reaction, especially if the individual had low occupational self-esteem. However, the notion that all appraisees are going to react the same way to appraisal is as unsafe as the proposition that appraisers are all going to adhere rigidly to the organisation's appraisal agenda and try to give an objective and accurate performance rating. A number of papers on appraisal have advocated a contingency approach, with the AI being tailored to the circumstances and make-up of the particular employee (Cummings & Schwab, 1973; Cederblom, 1982; Ilgen, Barnes-Farrell, & McKellin, 1993; Klein & Snell, 1994). Again, there are a number of personality and other attributes which might be expected to influence an individual's reactions to being appraised, including motivation, self-awareness and self-esteem, locus of control and attributional style, and feedback attitudes.

Motivation

Just as the appraiser can have a variety of motives in arriving at an assessment of a subordinate, the latter may also enter the appraisal process with a wide and mixed agenda:

- The appraisee may wish to know how he/she is viewed by the manager, without necessarily being committed to accept it—in other words, his/her orientation may be chiefly protective and designed to maintain self-esteem.
- Following on from this, he/she may wish to present a counter point of view and seek to persuade the appraiser to accept his/her self-evaluation, to either maintain present levels of reward or to enhance them; it is an impression management exercise.
- The appraisee may wish to use to the appraisal as a springboard to development, getting his/her manager to support and arrange specific training and development steps.
- The appraisee may wish to solve job problems and to improve performance as a result.
- It may be important to use the AI as a vehicle for "upward management", trying to persuade the appraiser to manage the appraisee in a different manner, or to modify the performance goals set.
- The AI can be an opportunity to express grievances against colleagues or to make the appraiser aware of personal issues and difficulties.

While many of these needs could be accommodated within an organisational PA scheme, the degree of emphasis placed on any one or combination of these may vary from one individual to another or for the same individual on different occasions.

The pattern and strength of an appraisee's needs may be influenced by a number of factors, but one of the most important is likely to be the appraisee's Need for Achievement or "N.Ach" (McClelland, 1961). This attribute has been found to be a significant influence in determining many work outcomes, one of which is the level of goal difficulty the individual prefers (Spangler, 1992; Sagie, Elizur, & Yamauchi, 1996). Cassidy and Lynn (1989) identify seven elements of N.Ach:

- *Work Ethic*—motivation to achieve based on finding reinforcement in the performance itself; the desire to work hard.
- *Acquisitiveness*—motivation based on the reinforcing properties of financial reward.
- *Dominance*—the desire to lead or to be in a position of dominance.
- *Pursuit of Excellence*—motivation that finds reward in performing to the best of one's ability.
- *Competitiveness*—enjoyment of competition with the aim of winning.
- *Status Aspiration*—motivation reinforced by climbing the social hierarchy.
- *Mastery*—reinforcement gained from success in the face of difficulty.

All, except perhaps Dominance, would seem to have potential relevance to understanding an individual's orientation to appraisal. For example, individuals high on Work Ethic, Pursuit of Excellence, and Mastery might be expected to have relatively little need for external recognition or encouragement to do better, though they might welcome development opportunities and challenging objectives. However, individuals high on Work Ethic but low on Mastery may feel most comfortable with objectives that emphasise amount of work rather than qualitative difficulty. The pay links to appraisal would obviously be a focus for appraisees high on Acquisitiveness, while emphasising how the individual is doing relative to peers might be important with those who are Competitive.

A more recent stream of literature relating to motivation and which bears some relation to need for achievement is that dealing with the concept of Goal Orientation, which may be defined as an orientation towards developing or demonstrating one's ability (VandeWalle & Cummings, 1997). Dweck and Leggett (1988) and other writers have described two general groups of underlying goals that individuals pursue in achievement situations; one is usually referred to as Learning Goal Orientation (LGO) and the other as Performance Goal Orientation (PGO). The former is an orientation towards developing competence by acquiring new skills and mastering new problems and tasks while the latter is concerned with an orientation to demonstrate and prove the adequacy of one's competence by seeking favourable assessments and avoiding criticism. VandeWalle and Cummings (1997) found that LGO was positively related to feedback seeking but PGO was negatively related to feedback seeking. In the context of appraisal, one would expect that individuals characterised by LGO would be much more positive in attitude to genuine feedback, development suggestions and challenging goals; individuals demonstrating PGO might show less tolerance of anything but positive feedback and might tend to focus their efforts on maintaining their performance in areas in which they had already proved their effectiveness. Phillips and Gully (1997) have demonstrated that goal orientation is related to self-efficacy (see below).

Self-awareness, self-esteem, and self-efficacy

An individual's level of self-objectivity is likely to exert some effect on his/her reaction to PA. If the individual is able to stand back from his/her own feelings and needs, and to assess his/her performance in an unbiased manner, it will perhaps make the task of the appraiser somewhat easier when it comes to conveying an assessment (assuming that the assessment is itself a fair one). The extent to which self-assessments are congruent with assessments made by others has been termed 'self-awareness' and has been the subject of a growing body of research (London & Smither, 1995; Fletcher & Baldry, 1999). The evidence, from a variety of settings, suggests that those higher in self-awareness are found on independent measures to be higher performers (Fletcher, 1997c). Self-awareness is, as was noted above, also recognised as a component of emotional intelligence. It thus seems very likely that the more self-aware an individual is, the more positive is his/her reaction likely to be in the PA situation. In part, this is because any assessment made in PA should not come as a surprise to the person appraised, will tend to be consistent with his/her self-picture and may be positive—or, at least, not less positive than the appraisee's self-assessment. Though there are a number of studies in relation to 360 degree feedback that have examined self-awareness (e.g. Furnham & Stringfield, 1994), so far none has related it directly to reactions to PA more generally. Some findings show a gender difference on self-awareness and self-assessment, suggesting that women may be more modest in their self-assessment and more congruent with others' assessments of them (Fletcher, 1999) which may in turn imply a greater likelihood of a positive appraisal response on their part.

More generally, however, self-assessment is likely to be influenced by self-esteem. Fahr and Dobbins (1989) investigated the relationship between self-esteem and self-assessments and found that individuals with high self-esteem evaluated themselves more favourably than people with low self-esteem. There is a substantial literature on self-esteem levels and responses to feedback (Swann, 1987), offering two alternative hypotheses. The first is the self-consistency position, which asserts that individuals with low self-esteem will prefer less positive feedback (because it fits with their self-image) while people with high self-esteem will want more positive feedback (for the same reason). The self-enhancement position, on the other hand, suggests that both high and low self-esteem individuals will want positive feedback, and that the latter will be especially motivated to seek it out. Neither position has achieved consistently greater support over the other. It may be that one principle holds in some situations but not in others (Shrauger, 1975). Unfortunately, little of the research in this area has been done on appraisal in a field context; however, it seems clear that self-esteem is frequently related to self-assessment and feedback responses.

Another highly relevant aspect of how the individual views himself is provided by Self-efficacy theory (Bandura, 1977). This defines Self-efficacy as a person's belief in his capabilities to meet the demands of a given situation, and there are numerous studies in the organisational field showing its relationship to variables such as managerial ambition (Van Vianen, 1999) and ratings of work performance made by others (Robertson & Sadri, 1993). Again, though largely ignored in the appraisal literature, it seems very likely that self-efficacy has an impact on numerous aspects of the appraisal situation. For example, Locke and Latham (1990) give it a central place in goal theory, and it has also been shown to related to feedback responses (Waldersee, 1994). Thus, setting objectives that represent tasks for which the individual has a low level of self-efficacy is unlikely to be a productive strategy in an appraisal.

Locus of control and attributional style

Spector (1982) reviewing the literature on locus of control cited evidence of its correlation with many organisational variables highly relevant to the appraisal situation, including effort, performance, job satisfaction and compliance with authority. Among other things, internals show a preference for participative bosses and respond more positively to incentive systems. More recently, Tang, Baldwin and Frost (1997) hypothesised that internals would be less affected by appraisal feedback than externals, and found results in line with this; perceived feedback showed no significant impact on an area of organisational commitment for internals whereas it did for externals. The interpretation of feedback and willingness to act on it are both likely to be influenced by the attributional style of the person appraised, which in turn is related to a number of personality variables (Mitchell, 1989) including self-esteem (see also the work of Herold et al., cited below). It is also related to gender. Women have been consistently found to attribute success more externally than men, thereby taking less credit for their performance, and have lower self-esteem (Beyer, 1990; Feingold, 1994). In an appraisal context, where an appraisee might need to project a positive self-image to some extent, this could clearly work against female appraisees, despite the possibility of a more positive appraisal response on their part noted earlier (Fletcher, 1999).

Feedback attitudes

There are several aspects of feedback that may impact orientation to PA. Perhaps the most fundamental is that feedback seeking is an individual difference variable in its own right (Ashford, 1986; Ashford & Cummings, 1983). Some individuals characteristically want and seek more feedback than others. However, there are further differences in the source of that feedback. Herold, Parsons, and Rensvold (1996) developed three domain-specific measures of individual differences in what they refer to as feedback propensities—internal propensity, internal ability and external propensity. The first of these reflects self-reliance, a lack of trust in other people's evaluations, and valuing internal feedback. The second, internal ability, reflects the ability to self-assess, to know what is required by way of performance and the ability to judge one's progress towards it—irrespective of preference for internal or externally generated feedback. External propensity is a preference for, and greater trust in, performance feedback from outside sources. Herold et al. (1996) found that internal ability was quite strongly related to positive self-esteem (r-values of around .4 to .5) and also to N.Ach and self-assurance; internal propensity showed a similar pattern. External propensity showed more or less the reverse pattern and was negatively correlated with tolerance for ambiguity. It seems very possible that differences in these three variables may have implications for reactions to PA. Thus, those with high external propensity may value traditional top-down appraisal, and possibly elements of 360-degree feedback, while those who are high on internal propensity and internal ability will respond best where appraisal is initiated and led by their self-assessment.

The genesis of self-awareness may lie in these feedback-seeking differences, but as indicated by the work of Herold et al., there are some underlying personality factors at work that may be relevant to both feedback attitudes and self-awareness. A number of studies support this suggestion. Roush and Atwater (1992) found that introverts and sensing types (as measured by the MBTI) had more accurate self-perceptions than those classified as other types. Nydegger (1975) found that individuals scoring highly on a cognitive complexity measure made better use of feedback cues, and were less likely to inflate their self-evaluations. Mabe and West (1982), in their meta-analysis of self-assessment, reported that individuals higher in need for achievement and intelligence tend to provide more accurate self-evaluations. Fletcher and Baldry (2000) found that individuals whose self-ratings were congruent with ratings made of them by their superiors were more reserved, shrewd, open-minded, conscientious and careful, and serious-minded as measured by the 16PF (note that some of these are also linked to the second-order factor of Introversion). Presenting the reverse side of the coin, managers who did not see themselves in the same way as their bosses were more outgoing, impulsive, forthright and artless, conservative, and expedient. It is not difficult to see how such differences could influence sensitivity to, and interpretation of, feedback from superiors, and hence affect responses to PA.

Finally, in relation to feedback, it has frequently been observed that the credibility of the source of the feedback is crucial to its acceptance (Ilgen, Fisher, & Taylor, 1979; Taylor, Fisher, & Ilgen, 1984; Bastos & Fletcher, 1995). While in some ways this may be viewed as an attribute of the appraiser, its perception resides in the appraisee. If appraisees do not find the PA system a credible source of feedback, then their reaction to it will be indifferent if not negative. Lack of perceived credibility may stem from deficiencies in the rating instrument, inadequate observation of the individual's performance by the supervisor, procedural justice concerns, and doubts about the motivation or other attributes of the appraiser (though these may in turn reflect the personality of the appraisee—lack of objectivity, high aggression leading to low levels of interpersonal trust, etc.).

The personality and personality-related variables mentioned here as influencing appraisee orientation to appraisal are not suggested as an exhaustive list, but they are perhaps among the more prominent ones. It will be obvious from the above that they are also interrelated. For example, internal vs. external locus is a fundamental element in attributional style and is the cornerstone of the feedback attitudes identified by Herold et al. (1996). Their Internal Ability factor links self-assessment ability with N.Ach—identified by Mabe and West (1982) as a correlate of self-assessment accuracy—and self-esteem, which has been noted above as being associated with self-evaluation (Fahr & Dobbins, 1989). Herold et al.'s External Propensity factor was correlated with low tolerance of ambiguity, which has an echo in some of the individual differences mentioned earlier as correlating with high self-awareness or self-assessment accuracy, namely cognitive complexity and open-mindedness. Phillips and Gully (1997) found that both goal orientation and locus of control influenced self-efficacy, and that the latter along with Need for Achievement influenced self-set goals.

As has been suggested, between them these variables have a considerable potential to influence many core aspects of the AI:

- Both N.Ach and self-efficacy will influence the appraisees' preferences for the degree of difficulty and challenge presented by the goals set—either those set by the appraiser or by themselves.
- Self-esteem and goal orientation seem to relate to preferences for amount and type of feedback.
- Self-awareness is likely to impact on reactions to feedback and to tolerance of negative feedback.
- Internality–externality differences affect choice of feedback source and perceptions of source credibility, preferences for participation level and the degree of ambiguity tolerated (i.e. amount of feedback).
- N.Ach and internality–externality are likely to influence reward preferences.

Finally, because these personality variables are likely to impact on individuals' reactions to assessments made of them and the feedback conveyed as a result, they are also likely to strongly influence perceptions of procedural justice. Any contingency approach to conducting or (in research model terms) explaining appraisal should presumably take account of them.

THE RELATIONSHIP BETWEEN APPRAISER AND APPRAISEE

While many of the attributes of appraiser and appraisee already mentioned are obviously relevant here in that they contribute to the relationship between both parties, some research has specifically focused on the nature of the relationship and it is to this that we now turn. A number of writers have highlighted this as a key factor in determining appraisal outcomes. Beer (1981) suggested that there was "no substitute" for the quality of the supervisor–subordinate relationship, and that without this being good no appraisal system could be effective. Similarly, Kikoski and Litterer (1983) identified the quality of the relationship as being a vital precondition for a successful appraisal interview. They went on to point out that psychotherapy research shows how the quality of the therapist–client relationship is more important, in terms of various criteria, than the actual kind of therapeutic approach taken.

Much of the research done in this area was carried out some time ago, and initially emphasised the amount and quality of communication between appraiser and appraisee, and the degree of similarity or congruence between them. On the first of these themes, Burke and Wilcox (1969) found that greater openness in communication between manager and subordinate was associated with higher satisfaction with the appraisal, with the job and with the company. Fletcher (1978) found that the frequency with which the manager and subordinate discussed work outside the appraisal situation was related to appraisal outcomes. Thus, of appraisees who reported that they rarely or never discussed work with their boss on a day-to-day basis, 26% said the appraisal led to increased job satisfaction, 32% said it led to better performance, and 21% of the interviews resulted in some kind of action recommendation being recorded; the equivalent figures for appraisees who frequently or sometimes discussed work outside the appraisal were 52%, 61% and 40%.

The research on similarity between appraiser and appraisee—including gender match—as a predictor of appraisal outcomes had mixed success, but that which examined congruence of attitudes showed some positive findings. Wexley, Alexander, Greenwalt, and Couch (1980) found that the more aware a manager was of subordinates' work-related attitudes, the more positive were the evaluations they gave, and the more congruent subordinates perceived the manager's attitudes to be to their own, the more satisfied they were with the supervision received. The authors conclude that seeing others as they see themselves allows one to better understand and predict their behaviour, and this is generally a rewarding experience. Although this was an experimental study, the findings were replicated by Wexley and Pulakos (1983) who also found that the effect was strongest in same-sex dyads.

Later work on appraiser–appraisee relationships has tended to focus on the overall quality of the relationship and on liking or affect. Following on Beer's (1981) suggestion that such factors as trust and loyalty were likely to influence the extent to which important issues were discussed in appraisal, Nathan, Mohrman, and Milliman (1991) measured the quality of the relationship using a series of semantic differential scales. They found that, even controlling for the favourableness of performance evaluations, appraisee reactions to the review process were significantly influenced by relationship quality. The implications of the quality of relationship for the effectiveness of *specific* appraisal content and method were examined by Klein and Snell (1994) in their study of 55 appraiser–appraisee dyads. They found that criticism had a positive effect where the individuals appraised had a good relationship with their line manager. They also found that goal setting had a greater impact on poor performers who reported a poor relationship with their supervisors.

Another way of viewing the appraiser–appraisee relationship is to focus on the degree of liking between the two parties. Numerous investigations have been published that address this, and Lefkowitz (2000) concluded from his review of 24 studies that supervisors' positive regard for subordinates is often found to relate to more lenient appraisal ratings, greater halo effects, reduced accuracy, less inclination to punish poor performance and—not surprisingly—better interpersonal relationships. The effect of liking has been observed even when ability or performance level has been controlled for (e.g. Harris & Sackett, 1988). Varma, Denisi, and Peters (1996) pointed out that although the effects of liking are well documented, the reasons for the influence of liking are not clear. They interpreted the findings from their own study as indicating that rather than affect being a biasing factor, it resulted from better performance in the first place.

Dobbins and Russell (1986) use attributional theory in their explanation, suggesting that when disliked individuals perform poorly, their behaviour is "in-character" and hence attributed to factors internal to them. On the other hand, when liked subordinates perform below expectation, this is "out-of-character" and is attributed to external factors. However, Lefkowitz (2000) identified a range of conceptual and methodological problems in studies on liking as an influence on PA. These include failure to take account of the duration of the relationship and the lack of fidelity to organisational appraisal systems (arising from the use of experimental research designs or studies carried out specifically for research purposes). His conclusion is that it is not justified to assume either that liking reflects bias or that it simply stems from a reaction to good performance. The influence of liking on ratings, for whatever the underlying reasons, is less where clear standards and observable performance information are available (Varma et al., 1996).

It would certainly be understandable if managers had more positive reactions towards subordinates whose performance was good—and who consequently helped the manager's position and produced fewer problems. This is the perspective taken by Hogan and Shelton (1998), though they approach it from a rather different angle. They assert that appraisal evaluations reflect supervisors' judgements of *Rewardingness*, which is described as the degree to which the appraisee meets or fulfils the boss's expectations regarding his or her performance. They cite the findings of Barrick and Mount (1991) that scores on measures of Conscientiousness and of Emotional Stability predict appraisal ratings and argue that this is because people who work hard, follow the rules, stay in a good mood and act in a consistent manner are rewarding to work with. Fletcher (1995) makes a similar point, based on findings that appraisees' scores on the Optimism scale of a personality inventory correlated with a wide range of appraisal ratings. Hogan and Shelton also point out that rewardingness is not necessarily about meeting organisational goals, it is primarily about meeting the boss's goals, which links back to the earlier discussion of appraiser motivation.

IMPROVING FUTURE RESEARCH AND PRACTICE IN PERFORMANCE APPRAISAL

The research described in the preceding section of this chapter has not sought to offer a comprehensive review of every possible psychological factor that might impact on those involved in the appraisal process. Rather, it has selected a number of variables that seem to be of particular relevance in understanding people's reactions to PA, some of which have attracted a good deal of research, and attempted to illustrate the importance of this more individually focused perspective on PA. There have been many studies done on major research themes such as participation in appraisal or on aspects of appraisal design. But while these tell us a lot about some of the general principles that relate to successful PA, it seems likely that at the end of the day the largest determinant of appraisal outcomes are the make-up and styles of the appraiser and appraisee, and the existing relationship between them. It is thus essential that we improve our knowledge of these factors and how they interact. This is likely to become even more imperative in view of the increasingly international nature of business and the growing diversity in the workforce. Kikoski (1999, p. 301), talking in an American context, observes that:

"the problems of face-to-face communication in an essentially monocultural workforce may be insignificant compared to the interpersonal communication difficulties
which may accompany the more culturally diverse workforce that is forecast."

While Kikoski is referring to the growing proportion US workers from Hispanic, Asian
or African backgrounds, the cultural diversity issue is likely to be even more marked in
the European Union, with its freedom of movement of labour. There is a double challenge
that this presents. First, the vast majority of research studies on PA have emanated from
the USA, and the extent to which the findings of these can generalise to other countries
is highly questionable; see Fletcher and Perry (2001) for an analysis of this. Second,
as already observed in this present chapter, relatively little contemporary research has
been directed towards the more psychological aspects of the handling of the appraisal
interaction. Again, Kikoski (1999) has something to offer on this point, advocating the
value of microskills training in interpersonal communications as relevant to appraisal.
But there is little empirical evidence of the effectiveness of such approaches to appraisal
interview training in the literature; nearly all the attention has been directed towards rater
training (Woehr & Huffcutt, 1994). Interestingly, however, there are some findings on
applying behaviour modelling training to appraisees (Stoffey & Reilly, 1997). However,
instruction on interview skills and the handling of the AI can only go so far without a better
knowledge of the effectiveness of different strategies with different kinds of appraisee.
In other words, a contingency approach of the kind described by Klein and Snell (1994),
some of whose findings were alluded to earlier in the chapter. Once a manager has been
trained in handling the AI and has been advised as to the most effective strategies to
adopt with appraisees of differing needs, personalities and so on, success will largely
rest on how well the manager concerned knows and understands his/her subordinates as
individuals and can tailor his/her style accordingly. Thus, in the future more PA research
based on a contingency model is likely to be helpful.

Performance appraisal and the context in which it operates does not stand still, and the
rapidly increasing use of 360-degree assessment systems for development and appraisal
purposes is another aspect of this. Multi-source appraisal is a topic that can take a chapter
or several books to itself, and yet many aspects of it are likely to be susceptible to exactly
the same kind of phenomena as traditional top-down appraisal. Certainly, using several
sources of assessment does not necessarily eliminate many of the problems so frequently
found in conventional appraisal (Fletcher, Baldry, & Cunningham-Snell, 1998). Using
this kind of assessment input as part of the appraisal system will still pose the same kind
of challenges inherent in communicating performance feedback more generally. For
example, there is still likely to be a threshold above which individuals become defensive
to critical feedback. While recognising there are some unique features of 360-degree
assessment, the lessons of research on PA do need to be applied to it also.

Apart from changes in appraisal methods, the nature of the work that they relate to is
also going to be transformed and this will no doubt have implications for how appraisal
operates (Cascio, 1995; Sulsky & Keown, 1998). The predictions made about the future
are inevitably vague and sometimes contradictory; for example, Pilon (1993) suggests
that advances in technology will lead to a need for fewer but smarter workers, while Prieto
and Simon (1997) emphasise that better information technology can make jobs easier!
Although computers will make possible new forms of performance monitoring and
feedback mechanisms (Kulik & Ambrose, 1993; McCune, 1997; Stanton, 2000), it seems
certain that some form of appraisal interview or equivalent interaction will continue to

take place—in which case the research need in this domain will continue. If work and organisational psychologists are to make a distinctive contribution to understanding and improving PA in the future, it would seem important that they do not devote as much time as in the past to "systems" perspectives (which has sometimes made their work indistinguishable from that of human resource and general management studies researchers) or to searching for the "perfect" rating scale. Instead, they might concentrate more on doing what they are uniquely qualified to do—trying to understand, describe and predict the appraisal interaction at an individual psychological level.

REFERENCES

Antonioni, D. (1996). Designing an effective 360-degree appraisal feedback process. *Organizational Dynamics*, **25**, 24–38.

Arvey, R. D., & Murphy, K. R. (1998). Performance evaluation in work settings. *Annual Review Psychology*, **49**, 141–168.

Ashford, S. J. (1989). Self-assessments in organizations: A literature review and integrative model. *Research in Organizational Behaviour*, **11**, 133–174.

Ashford, S. J., & Cummings, L. L. (1983). Feedback as an individual resource: Personal strategies of creating information. *Organizational Behavior and Human Performance*, **32**, 370–398.

Austin, J. T., & Villanova, P. (1992). The criterion problem, 1917–92. *Journal of Applied Psychology*, **77**, 836–74.

Bandura, A. (1977). Self-efficacy: Towards a unifying theory of behavioral change. *Psychological: Review*, **84**, 191–215.

Barrick, M. R., & Mount, M. K. (1991). The big five personality dimensions and job performance: A meta-analysis. *Personnel Psychology*, **44**, 1–26.

Bastos, M., & Fletcher, C. (1995). Exploring the individual's perception of sources and credibility of feedback in the work environment. *International Journal of Selection and Assessment*, **3**, 29–40.

Beer, M. (1981). Performance appraisal: Dilemmas and possibilities. *Organizational Dynamics*, **9**, 24–36.

Beyer, S. (1990). Gender differences in accuracy of self evaluations of performance. *Journal of Personality and Social Psychology*, **59**, 960–970.

Burke, R. J., & Wilcox, D. S. (1969). Effects of different patterns and degrees of openness in superior–subordinate communication of subordinate job satisfaction. *Academy of Management Journal*, **12**, 319–326.

Burke, R. J., Weitzel, W., & Weir, T. (1978). Characteristics of effective employee performance review and development interviews: Replication and extension. *Personnel Psychology*, **31**, 903–920.

Cascio, W. F. (1995). Whither industrial and organizational psychology in a changing world of work? *American Psychologist*, **50**, 928–939.

Cassidy, T., & Lynn, R. (1989). A multifactorial approach to achievement motivation: The development of a comprehensive measure. *Journal of Occupational Psychology*, **62**, 301–312.

Cawley, B. D., Keeping, L. M., & Levy, P. E. (1998). Participation in the performance appraisal process and employee reactions: A meta-analytic review of field investigations. *Journal of Applied Psychology*, **83**, 615–631.

Cederblom, D. (1982). The performance appraisal interview: A review, implications and suggestions. *Academy of Management Review*, **7**, 219–227.

Cleveland, J. N., & Murphy, K. R. (1992). Analyzing performance appraisal as goal-directed behavior. *Research in Personnel and Human Resources Management*, **10**, 121–185.

Cummings, L. L., & Schwab, D. P. (1973). *Performance in organizations: Determinants and appraisal*. Glenview, Illinois: Scott, Foresman & Co.

Cunningham-Snell, N., Anderson, N., Fletcher, C., & Gibb, A. (1998). *What influences candidates' perceptions of procedural fairness: Due process or final verdict?* Paper presented at the British Psychological Society Occupational Psychology Conference, Eastbourne.

DeNisi, A. S. (1997). *Cognitive approach to Performance Appraisal: A programme of research.* London: Routledge.

Dobbins, G. H., & Russell, J. M. (1986). The biasing effects of subordinate likeableness on leaders' responses to poor performers: A laboratory and a field study. *Personnel Psychology,* **39,** 759–777.

Dulewicz, S. V., & Fletcher, C. (1989). The context and dynamics of Performance Appraisal. In P. Herriot (Ed.), *Assessment and selection in organisations.* London: John Wiley & Sons.

Dweck, C. S., & Leggett, E. L. (1988). A social-cognitive approach to motivation and personality. *Psychological Review,* **95,** 256–27.

Fahr, J., & Dobbins, G. (1989). Effects of self esteem on leniency bias in self reports of performance: A structural equation model analysis. *Personnel Psychology,* **42,** 835–850.

Feingold, A. (1994). Gender differences in personality: A meta-analysis. *Psychological Bulletin,* **116,** 429–456.

Fletcher, C. (1978). Manager–subordinate communication and leadership style: A field study of their relationship to perceived outcomes of appraisal interviews. *Personnel Review,* **7,** 56–62.

Fletcher, C., & Williams, R. (1992). *Performance appraisal and career development* (2nd edn.). Cheltenham: Stanley Thornes.

Fletcher, C. (1994). The effects of performance review in appraisal: Evidence and implications. In C. Mabey & P. Iles (Eds.), *Managing learning.* London: Routledge/Open University.

Fletcher, C. (1995). New directions for Performance Appraisal: Some findings and observations. *International Journal of Selection and Assessment,* **3,** 191–196.

Fletcher, C. (1997a). *Appraisal: Routes to improved performance* (2nd edn.). London: Institute of Personnel & Development.

Fletcher, C. (1997b). Performance Appraisal in context: Organisational changes and their impact on practice. In P. Herriot & N. Anderson (Eds.), *Handbook of assessment and selection in organisations.* London: Wiley.

Fletcher, C. (1997c). Self-awareness: A neglected attribute in selection and assessment? *International Journal of Selection and Assessment,* **5**(3), 183–187.

Fletcher, C., Baldry, C., & Cunningham-Snell, N. (1998). The psychometric properties of 360 degree feedback: An empirical study and cautionary tale. *International Journal of Selection and Assessment,* **6,** 19–34.

Fletcher, C., & Baldry, C. (1999). Multi-source feedback systems: A research perspective. In C. Cooper & I. Robertson (Eds.), *International review of organizational and industrial psychology,* Vol. 14. New York & London: Wiley & Sons.

Fletcher, C. (1999). The implications of research on gender differences in self assessment and 360 degree appraisal. *Human Resource Management Journal,* **9**(1), 39–46.

Fletcher, C., & Baldry, C. (2000). A study of individual differences and self awareness in the context of multi-source feedback. *Journal of Occupational and Organisational Psychology,* **73,** 303–319.

Fletcher, C., & Perry, E. (2001). Performance appraisal: A cross-cultural and future-oriented perspective. In N. Anderson, D. Ones, H. Sinangil, & C. Viswesvaran (Eds.), *International handbook of work and organizational psychology.* Sage.

Foucault, M. (1981). *Power/Knowledge: Selected Interviews and other Writings.* Brighton: Harvester Press.

Furnham, A., & Stringfield, P. (1994). Congruence of self and subordinate ratings of managerial practices as a correlate of supervisor evaluation. *Journal of Occupational and Organizational Psychology,* **67,** 57–67.

Gioia, D. A., & Longenecker, C. O. (1994). Delving into the dark side: The politics of executive appraisal. *Organizational Dynamics,* **22,** 47–58.

Greenberg, J. (1986). Determinants of perceived fairness in performance evaluations. *Journal of Applied Psychology,* **71,** 340–342.

Greller, M. M. (1975). Subordinate participation and reactions to the appraisal interview. *Journal of Applied Psychology,* **60,** 554–559.

Harris, M. M., & Sackett, P. R. (1988). Interpersonal affect and performance rating level: An individual difference analysis. *Third Annual Conference of the Society of Industrial & Organizational Psychology,* Dallas, Texas.

Harris, M. M., Smith, D. E., & Champagne, D. (1995). A field study of performance appraisal purpose: Research-versus administrative-based ratings. *Personnel Psychology*, **48**, 151–160.

Herold, D. M., Parsons, C. K., & Rensvold, R. B. (1996). Individual differences in the generation and processing of performance feedback. *Educational and Psychological Measurement*, **56**, 1, 5–25.

Higgs, M., & Dulewicz, V. (1999). *Making sense of emotional intelligence*. Windsor: NFER–NELSON.

Hogan, E. A. (1987). Effects of prior expectations on performance ratings: A longitudinal study. *Academy of Management Journal*, **30**, 354–368.

Hogan, R., & Shelton, D. (1998). A socioanalytic perspective on job performance. *Human Performance*, **11**, 129–144.

Ilgen, D. R., Fisher, C. D., & Taylor, M. S. (1979). Consequences of individual feedback on behavior in organizations. *Journal of Applied Psychology*, **64**, 349–371.

Ilgen, D. R., Barnes-Farrell, J. L., & McKellin, D. B. (1993). Performance appraisal process research in the 1980s: What has it contributed to performance appraisals in use? *Organizational Behavior and Human Decision Processes*, **54**, 321–368.

Industrial Society (1997). *Appraisal*. Report no. 337. London: Industrial Society.

Kay, E., Meyer, H. H., & French, J. R. P. (1965). Effects of threat in a performance appraisal interview. *Journal of Applied Psychology*, **49**, 311–317.

Kikoski, J. F., & Litterer, J. A. (1983). Effective communication in the performance appraisal interview. *Public Personnel Management*, **22**, 33–42.

Kikoski, J. F. (1999). Effective communication in the performance appraisal interview: Face-to-face communication for public managers in the culturally diverse workplace. *Public Personnel Management*, **28**, 301–323.

Klein, H. J., & Snell, S. A. (1994). The impact of interview process and context on performance appraisal interview effectiveness. *Journal of Managerial Issues*, **VI**, 160–175.

Knowlton, W. A., & Mitchell, T. R. (1980). Effects of causal attributions on a supervisor's evaluation of subordinate performance. *Journal of Applied Psychology*, **65**, 459–466.

Korsgaard, M. A., & Roberson, L. (1995). Procedural justice in performance evaluation: The role of instrumental and non-instrumental voice in performance appraisal discussions. *Journal of Management*, **21**, 657–669.

Kulik, C. T., & Ambrose, M. L. (1993). The impact of computerized performance monitoring design features on the performance appraisal process. *Journal of Managerial Issues*, **5**, 182–197.

Landy, F. J., & Farr, J. L. (1980). Performance rating. *Psychological Bulletin*, **87**, 72–107.

Lefkowitz, J. (2000). The role of interpersonal affective regard in supervisory performance ratings: A literature review and proposed causal model. *Journal of Occupational and Organizational Pyschology*, **73**, 67–85.

Locke, E. A., & Latham, G. P. (1990). *A theory of goal setting and task performance*. Englewood Cliffs, NJ: Prentice-Hall.

London, M., & Smither, J. W. (1995). Can multi-source feedback change perceptions of goal accomplishment, self-evaluations and performance related outcomes? Theory-based applications and directions for research. *Personnel Psychology*, **48**, 803–839.

Longenecker, C. O. (1989). Truth or consequences: Politics and performance appraisals. *Business Horizons*, Nov./Dec., 1–7.

Longenecker, C. O., & Gioia, D. A. (1988). Neglected at the top: Executives talk about executive appraisal. *Sloan Management Review*, Winter, 41–47.

Longenecker, C. O., Gioia, D., & Sims, H. P., Jr. (1987). Behind the mask: The politics of employee appraisal. *The Academy of Management Executive*, **1**, 183–193.

Longenecker, C. O., Liverpool, P. R., & Wilson, K. A. (1988). An assessment of managerial/subordinate perceptions of performance appraisal effectiveness. *Journal of Business and Psychology*, **2**, 311–320.

Longenecker, C. O., & Ludwig, D. (1990). Ethical dilemmas in performance appraisal. *Journal of Business Ethics*, **9**, 961–969.

Mabe, P. A., & West, S. G. (1982). Validity of self-evluation of ability—a review and meta-analysis. *Journal of Applied Psychology*, **67**(3), 280–296.

Maier, N. R. F. (1958). Three types of appraisal interview. *Personnel*, March/April, 27–40.

McEvoy, G. M., & Buller, P. F. (1987). User acceptance of peer appraisals in an industrial setting. *Personnel Psychology*, **40**, 785–797.

McCune, J. C. (1997). Employee appraisals the electronic way. *Management Review*, **86**, 44–46.

McClelland, D. C. (1961). *The Achieving Society*. Princeton, NJ: Van Nostrand.

McGregor, D. (1957). An uneasy look at performance appraisal. *Harvard Business Review*, **35**, 89–94.

Meyer, H. H., Kay, E., & French, J. R. P. (1965). Split roles in performance appraisal. *Harvard Business Review*, **43**, 123–129.

Napier, N. K., & Latham, G. P. (1986). Outcome expectancies of people who conduct performance appraisals. *Personnel Psychology*, **39**, 827–837.

Nathan, B. R., Morhman, A. M., Jr., & Milliman, J. (1991). Interpersonal relations as a context for the effects of appraisal interviews on performance and satisfaction: A longitudinal study. *Academy of Management Journal*, **34**, 352–369.

Nemeroff, W. F., & Wexley, K. N. (1979). An exploration of the relationships between performance feedback interview characteristics and interview outcomes as perceived by managers and subordinates. *Journal of Occupational Psychology*, **52**, 25–34.

Newton, T., & Findlay, P. (1996). Playing God? The performance of appraisal. *Human Resource Management Journal*, **6**, 42–58.

Nydegger, R. V. (1975). Developmental changes in abstractness and moral reasoning. *Dissertation Abstracts International*, **32**, 4109A. University Microfilms, No. 72-03, 831.

Phillips, J. M., & Gully, S. M. (1997). Role of goal orientation, ability, need for achievement, and locus of control in the self efficacy and goal setting process. *Journal of Applied Psychology*, **82**, 792–802.

Pilon, L. J. (1993). Quoted in "Jobs, Jobs", *Business Week*, 22 February, page 74.

Pollack, D. M., & Pollack, L. J. (1996). Using 360 degree feedback in performance appraisal. *Public Personnel Management*, **25**, 507–528.

Prieto, J. M., & Simon, C. (1997). Network and its implications for assessment. In N. Anderson & P. Herriot (Eds.), *International Handbook of Selection and Assessment*. Chichester: Wiley & Sons.

Robertson, I. T., & Sadri, G. (1993). Managerial self-efficacy and managerial performance. *British Journal of Management*, **4**, 37–45.

Rothaus, P., Morton, R. B., & Hanson, P. G. (1965). Performance appraisal and psychological distance. *Journal of Applied Psychology*, **49**, 48–54.

Roush, P. E., & Atwater, L. (1992). Using the MBTI to understand transformational leadership and self-perception accuracy. *Military Psychology*, **4**, 1, 17–34.

Sagie, A., Elizur, D., & Yamauchi, A. (1996). The structure and strength of achievement motivation: A cross-cultural comparison. *Journal of Organizational Behaviour*, **17**, 431–444.

Salovey, P., & Mayer, J. D. (1990). Emotional intelligence. *Imagination, Cognition and Personality*, **9**, 185–211.

Shrauger, J. S. (1975). Responses to evaluations as a function of initial self-perceptions. *Psychological Bulletin*, **82**, 581–596.

Silverman, S. B., & Wexley, K. N. (1984). Reaction of emlpoyees to performance appraisal interviews as a function of their participation in rating scale development. *Personnel Psychology*, **37**, 703–710.

Spangler, W. D. (1992). Validity of questionnaire and TAT measures of need for achievement: Two meta-analyses. *Psychological Bulletin*, **112**, 140–154.

Spector, P. (1982). Behavior in organizations as a function of employee's locus of control. *Psychological Bulletin*, **91**, 482–497.

Stanton, J. M. (2000). Reactions to employee performance monitoring: Framework, review and research directions. *Human Performance*, **13**, 85–113.

Stoffey, R. W., & Reilly, R. R. (1997). Training appraisees to participate in appraisal: Effects on appraisers and appraisees. *Journal of Business and Psychology*, **12**, 219–239.

Sulsky, L. M., & Keown, J. L. (1998). Performance appraisal in the changing world of work: Implications for the meaning and measurement of work performance. *Canadian Psychology*, **39**, 52–59.

Swann, W. B. (1987). Identity negotiation: Where two roads meet. *Journal of Personality and Social Psychology*, **53**, 1038–1051.

Tang, T. L.-P., Baldwin, L., & Frost, A. G. (1997). Locus of control as a moderator of the self reported performance feedback–personal sacrifice relationship. *Personality and Individual Differences*, **22**, 201–211.

Taylor, M. S., Fisher, C. D., & Ilgen, D. R. (1984). Individuals' reactions to performance feedback in organizations: A control theory perspective. In K. M. Rowland & G. R. Ferris (Eds.), *Research in personnel and human resources management*. Greenwich, CT: JAI Press.

Townley, B. (1999). Practical reason and performance appraisal. *Journal of Management Studies*, **36**, 287–306.

Tziner, A., Latham, G. P., Price, B. S., & Haccoun, R. (1996). Development and validation of a questionnaire for measuring perceived political considerations in performance appraisal. *Journal of Organizational Behavior*, **17**, 179–190.

VandeWalle, D., & Cummings, L. L. (1997). A test of the influence of goal orientation on the feedback seeking process. *Journal of Applied Psychology*, **82**, 390–400.

Varma, A., Denisi, A. S., & Peters, L. H. (1996). Interpersonal affect and performance appraisal: A field study. *Personnel Psychology*, **49**, 341–360.

Van Vianen, A. E. M. (1999). Managerial self efficacy, outcome expectancies, and work-role salience as determinants of ambition for a managerial position. *Journal of Applied Social Psychology*, **29**, 639–665.

Waldersee, R. (1994). Self efficacy and performance as a function of feedback sign and anxiety: A service experiment. *Journal of Applied Behavioral Science*, **30**, 346–356.

Wexley, K. N., Alexander, R. A., Greenwalt, J. P., & Couch, M. A. (1980). Attitudinal congruence and similarity as related to interpersonal evaluations in manager-subordinate dyads. *Academy of Management Journal*, **23**, 320–330.

Wexley, K. N., & Pulakos, E. D. (1983). The effect of perceptual congruence and sex on subordinates' performance appraisals of their managers. *Academy of Management Journal*, **26**, 666–676.

Williams, R. (1998). *Performance Management*. London: International Thomson Business Press (Essential Business Psychology Series).

Woehr, D. J., & Huffcutt, A. I. (1994). Rater training for performance appraisal: A quantitative review. *Journal of Occupational and Organizational Psychology*, **67**, 189–206.

Performance Appraisal

Gesa Drewes
Dieter Strametz & Partner, Liederbach, Germany, and
Bernd Runde
University of Osnabrück, Osnabrück, Germany

SUMMARY

Annual performance appraisals present a field of conflict, which many managers attempt to avoid. The reasons why managers seem to be afraid may be seen in the various complications that arise in the introduction and further course of performance appraisal systems. This chapter attempts to give an answer to the questions that arise when trying to implement performance appraisal systems. What purpose do performance appraisal systems serve? What steps need to be considered before a performance appraisal systems is introduced? How can the quality of such a system be determined and which factors carry a positive influence as far as quality is concerned? Performance appraisal is not only applied 'from top to bottom' but on occasion also between coworkers at

Psychological Management of Individual Performance. Edited by Sabine Sonnentag.
© 2002 John Wiley & Sons, Ltd.

the same hierarchical level or when subordinates are appraising their superiors. A combination of the possible appraisal levels that can be found in a 360-degree feedback system will be presented from an implementation perspective.

INTRODUCTION

It is one of the most important tasks of personnel management to keep and support highly efficient and productive employees. In this context, performance appraisal is an important tool, which can be useful in order to evaluate an employee's performance, clearly encompassed in the form of an observable and describable result of that person's work. These results can then be compared to a nominal output. Throughout this chapter, the term "performance appraisal" is used whenever the following criteria are met:

- appraisals (of performance) take place at regular intervals
- a standardized method is used, on the grounds of previously agreed upon performance criteria
- either the employee's behaviour or outcome of performance is to be evaluated
- the employee is evaluated by the next higher-ranking superior, equally ranking colleagues, other coworkers or makes a self-appraisal.

In this chapter, we address performance appraisal from a practitioner's perspective. More specifically, we describe the functions of performance appraisal systems. Particulary with this practical focus posing as a background, the introduction process of a performance appraisal system is presented in detail. We name the core functions and elements of such a process and describe how mistakes can be prevented.

The chapter presents an overview of the relevant quality criteria that a performance appraisal system must meet in order to achieve a company's main aims: the reaction to the demands of a market that is altered and has gained in flexibility, and how the company can ascertain its ability to compete there. We take a closer look at the different ways to go about performance appraisal: Which methods exist? Which are put to use? This context also allows for the presentation of the conclusion why the characteristic or trait orientation of performance appraisals should be exchanged for a behavioural orientation. The comments become even more specific when one takes a look at a very recent performance appraisal system: the 360-degree feedback. On the basis of a study performed by one of the authors of this chapter, a closer look can be taken at the chances and risks, as well as success factors, for the introduction of this system.

DIFFERENT PURPOSES OF PERFORMANCE APPRAISAL

PERFORMANCE APPRAISAL AS A MANAGEMENT TOOL

A performance appraisal system can be used as a management tool to support personnel development and management. It is a major task of a superior to set goals in cooperation with the employees, to provide them with feedback about their performance and to help them to develop their skills.

When designed carefully, a performance appraisal system provides well-defined criteria for assessing an employee. The superiors are able to define the strengths and weaknesses of the employee on the grounds of these criteria. They give the employee feedback and agree with him/her on measures to develop his/her skills and competences and to reach his/her goals. These arrangements do not only include training but also advice for working habits and for being organized.

Of course a superior could manage these tasks even without an appraisal system. But there are some clear advantages for supporting this process by the means of an appraisal system: one of the most important advantages is the standardization of the evaluation process and the feedback dialogue. Without a performance appraisal system some superiors provide feedback to their employees and others do not, some do it in a detailed manner and others make only a general statement about the employee's performance. Also, in all probability, superiors will assess different criteria according to their preferences. Without a performance appraisal system, feedback—if feedback takes place at all—depends much more on the personal potential of the superior to pass assessment. Thus, one aim of a company for implementing a performance appraisal system can be to standardize the process: the superiors have fixed dimensions which they use to appraise. The appraisal is required regularly and can be controlled by the personnel department. Giving feedback is a difficult task for many superiors and they often try to avoid it. With a performance appraisal system the necessity of a feedback dialogue is set by the system and the superiors can be trained based upon its standards.

Because the performance appraisal system offers a standardized appraisal, it can ensure comparability of the appraisals. As a consequence, it becomes easier for employees to change to different business domains within a company. The aim of a company can be to ensure an optimal deployment of their staff. Especially large international companies try to build up skill databases of their employees. A successful and standardized performance appraisal system is one prerequisite for such a database. But the comparability of appraisals has to be regarded with care and can only be realized within a certain range. We will refer to this when we discuss rating scales.

A performance appraisal system can also be used to support goal achievement. Some companies implement goal setting together with the performance appraisal system. The superior and the employee define goals for a certain period of time. These goals should have certain criteria: they should be measurable, well defined, acceptable for the employee and within reach and timed. If the goals meet these criteria it can be judged whether they are achieved or not. Assessment of goal achievement may also be a part in the performance appraisal dialogue (see also Algera, Kleingeld, & van Tuijl in this volume).

PERFORMANCE APPRAISAL FOR SALARY DISTRIBUTION

A performance appraisal system can be used for salary adjustment. In addition to fixed salaries, many companies offer their management staff a bonus or specific type of flexible pay. This trend is increasing. This bonus is often related to individual performance. Thus, performance appraisal is used to determine the amount of the flexible salary. In general there are two possibilities to combine the compensation with the performance appraisal.

The first method is to define targets between superior and employee. If these targets are achieved the employee will gain a certain bonus. In this case, the employees know exactly which amount of money they can expect. The flexible part of the salary is defined in a fixed range. The expenses cannot exactly be estimated beforehand, which is a disadvantage for the company.

The second possibility is that the company fixes an amount for bonus salaries for a certain department. This amount has to be distributed in a fair method among the employees of the business unit. The dilemma for the superiors is that they cannot define a certain amount for each employee because it depends on the performance of all employees. The disadvantage for the employees is that they do not know exactly how much bonus they can get.

CAN PERFORMANCE APPRAISAL SYSTEMS BE USED FOR BOTH OBJECTIVES AT THE SAME TIME?

A performance appraisal system should not be used for personnel development and salary distribution at the same time, for the main reason that the employee will probably behave differently in a feedback dialogue according to its aim. If the aim is to appraise goal achievement in order to fix a bonus, employees will tend to highlight their achievements. It is then difficult to admit weaknesses. The goal of salary distribution dominates the developmental function of the appraisal system. In spite of this, in real life, performance appraisal systems are often used for both objectives at the same time.

There may be a compromise between these two purposes by combining the performance appraisal system with goal-setting, as the achievement of defined goals is another dimension on which the employee is appraised.

This can be used as one step on the way to a flexible pay or bonus system which is performance related. As goal setting can be used to define goals for the personal development of the employee, this also becomes a clear objective. That method may help to realize personal development, but it does not solve the problem of the employee being less willing to admit weaknesses when his or her bonus is going to be defined.

INTRODUCTION OF A PERFORMANCE APPRAISAL SYSTEM

ARGUMENTS FOR A PERFORMANCE APPRAISAL SYSTEM

When introducing a performance appraisal system in a company, it is necessary to have an influential advocate who supports the process. Someone from the corporate management or from the executive board has to be convinced of the benefits of performance appraisal and then support the introduction of such a system. If the appraisal system is only implemented by the initiative of the personnel department it is highly probable that it will not be successful. The introduction of an appraisal system should be a decision made as part of the business policy and not just as a service of the personnel department.

If the members of the corporate management are not convinced of the advantages of the appraisal system, it is the task of the human resources management to convince them. At this point the personnel manager should use more economical than "soft" arguments: it is not reasonable to use arguments such as "the employees will feel happier with feedback" or "corporate climate will improve". We have observed that people of the personnel department have a tendency to use these "soft" arguments, but are not very successful by exclusively referring to them.

Economical arguments for the use of a performance appraisal system are, for example:

- Superiors can train their employees more efficiently and can increase their performance.
- Goal achievement will improve because of the feedback, especially if specific goals are set.
- Employees show a better performance when they know what is expected of them. A performance management system makes the demands transparent to them.
- The productive potentials and abilities of the employees can be recognized and supported. Management positions can more often be staffed within the company and expensive external search can be reduced.
- Employees who have the potential to develop abilities and be promoted within the company have fewer reasons to leave the company. The turnover rate will decrease.

In practice, it is difficult to measure the impact of an appraisal system. The turnover rate can be an indicator, but this depends on many other factors as well. And if people do not leave their job you can only estimate how many would have done so had there not been a performance appraisal system.

COMMUNICATION

Communication has an important influence on the successful implementation of an appraisal system. A communication plan at the beginning of the process is absolutely necessary. The corporate management has to be involved in implementing the performance appraisal system and has to communicate its goals early during the implementation process. The announcement of a performance appraisal system usually causes fear and uncertainty. If the implementation is not well communicated in the beginning, rumours and resistance will easily arise among the staff. For this reason the management has to explain the aim of the performance appraisal system and the consequences related to it.

During the communication process the economical situation of the company has to be taken into account. In a company that has good economic conditions, the staff will have different fears and suspicions from those in a company with doubtful economic conditions. Particularly management staff must get information at an early stage and the use of the system should be described to them. Performance appraisal can be presented to them as a management technique for achieving goals and managing the performance of their employees, and as a tool for giving feedback to employees.

DEVELOPMENT OF THE APPRAISAL SYSTEM

The performance appraisal system must be developed according to the demands and characteristics of the company.

The **appraisal dimensions** can be defined by the corporate management in cooperation with the personnel department and possibly some external consultants. One possibility to define criteria is to start with the qualities that an employee needs to be a successful player. These criteria can be developed by interviewing "experts", i.e., employees who have been with the company for several years. This method derives the appraisal criteria from contemporary success factors of the company.

But perhaps a company wants to change its job demands and put more emphasis on qualities which were not decisive in the past but are now important because of changes in the market situation. For example, "initiative" was not demanded from employees in a company in the past but now it is necessary to have employees who show initiative. So this quality is encouraged and considered in the appraisal system. With this method, appraisal dimensions are based on strategic company goals and consideration should be given to those qualities that the employees must have to realize the corporate strategy and goals. For example, "customer orientation" or "flexibility" are characteristics that can be important if a company is to achieve its goals in the present situation. In the past an employee could perhaps progress without these qualities, but the company now demands these qualities of all employees. The experience shows that often the corporate strategy is not carefully fixed. The corporate goals are not defined in detail and so the demands on the employees cannot be derived accordingly.

A method of achieving employees' acceptance of the appraisal system can be the implementation of workshops. Such workshops are useful at the stage of determining the criteria. The employees can define specific behaviours for the dimensions. They can tell what "flexibility" means in their job. Permitting the employees to participate in the developmental process will depend on the size of the company. If it is a large company, representatives for each area should be chosen as there will be more identification if the employees are included in the process.

The appraisal system has to be adapted to the organizational demands. That is also an important success factor: for example, if the span of control is large, the appraisal should be as easy to handle as possible. Or, if a sales manager works mainly at headquarters while the sales representatives work in the field, then this has to be taken into account.

THE CORPORATE CULTURE

When introducing a performance appraisal system, it is important to consider the organization's corporate culture. For example, issues to be addressed include questions such as 'How frank is the culture?' and 'Are the employees used to feedback?' An appraisal system will probably not be successful if the corporate culture does not support it because of a lack of feedback culture and frankness. If a superior has never talked with his or her employees about performance or has never provided feedback because this is not common within the organization, then it will be difficult to implement feedback dialogues which are based on open questions ("What are the strengths of the employee?"). In this case the appraisal system has to be more structured and rating scales with a detailed description of the dimensions are recommended. In addition to the structure of the system there has to be more training and coaching for the superiors. If the employees of a company are used to feedback then the appraisal system can be less structured and open questions can be used.

Thus, the structure of the appraisal system has to take the corporate culture into account. It is important to realize that you cannot create a corporate culture with an appraisal system. If the culture is not prepared for an appraisal system then it is useful to start, for example, just with employee dialogues and to train dialogue culture and feedback. People should get used to talking to each other and expressing their opinions. An appraisal system can then be the next step.

INTEGRATION IN A PERSONNEL MANAGEMENT CONCEPT

The appraisal system should be regarded as part of the personnel management concept and should be integrated into it. The results of the appraisal must have consequences for the employees. These could be financial consequences if the appraisal system is used for salary distribution. If it is used as a management technique or for personnel development, these could be training, challenging tasks or projects which give the employee the chance to develop his or her abilities, skills, and competences. Apart from training these can be management development programs, but also tasks forces which are assigned to employees as a challenge.

TRAINING

An appraisal system has to be implemented by information workshops or training. It is not useful to give the information only by a user manual. Defects and loss of quality in the course of performance appraisals regularly appear when the superiors have to take on this task suddenly and unprepared. The majority of company superiors are not prepared to conduct a high-quality performance appraisal process without additional training. Effective training prepares the appraisers for their tasks. Such training consists of the following aspects:

- information for the appraiser as well as the person to be appraised about the goals, the use, and the risks of a performance appraisal system
- information about the appraisal criteria and how they were developed
- information about the evaluation process
- training on how to apply the evaluation criteria
- information about possible errors that can occur during appraisal or tendencies towards faulting (e.g. likeability effects, excessive weighting of single features)
- training of perception and evaluation skills
- training of communication skills, with respect to the performance evaluation and to the presentation of one's role and self-image to others
- study of the development of future goals of performance (as far as this is included in the process).

Manuals and textbooks for the use of a performance appraisal system as well as behaviour examples for performance standards frequently constitute necessary devices to help the appraiser.

Within the training, the appraisal system and the appraisal criteria should be explained. This is an important step to ensure the same standards of the appraisal—or at least a certain standard. Moreover, the appraisal procedure is described. The appraisal dialogue is discussed and at best is exercised in role plays. That is particularly important when there is no feedback culture in the organization. The experience shows that superiors try to avoid these role plays. The reasons are often that they are used to talking to their employees and they of course regard this as a part of their management role. But role plays show that even experienced managers have difficulties in giving feedback in a frank and constructive way. To tell someone what his or her strengths and weak points are is a very difficult task for many superiors.

When the performance appraisal is combined with goal setting, it is also important to train the superiors in defining measurable goals. As experience shows, this is easy for quantitative goals but is extremely difficult for qualitative goals. Goals should meet the criteria of being measurable, specific, acceptable, realistic, and time-bound.

Moreover, training is often seen as a 'kick-off' within the process of introducing a performance appraisal system. Training sets a starting point and the managers see during the training that everybody has now to do performance appraisals. Thus, training can also be an important motivational factor.

SUCCESS AND QUALITY FACTORS FOR PERFORMANCE APPRAISAL SYSTEMS

Which factors make a performance appraisal system successful? Which quality assurance has to be conducted? Of course, the success of performance appraisal systems also depends on the specific conditions within a company.

STRONG ADVOCATES AND ROLE MODELS

Support by the upper management is a very important success factor of a performance appraisal system. If this support is missing, the staff will recognize this quickly and will not accept the appraisal system. Additionally, successful superiors who obviously use the performance appraisal system and say that they find it useful can be strong promoters for the system.

INTEGRATION AND CONSEQUENCES: REALIZATION OF PERFORMANCE APPRAISAL RESULTS

Some of the questions to be answered early in the process of developing a performance appraisal system are: What happens with the results? How are those results translated into consequences? A clear-cut answer to these questions is an important success factor for a performance appraisal system. There must be a clear connection between the results of a performance appraisal and its consequences. Those who have done a better job first come out with a better evaluation. The consequences could include a higher wage, faster promotion, the chance for additional training, or other ways of appreciation. There has to be an apparent correlation between the appraisal scores and the measures of appreciation.

As mentioned before, the performance appraisal system has to be integrated into an overall personnel management concept. If the performance appraisal system is used for evaluating performance-oriented payment, it needs to be presented at least one or two months before the actual decision regarding the future wage is made. Appraiser and the person to be appraised should know how specific decisions have been made, i.e., which performance appraisal criteria have been taken into consideration.

TIME

The appropriate evaluation period can also be a success factor. Usually performance appraisal takes place once every year. Sometimes companies make an appraisal twice a year, which is also an appropriate evaluation period. The schedule for the appraisal should be set and checked by the personnel department. Especially when goals are defined, superior and employee have to talk about the achievement of milestones before the whole evaluation period has passed. A quarterly evaluation, which few companies want to establish, is often difficult to implement because superiors often lack the time to accomplish the appraisals. Thus, a quarterly appraisal can only be recommended if a superior has a small number of employees to appraise and if the performance appraisal process is not too time-consuming.

EASY TO HANDLE AND SPECIFIC

The performance appraisal system is more likely to be applied if it is easy to handle. This means that it should not be complicated to fill in the rating form. If the superiors have to read ten pages of a manual before they are able to make the evaluation, the appraisal system will have less chance to be used. Moreover, as stated above, the evaluation process should not be too time-consuming. An appraisal system with two sheets of paper to be filled in is better than one with five sheets.

The criteria of the appraisal system have to be as specific as possible. If many of the criteria are not appropriate for the employees, the use of the system is questionable. For this reason it is important that the appraisal system is developed specifically for the demands and tasks of the company. It has to be fitting for most job descriptions. A good idea is to have some modules for specific jobs. For example, for superiors there can be a module which covers their typical demands such as leadership or delegation and is not applicable to the appraisal of other employees.

CAREFUL IMPLEMENTATION WITH TRAINING TO PREPARE THE SUPERIORS

Training is an important tool for establishing a performance appraisal system. Within the training the appraisal system and the appraisal criteria have to be explained. Moreover, superiors have to be prepared to give feedback. The ability of the superiors to give feedback is a success factor.

The reluctance or lack of skill to give feedback is a serious problem. This is especially true for negative feedback cases because superiors often avoid giving negative feedback. Some of the reasons for this attitude are the fear of possible conflicts, deterioration of the relationship between the superior and the employee, and the lack of confidence in the validity of the evaluation results.

Still, employees wish to receive specific and thereby possibly negative feedback as frequently as possible. Research shows that the assessments as to what is really important for a specific and frequent feedback differ hugely between the appraisers and the persons to be appraised. Leading personnel judge the width and the quality of their feedback as adequate, whereas the employees' assessment shows apparent weak points (Taylor, Fisher, & Ilgen, 1984). While informal day-to-day feedback gives the employee information about the quality of specific task fulfilment, quarterly or half-yearly feedback discussions deal with goal achievement and the fulfilment of specific organization expectations. It all centres around problem solving, the perfection of existing strengths and surpassing of weaknesses.

As part of the feedback dialogue, the necessary support from the superiors as well as the called for measures of qualification in the work field are also discussed. That way, the employee receives impulses for future performance development.

QUALITY ASSURANCE: SUPERVISION OF THE APPRAISER AND ADAPTATION OF THE SCALES

Supervision of the appraiser

To ensure that performance appraisal takes place at a high quality level, the appraisal process itself has to be monitored. This can be accomplished by evaluating the appraisals and paying particular attention to possible rating errors because typical rating errors can quickly lead to problems. If the overall performance of members of one group is judged more positively than that of another group, the performance appraisal system is questioned. Unfairness and a lack of differentiation will be claimed, although the reason for this result could be found in individual rating errors.

In order to assess the validity of the evaluation, comparisons with other performance indicators are helpful (e.g. specific results, project progress).

Evaluation of the system

A performance appraisal system has to be reviewed after the first year. The feedback of the users has to be used for the improvement of the system. Fairness and transparency of a performance appraisal system are heightened by giving the employees the chance to voice their criticism against the system (Folger, Konovsky, & Cropanzano, 1992).

To be successful in the long run, a performance appraisal system has to be adapted to the changing tasks and demands within a company. For this reason a performance appraisal system has not only to be carefully implemented but also monitored on a regular basis.

APPRAISAL METHODS

A performance appraisal has to meet some specific demands. These demands can be based on the purpose of an appraisal system to ensure standardization in development of employees or to define a salary increase or bonus. Thus an appraisal system should have:

- well-defined criteria according to which the employee is assessed
- a method of how the employee is assessed according to these criteria (e.g., a rating scale)
- a defined appraisal process.

WELL-DEFINED CRITERIA

Within an appraisal system, appraisal criteria can be described in detail. If standardization of the appraisal process is important the description should ensure that everybody understands the criteria in the same way. For this reason the criteria should be behaviour-related.

For example, without further explanation the dimension "flexibility" can be interpreted as "flexibility to learn new tools" or "flexibility in working time" or maybe even "flexibility in working places". To avoid these ambiguous interpretations, a description can be provided, for example:

Flexibility means the ability of the employee to react in an appropriate way on different circumstances and to adapt easily to new task areas of responsibility.

Now it is more likely that each appraiser has the same idea of the term "flexibility". But how can "flexibility" be observed? Which specific behaviour is related to it? To realize standardization, behavioural examples for each dimension can be used. So the appraisers know exactly the grounds on which they can judge their employees' behaviour; for example:

Employee can easily switch to another theme; can adapt quickly to new tasks; produces good ideas to solve problems; reacts appropriately in different situations.

The disadvantage of this close description is that it is of course less abstract and has to be adapted to certain areas of responsibility. But for a successful appraisal system it is necessary that the dimensions are explained and connected with behavioural examples, otherwise there will be less standardization.

How to Assess: Ratings Scales or Not?

Now that the superiors understand the appraisal dimensions and know which behaviour they have to consider for each dimension, how do they express their evaluation? There are some methods but we will only refer to two possibilities which show the extremes. Performance appraisal systems may have a rating scales for every dimension, for example:

Achievement motivation

1	2	3	4	5

The superior decides on a score. The rating scales can have different ranges and often this is a well-discussed process to agree on a rating range. The general question is: should it be an equal number of alternatives or not? The number of alternatives varies in most cases between three and seven.

Moreover, it makes sense to divide the scale into three main levels: below level, level, and above level. So a rating scale of five alternatives can be divided as follows:

Team Working

1	2	3	4	5
below level	level			above level

How can it be ascertained that a rating of 4 is comparable between the different appraisers? For this purpose, brief descriptions of every level can be given, as shown below. Of course it would be best if every step had its own description. But it turns out to be very difficult to describe the difference between a 3 and a 4 with behavioural examples. To give an orientation to the appraiser and avoid complicated descriptions, it is often a good solution to provide behavioural descriptions for the three main levels.

Team Working

1	2	3	4	5
Should integrate better and demonstrate more cooperation; does not accept the opinion of others, criticises destructively; offers support seldomly; does not always pass information to others	Is integrated into the team; accepts the opinion of others, criticizes constructively, gives support to colleagues, gives information to others appropriately			Is important for the team, others ask for his/her opinion; is interested in other's point of view and asks actively for it; accepts opinion of others; critizises constructively; offers actively support to others; supports the exchange of information within the teams

There are other appraisal systems, which have no rating scales at all but use open questions which the superior has to answer in his or her own words; for example:

Which strength does the employee exhibit in fulfilling his present tasks?

Regarding the standardization and comparability aspects, rating scales are preferred. They are more concrete and well defined than open questions and, if combined with behavioural examples, they assure that different individuals understand the same terms in the same way.

In addition, the rating scale is the more comfortable tool. The handling of a rating scale is more convenient because the superior has no need to write whole sentences. Especially for less experienced executives, rating scales are easier to manage.

There is, however, one aspect about rating scales that should be taken into account: rating scales should not be regarded as an instrument for objective measurement. The rating scale gives an illusion of objectivity that does not exist. In former times, there was a tendency to sum up the results of the rating scale and use the results for benefit distribution. Such a procedure assumes a degree of objectivity that cannot normally be realized between different superiors. If used for salary distribution, a key has to be defined on how to transfer the evaluation results into benefits.

THE EVALUATION PROCESS

Appraisal systems should have a well-defined evaluation process: this implies that a specific evaluation period is defined. In the first appraisal dialogue the superiors have the task of explaining the appraisal system to the employees. The appraisal dimensions are to be clarified, so that the employee knows—at least from then on—what the superior expects of the individual and how his or her performance is being measured.

The appraisal dialogue can be more or less structured. If the appraisal system has some dimensions and rating scales, then the dialogue will probably be guided by this structure. The superiors give the employee feedback along these dimensions and hopefully explain their ratings and impressions. The employees have the opportunity to give their own views on their performance. It is often recommended that the employees make a self-appraisal before they are informed of the appraisal of the superior, and in this way the employees achieve a basic understanding of the system. It can be useful to integrate the employees' self-evaluations, especially to discuss their future development, but inexperienced superiors are often afraid of discussing ratings with their employees and have to be trained for this task.

When comparing the superior's evaluation with the self-evaluation, one can often detect obvious tendencies towards leniency in the self-evaluation. If it is clear from the start that in addition to the self-evaluation there is also an appraisal by others, this tendency fades. In this case, the self-evaluations are often critical and realistic.

In less formalized systems there is only a rough structure for feedback. In this case the discussion is more like an informal dialogue between superior and employee, where they discuss the strengths and weaknesses of the employee and his or her expectations for the future. It is more or less a career consulting dialogue. However, this less formalized procedure can only be recommended when the managers and the corporate culture have a tradition of giving and receiving feedback.

TREND TOWARDS A "BETTER" EVALUATION

When an organization is using an appraisal system, a tendency towards a "better" evaluation is a consequence of any such system; i.e., the appraisals are improving over the course of time. There are many reasons for this tendency:

- The employee makes progress.
- The dimensions of the appraisal system are well known and employees will oriented their behaviour according to these criteria.
- The superiors try to avoid conflicts with their employees and give better ratings.
- The superiors give better ratings because their goal is to develop their employees.
- The executives enforce the positive development of their employees.

There are several ways to deal with this problem, but none is really satisfactory. First, the superior or another person, whose task is to ensure quality of the evaluation, discusses the ratings with the appraiser and gives him or her feedback. The person who provides the feedback has to discover if the better evaluation is realistic or if the appraiser has avoided negative ratings.

Second, one can simplify the evaluation system as much as possible. In the simplest case scenario, the task of the appraiser is to assess whether or not the company's expectations were met. With this dichotomous appraisal, however, it is impossible to differentiate within the group of employees who meet the expectations and those who do not. Moreover it is not possible to have a detailed look at the strengths and weaknesses of the employees, which is the basis for personnel development. Therefore this type of simplification should not be applied.

Third, percentages for the distribution of each rating can be defined. For example, if there are five rating alternatives, the restriction is that 10% can be in the best category, 20% in the second best, 40% in the middle and 20% and 10%, respectively, in the last categories. This method is based on the basic assumption that levels follow a normal distribution. The rating may not be fair because in reality the employees may not follow this distribution.

360-DEGREE FEEDBACK

In the previous sections, we have concentrated on illustrating the success factors of a performance appraisal system and on introducing specific methods. The question remains, though, of how far those success factors and methods are taken into account in practical applications. Based on this question, we will present an innovative appraisal system which aims particularly at the inclusion of as many levels of a company as possible: the 360-degree feedback.

A 360-degree feedback is the formalized feedback system for personnel management. The results derive from the social process of perception in the daily work routine. The feedback ideally comes simultaneously from persons associated with the relevant internal (rarely external) customer segments (superiors, coworkers, colleagues). Thus, the evaluated person can be appraised by coworkers, colleagues, superiors and customers at the same time. The goal of such a system is to give the evaluated persons the chance for self-development. When feedback from all the named sources is presented within a framework that gives people the chance to practise key behaviours and plan for improvement, it can serve as a lever to bring about real, measurable changes in people's behaviour (McCall, Lombardo, & Morrison, 1988).

This section provides a requirement analysis from a practitioners' point of view for the intoduction of 360-degree feedback. Therefore, we will first introduce the advantages and disadvantages of this system then illustrate the relevant success factors of the 360-degree feedback system.

ADVANTAGES AND DISADVANTAGES

What advantages does the 360-degree feedback hold in comparison to the "classical" (person-oriented, dyadic, strictly structured top-bottom) system?

- Intensification of internal communication by means of follow-up workshops, discussions, etc.
- Strengthening of feelings of responsibility (both within the appraised and the appraising person). The involvement in the appraisal system is a first step against a resigned attitude ("That's just the way it is . . .").
- Open presentation of appraisal criteria. All those involved can relate to a certain appraisal result.
- Reason and basis for the development or implementation of management methods, business missions, etc. Those should usually present the base for a 360-degree feedback system.
- Basis for a specifically tailored and exact personal development.
- Increase of customer satisfaction, since customers are often found among the group of appraisers.
- Practice of courage: the appraised persons have to confront the task of dealing with unexpected negative feedback.
- The appraised persons are likely to feel disciplined because of the expectation of continuous all-around evaluation and their own resulting justification.
- Implementation of actions.

Those advantages should not unjustly overshadow the fact that a non-reflected acceptance of a 360-degree feedback system can lead to severe problems. Two of these problems will be outlined shortly at this point: 360-degree feedback systems are faced with a dilemma for which a solution is yet to be found: the evaluation dimensions of a performance appraisal system should always be situation specific and behaviour-focused. If the system fails at that, the appraiser will be forced to give a general evaluation of the person to be appraised, without any relation to specific behaviours. In contrast, the evaluation of specific behaviour is definitely more valid because it is certainly less liable to suffer from cognitive distortion. What does someone have to do in specific situations to enable colleagues, customers, and coworkers to say: That was "a good thing to do"?

Still, 360-degree feedback systems deal with differing configurations: situations that deal with the superior, the customer, the coworker, and the colleague as respective counterparts. One can observe quite different ways of behaving within each of these configuration. In order to meet the various demands, it is recommended that each configuration should have its own unique appraisal system.

That way, however, it is no longer possible to compare the different perspectives, which leads to the point of deciding between two alternatives: either one decides for a behaviour-related scale of evaluation, although aware of the disadvantage that the two perspectives can hardly be compared; or one decides for evaluation dimensions of a relatively abstract nature—and herein lies the advantage of comparability as far as the perspectives are concerned.

In reality, the favour often falls to the latter alternative. The results are dimensions which are too global (e.g., "he/she communicated in an open-minded fashion, he/she supported the common input for good achievement") and as a consequence it becomes rather difficult to arrive at a conclusion about the appraised person's developmental needs.

Another aspect carries major significance: the linkage of the potential components of 360-degree appraisal with obtaining and sustaining a firm's competitive advantage requires further research. The call for studies in which a systematic, all-encompassing control of a 360-degree feedback system was employed has become apparent. Many attempts at a 360-degree feedback system are not reported in an organizational or strategic context. The inclusion of external and internal customers can provide insight into the management behaviour–work unit relationship that may help to identify the leadership energy, roles, and behaviors essential for organizational survival.

These remarks should not lead to a harsh criticism of the 360-degree feedback system. The main issue is rather to evaluate the innovative structures of this system systematically and thereby add to its continuous improvement.

SUCCESS FACTORS OF 360-DEGREE FEEDBACK SYSTEMS

The introduction of a 360-degree feedback system calls for thorough planning and consideration of possible resistance beforehand. Because changes often lead to fears and might cause resistance, resistance against personnel management innovations, such as the 360-degree feedback system, are usual side-effects. This resistance should certainly be taken seriously by means of a thorough, careful planning of the process. Runde, Kirschbaum, and Wübbelmann (2000) have detected specific success factors for the introduction and sustained implementation of 360-degree feedback, which will be outlined in this section. For the detection of success factors, 15 heads of project from internationally active companies participated in a study. The study focused on dimensions relevant for the design of a 360-degree feedback system. In addition, the heads of project were to judge the success of the 360-degree project according to the following criteria:

- the extent of goal achievement
- subjective evaluation of those involved
- order of events/charge taking
- future of the 360-degree feedback in the company
- expense–use relation.

This evaluation allows us to draw conclusions concerning the influence of shaping dimensions on the success of a 360-degree feedback system. The random sample consists of persons who have been part to the introduction process of a 360-degree feedback system among the companies (mostly members of the board). The companies belong to the following branches: chemistry (6), automobile industry (2), IT (2), transportation (1), insurance (1), building material (1), electronics (1), tourism (1). The number of employees ranges between 500 and 400,000, and sales cover a range from $10 million to $250 million. The following success factors were found.

Inclusion in an overall personnel management strategy

A 360-degree feedback system is frequently introduced in parallel with other projects. This bears the possible risk that the employees misjudge their company's use of basically innovative concepts and methods as rather inflationary. Often, it is difficult for employees to perceive that the projects are interlaced and aim at a common goal. Therefore, it becomes necessary to include the feedback system in a general strategic concept, to integrate the different goals, and to make them visible for the participants.

Management

The 360-degree feedback should be introduced to many groups simultaneously in a level-overlapping manner. The 360-degree feedback can be regarded as a device for creating a more effective form of communication inside a company. If this device is employed by only a small number of persons at irregular intervals, it can lead to insecurity on the part of the feedback-giver. The response behaviour is accordingly overshadowed by insignificant questions (e.g. Why now? Why him? etc.). Moreover, it is necessary to ensure that participation in the feedback system is voluntary at all stages of the process.

Instrument

It is advisable to use company-specific instruments rather than a standardized one. It is hardly possible to integrate aspects of a specific leadership culture or of a change process into a standardized instrument. Feedback giver as well as feedback receiver, often justly criticize the lack of relevant evaluation dimensions and core competencies. In comparison to that, the advantage of standardized instruments lies in the test criteria (e.g. Scherm, 1999). The psychometric quality of company-specific instruments can only be discussed after they have been put to use several times. Obviously, this aspect wasn't regarded as very significant among the persons approached in the study.

Project organization

The question as to how the feedback system needs to be developed, can be answered point by point, applying three categories: (1) exclusive internal development, (2) exclusive external development (i.e. comparable to a completely standardized, organization-unspecific method, no involvement of an internal person or project) and, finally, (3) a combination of (1) and (2). In this case, the project should be planned and managed in cooperation with a professional, external partner. The tasks which call for the exact knowledge of the organization's internal processes should be in the hands of the responsible organization personnel (e.g., information management). It is thereby assured that both the methodological and the conceptual criteria fit the organization-specific conditions.

Information management

Informing employees extensively about the 360-degree feedback project as a whole, and at every single step, is connected closely to the success of the project. In the course of implementing successful 360-degree feedback systems, almost all channels of communication are used in order to inform the employees as thoroughly as possible: company brochures, info letters, information events (for that purpose only), conferences, personal talks in regular turns. The most essential prerequisite of a 360-degree feedback system is undoubtedly the participants' commitment. This commitment is also created by making each step of the project and the according goals transparent.

Feedback-giver

The feedback-giver, i.e. the appraiser, needs to be prepared thoroughly for his or her tasks. This includes, e.g., close knowledge about the instrument, a training for the appraisal, general personal competence and the skill to chair discussions. There are three possible ways for choosing a feedback-giver: (1) the feedback-receiver exclusively appoints the feedback-giver, (2) someone else (e.g., staff management, superior, project team) takes on this task, or (3) the individual is chosen randomly, but very few companies make use of this possibility.

Presentation of results

An all-inclusive presentation of the results to the feedback-receiver, along with an adequate chance for questioning the presenter, supports the success of a 360-degree feedback. The feedback report consists of the exact comparison of self-impression and general impression on the ground of the appraisal dimensions. Beside the written information there are also frequent oral explanations, with space for reference questions. After the result is presented it should be possible to claim support for the interpretation in the form of coaching or advice. Many companies like to add a "second level" of activities to the first, in the form of a feedback process among a team, i.e., a meeting of the appraised person with his or her appraiser. Since there is no longer anonymity during such a discussion and meeting process, these measures should only be applied if it is the feedback-receiver's explicit wish and if the feedback-giver also agrees.

Consequences

The participants of the 360-degree feedback process consider it extremely important to ensure the confidentiality of the result data. Neither the superior nor the staff management should be allowed to look into the personal results without the feedback-receiver's permission. The staff management, respectively the superior, can access the results indirectly if the feedback-receiver writes a summary report on the basis of the hard data, which he or she then forwards. In any case, specific follow-up measures should be decided in order to ascertain the project's success.

CONCLUSIONS

A performance appraisal system can be a useful instrument for a company to develop its employees and achieve its goals. Many organisations use it to define a flexible part of their employees' salary, often in combination with goal-setting. But to take full advantage of a performance appraisal system, some conditions have to be met otherwise it is not efficient or can even cause damage.

Often, the management board does not set strategic goals, in which case, goals and performance standards cannot be defined appropriately. Another problem is that the results of the performance appraisal have seldom any consequences for the employee. In this case the management of performance is introduced as a single measure and not integrated into an overall personnel management concept. The appraisal can then have negative effects on performance because the employees are frustrated. They learn not to take goals seriously and develop an indifferent attitude to them. Thus, to fully benefit from a performance appraisal system a careful implementation is necessary.

REFERENCES

Folger, R., Konovsky, M. A., & Cropanzano, R. (1992). A due process metaphor for performance appraisal. *Research in Organizational Behavior*, **14**, 129–177.

McCall, M. W., Lombardo, M. M., & Morrison, A. M. (1988). *The lessons of experience: How successful executives develop on the job*. Lexington, Mass. Lexington Books.

Runde, B., Kirschbaum, D., & Wübbelmann, K. (2001). 360-degree Feedback—Hinweise für ein best-practice—Modell. *Zeitschrift für Arbeits- und Organisationspsychologie*, **45**, 146–157.

Scherm, M. (1999). 360-Grad-Feedback: Das Multiratersystem "benchmarks" von Lombardo und McCauley (1996*). Zeitschrift für Arbeits- und Organisationspsychologie*, **43** (2), 102–106.

Taylor, M. S., Fisher, C. D., & Ilgen, D. R. (1984). Individual's reaction to performance feedback in organisations: A control theory perspective. *Research in Personnel and Human Resources Management*, **2**, 231–272.

CHAPTER 8

Analysis of Performance Potential

Daniela Lohaus

CMG Industrie GmbH, Eschborn, Germany, and

Martin Kleinmann

University of Marburg, Marburg, Germany

SUMMARY

Performance potential refers to the capability of an individual to perform at a certain level. The analysis of potential seeks to estimate the degree to which performance-related skills and abilities that already exist, or do not yet exist, will develop or could be developed. However, for potential to be actually transferred into performance, motivation has to supervene. Thus, the estimation of potential should include measures of motivation. Potential analyses are done for current employees as well as for job applicants—though, to a lesser extent for the latter. They follow a range of objectives whose achievement is more likely if procedures are fair and transparent for participants. Human resources personnel who develop a potential analysis system in order to predict future performance are faced with a number of methodological issues, each of which is of critical importance for the quality of the potential analysis. Various methods to analyze potential are used, with assessment centers (ACs; recently dynamic ACs have gained increasing popularity) probably being the most common. Although ACs suit best the needs to reconcile placement decisions with the company culture, there is evidence that general mental ability best predicts future performance.

Psychological Management of Individual Performance. Edited by Sabine Sonnentag.
© 2002 John Wiley & Sons, Ltd.

INTRODUCTION

In an industrial organization the expenditure for personnel amounts to sums of 20 to 25% of the turnover or 40 to 45% of the net product (turnover minus purchases; e.g., Agrevo, 1998; Hoechst, 1998; Novartis, 1998). Along with the organizations' aim of continual increases of their efficiency goes the demand of permanent cost-cutting exercises. It goes without saying that these efforts include expenses for human resources. A logical consequence of such a claim would be a cutback in personnel. However, if the performance level of the organization is to be sustained, a cutback is only feasible if the remaining staff works more efficiently. One possibility to attain this would be human resources development; another, the exchange of current personnel by new personnel which already possesses higher qualifications. In order to be cost-effective, both measures presuppose an analysis of the performance potential. A sound potential analysis is important because failures are costly for the organization.

The viewpoint of the organization is central in this chapter, which, however, is not the only possible perspective that stresses the fact that development of human resources is useful. For example, from the view of political economists, measures that aim at a high performance level are essential in order to guarantee the competitiveness of the whole economy of a country. And seen from the angle of the individual, a high performance level and the opportunity to develop one's capability lead to job satisfaction and could be a way of self-realization.

In this chapter a definition and delimitation of the term potential analysis is given before contexts are explained in which potential analyses are carried out. Then follows a description of the objectives of the procedures. The subsequent section focuses on methodological issues that are associated with the measurement of performance potential. The final section of the chapter comprises the most popular methods of potential analysis with the focus on assessment centers.

DELINEATION OF PERFORMANCE POTENTIAL ANALYSIS

DEFINITION OF CONSTITUENTS

Before expounding various definitions of potential analysis it is necessary to comprehend the meaning of the term's components "potential" and "performance". Campbell (1999, p. 402) defines performance

> "as behavior or action that is relevant for the organization's goals and that can be scaled (measured) in terms of the level of proficiency (or contribution to goals) that is represented by a particular action or set of actions. Performance is what employers (self or other) pay you to *do*, or what they should pay you to do."

The definition needs further specification for its application in the context of potential analysis. It should be mentioned that it is not organizations which have goals but rather human beings, i.e., the management as well as shareholders, employees, works councils, etc. In order to run the business more or less in accordance with such goals, certain functions (such as production, purchasing, sales, etc.) are specified. Within these functions several tasks are combined to a job position. These positions are filled by employees. Performance as contribution to the goals of the organization—which cannot be argued in length within the scope of this chapter—can thus be understood as the degree to which individuals fulfill their tasks which belong to their position and which should have been identified by job analysis techniques (Lohaus, 1998). According to Campbell (1999) performance comprises eight higher-order components which are: job-specific and non-job-specific task proficiency; communication proficiency; demonstration of effort; maintenance of personal discipline; facilitation of team and peer performance; supervision/leadership proficiency; as well as management/administration proficiency.

After having specified the meaning of the term performance, the attention is directed to the term potential. The word potential is Latin in origin and means ability, capacity, power. It is the total power of employable means to achieve a specific end. Potential clearly sets the upper limit of what a person can achieve. This definition includes a future-oriented aspect but does not comprise a reference to the individual's motivation to reach the aimed-at goal.

Pringle (1994) has defined potential for the context of individual performance and, according to him, potential comprises the physiological and the cognitive capability (that includes ability, knowledge, experience, intelligence, state of health, level of education, energy level, motor skills) to perform a task effectively. However, it does not cover a person's willingness to do so. Willingness refers to emotional and psychological factors that affect the degree to which a person is inclined to perform a task and includes motivation, job satisfaction, personality, norms of the individual, values, job involvement, etc. In Pringle's understanding motivation is a distinct aspect and not a component of potential. However, in contrast to the aforementioned lexical definition, Pringle's definition of potential does not refer to the future.

According to Sarges (1996), potential is not only the skill but also the will to develop or perform on a higher level in future. This definition explicitly includes motivation and refers to the future. This understanding cannot be directly derived from the term potential and it seems to be influenced by practical considerations. In the context of organizations and human resources development it might be useful to adopt this viewpoint, i.e., to assume an existing readiness in certain circumstances to enhance one's qualification and take on more responsibility.

As we see it, potential refers to the capability of an individual to perform on a certain level and, as such, it is the prerequisite for performance. It sets the upper limit of the achievable performance level. However, for the application in the context of organizations this definition is too restricted. For potential to be actually transferred into performance, motivation has to supervene. This motivation includes a personality-caused as well as a situation-caused aspect. Put simply, an individual who has the capability to perform on a high level but is not achievement-motivated or not ambitious might not use her or his potential and may actually perform on a moderate level. And this personality-caused motivation can well compensate for capability to a certain extent. Moreover, you can imagine an individual to have the capability and be ambitious and still perform on a moderate level. In this case one can assume that motivation is also determined by situational circumstances, such as the scope of action and the requirements of the task in general, or the reward contingencies in the organization and/or the work team. Further, potential is future-oriented in the way that it takes into account, that actual performance reflects typical behavior but needs not necessarily be the maximum that could be reached when job requirements change or different jobs are taken on.

In the context of organizations, potential is analyzed in order to predict future performance on a variety of jobs, i.e., potential assessment is not a goal for itself but is a means to reach a certain end. It is not future potential performance but future actual performance (i.e., observable behavior and/or its results) that the organization needs to know. Therefore, it should be made clear that observable performance behavior or its results are always a combination of potential (in the meaning of capability) and motivation, the exact proportions of which are difficult to determine. Thus, it is necessary to include the personality-caused aspect of motivation, i.e., a person's principal readiness to perform on a higher level.

DEFINITION OF POTENTIAL ANALYSIS

Now, what is potential analysis? Definitions of potential analysis vary according to several aspects. One aspect is the question: Where does the stimulation for development come from? A second is the question: Does potential analysis only refer to abilities and skills that have not yet come into existence or also to abilities and skills that already exist? A third aspect concerns the kind of individuals whose performance potential is measured. In the following, we provide an overview of the components that are included in the various definitions and add our compilation.

According to Lattmann (1994) potential analysis is the measurement of the degree and direction to which an individual could be developed. In this definition the drive for development comes exclusively from outside the individual, i.e., from the organization's side. It is our opinion that this is too mechanistic a view of people but has the great advantage of simplifying human resources development planning. However, the assumption that people always have a determined level of abilities that were given them by planful developmental measures seems unrealistic. In contrast to this position, other researchers (e.g., Becker, 1992; Deller & Kendelbacher, 1996) define potential analysis as the identification of abilities and skills of an individual that might develop or might be developed. This definition includes the possibility of spontaneous changes of the individual (e.g., from maturity or from situational influences which the individual adapts to) that are not initiated by purposeful human resources development measures. From the viewpoint of human resources personnel, who in the case of potential analysis represents the interests of the organization's management, it seems more useful and realistic to adopt this latter position. If spontaneous changes are likely to occur it is reasonable to consider them in order to avoid misdirections in the planning of employee development. It even seems reasonable to anticipate actively such changes because the investment in training courses which develop abilities that would have developed anyhow may be saved.

A second difference in definitions is whether the identification of abilities and skills is restricted to those that still do not exist (Lattmann, 1994; Obermann, 1996). For example, Obermann underlines that the potential of an individual is not determined for a person as a whole but for single abilities and skills that the person has not yet developed. In contrast, Schuler (1996) and Becker (1992) speak of existing as well as future qualifications. The difference in these theoretical approaches to potential analysis is significant.

In the first position the idea is inherent that potential analysis is restricted to skills and abilities a person has not shown to date. Strictly speaking, that means that the potential to supervise employees cannot be determined by means of potential analysis for a person that has already supervised someone. It is obvious that this strict understanding of the term potential makes potential analysis a difficult task. But this viewpoint not only has consequences for the scope of abilities and skills that can be included, but also for the methods. Two different approaches are reasonable for potential analysis according to the first position. One is the measurement of talents or predispositions of a person. This diagnosis can be performed by tests that are content-related to the skill or ability for which the potential should be estimated. For example, the potential of a person who does not speak French to speak French in future, could be measured by a test of grammar understanding and a test that measures the capability to reproduce information from memory, etc. Alternatively, the potential could be estimated (by means of correlations) from a set of predictors that do not necessarily have any content-relation to the skill or ability in question, e.g., the time someone spent outside the mother country, the number of siblings, etc.

The second theoretical position includes the first one and broadens it to existing skills and abilities. That means, potential analysis according to this viewpoint includes the possibilities of the aforementioned position in the case of non-existing skills and abilities. In the case of potential analysis of existing skills and abilities, of course, the identical measures can be used as for non-existing. Additionally, potential can be measured by means of interpersonal comparisons or comparisons against a norm. For example, the potential of a person to speak French in future who presently is on a certain level (fluency, vocabulary) after having studied French in school for five years can be determined in comparison to other persons who have studied French in school for five years as well. If the history of skill or ability development is not known exactly and there are no comparison groups or norms available (which is the rule rather than the exception), it is possible to estimate the potential by a time-spaced sequence of tests that allow the direct observation of the skill or ability in question (e.g., role plays). It is obvious that this approach to potential analysis offers more possibilities of measurement and refers to a wider scope of skills and abilities that might be captured.

Another nicety that should be mentioned is the group of individuals which participate in such a potential analysis. Some authors see potential analysis as restricted to current employees of the organization (Becker, 1992; Lattmann, 1994) while others refer to the prediction of future performance in general and thereby imply personnel selection procedures (Birkhan, 1996; Schuler, 1996; Schuler & Prochaska, 1992). Becker deals with this detail of the definition explicitly. He points out that potential analysis refers to current employees and should be distinguished from personnel selection measures as the data basis is different. The prediction of future performance for employees is based on first-hand knowledge of the individual's daily work performance and is there-fore more sound than in personnel selection. However, it might be useful to avoid such strict distinctions as the following example illustrates: The performance of a job app-licant having worked for a business partner of the organization in question is well known, whereas the performance of an employee who only recently has joined the organization may better be predicted from application documents or tests. Although it does not seem helpful to restrict the definition, still, when talking of potential analysis the majority of authors implicitly refer to current members of the organization rather than to job applicants.

On the basis of the aforementioned arguments we think that none of the existing definitions is sufficiently comprehensive. Therefore we have compiled a definition which we think provides a basis for a conscious and considerate application of potential analysis. We understand potential analysis to be an estimation of the degree to which performance-related skills and abilities that already exist, or do not yet exist, will develop or could be developed. Potential analysis can be performed in the contexts of personnel selection as well as human resources development.

DELIMITATION OF POTENTIAL ANALYSIS AGAINST PERFORMANCE APPRAISAL

For the human resources management to sustain a continuously high level of performance of the organization, it is necessary to measure and predict the performance of individuals. Methods of realizing these tasks are performance appraisal and potential analysis. Whereas the application of performance appraisals is restricted to current employees, potential analyses are also done for applicants (as discussed in the following section). The following delineates how performance appraisal differs from potential analysis.

Both, performance appraisal and potential analysis are concerned with the measurement of performance. Typically, performance appraisals are restricted to the measurement of actual performance and do not include performance predictions (Cascio, 1992). One reason for this is that actual performance is in part determined by the requirements of the current position and in this way reflects typical performance rather than the performance maximum. In contrast, potential analysis aims at determining the performance maximum of an individual. However, some appraisal systems include some kind of potential analysis in so far as the person who renders the performance appraisal is often asked to judge the performance potential without reference to the individual's actual performance. Such a statement is usually based on observations during the daily work and relies on an individual and supposedly subjective impression that does not involve a formal or systematic assessment. Potential analysis differs from performance appraisal in several ways. These differences concern the time span, the purposes of appraisals (Cleveland, Murphy, & Williams, 1989; Williams, DeNisi, Meglino, & Cafferty, 1986), the sources which are used to obtain the judgments (Murphy & Cleveland, 1995) as well as the dimensions of performance that are assessed (Cascio, 1991; Domsch & Gerpott, 1985). Other differences such as the frequency and regularity of performance evaluation, the kind and amount of feedback and the kind of participants are less clear-cut.

One crucial distinction is the time span to which the performance measurement refers. Performance appraisals reflect the degree to which the individual's past behavior in the current position meets the expectations of effective performance in that position. In this respect they make up only part of what performance measurement means as the latter is not necessarily restricted to performance dimensions that are related to the current position (Cascio, 1992). However, the more important aspect is that they focus on the performance the individual has shown in the past. In the case of potential analysis, statements referring to performance are focused on the judgement of future behavior of the individual. Usually they do not, or at least not only, refer to the current position but rather to the individual's potential to perform very effectively at higher levels in the organization or in different types of jobs. The focus of such an appraisal is not a specific position but rather a family of jobs that have relevant characteristics in common.

Purposes common to potential analysis and performance appraisal are the identification of strengths and weaknesses of the assessed personnel and the provision of feedback by the assessor in order to attain performance improvements and substantiate placement decisions. The major purpose of performance appraisals, however, is the controlling of behavior (Schuler, 1991) and the evaluation of goal attainment. Moreover, some crucial aspects of performance appraisals that do not hold for potential analyses are their use for salary administration (Harris, Gilbreath, & Sunday, 1998) and for decisions concerning employment retention or termination (Cleveland et al., 1989; Ilgen, Barnes-Farrell, & McKellin, 1993). In addition, a significant purpose of potential analysis is the identification of training needs which in contrast might be a minor matter in performance appraisals.

Further, potential analysis usually differs from performance appraisal in the sources which are used to obtain performance evaluations. Although in principle there are various sources for performance appraisals (see Fletcher in this volume; Landy, 1989), in most cases the immediate superior renders the judgment (Hentze, 1980; Moorhead & Griffin, 1995; Viswesvaran, Ones, & Schmidt, 1996). In contrast, potential assessments are usually obtained from multiple sources. Potential analysis involves not only an immediate superior as judge but also higher-level managers and human resources specialists. Sources used for potential analysis are dealt with in more detail later in this chapter and in the chapter by Altink and Verhagen (this volume).

Another major difference between potential analysis and performance appraisal is the kind of rating dimensions by which the performance is measured. The latter ranges from (a) non-judgmental measures or results of performance such as output, turnover and absenteeism to judgmental measures such as (b) observable job behavior, and (c) personal characteristics, i.e., traits, such as initiative, honesty, and flexibility (Landy & Farr, 1983; Latham, 1986). Behavioral dimensions and results are preferred in performance appraisals whereas personal characteristics are most common in performance prediction. Non-judgmental measures as the outcome of behavior are performance indicators which best meet the organizational goals; and it is these results which should be employed if work outcomes can be reached by two or more ways of behavior. For example, a reduction in costs (as a result criteria) for employees in the sales department may be reached by various behaviors. The employees could either reduce the period allowed for payment for one or several clients. Alternatively, they could reduce costs by using cheaper and less office equipment. Further, behavioral feedback is most easily understood by the individual and applicable to future behavior. Additionally, the dimensions which are used for performance appraisals are related to the current position, i.e., to what the individual actually does. However, as potential analysis aims at the prediction of behavior rather than the evaluation of past behavior, it should not apply to a specific position but rather to a family of jobs with requirements not yet known in detail. In this case, the use of personal traits as rating dimensions might be more favorable since they may offer the desired transsituational generalizability when an individual's performance with regard to a new situation is to be predicted (Landy & Farr, 1983). Moreover, Landy and Farr argue that personal traits may cause or limit performance levels and in this way relate to the performance maximum rather than to typical performance. Schuler (1991) points out that traits are more abstract than behavioral dimensions or outcome measures and therefore allow for better comparisons across individuals as well as different jobs. The latter refers exactly to what is required for potential analysis. It should be noted, however, that trait dimensions used in performance appraisals are normally inferred from the work behavior observed. The direct measurement of traits (by use of personality tests) is unusual. That would be a self-assessment and superiors would not accept non-involvement in the appraisal process as they are responsible for administrative decisions based on performance appraisals.

POTENTIAL ANALYSIS IN THE CONTEXT OF HRM FUNCTIONS

Potential analysis is embedded in the human resources management, the major function of which is to guarantee a continuously high performance level of the organization with regard to the workforce (Kraiger, 1999). The human resources management not only has to secure the smooth running of the daily business, but, following the strategic goals of the organization, it has to bridge the discrepancies between the vision of the desired future and the current situation. Necessary and operational means to fulfill this major function are the implementation of satisfactory inter-individual conditions and the effective and efficient planning of human resources with regard to members and would-be members of the organization (Ilgen & Pulakos, 1999). Creating satisfactory and motivating conditions involves securing a general fairness in dealing with employees (see Figure 8.1). The

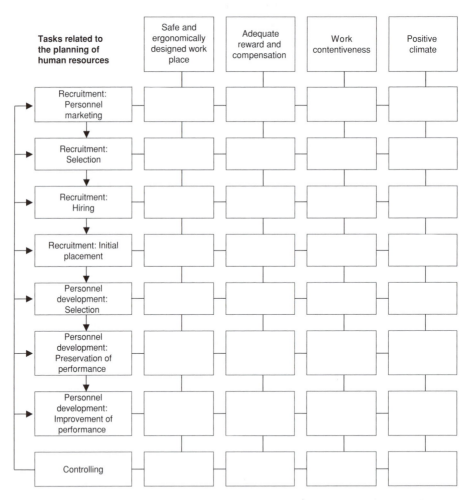

Figure 8.1 Overview of the Human Resources Functions: Satisfactory inter-individual conditions have to be realized throughout all human resources planning tasks in order to guarantee a continuously high performance level of the organization with regard to the work force. Controlling is a task that concerns all other planning tasks.

human resources planning refers to three tasks, namely, recruitment (with the phases personnel marketing, selection, hiring, and initial placement), personnel development (with the phases selection for new tasks, preservation of individual performance, and improvement of individual performance) and controlling of the performance of employees and the effects of personnel development (see also Miner, 1992). The inter-individual satisfactory conditions have to be considered for any phase of the planning process.

Except for the creation of motivating conditions there are different means to secure an appropriate level of performance and to fill the regularly evolving vacancies. One way is the recruitment from the labor market of individuals who already have the required qualifications. Another way is to match the incentives and rewards offered by the organization to the individual's needs and motives that are linked to the desired performance level. Third, appropriate placement decisions have to be taken that do not ask too much or too little of the job incumbent who, in that case, might leave the job. These placement decisions have to consider that executives themselves regularly strive for new tasks and challenges—a fact which may result in regular vacancies. Fourth, present employees can be trained to acquire the anticipated skills and knowledge. Regardless of the combination of measures that are taken to secure an appropriate performance level, but apart from performance appraisal systems, all measures require some kind of prediction of future performance, which can be performed as potential analysis.

A potential analysis which involves the identification of an individual's strengths and weaknesses with regard to previously stated job requirements should be, and widely is, applied in the planning process, especially in both selection phases. As explained earlier in this chapter, potential analysis should include an assessment of the individual's personality-caused motivation. However, the HRM does not intend to change an individual's personality (Neuberger, 1980a) just as, for example, it does not try to increase the intelligence of the individual by systematic measures. Nor does it have the task of creating a will in the individual to strive for higher positions.

Potential analyses are usually carried out for current employees. It should be mentioned, however, that an extensive potential analysis is not performed for the complete staff but is usually restricted to employees that are known to be high performers and are expected to hold executive positions in the future. Typically, employees are appointed for participation in the potential analysis on the basis of excellent former performance appraisals or nomination by their current supervisor (e.g., Shore, Tetrick, & Shore, 1998). This practice clearly shows the fact that for the HRM the distinction between potential (i.e., capability) and motivation to perform on a high level is peripheral. That is the prevailing idea of potential analyses by means of dynamic assessment centers. As will be described later, HRM does not strive to measure the actual weights of potential and motivation but rather to collect the combined data (i.e., actual performance) in order to predict future performance.

As was mentioned in connection with the definitions of potential analysis, the position to conduct potential analyses only for current members of the organization falls short of economically reasonable thinking. Rather, a potential analysis for job candidates could be just as profitable, as will be shown in this section.

Job analysis methods provide the profile of abilities, skills, and knowledge that are required from the job incumbent in order to perform effectively. However, it is not always possible in the recruitment process to identify, with desirable reliability, a person who already possesses all the necessary qualifications. Then, the selection process aims at finding a person who matches the profile as closely as possible and has the potential and the motivation to bridge the gap rapidly, either by training or by learning while doing the job. It is obvious that, in this case, selection procedures do not only comprise measures to determine the actual performance level but also involve methods to predict the future achievements of the individual. Even if it is possible to recruit people who exactly fulfill the job requirements from the beginning of the employment, the organization will seek to employ people who have the potential to develop or to be developed at least to the probable necessary extend to cope with the challenges the company will be faced with in future. The underlying assumption of this procedure is that no job remains the same over a longer period of time but that certain changes in kind and scope of knowledge and skills are inherent. In a technologically fast-paced environment the nature of the jobs to be done changes quickly and it would be rather expensive and not feasible for the organization to replace the present employee by a new recruit each time the job requirements change (Campbell, 1999). As a consequence, it is essential to hire people who have a certain potential to develop.

Thus, it is obvious that, on the one hand, it would be economic in any selection procedure not only to measure the present performance level but also to conduct a sound potential assessment for each candidate. On the other hand, an additional potential analysis is more costly (see also Schmidt & Hunter, 1998a) because present performance could well be measured using work sample tests of tasks which are crucial for the efficient execution of the job in question. In contrast, potential analysis would involve further diagnostic methods such as tests or learning potential assessment centers. These diagnostic measures might allow for the prediction of future behavior in certain content domains but will not necessarily result in concrete and specific statements concerning the individual's suitability for the job in question. Moreover, this additional investment would be wasted for those applicants who are not selected for the job.

OBJECTIVES OF POTENTIAL ANALYSIS

As was explained in the preceding paragraph, potential analysis is applied in the selection phases of the recruitment and the development function of the HRM. This section, however, will show that actions which follow potential analyses primarily serve to perform the functions of performance preservation, performance improvement, and control. Within that framework potential analysis follows various objectives.

First, information gathered in potential analyses is used for organizational decision-making about promotion (Lowry, 1994; Shore, 1992; Shore et al., 1998). The result of a potential analysis is a performance profile of the individual which gives a detailed picture of strengths and weaknesses. This profile can then be compared to the required profiles of the jobs the organization has to perform in the future. Assuming that no other HR actions, such as training, should be exerted, the potential analysis results in a list of jobs or positions the individual might fill in future (Kliem, 1987). On this basis, employees can be placed according to their capabilities and potential without expecting too much (or too little) of them and so sustain their capability.

Second, potential analyses are performed in order to enter into a joint process of planning the employee's career and to control human capabilities (Miner, 1992). Regardless of whether the reason for the potential analysis was the placement of an employee (see Shore, 1992) or the systematic development of knowledge and skills in order to prepare someone for a specific position, the results of this analysis should be communicated to the individual in an appropriate way, i.e., in a consultative process. The consultation deals with the question of which career development paths are available, which are suitable for this specific individual, and what measures (if any) are to be taken to achieve the personal goals.

A third objective of potential analysis is to justify expenses for training. A potential analysis is necessary to identify developmental objectives and derive personal training needs appropriately. That means that, on the basis of the profile of the individual's strengths and weaknesses, one can determine which positions at what levels in the organization, a specific employee might reach given that she or he is willing to develop the required qualifications. This delta analysis of actual qualifications and those required for an aimed-at position form the basis for the selection of a systematic training program. Training courses scheduled in this way aim at improving the performance of individuals in accordance with the setting of their individual developmental objectives. They are therefore much better recognized by the management than training requirements that are based solely on the employees' feelings of a lack in competence.

Fourth, an institutionalized potential analysis procedure also enables the HRM to justify personnel decisions with regard to rejected candidates (Kliem, 1987; Lattmann, 1994). Employees have the feeling that they could influence their fate and that decisions concerning their career are not arbitrary but founded on their actual performance in that assessment procedure which, anyway, involved multiple judges. That means that personnel decisions, regardless of whether they concern placements or training measures, are objectified. This creates a higher acceptance and might help to omit frustrations on the side of employees whose aspiration for a certain position was turned down.

Fifth, several authors stress the fact that potential analysis systems (and the participation in them) are a motivational or cultural asset of the organization (e.g., Becker, 1992; Deller & Kendelbacher, 1996). Although it is not the task of the human resources department to create the will in individuals to perform or develop (in the sense of achievement motivation, for example), it is their responsibility to create motivating conditions (see Figure 8.1) that further the development of an individual's abilities. These conditions include several aspects such as the existence of opportunities for promotion in general and various alternative routes to achieve higher positions. Employees who are motivated and performed well in the past, and who therefore are invited to participate in such a potential analysis, realize that commitment and efforts to perform effectively are perceived by the management and appreciated appropriately. They learn that high performance (rather than knowing the right people in the hierarchy) opens up opportunities to get on in one's job. Although surely genuinely designed as a tool to support the human resources planning, potential analysis in this way also serves individual purposes, because organizations are expected to provide opportunities for growth and further learning (Schein, 1988). A potential analysis system applied in this manner can also be an asset in supporting personnel marketing activities (see Figure 8.1).

Especially for these last two aspects to hold, it is absolutely essential that the potential analysis measure is transparent for everyone and conducted in a fair way. Seen from the level of the organization as a whole, potential analysis as a systematic approach serves to optimize future personnel decisions concerning succession planning (Gerpott & Domsch, 1995) and helps to realize a cost-effective investment of training and management development expenses. Concerning the level of the individual, the maximum objective of potential analysis is to identify for each employee (a) whether and which abilities and skills could develop and could be developed, (b) which positions on which level of the organization in what time could be filled, and (c) what qualifications, efforts, and expenses are required for the achievement.

METHODOLOGICAL ISSUES IN THE MEASUREMENT OF POTENTIAL

NEEDS ANALYSIS

Within the framework outlined above an appropriate potential analysis should follow a needs analysis which is performed in three steps, namely organizational analysis, analysis of future job functions, and qualifications required to fill the job functions as well as the person analysis. These steps resemble the analysis which is done in order to identify need for personnel development in general or training needs specifically (Goldstein, 1993; Patrick, 1992; Tannenbaum & Yukl, 1992; Wexley & Latham, 1991).

The organizational analysis starts with an examination of the organization's short-term and long-term objectives (Goldstein, 1993). The identification of long-term or strategic goals should take into consideration changes outside the organization that are to be expected (legal acts, the market situation in general, as well as the needs of customers and the behavior of competitors specifically, environmental changes, technological development, etc.).

On the basis of this review, the job functions which are required to enable the organization to survive in the future are determined (Patrick, 1992; Reid, Barrington, & Kenney, 1992). For each of these future jobs the criteria for success have to be identified—e.g., by critical incident technique (Flanagan, 1954)—and the required qualifications to perform successfully in that position may then be derived. Jochmann (1989) recommends the distinction between professional aspects, subject-specific aspects, and more general aspects. The latter cannot be part of a professional training but are acquired through job practice such as the competence to manage interpersonal relationships and the smooth running of the daily business. This process further involves the anticipation of internal changes such as scheduled retirements, expected promotions and organizational restructuring processes.

On the basis of this second step a person analysis (Goldstein, 1993; Tannenbaum & Yukl, 1992) is performed. It is checked for each employee or the candidates who are to be recruited, which of the relevant qualifications presently exist, and how probable the gap between actual qualifications and those required in future can be bridged either by training or by further job practice. If this probability for the current employees or the anticipated new staff is too low, a new run has to be set up. Of course, this analysis is not done on a one-by-one assignment of employees and future jobs; rather, the HRM will keep a register of all those highly qualified and, on a long-term basis, developed personnel who are suitable for different types of jobs.

A needs analysis performed in the aforementioned steps would be sound; however, it would still not be sufficient to guarantee successful performance of the organization in the future. There are various other methodological aspects to be taken into account which will be dealt with below.

IDENTIFICATION OF FUTURE JOB FUNCTIONS AND REQUIRED QUALIFICATIONS

Two major problems have to be considered with regard to the measurement of potential, i.e., the identification of future job functions and the qualification an individual needs to fill these functions adequately. First, even if the needs analysis was performed accurately, there is no guarantee that future tasks and the qualifications associated with them will not change within the supposedly covered period (Lattmann, 1994). The actual job requirements of executives have changed dramatically during the past few years, and these changes are caused primarily by the rapid implementation of new information technology applications in all functions of the company and the increased use of new work team designs (Campbell, 1999). For example, especially in the field of technological development, progress is moving so rapidly that the job functions that are identified might become obsolete soon after the needs analysis is completed.

As far as the required qualifications are concerned, this development suggests that the diagnosis of individuals' trainability (Robertson & Downs, 1989; Wexley, 1984), their motivation to learn, and their potential to develop and adapt are as crucial as the test of present capabilities (Obermann, 1996). It should be mentioned that certain personality characteristics that were important during the last few decades are no longer relevant in the selection and development of employees. While during the 1960s to 1980s organizations were searching for members who were loyal to the company and showed a high level of corporate identity, the opposite is now more accurate. Few if any organizations aim at life-time employment for their members. Rather, they seek "flexecutives" (Mahnkopf, 1999) who only identify with the next task they are asked to perform but not with the company as a whole. This change poses the great challenge for the field of human resources management to develop diagnostic instruments that allow for the measurement or prediction of the degree to which individuals are able to adapt their personality to the changing image of the ideal staff the management will seek, or will be coerced by market laws to look for. Campbell (1999) goes even further in that he not only attaches much importance to how well an employee adapts to new requirements but also to how well employees self-manage their continual learning. He suggests (p. 419) that

> "... assessment can focus on how well individuals assess their own training needs, how well they design or select training experiences to meet their own needs, how well they execute their own training experiences, and how well they evaluate whether they meet their own training objectives."

A second major problem in the identification of the required qualifications (Arvey, Salas, & Giallucca, 1992) is that the job functions can possibly be effectively performed with different kinds of qualifications. That means that, for all relevant job functions, the different combinations of skills and abilities that might enable an incumbent to perform effectively must be taken into account. With regard to practicability, however, it can be assumed that only certain combinations will be considered. This restriction could result in disadvantages for employees that do not fit one of the considered profiles. Put simply, needs analysis procedures could have provided the profile of a successful area sales manager being highly flexible, having excellent oral communication skills and an extrovert personality. Thus, potential analyses should strive to identify employees who are likely to develop that profile. One could imagine, however, that a high level of flexibility could well be compensated by good skills in planning, organizing, etc. However, in this case, an employee with good planning and organizing skills would not be considered.

STABILITY OF PERSONAL CHARACTERISTICS

Another methodological problem of potential analysis is the stability of personal characteristics which are said to determine range and executed or executable level of capabilities (Landy & Farr, 1983). Prediction of future job-related performance that refers to personal characteristics is based on the assumption that these characteristics are stable. Schmidt and Hunter (1998a) argue that the relevant characteristics of employees such as general mental ability or the ability to acquire job-relevant knowledge are in fact stable throughout a person's working life. This stability, however, does not refer to an absolute level (of performance) but to a person's rank within a reference group, as there may be and probably will be changes within a person as a result of learning through experience. If this fact was valid without restrictions, then it would be promising to measure the crucial characteristics and the performance of each employee on the present job in comparison to that of relevant reference groups. By this means the individual's rank and the degree of possible performance improvements could be determined. However, this procedure would not take into account that there might be other factors that cause inconsistency in an individual's behavior. That means that, even if the relevant characteristics are indeed stable, there is still the chance that other characteristics of the person will change. For example, motives and interests may vary according to experience with job, colleagues, and supervisors or the private situation of an employee drastically shifts and influences the observable behavior of that employee. Moreover, depending on the requirements of the present job some qualifications might increase due to their repetitious execution while others might stagnate or even degenerate (Lattmann, 1994) because of insufficient opportunities to practice them. Therefore, one would not necessarily gain an accurate picture of an individual by solely considering the present status of his or her personal characteristics.

UNCERTAINTY OF PREDICTIONS

A whole set of methodological issues of potential analysis is connected with the uncertainty of predictions of performance or development rather than their assessment. Research has shown that the best predictor of future performance is present or past performance (e.g., Gordon & Fitzgibbons, 1982; Ouellette & Wood, 1998; Schmidt & Hunter, 1998a) and that individuals with more abilities profit more from training (Vance, Coovert, MacCallum & Hedge, 1989). However, this prediction refers only to situations in which present job requirements and future ones are more or less identical. This knowledge is only applicable and usually applied when appointing job applicants whose application documents show that they have already done an equivalent job satisfactorily in another organization, rather than appointing someone who is supposed to have the potential to do the job in question but has never done it before. Potential analysis, however, seeks to predict performance in jobs which structurally differ from the present job, e.g., from a subject matter expert type job to an executive type job. This difference with regard to the selection procedures makes potential analysis more difficult because the relation between present and future job content is not so close, and less certain because of a lack of reliable predictors. Further, there is a prognostic uncertainty that the predicted and achievable development of a person will actually occur. Whether predicted and in fact existing potential is actually transferred into performance primarily depends on the motivation of the individual. Additionally, if the predicted development is communicated openly within the organization (i.e., to the assessee and the immediate superior), this communication can provoke a self-fulfilling prophecy (Becker, 1992) in stabilizing and, furthermore, enhancing motivational factors.

Prediction based on measurement procedures (which apply also to the measurement of characteristics) is dependent on the reliability of the chosen method. As Schmidt and Hunter (1998a) point out, measurements are never perfectly reliable but show a measurement error. Because this inaccuracy holds also for predictions with regard to personal features it decreases the possibility to predict future performance correctly. The authors therefore recommend the careful selection of those predictors of future job-related performance that can be measured more reliably.

RELIABILITY AND VALIDITY OF JUDGES' RATINGS

The quality of potential analyses strongly depends on the sources of assessment, i.e., on the raters who render the judgment of an individual's potential. In the context of performance appraisals Harris and Schaubroek (1988) found out that ratings by different sources correspond only moderately. The major reasons for this are the differences in perspectives on and knowledge of the incumbent's job. Therefore, the judges who assess the potential of employees should represent different stakeholders, i.e., different company functions and various levels of hierarchy. Thus, a higher amount of experience is employed to identify the required qualifications and to evaluate the individual's potential (Neuberger, 1980b). Further, the involvement of different kinds of judges is favorable as rater errors and effects of similarity and likability (Cardy & Dobbins, 1986; Schmitt, Pulakos, Nason, & Whitney, 1996) tend to neutralize each other. Moreover, the involvement of different raters might cause judges not to render over-optimistic predictions (see Reece & Matthews, 1993). Campbell (1999) identified accountability of judges as a critical aspect. Judges should justify their assessments of specific individuals in order to establish greater accuracy and fairness (Mero & Motowidlo, 1995; Motowidlo & Schmit, 1999). In any case, Woehr and Huffcutt (1994) suggest that the training of judges might be helpful in order to promote a common frame of reference.

The most important source are immediate superiors as they know best the employee's work performance and are able to rate the ability, knowledge, and technical proficiency (Borman, White, & Dorsey, 1995). However, Klimoski and Brickner (1987) argue that the judgment of the immediate supervisor might be biased in a potential analysis procedure. They fear that instead of assessing the performance the ratee shows during that procedure, the judgment will reflect the supervisor's opinion of the ratee's daily performance and thereby bypass the criteria of the potential analysis procedure. Moreover, the capability of the superior to assess the actual work performance of an employee is not necessarily in accordance with the requirements to correctly predict the future achievement of the ratee.

Higher-level managers are involved because they have greater knowledge of the overall functions the organization has to fulfill and the required qualifications. In addition, they have supposedly deeper insight into the ongoing changes of the company, its future structure, and the abilities, knowledge and skills related to the procedure. In contrast to the immediate superiors they are less likely expected to have own interests that might affect the evaluation of an employee (e.g., their own career objectives or they do not want to lose a competent employee).

Members of the human resources department should also be involved (Lattmann, 1994) as it is their task to organize the potential analysis system but, more importantly, to secure a high performance level of the organization by means of planning the succession. Additionally, their educational and professional background not only secures the state of the art with regard to the selection of the appropriate assessment procedures. Their participation is actually indispensable because their competence as interpreter and moderator in cases of contradicting judgments cannot be contributed by other observers. Moreover, a meta-analysis by Thornton and colleagues (Thornton, Gaugler, Rosenthal, & Bentson, 1992) showed that psychologists were able to give more valid predictions in assessment center ratings than line managers.

Peer evaluations are the second most commonly used source in performance appraisals (supervisory ratings being the most commonly used source; Viswesvaran et al., 1996), and can help to obtain certain behavioral information (such as cooperation). Although peers are capable of judging performance accurately in general (Fox, Ben-Nahum, & Yinon, 1989), the accuracy of their ratings depends on the similarity of their performance to the ratee's performance (Saavedra & Kwun, 1993) and the purpose of the evaluation (Farh, Cannella, & Bedeian, 1991). The influence of the relationship between colleagues on peer evaluation is not completely settled (Landy & Farr, 1986); for example, evaluations by peers might be lenient in case of a good personal relationship or too strict if the situation furthers feelings of competition (Jochum, 1991). However, there are studies which indicate that a positive relationship has no great effect on peer ratings (Borman et al., 1995; Love, 1981).

The employment of self-ratings is discussed controversially. Cawley, Keeping, and Levy (1998) report higher satisfaction of employees who participated in the performance appraisal process. However, self-appraisals were less strongly related to overall reactions (including satisfaction, motivation to improve, utility of appraisal, and fairness) than value-expressive participation (participation "for the sake of voicing one's opinion", p. 618) and participation intended to influence the appraisal. DeNisi and Shaw (1977) found that correlations of self-reports of abilities and tests of abilities were too small to have any practical significance and that self-reports could thus not substitute for ability tests. Shore et al. (1998) report that candidates who assessed their potential in an assessment center made use not only of their results in the exercises but also used their extensive self-knowledge about past performance. This source could well be a major benefit in predicting future performance. However, several researchers stress the fact that self-evaluations tend to be more lenient in accordance with the purpose they are made for (Heneman, 1974; Levine, 1980; Thornton, 1980; Zedeck & Cascio, 1982). Ashford (1990) sees the motive for such a leniency in the individuals' need to protect themselves and Fox, Caspy, and Reisler (1994) add the argument that self-ratings might be biased in order to reach a certain goal (e.g., a certain aimed-at position). See Moser (1999) for an up-to-date overview on moderators of self-ratings.

METHODS OF POTENTIAL ANALYSIS

Research over the past 85 years has tried to identify valid predictors for future job-related performance. Studies vary in the specificity of predictors (Cantwell, 1990: gender, needs and motivation; Gadzella, Ginther, & Bryant, 1997: learning style and critical thinking; Hojat, Vogel, Zeleznik, & Borenstein, 1988: psychological predictors such as stressful life events, test anxiety, etc.; Love & O'Hara, 1987: work maturity; Locke, Frederick, Lee, & Bobko, 1984; self-efficacy, goals, and task strategies; Stajkovic & Luthans, 1998: self-efficacy) as well as performance criteria (subjective, such as grade point average, Pringle, 1994; objective, such as job status, Martin & Bartol, 1985) and they usually hold only for specific groups of professionals.

Further, attempts to measure potential and to predict performance differ in the methods that are used. They range from appraisal interviews (Miner, 1970; Shahani, Dipboye, & Gehrlein, 1991), cognitive tests (Gordon, Charns, & Sherman, 1987; Shore et al., 1998), work sample tests (Mount, Muchinsky, & Hanser, 1977), and in-basket exercises (Hakstian, Woolsey, & Schroeder, 1986) to personality factors (Cook & Emler, 1999; Judge, Erez, & Bono, 1998; Linnehan, 1998), biodata (James, Ellison, Fox, & Taylor, 1974; Mael & Hirsch, 1993; McBride, Mendoza, & Carraher, 1997) and combinations of different methods (Jones, Joy, & Martin, 1990; Mayberry & Carey, 1997; Pössnecker, 1992) (for practical issues see the chapter of Altink and Verhagen in this volume). For each predictor there are a number of meta-analyses: Hunter and Hunter (1984), Hunter and Hirsh (1987), Gaugler, Rosenthal, Thornton, and Bentson (1987), Tett, Jackson, and Rothstein (1991), Robertson and Kinder (1993), Bliesener (1996), Salgado (1997). The extensive findings by Schmidt and Hunter (1998a) may serve to exemplify the research data (see Table 8.1). Their meta-analysis revealed that, with the exception of work sample tests (validity of .54), tests of general mental ability (GMA) have the highest validity. This predictor has a validity of .58 for job performance of managers and a validity of .51 for jobs of average demands. Assessment center show a validity of .37, biographical data measures have .35 validity, personality tests as well as conscientiousness tests have a validity of .31, and integrity tests have one of .41. Structured employment interviews have a validity of .51. The combination of two predictors shows that integrity tests in combination with intelligence tests make the best prediction (.65) whereas the combination of

TABLE 8.1 Predictive validity for overall job performance of general mental ability (GMA) scores combined with a second predictor using (standardized) multiple regression (Schmidt & Hunter, 1998b, p. 265)

Personnel measures	Validity (r)	Multiple R	Gain in validity from adding supplement	% increase in validity
GMA tests	.51			
Work sample tests	.54	.63	.12	24%
Integrity tests	.41	.65	.14	27%
Conscientiousness tests	.31	.60	.09	18%
Employment interviews (structured)	.51	.63	.12	24%
Biographical data measures	.35	.52	.01	2%
Assessment centers	.37	.53	.02	4%

intelligence tests with assessment center (.52) hardly helps to increase the validity that intelligence tests (.51) have when applied solely. These results show that the inclusion of motivational aspects (as are raised in tests of integrity and of conscientiousness) improve the prediction of performance.

In spite of these empirically distinct findings, intelligence tests in general are hardly accepted as instruments for potential analysis in Europe and the United States. A European study by Schuler, Frier, and Kauffmann (1993) as well as an internationally conducted study by Ryan, McFarland, Baron, and Page (1999), in which 959 companies within 20 world-wide countries were investigated, revealed that intelligence tests are not often used. In Germany, only 2% of the investigated companies apply intelligence tests in manager selection. As both studies show, Spain, Belgium, and the Netherlands, for example, make use of intelligence tests more often.

One of the most common methods to measure potential performance is the assessment center (AC) (Baumann-Lorch & Lotz, 1996; Baumann-Lorch, Millermann, & Lotz, 1994; Huck & Bray, 1976; Jochmann, 1989; Klein & Scheffler-Lipp, 1989; Kliem, 1987; Lowry, 1994; Sarges, 1996; Shore, 1992; Shore, Shore, & Thornton, 1992; Shore et al., 1998; Tziner & Dolan, 1982). ACs are used for the prediction of performance in both contexts, personnel selection and human resources development. As the procedure is costly (Schmidt & Hunter, 1998a), ACs are mainly used for potential assessment of higher management levels (for more practical details see the chapter of Altink and Verhagen, this volume).

Of course, the validity of ACs depends on their methodological standard. A study by Schmidt and Hunter (1998b) shows that the predictive validity of AC is reasonably good. Lievens (1998) and Kleinmann (1993, 1997a, 1997b) point out conditions under which predictive and construct validity can be increased.

However, two major objections are raised against the use of classical ACs. First, most of the traditional assessment centers measure status quo performance rather than performance potential. That means, the measured performance is influenced to a large extent by the experience of the candidate. For example, if candidates are not supervising any other employees, their knowledge of management and supervision will be dependent on their experience with the behavior of their direct supervisor. And if these candidates are asked to act as a supervisor in a role play during a classical AC, the probability is high that their behavior resembles the behavior of the direct supervisor. If we further assume that this supervisor is not very skillful, the management potential of the candidates in question will probably be judged to be rather poor. Thus, on the basis of status quo performance evaluations it is impossible to draw valid conclusions concerning the learning potential of a candidate in this performance domain (Obermann, 1996). In order to omit these shortcomings, several authors (e.g., Kleinmann, 1996; Obermann, 1996; Sarges, 1996) suggest the use of dynamic ACs that allow the candidate to show results of learning processes during the AC. The second major objection against classical ACs is that future job requirements are usually not known in such detail that the qualifications of candidates could be measured appropriately. There are of course exceptions where the position the candidate should fulfill is already known. Several researchers (e.g., Obermann, 1996; Sarges, 1996) argue that in times of a rapidly changing environment and the increased dynamic of technological and market developments, the capability of an individual to cope with these changes, to adapt to them and to structure them unerringly is most important. According to Sarges (1996) this capability is best represented by psychological constructs such as learning potential, which is the combination of willingness to learn and ability to learn. Obermann (1996) tried to specify especially the latter aspect and resumes that learning potential is not one homogeneous construct that holds for any task domain. Rather, he found that learning potential for one task (e.g., criticizing an employee in a constructive manner) correlates with similar tasks of that domain (e.g., motivating an employee). He therefore suggests the diagnosis of relevant parts of the whole range of qualification requirements of a manager.

Schmidt and Hunter (1998a) argue that the AC has little incremental validity over GMA, because they assume a high correlation between AC ratings and GMA. However, recent findings question this assumption because they show that GMA does not uniformly show a positive relationship with AC ratings (Lance et al., 2000). Future empirical research should further investigate this relationship to find the best predictors and predictor combinations for potential analysis.

REFERENCES

Agrevo (1998). *Geschaeftsbericht* [Business report]. Frankfurt/Main.

Arvey, R. D., Salas, E., & Giallucca, K. A. (1992). Using task inventories to forecast skills and abilities. *Human Performance*, **5**, 171–190.

Ashford, S. J. (1990). Self-assessment in organizations: A literature review and integrative model. In L. L. Cummings & B. M. Staw (Eds.), *Evaluation and employment in organizations* (pp. 59–100). Greenwich, CT: JAI Press.

Baumann-Lorch, E., & Lotz, J. (1996). Potential-Assessment für das obere Management [Potential assessment for top-level managers]. In W. Sarges (Ed.), *Weiterentwicklungen der Assessment-Center-Methode* (pp. 189–203). Göttingen: Verlag für Angewandte Psychologie.

Baumann-Lorch, E., Millermann, E. G., & Lotz, J. (1994). Internationales Potential-Assessment. Ein Diagnostikum für das obere Management [International potential assessment. A diagnostic tool for the upper management]. *Personal*, **46**, 577–581.

Becker, F. (1992). Potentialbeurteilung [Potential assessment]. In E. Gaugler, & W. Weber (Eds.), *Handwörterbuch des Personalwesens* (2nd edition) (pp. 1921–1930). Stuttgart: Poeschel.

Birkhan, G. (1998). Das Einzel-Assessment: Anatomie eines der wichtigsten Tage im Leben des Managers Herr Y [A single assessment: Anatomy of one of the most important days in the life of the manager Mr. Y]. In M. Kleinmann & B. Strauss (Eds.), *Potentialfeststellung und Personalentwicklung* (pp. 151–172). Göttingen: Verlag für Angewandte Psychologie.

Bliesener, T. (1996). Methodoligical moderators in validating biographical data in personnel selection. *Journal of Organizational and Occupational Psychology*, **69**, 107–120.

Borman, W. C., White, L. A., & Dorsey, D. W. (1995). Effects of ratee task performance and interpersonal factors on supervisor and peer performance ratings. *Journal of Applied Psychology*, **80**, 168–177.

Campbell, J. P. (1999). The definition and measurement of performance in the new age. In D. R. Ilgen & E. D. Pulakos (Eds.), *The changing nature of performance. Implications for staffing, motivation, and development* (pp. 399–429). San Francisco: Jossey-Bass Publishers.

Cantwell, Z. M. (1990). Predictors of performance in a field-based counselor education program. *Psychological Reports*, **66**, 151–159.

Cardy, R. L., & Dobbins, G. H. (1986). Affect and appraisal accuracy: Liking as an integral dimension in evaluating performance. *Journal of Applied Psychology*, **71**, 672–678.

Cascio, W. F. (1991). *Applied psychology in personnel management* (4th edition). Englewood Cliffs, NJ: Prentice Hall.

Cascio, W. F. (1992). *Managing human resources* (3rd edition). New York: McGraw-Hill.

Cawley, B. D., Keeping, L. M., & Levy, P. E. (1998). Participation in the performance appraisal process and employee reactions: A meta-analytic review of field investigations. *Journal of Applied Psychology*, **83**, 615–633.

Cleveland, J. N., Murphy, K. R., & Williams, R. E. (1989). Multiple uses of performance appraisal: Prevalence and correlates. *Journal of Applied Psychology*, **74**, 130–135.

Cook, T., & Emler, N. (1999). Bottom-up versus top-down evaluations of candidates' managerial potential: An experimental study. *Journal of Occupational and Organizational Psychology*, **72**, 423–439.

Deller, J., & Kendelbacher, I. (1998). Potentialeinschätzung von oberen Führungskräften im Daimler-Benz-Konzern [Evaluation of management personnel potentials at the Daimler Benz company]. In M. Kleinmann & B. Strauss (Eds.), *Potentialfeststellung und Personalentwicklung* (pp. 133–149). Göttingen: Verlag für Angewandte Psychologie.

DeNisi, A. S., & Shaw, J. B. (1977). Investigation of the uses of self-reports of abilities. *Journal of Applied Psychology*, **62**, 641–644.

Domsch, M., & Gerpott, T. J. (1985). Verhaltensorientierte Beurteilungsskalen [Behaviorally based rating scales]. *Die Betriebswirtschaft*, **45**, 666–680.

Farh, J. L., Cannella, A. A., & Bedeian, A. G. (1991). Peer ratings: The impact of purpose on rating quality and user acceptance. *Group and Organization Studies*, **16**, 367–386.

Flanagan, J. C. (1954). The critical incident technique. *Psychological Bulletin*, **54**, 327–358.

Fox, S., Ben-Nahum, Z., & Yinon, Y. (1989). Perceived similarity and accuracy of peer ratings. *Journal of Applied Psychology*, **74**, 781–786.

Fox, S., Caspy, T., & Reisler, A. (1994). Variables affecting leniency, halo and validity of self-appraisal. *Journal of Occupational and Organizational Psychology*, **67**, 45–56.

Gadzella, B. M., Ginther, D. W., & Bryant, G. W. (1997). Prediction of performance in academic course by scores on measures of learning style and critical thinking. *Psychological Reports*, **81**, 595–602.

Gaugler, B. B., Rosenthal, B. B., Thornton, G. C., & Bentson, C. (1987). Meta-analysis of assessment center validity. *Journal of Applied Psychology*, **72**, 493–511.

Gerpott, T. J., & Domsch, M. (1995). Personalbeurteilung von Führungskräften [Personnel assessment of managers]. In A. Kieser, G. Reber, & R. Wunderer (Eds.), *Handwörterbuch Führung* (2nd edition) (pp. 1694–1704). Stuttgart: Schäffer-Poeschel.

Goldstein, I. L. (1993). Training in organizations: Needs assessment, development and evaluation (3rd ed.). Pacific Grove, CA: Brooks/Cole.

Gordon, H. W., Charns, M. P., & Sherman, E. (1987). Management success as a function of performance on specialized cognitive tests. *Human Relations*, **40**, 671–698.

Gordon, M. E., & Fitzgibbons, W. J. (1982). Empirical test of the validity of seniority as a factor in staffing decisions. *Journal of Applied Psychology*, **67**, 311–319.

Hakstian, A. R., Woolsey, L. K., & Schroeder, M. L. (1986). Development and application of a quickly-scored in-basket exercise in an organizational setting. *Educational and Psychological Measurement*, **46**, 385–396.

Harris, M. M., Gilbreath, B., & Sunday, J. A. (1998). A longitudinal examination of a merit pay system: Relationships among performance ratings, merit increases, and total pay increases. *Journal of Applied Psychology*, **83**, 825–831.

Harris, M. H., & Schaubroek, J. (1988). A meta-analysis of self-supervisor, self-peer, and peer-supervisor ratings. *Personnel Psychology*, **41**, 43–62.

Heneman, H. G. (1974). Comparisons of self- and superior ratings of managerial performance. *Journal of Applied Psychology*, **59**, 638–642.

Hentze, J. (1980). *Arbeitsbewertung und Personalbeurteilung* [Performance rating and personnel assessment]. Stuttgart: Poeschel.

Hoechst (1998). *Geschaeftsbericht* [Business report]. Frankfurt/Main.

Hojat, M., Vogel, W. H., Zeleznik, C., & Borenstein, B. D. (1988). Effects of academic and psychological predictors of performance in medical school on coefficients of determination. *Psychological Reports*, **63**, 383–394.

Huck, J. R., & Bray, D. W. (1976). Management assessment center evaluations and subsequent job performance of white and black females. *Personnel Psychology*, **29**, 13–30.

Hunter, J. E., & Hunter, R. F. (1984). Validity and utility of alternative predictors of job performance. *Psychological Bulletin*, **96**, 72–98.

Hunter, J. E., & Hirsh, H. R. (1987). Applications of meta-analysis. In C. L. Cooper & I. T. Robertson (Eds.), *International review of industrial and organizational psychology* (Vol. 2, pp. 321–357). Chichester: Wiley.

Ilgen, D. R., Barnes-Farrell, J. L., & McKellin, D. B. (1993). Performance appraisal process research in the 1980s: What has it contributed to appraisals in use? *Organizational Behavior and Human Decision Processes*, **54**, 321–368.

Ilgen, D. R., & Pulakos, E. D. (1999). Introduction: Employee performance in today's organizations. In D. R. Ilgen & E. D. Pulakos (Eds.), *The changing nature of performance. Implications of staffing, motivation, and development* (pp. 1–18). San Francisco: Jossey-Bass Publishers.

James, L. R., Ellison, R. L., Fox, D. G., & Taylor, C. W. (1974). Prediction of artistic performance from biographical data. *Journal of Applied Psychology*, **59**, 84–86.

Jochmann, W. (1989). Die Management-Potenial-Analyse in der Praxis [Management potential analysis in practice]. In H. C. Riekhof (Ed.), *Strategien der Personalentwicklung* (2nd edition). Wiesbaden: Gabler.

Jochum, E. (1991). Gleichgestelltenbeurteilung—Ein Instrument der Personalführung und Teamentwicklung [Peer evaluation—An instrument of personnel management and team development]. In H. Schuler (Ed.), *Beurteilung und Förderung beruflicher Leistung. Beiträge zur Organisationspsychologie. Band 4* (pp. 107–134). Stuttgart: Verlag für Angewandte Psychologie.

Jones, J. W., Joy, D. S., & Martin, S. L. (1990). A multidimensional approach for selecting child care workers. *Psychological Reports*, **67**, 543–553.

Judge, T. A., Erez, A., & Bono, J. E. (1998). The power of being positive: The relation between positive self-concept and performance. *Human Performance*, **11**, 167–187.

Klein, K.-D., & Scheffler-Lipp, A. (1989). Die "Erweiterte Potentialanalyse" (EPA)—Ein Ansatz zur Optimierung des Assessment Center [The Erweiterte Potentialanalyse (EPA)—A way of improving assessment centers]. *Zeitschrift für Arbeits- und Organisationspsychologie*, **33**, 145–152.

Kleinmann, M. (1993). Are assessment center rating dimensions transparent for participants? Consequences for criterion and construct validity. *Journal of Applied Psychology*, **78**, 988–993.

Kleinmann, M. (1996). Assessment-Center [Assessment center]. In M. Kleinmann & B. Strauss (Eds.), *Potentialfeststellung und Personalentwicklung* (pp. 97–109). Göttingen: Verlag für Angewandte Psychologie.

Kleinmann, M. (1997a). *Assessment-Center: Stand der Forschung—Konsequenzen für die Praxis* [Assessment center: State of the art—consequences for practice]. Göttingen: Verlag für Angewandte Psychologie.

Kleinmann, M. (1997b). Transparenz der Anforderungsdimensionen: Ein Moderator der Konstrukt- und Kriteriumsvalidität des Assessment-Centers [Transparency of the required dimensions: A moderator of assessment centers' construct and criterion validity]. *Zeitschrift für Arbeits- und Organisationspsychologie*, **41**, 171–181.

Kliem, O. (1987). Zur Management-Potential-Analyse (MPS)—oder: wie man bereits heute Manager von morgen identifizieren könnte [On management potential analysis (MPS)—or: How to identify today who could be a manager tomorrow]. *Personal, Sonderheft*, 14–19.

Klimoski, R., & Brickner, M. (1987). Why do assessment centers work? The puzzle of assessment center validity. *Personnel Psychology*, **40**, 243–259.

Kraiger, K. (1999). Performance and employee development. In D. R. Ilgen & E. D. Pulakos (Eds.), *The changing nature of performance. Implications of staffing, motivation, and development* (pp. 366–396). San Francisco: Jossey-Bass Publishers.

Lance, C. E., Newbolt, W. H., Gatewood, R. D., Foster, M. R., French, N. R., & Smith, D. B. (2000). Assessment center exercise factors represent cross-situational specificity, not method bias. *Human Performance*, **13**, 323–353.

Landy, F. J. (1989). *Psychology of work behavior* (4th edition). Pacific Grove, CA: Brooks/Cole.

Landy, F. J., & Farr, J. L. (1983). *The measurement of work performance. Methods, theory, and applications*. San Diego, CA: Academic Press.

Latham, G. P. (1986). Job performance and appraisal. In D. L. Cooper & I. T. Robertson (Eds.), *International Review of Industrial and Organizational Psychology* (pp. 117–155). Chichester: Wiley & Sons.

Lattmann, C. (1994). *Die Leistungsbeurteilung als Führungsmittel* [Performance appraisal as a controlling means] (2nd edition). Heidelberg: Physica-Verlag.

Levine, E. L. (1980). Introductory remarks for the symposium "Organizational Applications of Self-Appraisal and Self-Assessment: Another look." *Personnel Psychology*, **33**, 259–262.

Lievens, F. (1998). Factors which improve the construct validity of assessment centers: A review. *International Journal of Selection and Assessment*, **6**, 141–152.

Linnehan, F. (1998). Examining selective determinants of job performance for entry and lower-level workers in Mexico. *Applied Psychology: An International Review*, **47**, 547–557.

Locke, E. A., Frederick, E., Lee, C., & Bobko, P. (1984). Effect of self-efficacy, goals, and task strategies on task performance. *Journal of Applied Psychology*, **69**, 241–251.

Lohaus, D. (1998). *Kontexteffekte bei der Leistungsbeurteilung* [Context effects in performance appraisal]. Hamburg: Kovac.

Love, K. G. (1981). Comparison of peer assessment methods: Reliability, validity, friendship bias, and user reaction. *Journal of Applied Psychology*, **66**, 451–457.

Love, K. G., & O'Hara, K. (1987). Predicting job performance of youth trainees under a job training partnership act program (JTPA): Criterion validation of a behavior-based measure of work maturity. *Personnel Psychology*, **40**, 323–340.

Lowry, P. E. (1994). Selection methods: Comparison of assessment centers with personnel records evaluations. *Public Personnel Management*, **23**, 383–395.

Mael, F. A., & Hirsch, A. C. (1993). Rainforest empiricism and quasi-rationality: Two approaches to objective biodata. *Personnel Psychology*, **46**, 719–738.

Mahnkopf, B. (1999). Von den Risiken des beschleunigten Wandels—oder: Grenzen der Flexibilisierung im Unternehmen [On the risks of speedy changes—or: Limits of flexibility in business]. In PASS IT-Consulting Group (Ed.), *Wandel als Herausforderung und Chance* (pp. 110–143). Muelheim, Germany: Bednarek-Druck.

Martin, D. C., & Bartol, K. M. (1985). Predictors of job status among trained economically disadvantaged persons. *Psychological Reports*, **57**, 719–734.

Mayberry, P. W., & Carey, N. B. (1997). The effect of aptitude and experience on mechanical job performance. *Educational and Psychological Measurement*, **57**, 131–149.

McBride, A. A., Mendoza, J. L., & Carraher, S. M. (1997). Development of a biodata index to measure service orientation. *Psychological Reports*, **81**, 1395–1407.

Mero, N. P., & Motowidlo, S. J. (1995). Effects of rater accountability on the accuracy and the favorability of performance ratings. *Journal of Applied Psychology*, **80**, 517–524.

Miner, J. B. (1970). Executive and personal interviews as predictors of consulting success. *Personnel Psychology*, **23**, 521–538.

Miner, J. B. (1992). *Industrial–organizational psychology*. New York: McGraw-Hill.

Moorhead, G., & Griffin, R. W. (1995). *Organizational behavior. Managing people and organizations* (4th edition). Boston, MA: Houghton Mifflin Company.

Moser, K. (1999). Selbstbeurteilung beruflicher Leistung: Überblick und offene Fragen [Self-assessment of vocational performance: A review and open issues]. *Psychologische Rundschau*, **50**, 14–25.

Motowidlo, S. J., & Schmit, M. J. (1999). Performance assessment in unique jobs. In D. R. Ilgen & E. D. Pulakos (Eds.), *The changing nature of performance. Implications of staffing, motivation, and development* (pp. 56–86). San Francisco: Jossey-Bass Publishers.

Mount, M. K., Muchinsky, P. M., & Hanser, L. M. (1977). The predictive validity of a work sample: A laboratory study. *Personnel Psychology*, **30**, 637–645.

Murphy, K. R., & Cleveland, J. N. (1995). *Understanding performance appraisal. Social, organizational, and goal-based perspectives*. Thousand Oaks, CA: Sage.

Neuberger, O. (1980a). *Personalentwicklung* [Personnel development]. Stuttgart: Enke.

Neuberger, O. (1980b). Rituelle (Selbst-)Täuschung. Kritik der irrationalen Praxis der Personalbeurteilung [Ritual (self-) delusion. Critique on the irrational practice of personnel assessment]. *Die Betriebswirtschaft*, **40**, 27–43.

Novartis (1998). *Geschaeftsbericht* [Business report]. Frankfurt/Main.

Obermann, C. (1996). Assessment Center als Prozeßdiagnostik [Assessment center as process diagnosis]. In W. Sarges (Ed.), *Weiterentwicklungen der Assessment-Center-Methode* (pp. 87–96). Göttingen: Verlag für Angewandte Psychologie.

Ouellette, J. A., & Wood, W. (1998). Habit and intention in everyday life: The multiple processes by which past behavior predicts future behavior. *Psychological Bulletin*, **124**, 54–74.

Patrick, J. (1992). *Training: Research and practice*. London: Academic Press.

Pössnecker, F. (1992). Potentialanalyse. Grundlagen der Identifikation und Förderung von Nachwuchskräften am Beispiel eines Industriebetriebs [Potential analysis. Principles of identification and promotion of trainees as demonstrated in an industrial firm]. *Zeitschrift für Arbeits- und Organisationspsychologie*, **36**, 37–42.

Pringle, C. D. (1994). An initial test of a theory of individual performance. *Psychological Reports*, **74**, 963–973.

Reece, W., & Matthews, L. (1993). Evidence and uncertainty in subjective prediction: Influences on optimistic judgment. *Psychological Reports*, **72**, 435–439.

Reid, M. A., Barrington, H., & Kenney, J. (1992). *Training interventions. Managing employee development* (3rd ed.). London: Institute of Personnel Management.

Robertson, I. T., & Downs, S. (1989). Work-sample tests of trainability: A meta-analysis. *Journal of Applied Psychology*, **74**, 402–410.

Robertson, I. T., & Kinder, A. (1993). Personality and job competences: The criterion-related validity of some personality variables. *Journal of Occupational and Organizational Psychology*, **66**, 225–244.

Ryan, A. M., McFarland, L., Baron, H., & Page, R. (1999). An international look at selection practices: Nation and culture as explanations for variability in practice. *Personnel Psychology*, **52**, 359–391.

Sarges, W. (1996). Lernpotential-Assessment Center [Learning potential assessment center]. In W. Sarges (Ed.), *Weiterentwicklungen der Assessment-Center-Methode* (pp. 97–108). Göttingen: Verlag für Angewandte Psychologie.

Saavedra, R., & Kwun, S. K. (1993). Peer evaluation in self-managing work groups. *Journal of Applied Psychology*, **78**, 450–462.

Salgado, J. F. (1997). The five factor model of personality and job performance in the European community. *Journal of Applied Psychology*, **82** (1), 30–43.

Schein, E. H. (1988). *Organizational Psychology* (3rd edition). Englewood Cliffs, NJ: Prentice-Hall.

Schmidt, F. L., & Hunter, J. E. (1998a). Meßbare Personmerkmale: Stabilität, Variabilität und Validität zur Vorhersage zukünftiger Berufsleistung und berufsbezogenen Lernens [Measurable personal traits: Stability, variability, and validity for the prediction of future job performance and job learning]. In M. Kleinmann & B. Strauß (Eds.), *Potentialfeststellung und Personalentwicklung*. Göttingen: Verlag für Angewandte Psychologie.

Schmidt, F. L., & Hunter, J. E. (1998b). The validity and utility of selection methods in personnel psychology: Practical and theoretical implications of 85 years of research findings. *Psychological Bulletin*, **124**, 262–274.

Schmitt, N., Pulakos, E. D., Nason, E., & Whitney, D. J. (1996). Likability and similarity as potential sources of predictor-related criterion bias in validation research. *Organizational Behavior and Human Decision Processes*, **68**, 272–286.

Schuler, H. (1991). Leistungsbeurteilung—Funktionen, Formen und Wirkungen [Performance appraisal—Functions, types, and effects]. In H. Schuler (Ed.), *Beurteilung und Förderung beruflicher Leistung. Beiträge zur Organisationspsychologie. Band 4* (pp. 11–40). Stuttgart: Verlag für Angewandte Psychologie.

Schuler, H. (1996). *Psychologische Personalauswahl. Einführung in die Berufseignungsdiagnostik* [Psychological personnel selection. Introduction to professional aptitude diagnosis]. Göttingen: Verlag für Angewandte Psychologie.

Schuler, H., Frier, D., & Kauffmann, M. (1993). *Personalauswahl im europäischen Vergleich* [Personnel selection in a European comparison]. Göttingen: Verlag für Angewandte Psychologie.

Schuler, H., & Prochaska, M. (1992). Ermittlung personaler Merkmale: Leistungs- und Potentialbeurteilung von Mitarbeitern [Determination of personal traits: Performance appraisal and potential assessment of employees]. In Kh. Sonntag (Ed.): *Personalentwicklung in Organisationen* (pp. 157–186). Göttingen: Hogrefe.

Shahani, C., Dipboye, R. L., & Gehrlein, T. M. (1991). The incremental contribution of an interview to college admission. *Educational and Psychological Measurement*, **51**, 1049–1061.

Shore, T. H. (1992). Subtle gender bias in the assessment of managerial potential. *Sex Roles*, **27**, 499–515.

Shore, T. H., Shore, L. M., & Thornton, G. C. (1992). Construct validity of self- and peer evaluations of performance dimensions in an assessment center. *Journal of Applied Psychology*, **77**, 42–54.

Shore, L. M., Tetrick, L. E., & Shore, T. H. (1998). A comparison of self-, peer, and assessor evaluations of managerial potential. *Journal of Social Behavior and Personality*, **13**, 85–101.

Stajkovic, A. D., & Luthans, F. (1998). Self-efficacy and work-related performance: A meta-analysis. *Psychological Bulletin*, **124**, 240–261.

Tannenbaum, S. I., & Yukl, G. (1992). Training and development in work organizations. *Annual Review of Psychology*, **43**, 399–441.

Tett, R. P., Jackson, D. N., & Rothstein, M. (1991). Personality measures as predictors of job performance: A meta-analytic review. *Personnel Psychology*, **44**, 703–742.

Thornton, G. C. (1980). Psychometric properties of self-appraisals of job performance. *Personnel Psychology*, **33**, 264–271.

Thornton, G. C., Gaugler, B., Rosenthal, D., & Bentson, C. (1992). Die Prädiktive Validität des AC—eine Metaanalyse [Predictive validity of assessment centers—a meta-analysis]. In H. Schuler & W. Stehle (Eds.), *Assessment-Center als Methode der Personalentwicklung* (pp. 36–60) (2nd edition). Stuttgart: Verlag für Angewandte Psychologie.

Tziner, A., & Dolan, S. (1982). Validity of an assessment center for identifying future female officers in the military. *Journal of Applied Psychology*, **67**, 728–736.

Vance, R. J., Coovert, M. D., MacCallum, R. C., & Hedge, J. W. (1989). Construct models of task performance. *Journal of Applied Psychology*, **74**, 447–455.

Viswesvaran, C., Ones, D. S., & Schmidt, F. L. (1996). Comparative analysis of the reliability of job performance ratings. *Journal of Applied Psychology*, **81**, 557–574.

Wexley, K. N. (1984). Personnel training. *Annual Review of Psychology*, **35**, 519–551.

Wexley, K. N., & Latham, G. P. (1991). *Developing and training human resources in organizations* (2nd ed.). New York: Harper Collins.

Williams, K. J., DeNisi, A. S., Meglino, B. M., & Cafferty, T. P. (1986). Initial decisions and subsequent performance ratings. *Journal of Applied Psychology*, **71**, 189–195.

Woehr, D. J., & Huffcutt, A. I. (1994). Rater training for performance appraisal: A quantitative review. *Journal of Occupational and Organizational Psychology*, **67**, 189–205.

Zedeck, S., & Cascio, W. F. (1982). Performance decisions as a function of purpose of rating and training. *Journal of Applied Psychology*, **67**, 752–758.

Assessing Potential and Future Performance

Wieby Altink
SHL Nederland B.V., Utrecht, The Netherlands, and
Helma Verhagen
Fuji Photo Film B.V., Tilburg, The Netherlands

SUMMARY

Due to developments within their contexts, organisations have to pay more attention to management development or actually human development (HD) for the entire work-force. One of the important issues regarding this is "how to measure high potential" and "how to manage high potential". First of all, the definition of high potential is dependent on contextual factors, and the measurement of high potential is not only related to intelligence. The measurement of progress that someone makes in personal development is one of the indicators of "potential" for the future; therefore, analyses of this potential should be measured at several times during a career path in relation to development plans and opportunities offered by learning experiences. We discuss methods and techniques to predict (high) potential that are frequently applied within organisations. Next, we offer an overview of modern methods and procedures that relate to the process of human development, for example 360-degree feedback and development centres. A practical case study indicates that an organisation should adjust the methods for assessing potential and future performance to their human resource management policy, the departmental culture and the motivation and values of the participants. Tailor-made solutions, and a HD policy that sustains the process around development appear to be the main practical solutions that incorporate new insights in the area of potential analysis and human development.

INTRODUCTION

Organisations pay more and more attention to the assessment and measurement of potential concerning human development and future performance. The reason for this is that, on the one hand, the market is changing in terms of the demand from customers and intermediaries. Being able to react more quickly, more flexibly and in a more result-oriented manner calls for an adjusted human resource policy. A future-oriented scope, the assessment of possibilities and a creative and result-oriented anticipation of these possibilities are demanded more and more from management. On the other hand, there are changes in the supply-side of the labour market. Due to demographic developments (reduction in birth rate, more elderly people because of improvement in health care) there is a great need for young people with potential now and this trend will continue in the future.[1] The globalisation of markets, due among other things to technical development (information technology) and economic growth (or the building of a new economy in areas where this is needed) requires not only a workforce with high potentials but one that possesses strong competencies. This change also demands management to have an adjusted policy on recruitment, assessment and development of the current or future employees, especially when it concerns people with high potentials, people at managerial levels or people in areas where innovation takes place. As a consequence, assessment and development techniques—being able to judge the employees by their competencies and the development of potential and future functioning—are becoming important tools for human resource management within organisations.

This chapter will handle the methods with which (management) potential and future performance can be measured, predicted and developed. We will aim at the perspectives in management development—and more generally human development—and the target groups within organisations that are often associated with high potential in practice. First of all, attention will be paid to several relevant developments that take place within organisations. It is also important to be able to distinguish between 'potential' and 'high potential'. We adopt the definition of potential that Lohaus and Kleinmann (this volume) introduced in their chapter, and will extend this to the competency approach that is now very popular within organisations today. Also, we will present a model that puts emphasis on process factors when measuring potential. Following, it is discussed which methods are available to measure and develop potential. Finally, we will illustrate an approach that is in our opinion very promising regarding the measurement and development of (management) potential.

INNOVATIONS WITHIN WORK AND ORGANISATIONAL CONTEXT AND THEIR IMPLICATIONS FOR MANAGEMENT/HUMAN DEVELOPMENT

HUMAN DEVELOPMENT AS THE BASIS OF MODERN HUMAN RESOURCE MANAGEMENT

Nowadays, a number of changes that follow one another rapidly are taking place within the context of work and organisation. In the many discussions that we have had with managers of organisations we have noticed that the opinions regarding the influence of all the technological, market and organisational changes differ considerably. These opinions can be divided into two, rather extreme, viewpoints. The first viewpoint is based on the idea that there are so many changes occurring so rapidly that within a short period of time a rather chaotic business context will emerge that is hard to manage. The other viewpoint supports the idea that this discussion has also been going on for some years, and although some changes have been implemented, none of them has been 'earth-shaking'. Based on this idea it is stated that the coming period will certainly bring about changes and innovations, but these will not have a profound impact on the organisation policy.

Part of the difference in viewpoints can be attributed to the position that the manager takes (as well as his/her organisation) in the anticipation on new developments. And indeed, considering that organisations are fairly classifiable in terms of 'conservative/reactive' and 'entrepreneurial/proactive', this need not always be correlated with the actual characteristics of the business context (Ansoff & McDonell, 1990; Quinn, 1992; Peters & Waterman, 1995). Consequently, managers and human resource specialists differ in their reactions to the developments that take place. Some are looking for new ways to retain talents in organisations, others are adhering to existing methods of recruitment, selection and development of potentials because these methods have proved their merits in the past (Capelli, 2000). To state in general that the one or the other is applying a more sensible strategy is not the case, because in strategies that relate to developments in economy, society and organisations, and thus also the attraction, development and retention of potentials actions, have always be attuned to the specific situation.

Despite this, the opinion that the activities on the development of organisation members should be the focus of human resources management in the next few decades is prevailing (see, among others, Dutch surveys, Haak, Jansen, & Mul, 1998). Concepts that have been only applicable to certain target groups in the past, such as managers, should be applied more broadly in 'human development'. In other words, organisations have to concern the development of a broader target group of potentials within the organisation in order to create 'competitive advantage' (e.g. Moingeon & Edmondson, 1996). As Lohaus and Kleinmann (this volume) argue, human development, and more specifically potential analysis, should be incorporated in human resource procedures in order to be effective within organisations. In addition to this we state that tailor-made solutions specific to the organisational context are needed to yield the desired results from human development activities.

TRENDS THAT INFLUENCE MANAGEMENT/HUMAN DEVELOPMENT

The developments that are taking place in the context of an organisation or institute are partly dependent on, for example, the nature of the organisation and its goals, the location (country) of the organisation, the development phase, etc. The fact still remains, however, that some general trends can be detected which will affect every organisation sooner or later. Since potential implies a prediction of future performance, not only the future (managerial) job but also future organisational goals define the concept of 'potential'. Some general factors that may influence the goals of an organisation are summarised in Figure 9.1. They represent the context within which human development takes place, or has to take place.

In our point of view the influence of these contextual factors on human development, and therefore the measurement of potential, cannot be ignored. The current rapid technological changes and all the evolvements in the environment of an organisation (see Figure 9.1) ask for alert reactions and flexibility in order to be able to implement the desired manageral direction. In human development, certain competencies will become

---

I. *External sociopolitical environment:*
- Technological developments
- Demographic developments
- Political development (including law regulations)
- Environmental developments
- Innovation and growth

II. *Geographic perspective*
- World/region/ or nation state
- Labour-market challenges
- Pressures for social responsibility versus business power
- Work ethic, attitudes towards organisations and work

III. *Product markets*
- Life-cycle
- Saturation/generation of markets
- National/international markets
- Constraints/opportunities for innovation and growth

IV. *Internal environment*
- Structure
- Culture
- Power relations
- Management and Human Resource policy

FIGURE 9.1 Influences on organisations and management/human development (based on, a.o. Ansoff & McDonell; 1990)

more important, for example innovation, creativity and the overview of complex and broad developments. Due to the globalisation of markets, an increasing degree of fierce competition takes place. The need to be able to cope with this competition is sometimes at odds with the labour supply of managers and employees able to do so. Furthermore, it is even more difficult to find managers and employees who are able to deal with complex issues and still find sufficient time for family life. Thus, development and learning will need to be emphasised in human development. Methods and instruments are needed that 'trigger' development and learning in a rather automatically way. After all, concepts such as 'life-time employment' are becoming more and more outdated.

Furthermore, changes in product/market combinations require a closer cooperation between the diverse disciplines within an organisation. The target groups of management development are therefore broadened, as in addition to general managers, managers with, for example, a technical, marketing or HR background are needed in order to guarantee interdisciplinary cooperation. And this also applies to other organisational members. Thus, the estimation of potential will need to be applicable to all these target groups.

Delayering trends and more self-conscious and mature employees require different managerial processes to continuously develop organisational members. Management principles that should anticipate these trends are being introduced at a rapid pace (such as the development of self-steering teams, empowerment, etc.). Thus, it is important for the future manager and employee to be aware of these trends at all times and to evaluate them on their merits for the situation at hand. An important question in the field of human development is how to stimulate this awareness. Thus, besides the measurement of potential, attention should be paid to the possibilities of feeding and developing this potential, and also to the way people benefit from the development possibilities that are offered.

It is difficult to give a general overview of competencies that will prevail in the next decades. As we argued, this depends on the technological and societal developments, the developments within specific labour areas and markets, and within job families. However, nowadays competencies that are popular in (at least) west European countries are empowering, coaching, innovation, motivating people, being flexible and open to new developments, but two decades ago the focus was placed on steering, planning and organisation, being able to attain discipline and order together with content-related knowledge. In other countries or in particular organisations the emphasis may be put on just the latter competencies. What one may conclude is that job and organisational analysis is very important in applying a suitable policy on the development of potentials and the human workforce. It is more or less inherent to the definition of a potential that he or she is able to develop the competencies that are necessary to fulfil the job, the organisation and—in a broader sense—the societal goals that are at a particular moment (and in the coming future) prevailing.[2]

In other words, the present developments that are taking place within and outside organisations ask for a human development policy in which the following issues are of crucial importance: the development of (new) competencies, the offer of challenges, the broadening of target groups and continuous learning on both group and individual level (also see Vogelaar, 1997). This has far-reaching consequences for the definition of what should be known as "potential". A person who was regarded to have high potential ten years ago need not necessarily fall into this category today.

THE CONCEPT OF POTENTIAL AND FUTURE PERFORMANCE: THE RELEVANCE OF THE COMPETENCY APPROACH IN PRACTICAL APPLICATIONS

WHICH FACTORS DETERMINE THE CONCEPT 'POTENTIAL'?

Lohaus and Kleinmann (this volume) give a broad overview on the constituents and definitions of potential analysis. We adhere to this by stating that ample support has been found for the role of intellectual qualities and personality factors in predicting (managerial) success (Schmidt & Hunter, 1998; Barrick, Mount, & Judge, 1999).

Other factors have also received much attention in the practise of management (or more broadly human) development, particularly managerial competencies (e.g. Boyatzis, 1982); and when talking about competencies, this concerns behavioural dimensions on a relatively low abstraction level, for example, 'steering', 'building and containing relationships' and 'strategic vision' (from the PMC model, SHL, 1996). The advantage of the competency approach is that a more direct link is possible between the predictors and the criterion behaviour that needs to be predicted. In this way, competencies can be considered to be concrete expressions of underlying factors, such as intellectual capacities, personality, norms and values. In practising human resources management today, competency measurements have become very popular for the determination of potential (SHL, survey competency management 1997). This, to a large extent, is due to the fact that these can be coupled to follow-up measurements and activities within management/human development as well as other HRM activities, such as the 360-degrees feedback method and coaching on competencies.

In the competency approach several aspects are taken together: a competency is a result of intellectual qualities, personality factors, motivational factors, values and environmental influences—aspects that can measured by several methods (see below). Competencies, as defined nowadays, are the result of many factors, but they can be described in such a concrete way that they can be just as related equally to organisational goals as they can to personal goals and job descriptions (SHL, 1996). Thus, starting with Boyatzis (1982), the concept of competency has undergone a development in itself. Most important in this respect is the fact that competencies provide a common language in the job expectations and the direction to develop (Altink, Visser, & Castelijns, 1997). This might explain the popularity of this approach within organisations when dealing with questions in the area of management and human development.

Before we go into the factors that relate to measuring potential, an important question is whether competencies can be developed. Lohaus and Kleinmann (this volume) discuss this issue in the context of the concepts and factors that make up competencies. In addition to this we present a model that takes into account the importance of a process approach.

THE ROLE OF PROCESS FACTORS WHEN MEASURING POTENTIAL

In the day-to-day life within organisations potential is also determined by that what an individual contributes in the process of experiences that are offered to him/her. Odiorne (1984) had depicted this in his portfolio analysis in which high potentials (or 'stars') are considered persons that score high on potential and high on performance

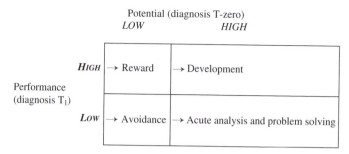

FIGURE 9.2 Human Resources Portfolio (Odiorne, 1984) in relation to human development actions

(see Figure 9.2). In this analysis, a high potential is someone that generates success with his/her underlying qualifications in the field of intellect, personality, ambitions, values and the competencies that he/she carried in first instance. According to Odiorne, a different approach is needed for all the different categories of managers/employees that can be distinguished in the figure. For example, in order to motivate those who have a lower potential but who perform high, external motivating factors apply best. Particular attention should be applied to those who have a high potential, but who do not perform according to this potential. They need special learning activities that "trigger" their potential.

As stated by Lohaus and Kleinmann in this volume, the realised competency level and accompanying performances at a certain period in time, are also dependent on the learning experiences that someone goes through, as well as the learning possibilities offered and the person's own initiative to benefit from these possibilities (see also, Moingeon & Edmondson, 1996). Thus measurement of progress in personal development can be considered as an indicator of "potential" at a later stage, as well as an indicator of performance. In other words, in our point of view potential is a concept that can be measured at different points in time. This measurement takes into account not only content-related factors that can be seen as more or less stable (intellect, personality, competencies, etc.), but also process-related factors (realised learning experiences) which are partly dependent on numerous situational circumstances. This has particular practical implications; for example, imagine a person who can be considered a high potential at stage T-zero, for example on the basis of intellectual quality and personality, but is not given the opportunity to challenging learning environment with opportunities, and moments of experience. This person could be classified as 'hardly to develop' with the associated action 'avoidance' at stage T_1 according to Odiorne's model. This time the measurement does not take into account the offered learning opportunities, as well as the fact that in principle, according to the zero or origin-measurement, the potential in a future situation could be high. On the other hand, a high potential could be a 'star' in stage T_1 as the result of extreme efforts by the organisation to provide learning experiences— or because his/her qualifications were congruent with the current organisational goals. However, this 'star' may not remain a 'star' in a less ideal environment without challenges, opportunities and learning possibilities. Taking account of the new developments that are awaiting organisations, this seems an important fact which should be at least considered when determining potential. High potential must not be equated with a high performer!

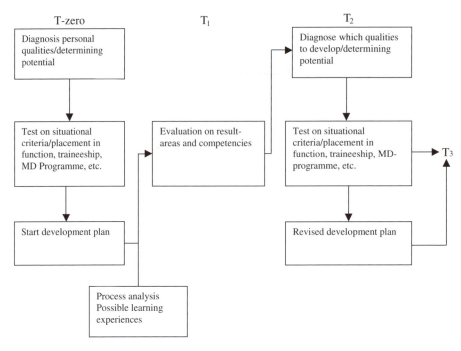

FIGURE 9.3   An interactive model in order to define potential and future performance

THE ROLE OF DEVELOPMENT AND ACTION PLANS WHEN DETERMINING POTENTIAL

We have summarised the train of thought on the measurement of numerous, successive moments in time mentioned in Figure 9.3. First of all, person-related factors are measured (e.g. intellect, competencies, performances, at different points in time). In addition, a test on the situation is also depicted, for example the placing in a more or less rigidly described position, a traineeship, participation in a management development programme, etc. This will lead to the beginning of a development plan.

The processes that take place between the different points in time are also taken into account. These processes are being influenced by numerous factors such as the position or programme a person is placed in, the developments an organisation goes through, the way someone deals with the learning opportunities offered, etc. Thus, this process determines which of the attention points that have been described in the development and action plans eventually have been realised. Although the role of the personal development plans is not new in human resource management (for example, in the Netherlands and a number of other counties they are extensively used), little attention is paid to the results of this method in the determination of potential at a later point in time (in terms of Figures 9.2 and 9.3, the determination of potential at T_1). This could take place more efficiently by the use of high-tech automated systems that are able to determine this information adequately. It should be clear by now that these systems still require a solid human development policy where the provision of the appropriate learning experiences and moments is concerned.

Finally, a comment on the difference between potential and high potential in this particular model simply concerns the 'norm': Where does one draw the line in determining that someone shows insufficient, sufficient, good or extremely good indicators that could contribute to and realise future organisation goals at a certain point in time? High potential is only one of many qualifications in this respect. However, this norm is situation-dependent, and is partly determined by the human development policy which, in turn, should be coupled to future organisation goals.

Therefore, an approach in which the development of persons and the possibilities to profit from this development is of relevance for the measurement of potential when relating this to human development and contextual influences. This has been used in practice for some considerable time by means of assessment methodology and development centres in combination of the 360-feedback method, in which more measurements are present (see below). Our approach therefore implies that more content related-factors (which individual characteristics determine the concept of potential) and process-related factors (possibilities to learn, being able to actively react on future changes, etc.) should both be considered when measuring potential.

The above-mentioned model implies that potential measurements are placed in a process in time in which continuous feedback and moments of prediction are present. It forms a practical elaboration on the (content-related) definition that Lohaus and Kleinmann (this volume) have given for the measurement of potential.

MEASURING AND DEVELOPING HIGH POTENTIAL

There are several activities directed towards the group of employees who form the so-called (high) potentials within the organisation. The main reason for these activities is to ensure an adequate number of senior employees in specialised positions, with good (top) management today and for the future. Development of (high) potential will therefore become an important part of company policy.

It must be realised that society is subject to many and, in particular, rapid changes that require flexible adjustments from both individuals and organisations. Organisations also want to retain their own "management philosophy" and their own "cultural pattern" of standards and values, which are subsequently translated into whatever "high potential" entails for their organisation. It is clear that through the development of personnel in general and management in particular, the company will not lose impetus. Pfeffer (1994, p. 210) described this as follows: "People and how we manage them are becoming more important because many other sources of competitive success are less powerful then they once were." Therefore the concept of competency is useful in communicating organisational and personal developments: it provides for a practical and goal-oriented language for "need analysis" (see also Lohaus & Kleinmann, this volume).

In this section, we first pay attention to the methods and techniques that are used to determine potential; then, in more detail, we discuss several HR activities which are of importance to the development and, finally, evaluation of the potential measured. According to the model described in the previous section, the achievement realised, and an evaluation of the process of development, form the basis of a new potential measurement, which can, in turn, eventually be supplemented by methods like those described in the following paragraphs.

FREQUENTLY APPLIED METHODS AND TECHNIQUES TO PREDICT (HIGH) POTENTIAL

We have already indicated that the measurement of potential in the general sense of the word simply involves the measurement of personal qualities. For, if a person has potential, this should, in principle, be regarded in isolation from contextual factors. The contextual factors are relevant to the question of what an organisation can and will do with this potential. It are, namely, often the contextual factors that make it easier, or more difficult, for someone to achieve a certain development or achievement. Subject to diverse developments on the market, the questions that are now at the forefront of discussions within many organisations are: Does this individual have any potential, and to what degree can this person develop certain competencies? This question will subsequently also have to be translated into a 'how' question, namely: How can this person develop in the manner specified?

What follows in this section is not an exhaustive overview, but an elaboration on several methods and techniques that are currently often deployed to predict if somebody possesses potential or not. These are:

- Intelligence measurements
- Personality measurements
- Assessment centre/development centre
- Value and motivation measurements.

Because potential is, generally, only measured when an organisation has an interest in the results of such a measurement (because of a vacancy, or a development plan), when determining which instruments are to be employed, several questions should already be answered, namely:

- What does the organisation understand by (high) potential?
- What criteria should the person meet, exactly? Is there a specific position available, or is the person concerned embarking on a career path. In other words, what are the middle and long-term expectations?
- What possibilities exist within the organisation for individuals to develop themselves?
- What is the situation on the labour market? What demands can the organisation afford to make?
- What is the long-term policy with regard to Human Development and Organisational Development?

On the basis of the answers given to these questions, the organisation can decide upon the most suitable measurement instrument or the correct measurement methods. It is, in any case, evident that there must be clarity with regard to what exactly the objective is and what is to be measured or assessed.

Intelligence measurements

Intelligence tests may be oriented towards the assessment of a candidate's abstractive capabilities, verbal reasoning, numerical and spatial insight, and so forth. These deal explicitly with the measurement of cognitive ability. Intelligence tests often form a basic measurement, particularly for the group of more senior employees or (high) potentials.

When the labour market is tight organisations are more inclined to base their decision purely on intelligence. This is often a conscious management decision whereby intelligence is regarded as a basic condition indicative of whether someone has the capacity to develop further or not. Although intelligence measurements do have a considerable predictive value (Schmidt & Hunter, 1998), there are enough documented cases of "the little boy who was the best in the class, but who was prevented from 'making' it because of circumstances". Sometimes this is due to environmental factors, but it may also be that "this boy" lacks specific competencies or motivation. A one-sided focus on intelligence measurement is then, in our opinion, not to be recommended.

Personality measurements

Besides cognitive skills, companies are increasingly also considering personality factors as contributing to the success of somebody within an organisation. In the first place personality questionnaires are used, which are available on the market in various forms. A personality questionnaire tries to identify an individual's more or less stable traits. Although it is often the case that people are able and/or prepared to adapt their behaviour to the circumstances that arise, there are still certain personality traits that recur in different situations, and are, thus, characteristic of somebody's attitude or behaviour (Barrick, Mount, & Judge, 1999). These personality traits may be relevant to the manner in which the organisation wishes the position(s) to be exercised, or career development within the organisation. Such tests also offer additional information which can be used to determine whether the person fits in the organisation, department or team that he or she will become part of (among others: Altink & Verhagen, 1999). A specific example of the latter is the Occupational Personality Questionnaire (SHL, 1978) which, in addition to a profile based on a number of specific behavioural dimensions, also gives a verdict on team roles, management styles and the management tasks suitable for the person in question. A translation to competencies (by means of an expert system) is also possible. As was observed above with regard to intelligence measurements, a too one-sided interest in personality factors is not to be recommended when the determination of potential is the objective. If people do not possess a number of essential skills (*competencies*) which are of importance for employment or promotion, the "perfect personality" will show little development.

Values and motivation measurements

In the past, values and motivation measurements were often used to determine potential. The idea behind this was that somebody who has to develop, must also possess a certain drive. If the development is to be successful, this person should also fit in with the value pattern that is specific to the organisation in question. Values also influence individuals in the choices they make and, therefore, form motives. Until recently, these measurements particularly concerned clinical instruments, which are less suitable for the determination of potential. Not only because the validity was not normally that high, but also because it was less acceptable for the target group concerned. At the present time, questionnaires are available that are more modern and more valid. An example of this is *Values at Work* (SHL, 2000), with which values can be measured on the basis of the person, group, organisation and national level. Subsequently, all kinds of comparisons can be made: person versus organisation, or the comparison of the ideal situation with the actual situation at the level of the person. As an addition to the above-mentioned methods and techniques, values and motivation measurements are useful when wanting to determine potential and how it can best be developed. Attention will, however, still have to be paid to the actual predictive value of various comparative methodologies, given that, from a psychometric point of view, these call for a number of difficult analyses for which, from a technical viewpoint, a good solution is not always available.

Assessment and development centre

Therefore, at the present time, a combination of measurement methods and/or instruments is utilised during a selection procedure at the start of a career, or during a potential assessment. These are so-called assessment centres or development centres, which may also include intelligence and personality measurements. In practice, an assessment or development centre normally refers to situational tests, often also called exercises or practical cases. These methods consist of a series of measurement instruments (realistic practice simulations which lend themselves to a considerable objective measurement) with which individuals' relevant skills and competencies can be identified. This could be a 3-way conversation whereby agreement has to be reached between two conflicting parties, the solution of a (fictional) company dilemma, the giving of a presentation, a group discussion, or an in-tray exercise. The assessment of explicit work-related behaviour on the basis of pre-formulated (position specific) competencies is always central here. Questions that can be answered in this way are: "To what degree does the person concerned possess the potential to show a certain desired behaviour in specific situations?", "Is the person concerned able to react and act in the desired way in an unfamiliar situation?", but also "To what degree can a certain competency be developed in the person concerned, and what is the assessment of his/her career potential?" It now appears to be possible to answer these questions with a considerable degree of validity, although this does depend on the exact organisation of the assessment and development centre (Altink & Verhagen, 1999).

The above-mentioned questions also illustrate the difference between the applicability of an assessment centre or a development centre. At an assessment centre, the emphasis is on the measurement and assessment of competencies in relation to an explicit function profile. This is often applicable in selection situations. At a development centre, the emphasis lies emphatically on developmental possibilities and the potential, or degree to which it is possible for the person concerned to develop. In general, the result is an analysis of strong and weak points in somebody's performance, development requirements and a personal development plan for the mid-term or long term. Within organisations, this information is often combined with internal performance or potential assessments and possibly the 360 degree feedback method.

DEVELOPING POTENTIAL AND FUTURE PERFORMANCE: THE PROCESS

The measurement of potential is the first step, but this cannot be seen separately from step two: the determination of what an organisation and the individual are going to "do" with the potential measured. In the past, when the potential to progress to a management position was being assessed, allowance was made, particularly, for a person's service record. The specialised employees who were the best achievers were appointed to management positions. In the present situation, where the success of a company seems increasingly to be directly determined by the human resources, given the high demands made by the market, more account is increasingly being taken of the (development) potential of the personnel in those areas in which the organisation pursues its goals. In order to keep the organisation moving, a considerable amount of attention is paid to developing the "human factor" within the organisation. Here, assessment is a crucial instrument to determine an employee's development and indicate his/her career perspectives (Schoenmaker & Geerdink, 1991). Whereas in the traditional situation assessment was used to 'reflect' on the performance of the employee, in the present trend of Human Development management, a combination of reflection and potential prognosis is the case. It is exactly this potential prognosis that is of importance because, in the interests of the organisation and the employee, a career path must be outlined. It goes without saying that personal development plans (see Figure 9.3) form the connection between measurement and actions to be taken.

Within the policy area of Human Development, a number of activities exist that are directed towards the development of the potential that exists within the organisation. The activities that we most often encounter in organisations are:

- Traineeship
- Management development activities/leadership development
- Job rotation
- 360-degree feedback.

Traineeship

To date, traineeship has always been directed towards offering an extensive training and developmental programme for a target group which is explicitly described as "high potentials". In general, a trainee training programme consists of a three- or four-year process in which a participant, in addition to a quite comprehensive and in-depth training component, gains hands-on experience at various locations within the organisation. The aim of a traineeship is ultimately to obtain a (higher) management position. The selection of this target group therefore requires extra care. On the other hand, labour shortage entails that other and specific forms of recruitment and selection, such as headhunting and search, must be used to attract highly qualified people from the labour market. These people are subsequently increasingly offered a career or, as referred to here, traineeship instead of a position within the organisation. Companies will then have to ask themselves how they can trigger the target group to apply and, more importantly, what they can do to keep this target group motivated to develop within the company. Young, highly educated people, new to the labour market, increasingly select companies on the basis of the training programmes on offer and possibilities with regard to individual development.

The latter factors, but also the other developments which were identified earlier in this chapter, demand a review of the structure of the traditional traineeship. It is our experience that organisations are at present striving to create a breeding ground for the fairly broad "highly educated" target groups. Only later is a decision made with regard to which positions they will be appointed and whether, taking into consideration the goals pursued by the organisation, they are actually high potentials or not. The fact that employment of this target group should be guaranteed not only in terms of quantity, but also in terms of quality, is not separate to, but does fall largely outside of, this discussion. However, a traineeship does also entail a considerable investment for the organisation in terms of training funds, time and salary expenses. The profit generated during the traineeship often amounts to little more than that gained from a student taken on for the purpose of a Master's research project or work experience. This makes a measurement of the real potential that somebody possesses in the light of the organisation's goals extremely desirable. A correct selection of the trainee pool requires a serious approach to how the selection and assessment of the competencies and the potential of this group is handled.

Management development activities/leadership development

Management development is the area of HR activity with the greatest potential for determining the strategic capability of organisational management teams (Purcell & Ahlstrand, 1994; Mumford, 1988; Storey, 1989). The central objective of Management Development (MD) is, first of all, the occupation of key positions within the organisation, and the maintenance of the present (top) management. The policy of many organisations in relation to "high" potential is then completely oriented towards the development of its future managers. In addition, MD offers scope for training and developing so that employees continue to be challenged and are allowed to learn, and potential is bonded to the organisation. The focus of a MD programme then shifts from structured training programmes for the various layers of managers to individual development plans and the support of career development by means of coaching in the workplace. Organisations increasingly define this field as leadership development, partly because the target groups are not usually those who have just graduated from university or college.

The underlying principle, introduced in the previous paragraph, is also that the best executives are not necessarily those who possess a previously identified, generous list of traits or who have risen to the top through 'survival of the fittest' (McCall, 1998). Rather, the real leaders of the future are those who have the ability to learn from their experiences and remain open to continual learning. If these people get the right experience on the job, they will have the ultimate opportunity to learn new executive skills. In the case of MD, the target groups in larger organisations follow structured training programmes which usually focus on the transfer of knowledge and skills with regard to management methods and techniques. This traditional MD approach has encountered a lot of criticism. In view of the current insecurity about the future in customer and labour markets, MD programmes are being perceived as formalistic and rigid. Especially with a view to the development of knowledge and competencies, two major points of criticism are encountered. Firstly, MD activities are often too far removed from daily management problems and the real experiences of management tasks. Secondly, due to a too heavy workload, insufficient opportunities exist in the work setting to apply the relevant knowledge and skills gained; as a result, these skills fade away. Thus, in most instances the programmes used only generate a small amount of practically applicable knowledge. People who have just become managers often feel that they are not prepared for their task. They are prepared for the technical aspects of their job, such as keeping track of the budget, but cannot handle other 'softer' aspects, such as their identity as a manager (Hill, 1992).

The essence of the above is that the knowledge and skills that are acquired by means of traditional approaches are, for various reasons, not adequate or it is not possible to put them into practice (Thompson & Henningsen, 1996). That knowledge can only be applied to an insufficient extent and that new skills can only be experimented with unsatisfactorily is a fundamental error of the organisation system, given that knowledge and skills only have value in an organisation when they are applied. There already is a long-standing interest in the use of the workplace as an effective development resource for managers. Mumford (1988), who investigated this in the context of enhancing individual learning styles, and Revans (1982), who pioneered 'action learning', are two early advocates of the workplace as a superior source of managerial learning compared with college or structured training programmes. Management Development activities are now partly motivated by the labour market and are being extended to include the workplace of the manager.

Job rotation

Job rotation is a tool which aims to contribute to broader employability and the possibility of further developing management potential on the one hand, and offering the challenges desired by the individual employee on the other. By gaining experience in different locations within the organisation, a broad basis is formed and competencies relating to different positions are combined. It is exactly by presenting new challenges when they are required that someone will remain motivated and challenged to function well (among others: Vogelaar, 1997). Another advantage is that the mobility of the person concerned is enlarged, which has a positive effect on both the organisation and the individual. Job rotation thus contributes to the possibility of promoting "employability", by which, simultaneously, the so-called "psychological contract" between the employee and the employer also receives a new impulse (Gaspersz & Ott, 1996). Job rotation appears, furthermore, to be a good instrument that is implemented in order to achieve the goal of continuous learning experiences. In addition to this, another goal of job rotation is knowledge management; participants gain insight into all the primary processes at work in an organisation in a short time.

Job rotation does not, however, appear to be unproblematic in all cases. Such areas as production process technology and the essential specialist knowledge required for certain tasks, often stand in the way of job rotation. Managers, on the other hand, who increasingly define their position according to the mottos of "empowerment" and "coaching", have the advantage that at higher management levels the management and steering of processes is increasingly at the forefront in contradistinction to specialist support. In various literature relating to the field of Management Development warning is given of the very short cycles in which the development of employees is set. Analysis shows (among others: Lynn, Piehler, & Kieler, 1993) that the gradual competency development pattern (whereby it is possible to broaden knowledge and skills) allows employees to achieve substantially better when challenging but rapid and large steps are taken. There are also other more specific obstacles to job rotation which could be indicated. The subject here is the complexity of the production process versus the possibilities to actually have people rotate. So-called high potentials who are very strong as (super) specialists are exactly the employees who are difficult to rotate to functions within another field. Often the career paths for this group are fairly stable, and can be identified beforehand (an eventual progression from junior to senior), and rotation usually has more disadvantages than advantages. The organisational structure can also form an obstacle. The development of potential often starts within a certain business unit, where there is the possibility and aim to progress to positions within other units. However, managers often actually want to retain these people within their own unit and, for this reason, political considerations often play more of a role than is desirable in job rotation (Vogelaar, 1997).

360-degree feedback

Another instrument that can be deployed for the development of potential is the 360-degree feedback. This method has already long been in use in such countries as the United Kingdom, the United States and Japan. Large companies such as AT&T and General Electrics have already been using this method for a number of years, and in The Netherlands increasing numbers of companies are showing an interest in this feedback method. In global terms, the 360-degree feedback method entails the feedback of opinions about the performance and (work) achievements of individual employees in organisations (Mulder & Martens, 1998). It is a methodology whereby all those parties who are concerned with the achievements gained by someone, can give their comments and feedback.

Feedback is given by persons holding various senior, peer and subordinate positions who have an insight into the performance and achievement of the employee concerned. This insight is an important condition, if a valid assessment is to be arrived at. The assessors are often employee's manager, subordinate(s), colleagues, customers, or even suppliers. The major advantage of this method is that input is supplied from different perspectives and reference points. In addition to the insight required into someone's performance, the success of this methodology is also dependent on a situation in which open communication exists around the process of giving feedback. In many companies this is, however, definitely not yet the case. The 360-degree feedback method is sometimes linked to remuneration, with all its consequences with regard to objectivity and integrity.

The method does, however, offer good perspectives, especially if it is used as a development instrument. Employees and managers receive feedback on their performance from different points of view, and very concrete development points can be identified and subsequently included in a personal development plan. In the role of manager or (high) potential, self-awareness is a very important asset to choose the correct route, or determine which items to set to work on, in order to undergo a certain development. It also leads to a process that is vital to development: reflection (Hill, 1992). After some time you can again use a 360-feedback questionnaire to get information about the progresses.

Below, we will describe an example from practice in which, in the framework of the issue of leadership development, attention is paid to the development of management potential as described above. The case is a general description of an approach within a large production organisation and is part of a far more elaborated HR policy of the entire organisation.

PRACTICAL CASE STUDY

HUMAN DEVELOPMENT AT FUJI PHOTO FILM B.V.

Fuji Photo Film B.V. Tilburg—the Netherlands—is a large production company, with about 1,500 employees, that develops, produces and distributes photosensitive products: colour paper, colour negative film and presensitised plates. Fuji Tilburg's mission is to increase the market share of these three product groups on the European market and to become the overall profitable leading European brand. The slogan of the organisation is 'Going to the top as a creative team'.

Considering this development Fuji wants to it seems to be necessary (among other things) to implement a different leadership style within the organisation. This demands a different profile with other or additional competencies of the managers in all managerial layers of the organisation. Consequently, the issue of 'leadership development' has been integrated in the HR policy in order to develop a management profile that fits the future organisational developments and to give management potentials an impulse in their development to manager according to the desired profile.

In order to do so, the top of the organisation firstly defined a new management profile. Instead of a content-related, task-oriented approach of leadership and its associated hierarchical structure, the organisation wants to change to the concept of coaching and self-steering. This eventually resulted in the description of the 'result-oriented people manager'. This means that the managers need to move beyond their traditional focus on functional excellence towards the coach in a supporting role, who is able to provide visibility (of customer, company objectives and employees) and recognition and has the ability to remove barriers to progress.

First of all the entire Management Team took part in a development centre to make an analysis of their competencies on general management skills and to realise a personal development or coaching plan.

Next step in the plan of approach is conducting a strengths and weaknesses analysis for section management (the layer just below MT-level) on the current functioning concerning the defined competencies in "section managers-profile" and the potential to develop in the desired direction. The tools that are used are the assessment/development centre method and the 360-degree feedback instrument. These should eventually lead to an 'individual development plan' for each manager. In practice both methods are being used, dependent on the preference of higher management of the particular group of (section) managers. In Japan the 360-degree feedback method has become quite common, which is the reason why these particular department managers have chosen for this method. The outcome, i.e. the realisation of development plans, was the most important issue for the organisation.

Most of the managers take part in a development centre in which they are confronted with a number of complex problems, which share analogue characteristics with daily managerial practice (but which are not the same because of the fact that, otherwise, knowledge and experience can influence the measurement). It became obvious that the managers mostly possessed general, theoretical knowledge on management and management techniques but in many instances lacked the appropriate skills to reach desired goals. High potentials showed both sides. This means that they had strong intellectual capabilities (analytical qualities) and content-related knowledge/skills, being good professionals (mostly in a technical field). Besides this they also had higher scores on (strategic) vision, management control and coaching competencies (motivating others).

In the first place, the result of the development centre gives an insight into one's own strengths and weaknesses. On the other hand, one receives concrete guidelines to develop according to one's individual development plan, taking into account one's ambitions, knowledge and skills. In practice coaching-on-the-job, intervision, training or job-rotation are being used to stimulate development.

A small group of managers (within the same department) follows the 360-degree feedback method in which they ask a number of persons in their own environment to assess their current performance. In many cases this concerns a superior, colleague-managers or subordinates.

This method also results in increasing the insight into the functioning in the present position in which "section managers profile" also was basic. According to this, taking into account the standard profile of a manager, the manager together with his/her superior develops a development plan. In the case of this group of managers, an analysis is made for the development needs of the entire team. In doing so, individual scores were discussed together at the beginning. Afterwards scores were also put together, averaged and compared to the standard of the preferred management style of the particular department, which is derived from the management style of Fuji Tilburg. Where the majority seem to show a weakness on certain competencies, a development programme can also take place at the group level—for example, by means of theme-related group sessions, intervision groups or workshops about certain items, such as motivation and motivating others.

After a period of about two years a further 360-degree feedback round takes place to test the extent to which the desired goals have been realised. This is also applicable to the group of managers that have participated in a development centre at an earlier stage. Although this mostly concerns the determination of an individual plan based on the person's own responsibility and voluntariness, the development of competencies is not entirely free of obligations. Fuji expects its managers to actively and continuously develop themselves and consider development as a serious item. By means of a development contract that is signed between the manager and his/her superior (and to which they both need to be committed) and by means of monitoring by a MD officer, the development becomes a continuous process.

In practice we have learned that this method of development is very successful, that it is particularly perceived as extremely practice and process-oriented, that it truly stimulates development and that managers are inspired to put effort into the process. The difficulty for the group that participated in a development centre was in translating the plan to the work setting and forming a concrete action plan in their practice. In the case of the group practising an internal 360-degree feedback, this followed more apparently from the feedback they received, especially because it was function-oriented. However, this approach lacks the more general character of a potential measurement besides the organisational context. A combination of both methods would certainly be worth considering despite the investment in time it demands from managers.

THE INTERACTIVE MODEL: FINAL COMMENTS

The interactive model that we discussed in this chapter seems to be a worthwhile tool in the area of human development. As the Fuji case illustrates, human development asks for a tailor-made solution that incorporates sound instruments and a human development policy that sustains the process around development. The management of psychological contracts is essential to this, but also the way in which use is made of the continuous feedback moments, the learning experiences of people and the choice of new learning methods (such as group learning, etc.).

In our opinion modern management development and human development are characterised by a serious attention for the choice of adequate techniques and instruments (content) and of adequate activities to sustain the working and successes of these techniques and instruments (process). The fact that development is an ongoing activity seems obvious in this instance.

NOTES

1. We realise that this situation may differ for the various countries in Europe and other parts of the world. Anyhow, one may conclude that developments (technical, markets, demographic) take place in a more rapid way compared to, e.g., several decades ago.

2. The SHL organisation, which works in 38 countries, has recently (i.e. 2001) developed a competency set that encompasses all possible competencies. The experience is that job competencies and competencies that apply for high potentials may differ over countries, organisations and jobs. So, unfortunately, no specific model can be generated about the competencies that high potentials should possess in the near future (irrespective to country or organisation).

REFERENCES

Altink, W. M. M., & Visser, C. F. (1996). Kennisontwikkeling bij management development als bron voor organisatiesucces. In J. von Grumbkow & P. W. G. Jansen (Eds.), *Management development; nieuwe ontwikkelingen en trends.* Deventer: Kluwer Bedrijfswetenschappen.

Altink, W. M. M., Visser, C. F., & Castelijns, M. (1997). Criterion development: The unknown power of criteria as communication tools. In N. Anderson & P. Herriot (Eds.), *International handbook of selection and assessment.* Chichester: Wiley.

Altink, W. M. M., & Verhagen, H. A. B. M. (1999). Werving en selectie. In *Handboek de directeur.* Amsterdam: Elsevier.

Ansoff, I., & McDonell, E. (1990). *Implanting strategic management* (2nd edn.). New York: Prentice Hall.

Barrick, Mount, M. K., & Judge, T. A. (1999). *The big five personality dimensions and job performance: A quantitative review of prior meta-analyses.* Paper presented at the Fourteenth Annual Conference of the Society for Industrial and Organizational Psychology, Atlanta, GA.

Boyatzis, R. E. (1982). *The competent manager. A model for effective performance.* New York: Wiley.

Capelli, P. (2000). A market-driven approach to retaining talents. *Harvard Business Review,* January–February (10 pp.).

Gaspersz, J., & Ott, M. (1996). *Management van employability; nieuwe kansen in arbeidsrelaties.* Den Haag: Stichting Management Studies.

Grumbkow, J. von, & Jansen, P. W. G. (1996). *Management development; nieuwe ontwikkelingen en trends.* Deventer: Kluwer Bedrijfswetenschappen.

Haak, T. W., Jansen, P. W. G., & Mul, W. C. M. (1998). *Management development in Nederland.* Amsterdam: KPMG Ebbinge.

Hamel, G., & Prahalad, C. K. (1994). *Competing for the future.* Boston, Massachusetts: Harvard Business School Press.

Hill, L. A. (1992). *Becoming a manager.* Boston, Massachusetts: Harvard Business School Press.

Lynn, L. H., Piehler, H. R., & Kieler, M. (1993). Engineering careers, job rotation and gatekeepers in Japan and the United States. *Journal of Engineering and Technology Management,* **10,** 53–72.

McCall, M. W. (1998). *High flyers: Developing the next generation of leaders.* Boston, Massachusetts: Harvard Business School Press.

McCall, M. W. (Jr.), Lombardo, M., & Morrison, A. (1988). *The lesson of experience: How successful executives develop on the job.* Massachusetts: Lexington.

Moingeon, B., & Edmondson, A. (Eds.) (1996). *Organizational learning and competitive advantage.* London: Sage.

Mulder, M., & Martens, J. (1998). 360 feedback in theorie en praktijk. *Art; Opleiding en* ontwikkeling 3-1998.

Mumford, A. (1988). *Management development: Strategies for action.* London: Institute of Personnel and Development.

Odiorne, G. S. (1984). *Strategic management of human resources: A portfolio approach.* San Francisco: Jossey-Bass.

Peters, T., & Waterman, R. (1995). *Excellente ondernemingen: kenmerken van succesvol management* (10th edn.). Amsterdam: Contact.

Pfeffer, J. (1994). *Competitive advantage through people: Unleasing the power of the work force.* Boston, Mass: Harvard Business School Press.

Purcell, J., & Ahlstrand, B. (1994). *Human resource management and the multi-divisional company.* Oxford: Oxford University Press.

Quinn, J. B. (1992). *Intelligence enterprise: A knowledge and service based paradigm for industry.* New York: The Free Press.

Revans, R. (1982). *The origins and growth of action learning.* Bromley: Chatwell-Bratt.

Schoenmaker, M. J. R., & Geerdink, T. (1991). *Human talent management.* Deventer: Kluwer Bedrijfswetenschappen.

SHL (1978). *Occupational Position Questionnaire.* London: Saville & Holdsworth.

SHL (1996). *PMC model.* London: Saville & Holdsworth Limited.

SHL (1997). *Survey competence management.* London: Saville & Holdsworth Limited.

SHL (2000). *Values at work.* London: Saville & Holdsworth Limited.

Schmidt, F. L., & Hunter, J. E. (1998). The validity and utility of selection methods in personnel psychology: Practical and theoretical implications of 85 years of research findings. *Psychological Bulletin,* **124,** 262–274.

Storey, J. (1989). Management development: a literature review and implications for future research: Part 1, Conceptualisations and practices. *Personnel Review,* **8**(6), 3–19.

Thompson, J. A., & Henningsen, C. A. (1990). *The portable executive, from corporate dependence to self-direction.* Simon & Schuster.

Vogelaar, V. (1997). Corporate support for work-based management development. *Human Resource Management,* **10**(1).

PART III

Enhancing Performance

CHAPTER 10

The High Performance Cycle: Standing the Test of Time

Gary P. Latham,
University of Toronto, Toronto, Canada

Edwin A. Locke
University of Maryland, College Park, USA, and

Neil E. Fassina
University of Toronto, Toronto, Canada

SUMMARY

Locke and Latham's (1990a, b) high performance cycle (HPC) states that specific difficult goals lead to high performance. High performance on enriched tasks is usually rewarding for the individual. Rewards generate satisfaction that subsequently encourages commitment to the organization. The literature from 1990 through the spring of 2000 was reviewed to determine whether the HPC has withstood the test of time. Significant advancements were made in understanding the physiology of goal setting. Moreover, research has identified the benefit of setting learning goals for complex tasks as well as the benefit of setting proximal goals in environments marked by uncertainty. An understanding of how the consequences of high performance affect satisfaction and subsequent organizational commitment requires additional research. Research conducted over the past decade generated unanswered questions regarding potential moderator variables influencing the effects of proximal and learning goals, as well as moderators influencing the effect of enriched tasks on the setting of and commitment to high goals.

Psychological Management of Individual Performance. Edited by Sabine Sonnentag.
© 2002 John Wiley & Sons, Ltd.

INTRODUCTION

In this chapter we discuss evidence regarding the validity of the high performance cycle (HPC) initially presented by Locke and Latham (1990a, b). Specifically, we focus on the historical background of issues that the HPC addresses, namely the relationships among motivation, job satisfaction and performance. The remainder of the chapter addresses the research published between 1990 and 2000 to determine the extent to which the HPC has withstood the test of time.

Historical Context

Two primary variables of interest to industrial/organizational psychologists throughout the twentieth century were job performance and job satisfaction. For the first half of that century, job satisfaction was investigated in the belief that it was the causal variable; it was the antecedent of job performance. The implicit, if not explicit, hypothesis of the human relations school was that happy employees are productive employees (Roethlisberger, 1941).

In the middle of the twentieth century, an enumerative review of the literature cast doubt on that hypothesis. Brayfield and Crockett (1955) found little empirical support for a causal relationship between satisfaction and performance. Rather, there was suggestive evidence for a causal arrow in the opposite direction. It appeared that job performance might lead to job satisfaction, rather than the other way around. People derive enjoyment from that which they do well and the inherent rewards that result. Perhaps the key to job satisfaction was to focus on ways to increase job performance.

To further confuse matters, in this same time period Herzberg et al. (1959) argued that job performance was defined too narrowly. When the definition of performance was broadened to include variables such as voluntary employee turnover and absenteeism, Herzberg stated that there was indeed evidence that by increasing job satisfaction, job performance was increased.

Herzberg's conclusions were based on his use of the critical incident technique (CIT) developed by his graduate school mentor, John Flanagan. Herzberg's data showed that the opposite of high job satisfaction is not dissatisfaction, but rather no satisfaction; conversely, the opposite of high job dissatisfaction is not satisfaction but no dissatisfaction. Hence he labeled his findings the two-factor theory. The CIT (Flanagan, 1954), as Herzberg used it, showed that the causes of job dissatisfaction were hygiene or job context variables, namely, the organization's policies, benefits, physical working conditions, equipment, pay, pension, etc. Hygiene variables, he argued, had little or no bearing on performance. Satisfaction with job content variables, he believed, did increase employee performance. His findings revealed that such variables as recognition, task variety, feedback, autonomy, and opportunities for advancement enriched the job and hence increased job performance. His 1968 article, "One more time, how do you motivate employees?" remains to this day among the most requested articles published in the *Harvard Business Review*.

Nevertheless, there was a critical flaw in Herzberg's two-factor theory, more commonly referred to as job enrichment. It was the methodology on which it was based, namely, the CIT that Flanagan had developed for conducting a job analysis.

As a graduate student, Herzberg was undecided as to whether to pursue a career in clinical or industrial psychology. Eventually, he decided in favor of studying ways to increase the mental health of the worker. When, in a graduate seminar, he proposed using the CIT as a method for measuring the causes of satisfaction and mental health, Flanagan (W. Ronan, personal communication) responded that this would be inappropriate, because employees would be likely to attribute positive incidents to what they themselves did while attributing the cause of negative incidents to factors in the environment outside their control. Herzberg did not heed this advice. A decade later, scholars (e.g., Dunnette, Campbell, & Hakel, 1967; King, 1970) showed that Flanagan was indeed correct. The emergence of the two factors was the result of a methodological artifact including the confusion of events with agents (Locke, 1976). Herzberg's findings could be replicated only if the same methodology, the CIT, was used. All other methods showed that job satisfaction–dissatisfaction were on the same continuum rather than two independent continua. Consequently, Herzberg's two-factor theory fell into disrepute. The negative findings of Brayfield and Crockett plus the problems inherent in Herzberg's methodology left the field in a state of chaos.

Nevertheless, Herzberg's work focused the attention of scientists and practitioners on the importance of challenging and meaningful growth-facilitating tasks. The problem became that of identifying the relationship between enriched jobs and job satisfaction as well as the relationship of these to job performance.

Enriching jobs, includes increasing performance feedback. This increase in feedback often leads people to set performance goals. Umstot, Bell, and Mitchell (1976) found that it was goal setting that directly increased performance, whereas task-enriching variables directly increased satisfaction.

THE HIGH PERFORMANCE CYCLE

At the end of the twentieth century, Locke and Latham (1990a, b) tried to bring order to these contradictory findings by formulating the concept of the high-performance cycle (HPC). It is an inductive theory based primarily on the accumulated findings of empirical research on goal-setting performance, satisfaction and organizational commitment conducted during the final quarter of that century. The theory, shown in Figure 10.1, states that specific difficult goals plus high self-efficacy for attaining them are the impetus for high performance. Goals and self-efficacy affect the direction of action, the effort exerted as well as persistence to attain the goal. In addition, the goals and self-efficacy motivate the discovery of strategies for effectively doing so. The effect of goals on performance is moderated by ability, the complexity of the tasks, situational constraints, the feedback provided in relation to the goal, and commitment to the goal.

High performance on tasks that are perceived as meaningful and growth facilitating, plus high external and internal rewards, lead to high job satisfaction. The consequence is a willingness to stay with the organization and accept future challenges, hence the high performance cycle.

The theoretical significance of the HPC is that it provides a comprehensive sequence of causal relationships that is consistent with research findings. The practical significance of the HPC is that it provides a model or blueprint for creating a high performing workforce that is also highly satisfied.

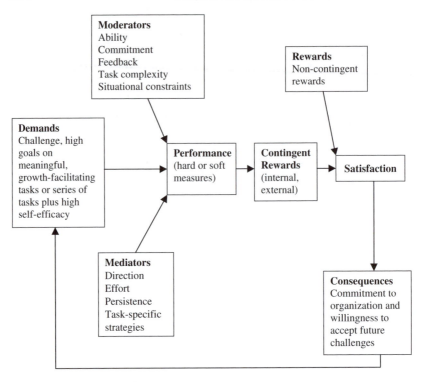

FIGURE 10.1 The high performance cycle

Because of the theoretical and practical importance of the HPC for the workforce in this new millennium, the literature from 1990 through the spring of 2000 was reviewed to see the extent to which the HPC has withstood the test of time. An electronic search was conducted through PsycInfo and Proquest using key words from the HPC. Approximately 105 empirical studies and literature reviews relevant to the HPC were located, and are summarized in Table 10.1.

DEMANDS INFLUENCE PERFORMANCE

GOALS

A goal is the object or aim of an action. In a study involving the performance appraisal of unionized employees, Brown and Latham (2000a) found that those who set specific, difficult goals for a subsequent evaluation of their behavior on behavioral observation scales had significantly higher evaluations than those who were urged to do their best. In a study of chronic musculoskeletal pain patients, Tan et al. (1997) discovered that the return to work goal was the single best predictor of a return to work. The positive effect of specific, high goals on behavior has also been obtained in the field of neuro-rehabilitation involving five studies of brain-damaged patients (Gauggel, 1999). No clinical or neuropsychological variable (e.g., time since onset of illness) was found to have a moderating influence. An interesting finding was that assigned goals led to better

TABLE 10.1   Articles reviewed for the update and revision of Locke and Latham's (1990a) high-performance cycle

Author(s) and publication date	Type of paper	Major findings
	DEMANDS	
Brown and Latham (2000a)	Laboratory	Specific difficult goals positively related to BOS performance evaluations.
Tan et al. (1997)	Field	A return to work goal was the strongest predictor of an individual's actual return to work.
Gauggel (1999)	Field	Specific difficult goals positively related to neurorehabilitation rate.
Hinsz (1991, 1995)	Laboratory	Self-set goals less challenging than assigned goals.
Von Bergen et al. (1996)	Laboratory	Self-esteem moderated the moderately difficult goal–performance relationship.
Tang and Reynolds (1993)	Field	Low self-esteem related to lower self-set goals and lower performance relative to high self-esteem.
O'Leary-Kelly et al. (1994)	Meta-analysis	Goal difficulty–performance relationship held for group contexts.
Klein and Mulvey (1995)	Laboratory	Difficulty level of self-set group goal positively related to group's performance.
Mulvey and Klein (1998)	Laboratory	Difficulty level of self-set group goal positively related to group's performance.
Crown and Rosse (1995)	Laboratory	On interdependent tasks, group goals held by committed members increased group performance.
Allscheid and Cellar (1996)	Laboratory	No main effect of goal difficulty. Null result linked to a restriction of range in goal-setting manipulation. Goal commitment had a direct effect on performance.
Bar-Eli et al. (1993)	Field	Very high goals not found to decrease individual motivation and performance.
Jones and Cale (1997)	Laboratory	Very high goals not found to decrease individual motivation and performance.
Weinberg et al. (1991)	Laboratory	Performance level determined by individual's perception of how he or she will perform on subsequent trials (self-efficacy).
	SELF-EFFICACY	
Bandura (1997)	Review	Performance is affected by individual confidence levels toward achieving a goal. Goal–performance relationship was influenced by external rewards only when people perceive the rewards to be attainable.
Lee and Bobko (1992)	Laboratory	The higher an individual's self-efficacy for a task, the lower his or her perception of goal difficulty.

continues overleaf

TABLE 10.1 (*continued*)

Author(s) and publication date	Type of paper	Major findings
Carson and Carson (1993a)	Laboratory	Self-efficacy and self-set goal difficulty was positively related to performance levels on a creative task.
Earley and Lituchy (1991)	Laboratory	Self-efficacy and self-set goal difficulty was positively related to performance levels.
Zimmerman et al. (1992)	Field	Self-efficacy and self-set goal difficulty was positively related to performance levels.
Lerner and Locke (1995)	Laboratory	Self-efficacy was positively related to an individual's personal goals.
Berry and West (1993)	Review	High self-efficacy was positively related to setting of high personal goals, selection of challenging tasks and high performance.
Hinsz and Matz (1997)	Laboratory	Low self-efficacy linked to poor performance.
Brown and Latham (2000b)	Field	Self-efficacy was positively related to goal level, goal commitment and team-playing behavior in study teams.
Seijts et al. (2000)	Laboratory	Reciprocal relationship found between group efficacy and group performance.
Seijts and Latham (2000a)	Laboratory	Group efficacy, group goal commitment, and outcome expectancies for cooperation were positively related to group performance. High personal goals that are comparable to a group's goal enhanced group performance, where as individual goals which contradicted the group goal had detrimental effects.
Silver and Bufanio (1996)	Laboratory	Group efficacy moderated the relationship between group goal difficulty and group performance.
Seijts and Latham (2001)	Laboratory	High self-efficacy was positively related to the discovery of task relevant strategies. Identification of strategies mediated the relationship between self-efficacy and performance. For complex tasks, distal learning goals led to high goal commitment and performance more so than assigned distal outcome goal. Self-efficacy increased over time with a learning goal, whereas it decreased with an outcome goal. Do-best condition led to higher performance than outcome goals. Goal commitment had a main effect on performance when all participants were trying to achieve a difficult goal.
Button et al. (1996)	Laboratory	Self-efficacy maintained a consistent effect on personal goals over time. Normative information became more influential on personal goals over time.

TABLE 10.1 (*continued*)

Author(s) and publication date	Type of paper	Major findings
Tabernero and Wood (1999)	Laboratory	High self-efficacy was related to an incremental perception of ability; low self-efficacy was related to a fixed view of ability. Substandard performance feedback increased performance for people with an incremental perception of ability but not for people with a fixed perception of ability.

GROWTH-FACILITATING TASKS

Roberson et al. (1990)	Laboratory	Personal goals and task attributes had independent effects on satisfaction.
Ambrose and Kulik (1999)	Review	Tasks that are perceived as enriched facilitated high performance.
Campion (1996)	Review	Tasks that are perceived as enriched facilitated high performance.
Mathieu and Zajac (1990)	Meta-analysis	Jobs that are perceived as enriched yielded high job satisfaction and high organizational commitment. Separation of job satisfaction into intrinsic satisfaction, extrinsic satisfaction and its components yielded significant correlations with organizational commitment.
Kirkpatrick (1992)	Laboratory	Enriching jobs through increasing responsibility was found to increase performance through self-set goals.
Cordery (1996, 1997)	Review	Increased performance through job enrichment depended on supervisors providing a goal structure, a method structure, the required KSAOs and goal feedback.

INDIVIDUAL DIFFERENCES

Phillips and Gully (1997)	Laboratory	Locus of control was positively related to self-efficacy and indirectly related to difficulty of self-set goals.
Lambert et al. (1999)	Field	Self-set goals were more strongly related to increase performance when individual has internal locus of control.
Harackiewicz and Elliot (1993)	Laboratory	Achievement oriented individuals were more responsive to performance than to learning goals.
Locke (2001)	Review	Effects of personality often mediated or partially mediated by goals and self-efficacy.
Button et al. (1996)	Laboratory	Goal orientation is composed of two distinguishable dimensions, learning and performance.
VandWalle et al. (1999)	Field	Learning goal orientation–sales performance relationship fully mediated by goal setting, effort and planning.

continues overleaf

TABLE 10.1 (*continued*)

Author(s) and publication date	Type of paper	Major findings
		MEDIATORS
		Direction
Wood and Locke (1990)	Review	Goals are proposed to stimulate the use one or more of stored universal plans, stored task specific plans, and new task specific plans. The effectiveness of goals in combination with the different types of plans or strategies is proposed to change as the complexity of the task increases.
Bagozzi and Warshaw (1990)	Laboratory	Direction was result of the decision made to attain a specific goal.
Hinsz and Ployhart (1998)	Laboratory	The direction of an individual's actions were the result of his or her decision to attain a specific goal.
Kernan and Lord (1990)	Laboratory	Valence, expectancies, and discrepancies strongly related to goal priority and resource allocation in multiple goal environments, but not in single goal environments.
Kanfer et al. (1994)	Laboratory	Motivation and performance was affected independently by goals and practice as well as the interaction between them.
Tubbs and Ekeberg (1991)	Review	Performance was highest when the individual could shift attention between levels of a multi-task hierarchy.
		Effort and persistence
Rasch and Tosi (1992)	Field	Goal difficulty was positively related to effort level which in turn was positively related to performance.
Multon et al. (1991)	Meta-analysis	Self-efficacy accounts for a significant amount of variance in persistence levels.
Theodorakis et al. (1998)	Laboratory	Effort, persistence and task strategies interacted to increase performance rather than acting in isolation.
Weingart and Weldon (1991)	Review	Effort, persistence, goal commitment, performance monitoring and the identification of strategies to attain group's goals mediated the effect of goal-performance relationship.
Weldon et al. (1991)	Laboratory	Effort, persistence, goal commitment, performance monitoring and the identification of strategies to attain group's goals mediated the effect of goal-performance relationship.
Gellatly and Meyer (1992)	Laboratory	Effort and persistence were associated with increased heart rate, which in turn mediated the goal difficulty performance relationship.
Duncan (1995)	Laboratory	Action was represented by goals and sub-goals in the prefrontal context.

TABLE 10.1 (*continued*)

Author(s) and publication date	Type of paper	Major findings
		Task-specific strategies
Chesney and Locke (1991)	Laboratory	For complex tasks, strategy had a stronger effect on performance than that of goals.
Earley et al. (1990)	Field	Individuals with a high goal setting composite (specific/difficult) were more likely to develop work strategies than those with a low goal setting composite.
Latham et al. (1994)	Laboratory	Participation in goal setting was completely mediated by task strategy and self-efficacy.
Smith et al. (1990)	Laboratory	Lagged improvement in performance for highly complex tasks was the result of strategy development.
Earley et al. (1992)	Laboratory	Lagged improvement in performance for highly complex tasks was the result of strategy development. Goal commitment was found to be a curvilinear function of goal difficulty.
Audia et al. (1996)	Laboratory	Lagged improvement in performance for highly complex tasks was the result of strategy development. Both learning and motivation were required for performance even for simple tasks that offer multiple paths to accomplishment.
Locke (2000)	Review	Performance was regulated by goals that lead to the discovery of task knowledge as well as task knowledge that was not associated with goals.
		MODERATORS
		Ability and task complexity
Mathieu and Button (1992)	Laboratory	Past performance as a proxy for ability influenced future self-set goals.
Boyce and Wayda (1994)	Laboratory	Assigned goals lead to higher performance than self-set goals on tasks where the requisite knowledge had not yet been acquired.
Kanfer (1990)	Laboratory	In the absence of requisite ability, specific difficult outcome goals decreased performance relative to those told to do their best.
Polzer and Neale (1995)	Laboratory	Specific difficult goals decreased an individuals' ability to integrate new information.
Bouffard et al. (1995)	Laboratory	For complex tasks, learning goals lead to increased performance through the development of effective self-regulating strategies.
Winters and Latham (1996)	Laboratory	For complex tasks, specific high learning goals were related to increased performance more so than urging people to do their best. Moreover, urging people to do their best generated higher performance than specific difficult outcome goals.

continues overleaf

TABLE 10.1   (*continued*)

Author(s) and publication date	Type of paper	Major findings
Newman (1998)	Field	Assigned learning goals to develop strategies was related to fewer requests for assistance than those with performance goals.
VandeWalle and Cummings (1997)	Field and Laboratory	Learning goals tended to induce feedback-seeking behavior.
Greene and Miller (1996)	Laboratory	Learning goals related to the development of a strategy portfolio for future complex tasks.
Situational constraints and uncertainty		
Lane and Karageorghis (1997)	Field	Learning goals were more effective than outcome goals in overcoming obstacles created by coworkers.
Latham and Seijts (1999)	Laboratory	In an environment marked by continual uncertainty distal goals in combination with proximal goals were related to higher performance than urging people to do their best, which in turn was related to higher performance than distal outcome goals.
Feedback		
Cellar et al. (1996)	Laboratory	Feedback in combination with a quantity goal led to higher performance than goal setting alone.
Neubert (1998)	Meta-analysis	Feedback in combination with goal setting leads to higher performance than goal setting alone.
Shoenfelt (1996)	Field	Specific behavioral feedback increased transfer of training effectiveness.
Siero et al. (1996)	Field	Performance was higher when normative feedback was given rather than individual feedback relative to arbitrary goal.
Carson and Carson (1993b)	Laboratory	On a creativity task, goal commitment increased with feedback.
Vance and Colella (1990)	Laboratory	Negative feedback in relation to a goal decreased goal commitment and difficulty of subsequently set personal goals.
Phillips et al. (1996)	Laboratory	Action does not stop when feedback indicates the goal has been achieved. Rather, a more difficult goal is set.
Goal commitment		
Wofford et al. (1992)	Meta-analysis	Without goal commitment, goal setting had little or no effect. Commitment was a function of the expectancy that a goal can be attained and the value attached to the goal.

TABLE 10.1 (*continued*)

Author(s) and publication date	Type of paper	Major findings
Klein and Kim (1998)	Field	Goal commitment was easily achieved with strong leader-member relations.
Klein et al. (1999)	Meta-analysis	Goal commitment moderated the relationship between goal difficulty and performance. Goal commitment was found to be unidimensional and 5 of the 9 measures on Hollenbeck et al.'s (1989) scale were robust and psychometrically sound measures of goal commitment.
Morin and Latham (2000)	Field	Goal commitment correlated positively with self-efficacy as well as performance.
Donovan and Radosevich (1998)	Meta-analysis	Goal commitment accounted for 3% of the variance in the goal-performance relationship.
DeShon and Landis (1997)	Laboratory	The Hollenbeck, Williams, and Klein (1989) measure of goal commitment assesses two factors on complex tasks: goal commitment and the likelihood of goal achievement.
Tubbs (1993, 1994)	Laboratory	Moderation effect of goal commitment was only valid for the concept of strength of intention.
Tubbs and Dahl (1992)	Laboratory	Commitment was a function of the expectancy that the goal can be achieved and the value attached to the goal.
Wright et al. (1994)	Re-analysis of data	After ability was partialled out, correlation between discrepancy measure of goal commitment and performance was significantly reduced.
Seijts et al. (1997)	Laboratory	For very difficult goals, higher performance was achieved by those that perceived the goal to be meaningful.
Hinsz et al. (1997)	Laboratory	An anchor affects goal level, which in turn affects self-efficacy and subsequent performance.
Seijts and Latham (2000b)	Review	Advances in the understanding of goal commitment regarding the interaction with goal difficulty, identification of appropriate measures and the effects of anchoring.

PERFORMANCE LEADS TO REWARDS THAT AFFECT SATISFACTION

Mento et al. (1992)	Laboratory	High goals were perceived as instrumental in gaining positive outcomes.
Eby et al. (1999)	Meta-analysis	Perceived competency as a proxy for success increased job satisfaction.
Anshel et al. (1992)	Laboratory	High goals lead to increased intrinsic motivation.
Kernan and Lord (1991)	Laboratory	Higher performance in relation to a goal created higher job satisfaction.

continues overleaf

TABLE 10.1   (*continued*)

Author(s) and publication date	Type of paper	Major findings
Farh et al. (1991)	Laboratory	Satisfaction was highest when individuals were allowed to choose their extrinsic rewards. High ability people chose piece rate; low ability people chose a fixed rate.
Lee et al. (1997)	Laboratory	Goal–performance relationship was influenced by external rewards only when people perceive the rewards to be attainable.
Doherty (1998)	Field	High dissatisfaction was related to rewards that are perceived as unfair, impersonal or as punishment.
Summers and Hendrix (1991)	Field	Positive relationship found between pay fairness and pay satisfaction.

SATISFACTION LEADS TO ORGANIZATIONAL COMMITMENT		
Tett and Meyer (1993)	Meta-analysis	Job satisfaction and organizational commitment are distinct concepts.
Cohen and Lowenberg (1990)	Meta-analysis	Satisfaction-commitment relationship higher in private than in the public sector, and for professional than for clerical workers.
Alnajjar (1996)	Field	No correlation found between job satisfaction and organizational commitment among people in the United Emirates.
O'Driscoll and Randall (1999)	Field	Satisfaction with intrinsic and extrinsic rewards was a significant predictor of affective organizational commitment.

performance than self-set goals, because the latter were not as difficult. Self-set goals have often been found to be less challenging than goals that are assigned to participants in the normal population (Hinsz, 1991, 1995).

Similarly, Von Bergen, Soper, and Rosenthal (1996) found a positive relationship between goal difficulty and performance. They also found that people with low self-esteem performed worse when the assigned goal was moderately difficult while those high in self-esteem performed best. Tang and Reynolds (1993) obtained the same finding. Those with low self-esteem had lower self-set goals and lower performance than those with high self-esteem. Self-esteem may have been a proxy variable for self-efficacy.

The finding that high goals lead to high performance is also true for groups. A meta-analysis revealed that the mean performance level of groups with specific high goals is almost one standard deviation higher than the performance of groups for which no goals are set (O'Leary-Kelly, Martocchio, & Frink, 1994). Klein and Mulvey (1995) and Mulvey and Klein (1998) showed that the difficulty level of a self-set group goal correlates positively with the group's performance. Crown and Rosse (1995) found that group goals for individual members who were committed to the group increased the group's performance on an interdependent task relative to any other condition.

In summary, the finding that specific, difficult goals lead to the highest level of performance for both individuals and groups continues to hold true when the proper methodology is used to detect the relationship. Only two studies have found non-significant direct relationships between goal difficulty and performance. Because they did not have either a low or a no-goal condition in their two laboratory experiments, Allscheid and Cellar (1996) concluded that the findings from their study were due to restriction in range. Nevertheless, they argued for the robustness of the relationship as they found a probability level of 0.066 for the main effect of goal difficulty in spite of not including a low or no-goal condition.

The concern that very high goals may lead to a decrease in motivation and performance has not received empirical support (Bar-Eli, Levy-Kolker, Tenenbaum, & Weinberg, 1993; Jones & Cale, 1997). Rather, it is the person's perception of how well he or she will perform on the subsequent trial or task that determines performance level (Weinberg, Fowler, Jackson, Bagnall, & Bruya, 1991). One's perception of one's ability to accomplish a specific task has been labeled by Bandura (1986, 1997) as self-efficacy.

SELF-EFFICACY

Performance is affected not only by one's goals, but by how confident one is of attaining them. Bandura's (1997) research has shown that it is not so much our ability that holds us back or propels us forward as it is our self-efficacy. Lee and Bobko (1992) found that the higher one's self-efficacy in performing well on a task, the less difficult the goal is perceived to be.

Carson and Carson (1993a) found that self-efficacy influences the personal goals that one sets. The strong positive relationship of self-efficacy to personal goals and their performance was also documented by Earley and Lituchy (1991) as well as Zimmerman, Bandura, and Martinez-Pons (1992). Lerner and Locke (1995) too found that self-efficacy affected the individual's personal goals.

In their review of the literature, Berry and West (1993) found that the consequences of high self-efficacy included the setting of high personal goals, the selection of challenging tasks, and high performance. Hinsz and Matz (1997) found that people with low task and self-efficacy had low personal goals and performed poorly. Brown and Latham (2000b) found that self-efficacy correlated positively with goal level, goal commitment, and the team playing behavior of MBA students in their respective study groups. Seijts, Latham, and Whyte (2000) found that group efficacy affects performance, and in turn, performance affects the group's efficacy. Seijts and Latham (2000a) found that a group's efficacy in making money, the group's goal commitment, and outcome expectancies that cooperation with others will lead to goal attainment correlated positively with the group's performance. Silver and Bufanio (1996) showed that group efficacy affects the group goal difficulty performance relationship. Seijts and Latham (2001) found that high self-efficacy led to the discovery of task relevant strategies.

Button, Mathieu, and Aikin (1996) found no support for their hypothesis that over time assigned goals become less influential than self-efficacy on personal goals. Rather, they found that the effect of self-efficacy remained relatively constant and that normative information, that is, feedback that could lead to goal-setting, became more influential as time progressed.

In summary, consistent with the findings obtained prior to 1990, individual and group efficacy are positively associated with the setting of high goals, with goal commitment, and with high performance. An intriguing discovery was made by Tabernero and Wood (1999). They found that people who have high self-efficacy have an incremental view of their ability and thus adjust their level of performance to negative feedback more effectively than do people who have low self-efficacy and who are more likely to hold a fixed entity belief.

GROWTH-FACILITATING TASKS

Roberson, Korsgaard, and Diddams (1990) found that personal goals and task attributes have independent effects on satisfaction; the former effect may be the result of goal success. Tasks that are perceived as enriched facilitate high performance (Ambrose & Kulik, 1999; Campion, 1996), probably through their effects on goals and/or organizational satisfaction and commitment. Meta-analyses conducted by Mathieu and Zajac (1990) revealed that jobs that are perceived as enriched, which are known to produce high satisfaction, also yield high organization commitment.

Kirkpatrick (1992), using a proof-reading task, manipulated autonomy and responsibility in order to determine the effect on performance. Increases in responsibility led to increases in the difficulty level and commitment to self-set goals. The goals in turn increased performance. Autonomy only affected feelings of responsibility. These results suggest that enriching jobs through increases in responsibility can increase performance through the process of goal setting.

Cordery (1996, 1997) argued that job enrichment alone does not improve performance. He found that the antecedents of effective job design/redesign outcomes are supervisory practices regarding (a) goal structure, the extent to which the supervisor ensures that the employee has specific attainable goals; (b) method structure, the extent to which the employee is able to exert control over work activity; (c) boundary protection, the extent to which the employee is provided the knowledge, skills and resources to perform effectively; and (d) goal feedback, the extent to which the supervisor ensures that the individual is given timely information on progress toward goal attainment. These supervisory practices affect employee perceptions of job content.

In summary, enriched or challenging jobs appear to increase job satisfaction directly and independently of goal setting. Goal attainment, however, also affects job satisfaction. The effect of job enrichment on employee performance is indirect, namely through its effects on goals, feedback, satisfaction and organizational commitment.

INDIVIDUAL DIFFERENCES

The assertion that specific high goals lead to high performance was based on findings from over 400 empirical studies at the time that the HPC was published in 1990. Thus there has been minimal interest in or need for replicating this finding in the past decade. Because goal-setting is a strong variable that masks individual differences (Adler, 1986), personality variables were not included in the HPC.

Individual differences, however, have been the focus of much research in the past decade. Phillips and Gully (1997) identified, in addition to ability, locus of control as having a positive relationship with self-efficacy and an indirect relationship with self-set goals. Lambert, Moore, and Dixon (1999) showed that self-set goals were more effective for gymnasts who have an internal rather than an external locus of control. Achievement-oriented individuals are more responsive to performance than to learning goals (Harackiewicz & Elliot, 1993). A review of personality research showed that personality effects were often mediated or partially mediated by goals and self-efficacy (Locke, 2001).

An individual difference concept that has received considerable attention in the past decade is that of a learning vs. a performance goal orientation. Confusion has arisen over these traits, in large part due to poorly chosen terminology. If one looks at the actual items in the scales, a learning goal orientation seems to refer to the desire to undertake challenging tasks and acquire new knowledge and skills, whereas a performance goal orientation refers to a desire to ensure success by choosing tasks or goals that one can easily master and hence get praise from others for success (e.g., Button, Mathieu, & Zajac, 1996; VandeWalle, Brown, Cron, & Slocum, 1999).

The evidence, as discussed subsequently in this chapter, suggests that people with a learning (challenge) goal orientation do better than those with a performance (success on easy tasks) goal orientation.

In summary, the relation of goals and personality traits when used to predict performance is neither fully understood nor extensively researched. However, there is evidence of both mediation and moderation (interaction) effects. This topic is in need of additional study.

MEDIATORS

As noted earlier, and shown in Figure 10.1, four mediators explain how or why goals increase job performance. The first three, labeled by Wood and Locke (1990) as universal task strategies, are primarily motivational, namely, direction, effort, and persistence. The fourth mediator, task specific strategies, is primarily cognitive.

DIRECTION

Bagozzi and Warshaw (1990) proposed a theory of goal pursuit based on behavioral intentions. Attention or direction is a result of the decision made to attain a specific goal. Empirical support for this assertion was obtained by Hinsz and Ployhart (1998).

Kernan and Lord (1990), as well as Kanfer and her colleagues (Kanfer, Ackerman, Murtha, Dugdale, & Nelson, 1994), drew upon the attentional resource allocation model to explain the relationship between goals and performance in multiple goal environments. Direction occurs through a prioritization process that is affected by situational cues, the personal importance of one goal relative to another, and feedback. Tubbs and Ekeberg (1991) found that performance is highest when an individual is adept at shifting attention between levels in a multi-task hierarchy.

EFFORT AND PERSISTENCE

In a study involving software engineers, Rasch and Tosi (1992) showed that goal difficulty affects the level of effort expended which in turn affects performance. With regard to persistence, Multon, Brown, and Lent (1991) found that some of the variance was accounted for by self-efficacy.

That mediators do not always operate in isolation is shown in a study by Theodorakis, Laparidis, Kioumourtzoglou and Goudas (1998). Effort, persistence, and task strategies jointly increased the performance of athletes on an endurance task relative to those with no goals. With regard to groups, Weldon and her colleagues (Weingart & Weldon, 1991; Weldon, Jehn, & Pradhan, 1991) found that effort, persistence, goal commitment, performance monitoring, and the identification of strategies to attain the group's goal mediated the effect of the goal–performance relationship.

Gellatly and Meyer (1992) found that attention, effort, and persistence are associated with arousal of the sympathetic nervous system, specifically changes in heart rate. Heart rate mediated the goal difficulty–performance relationship. Duncan (1995) found that action is represented by a hierarchy of goals and subgoals activated in the prefrontal cortex.

TASK-SPECIFIC STRATEGIES

Chesney and Locke (1991) found that, on a complex task, strategy had a stronger effect on performance than did the goal. This was because having the requisite knowledge is especially critical on such tasks. Similarly, Earley, Lee, and Hanson (1990) found that people with a high goal-setting composite (specific/difficult) were more likely to develop an effective work strategy whereas strategy development was lacking among those with a low goal composite.

On a task involving the scheduling of classes, Latham, Winters, and Locke (1994) found that participation in goal setting was completely mediated by task strategy and self-efficacy. Subsequent research revealed that the identification of strategies mediated the relationship between self-efficacy and performance (Seijts & Latham, 2001). Support continues to be found in the literature for the role that the HPC mediators play in explaining performance.

Numerous studies have indicated that difficult goals for tasks that are highly complex for a person may not be as detrimental to performance as once thought. The improvements are lagged as a result of strategy development on ways to attain the goal (Smith, Locke, & Barry, 1990; Earley, Shalley, & Northcraft, 1992; Audia, Kristof, Brown, & Locke, 1996).

In summary, there continues to be support for the mediators of the goal effect (direction, effort, persistence, and task strategies) identified by Locke and Latham (1990a, b). However, the relationship is sometimes one of moderation, especially with regard to the effect of goals and strategies. In some studies goals and strategies appear to have independent effects. To make sense of these inconsistent findings, Locke (2000) has provided a detailed review and analysis of the studies of task goals and knowledge. He showed that these findings can be subsumed under a single, dynamic model. The model shows that performance can be regulated by goals that arouse or lead to the discovery of relevant task knowledge and also by task knowledge that is not aroused by or associated with goals but rather other motives. The particular results observed in a given study (mediation, moderation, independent effects) are simply a function of the specific variables that were measured.

MODERATORS

Moderator or boundary variables can enhance or attenuate the effect of demands, shown in Figure 10.1, on the employee's performance. These moderators include: ability, task complexity, situational constraints, feedback, and goal commitment.

ABILITY AND TASK COMPLEXITY

Because goal setting is a motivational theory, ability was taken as a given in most studies conducted prior to 1990. The tasks that were used in those studies were usually ones that the person already had the requisite knowledge and skill to perform well. This was done to minimize confounding of learning with motivation. The difficulty for practitioners is that tasks in most field settings are inherently confounded in that both learning and motivation are required to excel on the job. This can be true for even easy tasks where there are multiple paths to accomplishment (Audia et al., 1996).

Mathieu and Button (1992) found that past performance, which is evidence of one's ability, influences the setting of future self-goals. Boyce and Wayda (1994) found that on tasks where the requisite skills to perform it have yet to be acquired, assigned goals lead to higher performance than self-set goals. As both Kiesler (1971) and Salancik (1977) noted years ago, the act of goal assignment, especially when the goal is high, increases self-efficacy in that it signals the belief by one's supervisor that the person has the ability to attain it.

Goals sometimes can be detrimental if individuals do not have the skill or knowledge required to attain them. In a simulation of air traffic controllers involving airforce cadets, Kanfer (Kanfer & Ackerman, 1989; Kanfer, 1990) found that in the absence of requisite ability, setting a specific difficult performance outcome goal, as had been done in the literally hundreds of previous goal-setting studies, led to a significant decrease rather than an increase in performance relative to those participants who were urged to do their best. This is because tasks that are complex for an individual require attentional resources for learning what is required to perform well. Individuals who are motivated to do well before they have acquired the ability to do so fail to quickly master the requisite knowledge and hence perform poorly.

Polzer and Neale (1995), in a simulated job interview, likewise found that a specific difficult outcome goal had a detrimental effect on negotiations. They attributed this finding to a failure on the part of the participants to integrate new information.

Elliott and Dweck (1986) labeled the performance benefit of "urging" children to increase their ability or master a new task, rather than attaining a specific performance outcome, a learning goal. Bouffard, Boisvet, Vezeau and Larouche (1995) found that on tasks, such as self-regulation, that are complex, a learning goal orientation increased performance as it led to the discovery of effective self-regulating strategies.

Winters and Latham (1996) found that setting a specific high learning goal, such as discover X ways to master this issue, leads to higher performance on a task that is complex for people than urging them to do their best; urging people to do their best on such tasks, consistent with the findings of both Dweck and Kanfer, leads to higher performance than setting a specific difficult performance outcome goal.

Newman (1998) found that assigned learning goals in terms of identifying problem-solving strategies led to fewer requests for assistance than was the case where students had performance outcome goals in terms of academic grades. VandeWalle and Cummings (1997) found that a primary benefit of learning goals is that they tend to induce feedback-seeking behavior. Greene and Miller (1996) found that people with a learning goal orientation developed a strategy portfolio so that they did not have to develop additional strategies whenever they encountered a task that was complex for them.

Seijts and Latham (2001) examined the effect of setting proximal goals in conjunction with either a distal learning or a distal outcome goal on a task that required learning in order to perform it correctly. As was found by Kanfer and Ackerman, the people in the "do your best" condition performed significantly better than those with a distal outcome goal. But, as was the case in the Winters and Latham study, performance was even higher when people were assigned a specific difficult learning goal. This is because a distal learning goal led to higher goal commitment than did the assignment of a distal outcome goal. Moreover, self-efficacy increased across trials in the distal learning goal condition whereas in the distal goal condition it decreased. People with high self-efficacy were more likely than those with low self-efficacy to discover task-relevant strategies. A mediator analysis showed that strategies had both a direct effect on self-efficacy as well as an indirect effect on performance.

Setting proximal goals led to the formulation of the largest number of strategies. That proximal goals did not have a direct effect on performance in this study may have been the result of the task, namely one of high certainty rather than uncertainty.

In summary, knowledge of how to perform a task includes strategy, tactics and ability (Locke, 2000). Important discoveries in this area within the past decade include the documentation of when to set a specific high learning goal rather than a performance outcome goal. When people lack the knowledge or skill to perform the task, a specific difficult learning goal should be set rather than an outcome goal; a specific difficult outcome goal should be set when people have the requisite knowledge or skill. Proximal goals are often more effective than distal goals in generating high performance on tasks that are complex for people.

SITUATIONAL CONSTRAINTS AND UNCERTAINTY

Related to the moderating influence of ability, as well as tasks that are complex, are situational constraints. In the study referred to above, Lane and Karageorghis (1997) found that learning goals were more effective than outcome goals in overcoming obstacles caused by coworkers.

Uncertainty can attenuate the relationship between demands and performance when what the person knows to be true at one point in time is no longer true at a later point in time due to the situation being in a state of flux. Using an assessment center simulation where high school students were paid on a piece-rate basis to make toys, Latham and Seijts (1999) found that urging people to do their best led to higher performance than setting a difficult, distal outcome goal. However, setting proximal in addition to distal goals led to the greatest monetary earnings in an ever-changing marketplace. This is because proximal goals, through self-efficacy and performance feedback, focused the person's attention on task appropriate strategies in coping effectively with uncertainty.

A social dilemma can be a situational constraint for the normally positive effects of goal setting. In addition, the size of the group is also a situational constraint in a social dilemma. In a money-making task, Seijts and Latham (2000a) obtained no main effect for goal setting. However, they found that high personal goals that are compatible with the group's goal enhances group performance; in contrast, a personal goal which contradicts the group goals has a detrimental effect. Individuals in 7-person groups were less cooperative, had lower collective efficacy, a lower commitment to the goal, and lower group performance than those in 3-person groups.

In summary, the Kanfer and Ackerman (1989) study may have done the field a disservice through the claim that goals have a detrimental effect in the learning stage of an activity. In point of fact, goals have a key role in the acquisition of knowledge and skill. Bandura and Schunk (1981) showed eight years prior to the Kanfer and Ackerman study that proximal goals on a task that requires learning increase perceived self-efficacy, intrinsic interest, as well as performance accomplishments whereas terminal or outcome performance goals have no effect.

Thus it appears that Kanfer and Ackerman assigned the wrong goal, that is, terminal product rather than proximal outcome or learning goals, and then issued an erroneous conclusion that goals are detrimental to learning. Research conducted in the past decade support Bandura's (1986) assertion that goals provide motivation and guidance for attentional and cognitive activities required for learning. The issue of importance for high performance is the type of goal that is set.

FEEDBACK

Cellar, Degrendel, Sidle, and Lavine (1996) found that feedback in relation to a quantity goal led to higher performance than goal-setting alone. A meta-analysis (Neubert, 1998) confirmed this finding. Specific behavioral feedback in relation to goal setting has also been found to increase transfer of training effectiveness (Shoenfelt, 1996).

Siero, Bakker, Dekker, and van den Berg (1996) obtained a large change in energy savings for industrial plants when feedback was given relative to the performance of other groups rather than in relation to a goal that was perceived by the employees as arbitrary. This may have led to competition with other groups that in turn increased goal commitment. On a creativity task, Carson and Carson (1993b) found that goal commitment increased as individuals tracked their progress toward the goal.

Vance and Colella (1990) found that negative feedback in relation to the goal not only decreased goal commitment, but led to a lowering of personal goals on subsequent trials. However, as noted earlier, Tabernero and Wood (1999) found that identifying substandard performance relative to goal attainment was highly effective in increasing the performance of those who have an incremental or dynamic belief about their ability; consistent with the finding of Vance and Colella, this increase did not occur for individuals who believed that their ability was a fixed entity. Undoubtedly these various beliefs have potent effects on self-efficacy.

The assertion by some that action stops when feedback indicates that the goal has been attained was shown to be incorrect by Phillips, Hollenbeck, and Ilgen (1996). Contrary to control theory, people actively create goal-performance discrepancies by setting a higher goal upon goal attainment. Seeking and striving are inherent in goal setting.

In summary, feedback allows people to track progress in relation to the goal and also to provide information bearing on one's degree of enactive mastery, which in turn affects self-efficacy.

GOAL COMMITMENT

When commitment is lacking, goals have little or no effect on behavior (Wofford, Goodwin, & Premack, 1992). Commitment is often easy to obtain in both laboratory and field settings because the goal is perceived as legitimate by the participants.

This is especially true when there are strong leader–member relations (Klein & Kim, 1998).

A meta-analysis showed that goal commitment moderates the relationship between goal difficulty and performance (Klein, Wesson, Hollenbeck, & Alge, 1999). The correlation between goal difficulty and performance is higher among individuals with high rather than low goal commitment. However, this analysis, as well as a study by Seijts and Latham (2001), revealed that goal commitment can have a main effect on performance when all participants are trying to attain reasonably difficult goals.

Allscheid and Cellar (1996) found that commitment had a direct effect on performance. Similarly, in a field experiment involving supervisors, Morin and Latham (2000) found that goal commitment correlated positively with both self-efficacy and performance.

Another meta-analysis revealed that goal commitment accounted for only 3% of the variance in the goal–performance relationship (Donovan & Radosevich, 1998). This is undoubtedly due to restriction of range, because as noted, most people readily accept assigned goals. A second reason for this finding is very likely the different operationalizations of goal commitment (DeShon & Landis, 1997; Seijts & Latham, 2000b). For example, Tubbs and his colleagues (Tubbs, 1993, 1994; Tubbs & Dahl, 1992; Tubbs & Ekeberg, 1991) operationalized goal commitment as the absolute discrepancy between assigned and self-set goals. They found that such a measure consistently moderated the relationship between assigned goals and performance. To the extent, however, that ability influences the choice of one's goals and one's subsequent performance, the observed relationship between the discrepancy measure and performance is partly spurious. When ability is partialled out, Wright and his colleagues (1994), in a re-analysis of Tubb's data, showed that the correlation between the discrepancy measure and performance was reduced significantly.

Klein et al. (1999), using meta-analysis and confirmatory factor analysis, found that goal commitment is unidimensional, and that 5 of the original 9 self-report measures on Hollenbeck et al.'s (1989) self-report attitudinal scale appear to be a robust psychometrically sound measure of goal commitment.

Seijts, Meertens, and Kok (1997) found that within very difficult goal conditions, participants who perceived the task as meaningful had higher performance than did those who viewed it as unimportant to them. Presumably meaningfulness was a proxy variable for goal commitment.

Earley, Shalley, and Northcraft (1992) found that goal commitment was a curvilinear function of goal difficulty. However, anchoring can dilute the decrease in commitment that can occur with very high goals. Hinsz, Kalnback, and Lorentz (1997) told participants to "set a challenging and specific goal for the number of uses you will generate this next period—for example 320" (p. 291). Consistent with findings in the decision-making literature, the anchor affected goal level, which in turn affected self-efficacy regarding goal attainment as well as subsequent performance. Commitment is a function of the expectancy that the goal can be attained and the value the individual attaches to its attainment (Locke & Latham, 1990a; Tubbs & Dahl, 1991; Wofford et al., 1992).

In summary, advances have been made regarding an understanding of goal commitment, specifically in documenting its interaction with goal difficulty, identifying the best items for measuring it, and showing the effect of anchoring on it (Seijts & Latham, 2000b). Goal commitment can affect performance directly when goal difficulty is held constant and is at a high level.

PERFORMANCE LEADS TO REWARDS THAT AFFECT SATISFACTION

That high performance leads to intrinsic and extrinsic rewards is axiomatic in western society. In a series of laboratory experiments, Mento, Locke, and Klein (1992) found that high goals were perceived as instrumental in gaining many positive outcomes, including a sense of pride in accomplishment, an increase in perceived competency, as well as career and life success. A series of meta-analyses by Eby et al. (1999) found that perceived competency, which implies success, increases job satisfaction.

Anshel, Weinberg, and Jackson (1992) found that high goals lead to increases in intrinsic motivation. Easy ones decrease it when rewards are not contingent on performance. Kernan and Lord (1991) found a positive relationship between goal–performance discrepancy and satisfaction; the higher the performance in relation to the goal the better. They concluded that it is the amount of the discrepancy rather than the person's absolute performance that influences satisfaction.

With extrinsic rewards, Farh, Griffeth, and Balkin (1991) found that satisfaction is high when people are allowed choice. High-ability people chose piece rate pay; those low in ability chose fixed pay. Their subsequent goals and performance were consistent with their selection. (Of course, satisfaction is also high when people actually get valued rewards.)

The goal–performance relationship is influenced by external rewards only when people believe that the rewards are attainable (Bandura, 1997; Lee, Locke, & Phan, 1997). High dissatisfaction occurs when rewards are perceived as unfair, as too impersonal, or as punishment, as can be the case when high performers are consistently assigned more work than low performers (Doherty, 1998).

Further support for the HPC is offered by Summers and Hendrix (1991) in their field study of restaurant managers. They found a positive relationship between reward (pay) fairness and pay satisfaction; pay satisfaction is a component of overall job satisfaction.

SATISFACTION LEADS TO ORGANIZATION COMMITMENT

Commitment to the organization is a key variable in the HPC, because it affects the willingness to remain in the organization and to continue to set and commit to high goals. A meta-analysis found that job satisfaction and organizational commitment, though related, are distinct concepts (Tett & Meyer, 1993). We view satisfaction as enhancing commitment. Another meta-analysis found that the satisfaction–commitment relationship was higher in the private than in the public sector, and for professional than for clerical workers (Cohen & Lowenberg, 1990).

Mathieu and Zajac (1990), using meta-analysis, found that separating job satisfaction into intrinsic satisfaction, extrinsic satisfaction, and its components yielded significant correlations with organization commitment. This supported their earlier finding that job satisfaction has a direct influence on level of organizational commitment (Mathieu & Hamel, 1989).

Unlike the external validity of goal-setting across countries (Locke & Latham, 1990a), culture may be a moderator variable of the above findings. No correlation was found between satisfaction with one's job and organizational commitment among people in the United Emirates (Alnajjar, 1996). However, a study of dairy workers in Ireland and New Zealand found that satisfaction with intrinsic and extrinsic rewards was a significant predictor of affective commitment to the organization (O'Driscoll & Randall, 1999).

DISCUSSION

The HPC appears to have withstood the test of time. Although the model would benefit from studies that use more elaborate statistical analyses, the extant empirical studies conducted during the past decade suggest that such tests would yield significant results. Specific high goals lead to high performance. High performance on enriched tasks often leads to high rewards which in turn promotes satisfaction which subsequently encourages commitment to the organization.

In the 10 years since the publication of the original HPC model, the findings reported in the present chapter show:

- that attention, effort and persistence are associated with arousal of the sympathetic nervous system, specifically changes in heart rate, and that action is represented by a hierarchy of goals and subgoals activated in the prefrontal cortex
- the relevance of goal-setting theory to neurorehabilitation and sports
- the differential effects of a learning vs. a performance goal orientation
- the benefit of setting specific difficult learning goals on tasks that are complex for the individual
- the benefit of assigning proximal goals as opposed to only a distal outcome goal on tasks that are characterized by high uncertainty
- the benefit of proximal learning goals on the generation of task strategies
- the role of goals (and self-efficacy) as mediators of the effect of such factors as personality, job enrichment and incentives on performance
- the significance of viewing task ability as an acquirable skill rather than a fixed entity
- the interaction between goal difficulty and goal commitment
- the refinement of the goal commitment scale
- a model of the relationship between motivation, task knowledge and performance
- the generalizability of goal-setting findings with individuals to groups.

Many questions remain unanswered. These include the following:

- Is a learning vs. a performance mastery goal orientation truly a trait? Are these orientations easily induced as states through instructions?
- How do people actually "translate" traits into situationally specific goals? Is this done consciously or subconsciously?
- How proximal should proximal goals be? Hourly? Daily? Weekly? Monthly? What context factors need to be taken into account?
- Under what specific conditions will enriched jobs lead to the setting of higher goals? Are the elements of enrichment that lead to higher goals (e.g., feedback) the same or different than the ones that lead to high goal commitment (e.g., task challenge)?
- What group process factors, other than those already discovered, facilitate vs. undermine the goal-directed behavior of groups?
- What is the relative importance of internal, self-administered rewards and external rewards provided by others to job satisfaction and organizational commitment? Do people differ in this regard? Is a particular trait involved?

- When an individual is more committed to an organization, does it follow that the person is more committed to work goals as opposed to when the person is less committed to the organization? Does type (e.g., affective, continuance, etc.) of organizational commitment matter?

These and related questions should keep investigators busy for decades to come.

ACKNOWLEDGEMENT

Robert Wood's comments on a preliminary draft of this chapter are appreciated. Preparation of this paper was funded in part through a Canada Social Sciences and Humanities Research Council grant to the first author.

REFERENCES

Adler, S. (1986). *Toward a role for personality in goal setting research*. Paper presented at the International Congress of Applied Psychology, Jerusalem.

Allscheid, S. P., & Cellar, D. F. (1996). An interactive approach to work motivation: The effects of competition, rewards, and goal difficulty on task performance. *Journal of Business and Psychology*, **11**, 219–237.

Alnajjar, A. A. (1996). Relationship between job satisfaction and organizational commitment among employees in the United Arab Emirates. *Psychological Reports*, **79**, 315–321.

Ambrose, M. L., & Kulik, C. T. (1999). Old friends, new faces: Motivation research in the 1990's. *Journal of Management*, **25** (3), 231–292.

Anshel, M. H., Weinberg, R. S., & Jackson, A. (1992). The effect of goal difficulty and task complexity on intrinsic motivation and motor performance. *Journal of Sport Behaviour*, **15**, 159–176.

Audia, G., Kristof, B., Brown, K., & Locke, E. A. (1996). Relationship of goals and microlevel work processes to performance on a mulitipath manual task. *Journal of Applied Psychology*, **81**, 483–497.

Bagozzi, R. P., & Warshaw, P. R. (1990). Trying to consume. *Journal of Consumer Research*, **17**, 127–140.

Bandura, A. (1986). *Social foundations of thought and action: A social cognitive theory*. Englewood Cliffs, NJ: Prentice-Hall.

Bandura, A. (1997). *Self-efficacy: The exercise of control*. New York: W. H. Freeman & Company.

Bandura, A., & Schunk, D.H. (1981). Cultivating competence, self-efficacy and intrinsic interest through proximal self-motivation. *Journal of Personality and Social Psychology*, **41**, 586–598.

Bar-Eli, M., Levy-Kolker, N., Tenenbaum, G., & Weinberg, R. S. (1993). Effect of goal difficulty on performance of aerobic, anaerobic and power tasks in laboratory and field settings. *Journal of Sport Behaviour*, **16**, 17–32.

Brayfield, A. H., & Crockett, W. H. (1955). Employee attitudes and employee performance. *Psychological Bulletin*, **52**, 396–424.

Berry, J. M., & West, R. L. (1993). Cognitive self-efficacy in relation to personal mastery and goal setting across the life span. *International Journal of Behavioural Development*, **16**, 351–379.

Bouffard, T., Boisvet, J., Vezeau, C., & Larouche, C. (1995). The impact of goal orientation of self-regulation and performance among college students. *British Journal of Educational Psychology*, **65**, 317–329.

Boyce, B. A., & Wayda, V. K. (1994). The effects of assigned and self-set goals on task performance. *Journal of Sport and Exercise Psychology*, **16**, 258–26.

Brown, T., & Latham, G. P. (2000a). The effects of goal setting and self-instruction training on the performance of union employees. *Relations Industrielles/Industrial Relations*, **55**, 80–91.

Brown, T., & Latham, G. P. (2000b, August). *The effects of training in verbal self-guidance and goal setting on team-playing behavior: A field experiment.* Paper presented at the meeting of the Academy of Management, Toronto, ON.

Button, S. B., Mathieu, J. E., & Aikin, K. J. (1996). An examination of the relative impact of assigned goals and self-efficacy on personal goals and performance over time. *Journal of Applied Social Psychology*, **26**, 1084–1103.

Button, S. B., Mathieu, J. E., & Zajac, D. M. (1996). Goal orientation in organizational research: A conceptual and empirical foundation. *Organizational Behavior and Human Decision Processes*, **67**, 26–48.

Campion, M. A. (1996). *Reinventing work: A new era of I/O research and practice.* Presidential address to the annual meeting of The Society of Industrial and Organizational Psychology, San Diego, CA.

Carson, K. D., & Carson, P. P. (1993a). The moderating effects of students' negative affectivity on goal-setting. *College Students Journal*, **27**, 65–74.

Carson, P. P., & Carson, K. D. (1993b). Managing creativity enhancement through goal setting and feedback. *Journal of Creative Behaviour*, **27** (1), 36–45.

Cellar, D. F., Degrendel, D., Sidle, S., & Lavine, K. (1996). Effects of goal type on performance, task interest, and affect over time. *Journal of Applied Social Psychology*, **26**, 804–824.

Chesney, A. A., & Locke, E. A. (1991). Relationships among goal difficulty, business strategies, and performance on a complex management simulation task. *Academy of Management Journal*, **34**, 400–424.

Cohen, A., & Lowenberg, G. (1990). A reexamination of the side-bet theory as applied to organizational commitment: A meta-analysis. *Human Relations*, **43**, 1015–1050.

Cordery, J. L. (1996). Autonomous work groups and quality circles. In M. West (Ed.), *Handbook of work and group psychology* (pp. 225–240). Chichester: Wiley.

Cordery, J. L. (1997). Reinventing work design theory and practice. *Australian Psychologist*, **32**, 185–189.

Crown, D. F., & Rosse, J. G. (1995). Yours, mine, and ours: Facilitating group productivity through the integration of individual and group goals. *Organizational Behaviour and Human Decision Processes*, **64**, 138–150.

DeShon, R. P., & Landis, R. S. (1997). The dimensionality of the Hollenbeck, Williams, and Klein (1989) measure of goal commitment on complex tasks. *Organizational Behaviour and Human Decision Processes*, **70**, 105–116.

Doherty, E. M. (1998). Emotional and outcome responses to experiences of negative rewards. *Psychological Reports*, **82**, 997–998.

Donovan, J. J., & Radosevich, D. J. (1998). The moderating role of goal commitment on the goal difficulty–performance relationship: A meta-analytic review and critical reanalysis. *Journal of Applied Psychology*, **83**, 308–315.

Duncan, J. (1995). Attention, intelligence, and the frontal lobes. In M. Gazzaniga (Ed.), *The cognitive neurosciences* (pp. 721–733). Cambridge, MA: A Bradford Book.

Dunnette, M. D., Campbell, J. P., & Hakel, M. D. (1967). Factors contributing to job satisfaction and job dissatisfaction in six occupational groups. *Organizational Behavior and Human Decision Processes*, **2**, 143–174.

Earley, C. P., Lee, C., & Hanson, L. A. (1990). Joint moderating effects of job experience and task component complexity: Relations among goal setting, task strategies, and performance. *Journal of Organizational Behaviour*, **11**, 3–15.

Earley, C. P., & Lituchy, T. R. (1991). Delineating goal and efficacy effects: A test of three models. *Journal of Applied Psychology*, **76**, 81–98.

Earley, P. C., Shalley, C. E., & Northcraft, G. B. (1992). I think I can, I think I can . . . processing time and strategy effects of goal acceptance/rejection decisions. *Organizational Behaviour and Human Decision Processes*, **53**, 1–13.

Eby, L. T., Freeman, D. M., Rush, M. C., & Lance, C. E. (1999). Motivational bases of affective organizational commitment: A partial test of an integrative theoretical model. *Journal of Occupational and Organizational Psychology*, **72**, 463–483.

Elliott, E. S., & Dweck, C. S. (1986). Goals: An approach to motivation and achievement. *Journal of Personality and Social Psychology*, **54**, 5–12.

Farh, J., Griffeth, R. W., & Balkin, D. B. (1991). Effects of choice of pay plans on satisfaction, goal setting, and performance. *Journal of Organizational Behaviour*, **12**, 55–62.

Flanagan, J. C. (1954). The critical incident technique. *Psychological Bulletin*, **51**, 327–358.

Gauggel, S. (1999). *Goal setting and its influence on the performance of brain-damaged patients.* Unpublished doctoral dissertation. Philipps University of Marburg, Germany.

Gellatly, I. R., & Meyer, J. P. (1992). The effects of goal difficulty on physiological arousal, cognition, and task performance. *Journal of Applied Psychology*, **77**, 694–704.

Greene, B. A., & Miller, R. B. (1996). Influences on achievement: Goals, perceived ability, and cognitive engagement. *Contemporary Educational Psychology*, **21**, 181–192.

Harackiewicz, J. M., & Elliot, A. J. (1993). Achievement goals and intrinsic motivation. *Journal of Personality and Social Psychology*, **65**, 904–915.

Harackiewicz, J. M., Barron, K. E., Carter, S. M., Lehto, A. T., & Elliot, A. J. (1997). Predictors and consequences of achievement goals in the college classroom: Maintaining interest and making the grade. *Journal of Personality and Social Psychology*, **73**, 1284–1295.

Herzberg, F. (1968). One more time: How do you motivate employees? *Harvard Business Review*, **46**, 53–62.

Herzberg, F., Mausner, B., & Snyderman, B. (1959). *The motivation to work.* New York: John Wiley.

Hinsz, V. B. (1995). Goal setting by groups performing an additive task: A comparison with individual goal setting. *Journal of Applied Social Psychology*, **25**, 965–990.

Hinsz, V. B. (1991). Individual versus group goal decision making: Social comparison in goals for individual task performance. *Journal of Applied Social Psychology*, **22**, 1296–1317.

Hinsz, V. B., & Matz, D. C. (1997). Self-evaluations involved in goal setting and task performance. *Social Behaviour and Personality*, **25**, 177–182.

Hinsz, V. B., & Ployhart, R. E. (1998). Trying, intentions, and the processes by which goals influence performance: An empirical test of the theory of goal pursuit. *Journal of Applied Social Psychology*, **28**, 1051–1066.

Hinsz, V. B., Kalnback, L. R., & Lorentz, N. R. (1997). Using judgmental anchors to establish challenging self-set goals without jeopardizing commitment. *Organizational Behaviour and Human Decision Processes*, **71**, 287–308.

Hollenbeck, J. R., Klein, H. J., O'Leary-Kelly, A. M., & Wright, P. M. (1989). Investigation of the concept validity of a self-report measure of goal commitment. *Journal of Applied Psychology*, **74**, 951–956.

Jones, G., & Cale, A. (1997). Goal difficulty, anxiety and performance. *Ergonomics*, **40**, 319–333.

Kanfer, R. (1990). Motivation theory and industrial and organizational psychology. In M. D. Dunnette & L. M. Hough (Eds.), *Handbook of industrial and organizational psychology.* (pp. 75–170). Palo Alto, CA: Consulting Psychologists Press.

Kanfer, R., & Ackerman, P. L. (1989). Motivation and cognitive abilities: An integrative/aptitude-treatment interaction approach to skill acquisition [Monograph]. *Journal of Applied Psychology*, **74**, 657–690.

Kanfer, R., Ackerman, P. L., Murtha, T. C., Dugdale, B., & Nelson, L. (1994). Goal setting, conditions of practice, and task performance: A resource allocation perspective. *Journal of Applied Psychology*, **79**, 826–835.

Kernan, M. C., & Lord, R. G. (1991). An application of control theory to understanding the relationship between performance and satisfaction. *Human Performance*, **4**, 173–185.

Kernan, M. C., & Lord, R. G. (1990). Effects of valence, expectancies, and goal-performance discrepancies in single and multiple environments. *Journal of Applied Psychology*, **75**, 194–203.

Kiesler, C. A. (1971). *The psychology of commitment.* New York: Academic Press.

King, N. (1970). Clarification and evaluation of the two-factor theory of job satisfaction. *Psychological Bulletin*, **74**, 18–31.

Kirkpatrick, S. (1992). *The effect of psychological variables on the job characteristics-work outcome relations.* Paper presented at the Eastern Academy of Management.

Klein, H. J., & Kim, J. S. (1998). A field study of the influence of situational constraints, leader-member exchange, and goal commitment on performance. *Academy of Management Journal*, **41**, 88–95.

Klein, H. J., & Mulvey, P. W. (1995). Two investigations of the relationship among group goals, goal commitment, cohesion, and performance. *Organizational Behavior and Human Decision Processes*, **61**, 44–53.

Klein, H. J., Wesson, M. J., Hollenbeck, J. R., & Alge, B. J. (1999). Goal commitment and the goal setting process: Conceptual clarification and empirical synthesis. *Journal of Applied Psychology*, **84**, 885–896.

Lambert, S. H., Moore, D. W., & Dixon, R. S. (1999). Gymnasts in training: The differential effects of self- and coach-set goals as a function of locus of control. *Journal of Applied Sport Psychology*, **11**, 72–82.

Lane, A. M., & Karageorghis, C. I. (1997). Goal confidence and difficulty as predictors of goal attainment in junior high school cross-country runners. *Perceptual and Motor Skills*, **84**, 747–752.

Latham, G. P., & Seijts, G. H. (1999). The effects of proximal and distal goals on performance on a moderately complex task. *Journal of Organizational Behaviour*, **20**, 421–429.

Latham, G. P., Winters, D. C., & Locke, E. A. (1994). Cognitive and motivational effects of participation: A mediator study. *Journal of Organizational Behaviour*, **15**, 49–63.

Lee, C., & Bobko, P. (1992). Exploring the meaning and usefulness of measures of subjective goal difficulty. *Journal of Applied Social Psychology*, **22**, 1417–1428.

Lee, T. W., Locke, E. A., & Phan, S. H. (1997). Explaining the assigned goal-incentive interaction: The role of self-efficacy and personal goals. *Journal of Management*, **23**, 541–559.

Lerner, B. S., & Locke, E. A. (1995). The effect of goal setting, self-efficacy, competition, and personal traits on the performance of an endurance task. *Journal of Sport and Exercise Psychology*, **17**, 138–152.

Locke, E. A. (1976). The nature and causes of job satisfaction, In M. D. Dunnette (Ed.), *Handbook of industrial and organizational Psychology*. Chicago: Rand McNally.

Locke, E. A. (2000). Motivation, cognition and action: An analysis of studies of task goals and knowledge. *Applied Psychology: An International Review*, **49**, 408–429.

Locke, E. A. (2001). Self-set goals and self-efficacy as mediators of incentives and personality. In M. Erez, U. Kleinbeck, & H. K. Thierry (Eds.), *Work motivation in the context of a globalizing economy*. Mahwah, NJ: Lawrence Erlbaum.

Locke, E. A., & Latham, G. P. (1990a). *A theory of goal setting and task performance*. Englewood Cliffs, NJ: Prentice-Hall.

Locke, E. A., & Latham, G. P. (1990b). Work motivation and satisfaction: Light at the end of the tunnel. *Psychological Science*, **1**, 240–246.

Mathieu, J. E., & Button, S. B. (1992). An examination of the relative impact of normative information and self-efficacy on personal goals and performance over time. *Journal of Applied Social Psychology*, **22**, 1758–1775.

Mathieu, J. E., & Hamel, K. (1989). A causal model of the antecedents of organizational commitment among professionals and non-professionals. *Journal of Vocational Behaviour*, **34**, 299–317.

Mathieu, J. E., & Zajac, D. M. (1990). A review and meta-analysis of the antecedents, correlates and consequences of organizational commitment. *Psychological Bulletin*, **108**, 171–194.

Mento, A. J., Locke, E. A., & Klein, H. J. (1992). Relationship of goal level to valence and instrumentality. *Journal of Applied Psychology*, **77**, 395–405.

Morin, L., & Latham, G. P. (2000). The effect of mental practice and goal setting as a transfer of training intervention on supervisor's self-efficacy and communication skills: An exploratory study. *Applied Psychology: An International Review*, **49**, 566–578.

Multon, K. D., Brown, S. D., & Lent, R. W. (1991). Relation of self-efficacy beliefs to academic outcomes: A meta-analytic investigation. *Journal of Counselling Psychology*, **38**, 30–38.

Mulvey, P. W., & Klein, H. J. (1998). The impact of perceived loafing and collective efficacy in group goal processes and group performance. *Organizational Behavior and Human Decision Processes*, **74**, 62–87.

Neubert, M. J. (1998). The value of feedback and goal setting over goal setting alone and potential moderators of this effect: A meta-analysis. *Human Performance*, **11**, 321–335.

Newman, R. S. (1998). Students' help seeking during problem solving: Influences of personal and contextual achievement goals. *Journal of Educational Psychology*, **90**, 644–658.

O'Driscoll, M. P., & Randall, D. M. (1999). Perceived organisational support, satisfaction with rewards, and employee job involvement and organizational commitment. *Applied Psychology: An International Review*, **48**, 197–209.

O'Leary-Kelly, A. M., Martocchio, J. J., & Frink, D. D. (1994). A review of the influence of group goals on performance. *Academy of Management Journal*, **37**, 1285–1301.

Phillips, J. M., & Gully, S. M. (1997). Role of goal orientation, ability, need for achievement, and locus of control in the self-efficacy and goal-setting process. *Journal of Applied Psychology*, **82**, 792–802.

Phillips, J. M., Hollenbeck, J. R., & Ilgen, D. R. (1996). Prevalence and prediction of positive discrepancy creation: Examining a discrepancy between two self-regulation theories. *Journal of Applied Psychology*, **81**, 498–511.

Polzer, J. T., & Neale, M. A. (1995). Constraints or catalysts? Reexamining goal setting with the context of negotiation. *Human Performance*, **8**, 3–26.

Rasch, R. H. & Tosi, H. L. (1992). Factors affecting software developers' performance: An integrated approach. *MIS Quarterly*, **16**, 395–413.

Renn, R. W. (1998). Participation's effect on task performance: Mediating roles of goal acceptance and procedural justice. *Journal of Business Research*, **41**, 115–125.

Roberson, L., Korsgaard, A. M., & Diddams, M. (1990). Goal characteristics and satisfaction: Personal goals as mediators of situational effects on task satisfaction. *Journal of Applied Social Psychology*, **20**, 920–941.

Roethlisberger, F. J. (1941). *Management and morale*. Cambridge: Harvard University Press.

Salancik, G. R. (1977). Commitment and the control of organizational behavior and belief. In B. M. Staw & G. R. Salancik (Eds.), *New directions in organizational behavior* (pp. 1–54). Chicago, IL: St. Claire Press.

Seijts, G. H., & Latham, G. P. (2001). The effect of distal learning, outcome, and proximal goals on a moderately complex task. *Journal of Organizational Behavior*.

Seijts, G. H., & Latham, G. P. (2000a). The effects of goal setting and group size on performance in a social dilemma. *Canadian Journal of Behavioural Science*.

Seijts, G. H., & Latham, G. P. (2000b). The concept of goal commitment: Measurement and relationships with task performance. In R. Goffin & E. Helmes (Eds.), *Problems and solutions in human assessment: Honoring Douglas N. Jackson at seventy*. Dordrecht, Kluwer Academic Publishers.

Seijts, G. H., Latham, G. P., & Whyte, G. (2000). The effect of self- and group-efficacy on group performance in a mixed-motive situation. *Human Performance*, **13**, 279–298.

Seijts, G. H., Meertens, R. M., & Kok, G. (1997). The effects of task importance and publicness on the relation between goal difficulty and performance. *Canadian Journal of Behavioural Science*, **29**, 54–62.

Shoenfelt, E. (1996). Goal setting and feedback as a posttraining strategy to increase the transfer of training. *Perceptual and Motor Skills*, **83**, 176–178.

Siero, F. W., Bakker, A. B., Dekker, G. B., & van den Berg, M. T. C. (1996). Changing organizational energy consumption behaviour through comparative feedback. *Journal of Environmental Psychology*, **16**, 235–246.

Silver, W. S., & Bufanio, K. M. (1996). The impact of group efficacy and group goals on group task performance. *Small Group Research*, **27**, 347–359.

Smith, K. G., Locke, E. A., & Barry, D. (1990). Goal setting, planning, and organizational performance: An experimental simulation. *Organizational Behaviour and Human Decision Processes*, **46**, 118–134.

Summers, T. P., & Hendrix, W. H. (1991). Modelling the role of pay equity perceptions: A field study. *Journal of Occupational Psychology*, **64**, 145–157.

Tabernero, C., & Wood, R. E. (1999). Implicit theories versus the social construal of ability in self-regulation and performance on a complex task. *Organizational Behaviour and Human Decision Processes*, **78**, 104–127.

Tan, V., Cheatle, M. D., Mackin, S., Moberg, P. J., & Esterhai, J. L. (1997). Goal setting as a predictor of return to work in a population of chronic musculoskeletal pain patients. *International Journal of Neuroscience*, **92**, 161–170.

Tang, T. L. P., & Reynolds, D. B. (1993). Effects of self-esteem and perceived goal difficulty on goal setting, certainty, task performance, and attributions. *Human Resource Development Quarterly*, **4**, 153–170.

Tett, R. P., & Meyer, J. P. (1993). Job satisfaction, organizational commitment, turnover intention, and turnover: Path analysis based on meta-analytic findings. *Personnel Psychology*, **46**, 259–293.

Theodorakis, Y., Laparidis, K., Kioumourtzoglou, E., & Goudas, M. (1998). Combined effects of goal setting and performance feedback on performance and physiological response on a maximum effort task. *Perceptual and Motor Skills*, **86** (3), 1035–1041.

Tubbs, M. E. (1993). Commitment as a moderator of the goal performance relation: A case for clearer concept definition. *Journal of Applied Psychology*, **78**, 86–97.

Tubbs, M. E. (1994). Commitment and the role of ability in motivation: Comment on Wright, O'Leary-Kelly, Cortina, Klein, and Hollenbeck (1994). *Journal of Applied Psychology*, **79**, 804–811.

Tubbs, M. E., & Dahl, J. G. (1992). An examination of individuals' information processing in the formation of goal commitment judgements. *Journal of Psychology*, **126**, 181–188.

Tubbs, M. E., & Ekeberg, S. E. (1991). The role of intentions in work motivation: Implications for goal setting theory and research. *Academy of Management Review*, **16**, 188–199.

Umstot, D. D., Bell, C. H., & Mitchell, T. R. (1976). Effects of job enrichment and task goals on satisfaction and productivity: Implications for job design. *Journal of Applied Psychology*, **61** (4), 379–394.

Vance, R. J., & Colella, A. (1990). Effects of two types of feedback on goal acceptance and personal goals. *Journal of Applied Psychology*, **75**, 68–76.

VandeWalle, D., Brown, S. P., Cron, W. L., & Slocum, J. W. (1999). The influence of goal orientation and self-regulation tactics on sales performance: A longitudinal field test. *Journal of Applied Psychology*, **84**, 249–259.

VandeWalle, D., & Cummings, L. L. (1997). A test of the influence of goal orientation on the feedback-seeking process. *Journal of Applied Psychology*, **82**, 390–400.

Von Bergen, C. W., Soper, B., & Rosenthal, G. T. (1996). The moderating effects of self-esteem and goal difficulty level on performance. *College Student Journal*, **30**, 22–267.

Weingart, L. R., & Weldon, E. (1991). Processes that mediate the relationship between a group goal and group member performance. *Human Performance*, **4**, 33–54.

Weinberg, R. S., Fowler, C., Jackson, A., Bagnall, J., & Bruya, L. (1991). Effect of goal difficulty on motor performance: A replication across tasks and subjects. *Journal of Sport and Exercise Psychology*, **13**, 160–173.

Weldon, E., Jehn, K. A., & Pradhan, P. (1991). Processes that mediate the relationship between group goal and improved group performance. *Journal of Personality and Social Psychology*, **61**, 555–569.

Winters, D., & Latham, G. P. (1996). The effect of learning versus outcome goals on a simple versus a complex task. *Group and Organization Management*, **21**, 236–250.

Wofford, J. C., Goodwin, V. L., & Premack, S. (1992). Meta-analysis of the antecedents of personal goal level and of the antecedents and consequences of goal commitment. *Journal of Management*, **18**, 595–615.

Wood, R. E., & Locke, E. A. (1990). Goal setting and strategy effects on complex tasks. In B. Staw & L. Cummings (Eds.), *Research in organizational behavior*, Vol. 12. Greenwich, CT: JAI Press.

Wright, P. M., O'Leary-Kelly, A. M., Cortina, J. M., Klein, H. J., & Hollenbeck, J. R. (1994). On the meaning and measurement of goal commitment. *Journal of Applied Psychology*, **79**, 795–803.

Zimmerman, B. J., Bandura, A., & Martinez-Pons, M. (1992). Self-motivation for academic attainment: The role of self-efficacy beliefs and personal goal setting. *American Educational Research Journal*, **29**, 663–676.

Enhancing Performance through Goal-Setting and Feedback Interventions

Jen A. Algera, Ad Kleingeld and **Harrie van Tuijl**
Technische Universiteit Eindhoven, Eindhoven, The Netherlands

SUMMARY

This chapter focuses on the *implementation* of goal-setting and feedback systems. The fit between the basic values of management and the other organisation members seems to be decisive for success or failure of the whole process of implementation. When problems arise, conflicts can often be interpreted as reflecting differences in these underlying values. The role of a facilitator is essential in helping the organisation to solve these conflicts. As such, the process is much more critical than the actual design of the elements of the system. Other organisational control systems to manage the human resources, e.g. reward systems, have to be made compatible to the goal setting and feedback system if it is supposed to be there for a long time. The last part of this chapter addresses the important role of the supervisor in assisting employees in problem solving and the development of better task strategies.

Psychological Management of Individual Performance. Edited by Sabine Sonnentag.
© 2002 John Wiley & Sons, Ltd.

INTRODUCTION

The primary focus of this chapter is on the *implementation* of goal-setting and feedback systems that aim for performance improvement. Although goal setting and feedback are very powerful motivational interventions (see, for example, Locke & Latham, 1990; Pritchard, 1995; Van Tuijl, Kleingeld, Schmidt, Kleinbeck, Pritchard, & Algera, 1997), installing feedback and goal-setting systems in practice turns out to be rather difficult. At least two important differences between studies on goal setting and feedback and the actual implementation should be mentioned.

First, actual implementation means that the goal-setting and feedback system is to be there for a long time. This implies a quite different perspective for the organisation than the situation of a field study in which the aim is to gather data to prove that goal-setting and feedback can be effective in practice. The main difference is that the goal-setting and feedback system has to be adopted by the organisation. One of the consequences is that it will have to fit with other organisational control systems, for example, reward systems (see, for example, Schmidt & Kleinbeck, 1997). Further, installing goal-setting and feedback systems can change the power relations in the organisation. For example, providing performance feedback directly to individual workers instead of to their boss could change the balance of power.

Second, actual implementation often means that a much greater part of the organisation will be involved than in a study. Field studies are mostly restricted to a single unit or department within an organisation. Locke and Latham (1990) present 395 goal-setting and/or feedback studies of which 156 are field studies. In general in these field studies the interventions are focused on rather narrowly defined behaviour domains. Mostly, these studies relate to one dimension of a task. In actual practice tasks are more complex and often multi-dimensional.

In this chapter we will discuss the implementation of goal-setting and feedback systems along the lines of the various phases that can be distinguished in the implementation process. In addition to describing the pitfalls in each stage of implementation, the focus will be on two themes. First, the problem of *adoption* of the goal-setting and feedback system will be covered. The second theme elaborates on the question of how to handle feedback data from the perspective of improving performance by developing better task strategies, i.e. *learning*.

PHASES IN THE IMPLEMENTATION PROCESS

The success of implementing goal-setting and feedback systems in practice is dependent on many factors. In each stage of the implementation process different factors can be more or less important. Actual implementations of goal-setting and feedback systems in practice have not too often been published, also because not too many well-described systematic approaches exist. An exception to this rule probably is the Productivity Measurement and Enhancement System (ProMES), as developed by Pritchard and others (see, for example, Pritchard, 1990, 1995; Van Tuijl et al., 1997; Algera & Kleinbeck, 1997; Schmidt & Kleinbeck, 1997). This system consists of four well-defined development steps and has been evaluated in a number of studies in many different countries. Although in most cases ProMES has been developed for work teams it has also been implemented for individual jobs (see Pritchard, 1995), for example, bank employees and university teachers. Looking in more detail to the implementation *process*, there seem to be no big differences between implementing ProMES for work teams compared to implementing ProMES for individual jobs. The main reason is that if a goal-setting and feedback system is developed for an individual job it pertains to jobs that are done by many job incumbents. Problems encountered in the implementation process are very much the same, such as the problem of adoption within the organisation, the problem of acceptance of a system that has been designed by colleagues in the design team, or the compatibility with other control systems. In addition to this, the distinction between individual tasks and group tasks is not always very clear. In the study of Kleingeld (1994), the maintenance technician job was composed of individual task components and group task components. A ProMES system was developed to cover both task components. In our discussion on the implementation process, we therefore will refer to findings from both group studies and individual studies.

The four phases that can be distinguished in implementing a goal-setting and feedback system are *starting conditions, system design, implementation* and *maintenance*. We will discuss possible pitfalls in each of the four phases. Table 11.1 presents an overview of the four implementation phases including the main issues that have to be dealt with.

PHASE 0: STARTING CONDITIONS

This phase precedes the actual design of a goal-setting and feedback system. It includes a check of the conditions as mentioned by Pritchard (1990), such as the full support of top management, the common feeling in the organisation that performance improvement is important but will take much effort and a mutual trust between management and the employees. Most important, however, is the implementation strategy. One of the basic characteristics of ProMES is the participation of employees in the design of the system (Pritchard, 1990), both for the cognitive benefits (i.e., generating ideas for valid performance indicators) and the motivational benefits (i.e., fostering feelings of employee

TABLE 11.1 Implementation model

Implementation phase	Main issues and/or pitfalls to be avoided
Phase 0: Starting conditions	• Check of the congruence between the principles underlying the goal-setting and feedback system, e.g. more autonomy for workers, and the basic values in the organisation
Phase 1: System development	• Participation by all individuals involved or participation by representation • Time span for development • Level of knowledge of workers • Visible support of top management
Phase 2: Implementation	• Availability of computerised information systems • Controllability of performance indicators • Links with other control systems, e.g. reward systems
Phase 3: Maintenance	• Management attitudes and skills in handling feedback data • Skills in problem solving to arrive at better task strategies

ownership of the system). Locke and Latham (1990) question the motivational benefits of participation, dependent on the existing leadership style or the more general cultural attitudes towards participation. Experiences with implementing ProMES suggest strongly that the participatory, bottom-up approach of this system can only be successful if the basic values within the organisation are congruent with this characteristic of the method (see, for example, Kleingeld, 1994). Thus, before starting the phase of system design one should check whether the basic values of organisation members, especially the managers, are fitting with the implementation strategy. Algera and Van den Hurk (1997) report on a feasibility study preceding the actual implementation of a goal-setting and feedback system. In this feasibility study both the cognitive elements (i.e., how to design valid performance indicators) and the motivational elements (i.e., are the consequences of adopting a bottom-up design approach) of the system became clear to all constituencies involved. As a result of this feasibility study a deliberate choice was made regarding the implementation strategy.

In the study of Kleingeld (1994), the mutual trust between employees and management was at stake regarding the possible use of ProMES data for pay for performance. This problem was handled by a document in which management stated that the ProMES data would not be used for pay for performance unless the employees would agree that it was better and more fair than the existing pay for performance procedures. After this issue had been dealt with the actual design could begin.

PHASE 1: SYSTEM DESIGN

In this phase the basic elements of the goal-setting and feedback system have to be designed, such as the key result areas, performance indicators for each key result area and the structure of the feedback data. An example of a key result area is "*improving quality*"; a performance indicator that could be used in this case is "*percentage of waste produced*". In structuring the feedback process, one of the most important decisions has to do with the time horizon of the feedback data. This could vary from one shift period of eight hours to one month or more, depending on the cycle time of the work process. Another important question is: Who should get (parts of) the feedback reports? In practice most often a design team is established to design the basic elements of the system. Members of the design team should have expertise in the task strategies that lead to performance of the job at hand. Thus the help of job incumbents is needed. In the usual design procedure of ProMES (Pritchard, 1990) a facilitator is responsible for managing the design process. A number of pitfalls can frustrate this design phase (see, for example, Algera, Van Tuijl, & Janssen, 1995).

A main problem is that the job incumbents participating in the design team are representing their colleagues for whom the system is to be developed. This can create problems of acceptance of the goal-setting and feedback system. Meeks (1994) presents empirical results on the difference between members and non-members of design teams in accepting the goal-setting and feedback system as being a valid system by which to express performance. As could be expected, members are more positive than non-members.

Another main problem is the time span needed for development of the system. Experience with designing ProMES systems reveals that between 8 and 20 design team meetings are required to design all elements of the complete system. Corresponding with this number of meetings, it can take 6 to 18 months to develop the system and there is a serious risk that the design team members may lose interest. This risk is even more serious for the non-members of the design team in the organisation. In particular, in situations where the complete system becomes rather complex (i.e., many performance indicators to cover all key result areas) a dilemma is faced. To solve this dilemma, a modular design strategy could be followed. For example, Van Tuijl et al. (1997) refer to a case in the chemical industry where quality performance was the most important key result area for the operators. The system was installed starting with this module, leaving aside other key result areas for the moment. Of course, the risk of this strategy is that other key result areas are getting less attention than needed for overall performance. Even for this single module, determining performance indicators turned out to be a rather complex endeavour. The relative importance of no less than some 25 quality indicators had to be determined. Eventually, this was done by using a financial criterion. Feedback was started with this quality performance result area, leading to a dramatic positive change in quality performance.

In another case referred to by Van Tuijl et al. (1997) a balance between the key result areas "quality" and "cost reduction" was also reached by using financial outcomes of weighting the relative importance of these result areas.

Support and commitment of top management remains important during the whole process of development. Even in the situation where top management delegates the "approval" of performance indicators, as suggested by design teams to lower management levels, the visible support of top management is needed. The results of the study of Rodgers and Hunter (1991) on the effectiveness of Management By Objectives programmes illustrate this point. Commitment of top management turns out to be an essential factor for performance improvement in the organisation.

PHASE 2: IMPLEMENTATION

After the design the actual implementation of the system can start. Looking at experiences with implementing ProMES systems, first feedback on the designed performance indicators is given. At this time the system has to prove its intended value: the proof of the pudding is in the eating. In many projects the reaction of job incumbents to feedback data give rise to serious discussions (see, e.g., Kleingeld, 1994; Janssen, Van Berkel, & Stolk, 1995), mainly on the controllability of the performance indicators. Controllability of performance indicators is rarely 100%. There are always external factors that more or less influence the scores on the performance indicators. For people to accept the feedback data as valid they should have the feeling that the performance scores indeed reflect their efforts to do a good job. In fact, sometimes parts of the design phase and, in particular, the definition of performance indicators have to be repeated (Kleingeld, 1994).

A very practical issue in the implementation phase is the availability of computerised information systems to provide the performance feedback data. Although these systems are have become widely available in organisations and data on performance are collected even before installing the goal-setting and feedback system, the performance indicators which have been designed often differ from the existing performance data. Thus, the reprogramming of computerised information systems is needed. For example, Kleingeld (1994) reports that it took about five weeks of programming to develop a system that was able to generate the feedback reports. In the study of Meeks (1994), implementation was severely hampered because of the lack of an information system to provide the feedback data at the start of the implementation phase.

In the implementation phase inconsistent links with other organisational control systems can arise. If the designed goal-setting and feedback system is not compatible with these other control systems it will probably not survive, unless the compatibility is actually improved. Algera, Monhemius and Wijnen (1997) report on the compatibility of ProMES and Statistical Process Control (SPC). The latter approach has its roots in quality management and has been developed in the area of industrial engineering. It is based on the concept of operator self-control supported by statistical tools. Both ProMES and SPC aim at improving the task strategies used by employees. At first sight, these two approaches are very different. For example, the primary goal of ProMES is productivity improvement, while SPC aims at reduction of process variation. Furthermore, ProMES is oriented to enhancing the motivation of employees and uses a bottom-up design approach, while SPC is focused on the identification of causes of process variation and uses an expert design approach. In addition to this there is a difference between ProMES and SPC in the time horizon for providing feedback. Algera et al. (1997) present a case in which these two systems are combined. It turns out that ProMES and SPC can be made compatible and even stronger: they can be designed to be supplementary. The focus of SPC on "out of control" situations can lead to clues for better task strategies. These clues are not usually provided by ProMES because of its focus on controllable performance indicators.

Schmidt and Kleinbeck (1997) refer to the compatibility of performance feedback data and organisational context factors. Important context factors are existing pay systems, supervisory behaviour and the level of interdependence of individual tasks in a work group setting. They conclude that incompatible constellations between goal-setting and feedback systems and the organisational context factors can have detrimental consequences for performance.

PHASE 3: MAINTENANCE

In this phase at least two important questions are at stake. The first question is how to continue the goal-setting and feedback system as time goes by and context factors change. For example, installing new technology may necessitate adaptations of performance evaluation to keep the system alive (see, for example, Kleingeld, 1994). Janssen et al. (1995) describe a case in which the initially designed ProMES system evolves, related to a change in the strategy of the organisation. In the beginning operators had rather restricted authority and responsibility but more and more self-management was introduced, and the performance indicators for the operators changed accordingly.

In addition to changes in context factors, getting experience with the goal-setting and feedback system leads to a higher employee awareness of performance constraints. A main issue is the attitude and skills of management in handling feedback data. Pritchard (1990) advocates a management attitude that can be expressed as "us against the figures", especially in situations of performance below expectations. Schmidt and Kleinbeck (1997) refer to the same phenomenon in discussing the style of supervisory behaviour that is needed to get a positive effect of performance feedback data. To enhance performance, a goal-setting and feedback system should not only provide outcome feedback but also provide suggestions how to change task strategies to improve performance. Many goal-setting and feedback systems as described in the literature (see, for example, Locke & Latham, 1990; Pritchard, 1990) only provide outcome feedback. Strictly speaking, people are much more inclined to improve performance by working harder than by working smarter (see Algera et al., 1997). Even when there is no lack of cues to improve task strategies it is not guaranteed that actual improvement will happen. Experience in practice shows that employees often lack problem-solving skills. Thus, to improve performance, additional interventions are needed.

The second question is how to expand the goal-setting and feedback system into the organisation. In the literature examples are very scarce. Janssen et al. (1995) report on an extension of a successful ProMES system to other departments in the organisation. In the study of Kleingeld (1994) the system has been introduced to all maintenance technicians in 13 units after the initial design and evaluation in two units. These two studies started in the early 1990s and the goal-setting and feedback systems are still alive in 2000. Many adaptations to the original systems have taken place in the meantime to survive in changing conditions. Information on the longevity of goal-setting and feedback systems is very scarce indeed. Probably these two examples mentioned above are exceptional. Locke and Latham (1990), reporting on 156 field studies, mention a maximum of 36 months of longevity. It illustrates at least that the maintenance of goal-setting and feedback systems probably takes even more effort by management and employees than the initial design and implementation. In addition, we conclude that to realise the potential performance improvement benefits of goal-setting and feedback systems in practice, context factors should be taken into account.

This statement implies that goal setting and feedback interventions can only be successful if embedded into the larger perspective of the organisation's strategy to improve organisational performance.

ADOPTION OF GOAL-SETTING AND FEEDBACK SYSTEMS

In this section we will focus on an important theme that pervades all phases of the implementation process. The adoption of a goal-setting and feedback system seems to be one of the most crucial factors for enhancing performance. By the term adoption is meant that not only the unit for which a system has been designed should accept the system but also the organisational context should be accommodated to get maximum performance benefits, as we have argued in the previous paragraphs. Locke and Latham (1990) refer to goal acceptance and goal commitment as similar terms, and prefer goal commitment "as the more inclusive concept in that it refers to one's attachment to or determination to reach a goal, regardless of where the goal came from" (p. 125). Much research exists on the effects of participation on goal commitment. Summarising apparently contradictory findings from previous studies, Locke and Latham (1990) conclude that assigned goal setting is as effective as participative goal setting to arrive at goal commitment. However these findings were mainly based on laboratory experiments. In these settings it even seems to be difficult to get non-commitment.

We believe that participation in the design of goal-setting and feedback systems in actual practice is important, provided that the organisational culture is not totally opposite to participation. Van Tuijl (1997) gives an overview of factors that can lead to "acceptance", "compliance" or "rejection" of goal-setting and feedback systems in practice. He concludes that in the end acceptance highly depends on the congruence of the basic values of management and the employees. By using a participative design method there are many chances to find out whether the basic values of management and employees are not too divergent to preclude the final acceptance of the system. A good example is the so-called "approval meetings" in the design process of ProMES (see Pritchard, 1990). The design team presents its proposal (i.e. key result areas, performance indicators, contingencies) to the management. Most often very serious discussions arise between management and the design team. These discussions reveal the basic expectations from both parties regarding their fundamental contribution to the organisation.

Another reason to use a participative design approach is the cognitive benefit of getting better ideas on how to define valid performance indicators and how to improve task strategies. Although Locke and Latham (1990) doubt the motivational (commitment) effect of participation they agree with a possible cognitive benefit. Kleingeld (1994) compared three experimental conditions in his study, using a quasi-experimental design: a participation condition, a transportation condition ("transporting" the same system to other units with only minimal participation) and a control condition. In the participation condition performance increases were substantial and significant compared to the control condition. Although performance in the transportation condition also increased significantly compared to the control condition, this increase was significantly smaller than the one obtained in the participation condition. He concludes that participation in the design of the system is the crucial factor. It should be noted that the units in the transportation condition after a long time (more than a year) reached about the same performance level as the units in the participation condition (however, attitudes towards the system and the feedback it provided remained more positive in the participation condition). It is not easy to disentangle the cognitive and the motivational effects of participation from his data, but nevertheless participation seemed to be crucial for both cognitive and motivational reasons.

Nowadays, in many organisations technology on the shop floor has become so complex that it is virtually impossible to design a goal-setting and feedback system without participation. This is simply because the expertise of shop floor employees is needed to design valid performance indicators.

Van Tuijl (1997) refers to possible sources of resistance during each implementation phase. He concludes that it is not easy to predict whether the reaction to a goal-setting and feedback system will be one of acceptance, compliance or rejection. However, a number of guidelines for the facilitator of the implementation process seem to be relevant:

- explain and share the necessity of performance improvement;
- demonstrate that people are a main source of performance variation;
- be sure that management really wants to invest in the system, e.g. by providing resources;
- bring differences of opinion to the surface;
- check whether the goal-setting and feedback system is compatible with other organisational control systems, e.g. the reward system;
- in case of lacking skills, provide training before and during development.

Following these guidelines can increase the chances of adoption of the goal-setting and feedback system in the organisation.

FACILITATING LEARNING IN THE IMPLEMENTATION PHASE OF PROMES

ProMES performance management systems are potentially effective tools for continuous improvement. One reason for that is that the core of such systems consists of valid performance indicators which are under the control of employees. Another reason is that employees, having participated in the design of their ProMES system, experience feelings of ownership towards it and, as a result, are willing to use the system as a control loop for self-regulation. However, participatory system design alone is not enough to sustain attempts towards productivity improvement in the long run. The latter requires that the system is actively, and again participatorily, used in an environment stimulating self-management and continuous learning and improvement.

In the phase of system design, the facilitator plays a crucial role in fostering employee participation. In the implementation phase, the immediate supervisor will have to take over this crucial role and adapt it to the demands of this new phase. The main difference between the two phases boils down to the different contents of the interaction among employees and between employees and the management. In the design phase, this inter-action is primarily concerned with the "what" of the performance to be delivered, i.e. the performance indicators and their relative importance. In the implementation phase, in-teraction largely concerns the "how" of the required performance, i.e. the question of effective task strategies. The supervisor will have to guide the employees through partici-patory problem-solving processes called for by ProMES feedback and aimed at directing employee attention towards applying available, or discovering new and more adequate task strategies. This section delineates effective supervisor behaviours for that purpose.

CRITICAL SUPERVISOR BEHAVIOUR DURING PROMES PERFORMANCE ENHANCEMENT SESSIONS

We will explore the ways in which supervisors should discuss a ProMES feedback report with their employees to achieve the desired effect, namely securing their willingness to work actively and self-managing on improving their performance.

Two kinds of supervisor behaviour will be looked at separately: supervisor behaviour in dealing with acceptance problems and supervisor behaviour aimed at achieving per-formance enhancement through the use of the feedback and goal setting. This twofold approach fits with the model of the accepted control loop (van Tuijl, 1997). The first question a supervisor should ask with regard to the performance of one of his employees reads: "Is there, in the eyes of this employee, an accepted discrepancy between feed-back and goals?" The second question is: "Given that there is an accepted discrepancy, does this person possess sufficient knowledge and skill to reduce the discrepancy?" Formulated in more simple terms: does the employee have a problem and if so does he or she have sufficient resources to solve the problem? The sets of critical supervisor behaviours designed to deal with these questions have been based on Latham and Saari (1979), Latham and Wexley (1981, 1994), Pritchard (1990), and on our own experiences in working with the ProMES method.

We will discuss these behaviours in the context of a ProMES system which has been developed in a service organisation. A short description of this ProMES system is given in the following case study.

CASE STUDY

A PROMES FEEDBACK SYSTEM FOR SERVICE TECHNICIANS

We will illustrate our experiences at the hand of one of the cases mentioned earlier, namely that of field service technicians in a region of a company that supplies and services photocopiers (Kleingeld, 1994). Each service region is headed by a supervisor and consists of approximately 20 service technicians, carrying out repairs and maintenance. Table 11.2 shows a feedback report which contains an overview of one technician's performance in a one-month period (as well as a six-month average).

TABLE 11.2   Example of a feedback report

ProMES feedback report page 1-Technician: Johan Karelse-Period: 01/99						
	Month			Moving average 6 months		
	Calls	Ind. score	Effect.	Calls	Ind. score	Effect.
1. Quality						
1.1. Mean Copies Between Calls (100)						
Copier model A	25	26300 copies	−1	164	23300 copies	−20
Copier model E	40	29500 copies	−24	226	27900 copies	−32
Average			**−15**			**−27**
1.2. % Repeat calls (70)						
Copier model A	25	8.0%	17	164	17.1%	−21
Copier model E	40	17.5%	−17	226	17.3%	−15
Average			**−4**			**−18**
2. Cost						
2.1. Labour time per call (50)						
Copier model A	25	97 min	12	164	87 min	22
Copier model E	40	90 min	17	226	90 min	17
Average			**15**			**19**
2.2. Parts cost per call (55)						
Copier model A	25	108,-	−20	164	75,-	0
Copier model E	40	123,-	6	226	121,-	5
Average			**−4**			**3**
Overall effectiveness			**−8**			**−23**

From the feedback report, it can be seen that the technicians consider themselves responsible for two responsibility areas: 'Quality' and 'Cost'. For each responsibility area, two performance indicators were developed. High-quality performance is demonstrated by a high average number of copies between two breakdowns (Mean Copies Between Calls) and by a low repeat call percentage (a repeat call refers to a breakdown followed by another breakdown within a very short space of time). A technician's performance on 'Cost' is measured by the average amount of time spent on each visit and the average price of spare parts used per visit.

A crucial element of each ProMES system is the performance effectiveness curve, also called 'contingency' (Pritchard, 1990). These curves are developed for each indicator

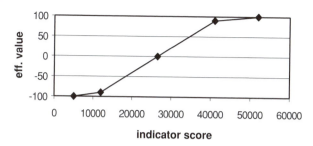

FIGURE 11.1 Example of a performance effectiveness curve (contingency) for the indicator: 'Mean Copies Between Calls'

included in a feedback report. Contingencies take into account the differences in importance between the indicators. Also, contingencies enable one to compare performance on different indicators and to obtain an overall score, summed across indicators. As an example, Figure 11.1 shows the contingency for the performance indicator 'Mean Copies Between Calls'. In this chapter, the actual construction of contingencies will not be dealt with (see, for a detailed discussion, Pritchard, 1990, and Pritchard & Roth, 1991). We will restrict ourselves to the following comments. Firstly, the relative importance of the indicators is reflected by the range of effectiveness scores on the vertical axis of the graph. Furthermore, on each performance indicator, the zero effectiveness level is attached to the indicator score that is assessed as 'not good but not bad either'. The effectiveness scores of different indicators can be added up, because they are all expressed in the same dimension.

A technician's work input involves different models of photocopiers with different characteristics (technical options, user intensity). Thus, the performance of a technician depends on the models of photocopying machines he or she has to service. From the report, one can see that the technician has realised on the indicator 'Mean Copies Between Calls', an average of 26,300 copies between two breakdowns for copier model A, equivalent to an effectiveness score of −1 (see Figure 11.1). For another model (copier model E), on which the technician has also worked, a higher indicator score but a lower effectiveness score has been realised. The reason is that the characteristics of model E are different from those of model A, which has been taken into account in the construction of the performance–effectiveness curves.

ALTERNATIVE APPROACHES TO PERFORMANCE FEEDBACK

The literature on performance appraisal (see, for example, Latham & Wexley, 1981, 1994) distinguishes three basic approaches a supervisor can adopt in performance appraisal sessions: 'tell and sell', 'tell and listen', and 'problem-solving'. The 'tell and sell' style is a one-way approach; the manager presents his[1] assessment of the performance achieved and explains what he wants to see in the future. This style does not fit in the ProMES approach which regards participation as a precondition for achieving consensus on the need for improvement. In the 'tell and listen' style, the supervisor not only presents his opinion, but also listens to the opinions of his employees on the subject. Although this approach gives the employees more opportunity to voice their opinions, the session is limited to an assessment of the performance achieved and lacks a future-oriented outlook. The 'problem-solving' style gives employees plenty of opportunity for active participation in developing ideas for improving performance in the future. This approach is, therefore, considered the most appropriate one for the ProMES performance enhancement sessions.

ELABORATION OF THE PROBLEM-SOLVING APPROACH

The discussions between supervisor and technician on feedback reports have the objective of stimulating the technician to use ProMES as a system for self-management. Performance enhancement sessions, most certainly at the start of the implementation phase, will consist of two parts. The first part of a performance enhancement session aims at overcoming resistance (resistance to attempts to performance improvement in general or resistance to specific components of the ProMES system), while the second part focuses on giving feedback and setting goals. For both parts, critical supervisor behaviours will be discussed. The reason for this division into two parts is that in all probability technicians' understanding of the purpose and technicalities of ProMES and of the discussions in which they are about to participate will vary considerably. Technicians may differ in the extent to which they endorse the objectives underlying the system, the extent to which they understand the system, and the extent to which they accept the system. Therefore, in the first part the supervisor must become aware of the attitudes of the person with whom he is dealing. For instance, a technician may come up with all sorts of complaints that actually stem from his resistance to or lack of understanding of the system or from both. Obstacles such as these will have to be removed before one can begin to work towards the concept of 'self-management' in performance enhancement sessions. Although the actual discussion topics in the two parts differ, the approach is rather similar, because both parts concentrate on the detection and solution of problems.

Consonant with the 'problem solving' style and with one of the main techniques of the ProMES method, a '*discussion until consensus*' approach is recommended for both parts. There are two steps in this approach: the joint generation and evaluation of ideas. The first step involves jointly listing all the issues considered relevant, while the evaluation step involves jointly sifting the wheat from the chaff. The discussion until consensus approach has general applicability. For example, in dealing with resistance, the sources of resistance are first identified and then discussed to ensure that everyone understands what is meant. The origins of each source of resistance are then listed and assessed and the main ones selected. The next step is to decide what to do about them. Actions are proposed and assessed and the most promising ones are selected.

The second part, that of providing feedback and setting targets, will start off in the same way, this time by identifying discrepancies between feedback and (explicit or implicit) goals. Next, causes of these discrepancies will be generated, and so on.

PART 1: CRITICAL BEHAVIOURS IN IDENTIFYING AND OVERCOMING RESISTANCE

Part 1 involves reaching agreement about the purpose (performance improvement) and the content (performance enhancement sessions based on ProMES feedback reports) of the new working method. In this part the objectives of the discussions are twofold: to make clear the reasons for introducing the new procedure (the crucial importance for the company to improve productivity) and to demonstrate how, through the new procedure (the ProMES feedback discussions), an individual can contribute to productivity improvement.

There is no point in actually starting the new procedure until consensus has been reached between supervisor and technician on the necessity, significance and feasibility of the new procedure. Well-reasoned arguments will have to be provided. These can follow the same lines as those used at the start of the development of the ProMES system: productivity improvement is a must for the company, and focusing on and working together on (in this instance) individual productivity is a justified activity. This can easily be done by discussing actual data on the technician's recent performance. The discussion should have a problem-solving character: technician and supervisor together analyse the technician's performance and reach conclusions as to how, if necessary, productivity improvement can be realised.

Eventual consequences of working according to the new procedure should also be examined. For example, if after serious and constructive attempts to apply the new procedure, it would appear that the technician should not be expected to be able to work more effectively or efficiently than he has already been doing (i.e. he has reached his ceiling), this situation should be accepted as a fact of life. Also, if agreements have been made with regard to payment by results, it should be explained in which way ProMES scores will be used to determine, for example, the amount of an annual performance bonus. Only after the technician and supervisor have solved all the problems that have come up during Part 1, i.e. only after the conclusion has been arrived that embarking on the new procedure is a justified and worthwhile step, Part 2 can be initiated, i.e. the sessions during which feedback is discussed and goals are set.

Critical supervisor behaviours for Part 1

- *Explain the necessity of the new procedure (productivity improvement is a must for the company).*
- *Explain the purpose of the new procedure (an aid to being able to work more effectively and efficiently).*
- *Clearly explain what the new procedure entails (working with ProMES feedback reports, employing a problem-solving approach).*
- *Explain that performance improvement is possible with ProMES ('there is always room for improvement', e.g. all technicians setting the priorities agreed upon in the ProMES system would already be a good start).*
- *Explain what the changes will actually mean for the individual technician; do not circumvent potential negative consequences, tell the truth ("no surprises"). It also follows that one should elaborate upon the advantages ("sell the benefits").*

Objective performance data will be made available and discussed. This could mean that the technician will find out that he has been performing less well than he had always thought. This can be hard to swallow and a supervisor should already at this moment be aware of a technician's need to save face. A discussion about task strategies can bring into the open the fact that the technician in some respects did not follow the prescribed strategies. This can be accepted in good spirit but with the proviso that it should not happen again. Eventual consequences of the continuation of bad practices will have to be explained too. It should be made clear for instance that such continuation will not improve the technician's position (it may have consequences for his performance appraisal). Furthermore, a number of conditions, such as working the required number of hours, should be set. In this way, the technician's normal activities will become more sharply defined and the impression might arise that his room to manoeuvre has been somewhat restricted. In a way that is true. On the other hand, role clarity will improve (as it already did for those who actively participated in the development of the system).

• *Ask the technician for his opinion (questions, misgivings, objections but also endorsement of the proposed new procedure) and listen to him with an open mind.*

It is very important to be able to empathise with the technician and show understanding of his present feelings. Moreover, new aspects that have not been thought of before may suddenly come up.

• *Ask the technician for his help in making the new procedure a success.*

This again can prompt him to think about the "ifs and the buts", which also helps in gaining insight into what he really thinks.

• *Ask the technician to think about solutions to the objections he may have raised about the new procedure.*
• *If, in this particular session, the technician cannot overcome his objections, even with your help, ask him to think matters through and arrange a date for a follow-up discussion.*
• *If the technician expresses his endorsement of the objectives, procedure and conditions, start up the actual feedback discussion.*

Part 2: Performance Enhancement through Feedback and Goal-Setting

Giving feedback

The main points of the structure of a feedback session are as follows. First, the supervisor should explain the purpose of the discussion to the technician. Then, the feedback reports from the preceding period(s) should be examined together with the technician to get a detailed picture of the performance realised and to find out whether it coincides with the technician's own idea of his performance. They should find out how this performance relates to the standards the technicians imposes on himself and to his abilities. They should then try to identify the causes of the scores obtained, for example, by looking at working methods the technician employed and comparing these to his colleagues' methods, and by looking at factors which help or hinder the technician to perform well. After bottlenecks have been identified, agreements can be made about contributions they both can make to overcoming these bottlenecks. At a following session, one should decide together whether the agreements have been kept.

Critical supervisor behaviours in giving feedback

Based on the above we propose the following supervisor behaviours for giving feedback:

- *Explain the purpose of the discussion: analysing feedback reports together, drawing up plans of action and making agreements will help the technician to use ProMES as a self-management system.*
- *Ask the technician to give a precise description of how his performance has been developing in the preceding period both overall and for each of the indicators.*

This is to establish whether the technician is fully aware of his main areas of responsibility, his performance in these areas and how his final score is obtained; allowing the technician to describe details of his feedback reports himself will show whether he clearly understands the system and can interpret his own scores.

- *Ask the technician if he recognises himself in the feedback report. Does the report reflect his own ideas about his performance?*

This question is not designed to find out whether he reacts rationally to what the report apparently says about his performance, but whether he accepts the image of himself ("yes, that's me") or rejects it ("that can't be me") or is not affected by it at all ("if it says so then it will be so, but it's all the same to me whatever it says"). Only the first response reflects real acceptance. The second response at least indicates that he cares; it might in the long run develop into acceptance. The last response is the most problematic one, because it signals indifference. To bring the technician into closer contact with his own performance, it may be wise to ask him to make some estimates of indicator scores. If the picture given in the report leads to acceptance, the estimates he is asked to make about, for example, the average labour time spent on a certain copier model, will be closely related to the real indicator scores. In case of rejection or a 'don't know' answer considerable discrepancies may become apparent. As long as the image presented is not really seen as a reflection of the technician's true performance, further progression is not possible. Quite likely the only thing to do is to arrange with the technician that in the coming period he keeps track of his own scores on a specific indicator for a certain copier model and compares his own observations with the scores in the feedback report. It should be kept in mind that indicator scores with positive effectiveness values will be more readily accepted compared to scores with negative effectiveness values.

- *Ask the technician to assess his overall performance and his performance on the various performance components in terms of the standards he imposes on himself: is he satisfied with the picture that is presented (assuming he considers the picture to be correct)?*

Again, a number of responses are possible: a technician who sets himself no goals has no basis whatsoever on which to answer the question and, if he is honest, will say he does not know. Because he does not know, he may also say that he is satisfied. So, satisfaction can indicate either that his own norms or goals have been met or that he has no norms or goals at all, and therefore accepts any outcome. Dissatisfaction can also result from different sources. A technician may have clear ideas about the level of performance he feels he ought to be able to attain and be dissatisfied with himself because he has not yet attained that level. He can also let himself be guided by the plus and minus scores of the ProMES system and be dissatisfied as long as he is in what he interprets as the danger zone (negative scores), or until he can positively distinguish himself from his colleagues (by scoring higher than the regional average).

A technician who is dissatisfied with his performance and who at the same time has positive expectations of improving his performance, has the right mindset for the next step: finding out about ways to improve his performance. The same applies to a technician who is satisfied with the fact that his performance shows an upward trend and who is thereby stimulated to try to improve again at the next occasion (see: Locke and Latham's High Performance Cycle (1990)). This also means that the time has come to ask the technician how he views his own potential (his expectations about possible improvements in the future and his ideas about his competencies).

- *Ask the technician if the performance results given in the feedback report are a valid reflection of his abilities.*

Does the technician believe that, given his present level of knowledge and skills, his performance in the preceding period is the maximum he can achieve, or does he consider himself capable of improving his overall score, within the constraints of the existing situation?

- *Ask the technician to explain his line of reasoning in answering the previous question and discuss his line of reasoning together.*
- *Ask the technician what he could change in his working methods to improve his productivity.*
- *Ask the technician what others could change in their working methods in order for him to improve his productivity.*
- *List all the ways in which productivity could be improved and rank them in order of feasibility (degree of difficulty, conditions that have to be met, etc.) and effect (how much productivity improvement can be expected).*
- *Choose the option that best combines feasibility and effect.*
- *Make arrangements about implementing this option ('who does what by when; when will effects become visible?').*

Setting goals

A peculiar aspect of this case study is that the performance effectiveness curves are based on average performance data of about 250 technicians from all over the country. Hence, maximums, minimums and 'zero points' reflect national averages which will not coincide with each and every technician's performance range. That implies that for some technicians negative scores will be difficult to accept and also that goals set in terms of positive scores will be considered altogether impossible to obtain by a substantial number of technicians. Therefore, setting specific, difficult but attainable goals for an individual technician against the background of that individual's performance range, should certainly be one of the features of the performance enhancement sessions of the supervisor and the technician.

Criteria for effective goals

Effective goals have the following features (e.g. Locke & Latham, 1990): they are specific, difficult and attainable. Above all, they should be accepted. To some extent, acceptance will be the result of the way in which the previous part of the performance enhancement sessions has been handled; discussing feedback and analysing the situation. If feedback is understood, recognised and accepted, and if a feeling of dissatisfaction exists about performance results (in the sense of 'it ought to be better' or 'could I still do better?'), and if, moreover, ideas exist about the way in which performance might be improved (if adequate task strategies are available) and the prospects for doing so are regarded with optimism, setting specific, difficult, and attainable goals may be no more than just the 'finishing touch'.

Critical supervisor behaviours in setting goals

In this case study, the following steps would be appropriate in setting goals:

- *Stimulate the technician to have a look at his performance during the past six months and ask him to make a suitable estimate of a reasonable performance for himself, (not good, not bad), a suitable estimate of a maximum performance and a suitable estimate of a minimum performance.*

This question can be asked at several levels, which are overall performance, performance on a specific indicator across copier models, overall performance per copier model, or indicator performance per copier model. Quite probably, it will not be immediately clear to every technician how his overall performance, expressed in terms of ProMES scores, has been arrived at. Also, he will probably not be able to understand which changes in behaviour will cause his performance to rise or fall on certain indicators. It might also not be immediately clear what consequences (through the contingencies) performance variations on separate indicators will have for his overall performance. Probably it would be best to start discussions at the lowest level possible, i.e. at the level of separate indicators per copier model. From there, and depending on the situation (see below), one can turn to either overall indicator level or to the level of overall performance per copier model.

In the previous part, discussions about the feedback reports should have resulted in the selection of one or two indicators which, at first sight, would seem to be the most suitable to direct 'improvement activities' to. Or one or two models should have been selected on which the technician frequently scores poorly, which suggests that 'improvement activities' are needed. Although Pritchard (1990, p. 170) advocates setting goals in terms of overall effectiveness scores, it is obvious that this is very difficult in this case study (as long as the technician does not understand how the overall scores have been arrived at).

Suppose the diagnosis reveals that the technician scores poorly on a certain indicator. In that event, a good starting point would be to assess the performance variation of the technician on the horizontal axis (indicator scores) of the performance effectiveness curve of the indicator in question (if necessary this can be done for each of the models under consideration). Then the question is asked: what do you consider 'not good, not bad', what is your maximum, what is your minimum?

- *Ask the technician if he can account for the performance fluctuations on the selected indicator.*

In most cases, there will be performance fluctuations. In the previous part, more obvious variations in performance have served as the criterion to select indicators for goal setting. Probably, the controllability of performance on the indicator in question will become a discussion item (as it should have been in the development phase), and perhaps that is a good thing. Is the top score due to pure luck and the lowest score due to bad luck, or do the variations depend on the technician's behaviour? If the latter is the case, one must ask what the technician actually did to achieve a high score and what he did not do, or what he did differently, when he got a low score? Perhaps, when he achieved a low score factors played a role which could be influenced by himself, the company, the supervisor or the customer. What were those factors that contributed to his low score and similarly, what factors contributed to his high score? In that case, what measures should the technician, company, supervisor or the customer take to ensure that the necessary conditions for achieving a high score are in place?

- *Ask the technician what sort of agreements could be made in order to fulfil the conditions necessary for consistently high scores in the coming period, or in order to change the technician's behaviour in such a way that consistently high scores would result.*

In fact, the way in which the technician and others influence the technician's performance is re-examined. The factors that have the greatest impact on the technician's performance are selected. The discussion is focused on what should be done, by whom, starting by when, in order to achieve constantly high scores. It is important to focus this discussion on the issues the technician is able to influence himself and to avoid the outcome of the discussion becoming a list of excuses or a lists of tasks for others. The question, "What is your influence on the performance variation on this indicator?" must therefore be the focal point.

- *Ask the technician what would be the specific ProMES score on the indicator in question in the coming period, if everybody kept entirely to the above agreements.*
- *Agree to set this ProMES score as a specific, difficult but attainable goal for the coming period, as this score should result if the technician kept entirely to the agreements (also assuming that others responsible for a number of conditions keep to theirs).*

A specific goal means that a target is formulated in terms of a specified score on a specific indicator, or on a set of indicators (relating to a certain area of responsibility), or on all indicators together: the overall ProMES score. Difficult but attainable means that the technician, on the basis of his insight into his competencies, gives himself a chance of at least 15% to attain the goal. If great uncertainty exists on the task-strategies required to achieve a higher performance, it is advisable not to decide on specific difficult goals but to introduce a period of experimentation to explore the relationships between cause and effect.

Use of the critical behaviours

In the case setting, the critical behaviours were discussed with the region supervisors and applied in the performance enhancement sessions that were conducted. There is some evidence of a positive relation between the degree to which a supervisor actually used the critical behaviours and the technicians' satisfaction with the usefulness of the ProMES system and the usefulness of the performance enhancement meetings (Kleingeld, 1994). The critical behaviours appear to be generalisable to other settings where ProMES feedback is used for enhancing the performance of individuals. The critical behaviours may also be employed with performance feedback generated from other sources (perhaps with a few alterations, for example if the weighting method differs from the contingencies ProMES uses). It does seem essential that the company's views on employee participation are in line with the approach chosen here (discussion until consensus, 'problem solving' supervisory style).

CONCLUSION

Implementing goal-setting and feedback systems in practice is not easy. Organisational context factors determine to a large extent the success of the implementation process. The fit between the basic values of management and the other organisation members seems to be decisive for success or failure of the implementation. When problems arise, in all four phases described, conflicts can often be interpreted as reflecting differences in these underlying values. The role of the facilitator is essential in helping the organisation to solve these conflicts. As such, the process is much more critical than the actual design of the elements of the system.

To sustain attempts towards productivity improvement in the long run, it is essential that the goal-setting and feedback system is used in an environment which motivates employees to actively engage in performance improvement activities. The last part of this chapter addressed the important role of the supervisor in assisting employees in problem solving and the development of better task strategies.

Looking back to the experiences of implementing goal-setting and feedback systems in practice, probably the most important issue is that installing these systems implies in fact a process of organisation development. Other systems to manage the human resources have to be made compatible to the goal-setting and feedback system if it is supposed to be there for a long time. Practitioners should therefore realise that the commitment of many organisation members, and in particular the management, is needed to make the implementation successful.

NOTE

1. To support the readability of this chapter, we have decided not to use references such as 'he or she' continuously. At the start of the twenty-first century, the number of men in management positions still exceeds the number of women. Even more so, all supervisors in the case study we will focus on were men. Therefore, we will use 'he', 'him', etc. The reader should read these as 'he and she', 'him and her', etc. To maintain consistency in the text, the same will be done for subordinates.

REFERENCES

Algera, J. A., & Kleinbeck, U. (1997). Performance improvement programmes in Europe (foreword). *European Journal of Work and Organizational Psychology*, **6**, 257–260.

Algera, J. A., Monhemius, L., & Wijnen, C. J. D. (1997). Quality improvement: Combining ProMES and SPC to work smarter. *European Journal of Work and Organizational Psychology*, **6**, 261–278.

Algera, J. A., & Van den Hurk, A. M. C. M. (1997). Testing the feasibility of ProMES before implementation: A case study in the Dutch steel industry. In R. D. Pritchard (Ed.), *Productivity measurement and improvement: Organizational case studies*. New York: Praeger.

Algera, J. A., Van Tuijl, H. F. J. M., & Janssen, P. M. (1995). *Pitfalls in implementing participative management of work groups: Dutch experiences in the design process of ProMES*. Paper presented at the conference on participative management of work groups, October 19–20, Dortmund, Germany.

Janssen, P. M., Van Berkel, A., & Stolk, J. (1995). ProMES as part of a new management strategy. In R. D. Pritchard (Ed.), *Productivity measurement and improvement: Organizational case studies*. New York: Praeger.

Kleingeld, P. A. M. (1994). *Performance management in a field service department: Design and transportation of a productivity measurement and enhancement system (ProMES)*. Unpublished doctoral dissertation. Faculty of Technology Management, Eindhoven University of Technology.

Latham, G. P., & Saari, L. M. (1979). Application of social-learning theory to training supervisors through behaviour modelling. *Journal of Applied Psychology*, **64** (3), 239–246.

Latham, G. P., & Wexley, K. N. (1981, 1994). *Increasing productivity through performance appraisal*. Reading, Mass.: Addison-Wesley.

Locke, E. A., & Latham, G. P. (1990). *A theory of goal setting and task performance*. Englewood Cliffs: Prentice-Hall.

Meeks, M. (1994). *Continuous improvement through performance management: Application of a performance management system within section CGSM of OFS2, Hoogovens IJmuiden*. Unpublished masters thesis. Faculty of Technology Management, Eindhoven University of Technology.

Pritchard, R. D. (1990). *Measuring and improving organizational productivity: A practical guide*. New York: Praeger.

Pritchard, R. D. (Ed.) (1995). *Productivity measurement and improvement: Organizational case studies*. New York: Praeger.

Pritchard, R. D., & Roth, Ph. J. (1991). Accounting for non-linear utility functions in composite measures of productivity and performance. *Organisational Behaviour and Human Decision Processes*, **50**, 341–359.

Rodgers, R., & Hunter, J. E. (1991). Impact of Management By Objectives on organizational productivity. *Journal of Applied Psychology, Monograph*, **76**, 322–336.

Schmidt, K.-H., & Kleinbeck, U. (1997). Relationships between group-based performance measures, feedback and organizational context factors. *European Journal of Work and Organizational Psychology*, **6**, 303–319.

Van Tuijl, H. F. J. M. (1997). Critical success factors in developing ProMES: will the end result be an "accepted control loop"? *Leadership and Organisation Development Journal*, **18**, 346–354.

Van Tuijl, H. F. J. M., Kleingeld, A., Schmidt, K., Kleinbeck, U., Pritchard, R. D., & Algera, J. A. (1997). Measuring and enhancing organizational productivity by means of ProMES: Three practical implications. *European Journal of Work and Organizational Psychology*, **6**, 279–301.

CHAPTER 12

Enhancing Performance through Training

Beryl Hesketh and **Karolina Ivancic**
The University of Sydney, Sydney, Australia

SUMMARY

Organizations will increasingly need to select and train "expert" employees who can perform at the highest level if they are to maintain their competitive edge in the expanding global business environment. We argue that in demanding workplaces that are characterized by constant change, training for adaptive expertise provides a basis for developing the cognitive and metacognitive skills needed to deal with variable job requirements. Several approaches to training (instruction in rules and examples; behavioral modeling and role playing; simulation training; active learning) are discussed in relation to how well they accord with fundamental training principles that promote adaptability. Factors in the organizational environment that can influence transfer of training are also discussed. The complexity of the transfer process and the impact of moderating variables on training outcomes highlight the need for accurate assessment of training needs and ongoing evaluation of training effectiveness.

Psychological Management of Individual Performance. Edited by Sabine Sonnentag.
© 2002 John Wiley & Sons, Ltd.

INTRODUCTION

Globalization and the need to compete at international standards of performance means that effective organizational training is more important than ever before. Trainers are expected to develop a highly skilled "expert" workforce that will deliver to organizations a competitive edge, and are under pressure to demonstrate that their programs lead to genuine performance benefits. In line with these heightened expectations, modern training has become a sophisticated, technology-driven industry. However, it is essential that the applications of training aids and methodologies are in keeping with sound learning principles that are derived from the research literature. These principles need to be applied to the organizational training program and evaluated systematically to ensure that training meets research-based standards of best practice. In this chapter, we review findings from the literatures on expertise, cognition, and organizational psychology, that provide research benchmarks for designing and evaluating training.

IDENTIFYING TRAINING NEEDS

The usual starting point when designing training is to determine training needs based on an analysis of task or job requirements within the broader context of organizational goals (Tannenbaum & Yukl, 1992; see Table 12.1 for an overview of pre-training strategies for enhancing transfer). A good match between the perceived and actual training needs of employees is required to ensure that the course content is relevant to employees, thereby motivating participation in training activities (Smith-Jentsch, Jentsch, Payne, & Salas, 1996). During the training needs analysis (TNA), the knowledge, skills, and attitudes required for effective job performance can be identified using a variety of methods, including observing others performing the job, interviewing expert employees, conducting group discussions, or administering questionnaires.

   Although the TNA specifies the skills required to perform the task, it neglects the skills that are required to ensure the transfer of skills from training to the workplace that may be identified in a Transfer of Training Needs Analysis (TTNA) (Hesketh, 1997a, 1997b). The TTNA takes into account the context in which trainees will carry out their jobs, and the cognitive and meta-cognitive skills that are required to bridge the gap between training and on-the-job performance. For example, as part of the TTNA, consideration may be given to whether job requirements are consistent or inconsistent, and whether future change is likely (Tannenbaum, 1997). Where changing job requirements are apparent,

TABLE 12.1   Pre-training strategies for enchancing transfer

Training needs analysis (Tannenbaum & Yukl, 1992)
- Identify knowledge, skills and attitudes required by trainees for effective job performance
- Identify organizational training needs

Transfer of training needs analysis (Hesketh, 1997b)
- Identify meta-cognitive skills required for effective job performance (e.g., planning, monitoring, evaluation)
- Identify transfer dimensions (e.g., variability of task demands, the environment in which the task is to be performed, likelihood of future change)

---

then the cognitive and meta-cognitive skills required to cope with change may need to be identified. Where possible these should be identified as part of selection, but training may also be required. One of these skills may be an orientation toward effortful processing that motivates trainees to understand the principles underlying a task, thereby permitting them to adapt their skills appropriately when task demands vary.

Although the benefits of the TTNA are still speculative at this stage and require empirical verification and theoretical development, we suspect that an analysis of the dimensions of generalization (time, place, type of problem, context, etc.) along which transfer must occur will place a transfer frame over a traditional TNA. Future research should elaborate methods for doing this, although the data-gathering approaches are likely to be similar to those used for TNA, but within a different conceptual framework. The TNA and TTNA can in theory provide clear outcome goals and learning process goals respectively which influence the structure of the training evaluation, as discussed in detail later in this chapter.

The shift toward sophisticated training methods that utilize computer technology has been accompanied by a change in the nature of skills being trained, from procedural skills that can be acquired through rote memorization and over-learning, to cognitive skills such as strategic planning and decision-making that involve high-level meta-cognitive abilities. The new focus on cognitive and meta-cognitive skills is apparent also in current conceptions of the nature of expertise. The advantages conferred by expertise include the ability to overcome the usual capacity limits of working memory by "chunking" information into meaningful units (Chase & Simon, 1972; Feltovich, Spiro, & Coulson, 1997), the classification of problems based on their underlying solution (Chi, Feltovich, & Glaser, 1981), and the subsequent use of forward problem-solving strategies to attain the desired outcome (Patel & Groen, 1991). These abilities depend in part on the formation of relatively abstract representations such as schemata that are hierarchically structured to facilitate the storage, organization, and retrieval of information (Thorndyke, 1984). The schemata of novices differ from those of experts in that the latter are more likely to represent the structural, solution-relevant features of a problem (Novick, 1988). Because schemata contain relatively little task-specific information, they can be applied to a relatively broad range of problems (Hesketh, Andrews, & Chandler, 1989), but may lead to inflexible behavior if they are applied without sensitivity to the conditions for application of the schema (Feltovich et al., 1997). Another feature of expertise is the automatization of skills with extended practice (Shiffrin & Schneider, 1977). Automatization permits rapid, effortless skill execution while freeing attention for other tasks (Anderson, 1982), but creates inflexibility when task demands vary.

Recognition of the shortcomings of expert performance have led to the distinction between "routine expertise", where superior performance is limited largely to routine problems within the domain of one's expertise, and "adaptive expertise", where the ability to adapt to changing task demands and to invent solutions to novel problems permits the solution of non-routine problems or problems outside one's domain (Ford & Weissbein, 1997; Smith, Ford, & Kozlowski, 1997). Adaptive expertise depends on the development of meta-cognitive skills such as planning, monitoring, and evaluation for regulating cognitive functions (Kanfer & Kanfer, 1991). If existing schemata are inadequate for successful task completion, meta-cognitive activity enables individuals to recognize that a known schemata must be modified or that a new schemata must be developed, and to evaluate the effectiveness of the implemented solution. Given that in many work environments "the 'unusual' is becoming much more usual" (Feltovich et al., 1997, p. 141), training for adaptive expertise confers important advantages, although there may be circumstances in which the development of routine expertise is preferable. A thorough analysis of the organization's training needs will provide valuable information about whether training should be oriented toward promoting routine or adaptive expertise.

TRAINING DESIGN PRINCIPLES

General principles used in the design of training programs have been qualified by more recent experimental evidence indicating that the effectiveness of some training interventions depends to a large extent on the influence of moderating variables (see Table 12.2 for an overview of training design principles). The length of the delay between the training and evaluation is now known to be one such moderator of training outcomes. Some training methods which boost initial training performance do not promote longer-term skill retention and transfer, whereas other training methods that initially produce less favourable outcomes lead to better long-term results. Training methods which facilitate longer-term retention and transfer are often more challenging, and therefore depress initial performance even though the level of learning is increased (Druckman & Bjork, 1994; Schmidt & Bjork, 1992). The discrepancy between immediate versus delayed training outcomes may lead to the adoption of less effective training practices, either because trainers are unaware of the longer-term consequences or because they are under pressure to deliver short-term gains (Hesketh, 1997a). The sequencing of course content, the type of information-processing strategies that are encouraged by training methods, and practice and feedback schedules are all aspects of the training program that need to be considered when designing training for longer-term outcomes. Furthermore, there is a growing recognition of the need to practice during training those cognitive and meta-cognitive processes that are important for subsequent transfer, and that will facilitate the development of adaptive expertise.

Sequencing of Course Content

Course content is usually sequenced so that it progresses from easy to hard, or from general principles to specific instances. This approach ensures that fundamental concepts are acquired before moving on to higher-order concepts, and eliminates the confusion

TABLE **12.2**   Training design strategies for enhancing transfer

---

- Use variable training tasks and conditions (Schmidt & Bjork, 1992)
- Encourage transfer appropriate processing e.g., problem solving, factual retrieval (Morris et al., 1977)
- Provide extended practice with training sessions that are distributed over time (Ericsson et al., 1993; Schmidt & Bjork, 1992)
- Provide appropriate feedback in terms of timing, specificity, and frequency (Kluger & DeNisi, 1996)
- Provide abstract theory in terms of rules and principles accompanied by illustrative examples (Gick & Holyoak, 1983; Nisbett et al., 1987)
- Adopt training methods that provide opportunities for practice and active learning, e.g., behavioral modeling, role playing, simulation, learning by exploration (Frese, 1995; Ivancic & Hesketh, 1995/1996).

---

that is often encountered with a hard-to-easy or variable sequencing (Gick & Holyoak, 1987). It also allows trainees to experience success early in training, thereby enhancing perceptions of self-efficacy that are critical to positive training outcomes (Ford, Smith, Weissbein, Gully, & Salas, 1998). However, at some point more challenging problems need to be phased into the training program, as variability and difficulty are key conditions for transfer (Schmidt & Bjork, 1992). Studies of problem solving have shown that, in some cases, transfer problems are solved more easily when individuals practice on a harder problem in training (Reed, Ernst, & Banerji, 1974; Klaczynski & Laipple, 1993). In the same way in which athletes benefit from training under more difficult conditions than those under which they will eventually compete, employees too may benefit from training to a standard that is somewhat more demanding than that usually required in the workplace. Typically this requires effort on the part of the trainee, and hence motivation has to be high.

There are obvious limits to the benefits of increasing the difficulty of training. If training is too difficult, the capacity of employees will be exceeded and motivation to engage in further training will be reduced. An optimum sequencing of the course content appears to involve the initial mastery of several relatively easy problems, followed by increasingly harder problems that eventually meet or exceed the level of difficulty that will be encountered in the workplace. Computer-based training involving self-paced interactive exercises may be useful in ensuring that the level of difficulty of the training problem is appropriate for the current competence of individual trainees. Given that individual differences in rates of learning and learning capacity are usually quite large, it is not easy to ensure that the difficulty level is appropriate for all participants when training is undertaken in groups.

ENCOURAGE APPROPRIATE INFORMATION-PROCESSING

Current research on learning and memory demonstrates the importance of ensuring that trainees practice appropriate information-processing strategies during training. This idea is apparent in the work of Downs and Perry (1984) who suggested that different learning strategies (memorizing, understanding, doing) may be required depending on the type of material to be mastered (facts, concepts, or procedural tasks). A more specific hypothesis is that transfer will be achieved to the degree that processes involved in training and transfer overlap (Morris, Bransford, & Franks, 1977). Effective training, therefore, should create the same information-processing demands as the transfer environment, i.e., the transfer appropriate processing principle. Support for this hypothesis has been obtained by Needham and Begg (1991). They found that training based on rote memory facilitated the recall of factual information, whereas training based on problem solving facilitated solving an analogous problem. Similarly, Lockhart, Lamon, and Gick (1988) found that a clue word was used to solve a problem when the clue word was presented initially in puzzle form, but not when the clue word was memorized. More recently, using a driving simulator for the research, Ivancic and Hesketh (2000) found that drivers avoided accidents when training also required them to learn to actively develop strategies for preventing similar errors, but not when training involved watching a video of a driver demonstrating the correct strategies.

The similarity of training and transfer information-processing strategies appears to be critical because these processes establish the context in which training occurs. How the information is presented in training (as a fact to be learned or as a problem to be solved) is often encoded into its representation. Consequently, if the training and transfer contexts are represented differently, information acquired during training may not be accessed because it is not perceived as relevant (Holyoak, 1984). The need for appropriate information processing again highlights the importance of identifying the conditions of the transfer environment during the Transfer of Training Needs Analysis (Hesketh, 1997b). The extent to which effective work performance depends on processes such as memorization or problem solving should be identified, and training designed accordingly to provide practice opportunities.

PRACTICE SCHEDULES

Research on expertise points to the importance of sustained practice over extended periods for the attainment of high skill levels. Ericsson, Krampe, and Tesch-Roemer (1993) argue that deliberate practice over a ten-year period is usually required to achieve expert status. Although this degree of practice is outside the scope of most organizational training programs, training methods that provide practice opportunities, such as role playing or error training, should be used where possible to ensure that newly acquired skills are mastered during training.

Massed practice in a short period of time leads to rapid skill acquisition, whereas retention is improved when practice sessions are distributed over time (Schmidt & Bjork, 1992). Distributed practice not only prevents fatigue, but also provides additional opportunities for relearning aspects of the task that have been forgotten since the previous session. Similarly, although consistent practice produces high levels of performance during training, variable practice leads to better generalization (Gick & Holyoak, 1987; Schmidt & Bjork, 1992). Where the training needs analysis has identified change as a feature of the work environment, variable practice provides the opportunity to engage in transfer appropriate processes related to adapting to changing demands. Nevertheless, consistent practice may be appropriate in jobs where task demands are constant and a reasonably high level of performance is required relatively quickly. In fact, skill automatization (which is a feature of routine expertise) requires consistent task demands at some levels (Carlson & Lundy, 1992). Importantly, continued practice after training ends, in the form of opportunities to perform trained skills on the job, is essential—an issue discussed later in this chapter.

FEEDBACK

Although it is generally believed that feedback improves learning and performance, more recent research indicates that the effect of feedback is variable and may even impede learning. The timing, specificity, and frequency with which feedback is delivered all influence the degree to which trainees benefit from the intervention (Kluger & DeNisi, 1996). For example, training performance tends to improve as the frequency with which feedback is delivered increases. However, if feedback is given too frequently, trainees may come to rely on external feedback without developing internal methods for assessing their own performance, with the consequence that performance declines when the feedback is withdrawn under transfer conditions (Schmidt & Bjork, 1992).

Although overly frequent feedback can interfere with transfer, it is important to note that, in an organizational context, employees often suffer from too little rather than too much feedback (Ilgen, Fisher, & Taylor, 1979). Feedback serves important informational and motivational functions (Frese, 1995; Ivancic & Hesketh, 1995/1996), both of which can be used to enhance training and transfer. Positive feedback reinforces good performance and creates a supportive transfer climate (Tracey, Tannenbaum, & Kavanagh, 1995) whereas negative feedback motivates trainees to update and revise inadequate schemata (Frese, 1995). Although negative feedback plays an important corrective role, the benefits of learning from one's errors is often overlooked because of a reluctance on the part of trainers to deliver, and trainees to accept, negative feedback (Ilgen et al., 1979). Trainees may need to learn to develop an error-tolerant attitude by participating in training which promotes a mastery orientation (Hesketh & Frese, 2000). Mastery goals are associated with the tendency to view obstacles as "challenges" and to persevere in the face of failure (Dweck & Leggett, 1988), thereby focusing attention on the potential to learn from mistakes. Mastery goals are related to increased meta-cognitive activity, which in turn is related to increased knowledge, skill acquisition, and self-efficacy (Ford et al., 1998). Although mastery goals are particularly important early in training, performance goals that emphasize the expert, errorless execution of a skill may need to be given more prominence as training progresses (Kraiger, Ford & Salas, 1993).

TRAINING METHODS

One of the key decisions facing trainers when selecting a training method is the extent to which it permits the course content to be presented as specific to the task or more generic. Traditionally, rules and principles have been favoured because their generality provides a mechanism for transfer (Nisbett, Fong, Lehmann, & Cheng, 1987). However, recent years have seen an increase in the popularity of "situated learning" or "problem-based learning" which situates learning in a particular context. Problem-solving strategies and knowledge about a domain are assumed to develop concurrently during the course of solving actual or simulated problem situations (Greeno, 1997). The potential for transfer to similar situations is high because the requirements of the training activity are similar or identical to actual task requirements, thereby capitalizing on the number of "identical elements" (Thorndike & Woodworth, 1901). However, concerns have been raised over the degree to which subsequent knowledge is specific to the context in which it was acquired, or whether it can be applied more generally (Hesketh, 1997a). This issue is closely related to the ongoing debate over the relative benefits of rule-based versus exemplar-based learning in the cognitive psychology literature. It also relates to the issue of short-term versus long-term training outcomes in that "situated learning" may lead to short-term gains in terms of facilitating transfer to similar problems, but may not lead to adaptable performance if task demands change in the longer term.

RULES AND EXAMPLES

As noted previously, course content usually progresses from general rules and principles to specific examples, with the rules and principles acting as "advance organizers" (Mayer, 1979) for subsequent information. Rules and principles promote transfer because of their wide applicability to a range of problems, but their very generality reduces their apparent relevance to specific instances (Salomon & Perkins, 1989). Catrambone

(1990) showed that training involving general instructions for a word processor was less effective than when instructions were tailored to the specific system. However, the general instructions were transferred more easily to another word-processing system than the specific instructions. The gap between abstract theories and specific instances can be bridged to some extent by accompanying rules and principles with examples illustrating their application (Gick & Holyoak, 1983). Multiple and varied examples, and instructions to compare examples, appear to enhance schema abstraction (Catrambone & Holyoak, 1989; Elio & Anderson, 1984; Gick & Holyoak, 1987), presumably because these processes encourage learners to distinguish common structural features that should be included in the schema from irrelevant surface features that are particular to a specific example (Holyoak, 1984).

Despite the advantages of training in rules and principles, there may be times when training with examples alone is more beneficial. Where the underlying principles are complex or non-linear, trainees may find it easier to reason from similar training examples than on the basis of abstract principles (Neal, Hesketh, & Bamford, 1999). However, care needs to be taken that the training examples are representative of the range of likely problems and that an optimum number of examples are presented, as specific instances may be difficult to recall if too many examples are used in training (DeLosh, Busemeyer, & McDaniel, 1997). The shortcomings of relying on exemplar-based training strategies may be overcome to some extent by following examples with reflective questions designed to encourage elaboration (Lee & Hutchinson, 1998).

As with other design issues already discussed, the appropriate level of specificity or abstraction that needs to be acquired should be identified during the training needs analysis. In most cases, a "moderately abstract" level of representation may represent a workable compromise between reasoning at the highest level of abstraction and reasoning from a specific example (Zeitz, 1997).

INSTRUCTION VERSUS PRACTICE

Another issue to consider when choosing a training method is the degree to which key concepts are acquired through direct instruction versus active involvement on the part of the learner. Substantial direct instruction may be required during training if the subject matter is complex or if trainees have little background knowledge they can bring to bear on the current task. Direct instruction using rules and examples is one way of giving trainees a good grasp of the major theoretical issues involved in a particular domain. However, the importance of incorporating activities that promote "active" learning is increasingly recognised (Frese, 1995; Ivancic & Hesketh, 1995/1996), particularly in light of the capacity of these training methods to provide opportunities for transfer appropriate processing. The ways in which active forms of learning such as behavior modeling and role playing, computer simulation, and error training can be used in training to enhance expertise are discussed next.

BEHAVIOR MODELING AND ROLE PLAYING

The popularity of behavior modeling as a training method has been enhanced by recent research demonstrating its effectiveness in training technical computer skills (Simon & Werner, 1996), as well as more interpersonal skills such as active listening (May &

Kahnweiler, 2000). Behavior modeling usually involves giving a verbal explanation of the key behaviors required to perform a skill, followed by a live or recorded presentation of a model performing the skill. Following the presentation, trainees practice the skill and are given positive and negative feedback on aspects of their performance. The skill is then practiced repeatedly until it is performed adequately. This process has been shown to produce positive training outcomes in terms of trainee attitudes, domain knowledge, and on-the-job performance (Russ-Eft & Zenger, 1995).

Role playing is also a useful way of training interpersonal skills. Participants assume a role and then act out a situation involving human interaction. At the conclusion of the role play, participants provide feedback on each other's behaviour and discuss how the situation may have been handled more effectively. If desired, the roles can be reversed and the role play re-enacted. Analysis of the role play may be facilitated by videotaping the role play to provide an objective record of the events that occurred, and to document improvements in skill execution.

The combination of practice followed by feedback appears to underpin the effectiveness of these training methods. Importantly, sufficient practice needs to be given to ensure that the relevant skills are mastered and to prevent skill decay (May & Kahnweiler, 2000). Multiple examples which utilize several different models or which alternate between positive and negative models also appear to be beneficial (Russ-Eft & Zenger, 1995). Asking trainees to complete checklists evaluating how well they are applying the skills in the weeks after training has been completed assists retention and performance of the modeled skill (Werner, O'Leary-Kelly, Baldwin, & Wexley, 1994).

SIMULATION TRAINING

The use of simulation is becoming increasingly widespread as the fidelity of simulators improves and the cost of the technology reduces. Evidence is emerging that simulators can in fact capture some of the effects observed in real flying and driving behavior (Duncan, 1998; Salas, Bower, & Rhodenizer, 1998), which in turn has provided justification for the use of simulators as training tools in the transport industries and the military. In addition to technical skills training, there is also a trend toward using simulators for training in cognitive and decision-making skills, with business games already widespread in management training (Kozak, Hancock, Arthur, & Chrysler, 1993). Applications for training in decision making are also available in emergency response command and control where rapid decisions are required, often in the absence of complete information. For example, fire simulators are now being used extensively in the UK for training fire command officers. The simulators model the spread of the fire in real time, with the goal being to contain the blaze while reducing the incidence of fatality and injury. Trainees can strategically deploy personnel and firefighting appliances to combat the fire and conduct search and rescue operations. The simulators provide scope to create a variety of different training and transfer tasks by manipulating features of the scenario (e.g., type of building structure, intensity of the fire, weather conditions). The scenario can also be replayed so that the extent to which organizational operating procedures were adhered to can be evaluated, and effective command and control strategies discussed with the trainee.

One of the main advantages of simulations is the capacity to present infrequently occurring events, thereby allowing trainees to experiment with decisions and learn from errors (Alluisi, 1991). Despite the benefits of simulation, ongoing evaluation is essential to identify possible shortcomings of the technology. Although much of the difficulty lies in determining which aspects of the real and simulated task should be "identical", increasing fidelity may be achieved at the expense of generalizability. Knowledge and skills may tend to become embedded in a particular context as the realism of simulating specific situations increases, for the same reason that situated learning may lead to inert knowledge. Research on examples is instructive of the need to simulate a variety of situations that are representative of on-the-job demands, and to facilitate comparisons of similarities and differences among these situations.

ACTIVE LEARNING

A number of training methods have been developed that emphasize the role of the learner as an active participant in the acquisition of domain-related knowledge. Learning by exploration (Kamouri, Kamouri, & Smith, 1986) requires trainees to form and test hypotheses about a task as they search the problem space. Error training (Frese, 1995) is similar in that it also acknowledges the key role of the trainee in the learning process, but places a greater emphasis on learning from mistakes. Trainees are encouraged to test the limits of a task to capitalize on the feedback provided by errors, and are provided with motivational strategies to focus attention on the positive informational function of errors. Because trainees take primary responsibility for organizing their own learning activities, they also have the opportunity to practice meta-cognitive skills related to developing, implementing, and evaluating problem-solving strategies. Where the work environment requires employees to cope with new problems that fall outside the range of prior experience, error training and learning by exploration provide important opportunities for transfer appropriate processing that prepare the groundwork for developing adaptive expertise (Ivancic & Hesketh, 2000).

The effectiveness of training methods that emphasize active learning is limited by the complexity of the task. Trainees may require substantial direct instruction before they can explore complex tasks independently. Alternatively, trainers may need to provide some structure to the session by outlining an agenda of information to be discovered (Charney, Reder, & Kusbit, 1990). In addition, progress must be monitored carefully and corrective feedback provided if trainees' exploratory activities are unsuccessful (Needham & Begg, 1991). As with the other training methods described earlier, practice and feedback are essential components of active learning.

ORGANIZATIONAL FACTORS INFLUENCING TRANSFER

It is tempting for trainers to believe that their work is done once the training program is completed. However, events that occur when trainees return to the workplace can influence whether or not trained skills are eventually transferred (Tannenbaum & Yukl, 1992). Therefore trainers need to be aware of organizational factors, such as the opportunity to perform trained skills and the organizational culture/climate, that may impede transfer so that they may prepare employees for potential difficulties. Table 12.3 summarizes post-training strategies for enhancing transfer.

TABLE 12.3 Post-training strategies for enhancing transfer

- Organize opportunities to perform trained skills in the workplace to enhance skill retention and generalization (Ford et al., 1992; Quinones et al., 1995/1996; Tesluk et al., 1995)
- Implement situational cues to remind trainees of prior training (Rouiller & Goldstein, 1993)
- Develop a reward structure for positively reinforcing the application of trained skills (Rouiller & Goldstein, 1993)
- Promote an organizational culture (e.g., continuous learning culture, transfer climate) that encourages transfer (Tracey et al., 1995)
- Design a relapse prevention intervention to raise awareness of the relapse process and to facilitate the development of strategies for dealing with obstacles to transfer (Marx, 1982)
- Conduct training evaluation to evaluate the longer-term effectiveness of training using a variety of measures (Kraiger et al., 1993)

OPPORTUNITY TO PERFORM

A lack of opportunity to perform skills on the job can impede transfer by affecting the chance to practice learned skills. Ford, Quinones, Sego, and Sorra (1992) found that four months after completing training, trainees reported wide variations in terms of the range of trained skills they had applied to the job and the number of times that these skills were applied. Trainees who have more opportunities to perform trained skills tend to generalize these skills to other work-related tasks (Tesluk, Farr, Mathieu, & Vance, 1995). Supervisors play a key role in providing opportunities to perform, as they tend to assign challenging and interesting tasks that promote continued skill development to employees who they perceive as talented or motivated (Quinones, Ford, Sego, & Smith, 1995/1996).

ORGANIZATIONAL CULTURE AND CLIMATE

Organizational culture and climate can affect training outcomes by rewarding or punishing attempts to transfer. Rouiller and Goldstein (1993) defined transfer climate as the situations and consequences that either help or hinder the transfer of learned skills to the job. Situational cues remind trainees of their training and provide opportunities to use the skills (e.g., the setting of goals for trainees by supervisors). The consequences of applying the learned behaviors can also become cues that will influence further use of these skills (e.g., positive feedback from the supervisor). Both situational cues and consequences contribute to the transfer climate, with more positive climates associated with greater transfer (Rouiller & Goldstein, 1993).

Continuous-learning culture refers to the need for trainees to participate in ongoing knowledge and skill development. Continuous-learning culture, along with transfer climate, has been shown to influence the transfer of supervisory skills (Tracey et al., 1995). Social support for the application of skills from the employee's supervisor, as well as from work colleagues, is an important contributor to the organization's transfer climate and continuous-learning culture (Tracey et al., 1995). Where limited opportunities to perform skills and a lack of positive organizational culture or climate are apparent, incorporating a relapse prevention module into the training course may prepare trainees for difficulties they are likely to encounter when attempting to apply trained skills in the workplace.

RELAPSE PREVENTION INTERVENTIONS

Relapse prevention aims to assist skill maintenance by helping trainees to identify potential obstacles to transfer and develop appropriate coping responses. Marx (1982) recommended that as part of a relapse prevention program, trainees should be informed about the relapse process so that they are prepared for potential difficulties. Trainees should then identify high-risk situations where the new skills may not be maintained, e.g., a lack of opportunity to perform trained skills on the job may be identified as a potential impediment to transfer. Finally, coping responses for overcoming these obstacles need to be brainstormed and practiced. For examples, trainees who decide to enlist the assistance of their supervisor in finding practice opportunities may role play various ways of approaching their supervisor with such a request.

Current evidence suggests that relapse prevention interventions can in fact facilitate the generalization and maintenance of complex skills. Tziner, Haccoun, and Kadish (1991) found that including a relapse prevention component in an instructional design course led to more frequent application of the trained skills in the ten-week period following training than when the relapse prevention program was not available. Frayne and Latham (1987) reported on a self-management program for employees with high levels of absenteeism, that included writing contracts and setting goals, as well as relapse prevention-style interventions, such as brainstorming potential problems and solutions. Job attendance rates and the level of course knowledge demonstrated three months after the training program were retained significantly at a nine-month follow-up (Latham & Frayne, 1989). Similarly, Gist, Bavetta, and Stevens (1990) found that a self-management program including relapse prevention improved the generalization of negotiating skills.

EVALUATION AS AN INTEGRAL PART OF TRAINING

Carefully planned evaluation serves several purposes. First, the requirement to evaluate makes it even more necessary to carry out the needs analysis. Second, the evaluation grows from the TNA and the TTNA that provide a set of outcome and training process goals. Third, the follow-up implicit in an evaluation provides an opportunity to practice the skills learned during training. The follow-up performance tests that are included in the evaluation may provide a booster to skill retention and transfer, an issue that should be explored in future research. Fourth, the results of the evaluation provide feedback that can be used to decide whether training programs should be retained, modified, or abandoned (Kraiger & Jung, 1996). Finally, the process of following up to check whether transfer has occurred sends a clear signal to managers and trainees that the behaviours, skills and meta-cognitions addressed during training are considered important by the organization.

The benefits of conducting evaluations are well known, but in practice training programs are often not subjected to systematic scrutiny. Evaluation designs that incorporate the experimental principles of random allocation to groups, pre- and post-training measurement, and the use of control groups are often advocated to protect the validity of the evaluation. However, these strategies may be difficult to implement given the constraints often experienced by practitioners in the field. For example, statistical power may be reduced considerably if a control group is used when sample sizes are small (Sackett & Mullen, 1993). Evaluation is further hampered by a lack of an adequate theoretical framework that can be used to guide the design and implementation phases. Practitioners and researchers have traditionally adopted Kirkpatrick's (1976) hierarchy which specifies four levels of training criteria: *reactions*, which refers to trainees' satisfaction with training; *learning*, which relates to the acquisition of relevant knowledge and skills; *behavior*, or the transfer of trained skills to the job and; *results*, which concerns organizational indicators such as productivity. Kirkpatrick's (1976) model is useful in that it highlights the need to avoid relying on trainee reactions as the sole measure of training effectiveness and include other less subjective measures in the evaluation. In a meta-analysis of 34 studies, Alliger, Tannenbaum, Bennett, Traver, and Shotland (1997) reported weak correlations between the first three levels of Kirkpatrick's (1976) model, and a correlation of only .07 between reactions and knowledge tests conducted immediately at the end of training. These results reinforce concerns that trainee reactions may be a misleading indicator of training effectiveness (Druckman & Bjork, 1994; Hesketh, 1997a).

The dominance of the Kirkpatrick (1976) approach has been undermined by an increased awareness of the shortcomings of the model, and in particular the lack of evidence for the hypothesized causal connection between the four levels of evaluation criteria (Holton, 1996; Kraiger & Jung, 1996). Consequently, a number of alternative evaluation models have been proposed. Among these is the model by Kraiger, Ford, and Salas (1993), in which they argue that evaluation measures should be derived from learning outcomes that relate to cognitive (or knowedge-based), skill-based, and affective (attitudinal and motivational) domains. Importantly, the learning outcomes should be derived from the training objectives that in turn follow from the needs assessment, thereby ensuring a close correspondence between what is evaluated and what was learned. (Kraiger & Jung, 1996). Where possible, measures should be taken over an extended period, as some training methods which deliver impressive short-term results are less effective in the longer term than techniques which initially appear less favourable (Schmidt & Bjork, 1992). The availability of post-training discussion groups, via the Web, offers another way of extending training an incorporating evaluation into training. Carefully structured questions used as a basis for discussion can provide feedback about the extent to which ideas and information were acquired from training, while also providing an opportunity to process more deeply the content of the training course.

In summary, the benefits of conducting evaluations justify the effort required to conduct a thorough examination of the short- and longer-term effects of training. Where practical constraints preclude the use of full experimental designs, quasi-experimental designs that incorporate measures from a variety of domains will often be preferable to not evaluating training at all. Further research is required to establish whether newer models of evaluation overcome the problems associated with the Kirkpatrick (1976) approach and whether they provide a useful framework for guiding the activities of training practitioners.

CONCLUSIONS

This chapter has aimed to illustrate the importance of knowing what are the desired training outcomes and understanding the context in which the trained skills and behaviors are likely to be performed when designing training. The process of identifying training needs should involve specifying, not only key knowledge, skills, and attitudes, but also the higher level meta-cognitive skills that are required to perform the job. The information acquired during the needs analysis forms a basis for selecting training methods that provide opportunities for engaging in appropriate cognitive processes, as well as a structure for evaluating training. Importantly, the messages delivered in training need to be reinforced after training concludes, either at follow-up evaluations or through support from the supervisor in the workplace. Although organizational training has traditionally aimed to deliver the fast, efficient, errorless performance characteristic of routine expertise, we argue that in organizations dominated by ongoing change, the flexible responding exhibited by adaptive experts can boost organizational competitiveness by fostering continued transfer, even in the face of variable job demands.

REFERENCES

Alliger, G. M., Tannenbaum, S. I., Bennett, W., Traver, H., & Shotland, A. (1997). A meta-analysis of the relations among training criteria. *Personnel Psychology*, **50**, 341–358.
Alluisi, E. A. (1991). The development of technology for collective training: SIMNET, a case history. *Human Factors*, **33**, 343–362.
Anderson, J. R. (1982). Acquisition of cognitive skill. *Psychological Review*, **89**, 369–406.
Catrambone, R. (1990). Specific versus general procedures in instructions. *Human-Computer Interaction*, **5**, 49–93.
Carlson, R. A., & Lundy, D. H. (1992). Consistency and restructuring in learning cognitive procedural sequences. *Journal of Experimental Psychology: Learning, Memory, and Cognition*, **18**, 127–141.
Catrambone, R., & Holyoak, K. J. (1989). Overcoming contextual limitations on problem-solving transfer. *Journal of Experimental Psychology: Learning, Memory, and Cognition*, **15**, 1147–1156.
Charney, D., Reder, L., & Kusbit, G. W. (1990). Goal setting and procedure selection in acquiring computer skills: A comparison of tutorials, problem solving, and learner exploration. *Cognition and Instruction*, **7**, 323–342.
Chase, W. G., & Simon, H. A. (1972). Perception in chess. *Cognitive Psychology*, **4**, 55–81.
Chi, M. T. H., Feltovich, P. J., & Glaser, R. (1981). Categorization and representation of physics problems by experts and novices. *Cognitive Science*, **5**, 121–152.
DeLosh, E. L., Busemeyer, J. R., & McDaniel, M. A. (1997). Extrapolation: The sine qua non for abstraction in function learning. *Journal of Experimental Psychology: Learning, Memory, and Cognition*, **23**, 968–986.
Downs, S., & Perry, P. (1982). How do I learn? *Journal of European Industrial Trainng*, **8**, 21–26.
Druckman, D., & Bjork, R. A. (Eds.). (1994). *Learning, remembering, believing: Enhancing human performance*. Washington DC: National Academy Press.
Duncan, B. (1998). Calibration trials of TRL driving simulator. In A. G. Gale (Ed.), *Vision in vehicles VI* (pp. 105–113). Oxford, UK: Elsevier Science.
Dweck, C. S., & Leggett, E. L. (1988). A social-cognitive approach to motivation and personality. *Psychological Review*, **95**, 256–273.
Elio, R., & Anderson, J. R. (1984). The effect of infomraiton order and learning mode on schema absraction. *Memory and Cognition*, **12**, 20–30.
Ericsson, K. A., Krampe, R., & Tesch-Roemer, C. (1993). The role of deliberate practice in the acquisition of expert performance. *Psychological Review*, **100**, 363–406.
Feltovich, P. J., Spiro, R. J., & Coulson, R. L. (1997). Issues of expert flexibility in contexts characterized by complexity and change. In P. J. Feltovich, K. M. Ford, & R. R. Hoffman (Eds.), *Expertise in context: Human and machine* (pp. 125–146). Menlo Park, CA: AAAI Press.
Ford, J. K., & Weissbein, D. A. (1997). Transfer of training: An updated review and analysis. *Performance Improvement Quarterly*, **10**, 22–41.
Ford, J. K., Quinones, M. A., Sego, D. J., & Sorra, J. S. (1992). Factors affecting the opportunity to perform trained tasks on the job. *Personnel Psychology*, **45**, 511–527.

Ford, J. K., Smith, E. M., Weissbein, D. A., Gully, S. M., & Salas, E. (1998). Relationships of goal orientation, metacognitive activity, and practice strategies with learning outcomes and transfer. *Journal of Applied Psychology*, **83**, 218–233.

Frayne, C. A., & Latham, G. P. (1987). The application of social learning theory to employee self-management of attendance. *Journal of Applied Psychology*, **72**, 387–392.

Frese, M. (1995). Error management in training: Conceptual and empirical results. In C. Zuccermaglio, S. Bagnara, & S. U. Stuchy (Eds.), *Organizational learning and technological change* (pp. 112–124). New York: Springer-Verlag.

Gick, M. L., & Holyoak, K. J. (1983). Schema induction and analogical transfer. *Cognitive Psychology*, **15**, 1–38.

Gick, M. L., & Holyoak, K. J. (1987). The cognitive basis of knowledge transfer. In S. M. Cormier & J. D. Hagman (Eds.), *Transfer of learning: Contemporary research and applications* (pp. 9–46). San Diego, CA: Academic Press.

Gist, M. E., Bavetta, A. G., & Stevens, C. K. (1990). Transfer training method: Its influence on skill generalization, skill repetition, and performance level. *Personnel Psychology*, **43**, 501–523.

Greeno, J. G. (1997). Theories and practices of thinking and learning to think. *American Journal of Education*, **106**, 85–126.

Hesketh, B. (1997a). Dilemmas in training for transfer and retention. *Applied Psychology: An International Review*, **46**, 317–339.

Hesketh, B. (1997b). W(h)ither dilemmas in training for transfer. *Applied Psychology: An International Review*, **46**, 380–386.

Hesketh, B., Andrews, S., & Chandler, P. (1989). Training for transferable skills: The role of examples and schema. *Educational and Training Technology International*, **26**, 156–165.

Hesketh, B., & Frese, M. (2000). Simulation and training in work settings. International Encyclopaedia for Organizational Behaviour.

Holton, E. F. (1996). The flawed four-level evaluation model. *Human Resource Development Quarterly*, **7**, 5–21.

Holyoak, K. J. (1984). Analogical thinking and human intelligence. In R. J. Sternberg (Ed.), *Advances in the psychology of human intelligence* (Vol. 2, pp. 199–230). Hillsdale, New Jersey: Lawrence Erlbaum and associates.

Ilgen, D. R., Fisher, C. D., & Taylor, M. S. (1979). Consequences of individual feedback on behavior in organizations. *Journal of Applied Psychology*, **64**, 349–371.

Ivancic, K., & Hesketh, B. (1995/1996). Making the best of errors during training. *Training Research Journal*, **1**, 103–125.

Ivancic, K., & Hesketh, B. (2000). Learning from errors in a driving simulation: Effects on driving skill and self-confidence. *Ergonomics*, **43**, 1966–1984.

Kamouri, A. L., Kamouri, J., & Smith, K. H. (1986). Training by exploration: Facilitating the transfer of procedural knowledge through analogical reasoning. *International Journal of Man-Machine Studies*, **24**, 171–192.

Kanfer, R., & Kanfer, F. H. (1991). Goals and self-regulation: Applications of theory to work settings. In M. L. Maehr & P. R. Pintrich (Eds.), *Advances in motivation and achievement* (Vol. 7, pp. 287–326). Greenwich, CO: JAI Press.

Kirkpatrick, D. L. (1976). Evaluation of training. In R. L. Craig (Ed.), *Training and development handbook: A guide to human resource development*. New York: McGraw-Hill.

Klaczynski, P. A., & Laipple, J. S. (1993). Role of content domain, logic training, and IQ in rule acquisition and transfer. *Journal of Experimental Psychology: Learning, Memory, and Cognition*, **19**, 653–672.

Kluger, A. N., & DeNisi, A. (1996). The effects of feedback interventions on performance: A historical review, a meta-analysis, and a preliminary feedback intervention theory. *Psychological Bulletin*, **119**, 254–284.

Kozak, J. J., Hancock, P. A., Arthur, E. J., & Chrysler, S. T. (1993). Transfer of training from virtual reality. *Ergonomics*, **36**, 777–784.

Kraiger, K., Ford, J. K., & Salas, E. (1993). Application of cognitive, skill-based, and affective theories of learning outcomes to new methods of training evaluation. *Journal of Applied Psychology*, **78**, 311–328.

Kraiger, K., & Jung, K. M. (1996). Linking training objectives to evaluation criteria. In M. A. Quinones & A. Ehrenstein (Eds.), *Training for a rapidly changing workplace: Applications of psychological research*. Washington, DC: American Psychological Association.

Latham, G. P., & Frayne, C. A. (1989). Self-management training for increasing job attendance: A follow-up and a replication. *Journal of Applied Psychology*, **74**, 411–416.

Lee, A. Y., & Hutchison, L. (1998). Improving learning from examples through reflection. *Journal of Experimental Psychology: Applied*, **4**, 187–210.

Lockhart, R. S., Lamon, M., & Gick, M. L. (1988). Conceptual transfer in simple insight problems. *Memory and Cognition*, **16**, 36–44.

Marx, R. D. (1982). Relapse prevention for managerial training: A model for maintenance of behavior change. *Academy of Management Review*, **7**, 433–441.

May, G. L., & Kahnweiler, W. M. (2000). The effect of a mastery practice design on learning and transfer in behavior modeling training. *Personnel Psychology*, **53**, 353–373.

Mayer, R. (1979). Can advance organizers influence meaningful learning? *Review of Educational Research*, **49**, 371–383.

Morris, C. D., Bransford, J. D., & Franks, J. J. (1977). Levels of processing versus transfer appropriate processing. *Journal of Verbal Learning and Verbal Behavior*, **16**, 519–533.

Neal, A., Hesketh, B., & Bamford (1999). Learning from examples: Implications for training and transfer. Paper submitted for publication.

Needham, D. R., & Begg, I. M. (1991). Problem-oriented training promotes spontaneous analogical transfer: Memory-oriented training promotes memory for training. *Memory and Cognition*, **19**, 543–557.

Nisbett, R. E., Fong, G. T., Lehmann, D. R., & Cheng, P. W. (1987). Teaching reasoning. *Science*, **238**, 625–631.

Novick, L. R. (1988). Analogical transfer, problem similarity, and expertise. *Journal of Experimental Psychology: Learning, Memory, and Cognition*, **14**, 510–520.

Patel, V. L., & Groen, G. J. (1991). The nature of medical expertise: A critical look. In K. A. Ericsson & J. Smith (Eds.), *Toward a general theory of expertise: Prospects and limits* (pp. 93–125). Cambridge: Cambridge University Press.

Quinones, M. A., Ford, J. K., Sego, D. J., & Smith, E. M. (1995/1996). The effects of individual and transfer environment characteristics on the opportunity to perform trained tasks. *Training Research Journal*, **1**, 29–48.

Reed, S. K., Ernst, G. W., & Banerji, R. (1974). The role of analogy in transfer between similar problem states. *Cognitive Psychology*, **6**, 436–450.

Rouiller, J. Z., & Goldstein, I. L. (1993). The relationship between organizational transfer climate and positive transfer of training. *Human Resource Development Quarterly*, **4**, 337–390.

Russ-Eft, D. F., & Zenger, J. H. (1995). Behavior modeling training in North America: A research summary. In M. Mulder, W. J. Nijhof & R. O. Brinkerhoff (Eds.), *Corporate training for effective performance*. Boston, MA: Kluwer Academic Publishers.

Sackett, P. R., & Mullen, E. J. (1993). Beyond formal experimental design: Towards an expanded view of the training evaluation process. *Personnel Psychology*, **46**, 613–627.

Salas, E., Bower, C. A., & Rhodenizer, L. (1998). It is not how much you have but how you use it: Toward a rational use of simulation to support aviation training. *International Journal of Aviation Psychology*, **8**, 197–208.

Salomon, G., & Perkins, D. N. (1989). Rocky roads to transfer: Rethinking mechanisms of a neglected phenomenon. *Educational Psychologist*, **24**, 113–142.

Schmidt, R. A., & Bjork, R. A. (1992). New conceptualizations of practice: Common principles in three paradigms suggest new concepts for training. *Psychological Science*, **3**, 207–217.

Shiffrin, R. M., & Schneider, W. (1977). Controlled and automatic human information processing: II. Perceptual learning, automatic attending, and a general theory. *Psychological Review*, **84**, 127–190.

Simon, S. J., & Werner, J. M. (1996). Computer training through behavior modeling, self-paced, and instructional approaches: A field experiment. *Journal of Applied Psychology*, **81**, 648–659.

Smith, E. M., Ford, J. K., & Kozlowski, S. W. J. (1997). Building adaptive expertise: Implications for training design strategies. In M. A. Quinones & A. Ehrenstein (Eds.), *Training for a rapidly changing workplace: Applications of psychological research.* Washington, DC: American Psychological Association.

Smith-Jentsch, K. A., Jentsch, F. G., Payne, S. C., & Salas, E. (1996). Can pretraining experiences explain individual differences in learning? *Journal of Applied Psychology,* **81**, 110–116.

Tannenbaum, S. I. (1997). Resolving training dilemmas: An organisational perspective. *Applied Psychology: An International Review,* **46**, 376–379.

Tannenbaum, S. I., & Yukl, G. (1992). Training and development in work organizations. *Annual Review of Psychology,* **43**, 399–441.

Tesluk, P. E., Farr, J. L., Mathieu, J. E., & Vance, R. J. (1995). Generalization of employee involvement training to the job setting: Individual and situational effects. *Personnel Psychology,* **48**, 607–632,

Thorndike, E. L., & Woodworth, R. S. (1901). The influence of improvement in one mental function upon the efficiency of other functions. *Psychological Review,* **8**, 247–261.

Thorndyke, P. W. (1984). Applications of schema theory in cognitive research. In J. R. Anderson & S. M. Kosslyn (Eds.), *Tutorials in learning and memory: Essays in honor of Gordon Bower* (pp. 167–191). San Francisco, NY: W. H. Freeman and Co.

Tracey, J. B., Tannenbaum, S. I., & Kavanagh, M. J. (1995). Applying trained skills on the job: The importance of the work environment. *Journal of Applied Psychology,* **80**, 239–252.

Tziner, A., Haccoun, R. R., & Kadish, A. (1991). Personal and situational characteristics influencing the effectiveness of transfer of training improvement strategies. *Journal of Occupational Psychology,* **64**, 167–177.

Werner, J. M., O'Leary-Kelly, A. M., Baldwin, T. T., & Wexley, K. N. (1994). Augmenting behavior-modeling training: Testing the effects of pre- and post-training interventions. *Human Resource Development Quarterly,* **5**, 169–183.

Zeitz, C. M. (1997). Some concrete advantages of abstraction: How experts' representations facilitate reasoning. In P. J. Feltovich, K. M. Ford & R. R. Hoffman (Eds.), *Expertise in context: Human and machine* (pp. 43–65). Menlo Park, CA: AAAI Press.

Enhancing Performance through Training

Brigitte Winkler

Brigitte Winkler, A47 Consulting, Corporate Development and Management Diagnostic, Munich, Germany

Psychological Management of Individual Performance. Edited by Sabine Sonnentag.
© 2002 John Wiley & Sons, Ltd.

Summary

This chapter addresses the process of training development from a practitioner's point of view and analyses the various steps essential to the development and implementation of a successful training process. Taking the example of a successful management training programme for newly appointed managers at a large organisation, we illustrate how best to combine training development theory with the practitioner's first-hand experience. We describe the advantages and disadvantages of various methods for assessing training needs, the development of training content and objectives for the target group, the right structure and methods for training, and the development of a lesson plan. Furthermore, we consider the merits of internal/external trainers and the role of management in achieving successful implementation. We examine the application process itself and show how the first training sessions should be run. We present methods for calculating costs and benefits in order to evaluate the results of the training.

INTRODUCTION

In this chapter we will consider the process of training development from a practitioner's point of view and work through the various steps which are essential to the development and implementation of a successful training process. The process which we will be focusing on forms the underlying framework for a management training programme for newly appointed managers which has been running successfully at a large organisation—in the following called "the firm"—for almost 10 years. We will be drawing examples from the firm's training programme in order to enhance the theoretical aspects of training development with some of the practitioner's first-hand experience. These examples will be presented at the end of each section. In the following paragraph a short summary of the example used throughout the article is given.

DEVELOPMENT OF A MANAGEMENT TRAINING PROCESS FOR NEWLY APPOINTED MANAGERS: INTRODUCTORY-LEVEL LEADERSHIP TRAINING

A large organisation with 28,000 employees has an ever-increasing demand for managers who will be required to manage branches or supervise teams in all areas of the firm's business operations. There is a natural staff turnover incidence of 4% and on average managers remain in any given position for a period of three to five years. Each year, no less than 150 staff members are given the opportunity of assuming their first managerial position, in which they will be responsible for a team consisting of anywhere from 4 to 20 staff. In order to improve their management skills and to provide them with support in their new role as managers, the firm offers a management training programme designed to meet their particular needs. The aim of this training programme is twofold: it should serve to reinforce fundamental management skills such as delegating, conducting meetings and appraisal discussions, etc. and it should help newly appointed managers in defining their new roles and responsibilities.

There are several steps necessary to develop an effective training programme from the needs analysis through to the evaluation process. Figure 13.1 shows the main elements

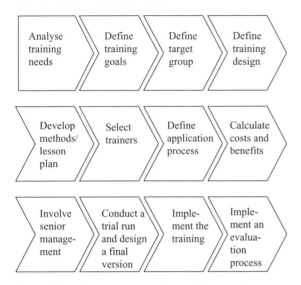

Analyse training needs ⟩ Define training goals ⟩ Define target group ⟩ Define training design

Develop methods/lesson plan ⟩ Select trainers ⟩ Define application process ⟩ Calculate costs and benefits

Involve senior management ⟩ Conduct a trial run and design a final version ⟩ Implement the training ⟩ Implement an evaluation process

FIGURE 13.1   Main elements of the training development process

of a training development process. Each element of this process will be described in this chapter by using the introductory-level leadership training programme as an example.

HOW TO IDENTIFY TRAINING NEEDS

Before designing and implementing a training programme it is important to identify which skills and areas of learning to focus on. Not infrequently a member of the senior management team will detect certain shortcomings in performance and then ask the internal training department to develop a training programme that will help to remedy these deficiencies.

Training in itself may very well serve as a possible solution in such a case, but by conducting a training needs analysis, you will be able to pinpoint a broader range of factors causing the performance deficiencies. Another frequent impetus for training needs analysis comes from the internal training department itself. They may have a number of training courses on offer and simply wish to find out if these courses are meeting the needs of the organisation. The internal training department will probably want to identify which skills are to be reinforced and strengthened within the organisation as a whole. There are several techniques which may be used to analyse an organisation's training needs.

INTERVIEWS

A popular and effective means of identifying training needs is the interview. Interviews provide you with an in-depth view of the specific working environment in which future training course candidates will be active, and they help to highlight those skills which are important for the success of a candidate's future performance. Interviews may be conducted with a number of different types of candidates:

- Managers who are highly successful in their first management position (subject matter experts) should be interviewed. The principal aim of the interview should be to find out which skills and areas of special know-how are crucial to successful performance in the candidate's workplace.
- Interviews could also be conducted with senior management to ascertain which strategic management skills they think should be implemented broadly throughout the organisation. Simple questions such as the following could help to underscore certain training needs which may be of great use: What are your people doing that new managers should not be doing? What aren't your people not doing that they should be doing?
- Future training course participants who have recently assumed their first management position and consequently are seen as prime candidates for a management training programme could also be interviewed to help to determine their own training needs. If they are given the opportunity to provide direct input for the development of a training course which, in essence, is being designed for them, then they may be much more receptive to the activity as a whole.
- Last, but by no means least, you might wish to interview customers to gain an outside perspective. For instance, you could have customers describe what is important to them when dealing with a branch manager of a firm, and have them list the kind of skills and knowledge they expect from such a person.

It is important to conduct interviews in a structured and systematic way if you wish to obtain accurate and reliable data. Interview questions are generally designed beforehand; but the interviewing process should remain flexible enough to allow the interviewer the opportunity of pursuing other pertinent issues should they arise during the course of an interview in order for him/her to gain a more complete understanding of the topics at hand. The interviewer can then return to the original questions. One very good interviewing technique is the *critical incident technique* (Flanagan, 1954). This technique stipulates that interviewees are asked to describe situations in their jobs which they consider critical as well as the skills necessary to respond properly to these situations.

After the interviews have been conducted the answers should be categorised by question, making it easier to extract the main results from the interview. Qualitative data is not as easy to summarise as quantitative data—but interpretation is easier because the answers are normally registered in full detail by the interviewer, thus facilitating a better understanding of the data.

SURVEYS

Surveys may be of use in an analysis of training needs if you are interested in asking a large representative sample of people about their training needs. A survey could be circulated among the same groups of people listed in the interview section.

Surveys are less time-consuming than interviews, since there is no need to arrange interview appointments. Quantitative data is easy to appraise and summarise, though it can become more difficult if you use open-ended questions like, "Please name the skills and knowledge areas, in which you feel further training is required." As with interview data, you will need to summarise and classify the answers to open-ended questions.

One disadvantage of surveys lies in the fact that quantitative data is more difficult to interpret than qualitative data, depending of course on the range and type of alternatives in the answer field (e.g. not at all/very much/yes or no). Another drawback is that the person surveyed generally cannot be asked follow-up questions because questionnaires are often submitted anonymously. Additional qualitative research is normally required.

APPRAISAL INTERVIEWS

Appraisal interviews allow managers and employees to assess training needs in a quiet and confidential setting. Both can sit down together and evaluate the employee's strengths and weaknesses and define further training needs (Hofbauer & Winkler, 1999). Once this has been done, measures are taken to develop the required skills. For instance, a newly appointed manager tells his/her manager in the appraisal interview that he/she would need training in facilitation and presentation skills. Manager and employee might then agree on a two-day training course offered by the internal training department.

ASSESSMENT CENTRES

Assessment centres are often used for selection purposes and internal development programmes. The aim may be to assess a person's potential for assuming a new role with higher responsibilities, or to evaluate a person's aptitude for a particular job. A profile of the candidate's strengths and weaknesses will help to determine recommendations for future career steps and to identify further areas that need to be developed. In this way, it is clear that assessment centres may be used for very specific training needs analysis with respect to important management skills. Feedback allows the person being assessed to gain valuable insight into his/her leadership potential (Thornton III, 1992). An overall analysis of the profiles of assessment centre candidates will help to determine if there are any skills within the organisation that require further attention (e.g. interpersonal skills).

OBSERVING MANAGERS IN ACTION

When asked which skills are required to cope with the demands of their jobs, managers will often overlook certain vital skills because, after years of experience, these skills have become second nature to them. Be that as it may, many of these skills, which can be identified through careful observation, may well be the ones which have been instrumental to a manager's professional success, and should therefore be taken into consideration when drawing up training programmes for newly appointed managers (Mintzberg, 1970). Well-structured observation charts are invaluable when recording your observations of skills and types of behaviour in various situations. When the observation session is followed up by an interview, it is then possible to learn more about action strategies and to ascertain why certain types of behaviour and skills are used in specific situations.

CUSTOMER FEEDBACK

Customer feedback is a source of highly credible data and is often taken very seriously by management. Customers are in an excellent position to appraise both the quality of service and the competence of the people with whom they interact. In certain circumstances they are also able to evaluate management behaviour, especially if they have occasion for direct interaction with a manager, for instance with the branch manager of a local firm. Managers can positively influence the quality of service and customer-orientation of their staff. Also, a positive working climate, created by effective management and team interactions, has a positive effect on customer treatment (Gebert et al., 1987).

USING FINANCIAL DATA TO IDENTIFY TRAINING NEEDS

Financial indicators may also reveal areas in need of improvement. Unsatisfactory sales figures are a clear indication that the sales part of a business is faltering. Training might be a way of indirectly improving sales figures through the improvement of sales skills. A thorough analysis is required to clarify all possible means of improving sales figures. Once this has been done, sales managers and employees could be interviewed in order to identify more accurately the reasons for the low sales figures (e.g. Are problems the result of product changes? . . . changes in customer needs? . . . the skills level of the sales team?).

NEW TRAINING MEASURES AS A RESULT OF NEW STRATEGIES

The implementation of a new strategy often necessitates the need for new skills and learning processes. Management might therefore find it beneficial to try to determine training needs from the perspective of someone attempting to change behaviour and company culture through the implementation of a new strategy. In the firm, for instance, changes in management behaviour were required when a new strategy which focused on more sales-driven behaviour was introduced. Instead of the top-down style of leadership, managers had to adopt the new role of coach in order to bring about an improvement in the sales-driven behaviour of their staff. The following paragraph highlights the needs analysis process used in our example.

INTRODUCTORY-LEVEL LEADERSHIP TRAINING NEEDS ANALYSIS

The training needs analysis for newly appointed managers was conducted in a variety of ways.

1. *Approximately 20 managers in their first management positions were systematically interviewed using the* critical incidents *technique (Flanagan, 1954), which revealed that many of the interviewees' responsibilities revolved around communication (e.g. giving feedback, facilitating meetings, helping their staff to solve problems); but planning and controlling were also cited, as well as representing the firm, dealing with difficult customers, and implementing both new work processes and structural changes.*
2. *An employee satisfaction survey revealed important areas where management skills were lacking. The employees pointed out inadequacies in the managers' communication*

skills, feedback skills, as well as in their ability to delegate responsibility, and they found shortcomings in staff development.

3. *A new strategy that changed the traditionally run firm into a sales-driven organisation was implemented. Senior management wanted to see a change in management style that would respond to the demands of a modern organisation. The old command-and-control management style was to be replaced by a style that was more cooperative, goal-oriented and sales-driven. The manager was expected to act as coach for his/her staff. This required him/her to be an exceptional communicator able to develop the strengths of his/her team through feedback and reinforcement. Not only did managers have to adopt a new role, but many had to learn new skills in order to meet the demands of these new roles. Senior management wanted this new leadership philosophy to be implemented throughout the organisation. Selection procedures for managers were brought into line with this philosophy and every newly appointed manager trained to fulfil the requirements of this new role.*

DEVELOPMENT OF TRAINING CONTENT

OUTLINE OF THE MAIN SKILLS THAT NEED TO BE TRAINED AND DEFINITION OF TRAINING OBJECTIVES

Once the training needs analysis has been completed you can then move on to defining the main areas of learning and to establishing the goals of the training programme. The more precisely you specify which skills and areas of knowledge you want developed by the training course the easier it will be to customise design.

Before the start of the training course, management, as well as the future participant, should be made aware of the main skills which will ultimately be the learning focus of the course. To the degree that learning can be specified, instructors have a better basis for making good decisions while teaching. Learners will get a better sense of why and how well they are learning and the organisation will have a better idea of what it is receiving from its training investment. The following example shows the learning objectives defined in the firm's introductory-level leadership training programme.

INTRODUCTORY-LEVEL LEADERSHIP TRAINING: OUTLINE OF THE MAIN SKILLS TO BE TRAINED AND DEFINITION OF TRAINING OBJECTIVES

Once the training needs analysis of newly appointed managers had been analysed several skills were identified that needed further development. Training goals were then defined with these development needs in mind.

Upon completion of the course, managers should . . .

1. *. . . have an understanding of what is expected of them as a manager within the organisation. They should be intimately familiar with the leadership philosophy of the firm, be able to identify their main responsibilities as a manager and know how to establish their priorities.*
2. *. . . have better communication skills (be active listeners, ask questions openly, hold presentations, and create a climate of honest and open communication).*
3. *. . . have a deeper understanding of team dynamics, know how to effectively resolve group conflicts and be familiar with a variety of intervention techniques which can be used to effectively build and strengthen their teams.*

4. ...*be aware of the strengths and weaknesses of their own management style. This will have been made clear through the intensive feedback sessions held during the training course. They will have been asked to work with individual action plans as a means to improving their weaknesses and to honing their strengths.*

5. ...*know how to conduct effective appraisal interviews, set goals, and delegate responsibility in keeping with the experience and abilities of the members of their teams. They should know how to give feedback constructively and be able to coach and encourage their staff. They should be familiar with the firm's main personnel development measures and know how to use them.*

6. ...*have learned how to run a goal-oriented team meeting.*

7. ...*know the principal leadership theories.*

8. ...*know the important areas and activities of the firm and have a sound understanding of the strategy and direction of the organisation as a whole.*

9. ...*be able to handle difficult leadership situations, learn from each other through feedback and be able to implement solutions in the workplace.*

10. ...*have learned the steps needed to implement changes successfully within their own organisational units.*

11. ...*have learned how to run their departments effectively from a sales and customer-oriented perspective.*

Networking between departments and business units as well as a strong focus on the applicability of newly acquired skills were considered to be very important requirements for the course.

DEFINING TARGET GROUPS

Properly defining the target group which you intend to train is important. If you wish to respond effectively to participants' training needs, it is often best that participants have similar levels of knowledge, skills and experience. In management training there are often notable differences between "beginners" who have limited expertise and more experienced managers.

Experienced managers might be interested in learning more about management theory, reflecting on their particular management style, and acquiring advanced management techniques, whereas newly appointed managers will need to focus on basic management skills such as delegating, organising, communicating in a team, etc. Practical training will be of greatest interest to them. The next paragraph describes how the target groups were defined in the firm's introductory-level leadership training programme.

INTRODUCTORY-LEVEL LEADERSHIP TRAINING: DEFINITION OF TARGET GROUPS

For the following training course the target group consisted of newly appointed managers and project managers who had been given management responsibilities in connection with a specific project. Participants had to have been active in a management position for at least 4 weeks before attending. Making these stipulations proved very successful as each participant was able to contribute examples from his/her own day-to-day experiences as a manager.

Employees who knew that they would be taking over a team in the near future, were given the opportunity for preparation in a two-day "management preparation course" which helped to give them focus during the first 100 days in their new roles as managers.

After the first month, they were expected to attend the first-level management course to provide them with support and the necessary skills required for success in their new positions.

TRAINING STRUCTURE AND DESIGN

Training courses are commonly designed as one-off, two- to three-day events which focus on a particular subject. A far more effective design is one that spaces out the various training sections and allows the participants time to practise newly acquired skills. Rather than running a three-day course without interruption, it is far more beneficial to plan a two-day training course, and to then organise a one-day follow-up training session a few weeks later. This gives managers the chance to practise new skills in their respective workplaces and to later discuss and exchange experiences with group members in the follow-up session.

Training courses are only one way of helping people to acquire new skills. There are other methods which are sometimes more suited to specific purposes and are more budget-friendly.

On-the-job training

People tend to learn most effectively if they are able to apply what they have learned to their day-to-day work. On-the-job training means that the trainees learn by observing more experienced people and by taking on greater responsibilities and new tasks in their jobs. This method is very cost-effective and saves a great deal of time as you avoid paying for training courses, travel expenses, etc. However, because training takes place in the workplace it is often not as structured as in a classical training environment due to inevitable interruptions. It is also difficult to gain insights into new working methods since training takes place in a familiar environment. To make sure that learning is possible it is important to allow enough spare time for the "on-the-job–trainer" to teach and for his or her trainee to learn. Often on-the-job–training must be carried out in addition to one's normal workload. This has the effect that the trainee is seen by the trainer as an additional burden rather than a person who needs to be taught the best way to create learning results.

Mentoring

Mentoring is a very effective method of giving junior personnel the chance to learn from more experienced members of staff. The mentoring contract defines the relationship between the employee and his/her mentor. The mentor has the explicit task of helping the employee to better understand decisive situations, and the employee's knowledge is enhanced by the mentor passing on some of his/her experience. The employee learns through observation, discussion, and by listening to the advice of his/her mentor. Mentoring is the most effective way of transferring experience-based, implicit knowledge to an employee.

Job rotation

Job rotation can be a useful method for developing multi-skilled employees. It familiarises them with other positions and broadens their perspectives. It can be a valuable method for preparing someone for a new position in which he/she needs to understand the basic workings of other jobs or departments.

Computer-based training

Some companies try to avoid high training costs by implementing specific computer-based training (CBT) modules. Although it is quite expensive to develop customised software which fulfils the specific requirements of a given organisation, once available these CBTs are very good at providing the theoretical aspects of a training course, e.g. product information, management theory, etc. Built-in question and answer sessions allow people to learn actively and at their own pace. Despite some of their advantages, CBTs cannot replace traditional learning techniques when it comes to behaviour-oriented skills training because they do not provide feedback on the participant's interpersonal behaviour in specific situations. Computer simulations of decision-making processes provide trainees with the opportunity to learn how to make decisions in complex situations. Although CBTs focus on general thinking processes and are good at the analysis and cross-referencing of information, they are of less use when dealing with communication aspects of the decision-making process such as negotiation or communicating a decision to the organisation.

Workshops

Workshops tend to focus on finding solutions to specific problems and allow people to concentrate their energies on a particular subject. Heterogeneity among workshop participants makes for a wider scope of ideas and perspectives which in turn could result in a greater number of possible solutions. Workshops best meet the expectations of the participants if the contents and agenda are developed together with the target group beforehand.

Coaching

Within an organisation, coaching is often applied as a training technique between members of senior management and employees because of the immediate pay-off. Coaching can be completely individualised to respond to the specific training needs of the employee. One-to-one communication allows for dynamic feedback and reappraisal of the learning objectives. Generally speaking, senior managers will require some training in coaching techniques before they are able to run effective coaching sessions. A senior manager–manager relationship based on trust is essential if this training technique is to work effectively (Whitmore, 1992).

The next paragraph describes the training structure and design chosen for the firm's introductory-level leadership training programme.

Introductory-Level Leadership Training: Training Structure and Design

The firm's analysis of training needs indicated that the course content should be practical and work-related. At the same time, many different training goals were drawn up for the programme. Because the participants had little experience as managers, it was

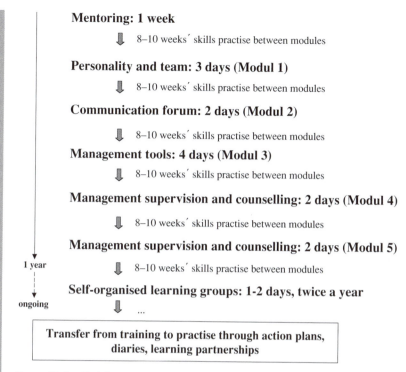

Mentoring: 1 week

⬇ 8–10 weeks' skills practise between modules

Personality and team: 3 days (Modul 1)

⬇ 8–10 weeks' skills practise between modules

Communication forum: 2 days (Modul 2)

⬇ 8–10 weeks' skills practise between modules

Management tools: 4 days (Modul 3)

⬇ 8–10 weeks' skills practise between modules

Management supervision and counselling: 2 days (Modul 4)

⬇ 8–10 weeks' skills practise between modules

Management supervision and counselling: 2 days (Modul 5)

1 year

⬇ 8–10 weeks' skills practise between modules

Self-organised learning groups: 1-2 days, twice a year

ongoing

⬇ ...

Transfer from training to practise through action plans, diaries, learning partnerships

FIGURE 13.2   Training modules

decided that a one-off training course alone would not suffice; they would require some degree of regular support during their first year. Therefore, a training course consisting of several modules, as shown in Figure 13.2, was designed. This allowed trainees time, between the modules, to practise newly acquired skills within their departments and to reflect on one's own management style. The training course was designed to accommodate 14 newly appointed managers who would stay together throughout the five-module training period, which reinforced a sense of trust and openness among the participants. The participants were drawn from all areas of the firm, providing an ideal platform for further networking with managers from different departments. Training modules were spread over 12 months. Participants were given the option of working with a mentor for approximately one week. Trainees were able to observe their mentor's behaviour in important management areas such as meetings, presentations, negotiations, discussions with employees, as well as in the handling of customer complaints, etc. Being provided with role models before taking on their new responsibilities turned out to be highly beneficial for the trainees. After the five training modules participants were given the option of working on a regular basis together on difficult management problems in self-organised learning groups twice a year.

DEVELOPMENT OF A TRAINING PLAN: METHODS AND INTERVENTIONS

Adults learn best when theory and practical knowledge are combined and adapted to their day-to-day job routine. All modern learning theories stress that adults have to be given a degree of responsibility over the learning process and opportunities to participate actively in the learning process. This sense of responsibility can best be achieved by

TABLE 13.1   Lesson plan

Time	Training goals	Instructor's activity	Students' activity	Methods
9.00–9.30	Goal setting	Short presentation of the goal-setting process (10 min.) Introduction of an example	Formulate a "measurable goal" according to the example	Brainstorming and group discussion

creating measures in which learners actively talk about what they have done in the past, or about what they are thinking and feeling as they experiment with new behaviour patterns during the course of the learning process. The design of a training course is usually structured according to a lesson plan, as shown in Table 13.1. The lesson plan details both the learners' as well as the instructor's activities.

A mixture of different training methods creates the best learning environment. The following list gives an overview of popular training methods, but is by no means complete (see Laird, 1985; Reid et al., 1992).

Lectures

A common way of imparting theory is by holding lectures as they offer an efficient means of delivering material. But theory is best understood if you can apply it to your area of work. Therefore lectures should always be accompanied by exercises, discussion or a reflection session which allows participants to reflect upon the theory in relation to their own jobs (House, 1996). Lecturers must be able to ascertain whether material is being absorbed in order for the method to be considered effectual.

Role plays

Role plays are an excellent method of training newly acquired skills in a safe setting, and they allow for "performance try-outs". They are particularly effective for practising interpersonal skills (Thiagarajan, 1996). For instance, appraisal conversations can easily be simulated in a role–play scenario. Trainees playing the roles of managers and employees are able to experience a rather authentic situation and managers can practise social skills and feedback techniques during the role play. If the role–play is videotaped, the managers are confronted with their behaviour and might learn a lot purely from observing themselves. The other training participants could support this learning process by providing valid feedback on strengths and weaknesses. The reverse role–play, whereby participants switch roles at a critical moment in the role–play, is a helpful method for gaining a better understanding of another person's viewpoint.

Behaviour modelling

Role models give insight into the possible form that ideal behaviour might take. Based on social learning theory (Bandura, 1977), imitation of a role model's behaviour is a way of learning new behavioural patterns (Latham & Saari, 1979). Learners discover which standards and types of action are expected of them, e.g. when negotiating with a customer. The role models could be presented through the use of video or by the instructor.

Case studies

In case studies participants are confronted with a complex work problem. It is a very good tool for training strategic thinking and decision-making abilities. If a whole group of managers works on a case study in a training course, then the group's own discussion and behaviour patterns can be observed and analysed and then improved upon. Case studies are usually worked on in small groups. The case study, along with a list of questions, is given to the group to solve. The desired output of the group might involve formulating a recommendation, a decision or the outline of an action plan (Winstanley & Woodall, 1992).

Outdoor activities

It has not yet been proved that outdoor training has any long-term effect on the strengthening of management behaviour or team building. It does, however, produce powerful experiences of teamwork and risk-taking activities (Conger, 1992). If the period allowed for reflection after an outdoor activity is put to good use and is applicable to the work situation, then outdoor activities can help to obtain a deeper understanding of group dynamics. For instance, during a merger situation it might be very helpful to provide outdoor activities for project teams which consist of employees from the different merging companies. It can help to facilitate team building and be of invaluable benefit during the whole post-merger integration process (Winkler & Dörr, 2001). The informal, action-oriented exercises of an outdoor training course can lead to breakthroughs in communication and form new patterns of team cooperation. In a training plan the right variety of learning methods (see Figure 13.3) guarantees learning results. The following example from the introductory-level leadership training programme shows how to combine different learning methods.

INTRODUCTORY-LEVEL LEADERSHIP TRAINING: DEVELOPMENT OF A TRAINING PLAN

Every year approximately 12 programmes were offered to groups of newly appointed managers, each group consisting of 14 participants. A detailed training plan was worked out and the trainers were trained to run the course so that there would be a high degree of consistency in terms of both content and learning objectives.

The training programme was designed so that various learning methods would be used (see Figure 13.3). The underlying principle was that the participants should not only hear about theory, but get an opportunity to learn by trial and error, through feedback processes and by means of the systematic training of skills in role–plays. Each participant received a diary for the use of self-reflection, the setting of learning goals and recording of important learning experiences. Learning partnerships (groups of two) were established during the course of the whole programme to enhance relationships built on trust and openness and to facilitate learning. Each participant chose a "learning partner" from among the other participants with whom he/she would form a closer relationship. The aims of the learning partnerships were to reflect together on learning experiences, to solve management problems together "outside" the training course, to give each other support in difficult situations, to visit each other in the workplace, and to provide important feedback on each other's behaviour.

Evening discussions with representatives from the firm, namely senior managers and board members, helped the participants to get a better understanding of the chief strategies and activities of the firm in areas outside their own technical expertise.

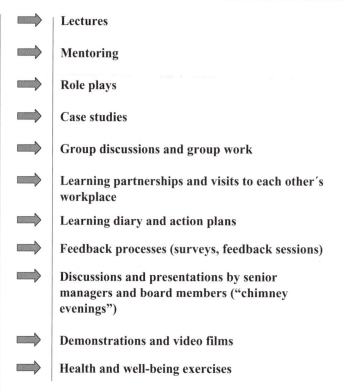

Lectures

Mentoring

Role plays

Case studies

Group discussions and group work

Learning partnerships and visits to each other´s workplace

Learning diary and action plans

Feedback processes (surveys, feedback sessions)

Discussions and presentations by senior managers and board members ("chimney evenings")

Demonstrations and video films

Health and well-being exercises

FIGURE 13.3   Learning methods used in the management training process

Each day started with a health and well-being activity, e.g. jogging, aerobics, relaxation, meditation. It was also the aim of the course to focus on the health and general well-being of the participants and to introduce them to relaxation techniques and to methods of restoring physical and mental power. Many of the participants were motivated by these health and well-being activities to become more physically active or to focus on relaxation techniques in order to improve their level of fitness and well-being both at work and in their private lives.

In the time between the various modules each participant planned a few activities and measures that he/she would carry out in his/her own working environment (e.g. to hold regular discussions with employees, to establish effective team meetings, etc.). This enhanced the learning process by giving participants the chance to put their learning into practice.

INTRODUCTORY-LEVEL LEADERSHIP TRAINING: DESCRIPTION OF THE DIFFERENT MODULES OF MANAGEMENT TRAINING (SEE FIGURE 13.2)

Module 1: Personality and team

*The first module is a three-day programme called **personality and team.** Participants not only learn about what is expected of them in their roles as managers, they also gain an understanding of the leadership principles of the organisation and they reflect upon their new roles in the context of their own departments. In addition to this, they practise effective communication skills, learn about group dynamics and how to chair a meeting successfully. Team intervention, presentation and facilitation skills are practised in* *role–plays and in simulations of difficult team meetings. The latest knowledge on leadership theory and on effective team processes is provided by the trainers. Theoretical knowledge is further discussed and applied to their own work situations through group work activities and role–plays, as well as through self-reflection and self-assessment exercises. By means of an intensive feedback process the participants learn more about the effects they have on others in groups. This process helps to identify important areas where there is a need for individual development and it helps to clarify those behaviour patterns and personal styles which could be modified in order to bring about greater effectiveness in facilitating constructive team discussions.*

Module 2: Communication forum

The second module, called **communication forum***, takes place 8–10 weeks after the first module and runs for two days. Two groups of Module 1 participants are put together into one training group for the second module. Module 2 is designed to provide participants with important information about the organisation.*

Members of important internal departments present their work to the managers, and contact is established in case the managers require assistance or further information.

The content of the different presentations are as follows:

- *Employment law for newly appointed managers, public relations, advertising and the press, the role of the works council, human resources development, handling difficult customer complaints, strategy and controlling, etc.*

It is possible to add new topics to Module 2 whenever the need to address new areas of strategy arises. The participants can also ask questions and discuss topics in further detail with the presenters.

Upon completion of this module, each participant is expected to have a better understanding of the organisation's strategy and to know who to call should special questions arise. Acquiring stronger networking abilities is also one of the objectives. A manager's ability to build up his/her own network within the organisation depends as much on personal skills as on knowing the right person to contact when information is required in any given situation.

Module 3: Management tools

The third module, called **management tools***, with the same 14 participants as in Module 1, runs for four days. As with Module 2, the assimilation period between modules was 8–10 weeks. Module 3 focuses on management tools which help managers to run their teams effectively. Through the use of practical role-plays, participants practise delegating responsibility and work on cultivating initiative and a sense of responsibility among their staff. They also focus on problem solving and conflict resolution, and learn how to coach and develop employees, to set and monitor goals, and to do the annual appraisal interviews. Participants also learn more about their own strengths and weaknesses by way of intensive feedback processes and open discussions with their learning partner.*

Modules 4 and 5: Management supervision and counselling

Modules 4 and 5, called **management supervision and counselling***, both run for two days and there is an 8–10 week assimilation period between modules.*

In these modules participants have the opportunity of working on real-life cases based on their own experience. A "supervision model" is introduced by the trainers who help the participants to reflect on their cases and find solutions in a very structured way. There is time allotted in each module to work through between four and six cases. These activities allow participants to put newly acquired skills into practice, and help them to find solutions to their management problems by way of structured discussion with colleagues. The supervision process is organised as follows:

1. *A participant presents a problem with which he/she is presently confronted (e.g. an unmotivated employee, a personal conflict, a complex project or assignment which needs to be implemented).*
2. *The other participants listen and ask questions in order to gain a better understanding of the issue.*
3. *Now it is the turn of the participant who reported the problem to listen. The other participants exchange their views on the issue and attempt to look at the problem from as many sides as possible.*
4. *Potential solutions to the problems are brainstormed.*
5. *In certain cases the solution might be practised in a role-play simulation (e.g. simulating a feedback session with an unmotivated employee).*

This method has proved very effective in helping managers to solve problems on their own. By Module 4, trust and confidence within the group has grown and it is easier for participants to admit to personal difficulties without losing face. The other participants provide coaching and offer valuable social support in helping to find solutions for specific problems.

Upon completion of the training course, all participants are given the opportunity to meet twice a year to work on "management cases" to encourage a continuous learning culture. The participants are responsible for taking the organisation of these meetings into their own hands (dates, hotel, etc.) and the firm bears the costs for travel and accommodation. This encourages a process whereby learners take responsibility for their own learning activities. At this point, the participants are no longer guided by a trainer, but the supervision model helps them to organise their learning activities. There are some groups of training participants at the firm who still meet on a regular basis some years after the original training course to work on difficult management problems. This demonstrates the degree to which the whole learning process has been accepted and shows how important social support from colleagues can be in solving leadership problems. It also confirms that the concept of keeping the same group of participants together for an extended period of training encourages an atmosphere of mutual trust and confidence and ultimately makes for a more effective learning environment.

HOW TO SELECT THE RIGHT TRAINER

Once the goals of the training process have been identified and a commitment from senior management for the training activity has been made, the right trainer or consultant for the training course must be selected.

INTERNAL VS. EXTERNAL TRAINERS

If the company has an internal training and development department an experienced management trainer may be selected internally to run the training course. If, on the other hand, the company decides that it is important to bring in new ideas and expertise, then an external trainer of excellent reputation should be hired. One advantage in selecting a trainer internally is that he/she will be readily familiar with the organisation and can more easily put theory into context by illustrating examples based on concrete aspects of the participants' workplace. One of the drawbacks is that internal trainers sometimes complain of a lack of acceptance by the participants because the latter feel that the internal trainer has nothing to teach them since he/she is one of them. An external consultant, specialised in management training, might bring fresh ideas and perspectives into the organisation by imparting his/her knowledge of management practices in other companies. External consultants are often more readily accepted because participants tend to have more faith in the expertise and unbiased approach of the external trainer. However, it is important to bear in mind that external consultants do not always find it easy to tailor their knowledge and use of examples to fit the business context of a specific company.

HOW TO ASSESS THE EXPERTISE AND ORGANISATIONAL FIT OF A TRAINER

Once the decision has been taken to hire a trainer, regardless of whether internally or externally, you still have to choose the right person. The following is a list of important selection criteria of what to look for in a trainer: specialist in the desired training area (e.g. management training); appropriate educational background (e.g. work experience and organisational psychologist); management expertise (it lends the trainer credibility in the eyes of the participants if he/she has gathered experience as a manager); personality (extroverted, motivating for others, etc.); communication style (e.g., is his/her communication style suitable for the participants or is the trainer too intellectual, too technical, too esoteric, etc.). It is always useful to check the way trainers work. It is advisable to ask for previous training evaluation forms, participant feedback and references from former clients. You might also consider discussing a trainer's methods and training style directly with him/her during the selection process.

DEFINING RESPONSIBILITIES AND GUIDELINES FOR TRAINERS

The next step is to define the responsibilities of both the organisation and the trainer. Is it important that the trainer works out the training concept, or is he/she only responsible for running a training course that has already been developed? Is he/she responsible for the logistical aspects of the course, e.g. organisation, invitations, etc.? Do both agree about evaluation procedures, e.g. participant feedback after each training module?

The following example illustrates the decision-making process that was used to select the right trainer for the firm's introductory-level leadership training programme.

INTRODUCTORY-LEVEL LEADERSHIP TRAINING: HOW TO SELECT THE RIGHT TRAINER

The firm decided on a training concept which emphasised two main areas: the training of social skills, and the familiarising of managers with important theoretical concepts of leadership behaviour. It was also considered vital to instruct managers in accordance with the firm's own management principles, whereby each managerial decision should dove-tail with the underlying strategy of the organisation as a whole. With these criteria in mind the training department sought to engage two trainers who matched the following profiles: The first, was to be an expert in leadership training, a specialist in the training of social skills and he/she was also expected to have a strong background in psychology. The second person was to act as a co-trainer, and the firm specifically wanted an experienced manager who would be able to share his/her experiences and recipes for successful management behaviour with the participants and who could help solve concrete problems.

For many managers the co-trainer role was to become an important aspect of their own management development. They were given the chance to broaden their skills through the training and development of others and they learned a lot about group dynamics by assuming an active role in the training process. A train-the-trainer preparation course was also made available to managers before the start of the training programme.

In this example, the firm's internal training and development department developed the training programme in conjunction with newly appointed and more experienced managers. The organisation wanted to be certain that the content of the programme was in keeping with the philosophy of the organisation and that the needs of newly appointed managers were being sufficiently met. All organisational aspects of the programme were handled by the internal training department for reasons of cost-effectiveness. The trainer was responsible for running the training course with an eye to developing and improving future courses through an analysis of his/her own experiences and participant feedback on the programme. To this effect, meetings were held twice annually to discuss possible improvements to the existing course.

APPLICATION PROCESS AND COURSE ORGANISATION

A sound application process is necessary if the right people are to be chosen for a training course. During the appraisal interview the employee and manager might agree on measures to respond to existing training needs. Most companies have internal training departments or external training providers who act as consultants and give advice on how to best match training needs and the right training programme. Normally a description of the format and content of the most important in-house and external training courses are available through training brochures or the intranet. In-house training courses are often organised by the internal training department. This involves organising hotels, technical equipment, training material, scheduling the training programmes, inviting the participants and contracting the internal or external trainer—in a cost-effective manner. A formalised application process with clear terms and conditions ensures that staff get the right training at the right time. In recent years awareness of training as a major cost factor has increased. Therefore most training departments act as an internal cost centre and make managers pay for their staff's training activities. Most training departments suffer as a result of training being cancelled by participants at short notice due to illness or increased workload. To avoid such cancellations, they invoice the manager for the training activity, even if their staff have not participated in the training. These terms and conditions are normally printed on the application form itself. The following example shows the application process chosen for the firm's introductory-level leadership training programme.

INTRODUCTORY-LEVEL LEADERSHIP TRAINING: APPLICATION PROCESS

In the annual appraisal interviews at the firm a development plan is agreed upon by employees and their managers. In the case of staff seeking to become managers, it is highly recommended that they participate in a management training course (during the pioneering days of this programme, attendance for newly appointed managers was mandatory, and although obligation to attend has since been lifted the popularity of the course has in no way suffered). In the appraisal interview, both employee and manager fill out the requisite training application form and the manager then puts his/her signature to it, thereby making a commitment to invest both the time and money required for the employee's development. The internal training department does its part to quickly accommodate the employee. Once placement in a course has been arranged, the supervisor receives an invitation on behalf of his/her employee and he/she then goes over the preparatory material with the employee and together they set some specific goals to be achieved by the end of the course.

MEASURING COSTS AND BENEFITS

Training costs need to be carefully planned and calculated. Training is a relatively expensive solution for performance problems. It contrasts sharply with the cost of other solutions such as feedback from the manager, quality circles, job aides and checklists, job rotation, mentoring. The following should be taken into consideration when calculating a training budget:

- Costs for consulting, designing, conducting, and evaluating the training programme (e.g. salary costs, fees)
- Training materials (manuals, slides, videotapes, overhead transparencies, television monitors and video equipment)
- Travel and hotel expenses
- Lost work time of trainees and management (pre- and post-training discussions, etc.).

Interestingly, for many companies, the net costs for trainers and training development are often moderate in comparison with hotel and travel expenses. It makes little sense to economise on trainers when you consider that administrative costs consume the greatest share of the training budget. Time and money spent on sub-standard training is far worse than investing a few 100 dollars more per day for an excellent trainer.

The benefits of a good employee development programme are evident but they are difficult to put into figures. Unfortunately, there are too many influencing factors to allow accurate measurement of the positive effects that training obviously has in areas such as: productivity and performance, increased staff competence, greater customer satisfaction, improved goal-oriented behaviour among managers and employees, increased morale, reductions in staff turnover, and so on. In the end, it is easier to calculate the costs of a training programme than it is to calculate its benefits. The following example shows how this was done in the firm.

Introductory-Level Leadership Training: Calculation of Estimated Costs and Benefits

The estimated costs for one training course (13 days over the course of a year) consisted of:

- *Costs for course planning, organisation, development and evaluation (salaries, fees)*
- *Trainer's fees*
- *Travel and hotel expenses*
- *Lost work time of participants*
- *Management time (co-trainer's salary divided by number of training days, time for pre- and post-training discussions).*

The internal training department calculated the overall costs of the programme and established a price for each training place in order to recoup the costs of the training course. The cost of lost work time was not calculated. The cost per participant was set at ca. $5000. This included hotel and travel expenses and was taken from the senior manager's "training and development" budget. Fortunately, senior management viewed the training programme as being highly beneficial. They shared the philosophy that money invested in human resources ultimately leads to greater cost-effectiveness for the organisation in the long run and saw the training programme as an investment in management development as a whole. Compared to the costs involved in recruiting an external, experienced manager through a head-hunter or a recruitment agency it showed that it is far less expensive to invest in the development of the leadership skills of existing staff than to pay recruitment costs, and to invest the time training an external manager to work effectively in the new company.

HOW TO INVOLVE AND CONVINCE SENIOR MANAGEMENT

Senior management is an integral partner in the training process. Training initiatives easily become a waste of time and money if the entire learning process is not in line with the senior management's overall strategy for the organisation.

Once the training needs analysis has been completed and the training goals and design have been established, then it is time to present the concept to senior management in an effort to gain their commitment. They will need to see the main benefits of the training programme, the amount of time it will take, the costs, and what their role will be in ensuring that the whole programme is a success.

Management has several responsibilities in ensuring that the programme runs successfully. First of all, they need to send the right people for training, which means that they have to be familiar with the programme content as well as the requirements of the future participants. They have to commit time and money in order for future participants to be able to attend the training course. In addition, they have to initiate pre-training discussions with future participants to discuss learning goals and expectations. Furthermore, they need to arrange a follow-up session in order to reflect upon the main learning experiences with the employee, evaluate progress and to agree upon new areas of responsibility in which the participant can practise his/her newly acquired skills.

If the newly appointed manager cannot practise newly acquired skills, and if there is no feedback on his/her improvement, then the effects of the training course will be minimal. Figure 13.4 shows the different responsibilities of a senior manager as a coach in the training process.

Some management courses involve senior managers directly in the training process. They enter into discussion with participants, talk about the participants' new roles as

Appraisal Interview
Feedback on training needs, agreement on development plan,
application for a training course

Pre-Training Discussion
Definition of training and learning goals, feedback on
development needs

Training Intervention
Employee visits training course: Senior manager allots time and
money for the activity

Post-training Discussion
Reflection on training results and how to best practise newly
learned skills

Delegation of New Tasks
Observation of the employee's performance progress

**The senior manager and his/her manager discuss and continously assess
training needs and the manager's learning progress**

FIGURE **13.4**   The senior manager's role as a coach in the training process

managers, or give presentations on the organisation's principal strategies. This method was also used in the firm.

INTRODUCTORY-LEVEL LEADERSHIP TRAINING: MANAGEMENT INVOLVEMENT

Involvement by senior management in the firm's training process takes on many forms. So-called "chimney evenings", as the name implies, are held in the evenings during a training course. These evenings allow participants to ask invited board members or senior managers questions and to discuss strategic issues. Presentations on specific topics are given by senior managers. Management also benefits from this experience by getting important, bottom-up feedback on a regular basis. There is always a senior manager involved in the training course as a co-trainer. Management has an important role in the pre-training and post-training discussions with employees.

THE FIRST TRAINING SESSION: THE TRIAL RUN

Each training course will inevitably improve with time. A trial run is a good way of accelerating the process and finding out the strengths and weaknesses of a training programme. One should be very selective when choosing participants for the trial run, because valid and relevant feedback can make for significant improvements in a training programme. One might wish to select a mixture of participants which includes an equal number of both newly appointed managers (to see if their needs are being fulfilled) and experienced managers (to find out if they feel that their management experience is well represented in the course).

PARTICIPANT FEEDBACK

It is useful to get feedback at the end of each training module in order to verify if the main learning goals have been met, to see if the learning methods were effective and appealing and to find out if there was sufficient opportunity to apply the content to real-life situations.

Open feedback methods like group discussions, in which the participants verbally evaluate the above-mentioned aspects of the training module, might be useful. Surveys might help to standardise the evaluation process by asking key questions in the main areas of evaluation. Brainstorming sessions should be used for both problem solving and the gathering of new ideas for improvement from the whole group. An overall exchange of feedback at the end of the training programme will hopefully clarify those areas of the training module that require further development. An interview with the initial participants after three months should help to determine whether the training content can in fact be applied in practice.

The final version of the training programme should be designed to include the trial participants' suggestions.

EVALUATION PROCESS

Despite spending millions of dollars on management training, few companies invest money to have their efforts evaluated. Once companies have decided to spend the money on management training, it seems that mere surface indicators are taken as sufficient proof that a company's investment is being put to good use. However, evaluations are only a small fraction of the overall cost of management training and they are not overly difficult to do. Universities are often very keen to gather research data from practitioners and are therefore an excellent evaluation resource. Evaluation might be of help in measuring the results and long-term effects of management training courses.

Taking a baseline measurement before the training course is essential if you are to derive an accurate understanding of the effects of training from post-training analysis. Post-training analysis can be done directly after a training session or after a short waiting period (e.g. 3 months)—once enough time has elapsed allowing for the application of the acquired skills.

The tools used for evaluations are surveys, interviews and performance data. You could evaluate the effects of a training course by asking participants, customers, colleagues, employees, managers and trainers about the results and effects of learning through interviews and surveys.

Although training evaluation can give valuable feedback on the success of a training programme it is not used throughout each training activity. One of the reasons for the frequent lack of systematic training evaluations is that it is easier to get funding for a training programme than for its evaluation. To be able to prove the success and the learning

Time 1	**Baseline** Assessment of pre-training performance *Methods:* Interviews, surveys of superior's assessment, participant's assessment, performance data, customer feedback, assessment centre data
Time 2	**Course evaluation** Participant's and trainer's assessment of the effectiveness of the training course *Methods:* Interviews, survey, feedback workshops
Time 3	**Post-training evaluation** Assessment of short-term training effects, e.g. 3 months after the training course *Methods:* Interviews, surveys of superior's assessment, participant's assessment, performance data, customer feedback
Time 4	**Follow-up to post-training evaluation** Assessment of long-term training effects, e.g. 6–9 months after the training course *Methods:* Interviews, surveys of superior's assessment, participant's assessment, performance data, customer feedback assessment centre data

FIGURE 13.5 Framework for evaluation design

progress of participants evaluation is highly recommended. Very often evaluation is done but only half-heartedly. It is not uncommon to find that the necessary pre-training data is missing, or that the wrong questions have been asked, or that there has been contamination in the measurement process and key indicators have somehow gone missing. Statisticians may insist on a control group to see if there has been a change in the group which has undergone training as compared to the group which has not undergone training.

The criteria upon which training programmes are normally evaluated can be divided into three major categories: contribution to organisational goals, achievement of learning objectives, and/or perceptions of the trainees and their managers.

If you focus an organisation's priorities then you can evaluate the training programme as compared with the goals set prior to the training programme. It is useful to delineate a baseline before the training programme begins and after it has been completed to be able to identify the training programme's effect. To make effective evaluations, the evaluation design must specify not only what will be counted, but also when. This necessitates analysis of several areas: pre-training, post-training and post-training follow-up evaluations, as shown in Figure 13.5, are an indication of whether the criteria contribute to your goals. The process should continue until management is satisfied that problems no longer exist.

The following example shows the evaluation process conducted by the firm and the conclusions that can be drawn from it as to the effectiveness of the overall introductory-level leadership training programme.

INTRODUCTORY-LEVEL LEADERSHIP TRAINING: THE EVALUATION PROCESS OF THE MANAGEMENT TRAINING COURSE

There were various ways of evaluating the success of the training course. First of all, after each module the participants gave some written and oral feedback and completed a training evaluation form. This feedback enabled the training department to see if the learning goals had been achieved or if improvements were necessary in the content of the course. Participants evaluated the trainer's abilities, the organisation of the course and the overall applicability of the course.

The second source of evaluation was a survey done three months after the last module of each training programme. The entire training course was assessed by all former participants to find out how significant a contribution it had made in supporting them in their new leadership role, and how applicable the content had been in the context of their day-to-day working environment as well as to what extent they had been able to improve their own leadership behaviour.

In general the results indicated that the training course provided a valuable support system for newly appointed managers and that the content was extremely relevant to their work environment. Nevertheless there was room for improvement with regard to the support and encouragement offered by the managers of the newly appointed managers throughout the training programme.

*A third source of evaluation data came from the internal assessment centres. One of the requirements for becoming a third-level manager (middle manager) was to attend an assessment centre where strategic, leadership and sales skills were assessed. An evaluation of the people assessed at the centres revealed that the successful participants who had very good scores in the area of leadership behaviour had all attended the introductory-level leadership training programme. Those who had not attended this course displayed significantly lower scores in leadership behaviour. This represented a quasi-experimental design because one could take the group who had not attended the training course as a **control** group and the group that had as an **experimental** group. The experimental* *group showed statistically significant better scores in the assessment centres than the control group.*

A last source of evaluation was an anonymous employee survey carried out 4 years after the implementation of the training programme. This employee survey was completed by each employee in the organisation. One part of the survey dealt with management behaviour. Each employee was asked to assess the management behaviour of his/her own manager and top management. The results of that survey revealed a very positive attitude towards management behaviour. Although the employees criticised top management's behaviour and especially the strategic activities of the board, they showed respect for and satisfaction with the behaviour of their own managers. The results showed that a large majority of managers with a first management position (who were exactly the target group of the training sessions) and middle managers (who were trained as well as newly appointed managers a few years ago) were able to give and receive feedback, effectively handle customer complaints, act as partners and coaches in conflict situations, develop their staff, communicate effectively, set goals and measure them, and were approachable—even regarding personal matters. This survey indicated that compared with the previous survey carried out a few years earlier, there was a vast improvement in management skills. Efforts to improve the management skills of both third-(middle managers) and fourth-level managers (mainly managers with a first management role) throughout the firm were successful.

CONCLUSIONS

Practitioners often face the problem that they are hindered in the development of a training process by both time and financial constraints. They need to convince the organisation that training efforts are worth the money invested. But the best training courses are developed, tested, and evaluated over a longer period of time. An in-depth training needs assessment, a clear definition of the learning goals and the target group help when developing the training plan and choosing the right learning methods and trainers. It is crucial for the success of the whole training process that senior management is involved in the training process and take an active part in creating learning opportunities for their staff. As there is always pressure to provide training which is as cost-effective as possible, one should calculate in detail the costs involved and the benefits of the training programme. If the organisation of the training course is well thought out this can help to save money. In the same way a clear application process ensures that the right people get onto the training course. An evaluation of the training process ensures that the programme itself can be further developed and that the organisation gets some feedback on the effectiveness of their investment.

Training professionals should attempt to establish some balance between quick fixes and sound work. Joint projects with universities provide an excellent way of getting help with new training methods, of learning about the latest research knowledge and of gaining some expertise in evaluation techniques, all of which can lead to an improvement in the quality of training processes.

REFERENCES

Bandura, A. (1977). *Social learning theory*. New York: Holt, Rinehart & Winston.
Conger, J. A. (1992). *Learning to lead*. San Francisco: Jossey-Bass.
Flanagan, J. C. (1954). The critical incidents technique. *Psychological Bulletin*, **51**, 327–358.
Gebert, D., Steinkamp, T., & Wendler, E. (1987). *Führungsstil und Absatzerfolg in Kreditinstituten*. Wiesbaden: Gabler Verlag.

Goldstein, I. L. (1989) *Training and development in organisations*. San Francisco: Jossey-Bass.

Hofbauer, H., & Winkler, B. (1999). *Das Mitarbeitergespräch als Führungsinstrument*. München: Carl Hanser Verlag.

House, R. J. (1996). Classroom instruction. In R. L. Craig (Ed.), *The ASTD training and development handbook* (4th edn.). New York: McGraw-Hill.

Latham, G. P., & Saari, L. M. (1979). Application of social-learning theory to training supervisors through behavioral modeling. *Journal of Applied Psychology*, **74**, 411–416.

Laird, D. (1985). *Approaches to training and development*. Reading: Addison Wesley.

Mintzberg, H. (1970). Structured observation as a method to study managerial work. *The Journal of Management Studie*, **7**, 87–104.

Reid, M. A., Barrington, H., & Kenney, J. (1992). *Training Interventions*. London: Institute of Personnel Management.

Thornton III, C. (1992). Providing Feedback of Assessment Centre Results. In *Assessment Centres in Human Resource Management* (pp. 165–210). Reading: Addison Wesley.

Thiagarajan, S. (1996). Instructional games, simulations, and role-plays. In R. L. Craig (Ed.), *The ASTD training and development handbook* (4th edn.). New York: McGraw-Hill.

Whitmore, J. (1992). *Coaching for performance*. London: Nicholas Brealey Publishing.

Winkler, B., & Dörr, S. (2001). Fusioneu überlebeu. Strategien für Manager. München: Carl Hanser Verlag.

Winstanley, D., & Woodall, J. (1992). *Case studies in personnel*. London: Institute of Personnel Management.

CHAPTER 14

Enhancing Performance through Mentoring

Terri A. Scandura and **Betti A. Hamilton**
University of Miami, Coral Gables, USA

SUMMARY

The benefits of mentoring include enhanced performance not only for the individual, but also for the mentor and the organization. Interest in harnessing these benefits for improved performance at the individual, group, and organizational levels have increased tremendously. In this chapter, we review the concept of mentoring from an academic perspective and report on the empirical findings that provide evidence for mentoring's impact on performance. As research on mentoring continues, models of mentoring have gone beyond the one-on-one traditional model. Mentoring research on the relationship of mentoring into the learning process is taking the field into new directions. Though the overwhelming outcomes of mentoring on performance are positive, there are instances when the relationship may turn dysfunctional with detrimental effects. The implications of current perspectives for performance and training and development are reviewed and summarized.

Psychological Management of Individual Performance. Edited by Sabine Sonnentag.
© 2002 John Wiley & Sons, Ltd.

OVERVIEW: THE CONCEPT OF MENTORING

According to Greek mythological legend, Mentor, a friend and counselor to Odysseus, was entrusted with the education of Odysseus' son, Telemachus. As a trusted senior adviser, Mentor was responsible for raising Telemachus and instructing him in the ways of the world. Today, the term *mentor* has come to mean a person who takes a special concern in furthering the career and development of a new (or junior) person in the organization (Kram, 1985). By guiding the development of the junior person in various ways, mentors may unlock the potential of those under their guidance.

There is nothing necessarily mythical about the mentoring process. Research has shown that mentoring can be assessed, and related empirically to outcomes for mentors, protégés and the organizations they work for. Most research on mentoring to date has focused on protégés and the career-related benefits they accrue. However, as the field matures, research is examining the benefits to the mentor, as well as understanding different outcomes of the mentoring process. Mentoring models are changing. Recent research is looking at redefining mentoring from the intense one-on-one relationship to constellations, or networks, of mentors (Higgins & Kram, 1999; Ibarra, 1994). Research is also examining how mentoring is related to the learning process (Lankau, 1996) and mentoring in a team environment (Dansky, 1996; Williams, 2000). In addition, the impact of mentoring in the international arena is another area where research is just beginning (Scandura & Von Glinow, 1997). The benefits and outcomes of mentoring have such potential impact for individual performance that this concept has been considered as an organizational training and development tool (Hunt & Michael, 1983). For these reasons, interest in mentoring research expanded in the last two decades and continues today. In this chapter, we will review research on mentoring relationships in organizations with a focus on findings that have implications for individual performance. For each topic, we will note areas in need of further research.

MENTORING DEFINED

A general definition of a mentor is that of an influential individual, with advanced experience and knowledge, who is committed to providing upward support and mobility to his/her protégé's career (Levinson, Darrow, Klein, Levinson, & McKee, 1978). Mentoring is thus a one-to-one relationship between a more experienced senior person (the mentor) and a new entrant or less experienced person (his or her protégé) in the organization setting (Ragins & Scandura, 1994). This traditional definition of mentoring emphasizes an intense and emotional one-on-one relationship (Kram, 1985; Roche, 1979). The dyadic hierarchical mentoring relationship is often characterized as a supportive and trusting collaboration providing mutually beneficial outcomes to both mentor and protégé. The emergence of this relationship may be formalized through organizationally directed programs; however, it is often an informal pairing borne of respect and interpersonal connections that connote the most beneficial mentoring relationships (Chao, Walz, & Gardner, 1992; Fagenson-Eland, Marks, & Amendola, 1997; Kram, 1985; Noe, 1988; Ragins & Cotton, 1999). Informal mentoring relationships and the functions they provide have been related to the individual performance and career mobility of the protégé (Dreher & Ash, 1990; Scandura, 1992).

In addition to personal development and rewards, mentoring may promote organizationally desirable outcomes. For example, research findings show that mentoring supports organizational goals due to the beneficial effects of learning (Lankau, 1996). Realization of mentoring benefits takes place over time as the relationship progresses (Chao, 1997; Kram, 1983; Orpen, 1995). Therefore, mentoring has traditionally been regarded as a relatively long-term relationship, which moves through developmental phases and provides specific forms of assistance to the protégé, which have been labeled mentoring functions.

MENTORING FUNCTIONS

Mentoring has been categorized as providing two broad classes of functions: Career development and psychosocial support (Kram, 1985). In career development, mentors provide vocational support, such as coaching, advising and visibility for their protégés (Kram, 1985). As a career coach, the mentor counsels the protégé on how to pursue and develop his/her career. As a sponsor, a mentor may advance the protégé's career by nominating him or her for promotion. Through exposure and visibility, such as contact and interaction with key players in the organization, opportunities for the protégé to demonstrate competence and special talents are enhanced and opportunities for challenging work assignments are assured. The mentor may also be a protector and try to minimize protégé involvement in situations that may be political or controversial. The mentor may also provide technical support and advice on specific skill development. This advice may be either task-related or focus on interpersonal skills.

In the psychosocial role, the mentor provides social support, serving as a confidant and friend. Psychosocial functions address interpersonal aspects of the mentoring relationship and enhance a protégé's sense of competence, self-efficacy, and professional and personal development. Whereas career development functions focus on the protégé's career in the organization, psychosocial functions involve relating to the protégé on a more personal level and extend to other spheres of life, such as the protégé's personal development. Mentoring may thus serve as a buffer in alleviating work-related stress (Allen, McManus, & Russell, 1999; Baugh, Lankau, & Scandura, 1996).

The mentor may also serve as a role model providing inspiration to the protégé. As a role model, the protégé learns appropriate behavior by observing the mentor's conduct. Protégés have someone to measure their behavior against and a model of success to aspire toward in the future. Role modeling may be seen as a more passive form of psychosocial mentoring (as conceptualized by Kram, 1985). However, role modeling has been shown to emerge as a separate and distinct mentoring function in some studies (Burke, 1984; Fagenson-Eland et al., 1997; Lankau, 1996; Scandura, 1992; Williams, 1999).

MENTORING PHASES

Mentoring relationships are conceptualized to be relationships of long duration [up to 5 years or more according to Kram (1985)]. Research has shown that often there is substantial emotional commitment by both parties over this extended time, and that these relationships evolve in distinct phases. Kram (1983) identified four stages: initiation, cultivation, separation, and redefinition. The initiation phase is the first stage and typically lasts six months to one year. During this time, the relationship gets started and both the mentor and protégé define their roles. Typically in this phase, the mentor provides coaching, challenging work, and some visibility. The protégé's technical proficiency increases and he or she expresses the desire to be coached by the mentor. As the relationship matures, it moves into the cultivation phase. In cultivation, a period that may last from two to five years, both individuals continue to benefit and contribute in the relationship. As the protégé advances in career and responsibility, the mentoring relationship provides increasing opportunities for meaningful and more frequent interaction. This is considered to be the stage of mentorship during which most benefits accrue to the mentor and the protégé. As noted by Scandura (1998), most mentoring research has focused on issues in the cultivation phase. Finally, as the protégé advances beyond the need of the current mentoring relationship, the nature of the mentoring relationship begins to change. This signifies the separation phase. In this period, which may last from six months to two years, the protégé has moved on to another position either through job rotation or promotion which begins to limit opportunities for continued interaction (Ragins & Scandura, 1999). In the final phase, redefinition, a new relationship is taking place. After the separation phase, the existing mentoring relationship is no longer needed. The relationship either terminates or it is redefined into a peer-like friendship. Ragins and Scandura (1997) found that mentoring relationships might terminate for functional reasons such as physical separation or evolution of the relationship. Conversely, the termination of the mentoring relationship may be dysfunctional when one of the parties refuses to let go of the relationship and psychological issues such as over-dependency, competitiveness, or jealousy arise. Functional separations are more likely to evolve into peer friendships (Kram, 1985).

Viator and Scandura (1991) defined the mentor–protégé relationship along a continuum. At one end of the continuum is the intense paternalistic relationship; at the other end is the peerlike relationship, pal or "helper" (Kram & Isabella, 1985). In the middle of the continuum is the mentor–protégé relationship where the mentor is more of a "sponsor". A sponsor may provide visibility to the protégé, but less of the direct face-to-face coaching that is described in the prototypical mentor–protégé relationship. More research is needed to examine potential differences between these mentor roles and how they may impact the development of the protégé's individual performance and other attitudinal outcomes. Future research might explore a broader range of the mentoring modalities.

MENTORING AND INDIVIDUAL PERFORMANCE

In today's work environment, mentoring is considered by many to be an important tool for enhancing career success, particularly upward mobility and compensation. However, the mentoring relationship offers additional benefits not only to the protégé but also to the mentor and additionally, may play an important role in the organizational socialization of new employees (Ostroff & Kozlowski, 1993; Wilson & Elman, 1990).

BENEFITS TO PROTÉGÉ

Research has found that mentoring provides many benefits to the protégé. Such benefits include higher rates of promotion (Dreher & Ash, 1990; Scandura, 1992), salary and compensation (Chao et al., 1992; Dreher & Ash, 1990; Scandura, 1992; Whiteley, Dougherty, & Dreher, 1991), and higher performance (Dreher & Ash, 1990; Scandura, 1992). Also, mentoring has been related to career and job satisfaction (Baugh et al., 1996;

Fagenson, 1989; Koberg, Boss, Chappell, & Ringer, 1994). Through the vocational mentoring function, mentors can create opportunities for protégés through special assignments and networking. These opportunities may lead to career advancement. In addition, protégés can get help and advice on career decisions from mentors, which is critical in managing a successful career. Mentoring has also been related to organizational socialization (Ostroff & Kozlowski, 1993) and reduced turnover intentions (Scandura & Viator, 1994). Protégés tended to feel more in tune with the organization's way of thinking and doing things, more nurtured and supported during the promotion process, and may be more aware of organizational politics (Dirsmith & Covaleski, 1985; Fagenson, 1988). Thus, as a learning forum, mentoring provides job-related and personal feedback, allowing protégés to test new ideas and learn new behaviors (Chao et al., 1992; Ostroff & Kozlowski, 1993). Lankau and Scandura (1997) found support for mentoring as a contributor to socialization and learning by providing a means of information dissemination and support for continuous learning. More research is needed to determine how the three mentoring aspects (vocational, psychosocial, and role modeling) relate to attitudinal outcomes and individual learning.

BENEFITS TO MENTORS

Ragins and Scandura (1994) also investigated the potential benefits that mentors may receive from the mentoring relationship. By contributing to future generations, mentors can get a sense of immortality (Erikson, 1963) believing that they have left a mark on the next generation as a result of the mentor–protégé relationship. Mentors also often feel the internal satisfaction of passing wisdom, knowledge and insight on to more junior persons in the organization (Levinson et al., 1978). In identifying and developing protégé talent, mentors receive recognition from peers and superiors. Additionally, mentors may engage in mentoring because they receive support from loyal protégés and advanced technical support. Kram (1985) considered these mentor benefits to be tangible support that provides a means from which the mentor may improve his or her own job performance. Mullen and Cooper (1994) found additional support for mentor benefits in the form of valuable work-related information from their protégés. Loyal protégés can also provide psychological support to the mentor (Kram, 1985). Managers may be more highly motivated to mentor others when the organization has a developmental culture (Aryee, Chay, & Chew, 1996). In a follow-up study, Ragins and Scandura (1999) found support that the formation of the mentoring relationship involves an intergenerational process. Mentors may thus base their decisions to mentor others on their own experiences as protégés; those who experienced positive experiences as a protégé may thus be more likely to become mentors in the future. Having protégés may positively impact the individual performance of the mentor. More research is needed to explore performance and other benefits that mentors may receive from the mentoring relationship.

BENEFITS TO THE ORGANIZATION

The benefits of mentoring to the organization are another area worthy of additional research. Zey (1984) proposed that the benefits of mentoring to the organization included better integration and socialization of employees, reduction in turnover, improved organizational communication, more effective management development, improved managerial succession, power, and productivity. The research literature has supported the linkages of many of these benefits and mentoring. In addition, Baugh et al. (1996) found that mentoring also reduced role stress. Kram and Hall (1991) also found support for mentoring as a stress reducer in organizational turmoil. Mentoring has also been related to perceptions of "fairness" at the work place (Scandura, 1997). In this study, those who were mentored were more likely to perceive the workplace as having greater distributive and procedural justice.

In integrating the individual and the organization, the mentor serves an important role in helping the protégé feel closer to the organization, and more aligned with its goals via the socialization process (Ostroff & Kozlowski, 1993). The protégé may have a greater sense of belonging, and be more committed to the organization (Baugh et al., 1996). Since mentoring relationships may prevent talented protégés from becoming lost in the organization, this may increase their tendency to remain in the organization, thereby reducing turnover (Dirsmith & Covaleski, 1985; Kram, 1985; Scandura & Viator, 1994). There is a need for additional studies on the role that mentoring may play in employee retention as an organizational performance outcome.

Communication between various organizational levels or departments can be promoted with the protégé serving as a "linking pin" (Likert & Likert, 1976). In addition, organizational communication may be facilitated because the protégé enjoys multi-tiered membership status as a result of the relationship with the mentor. By being in a position to transfer skills and knowledge to the protégé that might otherwise be denied, the mentor is an aid to improved management development. These transfer-of-training skills support the transformation of a technical worker to a full-fledged executive. Mentoring may reduce the haphazardness of management development and succession planning. By communicating corporate values and other key components of the corporate culture to the next generation of leaders, mentoring may facilitate the smooth transfer of the managerial reins from one generation of executives to the next. In the socialization and power area, mentoring produces managers who are comfortable with power and possess the ability to mobilize people and resources. In addition, mentoring may also be associated with increased cost-effectiveness of management development and training efforts. Mentoring may be particularly important in transfer-of-training since mentors may be able to provide coaching and feedback following a formal training intervention. More research is needed that links mentoring to the process of management development, training and executive succession.

DIMENSIONS OF PERFORMANCE

The dimensions of performance in mentoring include both performance and attitudinal variables. As noted above, mentoring has been linked to individual performance, career mobility, decreased intentions to leave, learning, job attitudes, lower stress and improved organizational socialization. These outcomes involve both performance indicators as well as work attitudes that may indirectly affect performance.

SUPERVISORY RATINGS AND OBJECTIVE PERFORMANCE INDICATORS

Research on mentoring needs to begin to link the mentoring functions to objective measures of productivity, in addition to supervisory performance ratings. The more coaching and instruction a mentor provides, the less uncertainty employees experience about their duties and what is expected of them on the job (Lankau & Scandura, 1997). In developing this linkage, new conceptualizations of mentoring may be needed which focus more on coaching for specific technical and interpersonal skills, rather than the mentoring literature's traditional focus on career development outcomes. Performance indicators of career success (promotions and salary, for example) have been linked to the vocational function of mentoring (Dreher & Ash, 1990; Scandura, 1992). These measures represent relatively more "objective" (i.e., non self-report) measures of individual performance.

ATTITUDINAL PERFORMANCE INDICATORS

Organizational socialization, professional development, personal learning, job satisfaction, and organizational commitment are all attitudes that have been linked to having a mentor and receiving mentoring functions (cf. Scandura, 1998, for review). Support from a mentor has also been related to lower levels of burnout from work (Lankau, 1996). Socialization of the protégé into the politics of the organization is also a potentially important process that may indirectly affect performance (Ostroff & Kozlowski, 1993). The more an employee knows about the history and rituals of the organization, and who the influential people are in the organization, the employee is likely to be more satisfied and experience less uncertainty with respect to his or her role in the organization.

LEARNING AND INNOVATION

Mentoring should support employees through coaching and support and allow employees to learn through their mistakes (Lankau & Scandura, 1997). This type of organization supports learning for all employees through its values, policies, practices and structure, and takes an active role in ensuring that new learning is disseminated throughout the organization so that it can gain insights and learn from mistakes (Bennett & O'Brien, 1994; Senge, 1990). In this knowledge era, organizational performance is dependent on the experience and capabilities of individuals (Carley, 1992; Clawson, 1996). Mentoring has increasingly become a forum for learning as it facilitates and promotes the growth and development of individuals in organizations (Hunt & Michael, 1983; Lankau, 1996). The development of a successful mentoring relationship reinforces the protégé's confidence in his or her ability to learn and may support risk taking and innovation (Lankau & Scandura, 1997). The more information, skills and knowledge an employee acquires, the more value he or she can contribute to the job, work group and organization. Lankau (1996) found that mentoring functions significantly impacted personal learning. Increased levels of role modeling provided by a mentor may be associated with increased personal learning through skill development, and the broadening of the protégé's repertoire of skills and abilities.

Zey (1984) postulated that the relationship between mentoring and creativity, though subtle, is quite powerful. The mentoring process facilitates the exchange of ideas between two partners, thus mentoring may act as a catalyst for innovation. A talented mentor will establish a safe, secure environment in which novel ideas are developed, nurtured, experimented with and successfully introduced into the corporate mainstream. It is the mentor's job to ensure that the protégé has ample time and freedom necessary to develop his or her ideas and innovations. Also, mentors or sponsors may serve as "champions" for the protégés' ideas while they are in the development stages. Thus, mentoring and innovation/creativity is yet another area that appears worthy of future research.

MENTORING MODELS FOR PERFORMANCE ENHANCEMENT

Mentoring may be formal or informal in nature. The degree of control exerted by the organization on the mentoring process typically characterizes where the mentoring process lies along a continuum. Formal programs are those which are planned, implemented and overseen by the organization, directed by written policy and guidelines, and required of all employees, particularly entry level staff (Burke & McKeen, 1989). Informal mentoring, on the other hand, usually lacks planning and specific guidelines. Responsibility for involvement is left to the individuals to make the right protégé–mentor match. There is no monitoring of the relationship or its outcomes. In between the two, an organization may encourage the mentoring process and perhaps even build mentoring into a formal reward system. The distinction between formal and informal mentoring is an important one, since research has called into question the effectiveness of formal mentoring (Chao et al., 1992; Fagenson-Eland et al., 1997; Noe, 1988; Ragins & Cotton, 1999).

The research literature has determined mentoring to be more effective as an informal process. Kram (1985) cited major advantages and disadvantages to formal mentoring. The major advantages of formal mentoring were that it (1) ensures that juniors and seniors find each other and that relationships are readily available; (2) increases the likelihood that matches will be good ones; (3) provides support to the individuals and helps to end incompatible relationships; and (4) changes attitudes and builds the necessary interpersonal skills required for individuals to initiate and manage the new relationships. However, Kram saw that formal mentoring had some disadvantages as well. The major disadvantages cited were that formal mentoring may (1) result in feelings of coercion and confusion about relationship responsibilities; (2) result in feelings of deprivation, resentfulness and pessimism about their futures by those not in the program; (3) set up an evaluation agenda which may put individuals in the program on the defensive; and (4) assume that all individuals can learn the necessary interpersonal skills though some may be ill-suited for these new responsibilities. Scandura and Williams (1998) echoed the results of other researchers finding that protégés in informal relationships experienced more career development and role modeling. Those in informal relationships also reported higher commitment and career expectations than non-mentored individuals. However, Scandura and Williams (1998) also found that mentoring relationships were most successful when both parties were invested in the initiation of the relationship. Thus, a potentially useful area of future research might examine how the matching process is conducted in formal programs and the degree to which both mentor and protégé are involved in the selection process.

In addition to how they are started, formal and informal mentoring relationships differ in the length of the relationship, with formal relationships usually shorter than informal relationships. Often, formal relationships are viewed as some form of organizational program which may last for the first two years of an employee's tenure in the organization. The goals of such programs are often to socialize the newcomer into the organizations (Forret, Turban, & Dougherty, 1996). Thus, the timeframe of the mentoring relationships set by the organization may affect the duration of mentoring in formal programs. Research is needed to examine if and why some relationships that were initiated by a formal program continue after the program terminates.

THE MENTORING DYAD

In the traditionally defined one-on-one mentoring relationship, a single mentor will most likely not be able carry an individual through a career. A more realistic approach is that of a succession of mentors over the course of an organizational career that will provide a range of critical career success factors at each phase of the career (Eby, 1997; Higgins & Kram, 1999; Ibarra, 1994; Kram, 1985).

The nature of the mentoring relationship has the mechanisms in place to challenge the individual beyond his or her own expectations. At the individual level, Scandura and Schriesheim (1991) found that mentoring had a positive impact on career progression and that the level of the mentor in the organizational hierarchy played a key role. Salary and promotions increased as a result of the individual's commitment to the firm. This commitment was evidenced by increased hours worked and jobs supervised as well as intent to remain with the organization. This study found that mentoring was enhanced if the mentor was a high-ranking individual. More research is needed to examine the performance impact of the level of mentor.

INDIVIDUAL DIFFERENCES AND MENTORING

Individual differences in personality such as internal locus of control, high self-monitoring, and high emotional stability measured as self-esteem and negative affectivity have been found to influence the development of mentoring relationships (Turban & Dougherty, 1994). High self-monitoring, emotional stability and positive affectivity traits may enhance the initiation of mentoring. In addition, recent work by Aryee, Lo, and Kang (1999) supports the addition of extraversion to the list. Protégés may be higher in need for achievement than non-protégés (Fagenson, 1992). In a follow-up study, Baugh and Fagenson-Eland (2000) identified the personality characteristics of need for dominance and self-esteem, in addition to need for achievement, as associated with protégé status in mentoring relationships. A one-to-one mentoring relationship facilitates dissemination of information, learning and feedback. Thus, mentoring may be enhanced by individual preferences for feedback seeking. Recent attention to the concept of emotional intelligence (Goleman, 1995; 1998) suggests that protégés (and mentors) may have higher levels of emotional intelligence. Emotional intelligence is defined by empathy, self-awareness, self-motivation, and social skills. When emotional intelligence is high, these characteristics reflect awareness of own emotions and the ability to competently deal with social situations. This would seem to be related to the ability to develop and maintain successful working relationships.

DIRECTIONS FOR FUTURE RESEARCH ON MENTORING AND PERFORMANCE

The traditional mentoring viewpoint of a one-on-one intense personal relationship is being modified as the workforce becomes more mobile and the nature of work itself is being redefined. Recognizing that organizations have downsized, the traditional, hierarchical view of mentoring may be changing (Kram & Hall, 1995; McManus & Russell, 1997). Along with changes in careers, mentors may now need to serve as promoters of the organizational vision. Bass (1985) describes a transformational leader as having charisma and the ability to get followers emotionally involved. Scandura and Williams (2000) studied the combination of transformational leadership and mentoring in the new workplace environment. They found support that mentoring enhances the effects of transformational leadership thereby supporting a complementary model of leadership and mentoring (Scandura & Schriesheim, 1994; Scandura & Williams, 2000). This new workplace is shaping emerging models of mentoring and coaching for individual development that can be further explored in future research.

MENTORING AND COACHING FOR INDIVIDUAL PERFORMANCE

Rapid changes in the work environment have increased the need for employees who can learn, unlearn, and relearn at a fast rate (Higgins, 1999; Jossi, 1997). Mentoring may be a means to facilitate learning, promote innovation, and increase productivity and performance. Mentoring may increase the effectiveness of the team leader thereby increasing the performance of the team (Williams, 1999). Future research needs to focus on how coaching may facilitate individual performance within a team concept (Williams & Scandura, 2000). In particular, the content of the coaching needs to be addressed: Is the focus on career development, technical skill building or interpersonal skill enhancement?

NEW DIRECTIONS IN MENTORING

Coaching teams

Teams and teamwork are being implemented in many organizations. Research suggests that the intellectual capacity of the team exceeds that of the average individual (Katzenbach & Smith, 1993). With the increasing information-processing requirements placed on firms, teams are proving to be a solution in managing information technology (Hackman & Walton, 1986). In extending the traditional mentoring model to teams, performance enhancements of the individual may also benefit the team. Team mentoring occurs when the leader serves as a team mentor and develops the team through career coaching, psychological support, and role modeling (Williams, 2000). This extension of the mentoring model into a team environment where members operate with a high degree of trust, cooperativeness, and information sharing broadens the role of mentoring. Williams (2000) additionally noted that team mentoring also occurs through the peer relationships that exist and in a way becomes the responsibility of each member of the team as they support the learning being promoted by the team leader/mentor.

Coaching peers and social networks

While more conventional (senior) mentors are deemed to be most important in early career development, Kram and Isabella (1985) found support that peers seem to play an important role at all stages of mentoring. They identified peer mentors as providing a source of information sharing and job-related feedback as well as effectively teaching corporate culture. This relationship may be more social and emotional (more of a friendship).

Peer relationships can provide complementary support to mentorship (Douglas & Schoorman, 1988). In a peer relationship, coworkers are at the same level in the organization, thus the psychosocial support and information-sharing functions of mentoring play key roles (Allen, Maetzke, & Russell, 1994). Higgins and Kram (1999) recently developed a model of mentoring in social networks that contrasts with the traditional dyadic mentoring relationships. The model developed is a reconceptualization of developmental relationships into different sets of constellations that may or may not include one or more mentors, senior colleagues, peers, family, and community members. This new concept builds upon the perception that individuals may rely on a series or a set of concurrent relationships or "networks", suggesting that mentoring is a multiple-relationship phenomenon. This approach adds levels of complexity that may pose challenges for data collection and empirical testing. More conceptual development and research on this mentoring networks concept is needed.

DYSFUNCTION IN MENTORING TERMINATIONS

Effective mentoring is characterized by a nurturing and supportive relationship between the mentor and the protégé yielding positive outcomes. However, not all mentoring relationships nurture, support, or provide positive benefits. Ragins and Scandura (1997) found that dysfunction may be present in the separation phase of mentoring relationships and results in termination of the relationship. Where relationships do not evolve in a mutually beneficial manner, either party may be dissatisfied and thus increase the probability of difficulty in the relationship, resulting in a termination process that is dysfunctional.

Dysfunctional mentoring styles

Further theoretical work by Scandura (1998) developed a typology of negative mentoring styles classified as dysfunctional. Mentors may abuse their power (negative relations), mentors and protégés may take revenge for negative actions (sabotage), value conflicts occur (difficulty), and feelings of regret or disappointment may emerge as vocational issues become problematic such as the mentor relocating or being fired (spoiling). Qualitative research conducted by Eby, McManus, Simon, and Russell (2000) supported the existence of dysfunction in mentoring and developed a grounded-theory typology of negative mentoring experiences. Such relationships are the exception rather than the rule, Scandura (1998) emphasized that most mentoring relationships are positive and productive. However, when dysfunction occurs, it may have serious impact on employee attitudes and work performance. The result may be increased stress and employee withdrawal in the forms of absenteeism and turnover.

Dysfunctional mentoring and performance decrements

Research is needed to examine the potential performance decrements that may occur due to dysfunctional mentoring experiences. Dysfunction in mentoring may be related to lower work satisfaction and turnover (Eby et al., 2000; Scandura, 1998). Dysfunctional mentoring may adversely affect mentors as well (McManus & Russell, 1999). One interesting question is whether relationships can produce high-performance outcomes, and yet result in lower job satisfaction and increased stress. Thus, the question of if and how dysfunction affects performance of mentors and protégés is an area worthy of future research.

INTERNATIONAL MENTORING

The concept of mentoring in the international context is a new and developing area. Global changes are placing increasing pressure on businesses to internationalize. As more business leaders are being thrust into the international arena, they are asked to operate in cultures with people who have different ideas about how work gets done. Competition in this arena focuses on having top managers who have had experience abroad. Through the process of mentoring, such managers may pass on necessary information to the protégés and thus to the organization. According to Scandura and Von Glinow (1997), the concept of mentoring in the international arena currently appears in the areas of training and development, the expatriate management literature, and career planning literature.

Failure rates for expatriates

Currently the failure rate for expatriates is between 16% and 50% and each of these failures may cost an organization up to $250,000 (Schaffer & Harrison, 1998). A pricier estimate is that the cost of one failure can be as much as $1 million if both direct and indirect costs are considered (Shannonhouse, 1996). Thus, the improvement of expatriate adjustment is an important area to target for performance enhancement, given current trends toward globalization, and the need to send managers abroad.

Performance enhancements for expatriates

In the area of expatriation, international assignments abroad, and repatriation, mentoring can play a key role in increasing performance levels and decreasing the failure rate of such ventures. Feldman and Thomas (1992) found that mentoring was related to better expatriate adjustment. Therefore mentoring may be able to improve organizational performance by allowing organizations to benefit more from expatriate assignments. This is also an area in which research on how expatriates use the internet to stay in contact with the home office while they are abroad may impact their individual performance. Expatriate managers abroad may need less technical skill coaching (they are usually selected because of the past track record of success in their home country) (Finney & Von Glinow, 1988). However, they may need more social support during their expatriate assignment. Finally, the network approach to viewing mentoring as a constellation of relationships may be an appropriate model for the expatriate (Higgins & Kram, 1999). Expatriates may need mentors from the host country to acclimatisee them to the culture, in addition to mentors in their home country to keep them informed of important matters in the home office.

CONCLUSIONS

The dynamics of mentoring reflect the processes of professional development, personal growth, organizational commitment, and improve the organization's ability to leverage human capital to improve organizational effectiveness. Mentoring may provide a key to career success and improved performance. Yet, there are many pieces to the puzzle of how mentoring relates to individual performance that are still missing. We have noted areas in need of future research throughout this chapter. There is a particular need for longitudinal research that examines how the process of mentoring unfolds over time. Also, program evaluation studies of formal mentoring programs are needed to assess the impact of mentoring programs which are very popular in organizations today (Murray, 1991). More research is needed on the role that mentoring may play in the employee withdrawal processes of absenteeism and turnover. And finally, further research is needed on the potential detrimental performance impacts when dysfunction occurs in the mentoring process (however rare this may be). The challenge of future research on mentoring will be to step beyond conventional wisdom and address the performance impacts of new mentoring models.

REFERENCES

Allen, T. D., McManus, S. E., & Russell, J. E. A. (1999). Newcomer socialization and stress: Formal peer relationships as a source of support. *Journal of Vocational Behavior*, **54**, 453–470.

Allen, T. D., Maetzke, S. B., & Russell, J. E. (1994). *Formal peer mentoring: Factors related to protégé's satisfaction and willingness to mentor others*. Paper presented at the Southern Management Association Meeting, New Orleans, LA.

Aryee, S., Lo, S., & Kang, I. (1999). Antecedents of early career stage mentoring among Chinese people. *Journal of Organizational Behavior*, **20**, 563–576.

Aryee, S., Chay, Y. W., & Chew, J. (1996). The motivation to mentor among managerial employees. *Group and Organization Management*, **21**, 261–277.

Bass, B. M. (1985). Leadership: Good, better, best. *Organizational Dynamics*, **13**, 26–41.

Baugh, S. G., & Fagenson-Eland, E. (2000). Protégé personality as a predictor of mentoring experience. Paper presented at the National Academy of Management Annual Meeting, Toronto, CA.

Baugh, S. G., Lankau, M. J., & Scandura, T. A. (1996). An investigation of the effects of protégé gender on responses to mentoring. *Journal of Vocational Behavior*, **49**, 309–323.

Bennett, J. K., & O'Brien, M. J. (1994). The building blocks of the learning organization. *Training*, **31**, 41–49.

Burke, R. J. (1984). Mentors in organizations. *Group and Organization Studies*, **9**, 353–372.

Burke, R. J., & McKeen, C. A. (1989). Developing formal mentoring programs in organizations. *Business Quarterly*, **53**, 76–79.

Carley, K. (1992). Organizational learning and personnel turnover. *Organization Science*, **3**, 20–46.

Chao, G. T. (1997). Mentoring phases and outcomes. *Journal of Vocational Behavior*, **51**, 15–28.

Chao, G. T., Walz, P. M., & Gardner, P. D. (1992). Formal and informal mentorships: A comparison of mentoring functions and contrast with nonmentored counterparts. *Personnel Psychology*, **45**, 1–16.

Clawson, J. G. (1996). Mentoring in the new information age. Special issue of *The Leadership and Organizational Development Journal*, "Developing the Leaders of Tomorrow through Mentoring," **17**, 6–15.

Dansky, K. H. (1996). The effect of group mentoring on career outcomes. *Group and Organization Management*, **21**, 5–21.

Dirsmith, M. W., & Covaleski, M. A. (1985). Informal communications, nonformal communications and mentoring in public accounting firms. *Accounting, Organizations and Society*, **10**, 149–169.

Douglas, C. A., & Schoorman, F. D. (1988). *The impact of career and psychosocial mentoring by supervisors and peers*. Paper presented at the meeting of the National Academy of Management Annual Meeting, Anaheim, CA.

Dreher, G. F., & Ash, R. A. (1990). A comparative study of mentoring among men and women in managerial, professional, and technical positions. *Journal of Applied Psychology*, **75**, 539–546.

Eby, L. T. (1997). Alternative forms of mentoring in changing organizational environments: A conceptual extension of the mentoring literature. *Journal of Vocational Behavior*, **51**, 125–144.

Eby, L. T., McManus, S., Simon, S. A., & Russell, J. E. A. (2000). The protege's perspective regarding negative mentoring experiences: The development of taxonomy. *Journal of Vocational Behavior*.

Erikson, E. H. (1963). *Childhood and society* (2nd edn.). New York: W. W. Norton.

Fagenson, E. A. (1992). Mentoring—Who needs it? A comparison of protégés' and nonprotégés' needs for power, achievement, affiliation, and autonomy. *Journal of Vocational Behavior*, **41**, 48–60.

Fagenson, E. (1989). The mentor advantage: Perceived career/job experiences of protégés versus nonprotégés. *Journal of Organizational Behavior*, **10**, 309–320.

Fagenson, E. A. (1988). The power of a mentor: Protégés' and nonprotégés, perceptions of their own power in organizations. *Group and Organizational Studies*, **13**, 182–194.

Fagenson-Eland, E. A., Marks, M. A., & Amendola, K. (1997). Perceptions of mentoring relationships. *Journal of Vocational Behavior*, **51**, 29–42.

Feldman, D. C., & Thomas, D. A. (1992). Career management issues facing expatriates. *Journal of International Business Studies, Second quarter*, 271–293.

Finney, M., & Von Glinow, M. A. (1988). Integrating academic and organisational approaches to developing the international manager. *Journal of Management Development*, **7**, 16–27.

Forret, M. L, Turban, D. B., & Dougherty, T. W. (1996). Issues facing organizations when implementing formal mentoring programs. *Leadership and Organization Development Journal*, **17**, 27–30.

Goleman, D. (1995). *Emotional intelligence*. New York: Bantam.

Goleman, D. (1998). *Working with emotional intelligence*. New York: Bantam.

Hackman, J. R., & Walton, R. E. (1986). Leading groups in organizations. In P. S. Goodman (Ed.), *Designing effective work groups* (pp. 72–119). San Francisco: Jossey-Bass Publishers.

Higgins, M. C. (1999). *Changing careers: The effects of social context*. Working paper no. 98-016, Harvard Business School, Boston, MA.

Higgins, M. C., & Kram, K. E. (1999). *Reconceptualizing mentoring at work: A developmental network perspective*. Working paper, Harvard Business School, Boston, MA.

Hunt, D. M., & Michael, C. (1983). Mentorship: A career training and development tool. *Academy of Management Review*, **8**, 475–485.

Ibarra, H. (1994). *The structure of mentoring: A network perspective on race and gender differences in developmental relationships*. Paper presented at the National Academy of Management Annual Meeting, Dallas, TX.

Jossi, F. (1997). Mentoring in changing times. *Training*, **34**, 50–54.

Katzenbach, J. R., & Smith, D. K. (1993). *The wisdom of teams: Creating the high-performance organization*. Boston: Harvard Business School Press.

Koberg, C. S., Boss, R. W., Chappell, D., & Ringer, R. C. (1994). Correlates and consequences of protégé mentoring in a large hospital. *Group and Organization Management*, **19**, 219–239.

Kram, K. E. (1983). Phases of the mentoring relationship. *Academy of Management Journal*, **26**, 608–625.

Kram, K. E. (1985). *Mentoring at work: Developmental relationships in organizational life*. Glenview, IL: Scott, Foresman, & Company.

Kram, K. E., & Hall, D. T. (1991). Mentoring as an antidote to stress during corporate trauma. *Human Resource Management*, **28**, 493–510.

Kram, K. E., & Hall, D. T. (1995). Mentoring in a context of diversity and turbulence. In S. Lobel & E. Kossek (Eds.), *Human Resource Strategies for Managing Diversity*. London: Blackwell Publishers.

Kram, K. E., & Isabella, L. A. (1985). Mentoring alternatives: The role of peer relationships in career development. *Academy of Management Journal*, **28**, 110–132.

Lankau, M. J. (1996). *An examination of mentoring, peer developmental relationships, and team participation as sources of learning in an organization*. Unpublished doctoral dissertation. University of Miami.

Lankau, M. J., & Scandura, T. A. (1997). *Mentoring as a learning forum: An examination of mentoring functions, socialization, personal learning, and job attitudes*. Presented at the National Academy of Management Annual Meeting, Boston, MA.

Levinson, D. J., Darrow, C. N., Klein, E. B., Levinson, M. A., & McKee, B. (1978). *Seasons of a man's life*. New York: Knopf.

Likert, R., & Likert, J. (1976). *New ways of managing conflict*. New York: McGraw-Hill.

McManus, S. E., & Russell, J. E. A. (1997). New directions for mentoring research: An examination of related constructs. *Journal of Vocational Behavior*, **51**, 145–161.

McManus, S. E., & Russell, J. E. A. (1999). *Stormy weather: Dysfunctional mentoring experiences from the mentor's perspective*. Paper presented at the National Academy of Management Annual Meeting, Chicago, IL.

Mullen, B., & Cooper, C. (1994). The relation between group cohesiveness and performance: An integration. *Psychological Bulletin*, **115**, 210–227.

Murray, M. (1991). *Beyond the myths and magic of mentoring: How to facilitate an effective mentoring program*. San Francisco, CA: Jossey-Bass.

Noe, R. A. (1988). An investigation of the determinants of successful assigned mentoring relationships. *Personnel Psychology*, **41**, 457–479.

Orpen, C. (1995). The effects of mentoring on employees' career success. *Journal of Social Psychology*, **135**, 667–668.

Ostroff, C., & Kozlowski, S. (1993). The role of mentoring in the information gathering processes of newcomers during early organizational socialization. *Journal of Vocational Behavior*, **42**, 170–183.

Ragins, B. R., & Cotton, J. L. (1999). Mentoring functions and outcomes: A comparison of men and women in formal and informal relationships. *Journal of Applied Psychology*, **84**, 529–550.

Ragins, B. R., & Scandura, T. A. (1994). Gender differences in expected outcomes of mentoring relationships. *Academy of Management Journal*, **37**, 957–971.

Ragins, B. R., & Scandura, T. A. (1997). The way we were: Gender differences in expected outcomes of mentoring relationships. *Journal of Applied Psychology*, **82**, 945–953.

Ragins, B. R., & Scandura, T. A. (1999). Burden or Blessing? Expected costs and benefits of being a mentor. *Journal of Organizational Behavior*, **20**, 493–509.

Roche, G. R. (1979). Much ado about mentors. *Harvard Business Review*, **59**, 1418.

Scandura, T. A. (1992). Mentorship and career mobility: An empirical investigation. *Journal of Organizational Behavior*, **13**, 169–174.

Scandura, T. A. (1997). Mentoring and organizational justice: An empirical investigation. *Journal of Vocational Behavior*, **51**, 58–69.

Scandura, T. A. (1998). Dysfunctional mentoring relationships and outcomes. *Journal of Management*, **24**, 449–467.

Scandura, T. A., & Schriesheim, C. A. (1991). *Effects of structural characteristics of mentoring dyads on protege outcomes*. Proceedings of the Southern Management Association Meeting, Atlanta, GA.

Scandura, T. A., & Schriesheim, C. A. (1994). Leader–member exchange (LMX) and Supervisor Career Mentoring (SCM) as complementary constructs in leadership research. *Academy of Management Journal*, **37**, 1588–1602.

Scandura, T. A., & Viator, R. (1994). Mentoring in public accounting firms: An analysis of mentor–protégé relationships, mentorship functions, and protégé turnover intentions. *Accounting, Organizations, and Society*, **19**, 717–734.

Scandura, T. A., & Von Glinow, M. (1997). Development of the international manager: The role of mentoring. *Business and the Contemporary World*, **9**, 95–115.

Scandura, T. A., & Williams, E. A. (1998). *Initiating mentoring: Contrasting the reports of protégés in assigned and informal relationships*. Proceedings of the Southern Management Association, New Orleans, LA.

Scandura, T. A., & Williams, E. A. (2000). *Relationships as tutorials in new career contracts: Augmenting effects of mentoring on transformational leadership*. Working paper, University of Miami.

Schaffer, M. A., & Harrison, D. A. (1998). Expatriates' psychological withdrawal from international assignments: Work, nonwork, and family influences. *Personnel Psychology*, **51**, 87–118.

Senge, P. M. (1990). *The fifth discipline: The art and practice of the learning organization*. New York: Doubleday Currency.

Shannonhouse, R. (1996, November 8). Overseas assignment failures. *USA Today/International Edition*, p. 84.

Turban, D. B., & Dougherty, T. W. (1994). Role of protégé personality in receipt of mentoring and career success. *Academy of Management Journal*, **37**, 688–702.

Viator, R., & Scandura, T. A. (1991). A study of mentor-protégé relationships in large public accounting firms. *Accounting Horizons*, **5**, 20–30.

Whiteley, W., Dougherty, T. W., & Dreher, G. F. (1991). Relationship of career mentoring and socioeconomic origin to managers' and professionals' early career progress. *Academy of Management Journal*, **34**, 331–351.

Williams, E. A. (1999). *A field experimental investigation of relationship-based mentoring training in team settings and team characteristics: Effects on employee attitudes and outcomes*. Unpublished Dissertation. University of Miami.

Williams, E. A. (2000). *Team mentoring: New directions for research on employee development in organizations*. Paper presented at the National Academy of Management Annual Meeting, Toronto, Canada.

Williams, E. A., & Scandura, T. A. (2000). *Team leader coaching and personal learning: tools and indicators of individual development*. Paper presented at the SIOP Annual Meeting, New Orleans, LA.

Wilson, J. A., & Elman, N. S. (1990). Organizational benefits of mentoring. *Academy of Management Executive*, **4**, 88–94.

Zey, M. G. (1984). *The Mentor Connection*. Homewood, IL: Dow Jones-Irwin.

Mentoring for World-Class Performance

James G. Clawson and **Douglas S. Newburg**
University of Virginia, Charlottesville, USA

SUMMARY

This chapter outlines some common features of traditional mentoring programs in corporations. While few corporations use all of these features, the issues related to effectively managing each one are presented. The chapter also introduces an alternative perspective on mentoring that focuses on the role of a person's experience (feelings) in world-class performance and encourages practicing managers to pay attention to both external achievements and internal experiencing as a path to effective mentoring.

INTRODUCTION

Mentoring is an enduring concept that ebbs and flows in its popularity and utility. That it endures suggests that there is a natural tendency in organized humans for mentoring and being mentored. That it ebbs and flows in its utilization suggests that our attempts to formalize the mentoring process and capitalize on its strengths have not yet been uniformly successful. Despite the fact that "mentoring" as a topic has a rich and growing theoretical literature and a broad scope (senior–junior, peer-to-peer, networking and

Psychological Management of Individual Performance. Edited by Sabine Sonnentag.
© 2002 John Wiley & Sons, Ltd.

team-based, functional, social-psychological), mentoring is rather difficult to plan and execute. Designing and implementing an intentional mentoring program for improving individual and organizational performance is a challenging task that often meets with mediocre results or clear-cut failure. In part, this is because mentoring is a complex, organic, highly variable process that is not easily modeled. In part, it is because we focus too much on results and not enough on experience as we will show below. This chapter will build on the chapter by Scandura and Hamilton (this volume) to suggest design principles that mentoring program administrators should consider in their work—and offer a somewhat radical approach to thinking about the content and design of applied, intentional mentoring programs. This chapter also provides a proven practical focal point for the psychological management of individual performance, the theme of this volume.

Definitions of mentoring abound. As the chapter by Scandura and Hamilton implies, the term is so widely used nowadays, it is almost synonymous with learning. Our view is that mentoring represents something more particular, that it is one of a range of developmental relationships. A developmental relationship (DR) is any relationship in which one or both parties learn from the other. These include supervisory (superior–subordinate relationships), coaching, quasi-mentoring, and mentoring relationships among others. Sometimes the learning is unilateral (the protégé learning from the mentor), sometimes it is bilateral (each learning from the other), and sometimes the learning is counterproductive (negative role modeling). A mentoring relationship is a special kind of developmental relationship in which the learning occurs on a wide range of topics from professional to personal and which includes a deep-seated caring for the other. Supervising is not necessarily coaching or mentoring, and coaching is not necessarily mentoring. Superiors who focus their efforts on teaching professional activity only may well be good coaches, or even quasi-mentors, but they are not, strictly speaking, mentors (Clawson, 1980; Shapiro, Hazeltine, & Rowe, 1978). Program administrators concerned with designing and implementing so-called "mentoring" systems should not overlook the developmental aspects of all of the superior–subordinate relationships naturally established in the organization. Many of these may already be mentor–protégé relationships (MPRs) (Clawson, 1984).

Scandura and Hamilton (this volume) suggest a range of strategies that administrators might take from informal to semi-formal to formal.[1] These alternatives represent strategic choices an administrator must make about how to approach the design of a mentoring program. One might choose to depend on the naturally occurring informal MPRs that grow in any organization; one might choose to enhance that natural development with various kinds of encouragement along the way; or one might determine to design and implement a formal mentoring program. We encourage administrators to pay attention to all points on that spectrum, acknowledging informal mentoring when it occurs, encouraging all supervisors to become better mentors, and where appropriate, implementing explicitly the principles we have learned about mentoring through research over the last

---

[1] "Administrators" here will mean either line executives or staff human resource executives who have been charged with or taken on the goal of designing and implementing socially based performance enhancement systems. In this context, every organization already has a form of a "mentoring" system in place in its regular supervisory and performance management system. Every boss is a potential "mentor". Each boss may be classified on a continuum of strength of developmental impact from low to high as a simple supervisor, a trainer, a coach, a quasi-mentor, or a fully-fledged mentor. Clearly, with interest, training and encouragement, superiors may develop their mentoring skills.

thirty years. Treating development as the focus of a separate mentoring program without including and acknowledging the informal and mid-range influences one can have is a mistake. That said, henceforth our use of the term "mentoring" will focus on the formal end of the spectrum and programs intentionally designed to enhance performance. First, we will outline typical objectives, design features, and pitfalls of formal mentoring programs, and then describe an unusual approach taken by the thoracic surgery department of a major teaching university.

OBJECTIVES OF TYPICAL MENTORING PROGRAMS

Mentoring program administrators first need to determine their objectives for a mentoring program. Fuzzy objectives lead to fuzzy results. Organizations, typically for-profit corporations, establish mentoring programs in the hope that they will help to improve performance in the company both by raising the standard of performance to that of senior levels and beyond (effectiveness measure) and by getting to that higher standard sooner (efficiency measure). The common objectives of applied mentoring programs include the following: developing young talent quickly in order to compete more effectively in the marketplace, socializing young talent quickly to the ways and means of the organization, developing leadership skills in the organization, strengthening the corporate culture in the midst of rapid change, reducing the need for supervision, more effective achievement of corporate objectives, and to provide experience that is likely to retain expensive talent.

DEVELOPING YOUNG TALENT

The most common objective of mentoring programs is to develop young talent quickly so that the company may compete in a rapidly changing environment. In more 'traditional' times, industrial age bureaucracies had established career tracks and patterns that insured significant experience in a variety of jobs at a variety of responsibility levels. These career tracks shaped and developed young talent largely through on-the-job training and experience. In the Information Age with rapidly changing conditions and competitive configurations, companies are feeling pressured to develop their young talent more quickly. They hope to utilize the wisdom and judgment of their senior leadership in mentoring programs that will accelerate the development process and leave younger people ready for more senior responsibilities sooner.

SOCIALIZING YOUNG TALENT

Another common objective of mentoring programs is to accelerate the socialization process of young talent. When, by necessity, young people are put into positions of responsibility perhaps earlier than their years and experience would indicate, senior management seeks some kind of assurance that the decisions that they will make will be consistent with the core values of the organization and with the decisions senior management would make if they were involved. While control systems, information systems, signature systems, and other means provide much of this control, mentoring programs are a means for explicitly encouraging young people to "do things the way we do them around here". By bringing protégés along on business trips, to conferences, to meetings with clients, mentors are signaling to them how to dress, speak, conduct business, make decisions, and carry themselves as representatives of that organization. Rapid growth and its attendant hiring complicate this process and often force administrators to find ways to accelerate the socialization process.

DEVELOPING LEADERSHIP

Many organizations today find themselves wrestling with shortages of leadership. Many of our clients are constantly searching for more rapid ways to develop the next generation of leadership. Mentoring programs are seen as one way of addressing this issue and linking it directly with current senior management practice. There are obvious concerns with this approach in that recreating the values of current leadership may *not* be what the corporation needs; however, most management teams are naturally likely to recreate the values and style they are comfortable with and mentoring programs are seen as a way of speeding up that process.

STRENGTHENING THE CORPORATE CULTURE

With the rate of change evident in today's business world, many corporations are concerned about maintaining their core values and beliefs (Collins & Porras, 1997). As companies grow rapidly either internally or through acquisition, promulgating and inculcating the companies' core values to new employees has become a growing and difficult concern. How do thousands of new employees (in larger companies) or 100% employee growth (in smaller companies) learn the core principles of how that company does business? Training programs help, on-the-job experience and supervision helps, and mentoring programs are another means of encouraging employee triangulation on a single set of core beliefs and values.

REDUCING NEED FOR SUPERVISION

The larger companies grow, and the more diverse and distributed they become, and the flatter they become, the more difficult it is to supervise and oversee them. Many organizations are turning to core values rather than standard operating procedures manuals as a means to controlling organization behavior. Mentoring programs are a means of passing on management values relatively quickly. If new employees, particularly those labeled for rapid advancement, can learn the underlying principles of the business, the need to write and police operating procedures dissolves. While less defined, values-based management systems are more enduring and require less supervision.

RETENTION OF EXPENSIVE TALENT

The low unemployment rate combined with booming business trends at the onset of the new century make it difficult to retain young talent. Employee retention at all ranks is, for many organizations, *the* major human resource management challenge. Wage earners can and do shop continuously for better benefits, working conditions, and wages. Salaried professionals are constantly on the search for more interesting work, better compensation, and a better work/lifestyle balance. Mentoring programs that promise and deliver access to senior ranks regularly provide a means of attracting and retaining younger talent. People who are stuck in what may be or may appear to be a traditional bureaucratic slow-climb career path may jump to organizations that offer more direct access to senior management and the likely increases in responsibility that this access implies.

Administrators designing a mentoring program should be clear and specific about their objectives in the program. Reviewing these objectives frequently will help to overcome obstacles and ensure that efforts to implement the program will have sufficient energy to do so. Armed with a set of objectives, administrators are then faced with designing a program to meet those objectives.

TYPICAL MENTORING PROGRAM DESIGN

After selecting a strategy and establishing a set of objectives, the typical elements in a designed mentoring program include: (a) identifying the target population, typically "high potentials", (b) identifying the resource population, typically older, senior mentors-to-be, (c) assigning connections between the two, (d) brief orientation and perhaps training activities, and (e) follow-up reviews and reassessments (Clawson, 1984).

IDENTIFYING THE TARGET POPULATION

While mentoring has been shown to have positive effects for both mentor and protégé, most intentional, that is, designed mentoring programs target a younger pool of talent for development. These "high potentials" or "high pots" are identified and invited to join a program. As Scandura and Hamilton (this volume) noted, research has shown that the mere identification of the "high pots" can poison a working environment. Those not chosen often feel like second-class citizens. Administrators who pay attention to the encouraging and informal aspects of mentoring can do much to overcome this jealousy. The accelerated development programs may include special training courses (on site and off site) and often a formalized mentoring relationship. Obviously, companies will choose those young people who, in their estimation, show the most promise for developing into senior management quickly. Typical criteria for choosing the protégé list include energy, intelligence, maturity of behavior, decision-making judgment, dependability, team skills, and loyalty. Sometimes it may be only educational credentials. Often overlooked yet seemingly important criteria would include willingness to learn, emotional intelligence, and a self-determination that can, if necessary, get one to think beyond what a mentor may suggest.

IDENTIFYING THE RESOURCE POPULATION

The other identification challenge is finding the right mentors. Not every senior manager is suited for mentoring roles. Many formalized programs falter on this point: they assume that any senior manager by virtue of that person's experience and position must be worthy of mentoring assignments. The data shows that skills in sharing, coaching, teaching, following-up, caring, and spending time with junior people are not necessarily directly correlated with title. The challenge is to select carefully the kind of senior manager that the company wants to coach its junior people. Some companies work hard at this, trying to avoid offending those not invited and making sure that those who accept the assignment are going to follow it through. Administrators may wish to interview prospective mentors and their colleagues to determine which senior managers would make the best mentors.

ASSIGNING CONNECTIONS BETWEEN MENTOR AND PROTÉGÉ

Having identified a target pool (protégés) and a resource pool (mentors), administrators must then find a way to assign them to relationships. Those who give relatively little thought to this ignore the research that shows that the effectiveness of the developmental aspects of the relationships depend heavily on the mutual respect and trust in them (Clawson & Blank, 1987). Random or superficial MPR assignments have led to the downfall of many well-intentioned mentoring programs and relationships. One alternative to administrator assignment is to approximate the informal mentoring realities by providing a planned series of social/training events in which the mentors and protégés can mingle and become acquainted and through that process begin to self-identify the counterpart with whom they would feel most comfortable working. While assignments are "quick" and avoid the discomfort of finding a counterpart, they also greatly risk superficiality and the passage of time without much result. Part of this issue has to do with how each party defines its roles, about which we will say more below.

ORIENTATION AND TRAINING

A well-designed program would include training for the protégés in how to be protégés, that is: introducing them to the social, psychological, and professional dilemmas associated with being in a learning model (Dalton, Thompson, & Price, 1977); coaching them in how to give and receive feedback (Anderson, 1966; Clawson, 1986); showing them how to communicate without using title or prestige as a means of persuasion (Cohen & Bradford, 1991); and guiding them in personal career awareness, and how to keep touch in appropriately assertive ways. Readings from the burgeoning mentoring literature may also help them to see the range of mentoring relationships and determine what they hope to achieve and contribute to such a relationship.

Well-designed programs will also include a training program for the mentors. Programs that assume that senior managers know how to mentor and coach often crumble. In addition to specific industry or organizational knowledge, mentors need to be cognizant of, and skilled with, giving and receiving feedback, understanding career alternatives, managing alternative learning styles (Kolb, 1981), and managing emotions (Goleman, 1995; Fassel, 1990). Training for mentoring is often a sticking point for senior management. Already busy, they profess schedules too full to learn how to coach or mentor more effectively and efficiently. Or they may just not believe they have anything to learn (Argyris, 1991). The sad paradox here is that this unwillingness to learn manifests in their relationships with protégés may be what they unintentionally pass on. Administrators who deal with executives who are unwilling to spend any time learning how to be more effective mentors ought to rethink including them in the program—since they may unintentionally set the program back rather than move it forward.

FOLLOW-UP AND REVIEW

Administrators of mentoring programs often complain of not being able to get their mentors to follow through. Protégés are often eager for more contact than they get including perhaps even repeatedly postponed appointments with mentors. When assigned mentors push their mentoring responsibilities lower in their priority stack and miss deadlines, push back commitments, and even ignore altogether their mentoring responsibilities and commitments, the relationship and the program may be gutted.

Mentoring program administrators often wrestle to keep in touch with the protégés, the mentors, and to manage the process to a successful conclusion—if in fact, a good mentoring relationship ever ends (Scandura & Hamilton, this volume). Periodic assessments of the protégés' and the mentors' experiences will help the administrator to keep abreast of the strength of individual relationships in the program and suggest where to spend time and effort. For mentors that are lagging behind, the administrator must face the challenge of coaching the coach to be a better coach. If the company is in the midst of merger negotiations or some other time-consuming and challenging business venture, mentoring junior talent may be squeezed out of the mentor's monthly routine. Unless senior management sees and continues to see mentoring as a powerful tool for developing the organization, the administrator's job will be very difficult to accomplish.

PROBLEMS WITH THE TYPICAL MENTORING DESIGN STRUCTURE

It would be nice if one could just outline these five general domains of attention and predict that the rate of development of next generation leadership would improve. Unfortunately, there are several problems with this traditional approach, including:

- unclear goals
- varying expectations of the target population
- varying expectations of the resource population
- inappropriate assignments between the two
- weak or insufficient orientation and training programs
- weak or non-existent monitoring and coaching during the process
- weak or non-existent reviews and assessments when the programmed relationship comes to an "end".

UNCLEAR GOALS

One of the difficulties with many mentoring programs is the lack of clear objectives. Goals like "developing leaders" or "realizing our high potentials sooner" are so general and vague that it is difficult to determine whether or not the programs are succeeding. More specific goals may help mentoring program administrators to track their progress. These might include "getting 70% of the high potential group promoted within one year" or "retaining 80% of the high potential group" or "filling in a succession plan for the organization within a year's time". Clear goals will help the program administrator to sell the program to management and keep the program on track.

Expectations of the Target Population

Protégés, whose introduction to the company may have included a glowing description of the mentoring program as a means of attraction, often have high expectations. They expect mentors to follow through, they expect to be courted after signing on (as they were during recruitment), they expect to be listened to, and they expect to have relatively short review and promotion cycles. Some expect that they were hired in part to make changes and therefore *not* to learn current practice but to lead change within it—influencing their seniors instead of the other way around (Ibarra, 2000). This perspective, perhaps viewed as arrogance by senior people, is increasingly strong in today's Information Age market-place. Further, some protégés are clear that they only want to learn a relatively narrow and specific range of professional activities from their "mentors". In this, they desire to participate in what we would call a quasi-mentoring or coaching program—limiting their development to professional activities—rather than a broader mentoring program. Mentors who are taking a broader and longer-term perspective of their role and of the relationship might view protégés with this mindset as obstreperous, arrogant, narrow-minded or overly ambitious. Wise mentoring program designers and administrators will be careful to be aware of and manage the expectations of new protégés so that they can hope to deliver on those expectations during the program.

Expectations of the Resource Population

Mentors often come to a mentoring program assignment with different expectations about how much time they are planning to allocate to the program, about the talent of the protégés, about their own skills as a mentor, and about who is to be teaching whom. Unless the program administrators manage the expectations of the mentors, the mentors may become irritated or even frustrated when protégés begin calling them unexpectedly, sending them documents for review, or reminding them of meetings that have been repeatedly postponed. This tendency underscores the need to have a strong, well-defined orientation/mentoring program for the mentors.

Inappropriate Assignments

The strength of mentoring programs depends largely on the quality of the relationship between the two parties in each relationship. Unless the relationship is characterized first by respect, then trust, followed by consistency and commitment, little development is likely to take place. Personal characteristics, expectations, and relationship skills of both protégé and the mentor are essential to establishing these relationships. Perhaps the mentor and the protégé do not fit in communication style, objectives, interpersonal style, orientation to work or any number of factors. These differences can undermine and even prevent the development of a strong mentor–protégé relationship. While the level of trust and respect in developmental relationships has been shown to be critical (Clawson & Blank, 1990) the underlying basis for that trust and respect likely varies from relationship to relationship. This conclusion suggests that mentor and protégé need to be a system that will allow each of them to draw his or her own conclusions before being formally assigned to each other. Program administrators need to ensure that the assignment process maximizes trust and respect in the developmental relationships, and to do that they need to allow each party to participate in the matching process.

WEAK OR INSUFFICIENT ORIENTATION

Mentoring programs that overlook the importance of orienting and perhaps training both the mentors and the protégés are subject to the random effects of the experiences of both parties. Without program-based clarification of the roles of both the mentor and the protégé, participants will exert and behave their own perspectives. This can lead to misunderstandings, disappointments, and ultimately program collapse.

WEAK OR NON-EXISTENT COACHING AND MONITORING DURING THE PROCESS

Even if a mentoring program has been introduced carefully and participants understand what their roles in it may be, the lack of ongoing coaching and encouraging during the program can be fatal to its purposes. Mentoring program administrators who check in regularly with both mentors and protégés, solicit their experience and suggestions, and offer counsel and advice about handling the relationships can have a powerful effect on relationship outcomes. Checking in, like management oversight, needs to be specific rather than general. Asking a mentor, "how is it going?" may result in a "fine" response that is useless. One might ask instead, "tell me about the last time you met or communicated with your protégé". Frequency, content, commitments, and development plans are more likely to come out of this opening than the more general one.

WEAK OR NON-EXISTENT REVIEWS AFTER THE PROCESS

Mentoring program administrators should review the results of their programs regularly. Having clear objectives helps enormously in this regard. Having solid and trusting relationships with both mentors and protégés is also essential. Tracking the careers of program alumni also helps designers to test their assumptions about the strength of the program. A database that tracks program alumni and charts their promotions and career moves can help administrators to realize the strength of their programs. Mentoring programs without empirical data to support their claims for effectiveness are likely to continue only at the whim of each successive human resource or line senior manager.

A RADICAL ALTERNATIVE

Having outlined common objectives for practical mentoring programs, described the typical program design, and identified some common pitfalls, we now wish to offer a somewhat radical alternative to the traditional, planned mentoring approach. This alternative is grounded in the experience of the thoracic surgery department of the University of Virginia (UVA) Medical Center, Charlottesville, Virginia. We recognize that thoracic surgery is not the same as manufacturing automobiles or making loans on the web; however, several features of the approach taken by this organization may be instructive to those contemplating designing and implementing mentoring programs in the for-profit private or the not-for-profit sectors. This approach is "radical" in that while it includes many of the objectives and design features outlined above, it pays much more attention to the internal experiencing, that is, the feelings and emotions, of protégés than typical, achievement-oriented development programs.

First, we highlight, in order to examine, what seems to be a pervasive underlying assumption of traditional performance management systems, namely, that performance is enhanced by focusing on goal setting, practicing technique and working for results. This model is implied in the chapter earlier in this volume on goal setting (Latham, Locke, & Fassina, this volume). Performance, many assume by definition, implies paying attention to goal setting and outcomes. There is much truth in this assumption. Indeed, Timothy Gallwey in his popular books on the "inner game of . . . " (Gallwey, 2000) points out that simply paying attention to the right measure without even identifying what to do about it becomes a performance intervention that can have dramatic results. He tells a story, for example, of significantly changing the waiting time in a professional office merely by asking people in the office to measure waiting time.

At the same time, research conducted by Newburg on world-class performance suggests that people recognized globally in a variety of professions have learned to focus on more than results (Clawson, 1999; Newburg, 1998). In fact, the focus on something other than results, paradoxically can, and often does, enhance results. Newburg calls this the Resonance Model of Performance. Newburg inferred a common model from the reflections of over 350 people in four professions—athletics, music, medicine, and business. These subjects included world record holders in a variety of sports, Olympic gold medallists, highly successful touring musicians, heart surgeons, and senior executives in rapidly growing businesses. They were all, in their own way, at the top of their careers and professions, all representatives of world-class performance. Newburg's model is reminiscent of Mihalyi Csikszentmihalyi's work on "flow", as noted below.

THE RESONANCE MODEL

The model Newburg developed from these interviews acknowledges a common cycle that many professionals fall into: practice → try and fail → practice harder → try again. This cycle is initiated when one tries to do one's best but encounters a setback, a failure, an obstacle that prevents one from achieving the desired results or outcomes. Typically at this point, most people will go back to practicing, preparing, doing the "work" they think they have to do to improve. Therein is a key: the work they *have* to do to improve. This "obligatory" mindset[2] creates tension, pressure, and frustration that can be and often is counterproductive; it gets in the way of improving performance. It is an external definition of performance that oddly enough can get in the way of performing better. In our experience, many organizational employees, including highly talented ones, get caught in this cycle, working ever harder when faced with setbacks, and in a way can leave them with the career blues (Clawson & Haskins, 2000). In this cycle, performance declines rather than improves.

On the other hand, the successful athletes, musicians, surgeons, and executives in Newburg's study instead refer to a drive toward freedom, a freedom cycle if you will, that frees them from this duty cycle. The freedom cycle evolves from taking an experiential

---

[2] We sometimes call this the "duty cycle" because the underlying thought process and language used by people in it suggest this obligatory mentality.

view of one's dreams rather than a goal-oriented one. It means focusing on the way it feels to perform rather than just on the results of one's performance. This shift in focus is antithetical to the way most professionals think about their work; nevertheless, in our experience, it is very powerful. It means learning to pay attention to, and target, a set of feelings with equal or superior priority to goal outcomes. The paradox is that when one does this, performance often improves dramatically.

Consider the statement of one Olympic gold medallist, for instance, describing coming in second in his event in his first Olympics. He said that he was so focused on winning that he forgot how he liked to perform, with "easy speed". The next day, in a relay race and focused on this experiential aspect of his performance, that is, on swimming with easy speed rather than trying to win, he set a new world record. In Newburg's language, this freedom cycle consists of "revisiting one's dream", that is, focusing on how one wants to *feel* rather than on what one needs to *do*. This implies that one is clear about one's experientially defined dream in the first place. "Dreams" in the resonance model refers to a state of experience rather than to specific, momentary, and external, outcomes. Most people have "dreams" like "become a senator", "become CEO", or "be wealthy". We view these as false dreams because the real issue is not being that goal-target, rather it is how we experience being in that role. The question is not whether or not you want to be a senator, but rather whether or not you *enjoy doing* what senators do, or more specifically, what politicians do whether or not you become a senator.

It is this internal, experienced-based perspective that is "radical" to most practicing managers in our executive education teaching experience. This is a profound and often overlooked different way of approaching performance management and mentoring. Most of the industrial world is goal-oriented. We set up entire management systems, leadership philosophies, and control structures around the underlying assumption of the importance of achieving goals. In so doing, we tend to overlook how it feels while we are working along the way. Consider the statement made by Maurice Herzog, a Frenchman generally credited with climbing the first 8,000-meter peak (Annapurna) in 1952. He wrote in his memoirs of a day's climb at 19,000 feet, still far below the 28,504-foot summit:

> ... we still had a long way to go. Like ants getting over an enormous obstacle we climbed up without appearing to make any progress. The slope was very steep. . . . The air was luminous, and the light was tinged with the most delicate blue. On the other side of the couloir, ridges of bare ice refracted the light like prisms and sparkled with rainbow hues. The weather was still set fine—not a single cloud—and the air was dry. I felt in splendid form and as if, somehow, I had found a perfect balance within myself—was this, I wondered, the essence of happiness.
>
> (Maurice Herzog, *Annapurna*, p. 166)

What is evident in this comment is a fact that many of us overlook far too easily: the resonance of life is in the climbing not in the momentary goal-satisfaction of standing on the peak. What resonates for each of us will vary. In our MBA and executive education classes, we find people who have experienced resonance in a wide variety of activities including running, sewing, project management, public speaking, giving birth, doing calculus (yes, calculus), and building a business. Whatever it is for each person, the discovery and cultivation of that resonance producing activities becomes a central purpose in life. As Steve McQueen's character in the film *LeMans* said, "Racing is life. Everything else in between is just waiting." But "it" is not racing for everyone.

Over-focus on goals, paradoxically, may make less probable their achievement. Consider the case of one senior executive from a global financial services firm that had designed a week-long leadership development seminar. This executive visited the seminar on a Thursday afternoon to talk to the participants. His message? "It's June and the stock price is $95. If the stock price isn't $125 by December, the president and I don't get our options, so you need to get moving!" His approach was decidedly honest, direct, goal-oriented, and financially motivated, AND it was enormously *de*-motivating to the fifty people assembled in the room. Contrast this episode with the statement of an Olympic gold medallist who commented on her mindset in playing basketball. After some encouragement to comment about the gold medal, she finally pounded the table and said, "Look, winning the gold medal is my goal, but it's *not* why I play. My *dream* is to play to win at the highest level." She understood an important fact: that she experienced resonance on the court not on the medal stand.

Think about it. When do we experience the thrill of creation, of winning, of building, of realizing our potential? It is not after the deal is done, after the race is won, after the merger is consummated. Resonance is found in the doing, in the running, in the negotiating, in the striving, not in the momentary self-satisfaction that comes standing on the medal stand receiving the reward, or in the letter confirming our promotion, or in the moving into a new office. If we recognized this fact, we would design our mentoring programs with much greater emphasis on the experience of both the mentor and the protégé. We noted above that it is important to follow-up and track the results of a mentoring program. We believe it is even more important to track and manage the experience of the participants *during* the program.

The resonance model of performance by design (Figure 15.1) therefore looks like this: a clear awareness of one's "dream" (defined here in experiential not position-related terms) provides an avenue to work and preparation motivated by positive energy rather than the rebound, duty-cycle motivation created when one fails and goes, mentally, immediately back to work. When one develops the mental discipline—either by coaching or mentoring, or by personal experience—to revisit one's experientially defined dreams before going back to work, the outcomes tend to be much better.

The resonance model builds on the work of Mihalyi Csikszentmihalyi (1990) in which he identifies a "flow" phenomenon characterized in part by time warps (time either speeds up or slows down), loss of self-consciousness, due to intense focus, peak performance,

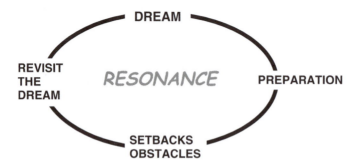

FIGURE 15.1   The resonance model of world-class performance

that occurs in a paradoxically effortless way (flow), that is intensely internally satisfying, and leaves one feeling larger and better grounded in the world. Most people in our experience in a large number of seminars seem to feel that flow is an ethereal thing that comes and goes all too infrequently. What Newburg has discovered is that many people in highly demanding professions are designing their lives and their work in ways that recreate this peak performance phenomenon on demand, if not every time, certainly with regularity. Focusing on, not losing sight of, one's experiential dream is central to that process.

Mentoring programs that focus on results at the expense of experience risk losing highly talented people to other organizations, especially in today's labor market. Programs that recognize the importance of experience as well as results will likely produce stronger loyalties AND better results.

The resonance model definition of a 'dream' recognizes the importance of feelings as well as actions. In other words, it is as important how you feel as what you do. In fact, how you feel has a huge impact on how you perform. Figure 15.2 depicts the interconnectedness of experience (feelings) and actions (behavior) in defining the resonance-based dream. The implications of this for mentoring programs are potentially enormous. The most central of these has to do with the training programs for both mentors and protégés. While these programs should include information on social learning as outlined above, they should also help both sides to focus on the importance of experience in producing results.

Newburg uses four basic questions, each associated with the four sides of the model, to introduce the basic elements of the resonance model to students and clients. The first question associated with the 'dream' is: "How do you want to feel today?" The second, is: "What will it take to get that feeling?" The third is: "What keeps you from getting it?" And fourth: "How can you get that feeling back?" This perspective contrasts sharply with the common goal-oriented questions that people often ask, "what are you going to do today?" or perhaps "what are you going to accomplish or achieve today?" The experiential approach is very counter-intuitive for most business managers. Trained to focus on results, they tend to ignore how one is feeling when one is performing at one's best. In our experience, the more mentoring relationships include this domain in their conversations, the more likely performance is to improve.

FIGURE 15.2 The interconnectedness of activities and feelings in experiencing resonance

THE THORACIC SURGERY DEPARTMENT EXPERIENCE

Let us explain how this model was used to transform the performance of a medical surgery department at the University of Virginia. In 1995, the thoracic surgery department at the UVA medical center was rated 23rd out of 23 departments by its residents. The department accepted only three residents annually at the time, had difficulty attracting new residents, and was viewed by its current residents as poor in its educational mission and method. About this time, the department chair appointed a new director of resident education. This man was an excellent surgeon and committed to learning whatever was necessary to strengthen the education of the department's residents—high-potential subordinates, new to the field, with lots to learn. Five years later, the thoracic surgery department was rated 2nd out of 23 departments and generally recognized as one of the superior educational programs in the school and the country. The department chair, the director of education and his associate were often called on to design, lead, and deliver seminars at national conferences teaching other medical schools how to do what they did.

What did they do? First, the new director of education hired a newly minted Ph.D. in sports psychology to be a performance counselor to the young heart surgeons. To date, we are unaware of any similar arrangement elsewhere. Gradually, the counselor began working with the residents and the surgeons, introducing them to his research on resonance-based performance management. When things did not go well in surgery, he was often called in to talk with the surgeons, but the conversations focused not on what they had done wrong, rather first, on why they had become surgeons. The gentle repetition of this "why" line of reasoning began to help surgeons focus not on technique (which they were practicing daily as they scrubbed and worked with senior surgeons day after day—clear coaching if not mentoring) rather on their experience when they were performing at their best and to connect that experience to their early dreams and goals about their profession.

In one case, a surgeon who had lost a patient was met by the counselor in his office. Although the surgeon did not see the value of it at the time, he allowed the counselor to enquire about his original interests in becoming a heart surgeon. At one point, after reflecting for some time, he related a story that occurred when he was about six years old. He had heard a commotion in the house about midnight and had left his room to see what was happening. He discovered his grandfather lying on the floor in the living room, his father kneeling over him trying to revive him, and his mother on the phone calling the rescue squad. He said he felt so helpless that right then and there he vowed he would never let that happen again. This constitutes a counselor-guided "revisiting of one's dream". With that vision in mind, the surgeon was able to refocus his preparation for his next patient that afternoon. Here is a profession in which the practitioners have to be at the world-class level on a daily basis, and by virtue of utilizing this experiential focus in their training, the thoracic surgery department at UVA has been able to catapult their performance individually and as a team over the course of five years.

What this approach invites is a perspective on mentoring that recognizes both external results and internal experience. There is precedent for this view. The Ohio State Leadership Studies, for example, concluded that there were two major dimensions of effective leadership: initiating structure (task) and consideration (process) (Yukl, 1998). Over-focus on either one was detrimental. Similarly, the classic book on organizational design by Lawrence and Lorsch pointed out that there must be a balance between differentiation (task) and integration (process) (Lawrence & Lorsch, 1967). Further, Harvard professors Mike Beer and Nitin Nohria conclude that the most effective change management programs recognize both economic (task) and organizational (process) approaches (Beer & Nohria, 2000). Even one of the most, if not *the* most, admired executive over the last twenty years, Jack Welch of General Electric, assesses his executives on two dimensions: results (task) and process in separate, equally powerful periodic review sessions. What Newburg has done is discover this same need for balance in managing performance. If one over-focuses on goals to the exclusion of focus on internal experience, performance suffers. Despite these precedents in the literature, the fact that most mentoring programs ignore this balance by focusing almost exclusively on external goals and results is what makes the resonance approach seem so "radical" to many.

CONCLUSION

Traditional, applied mentoring programs tend to have a common structure. Their objectives revolve around developing leaders more quickly. They assume that assigning highly talented young people to more senior experienced executives will enable them to meet this objective. Unfortunately, these programs often fail because they ignore the importance of the quality of the relationships between mentors and protégés and the role that well-designed orientation, training, coaching, and follow-up can have on those relationships. Further, they tend to take a goal-oriented approach that tends to ignore the experience of the protégés and the mentors.

The resonance model of world-class performance has provided an organizing framework for coaching young people that has produced dramatic results in at least one difficult setting, the thoracic surgery department of a major teaching hospital. By using a expert performance counselor to coach mentors and protégés, and by encouraging both to focus on experience as well as performance, the individual and team performance of the department improved dramatically over a five-year period.

One of the implications of this approach is that those who design and implement mentoring programs should pay particular attention to the experience of both mentors and protégés in their programs. This implies a more active role for mentoring program administrators than many companies have taken in the past. It also implies that the content of mentoring programs should be re-examined to include a strong awareness of and attention to experience as well as results. If one does this, one can expect lower turnover rates and higher promotion rates among the young high potentials that mentoring programs are designed to serve.

REFERENCES

Anderson, J. (1966). *Giving and receiving feedback*. Procter & Gamble internal company document, Cincinnati, OH.

Argyris, C. (1991). Teaching smart people how to learn. *Harvard Business Review*, reprint 91301.

Beer, M., & Nohria, N. (2000), Cracking the code of change. *Harvard Business Review*.

Brousseau, K. R., & Driver, M. J. (1996). *Career concepts: Roadmaps for career success*. Decision Dynamics Corporation, Los Angeles, CA.

Clawson, J. G. (1980). Mentoring in managerial careers. In C. B. Derr (Ed.), *Work, Family and the Career*. New York: Praeger Special Studies.

Clawson, J. G. (1984). Don't teach mentoring. *Exchange: The Journal of the Organizational Behavior Teaching Society*, 8.

Clawson, J. G. (1986). *Some principles of giving and receiving feedback*. Summarizes Anderson's 1966 note, Darden Educational Materials Services (UVA-OB-322), Charlottesville, VA.

Clawson, J. G., & Blank, M. (1987). Interpersonal style and mentoring. *International Journal of Mentoring*, 1.

Clawson, J. G., & Blank, M. B. (1990). What really counts in superior–subordinate relationships? Lessons from business. *Mentoring International*, 4.

Clawson, J. G. (1994). *A multi-pronged approach for building developmental relationships*. UVA Darden Educational Materials Services, UVA-OB-284, Charlottesville, VA.

Clawson, J. G. (1999). Leadership, resonance, and the purpose of life. *Level three leadership*. Upper Saddle River, NJ: Prentice-Hall.

Clawson, J. G., & Haskins, M. E. (2000). Beating the career blues. *Academy of Management Executive*.

Collins, J., & Porras, J. (1997). *Built to last*. New York: Harperbusiness.

Cohen, A. R., & Bradford, D. L. (1991). *Influence without authority*. New York: Wiley.

Csikszentmihalyi, M. (1990). *Flow: The psychology of optimal experience*. New York: Harper & Row.

Dalton, G. W., Thompson, P. H., & Price, R. L. (1977). The four stages of professional careers. A new look at performance by professionals. *Organizational Dynamics*, 19–42.

Fassel, D. (1990). *Working ourselves to death, and the rewards of recovery*. New York: Harper.

Gallwey, T. (2000). *The inner game of work*. New York: Random House.

Goleman, D. (1995). *Emotional intelligence*. New York: Bantam.

Ibarra, H. (2000). Making partner: A mentor's guide to the psychological journey. *Harvard Business Review*, 147 ff.

Kolb, D. (1985). *Learning style inventory*. Boston: McBer & Company.

Lawrence, P. R., & Lorsch, J. W. (1967). *Organization and environment*. Cambridge, MA: President and Fellows of Harvard College.

Newburg, D. S. (1998). *Resonance: A life by design: Develop your dream and mastering your fear*. Self-published, Charlottesville, VA.

Shapiro, E., Hazeltine, F., & Rowe, M. (1978). Moving up: Role models, mentors, and the 'Patron System'. *Sloan Management Review*, 51–58.

Yukl, G. A. (1998). *Leadership in organizations*. Upper Saddle River, NJ: Prentice-Hall.

CHAPTER 16

Enhancing Performance through Pay and Reward Systems

Henk Thierry

Tilburg University, Tilburg, The Netherlands

SUMMARY

A most obvious objective of the use of pay systems in organizations is to reward managers and employees for their contributions to achieving organizational goals. Moreover, it is hoped that through these contributions they serve their own particular interests as well. But do such well-known statements reflect what is actually occurring? This is the theme that is addressed in this chapter. First, various psychological theories on pay are discussed: they share the notion that remuneration may sizably affect an organization member's attitudes, cognitions and behavior at work. Thus, remuneration may impact the nature of the performance–outcome link, and the fairness of the relationship between somebody's investments in work and the returns received in comparison with one or more others or a referent norm. An important point is whether remuneration always facilitates or increases work motivation, which may be inferred from the meanings pay appears to have to organization members. Then some non-psychological theories on pay are touched on: they help to understand that the relative impact of pay in organizations is also determined by organizational characteristics and market forces. Second, a review is given of research on particular pay systems. These data show that a system like merit rating almost always leads to unfavourable results. Regarding other results-oriented pay systems it appears that a host of conditions ought to be fulfilled for reaching the objectives set. However, the latter observation also holds for fixed pay systems. In other words: pay systems should not be used as separate, autonomous action patterns, but rather be embedded in integrated Human Resource programs. Indeed, a pay system may fail to do what it is intended to achieve.

Psychological Management of Individual Performance. Edited by Sabine Sonnentag.
© 2002 John Wiley & Sons, Ltd.

INTRODUCTION

More than 10 years ago Kerr (1988) reviewed the evidence on one of the main objectives a compensation system ought to achieve (March & Simon, 1958; Gerhart, 2000): Do organizational reward and punishment systems effectively reinforce congruence between the goals of employees and those of the organization? Kerr's analysis was devastating. According to him many reward systems:

- lead to dysfunctional work behavior;
- negate or even punish functional work behavior;
- focus much too strongly on actions of individual employees instead of fostering mutual cooperation;
- make it difficult for employees to perceive a clear, unambiguous performance–reward relationship;
- intend to pay for performance, but pay in reality for attendance or membership;
- lead to behaviors that employees believe will be rewarded, but which are often at variance with the behaviors managers hoped to get.

Thus, compensation systems seem not to contribute to congruent goals within organizations. Moreover, employees have a hard time perceiving how the results of their efforts or performance affect a part of their pay. Interestingly, Kerr's analysis stresses primarily the 'instrumental' performance–outcome relationship, which is a vital component of expectancy theory's application on pay.

In the concluding section of this chapter we will consider whether the empirical evidence gained in the past 15 years is still in support of Kerr's arguments. Yet, compensation may also be tuned to objectives other than congruence in goals. Through compensation (e.g. Thierry, 1998a):

1. Applicants may be *attracted* on the labor market.
2. Qualified personnel may be *retained* within an organization.
3. Managers and employees may be *motivated* to perform well.
4. Managers and employees may be *alerted* to engage in different performance behaviors in times of drastic change.
5. Inconvenient working conditions may be '*balanced*' with an attractive reward.
6. Industrial conflicts may be *solved* (if not prevented).
7. Labor *costs* may be *cut down*.
8. A distinct, recognizable business unit or group *culture* may be furthered.

Throughout this chapter, terms like compensation, pay, and remuneration are used to refer to an employee's 'total compensation', i.e. the sum total of primary (wage, salary), secondary (e.g. health insurance), and tertiary (car lease, etc.) provisions. Obviously, each of the eight objectives requires a particular design of compensation components, not only regarding pay systems, but often also pay level (the amount of pay), and sometimes pay differentials as well (cf. Thierry, in press). Some evidence shows for instance that companies include base pay level and fringe benefits in their advertisements to attract employees (1), whereas they use a pay-for-performance system to reward excellent performance (3). It is also obvious that compensation does not operate in a 'vacuum', but should be aligned with the HRM and general business policy of a company. Still, it is apparently assumed that compensation is able to affect attitudes, cognitions, and behaviors of organization members effectively.

It is this assumption that is considered more in detail in the next section: How is compensation supposed to affect the behavior of people at work? Several psychological theories will be discussed subsequent to which various approaches from a few other disciplines will be outlined. In the third section research evidence regarding primarily the performance effects of several well-known compensation systems will be reported. In the concluding section the nature of contingent pay will be considered, in the context of which we return to Kerr's observation in the late 1980s—the failure of compensation systems to achieve congruence between goals—but now from the perspective of the available evidence at the beginning of the third millennium.

THEORIES ON COMPENSATION

Psychologists have not concerned themselves very much with research on compensation. Within social psychology most research in this domain has addressed equity and justice issues in laboratory settings. Industrial and organizational psychologists have largely neglected past and current compensation issues facing organizations and their members in practice (Cascio, 1998; Thierry, 1998b; Rynes & Bono, 2000). But also managers are rather hesitant to assess their compensation policies, for instance in terms of return on investments made, as Kanungo and Mendonca (1988) argue. These authors suggest that managers probably do not expect any motivational impact of these policies, due perhaps to the writings of Maslow (1954) and Herzberg, Mausner, and Snyderman (1959), which have been interpreted from the 1960s on as indicating that pay would not be important for motivating people in their work. Possibly, psychologists have been subject to the same mode of interpretation.

In this section several psychological theories on compensation are discussed (see Table 16.1). Some of these theories have been designed exclusively with regard to compensation, whereas others have been derived from more general psychological theories. They share with one another a focus upon the individual organization member as the primary subject affected by compensation. However, several relevant compensation characteristics are supposed to be affected by supra-individual levels, such as the labor market. Thus, also some compensation theories grounded in other disciplines will be touched on. The latter theories may help to better understand the organizational and environmental constraints and opportunities impacting upon individual managers and employees who are trying to make sense of their or others' compensation.

EXPECTANCY THEORY

In the domain of work motivation, expectancy theory is still rather popular. It gained momentum after Vroom's formalization of its main tenets (Vroom, 1964; Van Eerde & Thierry, 1996). Expectancy theory bears upon the situation in which an individual is confronted with the necessity or the opportunity to make a choice among alternative courses of action. Let's assume that an employee faces a choice whether to go for high performance or for a moderate, rather easy to reach performance level. Expectancy theory argues that three cognitions will jointly determine the employee's choice:

TABLE 16.1 Dynamics of compensation theories

Theory	Core elements
Expectancy	Extent to which pay is instrumental to satisfying motives Expectation on relationship between performance and pay
Organizational behavior modification	Reinforcement of performance through pay
Goal setting	Difficult self-set goals and high self-efficacy lead to high performance Expectation on relationship between performance and pay
Equity	Relationship between contributions (e.g. effort) and inducements (e.g. pay) as compared to referent Unfairness may result in negative performance effects
Cognitive evaluation	Intrinsic motivation causes feelings of competence and of internal locus of causality Contingent pay may decrease level of intrinsic motivation
Reflection	Pay meanings: motivational properties; relative position; control; spending More meaningful pay affects performance and pay satisfaction

1. The probability that a particular level of effort leads to a specific performance level.
2. The probability that this performance level causes the attainment of particular outcomes.
3. The attractiveness of these outcomes.

The alternative that gets the highest subjective utility for the employee is eventually chosen. Lawler (1971) has applied the last two components to compensation. Consequently, the relative importance of pay to an individual is a function of:

- the extent to which compensation is perceived to provide a means to satisfy particular needs (i.e. to reach particular goals);
- the importance of these needs (or goals) to the individual.

Thus, the more compensation is seen as 'instrumental' to gain more recognition from others, to get more security in (working) life, to learn more about one's own level of achievement—to mention a few examples—and the more these needs are important or attractive to a person, the more important is compensation. This instrumental character of compensation's importance illustrates that research data showing how organization members rate or rank the importance of compensation relative to other rewards, is not so informative per se. When pay is seen as very important, additional information (which is usually not available) ought to indicate the particular needs or goals to which pay is considered instrumental. High pay importance may also reflect that individuals do not appear to have other means available in their work to satisfy their needs (which occurs at lower hierarchical levels).

Pay-for-performance systems, discussed below, link one or more performance characteristics to a bonus or a salary increase. In order to be effective this requires an important additional instrumentality perception: the employee's or manager's belief that a particular performance outcome is related to a specified amount of pay. Research evidence shows that this belief contributes to the explanatory power of expectancy theory (e.g. Miedema, 1994; Van Silfhout, 2000). This belief is also affected by the quality of feedback, trust in the system, self-efficacy, and several other variables (e.g. Kanungo & Mendonca, 1988). Among the latter is cynicism. Wanous, Reichers, and Austin (2000) show that cynicism about the success of organizational change efforts has a negative impact upon the instrumentality belief. Cynicism appears to reduce the motivation of individual organization members to effect change through his/her own efforts. Importantly, the authors find the instrumentality belief to be much lower when a salary system with performance bonuses is applied than when a system of hourly wages (actually, a fixed pay system) exists. Cynicism seems to imply that the performance–pay relationship is reduced to zero, or is even perceived to have become negative in nature.

ORGANIZATIONAL BEHAVIOR MODIFICATION

Expectancy theory expresses also in its name the notion that expectations about behavior–outcome relationships shape the motivation to act. Yet, are 'conscious' expectations vital for the occurrence of behavior–outcome sequences? Not so, according to Skinner's operant conditioning concept (Skinner, 1969): particular behaviors are reinforced through effects that follow these behaviors. In terms of the Organizational Behavior Modification Model (Luthans & Kreitner, 1985; Komaki, Collins, & Temlock, 1987; Luthans & Stajkovic, 1999): behavior is a function of its contingent consequences. The model identifies five steps for changing performance behavior–consequences linkages:

- the *identification* of observable critical performance-related behaviors;
- the *measurement* of those behaviors' baseline frequencies;
- the *analysis* of antecedents (cues) and contingent consequences of these behaviors;
- the *intervention* to increase the frequencies of these behaviors;
- the *test* whether frequencies have increased.

Thus, a consequence is reinforcing when it strengthens a behavior–consequence linkage and increases its frequency. Pay may get reinforcing properties as it is tied directly and frequently to preceding performance behavior. Most organizational behavior modification research bears upon interventions as feedback, and pay. Luthans and Stajkovic (1999) report the results of a meta-analysis which covers all empirical data gained with this model: they show an average performance increase of 17%. Performance levels are much more affected in manufacturing than in service organizations. Feedback and pay are the most important reinforcers in manufacturing, whereas pay and getting recognition are most important in the services sector.

Yet, what happens when rewards follow preceding actions less directly and in varied frequency rates, i.e. when *partial reinforcement* is provided? Research on animal behavior has shown that partial reinforcement may cause stronger behaviors to occur: rats are running faster to the center of a maze where food might be available; pigeons are cooing for a longer time, etc.

Several field studies and experiments have applied the partial reinforcement concept to human behavior, for example planting seedlings, catching small beavers, being absent from work, and selling products to customers (e.g. Yukl & Latham, 1976; Latham & Huber, 1992; Mawhinney, 1986; Thierry, 1998a). Characteristically, in each setting hourly base pay was provided in addition to which 'Continuous Reinforcement' (CR) was given for each unit of performance. Thus, planters of seedlings got a CR-bonus for each bunch of 1,000 seedlings planted. Subsequently, a 'Variable Reinforcement' (VR) condition was introduced: after finishing the performance task employees had to guess the outcome of throwing dice with two (VR2), three (VR3), four (VR4) or more options. The more options at stake, the higher the bonus (linear relationship) when the guess was right. Usually, employees were successively subject to each experimental condition, whereas some employees constituted the control condition. The outcomes of these studies are slightly ambiguous: CR often resulted in high performance, but in some instances only when workers were still inexperienced. VR conditions produced diverging performance outcomes: for instance, VR4 caused higher performance in some and lower performance in other settings compared to CR. In all these examples higher performance resulted in a higher bonus, as is usual in field settings. Unfortunately, as Mawhinney (1986) has pointed out, this prevents any interpretation in terms of partial reinforcement: the effects of changing the frequency of a reward (the 'stretching' effect) can only be analysed when the amount of the reward remains unchanged. Another point is whether in practice a CR condition is not merely another VR mode: when performance results are continuously reinforced, it is essential that the reward is provided directly upon the performance delivered instead of later that day or that week. In organizational life this requirement can almost never be met: pay-for-performance bonuses are usually paid on a monthly or even annual basis. Thus, the data reported may be considered as illustrative of the application of pay-for-performance programs: performance levels in either the CR or VR condition were always higher than in the control condition.

Goal Setting

Goal-setting theory specifies the conditions under which an individual is motivated to perform on a high level. Generally, four conditions are crucial for high performance to occur (Locke & Latham, 1990a):

1. Goals should be set at a high, difficult level.
2. Goals ought to be very specific in terms of the result to be achieved.
3. Feedback has to be provided on a regular basis.
4. Employees must accept these goals.

In the High Performance Cycle Locke and Latham (1990b) specify various additional moderating (e.g. ability; commitment) and mediating (such as persistence; task-specific strategies) variables. In recent research, most emphasis is put upon self-set goals and self-efficacy (e.g. Bandura, 1997) as among the main determinants of the motivation for high performance.

How does compensation affect performance? Is it a trivial reward, once the conditions for high performance have been met? Would it stimulate to set the level of goals still higher, or could compensation be a substitute for inadequate feedback? Bartol and Locke (2000) argue that goal-setting theory's hypothesis about compensation runs similar to that accruing from expectancy theory (and of Bandura's social cognitive theory): pay-for-performance only motivates to act if the individual believes that this action for getting extra pay is feasible. Some studies found that bonus pay led to a higher level of goal commitment. Goal commitment might however be superfluous when personal goals and self-efficacy are separately measured. It is still inconclusive whether goals and self-efficacy mediate pay effects. In a study by Mowen, Middlemist, and Luther (1981) people with difficult goals performed best with a piece-rate system (i.e. each 'bit of performance' is paid for). People with moderate goals did best under a bonus system that paid only for goal success (i.e. having met the goal set). Bartol and Locke propose a threefold approach to pay-for-performance:

1. For people with difficult goals all-or-none bonuses should be used. Although this kind of bonus might increase the negative effects of failure, it might challenge highly motivated executives to find new methods to reach their goals.
2. Degree of success should be paid: performance pay is increasing proportionally as performance is getting better.
3. When self-set goals apply, rewards may be determined afterwards, for example, based upon the value of achieved performance to the organization.

The third suggestion is interesting, but its applicability seems to be doubtful. It may be combined with self-setting the proportional level of performance pay relative to the level of base pay. Anyway, at least some rules of the game ought to be specified in order to be confident that the system will be fairly administered—a subject that is discussed in the next section.

EQUITY AND JUSTICE

The compensation theories discussed in the previous sections all bear upon the relationship between performance behavior and outcomes (whatever the causal links hypothesized) and upon variables impacting upon this relationship. In the current section the focus is on the relationship between contributions and inducements regarding both the employee and the organization (usually represented by a line or HRM manager). Contributions and inducements are usually laid down formally in an individual labor contract. In (north-west) European countries Collective Labor Agreements may provide for a larger framework of working conditions to which the individual contracts refer. But contracts and agreements differ sizably from one another in, for instance, the scope of conditions covered, in specificity of arrangements, and in the provision of contributions and inducements that are 'silently' taken for granted. More important, individuals differ from one another in their perceptions of relevant and recognized contributions and inducements, and in the perceived fairness of the exchange. It is this perspective that is central to this section.

Adams' equity model (1963, 1965) holds that an individual tries to achieve balance between his/her inputs (contributions) and outcomes (inducements) relative to that individual's perception of the input–outcome ratio of a referent. A referent may be one or more other human beings, a particular group, the policy of an organization, and also the person earlier or later in his/her career. Inputs bear upon long-term investments and short-term costs, for instance, education, abilities, and effort. Examples of outcomes are task performance, recognition, compensation, and critique. Any attribute that the individual recognizes and considers to be relevant, may get input or outcome properties. Relevance also determines the choice of a referent. A feeling of equity results when the person's perceived input–outcome ratio is equal to the person's perception of the referent's ratio; inequity or dissonance manifests itself in the case of an unequal balance between ratios. Thus, as an employee perceives his or her effort to perform a task as high and the pay he or she gets as low, while believing that his or her colleague receives much more pay in exchange for the same effort level, the person experiences dissatisfaction as an effect of the resulting dissonance.

What happens when dissonance occurs? Generally, the person will try to restore the balance. But much evidence shows that it is rather difficult to predict which particular strategy will be chosen since a condition of 'under-reward' appears to elicit emotions that differ from an 'over-reward' condition. The person may try to change inputs and/or outcomes, he or she may cognitively reinterpret the situation (e.g. through adding attributes that were irrelevant until that moment), or may change the referent, and may withdraw from the situation (absenteeism; low commitment; turnover, etc.). Harder (1992) analysed the actions of over-rewarded and under-rewarded players in baseball and basketball tournaments. Over-rewarded subjects were supposed to improve their performance. Under-rewarded players were expected to lower their performance level; yet, it was also hypothesized that under-rewarded subjects with strong performance–reward expectancies would increase their performance, because they believe they could earn more eventually. Harder's evidence shows that most effects occurred in the under-rewarded condition: players tended to engage in utilitarian, egoistic behaviors that were expected to lead to future higher rewards; a lower performance level was seldom chosen.

The perceived unfairness may also lead to retaliation, as Skarlicki and Folger (1997) argue. Retaliation may take several forms, such as less commitment, less willingness to work more hours than agreed, thefts, and brief spells of illness. The authors hypothesize a three-way interaction between procedural, interactional, and distributive justice. Procedural justice bears upon the perceived fairness of the formal procedures a company is using. Interactional justice relates to the perceived quality of interpersonal relations and treatments going along with these formal procedures. Distributive justice addresses the perceived fairness of rewards received.

Accordingly, if a person experiences distributive dissatisfaction, then retaliation will occur when either procedural or interactional justice is low. If either procedural or interactional justice is high, no retaliation will take place. Data assembled in a manufacturing plant support these hypotheses. They also reported evidence that personality factors affect the incidence of retaliation (Skarlicki, Folger, & Tesluk, 1999). One factor was negative affectivity: persons with a higher score have more distress, discomfort, and dissatisfaction, whereas they keep thinking about their mistakes. Another factor was agreeableness: higher scores indicate persons being cooperative, sociable, and empathic. The authors found that the relationship between unfairness and retaliation is stronger for individuals with high negative affectivity than for those with low negative affectivity. Likewise, the unfairness–retaliation relationship was stronger for individuals with low agreeableness scores than for persons with high scores.

Perceptions of inequity and unfairness often bear (among others) upon the relationship between effort and compensation, and are thus affecting people's work attitudes, degree of satisfaction, commitment, organization citizenship, and the like. These in turn may lead to (negative) performance effects. Performance effects are also likely as an individual tries to restore equity or fairness, for instance, through increasing or decreasing the effort spent in the task. Violations of the perceived contributions—inducements contract (or, in terms of Rousseau, 1989: the psychological contract) do not necessarily imply an impairment of the organization's effectiveness (Rousseau & Ho, 2000). But violations tend to strengthen the person's focus upon his/her own interests, as also Harder (1992) noticed, and to increase the person's resistance against changing working conditions he/she considers to be vital. Consequently, also compensation is rendered less effective.

COGNITIVE EVALUATION THEORY

Many people seem to take it for granted that they are subject to deadlines at school and in their work, that they face competition from others, that their performance results may lead to sanctions or, on the contrary, to extra pay. But suppose that they are completely involved in their play, in learning or working: would pay and other 'extrinsic' outcomes possibly alter their motivation to engage in these activities? According to Deci (1975; Deci & Ryan, 1985), they certainly would decrease these people's intrinsic motivation. Intrinsic motivation results from two basic human needs: the need to be competent, and the need for an internal locus of causality of behavior. Thus, an intrinsically motivated human being is on the lookout for situations that are challenging.

What happens then when an employee is faced with an extrinsic reward like pay-for-performance (see also Thierry, 1990)? Deci and Ryan hold that any outcome may have one of three properties:

1. Informational: the outcome informs the person about his/her competence level, and causes intrinsic motivation to be continued.
2. Controlling: the outcome is perceived as controlling the person, i.e. by a source external to him or her. Consequently, intrinsic motivation is going to be less, since the locus of causality is now externally attributed.
3. Amotivational: the outcome contains a negative feedback message. Skills and competencies are poor; thus, intrinsic motivation decreases.

The nature of a particular reward contingency determines whether intrinsic motivation (IM) is going to be affected. Deci and Ryan distinguish five different kinds:

- Pay that comes unexpected: this is not affecting IM.
- Pay that is not task-contingent (i.e. pay for participating in a activity): it does not reduce IM.
- Task-contingent pay (that is, pay for engaging in a task, or for completing it): this has more negative than positive impact upon IM.
- Performance-contingent pay (i.e. for having met a target set): this reduces IM.
- Verbal rewards: they increase IM.

Recently, various meta-analytic studies have been published (Cameron & Pierce, 1994; Deci, Koestner, & Ryan, 1999; Eisenberger, Pierce, & Cameron, 1999). Several measures of IM were included, for instance, self-reported interest, performance during some free time, and willingness to return later to perform again (without pay). Most evidence shows that performance-contingent pay does *not* cause IM to decrease, unless performance goals set are rather vague.

Interestingly, various authors explain the supposed negative effect of contingent pay upon IM through the concept of *overjustification*: contrary to Cognitive Evaluation Theory, an extrinsic reward like pay is considered to be quite motivating. Yet, when task activities are motivating as well, the individual is faced with 'too many causes (justifications)' for its behavior; thus, IM gets lower. However, Eisenberger et al. (1999) argue that providing an employee with performance pay conveys to him/her the message that the manager is hardly capable to control his/her behavior. This causes the employee to get a stronger feeling of self-determination and, consequently, more IM; their research data are in support of their hypothesis. Cialdini et al. (1998) show that when an overjustification effect occurs, for instance, with children, the *relabeling* of an extrinsic reward into a personal disposition leads to positive performance effects.

REFLECTION THEORY

The theories addressed in the preceding sections outline, each in its own manner, how compensation may become important or meaningful to an individual. However, they do not clarify which meanings compensation may acquire. Only expectancy theory is more explicit in this respect. Reflection theory has been designed to fill this gap (e.g. Thierry, 1992a, 1992b; Miedema, 1994).

The root of reflection theory is the notion that the development and maintenance of *self-identity* is an essential characteristic of the human being. Through self-identity a person organizes his or her experiences, cognitions, emotions, interests, values, and preferences. Self-identity makes it possible to integrate past experience with current events, preparing the person to meet future challenges (more extensively in Thierry, 2001). Thus, he/she is alert on scanning work-related information, in particular for signals of change that may require the person's actions to effect internal or external change in order to reaffirm his/her self-identity. Compensation constitutes an important domain of information, the meanings of which are considered to be vital to a person's self-identity. Thus, compensation has no informational value and meaning on 'its own': it acquires significance through *reflecting* information about events in other fields. Four categories of meaning are distinguished:

1. *Motivational properties*. This category is derived from expectancy theory. It holds that pay is meaningful to the extent that pay is considered to be instrumental to satisfy a person's motives or goals.
2. *Relative position*. This category refers to the regulatory character of work, and distinguishes two aspects. One reflects feedback about task goals set: pay compares task performance with a standard or a goal. Thus, pay may signal whether particular (corrective?) actions are needed to reach set targets. The other aspect is social-comparative: pay reflects the evaluation of the person relative to significant social others. Pay may indicate how well an individual is doing compared to referents inside and outside the company.
3. *Control*. This category relates to the network of people and material means a person is dependent upon. In this respect pay reflects the exertion of control by as well as upon a person. Pay may reveal how effective an employee is influencing his/her superior as well as the extent to which others control that employee.
4. *Spending*. This category addresses the goods and services actually purchased through an employee's or manager's pay. In particular, pay reflects the extent to which motives and goals have been met through pay as well as the ease or hardship with which this occurred.

Obviously, the meaningfulness of pay to an organization member is affected by the particular pay systems in use; also, various other variables may have an impact (cf. Thierry, 1998a). Reflection theory now holds that as an employee is reading more meaning in his/her pay, his/her performance as well as satisfaction with pay is more affected. Recent and current research with the scales designed to measure the meanings shows that the structure of four meanings is usually supported, although relative position and control may merge in a few cases (e.g. Shaw, 1996). Moreover, pay meanings explain mostly quite some variance in pay satisfaction. Due to well-known problems in gathering reliable data on individual performance, there is scarce evidence in this respect. One study showed that the link between pay meanings and performance was moderated by pay satisfaction. Future research should focus on whether commitment moderates the relationship between pay meanings on the one hand and performance and pay satisfaction on the other. One hypothesis is that continuance commitment relates stronger to performance, whereas normative and affective commitment has a stronger relationship with satisfaction. Another hypothesis holds that when commitment is high, also rather low-pay-meaning scores affect performance and satisfaction.

AGENCY THEORY

This theory has a background in economics (Jensen & Meckling, 1976) and is dominating most current compensation research. The theory addresses the relationship between a principal (a more powerful individual, e.g. an owner) and an agent (a less powerful individual, say, a company president). The principal's concern is that an agent is abiding to the principal's interests (i.e. furthering the prosperity of the company). Yet, is it possible for the principal to monitor the actions of the agent in order to know whether the agent possibly is pursuing his own goals (called 'agency costs', such as when the agent tries to maximize his/her short-term earnings)? That depends: the agent might work in the vicinity of the principal, allowing the latter to assess the agent's work. In that case the principal will opt for a *behavior-based* contract with the agent without the need to make the agent's pay (partly) dependent upon performance. But the agent's work might require more expertise than the principal possesses, making it impossible to evaluate the agent's activities. Also, the agent might usually work at a client's site, or it might be too expensive to monitor the agent's actions. In these cases the principal will choose an *outcome-based* contract which includes a pay-for-performance system, transferring the risks the principal runs (i.e. not being able to assess the agent's action) to the agent (e.g. Eisenhardt, 1988). As the agent is supposed to be risk-aversive, he/she will counteract and bargain for a higher base salary (called: risk premium). Whether the agent is successful depends upon the agent's relative power position. Thus, agency theory offers a framework for explaining the choice of compensation systems and the level of compensation (Gomez-Mejia & Wiseman, 1997; Thierry, in press).

Current research bears, for example, upon determinants of risk-taking behavior, and also upon the relationship between monitoring instruments and performance pay. As to the latter, Prendergast (1999) holds that as performance measures contain more error, incentives and bonuses are less effective. Thus, whereas 'subjective' measures (performance appraisal by the superior) may have the advantage that a more global picture of an agent's performance is created, their main disadvantage is that agents alter their behavior. They engage in multi-tasking, implying the choice of tasks that are rewarded best, which resembles individual reactions to contract violation. They also seek to influence their superiors' ratings to the detriment of the firm's interests. Kowtha (1997) argues that an agent's skill level should be taken into account: the more skills, the more an agent is willing to carry risks since he/she is able to control a higher level of uncertainty.

MESO- AND MACRO-LEVEL THEORIES

Characteristic to the theories discussed previously is that compensation is supposed to affect emotions, cognitions and/or performance behaviors of the individual organization member. This emphasis is less prominent or even absent in a few theories to be outlined in this section. They throw some light on determinants of compensation inside and outside a company that are impacting upon how pay affects an individual at work. As will be seen, they differ in the extent to which managers or employees are understood to be able to exert any influence on the level, the systems or the significance of compensation, should they wish to do so.

The *resource dependence model* holds that the amount of control business units, groups or temporary coalitions have upon compensation is dependent upon the resources they are able to provide or withhold (cf. Pfeffer & Salancik, 1978; Pfeffer & Davis-Blake, 1987; Balkin & Bannister, 1993). A group that is able to regulate other members' access to information, expert knowledge, equipment, special support, etc., acquires a powerful position, and, as a result, may bargain for a comfortable pay pattern, for instance a high salary level without any performance pay. This model is often used to explain the rather sudden increase in compensation of specialists (e.g. information technology professionals), and the decrease of others.

Tournament theory conceives the company as an arena: on its playground members compete against one another in order to get a higher position. The differences in pay between positions should be large enough for incumbents and candidates to perceive these, and to motivate them to perform at their utmost to move up the career ladder. Thus, fixed rewards are set for successively higher jobs. The adequacy of an employee's performance level is not appraised in an absolute manner, but merely relative to that of competing employees (Prendergast, 1999). Becker and Huselid (1992) argue that tournament thinking is important when monitoring of employee's actions is difficult, or too expensive. Moreover, its self-enforcing reward structure makes managerial supervision superfluous: large pay differences should align employees' efforts to the company's interests. Interestingly, tournament theory and agency theory apparently address the same problem (monitoring), but the compensation design proposed to solve it differs considerably. Becker and Huselid show in a study with racing car drivers that there appear to be limits to the differences: too large differences are less motivating, and increase, moreover, risky behaviors. Bloom's evidence with baseball-players (1999) indirectly supports Becker and Huselid's result: the larger the pay differences, the lower the individual (and the group) performance level. Bloom also found a remarkable difference between players in the upper part of the pay distribution and those in the bottom part: the 'uppers' performed better with larger pay differences, whereas players at the bottom performed worse in the same condition.

Neo-classical labor market theory argues that the effective wage rate of an occupation depends on the point on the curve where labor supply (people looking for employment) and labor demand (vacant positions) meet. Thus, the more labor supply is abundant, the lower the wages are, etc. (cf. Gomez-Mejia & Balkin, 1992). Market forces determine pay levels; the individual company does not to have any control on these. What managers can do in this respect is merely to observe changes in market pay rates, and adjust pay levels accordingly. Gerhart (2000) states moreover that companies are not supposed to differ from one another in pay levels: if there would be unattractive job characteristics, extra pay would restore the balance.

Finally, the *efficiency wage model*. Pay levels ought not to conform to the effective wage rate (see the neo-classical labour market theory), but should be set at a higher level. With a relatively high pay level (base and performance pay) a company will attract more qualified employees and managers, not only since they have more abilities, skills, and experience, but also because of their stronger motivation and disinclination to shirk. Prendergast (1999) points out that it is difficult to prove unequivocally whether the tenets of efficiency wage theory hold.

THEORIES IN PERSPECTIVE

Several themes relevant to the relationship between compensation and performance run through the theories just described. They are mentioned in brief:

1. There must be a clear, unambiguous relationship between (individual) performance and compensation. This notion of *instrumentality* bears upon a particular performance result (usually on one or more indicators) which is linked to a specified amount of pay. Various theories, like expectancy theory, stress 'line of sight' in this respect, which means that an individual must perceive and understand the performance–pay linkage for making it effective. The Organizational Behavior Modification model emphasizes merely instrumentality. Clearly, these theories relate to pay for performance.
2. The balance between a person's effort (performance) and compensation must be fair relative to a referent. Under-rewarded individuals may engage in egoistic performance behaviors or acts of retaliation. This theme has implications for both base pay and performance pay.
3. If an individual perceives his/her pay as being controlled by others (intrinsic), motivation may decrease (and possibly also the level of performance). However, the use of performance pay may signify to the individual that he/she has got *more control*, the more so as skill levels are higher.
4. Aligning the interests of organization members with those of the organization (i.e. the owners) requires diligent monitoring of performance relative to the use of performance pay. Quantitative performance measures are needed, since subjective performance yardsticks are vulnerable as they may lead to *dysfunctional* employees' actions.
5. The higher the compensation level, the better motivation and performance will be. The larger the pay *differentials*, the stronger the risk that employees (with moderate performance goals and lower pay) will decrease their performance.

Let's see whether these themes are discernible in the empirical research on pay systems.

RESEARCH ON PAY SYSTEMS

THE LOGIC OF RESULTS-ORIENTED PAY

In most industrialized countries the total compensation of managers and employees is composed largely of base pay (salary or wage), and a rather small performance contingent

TABLE 16.2 Basic elements of results-oriented pay

Characteristics	Features
Performance	Critical factors to be affected by organization members' performance
	Tuned to individual, group and/or organization results
	Norms (average, adequate, superb results)
Payment	Link between results and pay (both actual and perceived)
	Frequency of feedback on results
	Bonus or higher position on salary scale
	Frequency of payout
Implementation	Extent of consultation/participation of employees
	Training of managers
	Selection effect?

part, in addition to which more or less secondary labor conditions are provided (e.g. health insurance; retirement provisions). Some companies offer also tertiary benefits (such as lower mortgage rates), which apply in various cases exclusively to middle and senior managers. Base pay is determined either through a system of job evaluation (Thierry & de Jong, 1998), the use of salary surveys, or estimates of market rates.

The introduction of performance-related pay requires many additional activities and is usually time-consuming (see Table 16.2 for an overview of the basic elements of result-oriented pay). First, one or more performance *characteristics* have to be defined. Requirements are that these characteristics are essential to the work to be remunerated, also in order to ensure that an employee's efforts are spent in the right direction. The scores on the characteristics should moreover reflect the discretion of the employee in executing the various tasks. Both requirements may necessitate a preceding analysis of the larger work process in the department or firm: often a part of the process is not running smoothly. When the performance characteristics have been set—for instance, the number of copiers leased, and clients' after-sales satisfaction—norms have to be determined. A norm signifies the level of average or good performance. An important point in this respect is how each characteristic is being assessed: an 'objective' (a better term is *quantitative*) appraisal would count (in the example given) the number of copiers leased over a certain period against the norm. A 'subjective' appraisal (as is often used in practice) would require a supervisor's account (and possibly from other sources as well) of, for instance, an employee's degree of initiative, or willingness to learn (also against a norm). Another very important issue is whether the performance of an *individual* employee or manager is at the right level for identifying the characteristics. Often, employees work for some part of their time in groups; moreover, groups or business units may be required to work closely together, for instance, when an aeroplane is being manufactured, or when patients are getting health care in a hospital. Characteristics should then relate to unit quality or to organizational effectiveness (e.g. sales value; return on investment; patient satisfaction). Thus, the term 'performance' would apply less in the latter cases; therefore, from now on we will use the word '*results-oriented pay*' (ROP).

Some *payment* issues must now be decided. One question concerns the nature of the link between results achieved (having met the norm) and pay. Often this link is proportional: one extra unit of performance (e.g. an extra copier leased) causes pay to increase by an extra unit. But assume that it would be easy each month to lease at least

10 copiers, but reaching a score of 15 copiers would need more effort, and the leasing of 20 copiers is only feasible with a lot of hard work. Company management may consider to pay less than proportional for a performance level of 10 or less, proportional between 11 and 15, and more than proportional from 16 and above. A second question relates to how pay is provided. It may be a bonus that is awarded each time the performance norm has been met. It is also possible to reward the employee with an extra step or grade on his/her salary scale: consequently, there is a permanent, 'structural' salary increase, whereas the bonus has to be earned each time.

A third issue is the *implementation* of the new system. An important point here is the extent to which organization members are consulted about the ROP plans and may change some of their features. Managers ought to be trained moreover in handling both the philosophy and the particular procedures of the new event. Also the strategies to attract and select applicants are a matter of serious concern: evidence shows that ROP may be attractive to high achievers. If the company would decide to pay more for most jobs than most competitors do, candidates with more qualifications ought to be hired. Thus, preparing a ROP system for application is a rather complicated event.

PIECE RATES

Employees subject to this system are usually paid a fixed hourly wage; additionally, each completed 'piece of performance' earns them a bonus. Examples of 'pieces' are: a slaughtered hog, an assembled electronic tube, a manufactured TV set, and a square meter of mowed lawn. These examples show that current production and information technology has largely made the concept of piece of performance outdated, although piece rates are still being applied on a modest scale. They also show that one performance characteristic is appraised and rewarded: quantity. Thus, the system is rather simple and easy to understand, which is reflecting its strengths. If also other features would be relevant, such as a product's quality, piece rates are not adequate.

In a review of research evidence covering some 40 years, more than 30 studies address the effects of piece rates upon performance (Thierry, 1987). In all cases higher performance levels are found. A few studies report less pay satisfaction. More recently, Paarsch and Shearer (2000) took payroll records of Canadian tree planters and estimated the productivity effects of piece rates compared to fixed rates. Piece rates were dependent upon soil conditions and steepness of the area. Their results show an increase in productivity of 22%. Since the quality of planting was not rewarded, a negative quality effect had to be accounted for (i.e. 8%), resulting in a net effect of 14% productivity gain.

MERIT RATING

Individual performance appraisal usually takes place once a year (in some cases semi-annually). Supervisors—and possibly others, as in the 360-degree appraisal method—communicate to their employees how well they have done on a variety of characteristics. Often, these characteristics are qualitative and rather abstract in nature, such as: initiative at work; dependability; willingness to learn; creative thinking, and the like. Also more quantitative measures may be included, like production quantity, and product quality. Merit rating implies that the appraisal result is taken as the basis for whether or not an employee gets some extra pay (bonus or salary increase) that year. The system is widely used in government institutions and in industry.

Unfortunately, research evidence is not abundantly available. Both older and more recent studies show however that merit rating is the sole system with respect to which almost exclusively negative results have been reported (cf. Thierry, 1987; Bannister & Balkin, 1990; Milkovich & Wigdor, 1991; Heneman, 1991; Marsden & Richardson, 1994). Merit rating appears not to have an impact upon individual performance or firm productivity. It affects however negatively the line of sight (perception of instrumentality) and the degree of satisfaction with the appraisal result–pay relationship. The overview of Campbell, Campbell, and Chia (1998) captures both older and more recent evidence. These authors argue that merit rating often leads to results—for instance, dissatisfaction, lower performance, and discouragement—which are opposite to the effects intended. Moreover, these results were also found some 30 years ago, so apparently nothing much has improved. The authors group their critique under five headings:

1. *Measurement problems.* Reliability and validity of the supervisory performance appraisal procedure are low. Characteristics used are vulnerable to distortion, deficiencies, contamination, bias, and the like. Moreover, the 'uniqueness' of individual contributions is not measurable.
2. *Feedback.* Employees often refuse to accept the appraisal result, since it is considered as inaccurate; thus, they will use defense mechanisms. Supervisors find it difficult to provide unambiguous feedback.
3. *Size of rewards.* Often, a separate budget is set for providing merit. Unfortunately, mostly a 'zero sum' condition exists: when outstanding performers are present, several 'under-performers' have to be found to meet budget constraints. Resulting pay differentials are too small.
4. *System noise.* An annual (or semi-annual) appraisal is much too infrequent, as an effect of which employees can hardly perceive a link between their behaviors and the appraisal result. Also, merit pay is influenced by non-performance factors, like an employee's current position on a salary scale, and the breadth of pay dispersion.
5. *Attribution.* The employee (actor) tends to attribute the causes for his/her actions to the situation, whereas the supervisor (observer) is inclined to locate these in an employee's personality characteristics. Thus, the employee and the supervisor may agree on the nature of a particular problem, but—due to the method used—not on its causes.

PERFORMANCE BONUS AND INCENTIVES

Instead of subjective characteristics, quantitative factors may be identified that are critical to the successful performance of a task. Whereas the usual merit rating aspects may be applied to all organization members, performance factors should always be tailored to the particular jobs in question. Obviously, the setting of these factors is a time-consuming process. ProMES—Productivity Measurement and Enhancement System (e.g. Pritchard, 1995)—is among the systems that identify critical factors, specify indicators per factor, and order those indicators according to importance. Several years ago ProMES data assembled in various countries showed an average effect size(d) on productivity of 2.3 (Pritchard, 1995, Ch. 18). Obviously, when work has been analysed in terms of critical factors and accompanying indices, results may be used for management information, performance appraisal, leadership practices, and also for compensation purposes.

Performance bonus systems generally follow the logic of results-oriented pay, as outlined in this chapter. Our review of earlier research (Thierry, 1987) reveals that studies showing positive performance effects outweigh those with negative effects sevenfold. Recently, Prendergast (1999) reported various studies with sizable positive effects. He warns, however, for attributing these effects exclusively to the performance bonus. His estimate is that around one-third of the performance effect has been caused by having attracted more qualified workers (in accordance with the efficiency wage theory). Other positive effects bear upon cooperation, higher pay, etc. Negative effects relate, for instance, to inaccurate task norms the maintenance of which was poor, and to problems with the line of sight.

By far most evidence on the performance bonus bears upon *individual* performance. Our 1987 review located more than 4,500 studies in which an individual bonus led to higher performance, whereas less than 20 studies related to a *group* bonus. Of the latter, 11 studies reported a higher performance, whereas 5 studies indicated a lower performance; also problems with understanding the performance–bonus link were mentioned repeatedly. Recently, a few companies are allowing their employees to self-setting their bonus percentage proportional to their base pay. Research data are not yet available.

Examples of group pay are still rather rare. Nonetheless, modern technologies require increasingly group work. What happens when task groups members who are getting equal pay perceive performance differences within their group? Would they choose to become 'free riders' or would they maintain their performance level?

Wilke (2000) found in an experiment in small groups with disjunctive tasks (i.e. only the performance of the best performing group member counts) that equal pay is considered to be less equitable as the other group member combines a low competence level with a low level of effort or, alternatively, as the other member is highly competent and spends much effort. Thus, equal pay is more equitable as competence level and effort level 'compensate', i.e. one is high and the other is low. Erez and Somech (1993) report evidence that social loafing does not tend to occur when group members are friends of one another, performance targets are clear, tasks are meaningful, and a group-supportive culture is favored.

A *company-wide* bonus system may be applied when various departments or business units within an organization are very much dependent upon one another and cooperation among them should be furthered. It may also be used in the context of promoting the involvement of all employees in the firm and the joint interests of owners and organization members (Lawler, 1986). Belonging to the category of gain-sharing systems, the Scanlon Plan seeks to involve all employees in contributing to the success of a firm and to let them share in the financial gains of their contributions (cf. Thierry & de Jong, 1979). Originally, in each department a small committee was installed to stimulate employees to send in ideas about how to improve the department's effectiveness. The committee has a budget, allowing them to implement those ideas that seem most worth while. A company-wide committee decides on ideas that have implications beyond one particular department. More recently, also other procedures to further employees' participation and involvement have been followed. Moreover, a financial index is chosen that should reflect the gains of the implemented ideas and proposals, e.g. the ratio of wages and salaries to total sales value. Achieved gains are distributed through a bonus to all members; part of the gains may be put in a collective fund (e.g. for welfare activities). Our review of earlier research (Thierry, 1987) shows that positive performance and attitudinal effects outweigh negative effects to a large extent. More recent evidence supports this trend (e.g. Hatcher, Ross, & Collins, 1991; Hanlon & Taylor, 1991; Hanlon, Meyer, & Taylor, 1994). Gain-sharing results for instance in better communication processes within the organization, and in extra pay. A gain-sharing pay-out has some (short-term) bonus and some (long-term) incentive properties. Dependent upon the frequency of feedback data extra pay (if gained) is awarded each month, each quarter, or, as in some cases, annually. One of the objectives of the collective fund is often to increase the involvement of managers and employees in the firm on the longer term.

The latter point qualifies gain sharing also as an *incentive* system. Incentives intend to establish financial bonds with executives, managers or employees for getting them to continue their relationship with the company. Examples of other incentive systems are profit sharing, employee stock owner plans (ESOPs), and options on shares. The sharing of profits involves that—whatever the particular definition of profit—an individual gets a percentage of the net annual financial result of the company. A particular problem associated with profit sharing is line of sight: many external and internal factors affect the level of profits; also, the time lag (between performance and profit announcement) is considerable. It is doubtful whether it affects performance and productivity; however, we found one study that established a positive relationship with productivity (Weitzman & Kruse, 1990). A particular objective of ESOPs is to gain employees' involvement through their co-ownership role. Options on company shares are awarded to managers and some qualified employees at a particular market rate, which may be used to purchase them and to sell them subsequently (if the company has performed well) after several years (e.g. Duffhues, Kabir, & Mertens, 1999). It is still an open issue whether ESOPs and options meet these objectives (Heneman, Ledford, & Gresham (2000), also since competing companies interested in attracting particular executives or professionals, are known to offer them still better financial packages.

FIXED AND SKILL-BASED PAY

As reported, results-oriented pay can have positive effects on performance or productivity and on cooperation, ideas for improvement, etc. Heneman et al. (2000) estimate that in general two-thirds of all ROP cases are successful; however, many failures have occurred as well, such as: the formula (i.e. the performance–pay link) is deficient; the bonus is much delayed; irrelevant behaviors are rewarded; impaired line of sight; low trust level. What would happen then when compensation is fixed without any contingence on results achieved? Our earlier research review (Thierry, 1987) identifies quite some studies in which subsequent to the introduction of flat rates performance levels more often improved than remained unchanged. However, there were more instances in which performance levels dropped. Satisfaction with the new system was apparent in many cases, yet preferences for ROP surfaced also.

When compensation is fixed, an employee is usually paid for job value. In order to challenge employees to improve their education level (and also to introduce some individual variable pay), *skill-based* pay (also called: competence pay) may be applied. According to this system it is specified which additional skills (and abilities) would be needed to keep up with expected changes in job content and/or to become eligible for a next career step. Upon having passed the terms of a class or training course, the employee's level of base compensation is increased; in cases where required skills and abilities are regularly changing, a skill bonus may be paid instead. Heneman et al. (2000) report rather positive experiences. These authors describe one case in which managerial attitudes on skill pay correlated positively with plant and regional performance figures. Crandall and Wallace (1998) warn that the costs for education and additional pay may be sizable. The gains may outweigh the costs, though, which makes timely adequate budgeting advisable.

IN CONCLUSION: THE CONTINGENCY OF CONTINGENT PAY

In discussing research evidence regarding compensation theories and effects of pay systems we have refrained where possible from including data which appeared to have a moderating effect. Many variables have been shown in studies to impact upon compensation and its consequences. Some of these refer to *pay system* characteristics, such as pay frequency, size of pay increase or decrease, benchmark referents (company internal or external), and previous pay raises (e.g. Rynes & Bono, 2000). Also managers' values regarding pay allocation principles may affect the size of a pay raise (Van Silfhout, 2000). Second, *personality* characteristics are found to be important: individuals higher on need for achievement tend to prefer individual ROP. Also more self-efficacious subjects tend to prefer individual rewards, whereas risk-aversive individuals prefer fixed compensation (e.g. Barber & Bretz, 2000). Thirdly, job and pay *(dis)satisfaction* may affect performance behaviors: pay dissatisfaction (whatever its causes) may lead not only to changes in perception of outcomes received, but also to behavioral changes like a different effort level, setting other goals, withdrawal, and the like (Heneman et al., 2000). Fourth, a company's *pay strategy* may have an important impact: some research indicates that the industrial sector relevant to a company, and company size determine the main compensation characteristics (Thierry, in press).

Nonetheless, the research described in this chapter clearly indicates that compensation may have an important impact upon performance. This conclusion holds primarily for individual performance, since group and company-wide compensation systems are still not very much in use. Yet, there is a host of conditions that ought to be met in order for this compensation–performance relationship to be positive. Current managerial thinking tends to group many of these together in concepts like performance culture and strategically oriented compensation. The positive relationship does not imply that a system of *performance* pay should always be applied: in particular when the work to be done is rather predictable, there seems to be no argument for performance pay. Possibly the positive performance effects of various cases of fixed pay apply to such work conditions.

The evidence also shows that results-oriented pay can have negative effects. Some of Kerr's (1988) arguments discussed in the Introductory section appear still to be valid. In particular the merit rating system appears to manifest consistently the same weaknesses over time. Various other pay systems show more promising results. Yet, there are still very few examples in which the performance behaviors of groups of employees, or even of larger units, are jointly rewarded. This should be a matter of serious concern, since task interdependencies among professionals and other employees are rapidly increasing.

There is still another reason to think in 'contingent' terms about performance pay. All studies known to this author that have been showing a positive relationship between the application of performance pay and (individual) performance—including studies with a control group, randomized designs, longitudinal data assembly, and adequate data analyses—have failed to demonstrate the '*causal agent*'. As described, the definition of performance characteristics, the analysis of work processes, the consultation with employees, the setting of goals, etc., are vital processes (that are undergoing change as well), which are directly preceding or going along with the introduction of performance pay. In other words: each of these processes may have acted as a causal agent. The performance–pay link is just one of the potential causes of the outcome effects. This should inspire researchers to design better studies for disentangling the particular role of compensation.

REFERENCES

Adams, J. S. (1963). Toward an understanding of inequity. *Journal of Abnormal and Social Psychology*, **67**, 422–436.

Adams, J. S. (1965). Inequity in social exchange. In L. Berkowitz (Ed.), *Advances in experimental social psychology*, vol. 2. New York: Academic Press.

Balkin, D. B., & Bannister, B. D. (1993). Explaining pay forms for strategic employee groups in organizations: A resource dependence perspective. *Journal of Occupational and Organizational Psychology*, **66**, 139–151.

Bandura, A. (1997). *Self-efficacy: The exercise of control*. New York: W. H. Freeman & Company.

Bannister, B. D., & Balkin, D. B. (1990). Performance evaluation and compensation feedback messages. *Journal of Occupational Psychology*, **63**, 97–111.

Barber, A. E., & Bretz, R. D. (2000). Compensation, attraction, and retention. In S. L. Rynes & B. Gerhart (Eds.), *Compensation in organizations* (pp. 32–60). San Francisco: Jossey-Bass.

Bartol, K. M., & Locke, E. A. (2000). Incentives and motivation. In S. L. Rynes & B. Gerhart (Eds.), *Compensation in organizations* (pp. 104–147). San Francisco: Jossey-Bass.

Becker, B. E., & Huselid, M. A. (1992). The incentive effects of tournament compensation systems. *Administrative Science Quarterly*, **37**, 336–350.

Bloom, M. (1999). The performance effects of pay dispersion on individuals and organizations. *Academy of Management Journal*, **42**, 25–40.

Cameron, J., & Pierce, W. D. (1994). Reinforcement, reward, and intrinsic motivation: A meta-analysis. *Review of Educational research*, **64**, 363–423.

Campbell, D. J., Campbell, K. M., & Chia, K. M. (1998). Merit pay, performance appraisal, and individual motivation: An analysis and alternative. *Human resource Management*, **37**, 131–146.

Cascio, W. F. (1998). Theory, research, and practice in American applied psychology. *Applied Psychology: An International Perspective*, **47**, 127–128.

Cialdini, R. B., Eisenberg, N., Green, B. L., Rhoads, K., & Bator, R. (1998). Undermining the undermining effect of reward on sustained effort. *Journal of Applied Social Psychology*, **28**, 249–263.

Crandall, N. F., & Wallace, M. J. (1998). *Work and rewards in the virtual workplace*. New York: American Management Association.

Deci, E. L. (1975). *Intrinsic motivation*. New York: Plenum Press.

Deci, E. L., & Ryan, R. M. (1985). *Intrinsic motivation and self-determination in human behavior*. New York: Plenum Press.

Deci, E. L., Koestner, R., & Ryan, R. M. (1999). A meta-analytic review of experiments examining the effects of extrinsic rewards on intrinsic motivation. *Psychological Bulletin*, **125**, 627–668.

Duffhues, P., Kabir, R., & Mertens, G. (1999). *Personeelsoptieregelingen in Nederland: theorie en praktijk* (Dutch Employee's Options Systems: Theory and Practice). Tilburg: Center, Applied Research.

Eerde, W. van, & Thierry, Hk. (1996). Vroom's expectancy models and work-related criteria: A meta-analysis. *Journal of Applied Psychology*, **81**, 575–586.

Eisenberger, R., Pierce, W. D., & Cameron, J. (1999). Effects of reward on intrinsic motivation—negative, neutral, and positive: Comment on Deci, Koestner, and Ryan (1999). *Psychological Bulletin*, **125**, 677–691.

Eisenhardt, K. (1988). Agency and institutional theory explanations: The case of retail sales compensation. *Academy of Management Journal*, **31**, 488–511.

Erez, M., & Somech, A. (1996). Is group productivity loss the rule or the exception? Effects of culture and group-based motivation. *Academy of Management Journal*, **39**, 1513–1537.

Gerhart, B. (2000). Compensation strategy and organizational performance. In S. L. Rynes & B. Gerhart (Eds.), *Compensation in organizations* (pp. 151–194). San Francisco: Jossey-Bass.

Gomez-Mejia, L. R., & Balkin, D. B. (1992). *Compensation, organizational strategy, and firm performance*. Cincinnati: South-Western Publishing Company.

Gomez-Mejia, L. R., & Wiseman, R. M. (1997). Reframing executive compensation: An assessment and outlook. *Journal of Management*, **23**, 291–374.

Hanlon, S. C., & Taylor, R. R. (1991). An examination of changes in work group communication behaviors following installation of a gainsharing plan. *Group and Organization Studies*, **16**, 238–267.

Hanlon, S. C., Meyer, D. G., & Taylor, R. R. (1994). Consequences of gainsharing: A field experiment revisited. *Group and Organization Studies*, **19**, 87–111.

Harder, J. W. (1992). Play for pay: Effects of inequity in a pay for performance context. *Administrative Science Quarterly*, **37**, 321–335.

Hatcher, L., Ross, T. L., & Collins, D. (1991). Attributions for participation and nonparticipation in gainsharing-plan involvement systems. *Group and Organization Studies*, **16**, 25–43.

Heneman, R. L. (1991). *Merit pay: Linking pay increases to performance ratings*. Reading: Addison-Wesley.

Heneman, R. L., Ledford, G. E., & Gresham, M. T. (2000). The changing nature of work and its effects on compensation design and delivery. In S. L. Rynes & B. Gerhart (Eds.), *Compensation in organizations* (pp. 195–240). San Francisco: Jossey-Bass.

Herzberg, F., Mausner, B., & Snyderman, B. B. (1959). The m*otivation to work*. New York: Wiley.

Jensen, M., & Meckling, W. (1976). Theory of the firm: Managerial behavior, agency costs, and ownership structure. *Journal of Financial Economics*, **3**, 305–360.

Kanungo, R. N., & Mendonca, M. (1988). Evaluating employee compensation. *California Management Review*, **31**, 23–39.

Kerr, S. (1988). Some characteristics and consequences of organizational reward. In F. D. Schoorman & B. Schneider (Eds.), *Facilitating work effectiveness*. Lexington: Heath & Co.

Komaki, J., Collins, R. L., & Temlock, S. (1987). An alternative performance measurement approach: Applied operant measurement in the service sector. *Applied Psychology: An International Review*, **36**, 71–89.

Kowtha, N. Rao (1997). Skills, incentives, and control: An integration of agency and transaction cost approaches. *Group and Organization Management*, **22**, 53–86.

Latham, G. P., & Huber, V. L. (1992). Schedules of reinforcement: Lessons from the past and issues for the future. *Journal of Organizational Behavior Management*, **12**, 125–149.

Lawler, E. E. (1971). *Pay and organizational effectiveness*. New York: McGraw-Hill.

Lawler, E. E. (1986). *High involvement management*. London: Addison-Wesley.

Locke, E. A., & Latham, G. P. (1990a). *A theory of goal setting and task performance*. Englewood Cliffs: Prentice-Hall.

Locke, E. A., & Latham, G. P. (1990b). Work motivation: The high performance cycle. In U. Kleinbeck, H. H. Quast, Hk. Thierry & H. Haecker (Eds.), *Work motivation* (pp. 3–25). Hillsdale: Lawrence Erlbaum.

Luthans, F., & Kreitner, R. (1985). *Organizational behavior modification and beyond*. Glenview: Scott, Foresman & Co.

Luthans, F., & Stajkovic, A. D. (1999). Reinforce for performance: The need to go beyond pay and even rewards. *Academy of Management Executive*, **13**, 49–57.

March, J. G., & Simon, H. A. (1958). *Organizations*. New York: Wiley.

Marsden, D., & Richardson, R. (1994). Performing for pay? The effects of 'merit pay' on motivation in a public service. *British Journal of Industrial Relations*, **32**, 243–261.

Maslow, A. H. (1954). *Motivation and personality*. New York: Harper & Row.

Mawhinney, T. C. (1986). Reinforcement schedule stretching effects. In E. A. Locke (Ed.), *Generalizing from laboratory to field settings* (pp. 181–186). Lexington: Heath & Co.

Miedema, H. (1994). *De Achterkant van het salaris* (The backside of salaries). Assen: Van Gorcum. Ph.D. Thesis.

Milkovich, G. T., & Wigdor, A. K. (Eds.) (1991). *Pay for performance: Evaluating performance appraisal and merit pay*. Washington: National Academy Press.

Mowen, J. C., Middlemist, R. D., & Luther, D. (1981). Joint effects of assigned goal level and incentive structure on task performance: A laboratory study. *Journal of Applied Psychology*, **66**, 598–603.

Paarsch, H. J., & Shearer, B. (2000). Piece rates, fixed wages, and incentive effects: Statistical evidence from payroll records. *International Economic Review*, **41**, 59–92.

Pfeffer, J., & Salancik, G. R. (1978). *The external control of organizations: A resource dependence perspective*. New York: Harper & Row.

Pfeffer, J., & Davis-Blake, A. (1987). Understanding organizational wage structures: A resource dependence approach. *Academy of Management Journal*, **30**, 437–455.

Prendergast, C. (1999). The provision of incentives in firms. *Journal of Economic Literature*, **37**, 7–63.

Pritchard, R. D. (Ed.) (1995). *Productivity measurement and improvement: Organizational case studies*. London: Praeger.

Rousseau, D. M. (1989). Psychological and implied contracts in organizations. *Employees Rights and Responsibilities Journal*, **2**, 121–139.

Rousseau, D. M., & Ho, V. T. (2000). Psychological contract issues in compensation. In S. L. Rynes & B. Gerhart (Eds.), *Compensation in organizations* (pp. 273–310). San Francisco: Jossey-Bass.

Rynes, S. L., & Bono, J. E. (2000). Psychological research on determinants of pay. In S. L. Rynes & B. Gerhart (Eds.), *Compensation in organizations* (pp. 3–31). San Francisco: Jossey-Bass.

Rynes, S. L., & Gerhart, B. (Eds.) (2000). *Compensation in organizations*. San Francisco: Jossey-Bass.

Shaw, J. D. (1996). *A confirmatory factor analysis of pay meaning dimensions on an english speaking sample*. Paper 1996, Southwest Academy of Management Conference.

Silfhout, R. K. van (2000). *Inequality in pay within organizations: Normative and instrumental perspectives*. Tilburg University: Human Resource Science. Ph.D. Thesis.

Skarlicki, D. P., & Folger, R. (1997). Retaliation in the workplace: The role of distributive, procedural, and interactional justice. *Journal of Applied Psychology*, **82**, 434–443.

Skarlicki, D. P., Folger, R., & Tesluk, P. (1999). Personality as a moderator in the relationship between fairness and retaliation. *Academy of Management Journal*, **42**, 100–108.

Skinner, B. F. (1969). *Contingencies of reinforcement*. Englewood Cliffs: Prentice-Hall.

Thierry, Hk. (1987). Payment by results systems: Review of research 1945–1985. *Applied Psychology: An International Review*, **36**, 91–108.

Thierry, Hk. (1990). Intrinsic motivation reconsidered. In U. Kleinbeck, H. H. Quast, Hk. Thierry, & H. Häcker (Eds.), *Work motivation* (pp. 67–82). Hillsdale: Lawrence Erlbaum.

Thierry, Hk. (1992a). Pay and payment systems. In J. Hartley & G. Stephenson (Eds.), *Employment relations: The psychology of influence and control at work* (pp. 136–160). Oxford: Blackwell.

Thierry, Hk. (1992b). Payment: Which meanings are rewarding? *American Behavioral Scientist*, **35**, 694–707.

Thierry, Hk. (1998a). Compensating work. In P. J. D. Drenth, Hk. Thierry, & Ch. J. De Wolff (Eds.), *Handbook of work and organizational psychology* (2nd edn., vol. 4, pp. 291–319). Hove: Psychology Press.

Thierry, Hk. (1998b). *Is financial compensation going to be a challenging issue in organizational psychology in the 21st century?* San Francisco: 24th IAAP Congress, Organizational Psychology Division. Invited Address.

Thierry, Hk. (in press). *Beter belonen in organisaties* (How to improve compensation in organisations). Assen: Van Gorcum.

Thierry, Hk. (2001). The reflection theory on compensation. In M. Erez, U. Kleinbeck, & Hk. Thierry (Eds.), *Work motivation in the context of a globalizing economy* (pp. 149–166). Mahwah: Lawrence Erlbaum.

Thierry, Hk., & Jong, J. R. de (1979). *Zeggenschap en beloning* (Participation in Pay). Assen: Van Gorcum.

Thierry, Hk., & Jong, J. R. de (1998). Job evaluation. In P. J. D. Drenth, Hk. Thierry, & Ch. J. de Wolff (Eds.), *Handbook of work and organizational psychology* (2nd edn., vol. 3, pp. 165–183). Hove: Psychology Press.

Vroom, V. H. (1964). *Work and motivation.* New York: McGraw-Hill.

Yukl, G. A., & Latham, G. P. (1976). Consequences of reinforcement and incentive magnitudes for employee performance: Problems encountered in an industrial setting. *Journal of Applied Psychology*, **29**, 221–231.

Wanous, J. P., Reichers, A. E., & Austin, J. T. (2000). Cynicism about organizational change. *Group and Organization Management*, **25**, 132–153.

Weitzman, M. L., & Kruse, D. L. (1990). Profit sharing and productivity. In A. S. Binder (Ed.), *Paying for productivity.* Washington: The Brookings Institute.

Wilke, M. J. C. (2000). *Billijkheid van prestatieverschillen in taakgroepen* (Equitability of performance differences in task groups). Nijmegen: Catholic University. Dissertation.

Performance Measurement and Pay for Performance

Harrie F. J. M. van Tuijl, Ad Kleingeld and **Jen A. Algera**
Technische Universiteit Eindhoven, Eindhoven, The Netherlands, and

Mariëlle L. Rutten
GITP Consultants, Nijmegen, The Netherlands

SUMMARY

This chapter, which takes a (re)design perspective, focuses on the management of employees' contributions to organisational goal attainment. The control loop for the self-regulation of task performance is used as a frame of reference. Several subsets of design requirements are described and related to the basic elements of a control loop, i.e. performance indicators, goals, feedback, and effector. Given that organisations use a number of control systems to further organisational performance, a special subset of design requirements emphasises the need of consistency between organisational control systems, such as the company's appraisal and reward system. To illustrate our approach, two case studies are presented. The first case study evaluates, in a qualitative way, a variable reward system linked to a ProMES performance management system. The second case study demonstrates quantitatively the relevance of several design requirements for the experienced procedural and distributive justice of and the satisfaction with a collective bonus system.

Psychological Management of Individual Performance. Edited by Sabine Sonnentag.
© 2002 John Wiley & Sons, Ltd.

INTRODUCTION

Performance measurement and pay for performance have their place in the context of performance management. Performance management deals with the question of how individuals, groups and departments can be encouraged to concentrate their efforts on the realisation of organisational goals. As an answer to this question, the literature on work motivation offers a number of principles with proven effectiveness, such as 'goal setting', 'feedback' and 'reinforcement'. These principles are coherently incorporated into performance management models such as the 'high performance cycle' of Locke and Latham (1990). For practical applications, a useful theoretical framework is also provided by control loop models for self-regulation (e.g. Bandura, 1991; Carver & Scheier, 1998; Locke, 1991). For the actual design of performance management systems, a method such as ProMES, Productivity Measurement and Enhancement System (Pritchard, 1990, 1995), is a very useful instrument. Nevertheless, although theory has a lot to offer to practice, it is still a rather large step from performance management principles of which the effectiveness has been demonstrated in laboratory and experimental field situations to performance management in the daily practice of complex field situations under 'uncontrolled' conditions. Even with the help of a rather practical instrument like ProMES, time and again, solutions must be found for problems that occur when general principles have to be applied in situations with unique characteristics: this is in essence the key problem in each design (Kleingeld, 1994; Raaijmakers, 1993; Schön, 1983). Experience gained during the implementation of theoretical insights seldom leads to new theoretical insights, but it does lead to application knowledge, i.e. steps that need to be taken into account when theoretical insights are made explicit by implementing them. By comparing applications in similar settings, generalisable application knowledge, i.e. design knowledge, can be obtained.

This chapter is written from such a (re)design perspective. We will first focus on the control loop model and propose a number of design requirements that control loops for self-regulation have to meet. These requirements are closely linked to the above-mentioned performance management principles in that they can be considered as their operational elaboration in practical situations. Next, two case studies are presented as illustrations of our approach.

DESIGN REQUIREMENTS TO BE MET BY CONTROL LOOPS FOR THE SELF-REGULATION OF TASK PERFORMANCE

The metaphor of the control loop as a model for human motivation has been put forward by, among others, Carver and Scheier (1981, 1998) and Klein (1989, 1991). The metaphor stems from cybernetics (Wiener, 1948) and the general idea runs as follows. A sensor receives input, in the form of information on some aspect of the system environment. The input is fed into a comparator, which judges the input against a pre-set target. If this comparison reveals a difference between input and target, this discrepancy is signalled to an effector, which triggers activities directed towards reduction of the discrepancy. The control loop can be used to model behaviour aimed at the attainment of positively evaluated states. The model can be expanded to include the avoidance of negative states (Carver & Scheier, 1998) and the production (instead of reduction) of discrepancies (Bandura, 1991). Producing discrepancies means that new, higher targets are set in cases where feedback informs the system that a strived for target level has been attained. Last but not least, the control loop model has been broadened to include multiple goals and goal hierarchies (Carver & Scheier, 1998).

As stated above, the focus of performance management is the contribution of individuals, groups or departments to organisational goal attainment. So, we are, by implication, interested in the control of the attainment of multiple goals and in the relationships between goals at different organisational levels. In particular, the above-mentioned extensions of the original simple control loop model make the expanded model a suitable metaphor for such complex behaviours as involved in the attainment of individual or group goals within the larger context of organisational goals.

The metaphor of the control loop has been used to model all kinds of goal-directed behaviour. As indicated, we use it specifically to model the self-regulation of task performance in the context of organisational goal attainment. In a control loop for the self-regulation of task performance, feedback on task performance is the equivalent of the input in the cybernetic model described above. Task goals fulfil the role of targets or set points. The function of the effector is executed by the person (or group) responsible for task performance. This person (or group) will in most cases also execute the functions of the sensor and comparator, but others (e.g. a supervisor or a support group) can fulfil these roles too.

Performing well on one's tasks can be considered to be one of several goals, which can be more or less prominent in the goal hierarchies of individuals or groups. Material gain is another obvious candidate for inclusion in such hierarchies (Austin & Vancouver, 1996). When we take the perspective of motivation being in essence a process of distributing effort across tasks or activities (Naylor, Pritchard, & Ilgen, 1980), the differential consequences which the expenditure of effort to certain activities will have for the attainment of different goals in a goal hierarchy will be the determining factor for effort distribution. In other words, several control loops, each directed towards the control of a different goal in the hierarchy, will signal actual or anticipated discrepancies and trigger activities to reduce these discrepancies. A particular activity may at the same time have a high chance of reducing discrepancy x, but a low chance of reducing discrepancy y. So, in the end the decision of how to distribute effort across activities becomes an optimisation problem.

Control loops for the self-regulation of task performance can be considered effective to the degree that employee contributions to the realisation of organisational goals are actually furthered by such control loops. In practice, this will mean the realisation of a previously specified target performance in well-defined areas, as well as continuous improvement of performance in those areas. Ineffectiveness would imply that the expected performance is not realised or that no attempts to improve performance are observed. Lawler (1976) has already mentioned several forms of ineffective or dysfunctional behaviour, specifically linked to design characteristics of control loops, a long time ago. Examples are bureaucratic behaviour, the provision of invalid data and, more generally, forms of resistance to the implementation of control loops. These dysfunctional behaviours can be understood from a perspective of multiple control loop design. The design requirements to be discussed hereafter take this perspective explicitly into account.

It is not easy to trace the exact origin of each of the design requirements to be discussed hereafter, because in generating them eclectic use is made of both content and process theories (Campbell & Pritchard, 1976) as well as of descriptions of intervention methods that are related to or derived from such theories (Connellan, 1978; Locke & Latham, 1984; Luthans & Kreitner, 1975; Pritchard, 1990).

The control loop model itself is used as a frame of reference within which several subsets of design requirements will be positioned, according to the main components of a control loop, i.e. performance indicators, goals, feedback, and effector. Apart from the meta-design requirement that all these four components must be present, each of the components has to meet a number of specific design requirements. In addition, one has to keep in mind that a control loop cannot exist outside a context. So, a second meta-design requirement concerns the issue that the design of control loop components must be adapted to characteristics of the context elements to which they are linked. To give an example, when in a particular context work outcomes are unpredictable, but work activities specifiable, performance indicators should be operationalised in terms of activities, not outcomes. In addition, control loops other than the one in focus can be part of the relevant context.

Hereafter, we will take the control loop for the self-regulation of task performance as the focal control loop, and give some examples of design requirements for each of the components of such a control loop. Pay for performance will be dealt with in terms of another control loop (i.e. a control loop for material gain) in the context of the control loop for the self-regulation of task performance. Obviously, both control loops are relevant from a performance management perspective.

It will not be possible to be exhaustive, but what we consider to be the most relevant design requirements will be dealt with shortly.

DESIGN REQUIREMENTS TO BE MET BY PERFORMANCE INDICATORS

As described above, the input of a control loop for the self-regulation of task performance consists of feedback in terms of specific performance levels attained on particular performance indicators. These performance indicators have to meet, among others, the following design requirements:

1. The performance indicators are operational definitions of the major responsibilities of the employees concerned, that is to say: they have to be specifically geared to what the people concerned stand for; in addition, there should be performance indicators for each major responsibility area.
2. The people concerned can control the performance measured by the indicators, that is to say: performance variation on the indicators concerned is mainly influenced by the people involved and only for a small part by external factors.
3. Good performance on the performance indicators is important for the organisation, both in the short run as well as in the long term; for example, short-term efficiency should not have an adverse effect on long-term effectiveness.

DESIGN REQUIREMENTS TO BE MET BY GOALS (TARGETS, STANDARDS)

Goals can be described as performance levels that people intend to achieve on performance indicators. This means that performance indicators, which meet the above-mentioned design requirements, have to be available before goals can be set at all. The goals themselves have to meet the following design requirements:

1. Goals have to be accepted by the people concerned; goals which are not accepted will probably not be strived for and there will most certainly be no attempts to improve

continuously; although participation is not a necessary condition for goal acceptance, it will often have a positive effect on it.

2. Within a context of simple, routine tasks, goals have to be 'specific and difficult, but attainable'; however, in case of complex tasks, one should realise that difficult goals have been demonstrated to have no or even negative effects on performance.
3. In order to be able to set attainable goals the range within which performance varies on the indicators concerned has to be established in a valid way.
4. For multi-dimensional tasks (one-dimensional tasks are rare in actual practice), goals have to be ordered according to priority (this can be done by weighing the performance indicators; when the ProMES method is used, the so-called 'contingencies', i.e. functions that translate indicator scores into effectiveness values, are very practical methods of realising this weighing).

Design Requirements to be Met by Feedback

What goes for goals also goes for feedback: it can only be specified in terms of performance on performance indicators. So, in order to give feedback, the availability of adequately designed performance indicators is a precondition. In addition, feedback has to meet the following design requirements:

1. Feedback has to be accepted by the people concerned; this will usually mean that the validity of the feedback is unquestionable.
2. Feedback has to be specific; that is to say, it has to be phrased in terms of degree of goal attainment on a specific performance indicator.
3. Depending on the context, feedback should be given either in terms of behaviour (process feedback) or in terms of results (outcome feedback); in situations in which results are significantly co-influenced by factors other than the behaviour of employees, process feedback is often more appropriate (because this feedback focuses on what can be influenced by the employees); in the case of direct (and known) relations between behaviour and results, outcome feedback is more appropriate.
4. Feedback should be given on all important indicators after each feedback period and also as soon as possible after the end of such a period.

Design Requirements to be Met by the Effector

The effector is that part of the control loop that, on the basis of a comparison of goals and realised performance levels, intervenes in order to either bring future performance levels more in line with the goals that are strived for or to set higher goals. In practice, the effector can be an individual, a duo (superior and employee) or a group (including the supervisor of that group). The design requirements that the effector has to meet are partly reformulations of the design requirements that performance indicators, goals, and feedback have to meet. To some extent, they follow naturally from these. The following design requirements are set for effectors:

1. The effector has to know about and must be able to apply effective work strategies; that is to say that the effector has to have a sufficient understanding of the relations between types of activities (behaviour) and types of results, and that he or she has to know how to apply this knowledge in attempts to realise goal attainment.

2. The effector must have the authority which enables him or her to switch from one type of work strategy to the other (on the basis of the above-mentioned understanding that such changes will lead to higher scores on one or more performance indicators and thus to a greater contribution to organisational effectiveness).

DESIGN REQUIREMENTS DEFINED FROM THE PERSPECTIVE OF THE CONTROL LOOP CONTEXT

The relevant context of a control loop for the self-regulation of task performance consists of a number of elements, including: the goods or services to be produced as well as the transformation processes through which those goods or services are produced; the inputs (e.g. people, equipment, materials) necessary for those transformation processes to take place; the part in these transformation processes played by people versus the part played by technology; the internal and external interdependencies of groups and departments resulting from the organisation structure (these interdependencies are important with regard to the controllability of performance); other control systems aimed at stimulating goal attainment (appraisal and reward systems are examples of such systems).

The prime design requirement with regard to context is consistency. In addition to examples of required consistency given above, the following can be added:

1. When groups or departments are interdependent, the performance asked from one of them has to be in line with the performance asked from the other(s); when this is not the case, suboptimisation will easily occur.
2. Rewards provided by the organisation have to correspond with the values of the employees concerned ("people work for rewards they value" (Cascio, 1991)).
3. Variable amounts of reward have to be proportional to employees' contributions to organisational effectiveness.
4. The culture prevailing within a group, department or organisation should be consonant with the culture required for performance management in a particular situation; for example, when goal attainment requires experimentation, the general atmosphere should be permissive with regard to failures or 'bad luck'. In other words, there should be a 'learning culture'; on the other hand, in many other situations a 'trial and error culture' could be detrimental.

PERFORMANCE MEASUREMENT AND PAY FOR PERFORMANCE AT THE INDIVIDUAL LEVEL: A FEEDBACK BASED APPRAISAL AND REWARD SYSTEM

To illustrate what is stated above, we will first present a case study in which the performance information generated by a ProMES performance management system is used for appraising and rewarding service technicians and supervisors. We will discuss successively: the organisational context, the ProMES system developed as a performance management tool for the service technicians, the use of ProMES information for appraising and rewarding service technicians, and the use of aggregated ProMES information for appraising and rewarding supervisors and middle managers.

CASE STUDY I

The organisational context

The organisation to be described is the service department of a large supplier of photocopying equipment in The Netherlands. The field service group of this department is geographically divided into 13 regions, each consisting of about 20 technicians and two senior technicians.

At the head of each service region is a supervisor who reports to one of two field service managers (each responsible for about half of the regions). Supporting groups within the service department are the service reception (which receives customers' phone calls regarding machine malfunctions), the planning group (which allocates service visits to technicians) and the product support group (which provides technical advice). Head of the service department is the managing director Service who is a member of the organisation's management team.

The ProMES system

By using ProMES (Pritchard, 1990, 1995), a group can develop a system with which its work performance can be measured. The measured performance can then be fed back to the group, so that the measurement system becomes the backbone of a control loop. This control loop contains the following: descriptions of the fields the group is responsible for (so-called 'products'), performance indicators for each field, statements about the relative importance of performance for each indicator and statements on minimal, expected and maximal levels of performance per indicator (combining the latter two results into the so-called 'contingencies'), performance data per indicator per measurement period, translations of these performance data (by means of the 'contingencies') into effectiveness scores (called later on 'ProMES scores') per indicator, per field of responsibility and summed across fields of responsibility. ProMES measurement and feedback systems are designed according to the following basic principles: participative bottom-up development, decision making via discussion until consensus is reached, and coordinating the designed system with the management responsible (Van Tuijl, 1997).

The company decided to develop a ProMES system for the field service department for the following three reasons. First, since service quality was considered the company's competitive edge, ProMES was expected to be a powerful tool to help direct technicians' attention towards this service quality objective. Secondly, although a large amount of performance data had already been gathered for a long time, the company never had been able to transform this data into effective feedback (notwithstanding urgent requests by the technicians to do so). Thirdly, due to the isolated work of the service technicians, it had always been difficult to gather valid and acceptable information for performance evaluation purposes. It was management's hope that a performance measurement system, developed according to the ProMES method, could provide such information (Kleingeld, 1994). It should be noted that, at the start of the project, potential negative consequences of this last objective were explicitly neutralised by a management statement, saying that the ProMES measurement system would only be used for appraisal or reward purposes if all constituencies would consider that such would be a good idea.

ProMES was introduced in the field service department in two phases. First, ProMES was developed and implemented in a participative manner in two service regions. The system developed by the two regions was subsequently 'transported' without any modifications to the other regions. The supervisors played an important role in making the technicians understand and accept the 'transported' system.

As technicians perform their tasks, i.e. the repair and maintenance of photo copiers in clients' offices, to a large degree independently from one another, the service technicians' ProMES system mainly measures the performance of individual technicians. The two most important areas of responsibility are 'Quality' and 'Costs'. Performance indicators for quality are 'Mean Copies Between Calls' (the average number of copies made on a photo copier between two successive repair calls) and 'Percentage Repeat Calls' (the percentage of service calls that result in a machine failure within a period of five working days after the original call). Indicators for costs are 'Mean Cost of Spare Parts Per Call' and 'Mean Labour Time Per Call'.

Periodically, bilateral feedback meetings take place in which a supervisor discusses the feedback reports of the past period with his technicians individually. These meetings aim to improve productivity through discussing the ProMES feedback in a problem-solving way. For a more detailed description of the development, implementation, and application of the ProMES system of this service department, see Kleingeld (1994).

An appraisal-based bonus for technicians

After system development, technicians were provided with ProMES feedback every month. For several reasons, which became apparent during discussions with the technicians, this feedback did not have the intended positive effect on their performance. One of the reasons was the (agreed! see above) absence of a linkage between performance as measured by ProMES and formal appraisals of the technicians' performance. According to Lawler (1976), even dysfunctional effects might occur (Lawler, 1976)—such as disregard of responsibility fields in favour of areas that do get recognition ('bureaucratic behaviour' in Lawler's terms)—if these responsibility fields or their operationalisations in terms of performance indicators are not well integrated into the appraisal and reward system. In order to prevent any of such dysfunctional effects and to stimulate performance improvement, a direct link was established between the ProMES system and the appraisal and reward system used in the company. An additional, pragmatic argument was provided by the fact that the supervisors, who had to appraise the technicians, were well informed on all the details of their technicians' ProMES feedback reports. So, ultimately it would hardly have been possible to live up with the original management statement and to ignore the ProMES information when appraising the technicians' performance. For these reasons, it was decided to develop a procedure which would guarantee a uniform and fair use of ProMES performance information in the technicians' year-end appraisal and the resulting grant of a year-end bonus.

Characteristics of the appraisal and reward system in use

Some elements of the company's appraisal system did not conform to generally accepted prescriptions (see, e.g., Latham & Wexley, 1981), thereby limiting its effectiveness. For example, the appraisal dimensions were formulated in general, non-function-specific terms, which complicates the provision of specific feedback and the setting of specific goals. This was made worse by the fact that appraisal scales were predominantly stated in terms of traits instead of specific behaviours or specific results. Moreover, the system did not provide explicit standards (for example, it was not clear when performance should be marked 'as expected' or as 'above expectation'). Finally, the dimensions were not weighted. As a result, each assessor could apply his own subjective weighting.

Not only the appraisal system, but also the appraisal process was far from optimal. For example, there was no uniform, systematic registration of performance data. Therefore, recent events might very well get too much emphasis. In addition, appraisals were only once a year. This low frequency can be expected to heighten the risk of biased sampling of performance data. Also, only short-term effects on working behaviour will probably result from such an infrequent intervention.

With regard to the consequences of appraisal, the lack of differentiation in rewards was striking: the amount of bonus granted was the same for 70% of the technicians. This is a typical finding for merit rating systems, because in those systems performance dimensions are described in very general terms, making it difficult to defend differences between the appraisal scores of different employees. Consequently, differentiation only takes place in extreme cases. The fixed budget available for bonuses made matters even worse: a higher bonus for one employee resulted almost automatically in a lower bonus for another. This aspect of the system might be expected to result in considerable resistance, particularly given the combination with the already-mentioned vague dimensions (Thierry, 1987).

Redesign of the appraisal and reward system

On the basis of the above evaluation, three elements of the appraisal system were adjusted. First, weights were added to the appraisal dimensions. In addition, for the job of technician and that of senior technician, separate sets of weighting factors were developed. Dimensions considered important (such as task conception, quality of work, quantity of work), were given a higher weight compared with dimensions considered less important (such as vertical communication). Some appraisal dimensions were removed from the system because they were considered irrelevant to the job of technician (i.e. leadership, helicopter view) or senior technician (i.e. leadership). Second, a behavioural description was added to the appraisal dimensions, to elucidate the meaning of the dimensions.

The third improvement concerned a differentiation of the amount of bonus to be granted on the basis of the appraisal results. In the old system, five bonus levels were distinguished (i.e. 0, 2, 4, 6 and 8% of the annual salary, corresponding with five possible overall appraisal scores). The low level of actual bonus differentiation observed seemed to be caused by the large difference between the appraisal categories 'performance as expected' (4%) and 'performance above expectation' (6%). The number of bonus levels was therefore increased to nine (0, 1, 2, 3, . . . , 8%). Particularly the addition of the 3% and 5% levels would enable more differentiation between technicians who, until then, all received a 4% bonus.

ProMES performance feedback as a basis for appraisal and reward

The following procedure for the use of ProMES feedback information in the year-end appraisal and year-end bonus was agreed upon. First, it was decided that ProMES performance information would play no role in the discussions on yearly salary increases. This decision is consonant with the idea that fixed salary increases should reflect employees' steady growth in terms of competencies, whereas variation in actual performance which can be of a more temporary and volatile nature, should be reflected in a variable reward component (MacLean, 1990).

From an analysis of the dimensions of the appraisal system, it followed that seven of these dimensions were directly or indirectly related to performance as measured by the ProMES indicators. Taking their weights into account, these appraisal dimensions determined about 80% of total appraisal. It was decided to give equal weight (i.e. 40%) to each of the two ways in which these seven appraisal dimensions were measured. So, both the supervisor judgements on the seven appraisal dimensions as well as the ProMES scores were given a weight of 40% in the final appraisal of task accomplishment. The 40% weight of the ProMES scores was further subdivided into two portions of 20% each (see below for explication). The three dimensions of the appraisal system not related to ProMES (making up about 20% of the final appraisal of task accomplishment) would only be appraised by supervisor judgements. So, in all, 60% of the bonus would be determined by supervisor judgements and 40% by technicians' scores on ProMES indicators.

Figure 17.1 shows the relation between the appraisal dimensions and the ProMES indicators.

It was also decided that half of the ProMES appraisal would be based on a technician's position in the distribution of 'absolute' performance scores of all technicians. The other half would be based on his position in the distribution of the 'relative' performance scores of all technicians (i.e. the distribution of scores calculated by taking the differences between the scores from the appraisal period and the scores from the previous appraisal period). Technicians are thus rewarded for their absolute performance level in the appraisal period and for the extent in which they have been able to improve themselves compared with the previous period.

If only the absolute score would be used (which is partly dependent on a technician's knowledge and experience), highly motivated but less experienced technicians would not

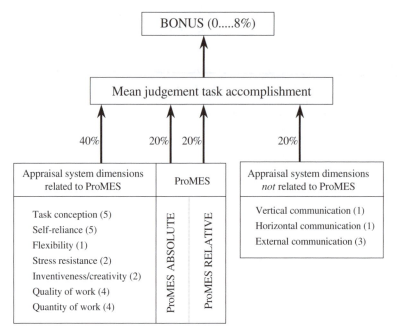

The numbers in brackets are the weights attached to the appraisal dimensions

FIGURE 17.1   Contribution of appraisal system dimensions and ProMES indicators to year-end appraisal.

be able to obtain an average or a high bonus. At the other hand, the use of only the relative score would be demotivating for technicians who already perform at a high level. The combination of the absolute and relative scores reduces the disadvantages of using only one of the alternatives.

   In negotiations with the union, it was determined that the average amount of bonus per department would be limited to 5% of the gross annual income of the employees in each department. As a result, the average bonus for the technicians could not exceed this percentage whatever the actual performance level realised. This meant that ProMES could only contribute to a more equitable distribution of the fixed total amount of bonus and not to an increase of the total amount (e.g. as a result of an increase in productivity). This was the main reason behind the elaboration of the 'absolute' and 'relative' performance distributions described above. Because of the upper limit on the total amount of money available for bonuses, it could not be avoided to base bonus allocation decisions on a system which compared employees with one another, instead of rewarding the attainment of individually agreed targets.

EVALUATION

From the perspective of the design requirement of consistency between control systems, the above-described linkage between the ProMES performance management system of the service technicians and their appraisal and reward system is nothing less than a logical choice. A significant performance increase was observed after implementation of the redesigned ProMES system in two service regions, compared with the performance of the other regions which were used as control groups (see Kleingeld, 1994). However, given that the redesign differed from the original design in a number of respects, it is not possible to attribute the performance increase of the two experimental regions entirely or even partly to the established linkage between ProMES and the technicians' appraisal and reward system. Even if such would be the case, we would still recommend to apply the design requirement of consistency between control systems in a differentiated way for reasons to discuss hereafter.

In theory, both control systems (performance management and appraisal/reward) have the same objective: to encourage employees to focus their attention on accomplishing the performance required by the organisation and to stimulate them to develop effective and efficient strategies to realise the required performance. As it comes to practice, however, this general principle may work out differently for the two systems.

Within the context of performance management, the practical objective simply is to provide comprehensive and accurate performance feedback about all areas of responsibility. Such information enables employees to realise, preferably by worker smarter, a performance improvement that is intrinsically satisfying for them. In contrast to this, within an appraisal/reward context, the financial exchange relationship between an individual employee and the organisation is the focal issue. Now, the prime interest is not so much how to improve performance as well as how to get the highest possible financial compensation in return for your performance. In order to maximise the chances of high financial returns, it is most helpful to have your performance measured in terms of easily controllable indicators. A set of indicators which cover your performance more completely, but in terms of less-well-controllable indicators might be more informative. The point is that in order to develop a set of performance indicators which has high content validity, one often has to include indicators with less than perfect controllability. As the above case study showed, when employees know or surmise that the measurements will be used for reward purposes, they will resist being measured in terms of less controllable indicators. When indicators are eliminated for that reason, one runs the risk of throwing away feedback with a high utility from a performance improvement perspective.

When the system went operational, in some instances dysfunctional effects occurred as a result of the link between the performance management system and the appraisal system. These effects can be described in terms of the dysfunctions mentioned by Lawler (1976). For example, although the amount of bonus to be earned was not large, getting a high bonus was very much appreciated by the technicians. This can lead to 'bureaucratic behaviour', i.e. striving rather rigidly for good performance on the ProMES indicators while forgetting about long-term organisational effectiveness.

A somewhat weak point of the linkage between the ProMES system and the appraisal/reward system in this particular case is the fact that some available performance indicators, which intend to stimulate cooperation between technicians, are not included in the appraisal of individual technicians. The reason is that the way in which information is gathered on these indicators, i.e. random sampling of instances from the whole group of service technicians, does not allow for reliable individual scores on these indicators. So, when technicians concentrate rather 'bureaucratically' on the performance indicators included in their appraisal/reward system, cooperation will suffer (and so will organisational effectiveness), and their behaviour may be described as dysfunctional. One concrete example of this concerns the obligation to adhere to the procedures for preventive maintenance (one of the indicators measured by random sampling from the whole group). A technician may choose to neglect preventive maintenance and, by doing so, to save time and spare parts. So, he will get positive scores on the 'costs' indicators, without any negative effects on his 'quality' indicator scores. Quality will not suffer on the short run, only on the longer run, but this falls outside the perspective of most technicians, because the chance that the same technician will be sent to the same photo copier at two or more consecutive occasions is rather low. So, the negative consequences of neglecting preventive maintenance are left to the colleague who has to do the next repair of the machine concerned (he will have to do the extra maintenance, which at that time may have become unavoidable, or he will do it because he feels responsible). Of course, the performance of the group as a whole, and through that the performance of the organisation as a whole (confronted as it will be with bad photo copier performance on the long run), would suffer, when this strategy would become generally followed by a majority of technicians.

There is also the risk that invalid data are provided, because the technicians provide a large part of the basic data on which the performance indicator scores are based. So, for instance, each day, technicians report the counter readings of the machines they have serviced, the spare parts they have replaced, and the number of working hours they have spent per call. It might be tempting to cheat a little bit in one's favour when reporting those data. Therefore, it is recommended—in case of a link between performance measurement information and appraisal/reward decisions—to use checks and balances in order to prevent possible improper use of the system. It should be noted that where instances of bureaucratic behaviour and invalid data were found, they mainly occurred in regions which had not participated in the development of the ProMES system. This underlines the importance of participation for the reduction of 'resistance to control'.

It will be clear that a better solution for these problems than checks and balances, consists in an appraisal and reward system that is designed in such a way that it stimulates cooperation where needed and prevents improductive competition. Proposals for such a system will be developed in the near future in a participative way by a design team consisting of representatives from all service regions and facilitated by two of the authors.

THE APPRAISAL AND REWARD SYSTEM FOR SUPERVISORS AND MIDDLE MANAGERS

In this section, we will describe how a connection was realised between the service technicians' ProMES system and the pay-for-performance system for supervisors and middle managers in the service department.

Redesign of the original merit rating system for supervisors and middle managers

In the same period in which the ProMES system was introduced nation-wide, the supervisors and field service managers of the service department had gained some experience with a merit rating system developed by the company. A number of result areas had been defined, indicators had been drawn up for each of these areas, and targets had been set with increasing levels of difficulty which corresponded with three bonus levels.

Examples of the indicators used in the system for the supervisors, all defined at the regional level, are: percentage repeat calls, mean number of calls per technician per day, time expenditure per million copies, and the number of repair visits carried out by the supervisor (for the purpose of not losing touch with the reality of the technician's job). Performance on such indicators determined the height of a year-end bonus that could in principle be rather substantial (between 0 and 150% of a monthly salary).

The experiences with this appraisal system for supervisors were not very satisfying. The measuring system, for example, did not take into account the differences in the machine population per region. Such differences could cause a completely distorted image of the actual results, at least on some of the indicators. Moreover, as unpredictable external developments had complicated the setting of realistic targets, it had therefore been necessary to adjust some of the targets during and even after the measurement period.

Service management and supervisors were of the opinion that ProMES might provide more valid information for a number of the indicators, because the ProMES system could, by means of the contingencies, take into account differences in machine population between regions adequately. In addition, using the ProMES measurements of the technicians' performance (for which supervisors were held responsible) as part of the appraisal/reward system of the supervisors, would lead implicitly to a high consistency between the two systems. The intended consequence, of course, was that technicians and supervisors would become goal interdependent and therefore would cooperatively strive for the same goals. One of the means of the supervisors to provide the technicians with support are the periodic ProMES feedback meetings of supervisors and technicians. To stimulate supervisors to fully support their technicians in those meetings with advice helpful to improve their performance, it was obviously best to incorporate the technicians' ProMES performance scores into the supervisors' performance appraisal system. Because ProMES scores allow for easy addition, total performance of the technicians of a particular region could be determined in a rather straightforward way. Table 17.1 illustrates how this was done at the hand of the example of region K. So, the regional overall ProMES score of 17 in Table 17.1 is considered to represent the effectiveness of region K's supervisor in coaching his technicians towards high performance.

TABLE 17.1 Overall regional ProMES score (region K)

Technician	MCBC	Percentage repeat calls	Cost of parts	Labour time	Sum score
1	−2	21	16	14	49
2	−38	65	−14	5	18
3	1	19	−20	−39	−39
⋮	⋮	⋮	⋮	⋮	⋮
19	1	36	10	26	73
20	−10	32	−21	25	26
21	−8	11	−7	20	16
Regional score	−2	17	−4	6	17

Notes:
1. The regional score for each indicator is the mean of the technicians' indicator scores.
2. The regional overall ProMES score is the sum of the regional scores on the four ProMES indicators.
3. MCBC = Mean Copies Between Calls.

TABLE 17.2 Determination of supervisors' bonuses

ProMES—Management By Results—SUPERVISORS—FINAL RESULT

	Absolute		Relative			
	Score	Rank	Score	Rank	Mean rank	Bonus (%)
Region A	21	5	+19	1	3	150
Region B	31	1	+7	5	3	150
Region C	20	6	+15	2	4	125
Region D	24	2	+4	8	5	125
Region E	18	7	+12	4	5.5	125
Region F	17	8.5	+13	3	5.75	125
Region G	22	4	−1	9	6.5	100
Region H	23	3	−8	12	7.5	100
Region I	16	10	+6	6.5	8.25	100
Region J	12	11	+6	6.5	8.75	100
Region K	17	8.5	−19	13	10.75	80%
Region L	2	12.5	−6	10.5	11.5	80%
Region M	2	12.5	−6	10.5	11.5	80%
Mean:	17	+3				

Given that supervisors have other responsibilities in addition to supervising their technicians, it was decided to make 25% of the supervisors' bonus dependent on their regional overall ProMES score. This percentage may be considered low, but it should be kept in mind that supervisors at that time were involved in a lot of projects, such as ISO quality certification, which were very important to the company. Given less turbulent times, the percentage would have been higher, and of course it can be adapted, on a yearly basis, to the circumstances at hand.

To limit the influence of external developments, it was decided that no absolute targets would be set, but to let the bonus of each supervisor depend on his position in a rank order of colleagues. This could be done because unproductive competition between supervisors was considered unlikely. Analogous to the system of the technicians, one half of this position was determined by the 'absolute' regional score and the other half by the 'relative' regional score. Table 17.2 illustrates how this was done.

As a final step, the technicians' performance as measured with ProMES was also, and in a comparable way, incorporated into the appraisal/reward system of the field service managers and the product support manager.

Evaluation

In general, the supervisors were satisfied with the way in which the ProMES information had been incorporated into the redesign of their appraisal/reward system. The main reason seemed to be the improved validity of the system compared with the old one. Supervisors considered the ProMES indicators to be more valid than the indicators of their former system, because now the relative importance of the indicators was taken into account as well as the differences between the performance characteristics of different types of photocopiers.

Given a rather low interdependence between service regions (compared to the interdependence between the technicians of one and the same region), there is no large risk of dysfunctional effects caused by increased competition between supervisors, which the newly designed system might provoke. However, one should keep in mind that a supervisor might close his eyes to invalid data supplied by technicians, because the regional score would gain from that. Phenomena like this have indeed been observed. So we have seen some supervisors introduce a new definition of labour time in their region. This resulted in a shorter average labour time per call and in longer travelling hours on paper, although nothing had actually changed in practice.

Another remarkable observation was that, unlike before, many supervisors did not allow their technicians to take half a day off, whereas a whole day off was no problem. The reason appeared to be that half a day off was not registered as a decrease in available capacity, whereas a whole day off was. So, a negative effect on the indicator 'Efficient use of capacity', one of the indicators used in addition to the ProMES indicators, was prevented by this strategy.

Some of these dysfunctional effects may have been strengthened by an incidental addition to the appraisal/reward system in the form of an incentive for the three highest scoring supervisors. They would get a free visit to a maintenance congress in the USA, together with the service director. Maybe this was an attractive incentive for some supervisors, but others evidently did not appreciate the prospective reward. The most extreme example of this was a supervisor who was so shocked by finding out that he—after three months—had realised the highest score on the ProMES indicator, that he was able to realise a spectacular decrease in the fourth month!

PERFORMANCE MEASUREMENT AND PAY FOR PERFORMANCE AT THE PLANT LEVEL: EVALUATION OF A COLLECTIVE BONUS SYSTEM

As a second example, we will describe in some detail the evaluation and redesign of the collective bonus system of a medium-sized company in the chemical process industry. This collective bonus system, which at the time of the evaluation had already been in use for more than five years, was the main component of a variable reward system that in addition to this collective component also consisted of an individual component. We will not go into the details of the individual part of the bonus system.

CASE STUDY 2

General background

The bonus system was said to be much resented by many of the employees. This resentment became apparent when a planned minor extension of the system was negotiated with the union. The union only agreed with the planned extension on condition of a thorough evaluation of the whole system. Two of the authors of this chapter were asked for advice on the evaluation and eventual redesign of the bonus system.

The core of the collective bonus system consisted of a set of plant performance indicators. Examples are 'number of client complaints', 'number of man-hours invested per ton produced', 'percentage of sickness leave', 'resource (gas, electricity) use', and so on. In total there were nine plant performance indicators. Based on past experience, for each performance indicator an upper and lower performance level had been defined and bonus percentages of 0 and 5% had been connected to these extremes. Upper and lower limits were adapted based on running averages of the actual performance on an indicator over a three-year period. Each month, the performance on each indicator was measured and transformed into a bonus percentage for that indicator. Monthly scores were fed back to all employees in the form of tables and graphs presented at monthly meetings. The yearly bonus score on an indicator consisted of the average of the monthly scores. The yearly grand total bonus percentage was calculated by averaging the indicator bonus percentages, meaning that all indicators got an equal weight in the resulting grand total bonus percentage, which could vary between 0 and 5%. The amount of money available for bonuses was calculated by taking this bonus percentage of the total wage sum of all plant employees. Seventy-five per cent of the resulting amount was then paid in the form of collective bonuses to all plant employees, to each in proportion to his or her yearly salary. The remaining 25% was paid in the form of individual bonuses on the basis of performance appraisals by immediate supervisors. The negotiations with the union concerned the maximum bonus percentage. Management had the intention to increase this maximum by 0.5%, i.e. to increase the variable reward component relative to the fixed reward component.

Main concepts and research hypothesis

The researchers agreed with the managing director to set up a thorough evaluation study in order to pinpoint the causes of the assumed dissatisfaction with the bonus system and, by doing so, to increase the chances of effective redesign. To that end, a questionnaire was developed and sent to the home address of all employees, with a stamped return envelope addressed to the researchers to guarantee anonymity. Hereafter, we will describe the parts of the questionnaire relevant for the evaluation of the collective component of the bonus system.

Based on considerations mentioned in the introductory part of this chapter, our hypothesis was that employees would be more satisfied with their company's bonus system to the degree that the system, in their opinion, conformed better to design requirements crucial for control loops in the area of performance management. More specifically, employees will be more satisfied with their company's bonus system to the degree that the performance indicators, goals, and feedback, which form the basis of that system, conform better to these elements' design requirements. A plausible alternative hypothesis would be that, instead of a direct relationship between design requirements and satisfaction, as would be predicted on the basis of a model such as the high performance cycle (Locke & Latham, 1990), the relationship between these variables is mediated by procedural and distributive justice, which concepts have been demonstrated to play an important role in reward issues (see, e.g., Sweeney & McFarlin, 1993).

Based on the above considerations and some aspects of the situation under study, the following concepts seemed most relevant for inclusion in the questionnaire study.

- *Controllability of performance indicators*. Controllability is a prime design requirement for performance indicators anyway, but when rewards are linked to performance, the importance of controllability becomes even more plausible, assuming that employees want to have as much influence on their rewards as possible. The controllability of performance was measured by means of questionnaire items such as 'Our department has a lot of influence on our company's performance on indicator x (name of performance indicator)'.
- *Goal attainability*. Given that no specific performance targets were set by the company on the performance indicators used to determine the collective bonus percentage, but that instead a performance range with upper and lower limits was used, we could not include questions on goal specificity in the questionnaire, but the attainability of the performance levels indicated by the upper and lower limits could be measured. This was done by items such as 'The upper and lower limits of the performance indicators are well chosen', and 'The upper (lower) limits of the performance indicators are attainable performance levels'.
- *Feedback informativeness*. Because feedback was given to inform employees on how well they were doing as a company, several aspects of the feedback provided, which might

be expected to contribute to that, were included in the questionnaire by means of items such as 'We get sufficient information on how well the company scores on the performance indicators', and 'Getting feedback on our company's scores on the performance indicators once a month is sufficient'.

- *Procedural justice.* Given that the core of the collective bonus system consisted of the performance indicators, we considered these indicators as the main element of the procedure involved. Therefore, we measured procedural justice in a rather direct, tailor-made way by asking respondents to evaluate the equitability of the inclusion of each of the performance indicators in the total set. Items read like 'I consider it as equitable that our performance on indicator *x* (name of performance indicator) co-determines the amount of collective bonus we get'.

- *Distributive justice.* Distributive justice was measured by three items from a longer list by Price and Mueller (1986), which were adapted to the specific situation of the evaluation of the collective bonus system under study. Items read like 'The amount of collective bonus in the past years was proportioned to my responsibilities'.

- *Satisfaction with the bonus system.* Given that the impetus for the study was the alleged dissatisfaction with the bonus system in general, several items were included to measure this satisfaction in general terms, i.e. irrespective of the collective or the individual component of the system. Examples of items are 'I am satisfied with our present bonus system', and 'Our company's bonus system is preferable to other systems I know of'.

For all items, seven category answer scales were used, the categories ranging from 'complete agreement' to 'complete disagreement'.

Results of the evaluation study

Forty-nine per cent of all employees returned the questionnaire, which resulted in a number of 115 questionnaires useful for analysis. Descriptive statistics of interest to the company were reported back to them. For the purpose of testing our main hypothesis—i.e. the existence of a direct relationship between the conformance of a bonus system to several design requirements set for performance indicators, goals, and feedback, and the satisfaction of employees with that system—a subset of 20 items, measuring the above six concepts, was taken out for a more detailed analysis.

Our first question was whether we had been able to devise adequate measurements of the six concepts described above, given that apart from the items taken from Price and Mueller (1986), all items had been written specifically for this study. To that end, a confirmatory factor analysis was done on the inter-item correlation matrix. All together there were 20 items: three items for each of the concepts 'controllability', 'goal attainability', 'procedural justice', and 'distributive justice', and there were four items for the concepts 'feedback informativeness' and 'satisfaction with bonus system'. The 20 items were modelled in conformance to the expectation that each item would only be related to its 'own' concept. Given an RMSEA value of .045 and a CFI (comparative fit index) of .97, we consider the resulting model fit satisfying, although the Normal Theory Weighted Least Squares Chi-Square is significant at the 5% level ($p = .027$). All items contribute significantly and substantially to their corresponding concept. No further improvement of the model, by setting free any relationships between items and non-corresponding concepts, appeared to be possible. So, taken together, these results seem to justify the conclusion that we have indeed six concepts, measured in a rather independent way by 'own' items.

As a next step, we devised scales for each concept by averaging the scores on the items, which measured each concept, and then determined each scale's internal consistency by calculating its Cronbach alpha coefficient. These Cronbach alpha coefficients are given at the diagonal of Table 17.3, which also presents the correlations between the six scales. It can be seen from the table that the scales' internal consistencies are generally quite satisfying, i.e. well above .80, except for the 'goal attainability' scale of which the internal consistency only reaches a value of .77.

TABLE **17.3**   Internal consistency of the six scales and inter-scale correlations

	(1)	(2)	(3)	(4)	(5)	(6)
1. Controllability	.83					
2. Goal attainability	.30**	.77				
3. Feedback informativeness	.07	.55**	.83			
4. Procedural justice	.51**	.56**	.39**	.87		
5. Distributive justice	.27**	.58**	.38**	.55**	.98	
6. Satisfaction with bonus system	.23*	.54**	.33**	.44**	.57**	.89

$** = p < .01$
$* = p < .05$

In order to test our main hypothesis, i.e. the direct relevance of design requirements for performance indicators, goals, and feedback, to satisfaction with the bonus system, we included 'controllability', 'goal attainability' and 'feedback informativeness' in a path model as exogenous variables, and 'procedural justice', 'distributive justice' and 'satisfaction with bonus system' as endogenous variables. A direct test of the hypothesis by setting free only the paths from the three exogenous variables to the endogenous variable 'satisfaction with bonus system' resulted in a very unsatisfactory model fit (RMSEA = .308; Normal Theory Weighted Least Squares Chi-Square = 138.45 with df = 12 and p = .000).

Our alternative hypothesis ran as follows: the higher the conformance of performance indicators, goals, and feedback to design requirements, the higher employees' feelings of procedural justice; the higher employees' feelings of procedural justice, the higher will be their feelings of distributive justice; the higher employees' feelings of distributive justice, the higher will be their satisfaction with the bonus system. This alternative hypothesis was tested by setting free the paths between the three exogenous variables and 'procedural justice', the path from 'procedural justice' to 'distributive justice' and the path from 'distributive justice' to 'satisfaction with bonus system'.

This resulted in a better, but still not acceptably fitting model (RMSEA = .121; Normal Theory Weighted Least Squares Chi-Square = 26.21 with df = 10 and p = .00347). Figure 17.2 shows a graphic presentation of this model together with the path coefficients, which are all significant. The percentages variance explained vary from 46% for 'procedural justice', to 30% for 'distributive justice', and 33% for 'satisfaction with bonus system'.

It was decided to further expand the model in an exploratory way, guided by some modification indices provided by LISREL. On the basis of these indications, direct paths

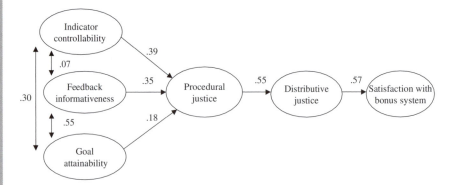

FIGURE **17.2**   Results of first, unsuccessful attempt to model the relationships between design requirements set to components of control loops in the area of performance management, and three dependent variables.

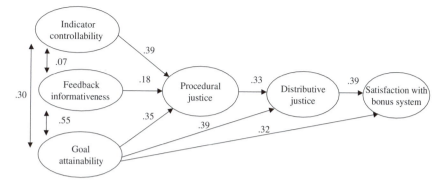

FIGURE 17.3   Relationships between design requirements set to components of control loops in the area of performance management, and three dependent variables. Results from a model with a good fit.

from 'goal attainability' to both 'distributive justice' and 'satisfaction with bonus system' were successively included in the model. The first of these extensions resulted in a more acceptably fitting model (RMSEA = .058; Normal Theory Weighted Least Squares Chi-Square = 12.41 with df = 9 and p = .19128). Variance explained for 'distributive justice' increases to 40%. Adding the second path mentioned resulted in to an almost perfect model (RMSEA = 0.000; Normal Theory Weighted Least Squares Chi-Square = 1.07 with df = 8 and p = .99773). Variance explained for 'satisfaction with bonus system' increases to 40%. Figure 17.3 shows a graphic presentation of the latter model including path coefficients.

CONCLUSIONS AND RECOMMENDATIONS

The starting point of this case study was the hypothesis, that satisfaction with the bonus system would be directly determined by the conformance of performance indicators, goals, and feedback, to such design requirements as 'controllability', 'goal attainability', and 'feedback informativeness'. The results show that all three types of design require-ments are related to employees' satisfaction with the bonus system, but that these relations are mediated by procedural and distributive justice. Of the three types of design require-ments, only 'goal attainability' is also directly related to satisfaction with the bonus system, and, in addition, to 'distributive justice'.

When the observed relations were of a causal nature, controllable performance indi-cators combined with attainable goals on those indicators would form the clue when one would like to try to influence satisfaction with the bonus system, be it that the supposed effects are mediated for a large part by constructs such as procedural and distributive justice. Feedback seems to play a significant role too, but its effect is rather small com-pared with the effects of controllability of indicators and attainability of goals. The latter finding makes sense when one considers the fact that satisfaction is the prime dependent variable, not performance. Having informative feedback once a month on the company's performance on the indicators would be especially helpful when the issue would be to increase one's rewards as much as possible through improving the company's perfor-mance. However, when it comes to satisfaction with a bonus system, it is imaginable that only the conviction that one's rewards are determined by (un-)attainable goals on (un-)controllable indicators is sufficient to feel (dis-)satisfied with such a system. Feedback could play a role too, of course, but probably mainly through the confirmation of such convictions about the bonus system, by demonstrating that actual performance scores lie, in accordance with or contrary to expectations, at certain points between the upper and lower performance limits. The relatively high correlation ($r = .55$) between 'feedback informativeness' and 'goal attainability' is consistent with such an interpretation. Of the three exogenous variables, 'goal attainability' evidently plays the more important role in explaining variation of employee satisfaction with the bonus system, followed by 'indicator controllability'. This is understandable from anecdotal information gathered on employee grievances with the bonus system. Many complaints referred to the felt injustice of the fact that the upper limit, i.e. a collective bonus of 5%, had never been reached in the past, and of the fact that performance on some indicators could not be influenced. The most controversial issue with regard to the latter point was long duration sickness leave.

Based on the above considerations, the company decided to first have a closer look at the controllability of the performance indicators, which together formed the basis of the collective bonus system. On the basis of the descriptive statistical information derived from the questionnaire, the controllability of a subset of these performance indicators could indeed be considered rather low. Examples are 'percentage of sickness leave' and 'resource (gas, electricity) utilisation'. The company decided to install a design team, consisting of representatives from all layers of the organisation, with the assignment to generate a new set of performance indicators, which had to fulfil the design requirement of controllability. In addition, it was realised that the upper limits of the yearly adapted performance ranges were misinterpreted by many employees as performance levels that ought to be attainable, and that something should be done about that.

EPILOGUE

This chapter has primarily been written from a (re)design perspective. In the introduction, a number of design requirements to be set to components of control loops for the self-regulation of task performance have been put forward. Next, two cases have been presented with the aim of demonstrating the practical relevance of at least some of those design requirements. In the first case, this has been done by describing in detail the elements of an appraisal and reward system and by evaluating the system's elements in terms of the relevant design requirements. System elements, which did not conform to design requirements have been replaced by more adequately designed alternatives. The case demonstrates that variable pay can be combined with a control loop for the self-regulation of task performance in a consistent way, but at the same time it becomes evident that one has to take into account a diversity of factors.

Whereas the first case is of a rather descriptive, anecdotal character, the second case is an attempt to present empirical evidence for the relevance of, be it a small subset of the design requirements presented in the introduction. It has been shown that in evaluating procedural and distributive justice of the collective part of a bonus system, conformance to a number of design requirements plays a significant role. The type of evaluation study presented appears to be a helpful tool in providing a company with useful insights as to what to change in order to improve employees, satisfaction with, in this case, a bonus system.

REFERENCES

Austin, J. T., & Vancouver, J. B. (1996). Goal constructs in psychology: Structure, process, and content. *Psychological Bulletin*, **120**, 338–375.
Bandura, A. (1991). Social cognitive theory of self-regulation. *Organisational Behaviour and Human Decision Processes*, **50**, 248–287.
Cascio, W. (1991). *Applied psychology in personnel management*. Englewood Cliffs, New Jersey: Prentice Hall.
Carver, C. S., & Scheier, M. F. (1981). *Attention and self-regulation: A control theory approach to human behaviour.* New York: Springer-Verlag.
Carver, C. S., & Scheier, M. F. (1998). *On the self-regulation of behaviour*. Cambridge: Cambridge University Press.
Connellan, T. K. (1978). *How to improve human performance*. New York: Harper & Row.
Campbell, J. P., & Pritchard, R. D. (1976). Motivation theory in industrial and organisational psychology. In M. D. Dunnette, (Ed.), *Handbook of industrial and organisational psychology* (pp. 63–130). Chicago: Rand McNally.
Jöreskog, K., & Sörbom (1996). *LISREL 8*. Chicago, IL: Scientific Software International.
Klein, H. J. (1989). An integrated control theory model of work motivation. *Academy of Management Review*, **14**, 150–172.
Klein, H. J. (1991). Control theory and understanding motivated behaviour: A different conclusion. *Motivation and Emotion*, **15**, 29–44.
Kleingeld, P. A. M. (1994). *Performance management in a field service department: Design and transportation of a productivity measurement and enhancement system (ProMES)*. PhD Thesis, Eindhoven University of Technology, Eindhoven, The Netherlands.
Latham, G. P., & Wexley, K. N. (1981). *Increasing productivity through performance appraisal*. Reading, MA: Addison-Wesley.
Lawler, E. E. (1976). Control systems in organisations. In M. D. Dunnette (Ed.), *Handbook of industrial and organisational psychology* (pp. 1247–1291). Chicago: Rand McNally.
Locke, E. (1991). The motivation sequence, the motivation hub, and the motivation core. *Organisational Behaviour and Human Decision Processes*, **50**, 288–299.
Locke, E. A., & Latham, G. P. (1984). *Goal setting: A motivational technique that works*. Englewood Cliffs, New Jersey: Prentice Hall.
Locke, E. A., & Latham, G. P. (1990). *A theory of goal setting and task performance*. Englewood Cliffs, New Jersey: Prentice Hall.
Luthans, F., & Kreitner, R. (1975). *Organisational behaviour modification*. Glenview, Illinois: Scott Foresman.
MacLean, B. P. (1990). Compensation: Value-added pay beats traditional merit programs. *Personnel Journal*, September, 46–52.
Naylor, J. C., Pritchard, R. D., & Ilgen, D. R. (1980). *A theory of behaviour in organisations*. New York: Academic Press.
Price, J. L., & Mueller, C. W. (1986). *Handbook of organisational measurement*. Marshfield, MA: Pitman.
Pritchard, R. D. (1990). *Measuring and improving organisational productivity: A practical guide*. New York: Praeger.
Pritchard, R. D. (Ed.) (1995). *Productivity measurement and improvement: Organisational case studies*. New York: Praeger.
Raaijmakers, J. G. W. (1993). *The psychologist as an engineer: On applied research in experimental psychology*. Inaugural Lecture, University of Amsterdam (in Dutch).
Schön, D. A. (1983). *The reflective practitioner: How professionals think in action*. New York: Basic Books.

Sweeney, P. D., & McFarlin, D. B. (1993). Worker's evaluations of the "ends" and the "means": An examination of four models of distributive and procedural justice. *Organisational Behaviour and Human Decision Processes*, **55**, 23–40.

Thierry, Hk. (1987). Payment by results systems: A review of research 1945–1985. *Applied Psychology: An International Review*, **36**, 91–108.

Tuijl, H. F. J. M. van (1997). ProMES: A method for 'accepted control loops'. *Leadership and Organisation Development Journal*, **18**, 295–303.

Wiener, N. (1948). *Cybernetics: Control and communication in the animal and the machine.* Cambridge, MA: MIT Press.

CHAPTER 18

Managing Individual Performance: A Strategic Perspective

Susan E. Jackson and **Randall S. Schuler**
Rutgers University, New Brunswick, NJ, USA
GSBA-Zürich, Switzerland

SUMMARY

Designing and implementing an approach to managing employees that ensures they are a source of sustainable competitive advantage is the objective of "strategic human resource management". A strategic human resource management system reflects the concerns of multiple stakeholders, is linked to the organization's specific business strategy, represents an integrated and coherent set of HR practices, and it is continuously monitored, evaluated and revised. This chapter describes the implications of these four features of strategic human resource management (HRM) systems, focusing on organizations pursuing strategies that require innovation. We show how an integrated HRM system addresses four major tasks: managing behaviors, managing motivation, managing competencies, and managing opportunities. After illustrating how these tasks are shaped by a strategy of innovation, we consider some of the key challenges that arise when applying this framework. Finally, we note that the performance management system should be monitored and evaluated to assess how effectively it (a) sends a clear, consistent message to employees and (b) represents the concerns of multiple stakeholders. Taking corrective action based on performance against these goals is essential for the organization's continuous learning and improvement.

Psychological Management of Individual Performance. Edited by Sabine Sonnentag.
© 2002 John Wiley & Sons, Ltd.

INTRODUCTION

A firm has a competitive advantage when all or part of the market prefers the firm's products and/or services. Because competition is the name of the game, companies seek ways to compete that can last a long time and cannot easily be imitated by competitors. That is, they seek to gain a sustainable competitive advantage (Barney, 1991; Porter, 1985; Schuler, Jackson, & Storey, 2001).

Some firms use their human resource management systems to gain a sustainable competitive advantage. Several conditions must be met if an organization is to gain a sustainable competitive advantage through human resource management. Perhaps the most obvious condition needed is that the firm's human resources—employees—must be a source of added value. Employees can add value in a variety ways: through their interactions with customers, by attracting other talent to the firm, by adapting quickly to changing conditions and so on. A human resource management system that encourages employee behaviors such as these can therefore be a source of competitive advantage.

If the employees in competing firms add similar value, no advantage is gained. Thus, rarity is another condition required in order for human resources to be a source of competitive advantage. One way in which employees might be rare is that they have unusually high levels of skill or knowledge. Employees who are unusually committed to the organization and its goals could help the organization to gain competitive advantage by keeping down the costs associated with high turnover. Employees with unusually high levels of organization-specific knowledge may be less likely to repeat past mistakes and be better able to recommend changes that will improve the operation of the total system. By helping an organization acquire, develop and retain employees such as these, a firm's human resource management system contributes to its competitive advantage.

Finally, in order for a firm's human resources to be a source of sustainable competitive advantage, they must be difficult to copy and there must be no other substitutable resources that competitors can rely on. The most difficult human resource to imitate is a corporate culture that has evolved over a period to suit the specific needs of the organization. Thus, a human resource management system plays a strategic role when it supports the development and continuous evolution of a unique corporate culture that is tailored to the needs of the organization.

Designing and implementing an approach to managing employees that ensures they are a source of sustainable competitive advantage is the objective of "strategic human resource management". To be strategic, a human resource management system must

- reflect the concerns of multiple stakeholders,
- be linked to the organization's specific business strategy,
- represent an integrated and coherent set of HR practices, and
- be continuously monitored, evaluated and revised.

By implication, a strategic approach to managing individual performance requires that these same issues be addressed. In the remainder of this chapter, we discuss the implications of these four features of strategic human resource management (HRM) systems, focusing specifically on the implications for managing individual performance. Throughout this chapter, we use the term *performance management system* to refer to those human resource practices that together can affect employee performance. As will be described in more detail later, several HR practices that can be considered to be part of a performance management system, including aspects of the selection process, socialization and training, performance measurement, as well as rewards and recognition programs. To the extent that any particular HR practice can have a meaningful impact on employee performance, we consider the practice to be part of an organization's performance management system.

Although managing individual performance is one of the primary goals of most HRM systems, it is not the only goal. For example, another important objective of an HRM system is to manage the flow of employees into and through the organization. Recruitment, career planning, terminations and retirement planning are examples of practices that are particularly relevant to managing employee flows. As another example, in some organizations, the goal of managing labor costs is particularly important. In such organizations, reducing the costs of employee benefits may be especially important.

ADDRESSING THE CONCERNS OF MULTIPLE STAKEHOLDERS

Stakeholders are individuals or groups that have interests, rights, or ownership in an organization and its activities. Stakeholders who have similar interests and rights are said to belong to the same stakeholder group. Customers, suppliers, employees, and strategic partners are all examples of stakeholder groups (Clarkson, 1995; Freeman, 1994; Jones, 1995).

CUSTOMERS

Customers may be seeking goods and services that are low in cost, high in quality, or simply unique. Their concerns can be addressed by performance management systems that incorporate customers' perspectives into performance definitions and employee evaluation measures. For example, customers' views can be used when developing job descriptions, designing training programs, and appraising individual employees.

EMPLOYEES

Most employees are concerned about being treated fairly and paid well. These concerns can be addressed by transparent and fair performance management systems that allow all employees to translate their efforts into rewards that they value. Increasingly, organizations are finding that employees also are concerned about balancing their work and nonwork roles. Designing policies and practices that make it easier for employees to perform well in all of their life roles is one way that performance management practices can address the concerns of employees. For example, a performance management system that emphasizes the specific number of hours and the schedule of work can create time conflicts that make it difficult to perform nonwork roles. In contrast, a system that emphasizes performance results and accepts variation among employees regarding workload and scheduling may improve employees' ability to successfully juggle multiple roles.

OWNERS AND SHAREHOLDERS

Most owners and shareholders invest their money in companies for financial reasons. Their concerns are addressed when a firm evaluates the cost-effectiveness of its performance management practices. This implies that organizations should evaluate their performance management systems to assess their economic utility. Owners and shareholders may also be interested in the long-term survival of the firm, however. This implies that short-term cost considerations and short-term performance gains should not be the primary drivers of performance management practices. Effective practices produce high levels of *sustainable* individual performance. They also minimize negative behavioral side-effects (e.g., absenteeism and turnover) that contribute to higher labor costs in the longer term.

COMMUNITIES AND SOCIETY

Local communities and society as a whole are concerned that business organizations comply with laws and regulations, contribute to the well-being of their communities, and protect and preserve the natural environment. Legal compliance and socially responsible behavior establish legitimacy and help businesses to gain acceptance and support from the community. Ultimately, this increases their chances for long-term survival (Meyer & Rowan, 1977; Scott, 1987; Zucker, 1987). Societal concerns can be addressed by performance management systems that reward employees for advancing the interests of society and punish employees who ignore these interests. For example, employee recognition programs can be used to reward employees for using their work-related expertise to help charitable or public service organizations to achieve their goals. Administering swift and severe sanctions to employees who engage in unethical or illegal behavior is another means through which organizations can use their performance management practices to address societal concerns.

The concerns of stakeholders define the social context within which strategic human resource management occurs. A strategic approach to performance management asserts that effective performance management systems are responsive to this social context. Sometimes the concerns of different stakeholders seem to conflict with each other. In that case, the management challenge is to find creative approaches to resolving these conflicts. Some evidence suggests that this is indeed possible. For example, satisfying employees also appears to contribute to satisfying shareholders and investors (e.g., see Fryzell & Wang, 1994; Richard, 2000; Welbourne & Andrews, 1996).

Responding to stakeholders' concerns is just one aspect of the strategic approach. As the term implies, the strategic approach also involves designing a performance management system that is linked to the organization's competitive strategy. We discuss this linkage next.

LINKING PERFORMANCE MANAGEMENT PRACTICES TO BUSINESS STRATEGY

A corporate level strategy describes how the corporation will select and manage a portfolio of businesses to ensure that the whole is greater than the sum of its parts (Porter, 1987). The central issue addressed is usually how much diversification (low, high) and what type of diversification (related, unrelated) to pursue. Corporate level strategies often have implications for how the human resources function is structured. More relevant to the development of specific performance management practices is the business strategy. A business strategy is specific to a particular company or business division. Business strategies describe how a company competes against other direct rivals offering the same products and services.

BASIC TYPES OF STRATEGIES

Firms describe their business strategies using a variety of terms, but basically these strategies reflect two decisions: Who are the customers? What is the *relative* importance attached to innovation, quality, and cost? (Miller, 1992; Campbell-Hunt, 2000). By specifying their target customers, firms clarify their primary stakeholders. By prioritizing the relative importance attached to innovation, quality and cost, they begin to clarify the behaviors needed from employees. Understanding the answer to the second question is essential to the design of effective practices for managing individual performance.

Innovation

Innovation is a strategy that involves differentiating the firm's products and services from those of competitors by having something new that competitors cannot offer, usually because the new product or service is protected by trademarks, copyrights or patents. When a desirable new product or service is created, its uniqueness and limited availability mean that a company can charge a premium price and a sufficiently large number of customers will be willing to pay it.

Quality

Offering excellent quality is another basic way to differentiate one's products and services from those of others. In the international arena, the standards of quality keep going up; an acceptable quality yesterday may be unacceptable today. Thus, organizations that compete on the basis of quality pursue continuous improvement with a vengeance. Delivering total quality depends on all parts of the organization working together based on feedback from customers, because quality is in the eyes, ears, hands and taste buds of customers.

Cost

A cost leadership strategy involves offering no-frills, standardized products and services with acceptable features at the lowest price. The most common approach to pursing a low-cost strategy is to generate a high volume of sales to make up for the low margin associated with each sale. To achieve high volume, companies competing on cost usually seek the broadest possible customer base. Efficient production systems, tight cost monitoring and controls, low investment in R&D, and a minimal salesforce are characteristic of this strategy.

STRATEGY IMPLEMENTATION

To be successful, an organization's competitive strategy must be effectively implemented. Effective strategy implementation is a complex, dynamic and never-ending process that touches all aspects of organizational life. Perhaps most important for managing performance, competitive strategies partly determine the structure of work, the objectives to be achieved, and the behaviors that are needed and considered acceptable means for achieving those objectives. Here we illustrate some of the implications for performance management practices of a strategy that gives high priority to innovation.

The structure of work

Innovation occurs when people juxtapose existing ideas and information in new ways. Thus, effective performance management practices increase the chances of information coming together. These practices must also be embedded within an appropriate organization structure. Functional structures, which are common in bureaucratic organizations, tend to prevent the flow of information across boundaries. By segmenting the workforce into groups with domain-specific knowledge and skills, functional structures create barriers to the juxtaposing of ideas in new ways. Even when new ways of doing things are discovered, rigid functional structures make adopting these new ways difficult because they give employees little autonomy to change the way they perform their individual jobs.

Innovative organizations eschew bureaucratic designs. Instead, they are structured to support the proliferation of teams that can be formed and disbanded as needed. Rather than grouping people together primarily on the basis of similar functional expertise, innovative organizations bring employees with dissimilar expertise together to form multi-disciplinary teams. Team members have considerable autonomy to make key decisions, and can take action without waiting for requests to crawl through a bureaucratic decision-making process (Burns & Stalker, 1995; Quinn, Anderson, & Finkelstein, 1996). Compared to functional structures, team-based structures are more flexible and fluid. Knowledge flows more easily among members of the organization, which contributes to learning and creates opportunities for innovation (Bontis & Crossan, 1999). Thus, the way work is structured is an essential aspect of strategic performance management.

Just as innovative organizations tend to have fuzzy internal boundaries, they have a fuzzy external boundary. Just as they use teams to bring together dissimilar expertise located internally, they use teams to bring together expertise located in other organizations. Strategic alliances and network forms of organization support innovation by encouraging knowledge flows between companies. Prevalent in high-tech industries, strategic alliances and network structures allow older, established firms to gain access to new discoveries made by scientists in universities and in small, creative organizations (Liebeskind, Oliver, Zucker, & Brewer, 1996). Thus, for innovative firms, a key strategic task is managing the performance of employees who cross organizational boundaries.

Prioritization of objectives

Companies whose managers set specific objectives and then aggressively pursue actions calculated to achieve their performance targets typically outperform companies whose managers have good intentions, try hard, and hope for success (Brews & Hunt, 1999). This relationship is captured in the old adage, "you cannot manage what you cannot measure". When success is defined as effectively serving the interests of stakeholders, their needs define a firm's fundamental objectives. These objectives, in turn, drive approaches to managing employee performance.

Profit-oriented businesses are often criticized for focusing too much on objectives that reflect the concerns of owners and shareholders and paying too little attention to objectives that reflect the concerns of other stakeholders, such as employees. If performance management practices are used simply as tools to achieve short-term business goals, they are likely to give undue weight to economic concerns at the expense of other stakeholders' concerns. Unfortunately, the strategic human resource management perspective is sometimes misconstrued as simply using human resource management practices to ensure that business objectives are met. In our view, considering only business success when designing performance management practices does not constitute a strategic approach. A truly strategic approach presumes that the concerns of employees and other key stakeholders also are addressed by the performance management system.

Establishing norms for employee behavior

In the strategic HRM literature, several alternative models have been proposed for explaining the means through which human resource management systems contribute to a firm's competitive advantage (e.g., see Arthur, 1994; Becker & Huselid, 1998; Jackson & Schuler, 1995). One such model is referred to as the behavioral perspective (Schuler & Jackson, 1987). According to the behavioral perspective, human resource management practices are an organization's primary means for energizing and directing employee behaviors. This perspective recognizes that many external forces, which are beyond the control of individual employees, have significant consequences for the ultimate success and survival of the firm. But having stated that caveat, it asserts that the aggregated effects of individual employee behaviors are primary determinants of organizational effectiveness. Specifically, performance management practices communicate the expectations that members of the organization have for how people should behave; they shape the aspirations of organizational members and also facilitate the achievement of those aspirations through formal and informal rewards and punishment.

DESIGNING AN INTEGRATED AND COHERENT HUMAN RESOURCE MANAGEMENT SYSTEM

A strategic perspective assumes that an organization's approach to managing performance includes a complex array of many elements. As already explained, these elements should be aligned with the organization's unique conditions, especially conditions created by the concerns of major stakeholders. Equally important are the degree of integration and internal alignment among all of the elements that comprise the total HR system. For example, an international study of 62 automobile plants found that flexible production systems enhanced production speed and quality the most when they were part of an integrated set of HR practices (MacDuffie & Krafcik, 1992).

During the past decade, researchers have attempted to identify a small number of unique bundles of HR practices that comprise integrated and coherent HR systems (Becker & Huselid, 1998). Implicit in such research is the assumption that the many varieties of HR systems being used in organizations can be reduced to a small number of archetypes. These efforts have been of limited success. One potential problem with this structural approach to assessing HR systems is that it underestimates the complex effects of the external and internal environments of organizations (see Jackson & Schuler, 1995).

For example, in looking for bundles that fit particular business strategies, researchers (and we include ourselves) tended to ignore concrete differences among firms regarding employees' concerns or the technologies in use.

A process-based approach to the design of integrated HR systems represents an alternative perspective. A process-based approach does not attempt to specify the practices that fit specific organizational conditions; instead, it presumes that the process through which an HR system evolves determines the degree of coherence and integration among specific practices. Some processes are very likely to yield integrated HR systems. The process we describe in this chapter is one that we believe would be relatively more likely to yield an integrated system. Other processes for creating HR systems may be less likely to result in coherence and integration. For example, if a firm chooses to outsource the design and/or implementation of its staffing to one external vendor and outsource the design and implementation of its training programs to another vendor, there is likely to be little integration between these aspects of the HR system. Another popular approach to developing HR systems is to conduct "benchmarking" studies to learn what other firms are doing, and then imitate the so-called "best practices". Relying on the benchmarking approach, a firm might imitate the staffing practices in one organization, the training practices in another, and the pay practices in a third. The degree of integration and coherence among these practices would most likely be quite low.

The development of an integrated and coherent HR system is more likely to occur when an organization begins by stating this as an objective. Having stated the objective, the organization also must have a method for achieving it. In the remainder of this section, we argue that the development of an integrated HR system requires an understanding of the major HR tasks to be achieved, and the use of HR practices in creative ways to achieve these tasks. Figure 18.1 illustrates this general framework.

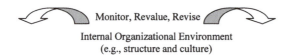

Monitor, Revalue, Revise

Internal Organizational Environment
(e.g., structure and culture)

HR Practices for Managing Performance	Major HR Tasks	Stakeholder Satisfaction
♦ Staffing	♦ Managing behaviors	♦ Customers
♦ Training and development	♦ Managing motivation	♦ Employees
♦ Performance measurement and feedback	♦ Managing competencies	♦ Owners and shareholders
♦ Recognition and monetary rewards	♦ Managing opportunities	♦ Community and society

FIGURE 18.1 Framework for Managing Human Resources for Learning and Innovation (adapted from Jackson & Schuler, 2000b)

In general, the four major tasks of any HR system involve: managing behaviors, managing motivation, managing competencies, and managing opportunities.[1] After illustrating how these tasks are shaped by a strategy that emphasizes innovation, we illustrate some of the implications for developing internally consistent performance management practices.

THE MAJOR TASKS OF HUMAN RESOURCE MANAGEMENT

Effective individual and organizational performance occurs when the organization succeeds in generating the behaviors, motivation, competencies, and opportunities needed to implement the business strategy and satisfy the needs of the organization's primary stakeholders. Behaviors are the most proximal determinants of performance, and identifying the behaviors that are needed is perhaps the most fundamental challenge of effective performance management. The task of managing behaviors is supported by the remaining tasks: managing competencies, managing motivation, and managing opportunities.

Managing behaviors

In order to effectively manage employee performance to support innovation, it is necessary to first specify the behaviors needed for innovation to flourish. (Alternatively, effectively managing performance given a strategy based on customer service requires specifying the behaviors needed to meet and exceed the expectations of customers.) Behaviors that facilitate (or impede) innovation include sharing information, and finding and solving problems. Consequently, performance management involves more than simply directing and motivating individual employees working on individual tasks. It also involves managing social interactions (Murphy & Jackson, 1999).

By sharing information about the problems they face and the solutions they discover, employees minimize the number of times they reinvent the wheel. Information sharing speeds up the process of organizational learning. As Bontis and Crossan (1999) explain, sharing information can support two types of learning flows. Feed-forward learning can occur when the knowledge and experiences of individuals and work groups is used to inform strategic decisions. Feed-back learning occurs when organizational practices provide employees with information that is useful in doing their work. Communication of company goals, policies and procedures as well as feedback about individual performance all support feed-back learning flows. Traditionally, performance management systems have emphasized feed-back learning flows and ignored feed-forward learning flows.

Innovation and learning occur when employees actively engage in problem finding and creative problem solving. Sheremata's (2000) model of the problem-solving processes required for new product development describes the importance of centrifugal and centripetal behavior patterns. Centrifugal actions are those related to reaching for and gathering new and relevant information. Such actions locate problems that need solutions and they also locate information that can be used during problem solving. Centripetal behaviors facilitate the integration of information and ideas.

---

[1] Elements of the process-based approach we describe here have also been presented in Jackson and Schuler (2000a) and Schuler, Jackson, and Storey (2001).

As described next, employees are most likely to engage in these behaviors when they are motivated to do so, when they have the competencies needed to do so, and when they have opportunities to do so.

Managing motivation

Motivational forces influence which behaviors employees choose to engage in as well as how much effort they put into those behaviors in the short–term and in the long–term. That is, the task of motivating employees involves influencing both the direction and persistence of behaviors.

Psychologists have long recognized that the direction and persistence of behaviors are influenced by both personal and situational factors. Typically, the task of performance management has been construed as shaping the situation. Research on creative organizational climates suggests that when innovation is the goal, motivation is enhanced by challenging work and freedom in how to carry out the work. Creativity is impeded by harsh criticism of ideas, internal competition, and protecting the status quo. Too much emphasis on productivity and excessive workloads also appear to reduce creativity (Amabile, Conti, Coon, Lazenby, & Herron, 1996). For firms that emphasize innovation, effective performance management does not take as its only goal creating these conditions, however. An effective approach also recognizes that some types of people—including those who are individual contributors and those who are managers—may enjoy and be motivated by working in the types of environments that support innovation and creativity. But others may be more motivated in an environment where the work is routine and predictable and where expectations and deadlines are specific and clear. The strategic approach to performance management is consistent with the psychological literature showing the importance of taking both situational and personal factors into account as explanations for motivation.

Managing competencies

Managing competencies involves ensuring that individual employees and the teams they work in have the skills, knowledge and attitudes that are required to carry out their work. A strategic approach to managing human resources recognizes two types of competencies that need to be managed: (a) competencies that support the behaviors *needed currently* and (b) competencies that ensure that the workforce is prepared to quickly begin performing new tasks as *needed in the future* (Wright & Snell, 1998). Some of the basic skills, knowledge and attitudes that an organization needs in the present will also likely be useful in the future. Some will become obsolete, and some will be transformed. Recent studies of knowledge-based organizations highlight the dynamic aspects of managing the competencies needed for innovation.

Bontis and Crossan (1999) use the term "knowledge stocks" to refer to the store of knowledge and information in organizations. As the level of a firm's knowledge stock increases, so does the firm's potential for creativity and innovation. Individual-level knowledge stocks refer to the knowledge and abilities of an employee. Group-level knowledge stocks develop when individuals interact to share knowledge and engage in creative problem solving (Levine & Moreland, 1999; Liebeskind et al., 1996).

Performance management practices that support the development and retention of knowledge stocks within the organization increase its capacity for innovation. Ultimately, the stock of any type of competency is determined by investments in competency development and by competency flows. Knowledge stocks can be increased by performance management practices that encourage employees to invest in continuously learning, e.g., providing incentives for training and professional development. By developing a reputation for being an employer of choice, an organization can more easily import the competencies it needs. In this way, competency flows into the organization. And by retaining that talent, the firm prevents competencies from flowing out to competitors.

Managing opportunities

If a workforce has both the motivation and the competencies needed to innovate, is it possible that they will fail to do so? Yes. They also need the right opportunities. Considerable research on creativity and innovation documents the importance of having contact with people who have information, perspectives and experiences that are dissimilar to one's own. As we have already noted, flat, team-based structures facilitate innovation by involving employees in a broad range of activities and exposing them to others from whom they can learn. But simply organizing around teams does not ensure that everyone will have opportunities to be creative or learn from others. The teams must be intentionally staffed to bring together diverse perspectives and talents (Jackson, 1996).

Furthermore, many opportunities for innovation and learning arise beyond the boundaries of work teams, and even beyond the boundaries of the organization. Many times employees in different parts of an organization are working on the same challenge, but are completely unaware of each other. They do not discuss common problems as they try to solve them, and they do not share solutions once they have been discovered because they have no opportunities to do so. Innovative organizations find ways to prevent this by creating opportunities for people to cross or span boundaries that might otherwise be barriers to information flow (Bouty, 2000).

Organizations create opportunities for innovation when they make it easy to share ideas, experiences and knowledge. Major innovations arise when people engage in meaningful dialogue and conversation. Electronic "knowledge management" systems can facilitate knowledge storage and distribution, but these systems appear to be less useful in stimulating the creative processes associated with innovation. When innovation is the objective, person-to-person exchanges appear to be more useful than document exchanges (Hansen, Nohria, & Tierney, 1999). Thus, performance management systems that create opportunities for person-to-person exchanges can facilitate innovation and learning.

Using HR Practices to Accomplish the Major HR Tasks: Key Challenges

Human resource management practices enable organizations to successfully carry out the four HR tasks of managing behaviors, managing motivation, managing competencies, and managing opportunities. The primary categories of practices are: staffing; training and development; performance measurement and feedback; and recognition and monetary reward systems. Under the traditional model of personnel management, each subset of practices was closely tied to, at most, two particular tasks. For example, staffing and training practices were viewed as relevant primarily for managing competencies.

Performance measurement and feedback were viewed as relevant primarily for managing behavior, and recognition and monetary reward systems were viewed as relevant primarily for managing motivation.

A strategic perspective assumes that all available HR practices can and should be used in unison to achieve the four major HR tasks. We are suggesting here that managing individual performance is also best understood as an objective that can be achieved through the systematic design of an *entire system* of human resource management practices. That is, successfully managing individual performance requires effectively using the entire set of available HR practices. Stakeholders' interests, in turn, should determine both the performance criteria of most importance and the acceptability of the organization's approach to achieving excellent individual performances.

Organizations that compete by offering low-cost, standardized services may use HR tools differently than organizations that compete by creating innovative solutions that address their customers' unique needs. A strategic perspective assumes that there is no "one best way". Rather, the available HR tools should be used creatively to achieve the four tasks of managing behavior, managing motivation, managing competencies, and managing opportunities in a given organizational context.

Years of research on how to develop performance measures has produced extensive technical knowledge that can be applied to measuring the performance of individual employees. Various employment laws and legal guidelines strongly encourage employers to use this knowledge in order to ensure that employees are treated "fairly". In US culture, "fair" treatment often translates into using performance information as the basis for making important employment decisions. Unfortunately, many of these technical and legal guidelines for performance measurement are grounded in an outdated bureaucratic model of organizations. As a result, they fail to address some of the more difficult issues faced by organizations that seek to continuously innovate. Here we discuss four of these issues: role instability, team-based work structures, involvement of multiple stakeholders, and balancing competing objectives.

Role instability

Employees with broadly defined jobs and who participate as members of multiple project teams often find themselves taking on a diversity of roles and being subjected to shifting role expectations. On one project such a person may serve as team leader, while in another he or she may be called upon as an expert adviser in a narrowly defined area. One project may require frequent meetings and close working relationships. Another may require individuals to make significant progress working alone, with meetings occurring only occasionally in order to report on each person's progress. Within the span of a typical day or week, an employee may repeatedly move between these diverse sets of expectations, adapting to the demands of each with varying degrees of ease. To perform well in such environments requires role flexibility.

Increasingly, employees are expected to demonstrate role flexibility, either because they are managing multiple roles simultaneously or because their roles are shifting rapidly across time. Consequently, their willingness and ability to adapt to diverse and changing expectations is becoming an important aspect of performance (Hesketh & Neal, 1999; Murphy & Jackson, 1999). The inclusion of measures of adaptive performance as criteria for hiring, training and rewarding employees may be one approach toward developing a workforce of employees who easily learn new tasks, are confident in approaching new tasks, and have the capacity to cope with the changes that innovation inevitably demands.

Team-based work structures

When work is organized around teams, as required by innovation, the objective of performance management shifts from managing individual performance to managing team performance. What do effective teams look like? As Figure 18.2 shows, there are many aspects to team performance; effective functioning includes many things (Jackson & Schuler, 2000a). No team is likely to be outstanding on all of the performance dimensions that might be measured. In order to decide which aspects of team performance to measure, goals for the teams must first be established. These goals, in turn, should reflect strategic concerns. If reducing cost and speeding up order fulfillment are important to the strategy, one set of measures might be suggested. But if the strategy calls for teams that can develop creative solutions, a very different set of measures would be appropriate. Or, perhaps the vision is to become a learning organization, and teams are viewed as a vehicle to facilitate learning. Then goals that indicate learning at the organizational and/or individual level should be specified. Measures of learning might then be developed (e.g., product and customer knowledge) or the outcomes that learning should affect might be measured (e.g., speed of new product development or customer satisfaction). Because it is based in a systems view, the strategic approach to managing performance recognizes that individual performance measurement should be considered in the context of team performance measurement. Team performance measures, in turn, should be considered in the context of larger organizational units.

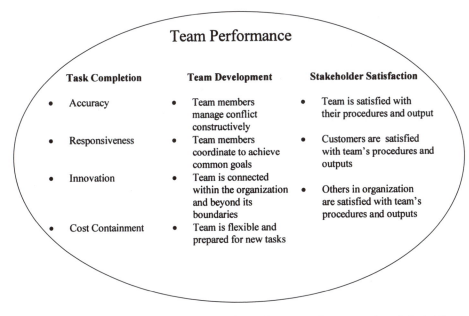

FIGURE 18.2   Possible performance indicators for work teams and team members (adapted from Jackson & Schuler, 2000a)

Involvement of multiple stakeholders

A strategic perspective suggests that performance measures at all levels of analysis (individuals, teams, business units, and so on) should reflect the perspectives of multiple stakeholders. In team-based and highly-networked organizational structures, definitions and measures of performance take into account the perspectives of many role partners. Consequently feedback processes become more complex. At a minimum, formal feedback is likely to reflect the views of a variety of different constituents.

One way to provide employees with feedback from many stakeholders is through the use of 360-degree feedback systems. In the traditional approach, feedback about performance emphasizes the views of a single person—usually a supervisor—to the exclusion of almost all other views. In contrast, 360-degree systems collect perceptions of an employee's performance from a set of colleagues and internal customers who form a circle around the employee.

Whereas traditional performance appraisals were developed for evaluating employees, 360-degree feedback was originally designed as a tool for employee development (Chappelow, 1998). Employees usually picked the people from whom they wanted to get feedback and the results were often completely confidential. The intent was to provide information to employees, who could then use it to improve their performance. Therefore, a feedback session would involve explaining how other people view the employee, comparing these perceptions to the employee's self-assessments, and developing action plans for how to improve in the future. Responsibility for communicating the feedback usually rests with supervisors, who are expected to help employees understand, integrate and act on the feedback.

Some organizations have begun using a variation of 360-degree assessments to conduct official performance appraisals. In those companies, the emphasis shifts from providing feedback for developmental purposes to making evaluations that can be used in personnel decisions related to promotion, compensation, and so on. The philosophy behind 360-degree feedback approaches fits well within the types of organizational cultures that are required for innovation and learning. In organizations where teamwork is the norm, feedback from multiple sources is perceived as more valid than single-source approaches because it involves a group of people who interact with the employee in many different ways.

Regardless of whether an organization uses a formal 360-degree feedback process, employees in innovative organizations are bombarded with feedback from a variety of sources, including teammates, customers and subordinates. This feedback is used continually in subtle negotiations about how one's role will be construed. Many of these other sources of feedback have neither the formal responsibility nor the resources needed to support and facilitate improvements in an employee's performance. Faced with potentially conflicting feedback information from different sources, employees may feel uncertain about the expectations they must meet in order to perform their roles satisfactorily. Practices such as 360-degree feedback and customer satisfaction surveys may confuse employees about the relative priority to be given to each member in their work role set. Multiple role senders, in turn, may be unaware of each other's conflicting expectations and hence unable to moderate their performance expectations. How do employees respond to this type of feedback environment? A typical response is to consider the reward system. If no recognition or rewards are tied to a source of available feedback, employees may conclude that the source and the feedback can safely be ignored.

Balancing competing objectives

Of all the HR tools available to support innovation and learning, recognition and rewards may be both the most powerful and the least understood. In particular, existing theories of motivation and performance do little to help organizations to design recognition and reward practices that effectively address the competing demands and paradoxes found within post-bureaucratic organizations, some of which are briefly noted below.

Short-term versus long-term considerations

The creative processes that result in significantly new innovations require that employees have cutting-edge knowledge in their fields. In addition, implementing innovation often requires employees to develop new skills. Maintaining cutting-edge skills, in turn, requires continuous learning. The need to motivate continuous learning requires that workers be rewarded today for developing the potential that may be needed in the future. As more and more companies consider paying for knowledge or skill acquisition, they come face-to-face with the question of how much value they should place on performance in the current job versus behaviors that prepare employees for future jobs.

Finding the appropriate balance between rewarding for current performance versus rewarding for long-term performance is a difficult balancing act. Many critics of performance-based incentive plans point to this as a common problem. Executive incentives that focus attention on short-term movements in the company's stock price, for example, may lead managers to make decisions that protect the stock price in the short–term but discourage the investments needed for longer-term innovation and learning. To address this problem, many executive pay packages include a mix of incentives that link pay to achieving both long- and short-term objectives. Although similar approaches may be useful at lower levels in the organization, they rarely are used.

Behaviors versus results

A large body of evidence shows that generally, organizations are more likely to achieve their stated goals when employees are rewarded for results that are consistent with those goals. Some authors have concluded that this general principle holds even when innovation is the stated goal. However, psychological research suggests that tying pay to results that require creativity and innovation may actually reduce employees' motivation to experiment and try new ideas (Amabile, 1979; Dweck & Leggett, 1988; Mumford & Gustafson, 1988). Experimentation is likely to involve some failure, especially in the short-run. When pay is linked to innovation results, it raises employees' concerns about the potential negative evaluations that may result from failure and thus actually reduces risk-taking and interferes with learning. Alternatively, it may send a message that any means to achieving results is acceptable, which is also problematic. These arguments suggest that it may be better to provide incentives for the *behaviors* thought to lead to innovation instead of paying for results, Of course, this approach works only if the organization can accurately specify and monitor those behaviors.

Individual versus team

If results form the basis for at least some recognition and rewards, a related issue is whether to reward and recognize individuals or teams or perhaps even larger work units. Currently, cultural norms rather than business objectives tend to drive this decision, with team recognition being more common in collectivist cultures and individual monetary rewards being more common in individualistic cultures. These cultural patterns may be breaking down, however, as companies around the world internationalize their workforces and join in the same race to develop innovative products and services. As US organizations restructure around teams to support innovation and adapt other HR practices to this new structure, interest in team-based recognition and rewards seems to be growing (Flannery, Hofrichter, & Patten, 1996). At the same time, as Japanese companies have begun competing in industries that require radical innovation rather than small engineering improvement, they have introduced elements of individual incentive pay. Matsushita was among the first to begin experimenting in this area. Their goal, it seems, is to encourage more of the risk taking and creativity that is needed to compete in industries such as software engineering and telecommunications (*The Economist*, 1999).

Monetary rewards and recognition are powerful tools for motivating employees, directing their behavior, and developing their potential. Perhaps this explains why so many US firms have been experimenting with new forms of pay in recent years. Like other areas of experimentation, the consequences of new pay systems are often difficult to predict accurately. They depend not only on design details but also on how managers administer the system and how well the system is aligned with other HR practices. Careful monitoring of the effects of new pay plans alerts managers to unintended behavioral consequences and speeds the organization's learning about how best to use these powerful tools.

CONTINUOUS MONITORING, EVALUATION, AND REVISION

The design and implementation of effective HR practices is a dynamic process, which unfolds in a unique way in each organization. Due to the complex interdependencies among all elements of a dynamic organization, it is impossible to fully and accurately predict how the introduction of one or more new HR practices will affect employees' behaviors or the longer-term consequences of those behaviors. Consequently, the creation of an effective HR system proceeds in an iterative manner and requires continual monitoring and evaluation. At the same time as the organization is adjusting to ongoing changes, it must be prepared to make revisions that will enable it to better address the future.

CONTINUOUS MONITORING AND EVALUATION

To judge improvement, an organization needs to know where it was before and where it is now. That is, in must engage in continuous monitoring. Continuous monitoring ensures that the organization and its employees learn from their mistakes and successes. Like any body of knowledge, our understanding of how to manage people effectively is based on what has worked in the past. As conditions change, some of our knowledge becomes obsolete. Organizations experiment with their approaches to managing human resources in order to replace obsolete knowledge and thereby improve performance. A strategic approach to managing human resources suggests that the design of *both* performance management practices *and* monitoring and evaluation practices should be driven by the same considerations. Our discussion of the strategic approach to managing human resources suggests that an organization's approach to monitoring and evaluating a performance management system should focus on assessing how effectively the system achieves two key goals: sending a clear, consistent message and representing the concerns of multiple stakeholders.

Clear, consistent message

When designing a performance management system, the intent is to develop policies and practices that are consistent and coordinated with each other in order to communicate a clear message to employees. Thus, evaluation and monitoring activities should assess what messages employees are receiving. If the intended message is not being received, then further diagnosis may be needed to determine which practice(s) account for the apparent communication interference (e.g., a 360-degree feedback system? an incentive system? a training program?). A performance appraisal system that evaluates employees on the basis of the attainment of long-term goals, coupled with a compensation system that rewards employees on the same basis, sends a clear message to employees. On the other hand, a human resource policy that describes employees as the firm's most valuable resource, coupled with constant layoffs and little training, sends conflicting messages.

Multiple stakeholders

In firms that manage their employees strategically, managers know why they lead their people the way they do. Their entire set of HR practices has been explicitly developed to match the needs of their employees, customers, owners, and so on. Consequently, monitoring and evaluation practices should provide feedback that reflects these diverse perspectives. The objective of monitoring and evaluation is not simply to assess whether plans have been carried out on schedule and within budget. Much more important is whether the actions taken have achieved the desired results. Table 18.1 illustrates several key stakeholders and the concerns they are likely to have (Jackson & Schuler, 2000a).

TAKING CORRECTIVE ACTION

The results of the evaluation process serve as input into decisions about how to revise existing performance management practices. Taking corrective action is essential for continuous learning and improvement. Where deficiencies are found, HR professionals must determine whether these are due to poor implementation of well-laid plans, or whether the system's design is itself flawed. Appropriate HR practices may be foiled by managers and subordinates who resist the changes needed. For example, managers may resist changing their leadership behaviors yet such changes may be essential to the successful implementation of new team-oriented HR practices and a culture of empowerment. Their subordinates may resist practices that require them to more actively evaluate and give feedback to their close colleagues and peers, fearing that this will disrupt friendships and create friction within the team.

TABLE 18.1   Examples of stakeholders' concerns for possible monitoring and evaluation

Stakeholder group	Examples of concerns
Owners, investors, or other financial supporters	Financial soundness Consistency in meeting shareholder expectations Sustained profitability Average return on assets over 5-year period Timely and accurate disclosure of financial information
Customers, clients, or patrons	Product/service quality, innovativeness, and availability Responsible management of defective or harmful products/services Safety records for products/services Pricing policies and practices Honest, accurate, and responsible advertising
Employees	Non-discriminatory, merit-based hiring and promotion Diversity of the workforce and quality of work life Wage and salary levels and equitable distribution Availability of training and development Workplace safety and privacy

Community	Environmental issues
	  Environmental sensitivity in packaging and product design
	  Recycling efforts and use of recycled materials
	  Pollution prevention
	  Global application of environmental standards
	Community involvement
	  Monetary charitable contributions
	  Innovation and creativity in philanthropic efforts
	  Product donations
	  Availability of facilities and other assets for community use
	  Support for employee volunteer efforts

Besides considering whether unmet objectives are due to the design or implementation of the performance management system, decisions about whether to make revisions must be sensitive to the dynamic nature of human reactions to change. On the one hand, early and frequent review can alert the organization to unanticipated disruptive reactions and enable early corrective action. On the other hand, however, it also is important to recognize that some deterioration in behavior and performance is normal and to be expected immediately after major changes are implemented. Initial performance deterioriation may be followed by rapid performance improvement. Thus, it is incumbent upon evaluators to construct models that illustrate the changing consequences that can be expected over time in order to prevent incorrect evaluations and prevent premature revisions (Becker & Huselid, 1998).

REFERENCES

Amabile, T. M. (1979). Effects of external evaluation on artistic creativity. *Journal of Personality and Social Psychology*, **37**, 221–233.

Amabile, T. M., Conti, R., Coon, H., Lazenby, J., & Herron, M. (1996). Assessing the work environment for creativity. *Academy of Management Journal*, **39**, 1154–1184.

Arthur, J. B. (1994). Effects of human resource systems on manufacturing performance and turnover. *Academy of Management Journal*, **37**, 670–687.

Barney, J. (1991). Firm resources and sustained competitive advantage. *Journal of Management*, **17**, 99–120.

Becker, B. B., & Huselid, M. A. (1998). High performance work systems and firm performance: A synthesis of research and managerial implications. *Research in Personnel and Human Resource Management*, **16**, 53–101.

Bontis, N., & Crossan, M. M. (1999). *Managing an organizational learning system by aligning stocks and flows of knowledge*. Paper presented at the Conference on Organizational Learning: Lancaster, UK, June 6–9.

Bouty, I. (2000). Interpersonal and interaction influences on informal resource exchanges between R&D researchers across organizational boundaries. *Academy of Management Journal*, **43**, 50–65.

Brews, P. J., & Hunt, M. R. (1999). Learning to plan and planning to learn: Resolving the planning school/learning school debate, *Strategic Management Journal*, **20**, 889–913.

Chappelow, C. T. (1998). 360-degree feedback. In C. D. McCauley, R. S. Moxley & E. VanVelsor (Eds.), *Handbook for leadership development* (pp. 29–65). San Francisco: Jossey-Bass.

Clarkson, M. B. E. (1995). A stakeholder framework for analyzing and evaluating corporate social performance. *Academy of Management Review*, **20**, 92–117.

Dweck, C. S., & Leggett, E. L. (1988). A social-cognitive approach to personality and motivation. *Psychological Review*, **95**, 256–273.

Freeman, R. E. (1994). *Strategic management: A stakeholder approach*. Boston: Pittman/Ballinger.

Fryzell, G. E., & Wang, J. (1994). The *Fortune* corporation 'reputation' index: Reputation for what? *Journal of Management*, **20**, 1–14.

Hansen, M. T. Nohria, N., & Tierney, T. (1999). What's your strategy for managing knowledge? *Harvard Business Review*, **77** (March–April), 106–116.

Hesketh, B., & Neal, A. (1999). Technology and performance. In D. R. Ilgen & E. D. Pulakos (Eds.), *The changing nature of performance* (pp. 21–55). San Francisco: Jossey-Bass.

Jackson, S. E. (1996). The consequences of diversity in multidisciplinary teams. In M. A. West (Ed.), *Handbook of work group psychology* (pp. 53–76). New York: John Wiley.

Jackson, S. E., & Schuler, R. S. (1995). Human resource management in the context of organizations and their environments. *Annual Review of Psychology*, **46**, 237–264.

Jackson, S. E., & Schuler, R. S. (2000a). *Managing human resources: A partnership perspective*. Cincinnati: South-Western.

Jackson, S. E., & Schuler, R. S. (2000b). Managing human resources for innovation and learning. In R. Berndt (Ed.), *Innovatives management* (pp. 327–355). Berlin: Springer-Verlag.

Jones, T. M. (1995). Instrumental stakeholder theory: A synthesis of ethics and economics. *Academy of Management Review*, **20**, 404–437.

Levine, J., & Moreland, R. L. (1999). Knowledge transmission in work groups: Helping newcomers to succeed. In L. L. Thompson, J. M. Levine, & D. M. Messick (Eds.), *Shared cognition in organizations* (pp. 267–297). Mahwah, NJ: Lawrance Erlbaum.

Liebeskind, J. P., Oliver, A. L., Zucker, L., & Brewer, M. (1996). Social networks, learning, and flexibility: Sourcing scientific knowledge in new biotechnology firms. *Organization Science*, **7**, 428–443.

MacDuffie, J. P., & Krafcik, J. (1992). Integrating technology and human resources for high performance manufacturing. In T. Kochan & M. Useem (Eds.), *Transforming organizations* (pp. 210–226). New York: Oxford University Press.

Meyer, W., & Rowan, B. (1977). Institutionalized organizations: Formal structure as myth and ceremony. *American Journal of Sociology*, **83**, 340–363.

Mumford, M., & Gustafson, S. (1988). Creativity syndrome: Integration, application, and innovation. *Psychological Bulletin*, **103**, 27–43.

Murphy, P. R., & Jackson, S. E. (1999). Managing work role performance: Challenges for twenty-first century organizations and their employees. In D. R. Ilgen & E. D. Pulakos (Eds.), *The changing nature of performance* (pp. 325–365). San Francisco: Jossey-Bass.

Porter, M. E. (1985). *Competitive advantage*. New York: Free Press.

Porter, M. E. (1987). From competitive advantage to corporate strategy. *Harvard Business Review*, **65** (3), 43–59.

The Economist (May 22, 1999). Putting the bounce back into Matsushita, pp. 67–67.

Richard, O. C. (2000). Racial diversity, business strategy, and firm performance: A resource-based view. *Academy of Management Journal*, **43**, 164–177.

Scott, W. R. (1987). The adolescence of institutional theory. *Administrative Science Quarterly*, **32**, 493–511.

Schuler, R. S., & Jackson, S. E. (1987). Linking competitive strategies with human resource management practices. *Academy of Management Executive*, **1** (August), 207–219.

Schuler, R. S., & Jackson, S. E. (1999). *Strategic human resource management*. Oxford, UK: Blackwell.

Schuler, R. S., Jackson, S. E., & Storey, J. (2001). HRM and its links with strategic management. In J. Storey (Ed.), *Human resource management: A critical text*. London and Boston: ITP.

Sheremata, W. (2000). Centrifugal and centripetal forces in radical new product development under time pressure. *Academy of Management Review*, **25**, 389–408.

Welbourne, T. M., & Andrews, A. O. (1996). Predicting the performance of initial public offerings: Should human resource management be in the equation? *Academy of Management Journal*, **39**, 891–919.

Wright, P. M., & Snell, S. A. (1998). Toward a unifying framework for exploring fit and flexibility in strategic human resource management. *Academy of Management Review*, **23**, 765–772.

Zucker, L. G. (1987). Institutional theories of organization. *Annual Review of Sociology*, **13**, 443–464.

Performance Improvement through Human Resource Management

Sabine Remdisch
University of Applied Sciences Lüneburg, Lüneburg, Germany

SUMMARY

This chapter describes the global Human Resource Management (HRM) concept of a large international automobile manufacturer. The HRM system is conceptualized as being part of the principles of a learning organization and realizes employee-centered qualification management. Strategic HRM is oriented toward the Business Plan goals of the company and company-specific qualification processes, such as transfer-oriented training control. Requirements for successful HRM are: an appropriate learning and error culture in the organization, innovative forms of learning, and support of the learning process by supervisors. The role of the HRM department today is that of a service center with the functions of counseling and promoting. The vision for future learning and knowledge management is an HRM system on a virtual campus.

Psychological Management of Individual Performance. Edited by Sabine Sonnentag.
© 2002 John Wiley & Sons, Ltd.

HRM IN A LEARNING ORGANIZATION

The key to economic success for every company is to develop the abilities of its employees and to secure their willingness to perform. The performance profile of each employee must be continuously adapted to meet current demands in the face of dynamic development of all areas of knowledge. Existing knowledge has a very short shelf-life. Life-long learning has become a question of professional survival. Investment in an efficient, responsive human resource management system is a measure taken for the security of the future.

The development of human resources is particularly important in the automobile industry, which has traditionally been a forerunner in new methods, techniques, organizational forms, and work practices. The economic setting of the automobile industry has drastically changed during the last few years, however, and several forces are driving the trend: global competition and market demands, increasing technological progress, accelerating rates of change, and exponential growth of knowledge. Companies must communicate and cooperate world wide, find answers to problems in record time, and continuously broaden their knowledge.

Aside from extensive technological changes in products and their production processes for which employees must be prepared, there are also organizational aspects making new demands. Take, for example, the breakdown of hierarchies, the decentralization of organizations, and the new structure of work processes. Employees, as well as organizational structures that are flexible and capable of change, are a necessity. In light of these developments stands the central and often competitively determining question of how a company can optimally design the continuous learning and further qualification of its employees.

An example of a modern human resource management system is that of Adam Opel AG (the German subsidiary of the General Motors Corporation). HRM and training are main branches under the auspices of the personnel department at Opel. They include all activities regarding personnel and organizational development: personnel selection, technical training, social competency training, leadership competency training, multimedia competency training, knowledge management, organizational diagnoses and development, as well as evaluation and training controlling.

HRM in the future must consider both personnel and economical aspects. Furthermore, HRM must be embedded in a visionary goal system that optimally prepares employees for increasing work demands. The goal direction of Opel's HRM system is reflected in its six characteristics: the global learning system, competency-based strategy, economy-driven and results-oriented direction, employee-centered training, controlling and continuous process evaluation, and cooperation and knowledge networks. Related to these characteristics there do exist guiding principles that are part of the official strategy at General Motors (GM).

THE GLOBAL LEARNING SYSTEM

The HRM system at Opel is conceptualized under the principles of a learning organization. This means developing a global network that can adapt to changing market situations, learn from past mistakes and successes, react to imminent threats, and is also experimental and innovative. Life-long learning is a major facet of tracking the dynamics of change and of coping with future challenges. *Learning is a vehicle to facilitate successful change* (see Guiding Principle in Table 19.1).

TABLE 19.1 The Opel HRM system: characteristics and guiding principles

Characteristics of the HRM system	Guiding principles
The global learning system	• *Learning is a vehicle to facilitate successful change.* • *It is the responsibility of General Motors' corporate leadership to integrate a learning culture.*
Competency-based strategy	• *Each learning experience must have a clear-set purpose and be tied directly to GM's vision, values and business competencies.*
Economy-driven and results-oriented direction	• *Learning strategies align the growth and developmental needs of GM employees in the framework of GM's overall business needs.* • *GM is heading towards becoming a learning organization able to compete in a world where knowledge truly is power.*
Employee-centered training	• *People learn and retain knowledge in different ways.* • *Learning is enhanced when it takes place in a creative, fun, and exciting environment.*
Controlling and continuous process evaluation	• *HRM is a process—from the identification of business demands to the adequate training of employees to completed training controlling that makes measurement of transfer success possible and secures quality.* • *An organization learns when its individuals have learned and changed.*
Cooperation and knowledge networks	• *New ideas and innovations are born from the exchange of knowledge.*

The basic requirement of every learning process is an organizational culture in which key elements are worldwide shared visions and goals, openness to new developments, an enthusiasm for learning, and development of learning-oriented models.

The management of a company plays an essential role in building a good organizational culture for learning. A motivating and potential-oriented leadership system is a necessity. Managers must analyze training needs, initiate attempts at the further education of his/her employees, accompany the learning process, and implement learning progress controls. Furthermore, in conjunction with employees, supervisors must establish the development of knowledge communities, initiate interdepartmental cooperation, and impart global thinking on their employees. *It is the responsibility of General Motors' corporate leadership to integrate global needs and capabilities.*

COMPETENCY-BASED STRATEGY

In flexible and innovative companies, it is important that employees are business-minded and have an entrepreneurial flair. Today, the individual employee must take increasing responsibility for the business process. Over the past few years the worker profile has changed. Essential abilities to possess now include: flexibility, initiative, willingness to take on responsibility, entrepreneurial thinking, team orientation, and cooperation. Consequently, employees must be interested in their own career development and must show initiative to be trained.

At Opel, certain company-specific core competencies are considered to be fundamental for their highly efficient and competitive new generation of executives. The core competencies are divided into four domains: *Interpersonal Effectiveness Domain, Leadership Domain, Management Domain,* and *Personal Qualities and Traits Domain.* Interpersonal effectiveness means appropriate interpersonal behavior and communication methods to facilitate one-on-one and group interactions, and to work effectively with business partners to meet mutual goals and objectives. The leadership/supervision domain intends for the use of leadership behaviors to guide subordinates in the execution of their assigned responsibilities and to facilitate effective performance. The application of *managerial behaviors* to guide the business unit is covered by the "managing the job" domain. The *personal qualities and traits domain* deals with traits that are part of an individual's overall personality and that are important in successfully addressing challenges of the job.

The company must internally advance and externally demand this profile of requirements.

The Opel HRM concept is not a single, isolated measure for continuing education, but rather an extensive HRM system of various connected building blocks. It is understood as a coherent system integrated in the organization's culture and strategic goals. The organization's HRM policy is consistent with other aspects of the Opel organization and strives for congruence between HRM practices and company strategies. *Each learning experience must have a clear-set purpose and be tied directly to GM's vision, values, and business competencies.* A good example is a coaching program for superiors that consists of role playing and behavior observation studies to train the interpersonal effectiveness competency. Another example are the performance appraisals that are oriented at the core competencies (meaning that the superior gives feedback according to the key actions in the core competencies).

ECONOMY-DRIVEN AND RESULTS-ORIENTED DIRECTION

The direction of HRM at Opel is clearly driven by the economy. With their strategic HRM system, Opel attempts to reach higher company goals. *GM is heading towards becoming a learning organization able to compete in a world where knowledge truly is power.*

Opel's HRM is a critical factor in assuring that employees are highly successful contributors to company performance, and that they possess the right skills for any circumstance. *Learning strategies align the growth and developmental needs of GM employees with the framework of GM's overall business needs.*

EMPLOYEE-CENTERED TRAINING

Not every employee must know or be able to do "everything" and not every employee learns in the same way. Each employee is an individual with regard to his/her learning type, learning motivation, work strategies, and initiative. There are also differences between employees with regard to learning success. Learning programs must meet employees' individual differences and must be developed for certain tasks and a target person. *People learn and retain knowledge in different ways.*

When designing learning programs, it is important to obtain the best possible match among employee-specific influences, organizational influences, and training methods; that is, to offer appropriate training measures for certain learning types while simultaneously taking environmental variables into consideration. Opel propagates the concept of various learning methods and spaces that the learning organization offers. The traditional seminar style is outdated. Workshops, simulations, case studies, coaching, team development measures, outdoor training, and the growing use of technology, such as internet and distance learning, make learning more interesting. Learning is becoming more flexible and diverse, and is thereby more oriented toward the individual learner. *Learning is enhanced when it takes place in a creative, fun, and exciting environment.*

CONTROLLING AND CONTINUOUS PROCESS EVALUATION

The effects of learning are expected and controlled on the individual level as well as on the organizational level. On the individual level, HRM improves employees' skills and flexibility, broadens employees' abilities, and increases motivation and job satisfaction. On the organizational level, the outcomes of successful HRM are high productivity and quality of work. When employees constantly further themselves, the entire organization is transformed. *An organization learns when its individuals have learned and changed.*

HRM is a process—from the identification of business demands and company goals, to the adequate training of employees, to completed training controlling that makes measurement of transfer success possible and secures quality.

COOPERATION AND KNOWLEDGE NETWORKS

One of the most important tasks of HRM has become the mobilization, processing, and integration of existing elements of knowledge on the organizational level and beyond the organization. Information must be quickly exchanged with customers and suppliers, as well as between departments. A focused acquirement of knowledge, the efficient communication of knowledge, and the professional handling of information all play a role in the success of a company. The task of the HRM department is to professionally support the process of knowledge management, and to strengthen the company through knowledge management. Intensive external contacts for the employees, for example, via journals, access to external data bases and internet, as well as cooperation with universities and participation in work communities, workshops, seminars, and conventions, are promoted. In addition, the HRM department regularly collects external feedback, for example, through surveys. Innovations are also effectively promoted by the HRM department through internal processes. *New ideas and innovations are born from the exchange of knowledge.*

ROLE OF THE HRM DEPARTMENT

During the last 10 years the role of the HRM department at Opel has developed into a *service center with the functions of counseling and promoting.* As a service center, the HRM department sees the employees and the supervisors as its "customers". The

Responsibilities within the Qualification Process

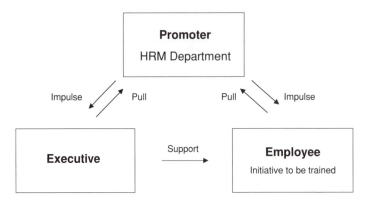

FIGURE 19.1   HR responsibilities and functions

customers communicate their training needs to the HRM department which gives support, but changes to a decentralization principle where people in the field lead the process. Two basic assumptions are responsible for the development of the role of the HRM department. First, each employee is responsible for actively promoting his/her own development, and second, human resource development is part of the supervisors' prescribed leadership role and must therefore not be delegated.

The main tasks of the HRM department are establishing an innovation-promoting learning environment and supporting change by developing an overall understanding and broad consciousness for problems. The guiding principle is the support for the attainment of the Business Plan goals and the security of quality through transfer-oriented training control.

The HRM department, executives, and employees all jointly carry out HRM functions (see Figure 19.1). The responsibilities of the executives are to lead personnel development discussions, to set developmental goals for their employees, and to monitor the realization of these goals. When leaders teach, they demonstrate their commitment and they learn through dialogue. They facilitate the learning process by selecting appropriate training topics or promoting employees via job rotation and formation of project work teams.

The "service center" approach illustrates the work philosophy of the HRM department at Opel. This service center adapts the learning program to the respective target group, involves employees in the development to optimize the learning programs, and designs solution-oriented workshops on change. Human resource management facilitates performance improvement through its products and services.

LIVING THE LEARNING ORGANIZATION: HRM PRODUCTS AND SERVICES

Training development, training, and evaluation support organizational learning at Opel, keeping competencies in focus. When there is a need for new training or development action, the development of the training is shared by the internal "customer" and the HRM department (see Figure 19.2). This customer expects solutions tailor-made to

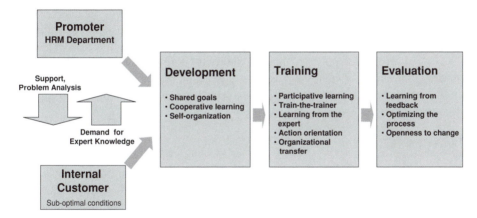

FIGURE 19.2 Training development and process

his/her needs rather than a "shopping list" answer to his/her problems. HRM at Opel is basically determined by going to the scene of the customer and, in conjunction with the customer, developing products and services that meet the customer's needs. This strong orientation towards demand means that project work on the scene takes precedent over standard training programs. Focusing on project work among the customer, the HRM department, and other expert sources not only ensures the development of solutions specifically designed for a certain department, but also supports the active role of the customer and the development of more global competencies, such as self-organization and cooperation.

PARTICIPATIVE LEARNING

Keeping the customer actively involved in the training development process is part of a bigger movement away from instructional learning toward a more participative training design. Under this auspice, learning is understood as being more active, self-propelled, constructive, situational, and social, while training programs focus on developing competencies via on-the-job training and action orientation. Action orientation gets away from teaching abstract "book knowledge" that neglects contexts and promotes a passive-receptive position by the learner, and focuses instead on relevant questions and authentic issues. By this, applicable content is shifted to the foreground of the training and becomes recognizable to trainees as a direct or indirect solution to everyday problems. Future relevance of the training material becomes especially clear when, during the training, employees are confronted with possible applications of the training content or develop these themselves.

One way to facilitate the social aspect of the participative training design is the use of expert models. Due to the increase in on-the-job training, superiors, experienced colleagues, or other expert sources who possess certain qualifications or skills play a critical role. These persons function as a model for learning employees by showing them how an expert would act. The employee observes the model person and learns in this way how to act "expertly".

Another social aspect of training is the emergence of networks. The goal of supporting networks in a training context is to promote important interpersonal relations and to use these in a positive way for the company. It is about using "good contacts" for the exchange of information, for shortening decision-paths, and for the application of non-bureaucratic means.

Collegial supervision provides another opportunity for building and maintaining personal relationships. Collegial supervisory groups are meetings of experts or leaders who discuss problems in the practice. These groups occur within a framework of equality. Participants profit from different opinions and views.

Train-the-Trainer

Aside from social aspects and participative learning, the train-the-trainer principle is an important training method. The principle calls for "learning through teaching", in which employees are further qualified on the scene so that they can, in turn, train their colleagues. Subsequent to a training session, an employee is assigned the implementation of a training measure. Then the employee becomes familiar with concepts of processing and imparting knowledge via an instructional program. Next, either alone or with a professional trainer, the "trainer" actively comes to terms with the topic and learns to apply techniques of processing and imparting knowledge. In this manner, he/she trains his/her didactic, communicative, and methodological skills, as well as presentation and visualization techniques. Finally, he/she learns important elements of group leadership, which can be useful in future management positions. The advantages of an in-house trainer are his/her familiarity with company values and norms and his/her acceptance by colleagues.

One special aspect of the train-the-trainer principle is the multiplier. Multipliers are employees that pass their expertise on to their colleagues. Changes in operation or current knowledge are imparted to multipliers, whose task it is then to further pass along the knowledge.

Evaluation and Transfer

As the final step of the training process, evaluation is crucial in determining whether the goal of the training program was reached, in identifying problem points, and in generating ideas for optimizing future training programs. The HRM department and customers together develop controlling instruments for the purpose of evaluating the success of the training program. The learning process and results are reflected upon and critically examined. However, the critical measure of the success of every type of training is the learning transfer.

Every qualifying attempt has as its core intent the use and generalization of acquired knowledge and trained behavior patterns. It is certainly not easy to transfer competencies gained in a training setting to daily routine, especially considering short-lived qualifications and knowledge and quickly changing work demands. Employee-centered training programs optimize transfer by realizing the optimal fit between the personality and performance characteristics of the employees and training contents and methods.

Transfer-Oriented Training Control: A Modern Example

At Opel, the controlling of a training session in a transfer-oriented manner involves various preparatory and post-evaluative measures (see Figure 19.3). First, a preparatory

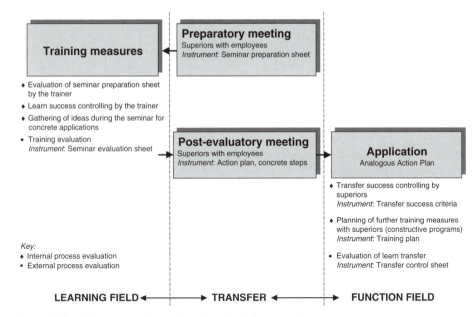

FIGURE 19.3 The process of transfer-oriented training control

meeting is held between supervisors and employees before the training session begins. At this time, participants write down their expectations of the training session and goals they hope to achieve by going through with the training session.

The next steps in controlling a training session occur during the session itself. The participants' expectations and goals are evaluated by the trainer. Participants and trainer also gather ideas for concrete applications of the material learned and develop an action plan, including a list of first steps to be taken. The seminar preparatory goals and expectations and the action plan, as well as transfer success criteria and a plan of future training measures, which will be discussed later, are all part of a one-page internal process evaluation. Finally, the trainer is responsible for controlling the learn success of the participants during the training session.

After the training session is complete, participants are asked to fill out a seminar evaluation sheet that has been developed by the HRM department and is part of the external process evaluation. This sheet asks participants to evaluate several aspects of the training session, including: preparation, organization, goals and contents, methods and course of events, and materials used, as well as an overall evaluation of the session. Then a post-evaluative meeting is held between superiors and employees where the action plan developed during the training session is discussed and concrete steps to be taken are finalized.

The final overall step in controlling the success of a training session is the development of an analogous action plan. First, the transfer success of the training session is evaluated internally using the transfer success criteria and can be evaluated externally by the HRM department using the transfer control form. Another criterion for evaluating transfer success is the observation of trainees at work and the determination as to what extent he/she is able to transfer the learned material into practice. An example would be after an English language training session to have the trainer call the trainee at their work place about two months later and speak to the trainee in English (using vocabulary that was taught during the training). The trainee would then be judged on how well he/she answered and how well he/she handled the situation. Finally, participants and superiors together develop a plan of constructive programs for future training sessions.

BARRIERS TO BECOMING A LEARNING ORGANIZATION

What are the problems and barriers to becoming a learning organization? First, a learning and error management culture must be present in an organization or a general fear may develop among employees of making mistakes. Bad experiences with previous processes of change or concerns about being overstrained by changes in work loads or responsibilities can also create a fear of change among employees. Furthermore, a problem arises when leaders, who are believed to have undergone many training programs, are assumed to be good trainers and are not further qualified to train other employees. Finally, insufficient training transfer can project an image of uselessness on training programs.

What has Opel done to anticipate these barriers? (see Table 19.2). Opel works continuously on building a learning culture that is unalterably for the furtherance and use of qualification potentials. The design of a learning culture requires the support of the HRM department. The HRM department looks after the participation of all organizational members in the learning process and ensures the inclusion of learning in internal career planning. The HRM department also plays an essential role in the development and testing of new design concepts and innovative forms of learning. In this context, Opel is leading an open practical–technological dialogue. Reflecting on theoretical basics and the controlled examination of preliminary measures are important elements. In cooperation

TABLE 19.2 Checklist of practical implications

• Learning and furtherance of potential must be seen as integral parts of company planning

• All members of the organization must participate in the learning process

• Orientation of organizational framework towards the demands of a learning organization: work in department-overlapping teams, formation of networks, avoidance of long-term appointments in favor of flexible job rotation principles

• Formation of a learning culture, an open error culture (error as a chance to learn rather than sanctions for errors). Development and trial of new design concepts and innovative learning forms

• Learning cultures need time

• Financial support of innovations, reward systems for creative ideas

• The roll of leadership: essential impulses for the furtherance of learning processes must go along with daily encounters with employees, the institution of leadership instruments, and leadership culture

• A future necessary task for leadership: developing and qualifying employees for the thinking in Human Resource, the strength of innovations, and the performance capabilities of the company with the HRM department, research is done on the scene, producing practicable, realistic concepts. Just as important as sources of learning are multi-faceted contacts and the exchange of experiences with other companies.

The effectiveness of skilled workers will be limited if they are not motivated to perform their jobs. The structure of the Opel HRM system affects employees in several ways. Opel has implemented an incentive compensation system that rewards employees for meeting specific goals. The employees are also directly involved in participation systems, e.g. team-based production systems or creativity teams. Furthermore, there is an internal labor market and job rotation system at Opel that provides an opportunity for employees to advance within the company. One example is the program for potential development, which trains participants with a focus on the core competencies. The program is characterized as target group-oriented qualification management that is tuned into learning and personality type. The program contains systematically coordinated independent and group activities.

To begin with, an individual performance profile is drawn up for each participant (*diagnosis phase*), out of which concrete development steps are derived. The individual development modules contain for each case substantiated information, transfer, and concrete applications with the chance to learn about and reflect upon individual behavior (*training phase*). The modules are based on learning by personal experience and incorporate situations from the concrete workaday routine (*transfer security*).

THE VISION FOR FUTURE LEARNING: HRM ON A VIRTUAL CAMPUS

Global cooperation is necessary to deal with the constantly increasing demands on companies and employees. Global cooperation also enhances the evolution of synergistic effects, the exchange of knowledge based on experience, and provides fertile ground for cooperative development of new ideas. Thus, the goal is to create a knowledge community for the future. Opel and GM have already achieved this with the GM University. GM University is a global corporate university aimed at focusing continuous learning activities under one virtual roof. It is a network of education and training opportunities targeted at achieving GM's business objectives. Like most universities, "GMU" consists of a series of colleges.

GMU has gone through different periods in history. In the beginning, the aim was to help people overcome cross-cultural barriers through awareness and discovery. Very quickly GMU moved on to creating better relations and understanding in a cooperative environment, thus improving effectiveness of key employees in multicultural operations and projects. Today, GMU is involved in assisting the formation of strategic alliances and international companies from a human resource point of view by employing information and communication technologies to their fullest potential. GMU's major goal is to establish new patterns and modes of cooperation in a virtual extended enterprise network of cooperating partners.

As a conclusion, the practical experiences described in this article show that successful HR function must have as its principal focus a set of properly aligned HR policies that solve business problems and support the company's strategic initiatives. HRM should be oriented toward the Business Plan goals of the company. More and more, the HRM department is playing a leading role within the organization, offering progressive HRM practices and innovative forms of learning. The future trends include employee-centered qualification management and participative learning. Also, flexibility in the training process must be maintained and could be reached through international connections by using worldwide knowledge networks in the field of HRM.

PART IV

Ensuring Performance
in a Wider Context

CHAPTER 20

Performance, Well-Being and Self-Regulation

Sabine Sonnentag

Technical University of Braunschweig, Braunschweig, Germany

SUMMARY

This chapter addresses the question: If, and how, is individual performance related to psychological well-being? It summarizes empirical studies showing that well-being is positively related to performance. In the chapter, it is argued that self-regulatory mechanisms—comprising goal setting, feedback processing and self-efficacy—play a crucial role in linking well-being and performance. It is suggested that self-regulatory mechanisms improve well-being similarly to their well-documented beneficial effects on performance. The chapter discusses various causal explanations for the well-being–performance relationship. It contrasts a 'self-regulation as a common source' model with a 'self-regulation as a mediator' model. The chapter specifies directions for future research.

Psychological Management of Individual Performance. Edited by Sabine Sonnentag.
© 2002 John Wiley & Sons, Ltd.

INTRODUCTION

Individual performance is one of the key factors contributing to organizational effectiveness. Organizations use a range of practices and procedures for ensuring high individual performance. These practices and procedures include personnel selection, performance appraisal, but also job design, training, and goal setting. When considering individuals within an organization, one must not focus exclusively on performance. Besides the improvement and maintenance of high performance the protection of individuals' health and well-being belong to the most important criteria of professional activities within work and organizational psychology.

This chapter addresses the relationship between performance and individual well-being. With respect to theory development, examining this relationship can contribute to our understanding of the correlates of performance, its predictors, and consequences. Also for practice-related reasons it is highly important to know whether there is any relationship between performance and individual well-being and whether this relationship is positive or negative—or whether it even follows a more complex pattern. If there was a negative relationship between performance and individual well-being, organizations would face a major problem because both criteria could not be optimized at the same time. Focusing on high performance would have detrimental effects on well-being—or vice versa. However, if a positive relationship between performance and individual well-being was found, the situation would be more favorable: Aiming at the improvement of these two criteria—or of the common underlying processes—would have beneficial effects on both criteria.

If we assume that there is a relationship between well-being and performance, we face a further question: How can we explain this relationship?

In the past, the hypothesized relationship was explained by the 'happy-productive worker hypothesis'. This hypothesis, which is closely linked to the assumptions of the Human Relations movement (Roethlisberger & Dickson, 1939), states that happy employees whose needs are met within their work settings show higher performance than unhappy employees. However, although the happy-productive worker hypothesis was—and still is—very popular it does not explain in detail *why* happiness and self-actualization lead to better performance. Thus, the reference to additional and more specific processes is needed to account for the assumed relationship between individual well-being and performance. In this chapter, I will argue, that self-regulatory processes might play a major role in explaining this relationship between individual well-being and performance (cf. George & Brief, 1996).

The chapter is organized as follows: First, I briefly describe the performance and well-being concepts. Then, I summarize empirical research on the relationship between individual well-being and performance. Subsequently, I report findings from empirical studies on self-regulation. More specifically, I describe how goal pursuit, feedback processing and self-efficacy as aspects of self-regulation are related to performance and well-being. Finally, I integrate the empirical findings on well-being, performance, and self-regulation into two causal models and suggest some directions for future research.

CONCEPTS OF PERFORMANCE AND WELL-BEING

The performance concept encompasses both action and outcome aspects (Campbell, McCloy, Oppler, & Sager, 1993; Roe, 1999). The action aspect refers to the behaviors of an individual, while the outcome aspect refers to the consequences or results of these behaviors. Campbell et al. suggested an influencial conceptualization of performance (cf. the discussion in Ilgen & Pulakos, 1999) and argued that only an individual's action should be labeled 'performance' because only the actions themselves, but not their outcomes, are under the control of the individual. Typical examples of performance comprise actions such as monitoring processes in the chemical industry, designing a computer program, or serving customers in a travel agency. Most authors agree that performance is a multi-dimensional concept which comprises both task and contextual performance (Borman & Motowidlo, 1993). In this chapter I will focus on task performance.

Diener, Suh, Lucas, and Smith (1999) described subjective well-being as "a broad category of phenomena that includes people's emotional responses, domain satisfactions, and global judgements of life satisfaction" (p. 277). Work-related well-being is one of the domain-specific aspects of well-being (cf. Warr, 1990). A broad conceptualization of work-related well-being includes phenomena such as job satisfaction and job morale as well as low levels of psychic complaints. A more narrow conceptualization of work-related well-being mainly refers to low levels of specific complaints. These complaints include job tension, depression, psychosomatic symptoms and burnout. Until now, well-being is mainly defined negatively, i.e., as the absence of complaints. In this chapter, I particularly refer to the more narrow conceptualization of work-related well-being.

Performance and well-being are two distinct criteria within work and organizational psychology. This is reflected in the relatively distinct literature on these two criteria. A more thorough examination of the literature on performance and well-being, however, suggests a partial overlap between the two concepts. Performance-related constructs can be conceptualized as parts of the well-being concept. The burnout concept is the most prominent example of such an inclusion of performance-related constructs within the well-being concept. Burnout has been conceptualized as an impairment of individual well-being characterized by three aspects: emotional exhaustion, depersonalization, and lack of personal accomplishment (Maslach & Jackson, 1981). Lack of personal accomplishment refers to feelings of not being competent (any longer) and of failing to perform successfully. Thus, lack of personal accomplishment is conceptually closely linked to low performance (cf. Dollard, Winefield, Winefield, & deJonge, 2000). More specifically, lack of personal accomplishment is the subjective experience of not being able to realize one's performance potential.

Despite the partial overlap between this specific burnout component and performance, individual well-being and performance are two distinct concepts. Therefore, it makes sense to examine their empirical relationship in more detail.

THE EMPIRICAL RELATIONSHIP BETWEEN PERFORMANCE AND WELL-BEING

Within work and organizational psychology, there is a long tradition to examine the relationship between job satisfaction and job performance. Meta-analyses of individual-level relationships resulted in effect sizes ranging between $r = .17$ and $r = .31$ (Iffaldano & Muchinsky, 1985; Petty, McGee, & Cavender, 1984). Based on these meta-analyses one can conclude that there is a consistent positive relationship between job satisfaction and performance, which is small to moderate in size.

Compared to the large number of studies on the relationship between job satisfaction and performance, research on the relationship between other, more narrowly defined well-being concepts and job performance is relatively limited. Nevertheless, there are studies which did examine this relationship. Within these studies, researchers addressed both general well-being concepts and more specific aspects of (poor) well-being such as depression, burnout, anxiety, and frustration.

CROSS-SECTIONAL STUDIES

The majority of studies on the relationship between well-being and job performance followed a cross-sectional research design with questionnaire measures of well-being and supervisory or coworker ratings of job performance. For example, Motowidlo, Packard, and Manning (1986) examined nurses who completed questionnaires on affect measures (i.e., anxiety, hostility, and depression). Supervisors and coworkers provided performance ratings. Path analyses showed negative effects of depression on various performance indicators. However, nearly no effects of anxiety or hostility on performance were found.

Spector, Dwyer, and Jex (1988) studied a sample of 191 secretaries. The authors gathered questionnaire measures on trait anxiety, frustration, and self-reported health symptoms as well as supervisory ratings of secretarial job performance. Analyses revealed a significant negative relationship between anxiety and performance. However, frustration and health symptoms were not significantly related to job performance.

Parker and Kulik (1995) examined the relationship between burnout and job performance in 73 registered nurses. Multiple regression analysis showed that the burnout factor 'emotional exhaustion' was a significant predictor of both self-rated and supervisor-rated performance. The other two burnout dimensions were no significant predictors.

In two studies with insurance sales personnel, Mughal, Walsh, and Wilding (1996) found positive relationships between trait anxiety and sales performance. Analyses showed that individuals high on trait anxiety exerted greater work effort. For example, they saw more potential clients—a behavior which could have resulted in higher performance.

Martin, Blum, Beach, and Roman (1996) examined the relationship between depressive symptoms and work performance in a sample of subclinical depression patients. Depressive symptoms were assessed by self-report. Measures of technical and social performance were based on supervisory and coworker performance ratings. The authors conducted multiple regression analyses in which additional factors were taken into account as control variables. Depressive symptoms were a significant predictor of both low technical and low social performance.

Wright and his colleagues conducted a number of studies on the relationship between well-being and job performance. In one of these studies, the researchers found a positive relationship between human service supervisory personnel's mental health and supervisory ratings of performance assessed one year later (Wright, Bonett, & Sweeney, 1993). In an other study, Wright and Bonett (1997) examined the relationship between well-being and job performance in criminal justice staff personnel. The authors reported a positive relationship between a pleasantness-based well-being measure and job performance as rated by the departmental managers. There was neither a significant linear nor a curvilinear relationship between emotional exhaustion and performance. However, in an additional study with a sample of social welfare workers, emotional exhaustion turned out to be a significant predictor of low job performance (ratings were provided by a top-ranking administrative officer). Emotional exhaustion remained a significant predictor in a regression equation with positive and negative affectivity as additional predictors (Wright & Cropanzano, 1998). Similarly, in studies with county agency personnel and juvenile probation officers, Wright and Cropanzano (2000) found a positive relationship between well-being and supervisory performance ratings. This relationship could not be explained by control variables such as age, gender, job tenure and—most interestingly—job satisfaction. This finding suggests that well-being is more important than job satisfaction when it comes to the prediction of job performance.

Leiter, Harview, and Frizzel (1998) took a somewhat different approach for studying the relationship between individual well-being and job performance. The authors assessed nurses' burnout scores and asked patients about their satisfaction with the care provided by the nurses. These satisfaction ratings can be regarded as a measure of nurses' job performance. Analysis showed strong negative correlations between nurses' exhaustion and cynicsm scores and their patients' satisfaction.

In summary, a fairly consistent pattern emerges from these cross-sectional studies. Depression is negatively related to job performance (for a further study, cf. Shaw & Weekley, 1985). Among the three burnout factors, only emotional exhaustion seems to have a significant negative relationship with job performance (cf. however, Wright & Bonett, 1997). Moreover, general well-being measures were found to be related to job performance. With respect to other aspects of well-being, the findings were inconsistent. This is particularly true for anxiety, for which both positive and negative relationships with performance were found.

Taken together, low depression, low emotional exhaustion and high general well-being are positively related to job performance ratings. However, one might argue that this relationship does not reflect a 'true' empirical relationship but is mainly caused by a rating bias. This rating bias would imply that an individual's mental health or well-being influences his or her supervisor's rating process independently of the individual's actual job performance (cf. Cardy & Dobbins, 1986). For example, supervisors might evaluate the performance of an individual with symptoms of burnout or depressivity more negatively than the performance of an individual with a better well-being. The same argument applies to ratings provided by other persons such as coworkers or patients.

To rule out the interpretation that the relationship between well-being and performance is based on rating bias, empirical studies with objective performance measures are needed. Such studies are still relatively rare and resulted in inconsistent findings. For example, in a study with 117 life insurance brokers, Bluen, Barling, and Burns (1990) found no substantial relationship between depression and the number of insurance polices sold. However, in a simulation of a data entry task, Glaser, Tatum, Nebeker, Sorenson, and Aiello (1999) found that experienced stress including worry and tension were negatively related to an objective measure of work performance. Similarly, Beehr, Jex, Stacy, and Murray (2000) reported significant negative relationships between well-being of door-to-door book sellers (i.e., low frustration and low depression) and a financial performance measure. Here, clearly more studies are needed which rely on objective performance measures. The cross-sectional designs of the studies reported so far do not allow for causal interpretations. However, there are a few longitudinal studies which examined the effect of well-being on performance.

LONGITUDINAL STUDIES

Staw, Sutton, and Pelled (1994) examined 272 employees over a period of 18 months. In this study, positive emotion (operationalized as lack of depression) was assessed at Time 1, supervisory performance ratings were gathered at two points in time (Time 1 and Time 2). Multiple regression analysis showed that positive emotion at Time 1 was a positive predictor of performance at Time 2, also when controlling for performance at Time 1 and a range of other control variables such as education, age, gender, and rated intelligence.

Wright and Staw (1999) reported two longitudinal studies in which they examined the effects of well-being on performance. In the first study, the authors gathered data from 53 social welfare workers at four points of time: Time 1 (year 1), Time 2 (year 3), Time 3 (year 4) and Time 4 (year $4\frac{1}{2}$). Multiple regression analysis showed that well-being at Time 1 and Time 2 predicted supervisory performance ratings at Time 3 and 4 with performance at Time 2 as a control variable. The second study was based on two measurement points, with the Time 2 measurement taking place one year after the Time 1 measurement. Study participants were 78 social services staff members. In this study, performance at Time 2 was regressed on the well-being scores averaged across Time 1 and Time 2, with performance at Time 1 and demographic factors as control variables. Average well-being at Time 1 and Time 2 was a significant predictor of performance at Time 2.

A similar procedure was followed by Cropanzano and Wright (1999) who gathered longitudinal data over a period of five years: Time 1 (year 1), Time 2 (year 1.5), Time 3 (year 4), and Time 4 (year 5). Study participants were 60 social welfare professionals. To test for possible longitudinal effects of well-being on performance, the authors regressed performance ratings provided by a department manager at Time 4 on a composite of well-being data measured at Time 3 and Time 4 with performance ratings at Time 3 and a composite of well-being data measured at Time 1 and Time 2 as a control variables. The composite of well-being data measured at Time 3 and Time 4 was found to be a significant predictor of performance at Time 4.

A study by Gorgievski-Duijvesteijn, Giesen, and Bakker (2000) provides additional evidence for a causal effect of individual health and well-being on performance. Gorgievski-Duijvesteijn et al. studied the relationship between health and financial problems in farm couples over a ten-year period. In the context of farm businesses, financial problems can be seen as a proxi for low performance. A structural equation modelling procedure showed that the husbands' mental and physical health complaints had a causal effect on the couples' financial problems ten years later.

To sum up, there is relatively consistent empirical evidence for a positive relationship between specific aspects of individual well-being and job performance. Moreover, longitudinal studies allow some conclusions about the direction of this relationship. Despite some methodological shortcomings in some of the studies these longitudinal studies suggest that there is a causal effect of well-being on job performance (Staw et al., 1994; Wright & Staw, 1999). However, these findings do not necessarily exclude alternative or additional causal processes which account for the empirical findings. Other causal interpretations will be discussed later in this chapter.

In addition, it has to be noted that the common variance in individual well-being and job performance is moderate in size. This implies that factors other than an individual's well-being contribute to this person's job performance. Nevertheless, focusing on the possible effects of well-being can improve our overall understanding of the determinants of high job performance.

With respect to practical implications, the positive relationship between well-being and performance is good news. This relationship implies that performance issues are not in conflict with well-being concerns. More specifically, organizations can feel encouraged to develop interventions which enhance individual performance without harming individual well-being.

SELF-REGULATION AND ITS RELATIONSHIP TO PERFORMANCE AND INDIVIDUAL WELL-BEING

THE SELF-REGULATION CONCEPT

Self-regulation refers to intrapersonal processes which are closely related to goal-directed behavior and which support goal attainment. Self-regulatory processes include the exercise of control over one's thinking, affect, behavior, and attention (Kanfer & Kanfer, 1991; Karoly, 1993). Taxonomies of self-regulation activities do not completely overlap across various theoretical frameworks (cf. Carver & Scheier, 1999). Nevertheless, authors agree that goal setting and goal attributes, self-monitoring, self-evaluations, and beliefs about the self, particularly self-efficacy, play a major role in self-regulation (Bandura, 1997; Kanfer & Kanfer, 1991; Karoly, 1993).

In the remainder of this chapter I will focus on three central aspects related to self-regulation: goal setting, feedback processing, and self-efficacy. There is extensive research which showed that goals, feedback processing, and self-efficacy are highly relevant for job performance (Kluger & DeNisi, 1996; Locke & Latham, 1990; Stajkovic & Luthans, 1998). In addition, there are studies which suggest that goals, feedback and self-efficacy are related to individual well-being (e.g., Brunstein, 1993; Jex & Bliese, 1999). Findings from this research are displayed in Table 20.1. Later, I will discuss whether self-regulatory processes can account for the relationship between individual well-being and job performance.

TABLE 20.1 Relationships of self-regulation with performance and well-being: Summary of empirical studies

Self-regulatory mechanism	Relationship with performance	Relationship with well-being
Goals	Positive, if • goals are difficult • goals are specific	Inconsistent; probably positive, if • goal attributes are positive • work situation is not adverse • probability for goal attainment is high
Feedback	Mainly positive, if • feedback is task-related	Probably positive
Self-efficacy	Positive	Positive Buffers negative effects of stressors

GOALS

On a very general level, goals can be defined as "internal representations of desired states" such as outcomes, events or processes (Austin & Vancouver, 1996, p. 338). Goals play an important role within self-regulatory processes (Latham & Locke, 1991).

Extensive research within work and organizational psychology has examined the effects of goal-setting interventions on job performance. Within goal-setting interventions high and specific goals are set for an individual. These goals are assumed to stimulate effort, persistence, direction and task-specific strategies as mediating processes. There is broad empirical support for the positive effect of goal setting on job performance (Locke & Latham, 1990; Latham, Locke, & Fassina this volume).

Within personality and social psychology, researchers addressed the question of whether personal goals have an effect on individual well-being (for reviews, cf. Brunstein, Schultheiss, & Maier, 1999; Emmons, 1996). Personal goals are "future-oriented representations of what individuals are striving for in their current life situations and what they try to attain or avoid in various life domains" (Brunstein et al., 1999, p. 171). Studies showed that the striving for personal goals is positively related to individual well-being (Emmons, 1986, 1991; Omodei & Wearing, 1990). In addition, perceived goal attainability was found to moderate this relationship (Brunstein, 1993). This finding suggests that it is not the mere existence of goals but the anticipation of achieving a desired state which is relevant for individual well-being.

Compared to the relatively unequivocal findings on the performance effects of goal-setting interventions, research on the effects of work-related goals on individual well-being is far less conclusive. Locke and Latham (1990) summarized laboratory and experimental field studies about the effects of goal setting interventions on individual affect, i.e., mainly satisfaction measures, but also tension and anxiety measures. Findings are inconsistent: in the majority of studies no effects of goal setting on individual affect were found. There were some studies which reported a positive effect of goal setting on affect, while others reported a negative effect. A meta-analysis by Rodgers, Hunter, and Rogers (1993) reported a small effect size of $d = .07$ between goal setting and affective reactions.

Correlational studies on the relationship between goal attributes and affect consistently revealed positive relationships. Individuals who assessed goal attributes as favorable were more satisfied than individuals experiencing the goal attributes as unfavorable. This suggests that goals and goal setting per se have no—or at least no strong—effects on individual well-being. Based on the findings summarized by Locke and Latham (1990) one can conclude that rather the attributes associated with the goal setting and goal pursuit process are more relevant for well-being. Individuals who experience goals as something positive will show better well-being than individuals who experience goals as negative and threatening. Because most of the studies which examined the relationship between attributes of work-related goals and individual well-being followed a cross-sectional design, a conclusive causal interpretation is not warranted.

If there is no or only a small direct effect of goals on individual well-being the question arises of whether there are specific factors which moderate the relationship between goals and individual well-being. Based on the transactional stress concept (Lazarus & Folkman, 1984) and an action theory approach (Frese & Zapf, 1994) it can be assumed that the threat of not attaining one's goal is experienced as stressful. For example, Semmer

(1996) stated that an anticipated or experienced thwart of goals is associated with a stress experience. Because perceived stress is known to have a negative effect on individual well-being—or even might be seen as an indicator of poor individual well-being (Kahn & Byosiere, 1992)—one can assume that the threat of not attaining one's goal has a negative impact on well-being. Typical threats to goal attainment are stressors in the work situation or lack of resources (e.g., lack of knowledge and skills or lack of support from others). Within this line of reasoning one would hypothesize that goals are positively related to individual well-being when the probability of goal attainment is high, i.e., when stressors are low and resources are high. In contrast, goals would be negatively related to individual well-being when stressors are high and resources are low.

A longitudinal study by Maier (1996) who studied newcomers in an organization supports this line of reasoning: Newcomers who showed a high commitment to their career goals and who received extensive coworker and supervisory support for goal attainment experienced increased satisfaction after a period of 9 months. Newcomers however, who also expressed high commitment to their career goals but did not receive extensive coworker and supervisory support reported a decrease in satisfaction. Additionally, Maier and Brunstein (2001) reported a similar interaction effect of goal commitment and goal attainability on satisfaction.

Goals might play an additional role in the well-being–performance relationship. Findings from experimental research suggest that mood and affective states have an effect on goal mechanisms. For example, Baron (1990) reported that study participants who were exposed to pleasant scents and therefore experienced a more positive affect set higher goals for themselves when working on a clerical task than did individuals not exposed to these scents.

Taken together, the pursuit of personal goals was shown to be beneficial for an individual's well-being. One can assume that the same is true for work-related goals—but only if these goals are associated with positive attributes, if they are not counteracted by an adverse work situation, and if the probability for goal attainment is high. Additionally, well-being might stimulate further goal setting.

FEEDBACK PROCESSING

Feedback processing refers to those aspects of action and self-regulatory processes in which an individual monitors and evaluates the present state of performance or other aspects relevant for the process under consideration. With respect to work contexts, one can differentiate between feedback interventions and proactive feedback-seeking behavior. Feedback interventions are "actions taken by (an) external agent(s) to provide information regarding some aspect(s) of one's task performance" (Kluger & DeNisi, 1996, p. 255). Feedback-seeking behavior refers to actions such as monitoring or inquiry by which an individual tries to acquire information about his or her own task performance (Ashford & Cummings, 1983).

Both feedback interventions and feedback-seeking behavior offer various types of feedback. On a very general level, feedback which addresses the task accomplishment process can be differentiated from feedback which is closely linked to meta-task and self-related issues. For example, with respect to feedback-seeking behavior, authors have pointed out that feedback seeking aims not only at competence improvement and uncertainty reduction (which are more task-related aims) but also at self-related issues such as ego protection and impression management (Ashford & Cummings, 1983; Morrison & Bies, 1991).

There is extensive research which examined the effect of feedback interventions on subsequent performance. Kluger and DeNisi (1996) conducted a meta-analysis in which they showed that feedback interventions which direct attention to the task have a positive effect on subsequent performance. However this positive effect of feedback interventions does not hold for interventions which mainly address meta-task processes.

With respect to feedback-seeking behavior, many studies revealed positive relationships between feedback seeking and performance (e.g., Ashford & Black, 1996; Ashford & Tsui, 1991; Battmann, 1988; Morrison & Weldon, 1990; Tsui, Ashford, St. Clair, & Xin, 1995). Interestingly, Asford and Tsui found that not all types of feedback-seeking behavior were uniformly positively related to performance (Ashford & Tsui, 1991; Tsui et al., 1995). In their studies, only 'negative feedback seeking' showed a positive effect on subsequent performance while 'positive feedback seeking' showed a negative effect. One could argue that 'negative feedback seeking' which aims at detailed, although potentially hurting evaluations, is a highly task-related feedback. Positive feedback seeking which aims at receiving 'good news' about oneself is highly self-related. Conceptualizing negative and positive feedback seeking in this way, the finding of these studies are pretty consistent with findings from feedback interventions studies summarized by Kluger and DeNisi (1996): Task-related feedback improves performance while self-related feedback has no or even a detrimental effect on performance.

With respect to the relationship between feedback processes and work-related well-being research is relatively scarce. However, there are good reasons to assume that feedback seeking has a positive effect on individual well-being. Individuals seek feedback in order to reduce uncertainty (Ashford & Cummings, 1983). This implies that successful feedback-seeking behavior should result in reduced role ambiguity. Role ambiguity is known to be negatively related to individual well-being (Jackson & Schuler, 1985). Thus, successful feedback-seeking behavior should improve well-being, mediated by reduced role ambiguity. Data reported by Morrison (1993a) partly support this assumption. The extent to which newcomers searched for information and feedback shortly after organizational entry predicted their subsequent role clarity (also when controlling for initial role clarity). Based on an additional analysis Morrison (1993b) reported a positive relationship between newcomer information seeking and subsequent job satisfaction. This study suggests that information and feedback seeking might have a positive effect on individual well-being. If this finding was replicated in future studies one might conclude that feedback-seeking behavior has a positive effect on both performance and well-being.

Research from social psychology offers a different perspective on how well-being and performance are linked via feedback-seeking processes. In an experimental study, Trope and Neter (1994) showed that individuals who experienced positive mood were more likely to ask for negative performance feedback than were individuals who experienced negative mood. This study suggests that positive mood and well-being stimulate an individual to search for negative feedback which in turn will have a positive impact on subsequent performance.

SELF-EFFICACY

Bandura (1997) defined self-efficacy as "beliefs in one's capabilities to organize and execute the courses of action required to produce given attainments" (p. 3). There is a large number of studies which examined the relationship between self-efficacy and job performance. Meta-analyses support the assumption that self-efficacy has a positive effect on job performance (Sadri & Robertson, 1993; Stajkovic & Luthans, 1998). In addition, self-efficacy has been found to be positively related to well-being and health in general (Bandura, 1997; Holden, 1991). Moreover, experimental studies showed a causal effect of mood on self-efficacy. Inducing positive mood increased self-efficacy whereas inducing negative mood decreased self-efficacy (Bandura, 1997).

Within the past decade there is increasing research on the relationship between self-efficacy and well-being at work. Authors suggested that self-efficacy is one important factor in work-related well-being and that poor well-being might be—at least partially—attributable to low self-efficacy. For example, Leiter (1992) conceptualized burnout as a 'crisis in self-efficacy'. Empirical research supports this idea. Several studies showed that low self-efficacy is positively related to burnout (e.g., Brouwers & Tomic, 1998; Chwalisz, Altmaier, & Russell, 1992). This negative relationship between self-efficacy and well-being seems not to be specific for burnout. For example, Jex and Gudanowski (1992) found that individuals with low self-efficacy experienced more frustration at work and more anxiety. In a sample of middle managers of a public sector organization, Terry, Tonge, and Callan (1995) reported negative relationships between self-efficacy and other well-being measures such as anxiety and depression. Also data assessed from air fleet staff in a post-merger situation indicated a positive relationship between self-efficacy and psychological well-being (Terry, Callan, & Sartori, 1996). Similarly, high self-efficacy predicted low psychological strain and physical symptoms in army soldiers (Jex & Bliese, 1999; cf. for similar findings Jex & Elacqua, 1999; Kahn & Long, 1988).

These results indicate that low self-efficacy is not only related to the specific burnout symptoms but that it is associated with a broader range of well-being impairments. Research furthers suggests that the relationship between self-efficacy and well-being is mediated by coping processes. More specifically, low self-efficacy was shown to be associated with emotion-focussed coping, escapism and self-blame which in turn were related to low psychological well-being (Chwalisz et al., 1992; Terry et al., 1995).

Additionally to the reported main effects researchers examined whether self-efficacy moderates the stressor-strain relationship. The general assumption in this line of research is that individuals high on self-efficacy will be more able to cope with stressful work situations and therefore will suffer less from strain than individuals low on self-efficacy. VanYperen (1998) examined this moderator hypothesis with a sample of maternity home nurses. More specifically, he tested whether self-efficacy moderates the relationship between low informational support and perceptions of inequity. He found no relationship between lack of informational support and perceptions of inequity in nurses high on self-efficacy. In nurses low on self-efficacy, however, lack of informational support was associated with perceptions of inequity—an experience which makes nurses more vulnerable to burnout.

Similarly, Jex and Bliese (1999) tested the moderator hypothesis with a large sample of army soldiers. Analyses revealed significant interaction effects. More specifically, long working hours, high work overload and low task significance were not substantially related to psychological strain in individuals high on self-efficacy. In individals low on self-efficacy, however, long working hours, high work overload and low task significance were related to psychological strain. In addition, individuals low on self-efficacy showed a high amount of physical symptoms in high work overload situations. This was not the case for individuals high on self-efficacy.

Jex and Elacqua (1999) examined the possible moderator effect of organization-based self-esteem, a construct closely related to self-efficacy. Low organization-based self-esteem enhanced the positive relationship between role ambiguity on the one hand and depression and physical symptoms on the other. However, in a previous study, Jex and Gudanowski (1992) had found no support for the assumption that self-efficacy moderates the stressor–strain relationship. This result might be explained by this study's relatively small sample size.

Taken together, there is strong empirical support for a positive relationship between self-efficacy and work-related individual well-being. However, because most studies are cross-sectional in nature, it would be premature to derive unequivocal causal interpretations. Additionally to the positive zero-order relationship between self-efficacy and individual well-being empirical research provided some support for the moderator effect of self-efficacy in the stressor–strain relationship. The general pattern within these studies is that stressful work situations were related to poor well-being in individuals low on self-efficacy. However, no such—or only a week—relationship was found in individuals high on self-efficacy.

Self-efficacy implies the belief that one can perform the task successfully, despite the stressors present in the situation. Compared to low self-efficacious persons, individuals high on self-efficacy perceive objectively stressful situations as less threatening because they still expect to accomplish the task successfully. As a consequence, stressors lose much of their detrimental effects and well-being does not suffer so much from the exposure to a stressful situation.

CAUSAL INTERPRETATIONS

PERFORMANCE AND WELL-BEING

The review of studies on the relationship between individual well-being and job performance showed that specific aspects of well-being are positively related to job performance. In addition, in longitudinal studies a lagged effect of initial well-being on subsequent job performance was found, also when controlling for initial job performance (Staw et al., 1994; Wright & Staw, 1999). These findings suggest that improved individual well-being has a causal effect on better job performance.

However, it has to be noted that the findings from longitudinal studies do not exclude other causal processes which account for the empirical relationship between well-being and job performance. Job performance might have a causal effect on well-being, i.e., high job performance might enhance an individual's well-being while low job performance might have a detrimental effect on well-being. It feels good having accomplished a task and having reached a goal (Locke & Latham, 1990). Therefore, an improved well-being will result. On the contrary, failing to meet performance requirements will be experienced as stressful—and therefore, well-being will be reduced. Moreover, individuals showing low performance might anticipate greater job insecurity—an experience which is known to be associated with poor well-being (Mohr, 2000).

In addition, it might be that the effects of well-being and job performance are not unidirectional. Rather, it might be that well-being has an effect on job performance and vice versa. The result would be a spiral effect with well-being enhancing job performance which in turn will enhance future well-being. One could conceptualize such a spiral effect in accordance to the efficacy-performance spirals suggested by Lindsley, Brass, and Thomas (1995) or the high performance cycle described by Locke and Latham (1990).

Additionally, there might be third variables which have both an effect on well-being and job performance. Among these potential third variables are job design factors and person variables. Most of the dominant job design theories, such as role theory (Kahn, Wolfe, Quinn, Snoek, & Rosenthal, 1964), job characteristics theory (Hackman & Oldham, 1976) and sociotechnical theory (Trist & Bamforth, 1951) argue that the job design principles they suggest will result both in better job performance and employee well-being. However, empirical support for this interpretation is less clear. Meta-analyses showed substantial relationships between job design variables (role stressors, job characteristics) and individual well-being (Fried & Ferris, 1987; Jackson & Schuler, 1985). However, the relationships between job design variables and performance were inconsistant across studies and low in size (Jackson & Schuler, 1985; Parker & Turner, this volume). Nevertheless, there are experimental and intervention studies which show that improvements in job design result in both higher performance and better individual well-being (Manning, Ismael, & Sherwood, 1981).

Additionally to work situation factors one might think of person factors as third variables which (partially) account for the relationship between well-being and job performance. In some studies, authors controlled for demographic and other person factors (e.g., negative affectivity). It turned out, that the relationship between well-being and job performance could neither be explained by demographic variables (Wright & Staw, 1999) nor by positive or negative affectivity (Wright & Cropanzano, 1998). However, there might be other factors which play a role in the relationship between well-being and job performance. For example, aspects of self-regulation might be prime candidates for such a person factors which act as third variables.

SELF-REGULATION, WELL-BEING, AND PERFORMANCE

There is clear empirical evidence that aspects of self-regulation have an effect on performance (Kluger & DeNisi, 1996; Locke & Latham, 1990; Stajkovic & Luthans, 1998). Moreover, empirical research summarized in this chapter showed that aspects of self-regulation are related to individual well-being. For example, individuals with extensive feedback-seeking behavior and high self-efficacy experience a better well-being than individuals low on feedback seeking and self-efficacy. However, direct relationships between goal setting and well-being are relatively small in size. Unfortunately, longitudinal studies in this area are still rare, thus the existing studies offer several causal interpretations.

A first plausible interpretation is that self-regulatory processes such as feedback seeking and self-efficacy have a positive impact on well-being. For example, feedback seeking reduces uncertainty and therefore well-being might increase. Possible mediating

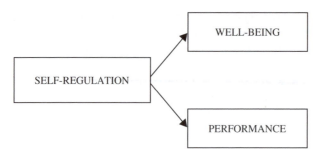

FIGURE 20.1   Self-regulation as the common source

mechanisms with respect to self-efficacy include favorable coping processes. Individuals high on self-efficacy will expect that they can sucessfully deal with the stressors at hand and therefore engage in more favorable coping behaviors which have a positive impact on individual well-being.

When linking this interpretation of a causal process of self-regulation on well-being to the finding that self-regulatory processes have an effect on job performance, one can consider self-regulation as a common source of both well-being and job performance. This implies that both well-being and job performance benefit from good self-regulatory processes, while poor self-regulation is detrimental both for well-being and job performance. Figure 20.1 shows this 'self-regulation as a common source' model graphically. How can we link this interpretation to the empirical finding that well-being has an effect on performance (e.g., Staw et al., 1994)? One would argue that self-regulation is the common source of performance and well-being, with well-being having an additional positive effect on performance—an effect which might not only be caused by self-regulation but also by others factors.

Assuming a causal effect of self-regulation on well-being, is not the only possible interpretation of the empirical relationship between self-regulation and well-being. There is some evidence from experimental studies that positive mood has a benefical effect on self-regulatory processes (Baron, 1990; Trope & Neter, 1994). Although induced positive mood is conceptually different from positive well-being as a relatively stable individual characteristic it might be that a similar effect exists for well-being. This would imply that well-being has a positive effect on self-regulation which in turn has a positive impact on job performance. Within this interpretation, self-regulation is the mediator in the well-being–performance relationship. This 'self-regulation as a mediator' model is displayed in Figure 20.2.

However, before arriving at far-reaching conclusions, a caveat is necessary. Findings about the effects of mood on self-regulation and related processes are not at all unequivocal. There is a large body of research which showed detrimental effects of positive mood on information processing (cf. for a review Schwarz & Bohner, 1996). It is only

FIGURE 20.2   Self-regulation as a mediator

recently that researchers question the negative effects of positive mood on information processing and self-regulation and rather focus on the potential benefits of positive mood (Aspinwall, 1998; Schwarz & Bohner, 1996).

These two models imply different practical implications: the 'self-regulation as a common source' model suggests a focus on individuals' self-regulatory processes as a means of increasing job performance and ensuring well-being. For example, one might design interventions which increase individuals' self-efficacy or one might encourage individuals to seek feedback more extensively. The 'self-regulation as a mediator' model suggests a start with improving individuals' well-being which in turn is expected to impact self-regulation and subsequently performance. Here, one might consider job design issues or specific intervention programs aiming at a direct improvement of individual well-being.

CONCLUSIONS

Without doubt more research is necessary in the area of well-being, performance, and self-regulation. Above all, longitudinal studies are highly needed. Future researchers might address three interrelated questions. First, they should examine the causal relationship between well-being and performance. In addition to the effect of well-being on performance, special attention should be paid to the possible positive effect of performance on well-being. Second, the effects of well-being on self-regulation and vice versa should be studied. Here, it is particularly important to examine whether the findings on the effects of induced mood may be generalized to habitual positive well-being and whether they hold in applied settings. Third, self-regulation in its relationship to both well-being and performance has to be studied. In this chapter, it was discussed whether self-regulation might be a common source of both well-being and performance. Framed in more technical terms, this would imply that self-regulation is a third variable which accounts for the relationship between well-being and performance. Alternatively, it might be that self-regulation is the mediator in the well-being–performance relationship.

To sum up, performance and individual well-being are two important outcome measures in work and organizational psychological research. Moreover, they are the major criteria of professional practice within work and organizational psychology. Although performance and well-being are distinct at the conceptual level they are linked empirically. This is good news from an applied perspective because enhancing performance does not contradict the improvement of individual well-being.

Self-regulatory processes play an important role both with repect to well-being and performance. Future research will reveal whether it is more appropriate to conceptualize self-regulation as the common source of both performance and well-being or to regard self-regulatory processes as the mediator and causal link between well-being and performance.

REFERENCES

Ashford, S. J., & Black, J. S. (1996). Proactivity during organizational entry: The role of desire for control. *Journal of Applied Psychology*, **81**, 199–214.

Ashford, S. J., & Cummings, L. L. (1983). Feedback as an individual resource: Personal strategies of creating information. *Organizational Behavior and Human Performance*, **32**, 370–398.

Ashford, S. J., & Tsui, S. A. (1991). Self-regulation for managerial effectiveness: The role of active feedback seeking. *Academy of Management Journal*, **34**, 251–280.

Aspinwall, L. G. (1998). Rethinking the role of positive affect in self-regulation. *Motivation and Emotion*, **22**, 1–32.

Austin, J. T., & Vancouver, J. B. (1996). Goal constructs in psychology: Structure, process, and content. *Psychological Bulletin*, **120**, 338–375.

Bandura, A. (1997). *Self-efficacy: The exercise of control*: Freeman.

Baron, R. A. (1990). Environmentally induced positive affect: Its impact on self-efficacy, task performance, negotiation, and conflict. *Journal of Applied Social Psychology*, **20**, 368–384.

Battmann, W. (1988). Feedback seeking as a means of self-assessment and affect optimization. *Motivation and Emotion*, **12**, 57–74.

Beehr, T. A., Jex, S. M., Stacy, B. A., & Murray, M. A. (2000). Work stressors and coworker support as predictors of individual strain and job performance. *Journal of Organizational Behavior*, **21**, 391–405.

Bluen, S. D., Barling, J., & Burns, W. (1990). Perdicting sales performance, job satisfaction, and depression by using the achievement strivings and impatience-irritability dimensions of Type A behavior. *Journal of Applied Psychology*, **75**, 212–216.

Borman, W. C., & Motowidlo, S. J. (1993). Expanding the criterion domain to include elements of contextual performance. In N. Schmitt & W. Borman (Eds.), *Personnel selection in organizations* (pp. 71–98). New York: Jossey-Bass.

Brouwers, A., & Tomic, W. (1998). Ordeverstorend gedrag van leerlingen, waargenomen eigen competentie en burnout onder leraren. *Nederlands Tijdschrift voor de Psychologie en haar Grensgebieden*, **54**, 173–183.

Brunstein, J. C. (1993). Personal goals and subjective well-being: A longitudinal study. *Journal of Personality and Social Psychology*, **65**, 1061–1070.

Brunstein, J. C., Schultheiss, O. C., & Maier, G. W. (1999). The pursuit of personal goals: A motivational approach to well-being and life adjustment. In J. Brandstätter & R. M. Lerner (Eds.), *Action and self-development: Theory and research through the life span* (pp. 169–196). Thousand Oaks, CA: Sage.

Campbell, J. P., McCloy, R. A., Oppler, S. H., & Sager, C. E. (1993). A theory of performance. In E. Schmitt, W. C. Borman, & Associates (Eds.), *Personnel selection in organizations* (pp. 35–70). San Francisco: Jossey-Bass.

Cardy, R. L., & Dobbins, G. H. (1986). Affect and appraisal accuracy: Liking as an integral dimension in evaluating performance. *Journal of Applied Psychology*, **71**, 672–678.

Carver, C. S., & Scheier, M. F. (1999). Themes and issues in the self-regulation of behavior. In R. S. Wyer (Ed.), *Perspectives on behavioral self-regulation* (pp. 1–105). Mahwah, NJ: Erlbaum.

Chwalisz, K., Altmaier, E. M., & Russell, D. W. (1992). Causal attributions, self-efficacy cognitions, and coping with stress. *Journal of Social and Clinical Psychology*, **11**, 377–400.

Cropanzano, R., & Wright, T. A. (1999). A 5-year study of change in the relationship between well-being and job performance. *Consulting Psychology Journal: Practice and Research*, **51**, 252–265.

Diener, E., Suh, E. M., Lucas, R. E., & Smith, H. L. (1999). Subjective well-being: Three decades of progress. *Psychological Bulletin*, **125**, 276–302.

Dollard, M. F., Winefield, H. R., Winefield, A. H., & deJonge, J. (2000). Psychosocial job straina and productivity in human service workers: A test of the demand–control–support model. *Journal of Occupational and Organizational Psychology*, **73**, 501–510.

Emmons, R. A. (1986). Personal strivings: An apporach to personality and subjective well-being. *Journal of Personality and Social Psychology*, **51**, 1058–1068.

Emmons, R. A. (1991). Personal strivings, daily life events, and psychological and physical well-being. *Journal of Personality*, **59**, 453–472.

Emmons, R. A. (1996). Striving and feeling: Personal goals and subjective well-being. In P. M. Gollwitzer & J. A. Bargh (Eds.), *The psychology of action: Linking cognition and motivation to behavior* (pp. 313–337). New York: Guilford.

Frese, M., & Zapf, D. (1994). Action as the core of work psychology: A german approach. In H. C. Triandis, M. D. Dunnette, & L. M. Hough (Eds.), *Handbook of industrial and organizational psychology* (2nd edn., vol. 4, pp. 271–340). Palo Alto, CA: Consulting Psychologists Press.

Fried, Y., & Ferris, G. R. (1987). The validity of the job characteristics model: A review and meta-analysis. *Personnel Psychology*, **40**, 287–322.

George, J. M., & Brief, A. P. (1996). Motivational agenda in the workplace: The effects of feelings on focus of attention and work motivation. In B. M. Staw & L. L. Cummings (Eds.), *Research in organizational behavior* (Vol. 19, pp. 75–109). Greenwich, CT: JAI Press.

Glaser, D. M., Tatum, B. C., Nebeker, D. M., Sorenson, R. C., & Aiello, J. R. (1999). Workload and social support: Effects on performance and stress. *Human Performance*, **12**, 155–176.

Gorgievski-Duijvesteijn, M. J., Giesen, C. W. M., & Bakker, A. B. (2000). Financial problems and health complaints among farm couples: Results of a 10-year follow-up study. *Journal of Occupational Health Psychology*, **5**, 359–373.

Hackman, J. R., & Oldham, G. R. (1976). Motivation through the design of work: Test of a theory. *Organizational Behavior and Human Performance*, **16**, 250–279.

Holden, G. (1991). The relationship of self-efficacy appraisals to subsequent health related outcomes: A meta-analysis. *Social Work in Health Care*, **16**, 53–93.

Iffaldano, M. T., & Muchinsky, P. M. (1985). Job satisfaction and job performance: A meta-analysis. *Psychological Bulletin*, **97**, 251–273.

Ilgen, D. R., & Pulakos, E. D. (Eds.) (1999). *The changing nature of performance: Implications for staffing, motivation, and development*. San Francisco: Jossey-Bass.

Jackson, S. E., & Schuler, R. S. (1985). A meta-analysis and conceptual critique of research on role ambiguity and role conflict in work settings. *Organizational Behavior and Human Performance*, **33**, 1–21.

Jex, S. M., & Bliese, P. D. (1999). Efficacy beliefs as a moderator of the impact of work-related stressors: A multilevel study. *Journal of Applied Psychology*, **84**, 349–361.

Jex, S. M., & Elacqua, T. C. (1999). Self-esteem as a moderator: A comparison of global and organization-based measures. *Journal of Occupational and Organizational Psychology*, **72**, 71–81.

Jex, S. M., & Gudanowski, D. M. (1992). efficacy beliefs and work stress: An exploratory study. *Journal of Occupational Behavior*, **13**, 509–517.

Kahn, R. L., & Byosiere, P. (1992). Stress in organizations. In M. D. Dunnette & L. M. Hough (Eds.), *Handbook of industrial and organizational psychology* (2nd edn., Vol. 3, pp. 571–650). Palo Alto, CA: Consulting Psychologists Press.

Kahn, R. L., Wolfe, D. M., Quinn, R. P., Snoek, J. D., & Rosenthal, R. A. (1964). *Organizational stress: Studies in role conflict and ambiguity*. New York: Wiley.

Kahn, S. E., & Long, B. C. (1988). Work-related stress, self-efficacy, and well-being of femal clerical workers. *Counselling Psychology Quarterly*, **1**, 145–153.

Kanfer, R., & Kanfer, F. H. (1991). Goals and self-regulation: Applications of theory to work settings. In M. L. Maehr & P. R. Pintrich (Eds.), *Advances in motivation* (Vol. 7, pp. 287–326). Greenwich, CT: JAI Press.

Karoly, P. (1993). Mechanisms of self-regulation: A systems view. *Annual Review of Psychology*, **44**, 23–52.

Kluger, A. N., & DeNisi, A. (1996). The effects of feedback interventions on performance: A historical review, a meta-analysis, and a preliminary feedback intervention theory. *Psychological Bulletin*, **119**, 254–284.

Latham, G. P., & Locke, E. A. (1991). Self-regulation through goal setting. *Organizational Behavior and Human Decision Processes*, **50**, 212–247.

Lazarus, R. S., & Folkman, S. (1984). *Stress, appraisal, and coping*. New York: Springer.

Leiter, M. P. (1992). Burn-out as a crisis in self-efficacy: Conceptual and practical implications. *Work and Stress*, **6**, 107–115.

Leiter, M. P., Harview, P., & Frizzel, C. (1998). The correspondence of patient satisfaction and nurse burnout. *Social Science and Medicine*, **47**, 1611–1617.

Lindsley, D. H., Brass, D. J., & Thomas, J. B. (1995). Efficacy-performance spirals: A multilevel perspective. *Academy of Management Review*, **20**, 645–678.

Locke, E. A., & Latham, G. O. (1990). *A theory of goal setting and task performance*. Englewood Cliffs, NJ: Prentice Hall.

Maier, G. W. (1996). *Perönliche Ziele im Unternehmen: Ergebnisse einrr Längsschnittstudie bei Berufseinsteigern*. Unpublished Dissertation, University of Munich, Munich.

Maier, G. W., & Brunstein, J. C. (2001). The role of personal work goald in newcomers' job satisfaction and organizational commitment: A longitudinal analysis. *Journal of Applied Psychology*, **86**, 1034–1042.

Manning, M. R., Ismael, A. H., & Sherwood, J. J. (1981). Effects of role conflict on selected physiological, affective, and performance variables. *Multivariate Behavioral Reserach*, **16**, 125–141.

Martin, J. K., Blum, T. C., Beach, S. R. H., & Roman, P. M. (1996). Subclinical depression and performance at work. *Social Psychiatry*, **31**, 3–9.

Maslach, C., & Jackson, S. E. (1981). The measurement of experienced burnout. *Journal of Organizational Behavior*, **2**, 99–113.

Mohr, G. B. (2000). The changing significance of different stressors after the announcement of bankruptcy: a longitudinal investigation with special emphasis on job insecurity. *Journal of Organizational Behavior*, **21**, 337–359.

Morrison, E. W. (1993a). Longitudinal study of the effects of information seeking on newcomer socialization. *Journal of Applied Psychology*, **78**, 173–183.

Morrison, E. W. (1993b). Newcomer information seeking: Exploring types, modes, sources, and outcomes. *Academy of Management Journal*, **36**, 557–589.

Morrison, E. W., & Bies, R. J. (1991). Impression management in the feedback-seeking process: A literature review and research agenda. *Academy of Management Review*, **16**, 522–541.

Morrison, E. W., & Weldon, E. (1990). The impact of an assigned performance goal on feedback seeking behavior. *Human Performance*, **3**, 37–50.

Motowidlo, S. J., Packard, J. S., & Manning, M. R. (1986). Occupational stress: Its causes and consequences on job performance. *Journal of Applied Psychology*, **71**, 618–629.

Mughal, S., Walsh, J., & Wilding, J. (1996). Stress and work performance: The role of traint anxiety. *Personality and Individual differences*, **20**, 685–691.

Omodei, M. M., & Wearing, A. J. (1990). Need satisfaction and involvement in personal projects: Toward an integrative model of subjective well-being. *Journal of Personality and Social Psychology*, **59**, 762–769.

Parker, P. A., & Kulik, J. A. (1995). Burnout, self- and supervisor-rated job performance, and absenteeism among nurses. *Journal of Behavioral Medicine*, **18**, 581–599.

Petty, M. M., McGee, G. W., & Cavender, J. W. (1984). A meta-analysis of the relationship between individual job satisfaction and individual performance. *Academy of Management Review*, **9**, 712–721.

Rodgers, R., Hunter, J. E., & Rogers, D. L. (1993). Influence of top management commitment on management program success. *Journal of Applied Psychology*, **78**, 151–155.

Roe, R. A. (1999). Work performance: A multiple regulation perspective. In C. L. Cooper & I. T. Robertson (Eds.), *International Review of Industrial and Organizational Psychology* (Vol. 14, pp. 231–335). Chichester: Wiley.

Roethlisberger, F. J., & Dickson, W. J. (1939). *Management and the worker*. Cambridge, MA: Harvard University Press.

Sadri, G., & Robertson, I. T. (1993). Self-efficacy and work-related behaviour: A review and meta-analysis. *Applied Psychology: An International Review*, **42**, 139–152.

Schwarz, N., & Bohner, G. (1996). Feelings and their motivational implications: Moods and the action sequence. In P. M. Gollwitzer & J. A. Bargh (Eds.), *The psychology of action: Linking cognition and motivation to behavior* (pp. 119–145). New York: Guilford.

Semmer, N. (1996). Individual differences, work stress and health. In M. J. Schabracq, J. A. M. Winnubst, & C. L. Cooper (Eds.), *Handbook of work and health psychology* (pp. 51–86). Chichester: Wiley.

Shaw, J. B., & Weekley, J. A. (1985). The effects of objective work-load variations of psychological strain and post-work-load performance. *Journal of Management*, **11**, 87–98.

Spector, P. E., Dwyer, D. J., & Jex, S. M. (1988). Relation of job stressors to affective, health, and performance outcomes: A comparison of multiple data sources. *Journal of Applied Psychology*, **73**, 11–19.

Stajkovic, A. D., & Luthans, F. (1998). Self-efficacy and work-related performance: A meta-analysis. *Psychological Bulletin*, **124**, 240–261.

Staw, B. M., Sutton, R. I., & Pelled, L. H. (1994). Employee positive emotion and favorable outcomes at the workplace. *Organization Science*, **5**, 51–71.

Terry, D. J., Callan, V. J., & Sartori, G. (1996). Employee adjustment to an organizational merger: Stress, coping and intergroup differences. *Stress Medicine*, **12**, 105–122.

Terry, D. J., Tonge, L., & Callan, V. J. (1995). Employee adjustment to stress: The role of coping resources, situational factors, and coping responses. *Anxiety, Stress, and Coping*, **8**, 1–24.

Trist, E. L., & Bamforth, K. W. (1951). Some social and psychological consequences of the long-wall method of coal-getting. *Human Relations*, **4**, 3–38.

Trope, Y., & Neter, E. (1994). Reconciling competing motives in self-evaluation: The role of self-control in feedback seeking. *Journal of Personality and Social Psychology*, **66**, 646–657.

Tsui, A. S., Ashford, S. J., St. Clair, L., & Xin, K. R. (1995). Dealing with discrepant expectations: Response strategies and managerial effectiveness. *Academy of Management Journal*, **38**, 1515–1543.

VanYperen, N. W. (1998). Informational support, equity and burnout: The moderating effect of self-efficacy. *Journal of Occupational and Organizational Psychology*, **71**, 29–33.

Warr, P. (1990). The measurement of well-being and other aspects of mental health. *Journal of Occupational Psychology*, **63**, 193–210.

Wright, T. A., & Bonett, D. G. (1997). The role of pleasantness and activation-based well-being in performance prediction. *Journal of Occupational Health Psychology*, **2**, 212–219.

Wright, T. A., Bonett, D. G., & Sweeney, D. A. (1993). Mental health and work performance. *Journal of Occupational and Organizational Psychology*, **66**, 277–284.

Wright, T. A., & Cropanzano, R. (1998). Emotional exhaustion as a predictor of job performance and voluntary turnover. *Journal of Applied Psychology*, **83**, 486–493.

Wright, T. A., & Cropanzano, R. (2000). Psychological well-being and job satisfaction as predictors of job performance. *Journal of Occupational Health Psychology*, **5**, 84–94.

Wright, T. A., & Staw, B. M. (1999). Affect and favorable work outcomes: two longitudinal tests of the happy-productive worker thesis. *Journal of Occupational Behavior*, **20**, 1–23.

Well-Being, Stress Management and Performance: From Analysis to Intervention

Rendel D. de Jong
Utrecht University, Utrecht, The Netherlands

SUMMARY

Traditional stress management approaches and their effectiveness are discussed. Stress management is relevant for job performance because of causal links between emotional states and job effectiveness. Stress management focused at the individual is moderately effective in the reduction of strains like anxiety and depression, with effect sizes of about .50. Cognitive-behavioral treatment is effective for employees in positions with high job control, relaxation for individuals with low job control. Interventions aimed at the level of the organization were, in general, ineffective. Several explanations are discussed, among them a lack of impact and specific focus, and a lack of attention to the behavior of leaders as focal persons. Implications for practice are discussed and practical examples are given. Individual approaches are likely to enhance effectiveness, possibly mediated by positive emotional states and self-regulatory processes. Interventions like management coaching and consultation are promising in the enhancement of emotional states and performance of teams and individuals.

Psychological Management of Individual Performance. Edited by Sabine Sonnentag.

INTRODUCTION

Indicators of individual well-being are related to performance. The results of cross-sectional and longitudinal studies suggest that depression and exhaustion may cause low performance, while, on the other hand, positive mood (rather than job satisfaction) enhances effectiveness in the job (Wright & Cropanzano, 2000; Sonnentag, this volume). Individual stress management interventions have been found effective in the reduction of complaints like depression and burnout and in fostering the development of psychological resources (Van der Klink, Blonk, Schene, & Van Dijk, 2001). These resources are also related directly to performance. As a consequence, not only the quality of life but also performance may benefit from individual stress management interventions. In addition, stress management can help to prevent the occurrence of negative long-term consequences of stress reactions like psychosomatic impairment and absence due to illness. Because of their potential for enhancing organizational quality of life and performance, an overview of individual stress management interventions is presented in this chapter.

Less obvious is the benefit of organization and team level stress interventions for individual well-being and performance. Surprisingly, Van der Klink et al. (2001) did not find much effect for organizationally focused interventions in their meta-analysis. Among other factors, a lack of an individually tailored focus was mentioned as a possible cause of their finding. In a similar vein, Briner and Reynolds (1999) conclude that organizational interventions cannot provide a simple solution to the complex problems of undesirable employee states and behaviors. Moreover, global interventions directed at the organization or department as a whole may simply not be powerful enough to have a real impact. Because of the strong impact of the actions of managers and supervisors at the various levels in the organization on the well-being and performance of the members, interventions directed at their behavior may be helpful.

As made clear by Sonnentag in Chapter 20, the individual differences moderating the effects of various interventions, like self-efficacy, are related to self-regulating processes. These variables are also very important as determinants of the stress-arousing effects of such performance-oriented procedures as goal setting. In the absence of self-efficacy, goal setting may have an adverse effect on performance and, moreover, on well-being.

It is the first aim of this chapter to discuss traditional individual and organization level stress management methods and their effectiveness. In addition, attention will be given to approaches aimed at the improvement of well-being and performance of individuals in groups and organizations through interventions directed at their managers and supervisors. Findings suggesting that the outcome of performance-enhancing actions like goal setting is dependent on self-efficacy will be mentioned. Finally, practical implications will be discussed.

STRESS MANAGEMENT INTERVENTIONS

STRESS: STRESSORS AND STRAINS

Stress can be conceptualized as a state of tension that is experienced as aversive (Semmer, 1996). In this conception, stress involves negative emotional states like anxiety, anger and depression, due to an imbalance between the demands or burden confronting the individual on the one hand and his or her ability to cope with them on the other. The negative consequences of the imbalance are indicated as *"strains"* or *"stress reactions"*, and typically consist of increases of negative states and a decrease of positive emotional states. In addition to emotional states, reactions can be somatic (illness) and behavioral, including performance. The demands or burdens are referred to as *"stressors"* and comprise many aspects such as work overload, ambiguity, insecurity, and dramatic changes in the circumstances of work and private life.

The ability to cope with stressors is indicated by a variety of individual difference variables. The impact of work-related stressors is moderated not only by personality factors and motivational tendencies like internal–external control, emotional stability, and involved striving (type A), but also by (subjective) competencies. Individual differences in needs and preferences may even determine if a certain environment is experienced as stressful at all.

Theoretically, all three aspects of stress—the stress reaction itself, individual differences in coping potential and, finally, the demanding environmental conditions (the stressors)—are potential targets for stress management interventions. However, the point of application of stress management techniques is rarely the stress reaction proper. Only substances like tranquilizers and antidepressants influence stress-related emotional states and physiological reactions directly. Individual psychological and behavioral interventions, as discussed in this chapter, are actually aimed at the individual's coping skills. Organization level interventions, on the other hand, attempt to modify some stressors in the (work) environment.

INDIVIDUAL STRESS MANAGEMENT: ENHANCING THE INDIVIDUAL'S COPING POTENTIAL

The expression "stress management" commonly refers to interventions aimed at the reduction of stress symptoms like tension, anxiety, depression, and exhaustion through the enhancement of the person's coping ability (Murphy, 1996). Following Folkman and Lazarus (1980) coping can be divided in two classes: emotion focused and problem focused. Emotion-focused coping is, of course, directed at the reduction of negative emotional states, while problem-focused coping refers to the individual's attempts to alter the undesirable, stress-inducing aspects of the situation. In other words, emotion-focused stress management methods attempt to help the individual to handle his or her bad feelings; problem-focused stress management teaches the individual how to change unpleasant work situations and to communicate with difficult people. Pure examples of the two kinds of stress management are, of course, rare. Effective social skill training, for example, is not only likely to enhance social skills but also to reduce social anxiety.

Relaxation training

The most direct attempt to attack stress symptoms is *relaxation training*, which was an important ingredient of various counter-conditioning techniques developed by behavior therapists in the 1950s (Wolpe, 1958). Relaxation training is based on the "progressive muscle relaxation" technique developed by Jacobson (1938). The underlying idea was that the relaxation of muscle tension would reduce "autonomic activity", and that this reduction, in turn, would cause a decrease in anxiety levels.

In this procedure, the client was seated in a comfortable (recliner) chair or lying on a couch, preferably in a quiet, softly lit room. The therapist was supposed to give instructions in a quiet, soft, and pleasant tone of voice. A session could start with the instruction to take a deep breath and hold it for about 10 seconds. After that, the client was asked to tense and then relax muscle groups in the body, working from a fist toward the feet. The original procedure designed by Jacobson (1938), taking 50 or more sessions, was shortened to about three in later versions. Any increased efficiency could be due to the introduction of "homework", requiring the client to practice relaxation twice a day with the help of an instructional tape.

In behavior therapy, relaxation is generally used as a tool within the process of desensitization or counter-conditioning. In this approach, the client is exposed to a series of increasingly anxiety-evoking stimuli. By employing relaxation as an antidote to anxiety, the client learns to master the threatening conditions.

In stress management, relaxation techniques are usually not combined with desensitization. Relaxation is one of the techniques included in the meta-study by Van der Klink et al. (in press), which shows that relaxation, as expected, has a significant effect on physiological reactions and psychological symptoms. The strength of the effects was expressed as a d-effect size, i.e., the difference of the means of the target variable in the treatment condition and in the control group, divided by the pooled standard deviations of the experimental and the control group. For both physiological reactions and psychological symptoms, the effect of the intervention was around .3. Interestingly, relaxation influenced the perception of working conditions (job control, job demand, social support) with an effect size of the same magnitude. The effect on psychological resources like self-esteem and coping skills was slightly smaller (.26).

However, the effectiveness of relaxation techniques was found to be dependent on work circumstances. The lower the person's control over his or her work situation, the stronger were the effects of relaxation training (Van der Klink et al., in press).

Cognitive-behavioral methods

Cognitive-behavioral approaches include a variety of methods. They aim at changing cognitions and subsequently reinforcing active coping skills. Traditionally, these methods are based on the idea that "faulty" thinking patters and appraisal habits make life more stressful than necessary and, as a consequence, require modification. In Rational Emotive Therapy (RET), developed by Albert Ellis, irrational philosophies or thinking patterns are the primary target of intervention. As Ellis put it, the modification of these thinking patterns can help people to remain sane in a crazy world (Ellis, 1962, 1973). Examples of these philosophies are:

- It is necessary to be loved and respected by all significant others.
- A person is only valuable when he or she is completely competent and successful.
- People are wicked and should be punished.

Thinking patterns are analyzed by means of the "ABC" paradigm. The clients are asked to describe a so-called problematic situation (A) in neutral terms, to take stock of the thoughts (B) evoked by that situation, and finally the emotions (C) that are caused by the thoughts. The thoughts are tested with respect to their "rationality", in other words, whether they are based on well-established facts and whether they are helpful in the accomplishments of the clients' goals. The clients are invited to substitute their "irrational" thinking patterns with more "rational" alternatives. After the modification of the thinking pattern, confrontation with difficult situations can be rehearsed symbolically and in reality.

In the stress inoculation approach of Meichenbaum (1972, 1985), primary and secondary appraisal patterns are considered as crucial in the development of undesirable stress reactions, and, as a consequence, an important therapeutic target. Basically, the client is taught, by means of coaching and modeling of adaptive "self-talk", to adopt more effective active coping patterns. The method has been used in the treatment of test anxiety and other less effective reactions in the confrontation with a variety of threatening situations.

In the meta-study, cognitive-behavioral methods were found to be very effective. With respect to the reduction of psychological complaints, the effect size was .52. An even stronger effect was found on psychological resources, .65. Also the perception of working conditions was changed remarkably, as indicated by an effect size of .48. Physiological reactions, however, did not change (Van der Klink et al., 2001). More specifically, Saunders, Driskell, Johnston, and Salas (1996) examined the impact of stress inoculation on anxiety levels and task performance in a meta-study. The effect size was .56 for performance anxiety, .39 for state anxiety, and .30 for task performance. It should be noted that most of the studies included in the meta-analysis related to tasks in educational and laboratory settings rather than to working conditions.

Multi-modal interventions

In multi-modal interventions, the focus is on a mix of coping skills. Recently, for instance, the impact of a stress management program consisting of a combination of muscle relaxation, problem-solving skills training, assertiveness training, and a training in awareness of stressors and coping style was examined in comparison to an assessment-only control group (de Jong & Emmelkamp, 2000). The training was delivered in eight $2\frac{1}{2}$-hour sessions. The training had a low to moderate effect on general symptoms and distress in situations requiring assertive responses, but no effect on the perception of working conditions.

Van Dierendonck, Schaufeli, and Buunk (1998) developed a burnout intervention program primarily designed to reduce feelings of inequity resulting from a discrepancy between the goals and expectations of the person and the degree that these wishes were fulfilled by the organization. In addition, the participants were stimulated to change some less satisfactory aspects of their work situation. The supervisors of the participants received a similar program. When compared to internal and external control groups, emotional exhaustion had been reduced in the intervention group 6 and 12 months after the end of the training. However, the outcome could partly be due to an increase in exhaustion in the control groups.

The results of the meta-analysis (Van der Klink et al., 2001) show a sizable effect of multi-modal interventions on complaints (.48) and on physiology (.36), but a heterogeneous effect on working conditions and no effect on psychological resources. It is self-evident that the effects of multi-modal approaches are dependent upon the specific mix of interventions that are employed.

STRESS MANAGEMENT AT THE LEVEL OF THE ORGANIZATION

A radical approach to occupational health is the creation of healthy work environments. According to the philosophy of preventive stress management, individual and organizational health are to be considered as interdependent, and the management has a responsibility for both. Optimistically, individual and organizational health are not seen as conflicting goals, but are both considered as the outcome of effective management practices (Quick, Paulus, Whittington, Larey, & Nelson, 1996).

The problem is to find ways to change the organization when it is not found to be a very healthy place to work. One way is to apply individual stress management methods organization wide. Another is to intervene in the occupational context, by means of the development of the organization as a whole in the removal of work-related stressors in the direct environment of the employee.

Individual stress management provided at the *organizational level* may be more than the equivalent of the sum of individual interventions. Just as negative mood appears to be contagious, so may be health. As a consequence, organization-wide programs may not just influence individual well-being, but organization level parameters as well. An example of the organization-wide application of individual stress management interventions is the Johnson & Johnson "Live for Life" program, including physical fitness training, cognitive restructuring, smoking cessation, and blood pressure and cholesterol management (Quick et al., 1996). Compared to a control group, the interventions resulted in reduced inpatient health care costs (reduction of hospital days), but did not affect outpatient treatment expenditure and other health care costs.

In intervening in the *occupational context*, various points of attack can be distinguished, varying from the person–work interface to the organization as a whole. At the direct *person–work interface*, work(over)load, role conflict, role ambiguity, and job insecurity have been found to be related to emotional symptoms and physiological reactions in studies in the Michigan tradition (Caplan & Jones, 1975, Winnubst, De Jong, & Schabracq, 1996). Lack of social support was related to stress reactions, while a high level of support could "buffer" the impact of other stressful conditions. Research in several traditions shows the effects of a lack of job autonomy or decision latitude on emotional symptoms. In addition, the results of research indicate the impact on well-being of the opportunity to make use of skills and to participate in decision making (Jones & Fletcher, 1996).

Based on theorizing and the outcome of stress research, a variety of procedures to reduce stress have been prescribed. It is suggested that jobs should be designed in such a way that they allow for skill development, job security, participation, and social support, but avoid repetitive, machine-paced work, role conflict, and role ambiguity. Greater control was advised with respect to various aspects of work (Landsbergis & Vivona-Vaughan, 1995).

Reports on interventions aimed at the *occupational context* are relatively scarce. In their review of 1990, Ivancevich, Matteson, Freedman, and Phillips identified only four studies that used organizational stressors as intervention targets. In only two of these studies was a control group included. These two studies (Jackson, 1983; Jones, Barge, Steffy, Fay, Kunz, & Wuebker, 1988) were also included in the meta-study by Van der Klink et al. (2001). In addition, two other publications that reported on studies that made use of control groups were included in their meta-study. Because of the scarcity

of information on interventions at the occupational level, the intervention methods employed, and their outcome, will be discussed more fully than studies on the effect of
interventions at the individual level.

In Jackson's (1983) study, hospital employees were offered (additional) opportunities
to participate in decisions. In the intervention condition, staff meetings of 12 semi-
autonomous units were increased in frequency from once a month to at least twice a
month, while the frequency remained the same in the 10 units in the control group. In
addition, all unit heads attended a 2-day training on leading group meetings and were
given a list of possible discussion topics for the meetings.

Indicators of job stressors, social support, and emotional strain were measured by
means of a questionnaire before the intervention and in two post-tests after three and six
months. The impact of the intervention is not easy to evaluate due to problems in the
design of the study. Because a Solomon four-group design was employed, a pre-test was
available for only half of the subjects. In addition, about 25% of the original 126 participants dropped out of the study at the three-month follow-up and an additional 20% at the
time of the second follow-up six months later, leaving only 55% of original sample available for analysis. Because all remaining subjects at each measurement were included in
the analysis, the cause of the significant difference in strain between the intervention and
the control group at the first and the second post-tests (effect sizes .4 and .3, respectively)
remains unclear. The results may be caused by the intervention but could also be due to
selective students dropping out. The same problem arises in the interpretation of the significant differences between the control and the intervention conditions with respect to
perceived influence, role conflict, and role ambiguity. Furthermore, differences between
the units were not taken into account. As a consequence, an important condition for the
statistical tests employed—i.e., independence of the individual scores—may not have
been met. Jackson mentioned supervisory style as one of the unmeasured variables that
might account for some of the unexplained variance in perceived influence.

In one of the studies reported by Jones et al. (1988), interventions took place at various
levels in a hospital organization. The intervention consisted of five steps. The first step
was to administer a stress survey to almost all 700 members of the organization and
communicate the results to senior management. In the second step the managers of the
departments with the highest stress levels worked with consultants on a series of policy
and procedural changes. These changes included the improvement of personnel policies,
organization, and interdepartmental communication, in order to reduce stress. In the
third step, senior management discussed the survey results in small group sessions with
the whole staff. Employee feedback was encouraged, and action plans to manage stress
were established. In the fourth step, video-cassette training modules were seen by all
employees. The purpose of these training modules was to give the employees instruction
in how to develop relaxation routines for coping with stresses, how to smoke less, and
how to eat more healthily. Finally, an employee assistance and counseling program to
combat work-related and personal problems was provided. The number of (self-reported)
medicine errors was significantly lower after the stress management program than before.
Unfortunately, the medicine errors were the only outcome measure, and no control group
was included in the study.

In a second study, the same stress management program was administered to 22 hospitals that responded positively to an offer to participate. It is not clear how many hospitals
were approached originally and in what way they might differ from the experimental

group. The control group of 22 comparable hospitals was selected from a group of 91. It is not known whether they had been invited to participate in the experimental program earlier.

In this study, outcome was measured with an indicator of performance: the number of malpractice claims, or complaints because of supposedly incompetent or inappropriate treatment. After the implementation of the program, the number of claims dropped significantly (31 to 9), while the number did not change in a non-equivalent control group (36 to 35). In an earlier study, Jones et al. (1988) established the relation between organizational stress and job stress on the one hand and malpractice claims on the other. Because individual stress management methods were used in addition to organization level interventions, it is not clear what the cause of the effects really was. Unfortunately, a post-test of work stressors and psychological strain variables was lacking. As a consequence, it could not be established whether a reduction in stress due to the intervention really took place and whether the effects of the intervention on the number of claims were mediated by a reduction of stress levels.

A stress management project in a public health agency was described by Landsbergis and Vivona-Vaughan (1995). The first step in this project was the administration of a stress survey among the employees and a report on the results, and the formulation of recommendations to the top management. Two pairs of intervention and control departments (consisting of 41–21 and 25–26 employees) were selected. In the two experimental departments, committees with a number of ten and six members, respectively, were selected by the employees. The committees met formally five times in a seven-month period. They developed proposals and action plans to reduce stressors, provided feedback to other employees, and encouraged and assisted management in implementing changes. The intervention did not affect psychological strain, but in one of the intervention departments where employees were less satisfied with their jobs, goal clarity, skill utilization, and decision latitude were *reduced*, while job demands increased. After the experiment, committee members were moderately positive about the effectiveness of the (their own!) intervention, but the other employees were not.

Heaney, Price, and Rafferty (1995) intended to induce changes at the organizational level and at the level of individual perceptions in care staff and home managers in group homes for the mentally disabled. The homes were randomly assigned to an intervention and a control condition. In the intervention condition, 1,247 employees in 157 homes participated, while the control condition consisted of 963 employees working in 124 homes. The intervention was based on the "train-the-trainer" approach. From each home, the house manager was invited to take part and invite a direct care staff member to join him or her in the training program. The program was designed with two goals in mind: (1) to teach the employees about the helping potential of social support systems and to build skills in mobilizing available support; and (2) to teach employees about participatory problem-solving approaches and to build skills in implementing such approaches in work team meetings. The program consisted of six 2-hourly sessions, spread over a 10-week period. Each group consisted of the employees from 10 homes and received the training from a pair of trainers. Small, but significant intervention effects (standardized regression effects between .04 and .07) were found for supportive feedback in the team, and work team functioning and work team climate. No change was found for supervisor support. Depressive symptoms did not change, but somatization was reduced and self-appraised coping potential was increased. A subgroup analysis revealed that the intervention was effective for the improvement on all dependent variables in the employees who partic-ipated in the training, but no effect at all was found for the others. In other words, the intervention had very little "trickle down" effect.

"CLASSICAL" STRESS MANAGEMENT INTERVENTIONS: CONCLUSION

The results of the meta-study by Van der Klink et al. (in press) show that individually fo-cused interventions are effective in the reduction of indicators of anxiety and depression. The effect sizes, around .50, are reasonable compared to the results found in meta-studies on the effectiveness of psychological therapies in clinical conditions, where the effect sizes were about .40 (Shadish, Matt, Navarro, & Phillips, 2000). Cognitive-behavioral treatment works very well with employees with high job control, but is probably less effective when job control is low. Unfortunately, only in one of the studies was cognitive-behavioral treatment given to a low control group of employees. For this group, relaxation training appears to be consistently effective. It is interesting to note the strong impact of the cognitive-behavioral methods on psychological resources, or, in other words, indi-vidual difference variables related to self-regulatory processes. As these self-regulatory processes are related to well-being as well as to performance (Sonnentag, this volume), these processes probably mediate the positive effects of the interventions on both types of outcome.

Surprising is the effect of the individually focused intervention on (the perception of) stressful job conditions, with an average effect size of .41. It is not clear how this finding has to be interpreted. One explanation is that the person, in a better psychological condition and becoming more resourceful, simply experiences the job conditions as less stressful, without any change in the "objective" situation. A second possibility is that an improvement in well-being and an increase in psychological resources enables the person to change job conditions, possibly aided by the coaching and guidance of the counselor. The possible importance of individual-level interventions for organization level change is suggested by the results of Jones et al. (1988), which, according to Van der Klink et al., was the most successful study in the organizational focus category.

Van der Klink et al. (2001) give several explanations for the disappointing results of most of the interventions at the organizational level. In the first place, all outcomes were assessed at the individual level, while the intervention was directed at a higher level and thus its impact may possibly be more significant by processes at an intermediate level. Van der Klink et al. reason that more time would be required to pass through this causal chain of beneficial effects than the period allowed between intervention and follow up. A period of initial deterioration may have preceded eventual improvement. However, exposure to experimental job conditions has been found to influence mood rather quickly (Ganster & Fuselier, 1989). Relief from stressful job conditions, for instance, resulted in a sizable reduction of burnout in less than a week, but on re-exposure to these conditions, the original level of burnout recurred in only a few weeks (Etzion, Eden, & Lapidot, 1998). In the second place, according to Van der Klink et al. an individually tailored focus is lacking in the interventions. The only exception is the study by Heaney and colleagues (1995). In this study, the intervention was found to have a relatively strong impact on employees who were prone to leave the organization. Van der Klink et al. observe that most interventions aim at the enhancement of job control, while not everybody will be able to cope with that. Additional training may be needed to enable employees to make effective use of the opportunity to control the work environment. They speculate that the effect in the study of Jones et al. (1988) may be attributed to the application of an individual training in coping skills in their intervention.

It can be added that the researchers, with Jones et al. as exceptions, were rather optimistic about the impact of the interventions in their studies. As Van der Klink et al. mentioned, global interventions, directed at the organization level, probably require a longer period to be effective. However, the lack of results may not be a matter of time but may rather be due to a lack of power of the interventions as such. One cannot be sure that a 6- or 10-member committee, meeting five times will be able to design and implement effective action plans for the reduction of tough and tenacious stressors, as expected by Landsbergis and Vivona-Vaugan (1995). The extent to which the employees in this intervention were exposed to any influence is dramatically small in comparison to the massive treatment provided in the studies of Jones et al. (1988). Not only is the strength of the treatment as such, in terms of contact time and quality of the intervention, likely to play a role, but also the involvement of influential persons in the organization. Top management commitment was found to be crucial for the success of management programs, for instance (Rodgers, Hunter, & Rogers, 1993). In the study of Jones et al., care was taken to involve (top) management from the very start of the project. As remarked by Jackson (1983), the style of leadership and management is a potentially important but unmeasured variable in the prediction of perceived influence of the employees.

Summarizing: it is important for the practitioner to know that research on the results of individual stress management indicates that cognitive–behavioral and multi–modal methods are not only effective in the clinical setting but also are helpful to combat stress, especially for employees enjoying high job control. These methods are probably effective because of their direct impact on both passive and active coping resources, and on (perceived) job conditions. Relaxation methods are effective in the reduction of symptoms, also in case of low job control.

The results of stress management research offer much less information and suggestions when it comes to intervention directed at the occupational context. Too few controlled studies are available to make any estimate of the effect size of the various interventions. Imperfections in the design of several studies limit the interpretation of the available data. The role of managers and supervisors received no explicit attention.

ADDITIONAL APPROACHES

It is the first aim of this section to discuss briefly the connections between leadership style, employee mood and performance as well as interventions at the level of managers and supervisors. The second aim is to give attention to the interaction between self-efficacy and performance-related interventions such as goal setting and their implications for practice.

LEADERSHIP, STRESS AND PERFORMANCE

Leadership styles have been found to be related to psychological strains and well-being directly as well as mediated by job characteristics. Leadership style is related to performance through the mood and attitudes of the employee.

Traditionally, two broad leadership factors can be distinguished: consideration and initiating structure (Fleishman, Harris, & Burt, 1955). Consideration is characterized by a friendly, approachable, and supportive conduct of the leader. A leader high in initiating structure makes clear what has to be done and how it has to be done, and also stresses the need for a high level of performance. In addition to consideration and initiating structure, a variety of other measures emerged; for example, participative or consultative leadership refers to the involvement of the follower in decision making and open communication (Mulder, de Jong, Koppelaar, & Verhage, 1986; Wofford & Liska, 1993): Leader–member exchange (LMX) theory proposes that leaders establish different relations with different followers. In high-quality LMX relations, followers receive their leader's support and consideration, and assist and support the leader in return. In low LMX relations, leader and followers are distant and only do what is necessary for each other (Howell & Hall-Merenda, 1999). Transactional leadership (reward, laissez-faire) can be distinguished from transformational leadership, and is characterized by charisma and individualized consideration (Bass, 1985). An important aspect of the behavior of management and supervision is the degree of fairness experienced by the employee (George, 1991). Related is the concept of psychological contract (Robinson & Rousseau, 1994).

Generally speaking, consideration and participative/consultative leadership were related positively to job satisfaction and negatively to emotional states like anxiety, depression and burnout (Seltzer & Numerof, 1988; Wofford & Liska, 1993; Offermann & Helmann, 1996; De Jong, Voorendonk, Boogaarts, Le Blanc, Den Ouden, & Spuijbroek, 1996; Stoker & De Jong, 1996). The relation between (supportive) leadership and negative emotional states was mediated by situational stressors, especially job ambiguity (O'Driscoll & Beehr, 1994). Perceived influence and stressful aspects of work, such as role conflict and ambiguity, are dependent upon the style of leadership. Role ambiguity, in particular, was found to mediate the connection between leadership and psychological symptoms (O'Driscoll & Beehr, 1994). The results of a meta-analysis by Salas, Rozell, Mullen, and Driskell (1999) suggest that role ambiguity is an important factor in the malfunctioning of teams. Among a number of different approaches like goal setting, interpersonal relations and problem solving, the only team-building intervention that was effective in the enhancement of team performance turned out to be role clarification.

Interactive effects among leadership styles were found in some cases. In a study of nurses, the highest level of burnout was related to a combination of low consideration and high structure. The least burnout was found in nurses who had a leader who was high in both consideration and initiating structure (Seltzer & Numerof, 1988).

With respect to performance, a pattern similar to the one discovered by Seltzer and Numerof (1988) was found by Tjosvold (1984). In an experimental study, four combinations of high and low consideration and structure were compared. In the first half of the experiment, the subjects worked under the guidance of a leader, and after a period, the leader left, asking the subjects to continue with the task as long as they could. Performance in the absence of the leader, who had displayed a combination of consideration and structure, was maximal. In their longitudinal study, Howell and Hall-Merenda (1999) found high-quality LMX positively related to follower performance. Interestingly, the impact of transformational leadership, an aggregation of charisma (communicating a vision for the future), intellectual stimulation and individualized consideration was dependent upon the physical distance, whether working in the same place as the leader or not. When the distance between leader and followers was small, the effect of transformational leadership on performance was positive, while the opposite was found when the physical distance was greater. In any event, charismatic behaviors may backfire when there is a discrepancy between the values of leader and followers.

It is not only leadership style, in the traditional sense, that is related to mood and mood-related performance. Perceptions of righteousness and fairness are also crucial. In organizations failing to fulfill one of some promised obligations, employees' trust, job satisfaction and performance suffer (Robinson & Rousseau, 1994). The fairness of the store management—even more than the fairness of the direct supervisor—was related to the positive mood in salespeople working for a large retailer (George, 1991). The positive emotions induced by a fair management were, in turn, related to the Organizational Citizenship Behavior (OCB) factor of altruism and also to customer service and sales performance in the retail store. OCB was found to be a predictor of the performance of teams (Podsakoff, Ahearne, & MacKenzie, 1997).

As suggested by the results of studies on stress management, the behavior of leaders is very important, but, of course, not easy to change. Research on the training of high LMX behaviors suggest some positive effect on the followers' performance (Scandura & Graen, 1984). The results of training in consideration, however, are not very consistent (Bass, 1990). The post-training context appears to be important. Gains in the level of consideration, for instance, were maintained only when the supervisor's boss was high in consideration. According to an earlier study (Wexley & Nemeroff, 1975), a combination of training and subsequent coaching appears to be effective. Only those supervisors who received a weekly coaching session after their leadership training showed any change toward a higher level of considerate behavior, and a subsequent increase in job satisfaction was also found in their followers (Wexley & Nemeroff, 1975).

WELL-BEING AND PERFORMANCE: SELF-EFFICACY SOLVING THE CONTRADICTIONS?

Generally speaking, goal setting is related positively to performance. Well-being also has a positive relation with performance, but the connection between goal setting an well-being may be either positive or negative. As a consequence, a gain in performance with the help of goal setting may be at the cost of personal well-being, depending on the person's attitude toward the goal (Sonnentag, this volume).

Also, performance itself may not benefit from goal setting in all cases. In their simulation of salary negotiations, Stevens and Gist (1997) found performance to be related positively to goal setting only in persons high in self-efficacy. In the case of low self-efficacy, a mastery-oriented training—teaching methods to cope with negative emotions and uncertainty—was effective in enhancing performance; and similar mechanisms may operate in goal-setting-related methods like management by objectives (MBO) (Rodgers et al., 1993). The functioning of management teams was found to be dependent upon the self-efficacy of their members when working in teams (De Jong, Bouhuys & Barnhoorn, 1999).

FINAL CONCLUSION AND IMPLICATIONS FOR PRACTICE

Implications for practice may be illustrated briefly with a case history.

Case Study

This case study concerns the manager/owner of a small business firm who is about 45 years old, is married and is the father of two daughters. He holds a BA in engineering. He was seeking assistance because of depressed mood and exhaustion. The main business of the firm was the leasing and maintenance of advanced measurement and regulation devices, and, if necessary, their adaptation. Customers were process industries in the area. The 15-member staff consisted mainly of specialized engineers. The client himself worked 60 to 70 hours per week, and was still not able to finish all his tasks. Apparently, quite a lot of time was needed to respond to the complaints of the customers due to errors made by his technical staff and lags in the delivery of goods and services. A critical incident analysis revealed that many errors were due to three sources: first, his tendency to attract work beyond the capacity of the organization; second, the lack of competence of the majority of his staff; and, third, his failure to give his workers proper instructions and guidance.

The client's tendency to attract too much work appeared to be related to his uncertainty about the future. The idea of having plenty of work set his mind at ease in the short run. Paradoxically, however, the thought of failure to meet these self-imposed demands evoked tension. Though the business was still profitable, the style of management was indeed endangering the future of the firm. Also, the long working hours were a threat to his marriage. Fear of failure played a part in the tendency to avoid a proper conversation with his staff about the work to be done. As he explained, he preferred to let his staff make errors rather than to do something wrong himself. Moreover, it was not very clear to the client what form an alternative style of leadership would take. It appeared that, due to unsystematic selection interviews, the wrong people had been attracted for the job at hand.

The intervention chosen can be characterized as multi-modal. Assertiveness training procedures were employed to develop the skills and self-confidence needed for a more consultative style of leadership and the ability to give clear instructions. In critical discussions of the client's opinions about the necessity to do more work than possible, and the (in)admissibility of failures, cognitive-behavioral methods were employed. Interventions in response to emerging problems appeared particularly fruitful. In a session taking place in a Friday afternoon, for instance, the client estimated that he would need about 40 hours to finish all the tasks to be completed before Monday. Unfortunately, one of his daughters was going to celebrate her birthday that weekend. Time management procedures and skills developed in that session (deciding about priorities, setting attainable goals) proved to be useful in a variety of other situations.

By mutual consent, a large part of the staff found a new job outside the company. In the selection of their replacements, the client was assisted by an experienced HRM professional. The aim of this assistance was twofold: to find new personnel fit for the specific tasks at hand, and give to the client, by means of modeling and guided practice, the opportunity to develop his communicative skills.

Relaxation methods were not employed, in agreement with the tentative conclusion that this approach would be less suitable for people in complex jobs (Van der Klink et al., in press).

In line with the literature discussed earlier, the client's well-being was improved after the intervention period. The performance of the firm as a whole was improved; and the organization was a healthier place to work in for the employees. It is probable that coaching the client in leadership and managerial skills was just as important as coaching in stress management.

To sum up, individual stress management interventions, especially behavioral-cognitive methods, have been shown to be effective in the reduction of psychological strain and the improvement of (perceived) job conditions. Moreover, they are promising as tools for the enhancement of individual effectiveness. The results of global, organization-wide interventions are not yet certain, but the coaching and mentoring of managers and supervisors can be expected to be effective as a method of improving the well-being and effectiveness of a larger group of people. In coaching, it is probably wise to take the client's level of self-efficacy into account, especially when goal setting is involved. In the case of low self-efficacy, attention has either to be given to the mastery of performance-related stress, or to the development of higher objective and subjective levels of competence.

REFERENCES

Bass, B. M. (1985). *Leadership beyond expectations*. New York: The Free Press.

Bass, B. M. (1990). *Bass & Stogdill's handbook of leadership*. New York: The Free Press.

Briner, R. B., & Reynolds, S. (1999). The costs, benefits, and limitations of organizational level stress interventions. *Journal of Organizational Behavior*, **20**, 647–664.

Caplan, R. D., & Jones, K. W. (1975). Effects of workload, role ambiguity, and type A personality on anxiety, depression and heart rate. *Journal of Applied Psychology*, **60**, 713–719.

De Jong, G. J., & Emmelkamp, P. M. G. (2000). Implementing stress management training: Comparative trainer effectiveness. *Journal of Occupational Health Psychology*, **5**, 309–320.

De Jong, R. D., Bouhuys, S. A., & Barnhoorn, J. C. (1999). Personality, self-efficacy and functioning in management teams: A contribution to validation. *International Journal of Selection and Assessment*, **7**, 46–49.

De Jong, R. D., Voorendonk, R. H., Boogaarts, F. P., Le Blanc, P. M., Den Ouden, M. D., & Spuijbroek, P. A. (1996). De situationele leiderschapstheorie. Garantie voor effectiviteit, satisfactie en gezondheid? (The situational leadership theory: guarantee for performance, satisfaction and health?) *Gedrag en Organisatie*, **9**, 401–415.

Ellis, A. (1962). *Reason and emotion in therapy*. New York: Lyle Stuart.

Ellis, A. (1973). Rational-emotive therapy. In R. Corsini (Ed.), *Current psychotherapies*. Ithaca (pp. 50–60): Peacock publishers.

Etzion, D., Eden, D., & Lapidot, Y. (1998). Relief from job stressors and burnout: Reserve service as a respite. *Journal of Applied Psychology*, **83**, 577–585.

Fleishman, E. A., Harris, E. F., & Burt, H. E. (1955). *Leadership and supervision in industry*. Ohio State University Studies, Bureau of Educational Research Monographs no. 33.

Folkman, S., & Lazarus, R. (1980). An analysis of coping in a middle-aged community sample. *Journal of Health and Social Behavior*, **21**, 219–239.

Ganster, D. C., & Fuselier, M. R. (1989). Control in the workplace. In C. L. Cooper & I. T. Robbertson (Eds.), *International review of industrial and organizational psychology*. Chichester: John Wiley & Sons.

George, J. M. (1991). State or trait: Effects of positive mood on prosocial behaviors at work. *Journal of Applied Psychology*, **76**, 299–298.

Heaney, C. A., Price, R. H., & Rafferty, J. (1995). Increasing coping resource at work: A field experiment to increase social support, improve team functioning, and enhance employee mental health. *Journal of Organizational Behavior*, **16**, 335–352.

Howell, J. M., & Hall-Merenda K. E. (1999). The ties that bind: The impact of leader–member exchange, transformational and transactional leadership, and distance on predicting follower performance. *Journal of Applied Psychology*, **84**, 650–694.

Ivancevich, J. M., Matteson, M. T., Freedman, S. M., & Phillips, J. S. (1980). Worksite stress management interventions. *American Psychologist*, **45**, 252–261.

Jackson, S. E. (1983). Participation in decision making as a strategy for reducing job-related strain. *Journal of Applied Psychology*, **68**, 3–19.

Jacobson, E. A. (1938). *Progressive relaxation*. Chicago: University of Chicago Press.

Jones, J. W., Barge, B. N., Steffy, B. D., Fay, L. M., Kuntz, L. K., & Wuebker, L. J. (1988). Stress and medical malpractice: Organizational risk assessment and intervention. *Journal of Applied Psychology*, **73**, 727–735.

Jones, F., & Fletcher, B. C. (1996). Job control and health. In M. J. Schabracq, J. A. M. Winnubst & C. L. Cooper (Eds.), *Handbook of work and health psychology* (pp. 33–50). Chichester: John Wiley & Sons.

Landsbergis, P. A., & Vivona-Vaughan, E. (1995). Evaluation of an occupational stress intervention in a public agency. *Journal of Organizational Behavior*, **16**, 29–48.

Meichenbaum, D. (1972). Cognitive modification of test anxious college students. *Journal of Consulting and Clinical Psychology*, **39**, 370–380.

Meichenbaum, D. (1985). *Stress inoculation training*. New York: Pergamon Press.

Mulder, M., de Jong, R. D, Koppelaar, L., & Verhage, J. (1986). Power, situation and leader's effectiveness. An organizational field study. *Journal of Applied Psychology*, **71**, 566–570.

Murphy, L. R. (1996). Stress management techniques: secondary prevention of stress. In M. J. Schabracq, J. A. M. Winnubst & C. L. Cooper (Eds.), *Handbook of work and health psychology* pp. 427–441. Chichester: John Wiley & Sons.

O'Driscoll, M. P., & Beehr, T. A. (1994). Supervisor behaviors, role stressors and uncertainty as predictors of personal outcomes for subordinates. *Journal of Organizational Behavior*, **15**, 141–155.

Offermann, L. R., & Helmann, P. S. (1996). Leadership behavior and subordinate stress: A 360 grades view. *Journal of Occupational Health Psychology*, **1**, 382–390.

Podsakoff, P. M., Ahearne, M., & MacKenzie, S. B. (1997). Organizational citizenship behavior and the quantity and quality of work group performance. *Journal of Applied Psychology*, **82**, 262–270.

Quick, J. C., Paulus, P. B., Whittington, J. L., Larey, T. S. & Nelson, D. L. (1996). Management development, well-being and health. In M. J. Schabracq, J. A. M. Winnubst & C. L. Cooper (Eds.), *Handbook of work and health psychology* pp. 369–387. Chichester: John Wiley & Sons.

Robinson, S. L., & Rousseau, D. M. (1994). Violating the psychological contract: Not the exception but the norm. *Journal of Organizational Behavior*, **15**, 245–259.

Rodgers, R., Hunter, J. E., & Rogers, D. (1993). Influence of top management commitment on management program success. *Journal of Applied Psychology*, **78**, 151–155.

Salas, E., Rozell, D., Mullen, B., & Driskell, J. E. (1999). The effect of team building on performance. *Small Group Research*, **30**, 309–329.

Saunders, T., Driskell, J. E., Johnston, J. H., & Salas, E. (1996). The effect of stress inoculation training on anxiety and performance. *Journal of Occupational Health Psychology*, **1**, 170–186.

Scandura, T. A., & Graen, G. (1984). Moderating effects of initial leader–member exchange status on the effects of a leadership intervention. *Journal of Applied Psychology*, **69**, 428–436.

Shadish, W. R., Matt, G. E., Navarro, A. M., & Phillips, G. (2000). The effects of psychological therapies under clinically representative conditions: A meta-analysis. *Psychological Bulletin*, **120**, 512–529.

Seltzer, J., & Numerof, R. E. (1988). Supervisory leadership and subordinate burnout. *Academy of Management Journal*, **31**, 439–446.

Semmer, N. (1996). Individual differences, work stress and health. In M. J. Schabracq, J. A. M. Winnubst, & C. L. Cooper (Eds.), *Handbook of work and health psychology*. Chichester: John Wiley and Sons.

Stevens, C. K., & Gist, M. E. (1997). Effects of self-efficacy, goal-orientation training on negotiation skill maintenance: What are the mechanisms? *Personnel Psychology*, **50**, 955–978.

Stoker, J. L., & de Jong, R. D. (1996). Leiding geven aan zelfstandige taakgroepen (Leading autonomous work groups). *Gedrag en Organisatie*, **9**, 401–413.

Tjosvold, D. (1984). Effects of leader warmth and directiveness on subordinate performance on a subsequent task. *Journal of Applied Psychology*, **69**, 422–427.

Van Dierendonck, D., Schaufeli, W. B., & Buunk, B. P. (1998). The evaluation of an individual burnout intervention program: The role of inequity and social support. *Journal of Applied Psychology*, **83**, 392–407.

Van der Klink, J. J. L., Blonk, R. W. B., Schene, A. H., & Van Dijk, F. J. H. (2001). The benefit of interventions for work related stress. *American Journal of Public Health*, **91**, 270–276.

Wexley, K. N., & Nemeroff, W. F. (1975). Effectiveness of positive reinforcement and goal setting as methods of management development. *Journal of Applied Psychology*, **60**, 446–450.

Winnubst, J. A. M., de Jong, R. D., & Schabracq, M. J. (1996). The diagnosis of role strains at work. In M. J. Schabracq, J. A. M. Winnubst & C. L. Cooper (Eds.), *Handbook of work and health psychology* pp. 87–125. Chichester: John Wiley & Sons.

Wofford, J. C., & Liska, L. Z. (1993). Path-goal theories of leadership: A meta-analysis. *Journal of Management*, **19**, 857–876.

Wolpe, J. (1958). *Reciprocal inhibition therapy*. Stanford, California: Stanford University Press.

Wright, T. A., & Cropanzano, R. (2000). Psychological well-being and job satisfaction as predictors of job performance. *Journal of Occupational Health Psychology*, **5**, 84–94.

CHAPTER 22

Integrating the Linkages between Organizational Culture and Individual Outcomes at Work

Paul Tesluk
University of Maryland, College Park, USA
David Hofmann,
Michigan State University, East Lansing, USA, and
Narda Quigley
University of Maryland, College Park, USA

SUMMARY

Organizational culture is frequently referenced as critical for achieving organizational effectiveness by directing and channeling employee effort and behavior in ways that are aligned with company goals and objectives. Yet there has been little systematic study on how organizational culture actually influences individual attitudes, affective states, behavior, and performance. This chapter attempts to describe these complex linkages by integrating the literatures on organizational culture and climate, leadership, normative contracts, and HR practices with relationships to employee attitudes and behavior. Differences between direct and indirect, or mediated, relationships are stressed. Extrapolating from the literature on culture and organizational performance using a competing values framework, we also propose four sets of cultural traits that appear particularly important in facilitating individual performance. We conclude by identifying future research issues that will require a meso perspective that integrates macro and micro perspectives to better understand the complex relationships between organizational culture and individual performance.

Psychological Management of Individual Performance. Edited by Sabine Sonnentag.
© 2002 John Wiley & Sons, Ltd.

INTRODUCTION

People are influenced by the environments in which they work. Spending time in companies such as Disney, Southwest Airlines, 3M, GE, or Intel, one realizes there is something about these settings that seems to create excitement, generate commitment, and foster behaviors that are congruent with specific strategic objectives. Everyone seems to be on the same page and moving in the same direction. In other words, members of these organizations seem to share similar values, beliefs, expectations, and behavioral norms; that is, there is a strong culture (Schein, 1990). Although organizational culture has been linked to organizational effectiveness in a broad sense (Deal & Kennedy, 1982; Denison, 1990), there has been less emphasis placed on how organizational culture can influence individual attitudes, affective states, behavior, and performance. The purpose of this chapter is to identify linkages between organizational culture and individual outcomes. In order to lay the foundation for these linkages, however, we must first discuss the critical role that culture plays in organizations as well as the need for an approach to understanding organizational culture that involves a merging of both macro and micro organizational factors.

IMPORTANCE OF ORGANIZATIONAL CULTURE FOR MANAGING INDIVIDUAL PERFORMANCE

Although organizational scholars have long recognized the importance of organizational culture as an important factor for promoting effectiveness (Barney, 1986; Deal & Kennedy, 1982; Denison, 1990; Denison & Mishra, 1995; Gordon & DiTomaso, 1992; Ouchi, 1981; Kilman, Saton, & Serpa, 1985; Peters & Waterman, 1982), it is perhaps becoming more important given the changing nature of organizations and the impact these changes have on the nature of work. Although a detailed treatment of these changes is beyond the scope of the present chapter, they include a rise in more flexible organizational forms, an increase in the use and integration of different forms of technology, and increases in global competition. These organizational changes produce fundamental changes in the design of work, jobs, and work roles (Cappelli, 1999; Howard, 1995). As a result, work is increasingly being characterized by performance expectations that are more ambiguous and dynamic where workers are required to be more adaptable and self-managing in their work roles and careers (Parker, Wall, & Jackson, 1997).

As modern organizations move away from traditional structures—typified by hierarchical control, stability, formal rules and regulations, clearly defined jobs, and well-specified performance expectations—to flexible and fluid structures that can readily adapt to changing competitive demands, new approaches to managing performance are needed (Murphy & Jackson, 1999). With respect to managing performance, one of the central questions is how to efficiently and effectively guide behavior in light of ambiguous job definitions and roles and where discretion is increasingly residing in the hands of front-line employees. In other words, the question is how to ensure, given this increased discretion, that front-line employees will make decisions consistent with broader organizational goals and values.

Although this is not necessarily a new question, we argue that it is becoming a more important one. Katz and Kahn, for example, more than 20 years ago recognized the importance of employee discretion when they stated:

> "The organizational need for actions of an innovative, relatively spontaneous sort is inevitable and unending. No organizational plan can foresee all contingencies within its own operation, can anticipate with accuracy all environmental changes, or can control perfectly all human variability . . . An organization that depends solely on its blueprints of prescribed behaviors is a very fragile system."
>
> (Katz & Kahn, 1978, pp. 403–404, as quoted in Schneider & Rentsch, 1988)

A fragile system indeed—for example, Galbraith (1977) illustrated how quickly traditional bureaucratic communication structures can become overloaded in light of increasing uncertainty. The increased uncertainty discussed by Galbraith over 20 years ago is now assumed, and more sophisticated organizational structures the norm. Thus, in more and more organizations, an increasing number of decisions cannot be anticipated or made in advance. The result is an increase in discretion required by front-line employees.

This increase in discretion not only changes the roles, responsibilities and requirements of these positions, but also changes the nature of managing these positions as well. Employees, for example, need to make decisions in real time and at the point where the uncertainty occurs (i.e., the level of the individual decision maker; Galbraith, 1977). The management of these positions, therefore, requires the development of a common set of decision premises that employees can rely on in response to complex and uncertain events with which they must cope. These decision premises, or implicit rules, that individuals use to develop and evaluate alternative solutions are in part a function of the organization's culture. Drawing on our initial examples, everyone seems to be on the right page and moving in the same direction in part because they share a coherent set of decision premises and implicit rules for evaluating alternative solutions, making decisions and taking action. An example of the importance of agreement on these implicit rules, assumptions, and decision premises (i.e., culture) in complex and changing performance conditions has been discussed in the context of Weick's (1987) work on high reliability organizations.

In addition to increased discretion and the resulting implications for management, another reason why organizational culture is becoming more important for managing individual performance is that the connection between individuals and organizations is becoming more critical. For example, Lawler and colleagues (Lawler, 1992; 1994) have argued that the changes confronting organizations make traditional job-based approaches to managing human resources obsolete (Lawler, 1994). Consequently, many scholars are now advocating that practices such as employee selection need to move away from approaches that seek to maximize person–job fit to using organizational context features, including culture, as a way to facilitate effective person–organization fit (Bowen, Ledford, & Nathan, 1991). As this trend occurs within organizations, the process of selection is also changing from the other side of the table. Specifically, job seekers seem to be shifting from considering the qualities of the job itself to a consideration of the broader work environment and culture (Judge & Cable, 1997; Stein, 2000).

THE NEED FOR A MESO APPROACH

Before stating the specific objectives of this chapter, we feel it is important at this point to restate an observation that has been made by others before. It has often been the case in the past that the macro literatures—in areas such as organizational structure, design, culture and organizational effectiveness—and the micro literatures that attempt to predict individual behavior and performance in organizational settings have historically not been well connected. The general consensus of the others who have made this observation (e.g., House, Rousseau, & Thomas-Hunt, 1995; Klein, Dansereau, & Hall, 1994; Kozlowski & Klein, 2000; Rousseau, 1985) as well as ourselves is that only a "meso" approach that integrates variables and perspectives that reside at different levels of analysis allows for a complete understanding of organizational behavior.

The relationship between organizational culture and individual performance at work seems to be an arena where a meso-perspective would be particularly beneficial. On the macro side, for example, organizational culture has often been considered a key factor for facilitating organizational effectiveness. The interest in culture as a means to promote effective organizations perhaps reached its height during the 1980s when a number of authors in the popular business literature encouraged organizations to turn their attention to culture as a way to regain their competitiveness (Baker, 1980; Deal & Kennedy, 1982; Ouchi, 1981; Kilman, Saton, & Serpa, 1985; Peters & Waterman, 1982). Into the 1990s, while the practitioner press maintained its interest in organizational culture (e.g., Goffee & Jones, 1998; Juechter & Fisher, 1998), a number of empirical studies began appearing that investigated the relationship between culture and organizational performance (e.g., Calori & Sarnin, 1991; Denison, 1990; Denison & Mishra, 1995; Gordon & DiTomaso, 1992; Marcoulides & Heck, 1993; Petty, Beadles, Lowrey, Chapman, & Connell, 1995).

However, the often stated axiom that "organizations do not behave, people do" holds for organizational culture as well. In particular, an implicit assumption that underlies both these practitioner and research literatures is that culture can influence an organization's performance by influencing individuals within the organization and, for example, their commitment, attitudes, interaction styles, motivation, behavior, and decisions. However, the way in which organizational culture contributes to organizational effectiveness through individual-level processes largely has been unspecified. Consequently, many questions remain regarding the nature of the culture–organizational effectiveness association and *how* they actually occur (Saffold, 1988; Siehl & Martin, 1990). Understanding more specifically how organizational culture influences *individuals* and which aspects or characteristics of culture are most important will help us understand how culture can be used as a means to positively impact organizational outcomes.

On the flip side of the equation, macro researchers have typically studied work performance without taking full account of the broader contextual influences. For example, the focus on the determinants of individual level attitudes, behavior, and performance has historically resided within the realm of individual differences (Cappelli & Sherer, 1991; Hattrup & Jackson, 1996). Understanding how macro factors influence individuals' attitudes and behaviors will help develop a more realistic and complete understanding of the factors that influence work performance and behavior in organizations. Organizational culture in particular, has been noticeably absent in industrial and organizational psychology and organizational behavior research (Schein, 1996). However, in those areas where it has been integrated—for example, in research on recruitment and retention (Cable & Judge, 1996; Chatman, 1991)—a more complete understanding of those micro phenomena has emerged.

In short, both the macro perspective focusing on organizational level outcomes and the micro area focusing an individual behavior and performance will benefit by developing a more complete understanding of the linkages relating organizational culture to individual performance. Despite the importance of organizational culture and its role in guiding member behavior, few attempts have been made to provide a framework for understanding the linkages between culture and individual level states such as attitudes, affect, behavior, and performance. In light of this, the specific objectives of this chapter are to: (1) offer a framework for relating organizational culture to individual performance, and ultimately, to organizational productivity and effectiveness; and (2) attempt to identify specific characteristics of cultures that foster high performance. In doing this, we also attempt to identify issues and areas that have been under-researched and attempt to provide direction for future work.

DEFINING ORGANIZATIONAL CULTURE

Understanding the ways in which organizational culture may influence individuals' work attitudes, affective responses, behavior, and performance requires an organizing framework that touches on a number of different factors such as strategy, structure, human resource management practices, leadership, and climate. However, before presenting a framework identifying linkages between organizational culture and individual outcomes, it is necessary to anchor this discussion with an explicit definition of organizational culture.

Organizational culture, particularly in the popular press, has been used to refer to almost every aspect of organizations. It is the case, however, that when a construct is used so broadly, it eventually loses its ability to uniquely identify anything. We, therefore, need to provide a precise definition of organizational culture to guide our discussion. Following Schein (1990), culture is defined as "(a) a pattern of basic assumptions, (b) invented, discovered, or delivered by a given group, (c) as it learns to cope with problems of external adaptation and internal integration, (d) that has worked well enough to be considered valid and, therefore (e) is to be taught to new members as the (f) correct way to perceive, think, and feel in relation to those problems" (p. 111). In short, culture refers to patterns of commonly held beliefs, values, and behavioral assumptions within the organization that are adapted in solving problems and that serve to guide and focus attitudes, perceptions, affect, and behavior.

It is an important feature of culture that it involves multiple layers of meaning ranging in their degree of abstraction (Rousseau, 1990). Schein's (1985, 1990, 1999) three-level framework is the most widely recognized organization of the different layers (see Table 22.1). At its deepest, least accessible, and most abstract level, culture consists of the shared, underlying, and largely unconscious *assumptions* that members use to make sense of issues and problems that arise as the organization copes with external adaptation and internal integration. Because organization members are generally not consciously unaware of these assumptions unless they are directly questioned or motivated to do intensive self-analysis, understanding and studying culture based on taken-for-granted

TABLE 22.1 Dynamic layers of organizational culture (Schein, 1985, 1990, 1999)

	Low	• Observable artifacts
Level of abstraction		• Values, norms, ideologies
	High	• Shared, underlying, unconscious assumptions

assumptions is difficult and requires intensive observation and focused questioning. For this reason, even though Schein (1990) argues that basic assumptions form the essence of organizational culture, most studies of culture tend to focus on the more readily observable and manifest layers.

The next level of abstraction includes the values, norms, and ideologies that define appropriate and inappropriate behavior and communicate the outcomes or states that are most highly regarded in the organization. An example might be the strong set of values for innovation at 3M and reinforcing norms that emphasize experimentation and individual creativity (Tesluk, Farr, & Klein, 1997). Understanding the values that define an organization's culture requires asking informants either through interviews or questionnaires what are the commonly held expectations in different circumstances. These values and lasting cultural norms guide behavior and decision making and influence members' motivation, performance, and attitudes (Cooke & Szumal, 1993).

The espoused values in turn shape the most immediately accessible, readily observable and most concrete aspects of culture, the observable *artifacts*. These are the material and physical manifestations that one observes when in the organization. They include the physical layout of the workplace, publicly displayed statements of the company's philosophy and mission, the dress code, the personnel manual, the use of titles, and other observable features that are consistent with and help to define the values and assumptions held by those in the organization. Although more immediately apparent to an outside observer, one of the limitations to using these artifacts to study an organization's culture is that observers can make invalid inferences if they do not fully understand the connections between these artifacts and the associated values and assumptions (Schein, 1990, 1999).

The three layers of culture in Schein's conceptualization are mutually reinforcing over time. The innermost aspects of culture influence the more outer layers which, in turn, reinforce the deeper cultural features. In this sense, culture can be viewed as dynamic process. In other words, culture can best be described as being continually "enacted" rather than a static thing that "exists" (Weick, 1979).

As culture becomes enacted over time it influences—and is ultimately embedded within and therefore defined by—other aspects of the organization, such as the chosen structures, strategies, routines, policies, and practices (Cooke & Rousseau, 1988; Tesluk et al., 1997). The content of these choices reflect the set of learned responses (i.e., culture) developed by the organization as it has learned to manage two critical processes, external adaptation and internal integration (Schein, 1985, 1999). The first process, external adaptation, is concerned with how the organization survives and thrives in its environment. This requires the development of the organization's: (a) mission, strategy, and goals, (b) structure, systems, and processes, and (c) the means by which the organization measures itself and detects and corrects errors. Beginning with the basic assumptions as well as the beliefs and values of the organization's founders and early leaders, the strategy and structure take hold as the primary mechanisms for managing the external environment. These basic assumptions, beliefs, and values then became enacted and articulated by subsequent organizational leaders through what leaders pay attention to, measure, and control.

The basic assumptions and values that define an organization's culture are also prominent in how the organization deals with the second fundamental process of internal integration. This process is concerned with (a) the development of common language and concepts designed to facilitate communication and coordination, (b) group boundaries and identity, (c) the nature of authority and relationships, and (d) the allocation of rewards and status. By addressing theses fundamental areas, the internal structure and systems of the organization become established. Examples include the compensation and promotion systems that organizations used to reward those who perform in ways that are consistent with the expectations and values of the organization's culture. Along with the means to manage external adaptation, these internal integration systems come to define an organization's culture.

LINKING ORGANIZATIONAL CULTURE TO INDIVIDUAL OUTCOMES

MODEL FOUNDATION

Our proposed model linking organizational culture to individual outcomes is adapted from work presented by others who have thought about similar linkages between macro and micro concepts (e.g., Ferris, Arthur, Berkson, Kaplan, Harrell-Cook, & Frink, 1998; James & Jones, 1976; Kopelman, Brief, & Guzzo, 1990; Ostroff & Bowen, 2000; Ulrich & LaFasto, 1995). We should note that our main focus is on the factors linking organizational culture to individual outcomes. Although we do include organizational-level factors, namely, the role of organization structure, strategy, and the founding leader as well as other subsequent leaders, our focus is on the mediating mechanisms that link culture to individual outcomes. We also do recognize that there are other antecedents to culture that reside outside the focus of this chapter (e.g., industry characteristics; Chatman & Jehn, 1994; Gordon, 1991).

FORMATIVE INFLUENCES ON ORGANIZATIONAL CULTURE: THE ROLE OF FOUNDING AND SUBSEQUENT LEADERS, STRATEGY AND STRUCTURE

Schein's (1985, 1990, 1999) work on organizational culture places a strong emphasis on the role of the founder and early organizational leaders. The personal values, beliefs, and assumptions of the founder (or founders) serve as a visible and articulated model for how people should behave and how the organization should function. As the personal beliefs of the founder are put into action members learn which beliefs are effective for the organization as a whole and which are not. Through experience and joint learning, members gradually create shared assumptions and an agreed upon system of values and beliefs. In addition to identifying and modeling the culture, early leaders determine and shape the culture by how they respond to critical incidents (e.g., crises, key events). As Schneider, Gunnarson, and Niles-Jolly (1994) emphasize, most important in the development of a strong culture is not what leaders say, but what they actually *do*. Their perspectives, responses, and the behaviors they demonstrate generate norms that can take hold and be acted on and reinforced over time.

Many views of organizational culture, especially those that link it to firm performance (e.g., Barney, 1986; Deal & Kennedy, 1982; Peters & Waterman, 1982), describe culture in terms of the set of values, beliefs, and assumptions that define how a firm is organized, how it operates (i.e., structure), what businesses it is in, and how it conducts its business (i.e., strategy). More broad-based perspectives on organizational functioning view the strategic, structural, and normative aspects of the organization as closely linked and highly interdependent (James & Jones, 1976). Any comprehensive approach to culture should recognize its relationship with strategy and structure, since the content of an organization's culture includes values, assumptions, and other learned responses shown to facilitate external adaptation and internal integration (Schein, 1990). In this way, culture could be considered the result of strategies and structures that ultimately are successful and take hold. At same time, however, the values, norms, and assumptions that define culture provide the tacit attitudinal and affective guidelines that managers and employees follow and support when formulating and implementing strategy (Lei, Slocum, & Slater, 1997; Schwartz & Davis, 1981). Thus, culture, strategy, and structure are intimately linked in dynamic and reciprocal cause-and-effect associations.

DIRECT EFFECTS: HOW ORGANIZATIONAL CULTURE CAN DIRECTLY IMPACT INDIVIDUAL ATTITUDINAL/AFFECTIVE STATES AND BEHAVIOR

In addition to specifying the formative influences on organizational culture, the model in Figure 22.1 also specifies both direct and mediated influences of culture on individual-level outcomes. Although we will discuss both of these linkages, we start with a discussion of the ways in which organizational culture can directly influence individual-level outcomes; namely, normative processes and person–organizational fit. These influences are summarized in Table 22.2 and discussed in detail below.

Normative processes

A number of organizational culture researchers have focused on behavioral norms as a critical component of culture (e.g., Cooke & Lafferty, 1986; Schwartz & Davis, 1981; Cooke & Szumal, 1993; Klein, Masi, & Weidner, 1995). Although numerous definitions of norms exist, they can be considered expectations of what are (and what are not) appropriate forms of thinking and behaving that are shared by members of a social unit (in this case, an organization) and that tend to endure or remain salient over time. They represent members' beliefs about the types of behaviors that are needed to "fit in" and be accepted within the organization (e.g., "work in the evenings on weekdays" or "wear 'business casual' on Fridays"). As social phenomena that regulate the behavior of members of the organization (Hackman, 1992), cultural norms are viewed as mechanisms that summarize and simplify the organization's influence on individuals' affective states, behavior, and performance (Cooke & Szumal, 1993).

   Although focused on group rather than organizational norms, Hackman (1992) provides a detailed description of the types of effects that norms exert on individuals and how these influences operate. Cultural norms can influence members' informational states, affective states, and behavior. *Informational states* include individuals' current beliefs (e.g., the importance of innovation for being an effective organization) and their accumulated knowledge about how to behave in certain situations and settings (e.g., in interactions with customers). *Affective states* refer to one's attitudes regarding different features of the work environment (e.g., the organization, one's job, the quality of supervision), level of emotional and psychological arousal (e.g., stress, positive affective state, mood), and personal values (e.g., the types of outcomes from doing one's job that are seen as important). Finally, cultural norms can also influence the *behavior* of organization members either directly, by rewarding or punishing engagement in certain

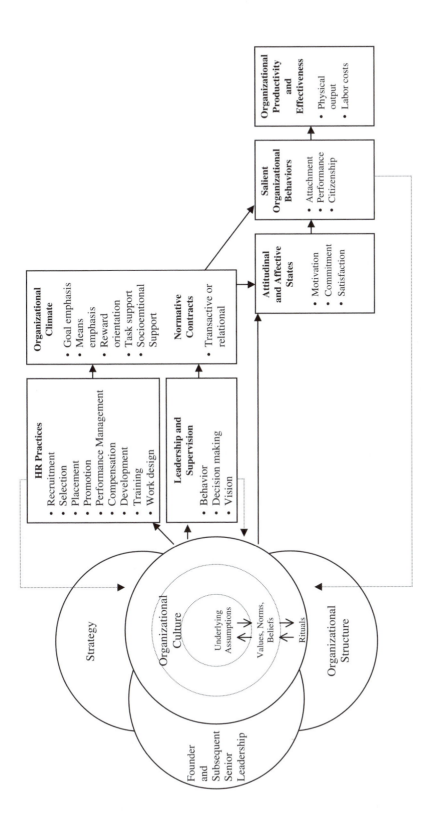

FIGURE 22.1 Model linking organizational culture to individual and organizational outcomes

TABLE 22.2   Direct impact of organizational culture on the individual

---

Normative processes
Expectations of what is acceptable, influences:

- **informational states** (current beliefs and knowledge about how to behave; Hackman, 1992)
- **affective states** (attitudes, emotions, and values)
- **behavior**

Person–organization fit
Congruence between personal values and belief systems and values inherent in organizational culture, influences:

- **job satisfaction** (Locke, 1976)
- **organizational commitment** (Bretz & Judge, 1993; Chatman, 1989, 1991; Meglino, Ravlin, & Adkins, 1989; O'Reilly, Chatman, & Caldwell, 1991; Posner, 1992)
- **turnover** (Bretz & Judge, 1993; Chatman, 1989, 1991; Meglino et al., 1989; O'Reilly et al., 1991; Posner, 1992)

---

actions (e.g., being praised in front of one's peers for coming up with a novel suggestion to improve a work process), or indirectly by influencing informational and affective states (e.g., staying late at work to finish a project in part because one feels a strong commitment to the company).

Norms influence individuals' informational and affective states as well as behavior through a variety of mechanisms. One is by cueing or making salient the types of values that can be fulfilled (Hackman, 1992). For instance, affiliative cultural norms (Cooke & Szumal, 1993), such as having lunch regularly with colleagues, alert members to whether or not the organization offers the opportunity to develop strong friendship ties with others at work. Hackman also notes that norms clarify behavior–outcome expectancies by making clear "what leads to what" in the organization. An employee who submits a draft report to his or her manager and receives very critical and chastising feedback regarding formatting and other details that the employee thought would be addressed in a future version quickly learns the importance of paying attention to detail and taking a perfectionistic approach.

One of the primary ways new members learn organizational norms is through socialization (Schein, 1990)—the "process by which an individual comes to appreciate the values, abilities, expected behaviors, and social knowledge essential for assuming an organizational role and for participating as an organizational member" (Louis, 1980, pp. 229–230). It is through socialization that the "cultural perspective" of the organization is conveyed to new members so that they learn the beliefs, values, orientations, and behaviors that are necessary for them to perform their roles and become effective organizational citizens (Van Maanen & Schein, 1979).

When we consider the role of socialization in the acculturation process of new organizational members, it is useful to consider two issues: (1) how the process occurs, and (2) the actual content (i.e., values, beliefs, assumptions) conveyed during the process. The most fully developed and researched model of socialization is Van Maanen and Schein's (1979) typology of six socialization dimensions that organizations use to structure the socialization experiences of new entrants. These experiences help new members to adopt preset roles and norms that are consistent with the organization's culture. Included in the socialization process are a common set of initiatory and learning experiences (collective) that occur outside the routine work setting (formal), are arranged into a fixed series of steps (sequential) with a specific timetable for progression in the organization (fixed), utilize role models (serial), and affirm the newcomer's identity (investiture). The common characteristic of these tactics is that they are more *institutionalized* or *structured* socialization processes (Ashforth & Saks, 1996).

Research has demonstrated that these institutionalized tactics can produce both desirable and somewhat undesirable outcomes. On the positive side, institutionalized tactics provide new members with information about both their new work role and the organization. This information can help both to reduce the anxiety and tension in starting a new job and simultaneously promote commitment to the organization and satisfaction with the job. In fact, research has shown these institutionalized tactics to be associated with reduced role conflict, role ambiguity, and other stress symptoms, "in addition to" increased job satisfaction and organizational commitment (Ashforth & Saks, 1996; Baker, 1992; Jones, 1986), and a greater sense of identification with the organization and its goals (Ashforth & Saks, 1996). One downside of these techniques is that, since institutionalized socialization practices encourage new members to passively accept established roles and procedures and support *a custodial role orientation*, they have been found to be negatively related to role innovation (Allen & Meyer, 1990; Ashforth & Saks, 1996; Jones, 1986).

In short, institutionalized socialization tactics provide newcomers with a more coherent sense of what the organization is about and how events should be viewed and interpreted and the types of behaviors that are appropriate. This encourages new members to approach their work in ways that are consistent with the existing culture, promotes a sense of attachment to the organization and greater organizational identification, and facilitates work adjustment. Although the use of more structured, institutionalized tactics may seem to imply a trade-off between promoting a loyal workforce while also discouraging role innovation and proactive performance (Allen & Meyer, 1990; Jones, 1986), that may not necessarily be the case (Nemeth & Staw, 1989). What appears more important is *what* is actually learned, not how the socialization experience is presented (Ashforth & Saks, 1996; Schein, 1968).

This leads to the second issue when considering the role of socialization in acculturating organizational members—that is the need to understand *what is actually learned* as part of socialization. Chao and her colleagues (1994) provided the following list of content areas of socialization based on the work of Schein (1968), Feldman (1976), Van Maanen (1975) and others.

- *Performance proficiency*—The extent to which the individual learns the tasks involved in the job.
- *People*—The degree to which the individual establishes successful and satisfying work relationships with other members of the organization.
- *Politics*—The extent to which the individual gains information regarding formal and informal work relationships and power structures within the organization.
- *Language*—The extent to which the individual becomes knowledgeable of the organization's and the profession's technical terminology as well as the acronyms, slang, and jargon unique to the organization.
- *Organizational goals and values*—The degree to which the individual understands the formal rules and principles of the organization as well as the informal, unspoken, and tacit rules, norms, goals, and values that are expected in the organization.
- *History*—The degree to which the individual is knowledgeable about the history of the organization and the backgrounds of key figures in the organization (e.g., founder, CEO).

As should be evident from the description of these dimensions of socialization, to greater and lesser degrees, each of the content areas serve to expose new members to the assumptions, values, and beliefs that form the essence of an organization's culture. Interestingly, Chao et al. (1994) found that changes in the extent to which individuals were socialized on the dimension of organizational goals and values dimension—arguably the dimension that most directly emphasizes the aspects of the organization's culture—was the best predictor of changes in career effectiveness outcomes. Specifically, individuals who indicated that they had become more familiar with the formal and informal rules, norms, goals, and expectations that were considered important in their organization reported significant improvements in job satisfaction and career involvement year-to-year over a 4-year period. Consistent with this finding, Klein and Weaver (2000) recently found that new employees attending an organizational orientation training program demonstrated significantly higher levels of commitment to the organization following the program, and that this was due to the socialization content dimensions of organizational goals and values and history.

It is important to note that while socialization is most often considered in terms of the new employee, socialization actually continues over the course of a career, especially as one experiences role changes stemming from promotions, transfers, or reassignments (Schein, 1971). Changes in socialization have been found to be related to changes in career outcomes for those who have been in the organization for several years (Chao et al., 1994). Thus, organizations should consider socialization practices as ways to communicate corporate culture not only for new employees, but for more tenured members as well.

Person–organizational fit

Another mechanism through which culture influences individuals' attitudes, affect, behavior, and performance is based on the congruence between one's personal values and belief systems and the values inherent in the organization's culture. As Locke (1976) proposed, the degree to which the work environment allows an individual to fulfill personally held values serves as an important influence on job satisfaction. Based on intuition alone, it is reasonable to conclude that when our priorities and values—whether they be for doing innovative work or acting in a way that is socially responsible—are consistent with those of the organization in which we work, we will experience greater satisfaction, stronger attachment to our organization, and be more willing to stay.

An important feature of both individuals and organizations is that both can be compared in terms of values—the enduring beliefs that a specific end-state or mode of conduct is desired where these beliefs guide attitudes, judgements and behaviors (Chatman, 1989, 1991; Meglino et al., 1989; O'Reilly et al., 1991; Schein, 1990). Values are a basic element in most definitions of organizational culture (e.g., Barley et al., 1988; Rousseau, 1990) and values also are central to notions of individual attitudes, motivation, and decision making in that they focus behavior beyond immediate goals to more distal, higher order objectives (Locke, 1976; Rokeach, 1973). In that sense, values have an isomorphic quality that enables a direct comparison between individuals and organizations.

Research on person-organizational (P–O) fit has demonstrated that the more individuals share the same values that are inherent in their organization's culture, the more likely they are to be satisfied with their jobs, committed to their organization, and less likely they are to want to leave (Bretz & Judge, 1993; Chatman, 1989, 1991; Meglino et al.,

1989; O'Reilly et al., 1991; Posner, 1992; Vandenberghe, 1999). Consistent with these findings, Chatman and Barsdale (1995) found that even though individualistic individuals working in cooperative settings recognized cultural norms indicting cooperation, they ignored them and behaved individualistically. In contrast, cooperative people working in a collectivistic organizational culture were the most cooperative, which is in line with the notion that outcomes are maximized when personal characteristics fit the organization's culture. Moreover, there is evidence that employees are directly aware of the extent to which their values are congruent with those of the organization (Cable & Judge, 1996).

The question then becomes how P–O fit is created and maintained. Schneider's (1987) attraction–selection–attrition (ASA) model provides a framework for understanding this process. To begin with, organizations seek out and select prospective employees whose traits are similar to those of successful members of the organization (Chatman, 1991). A self-selection process also is involved here whereby job seekers actively look for and pursue employment at organizations that have similar values and beliefs as their own (Cable & Judge, 1996). Subsequent to the job search/recruitment and selection phases of the employment relationship and upon organizational entry, socialization processes begin to make explicit the organization's values, norms, and beliefs. Upon learning these things explicitly, some individuals who do not possess strong fit with the organization may leave. Alternatively, there is also evidence that individuals' values and attitudes can change over time to be more consistent with those emphasized in their work environment (Kohn & Schooler, 1982; Wageman, 1995). Thus, over time, through ASA and socialization processes, P–O fit on values and beliefs increases (Ostroff & Rothausen, 1997; Schneider, Smith, Taylor, & Fleenor, 1998).

MEDIATING MECHANISMS: HR PRACTICES, LEADERSHIP, ORGANIZATIONAL CLIMATE AND NORMATIVE CONTRACTS

As shown in Figure 22.1, we propose that culture exerts several mediated, or indirect, influences on individual-level outcomes as well. One such indirect influence takes up the following sequence: organizational culture influences HR practices, these HR practices influence organizational climate, and then this organizational climate "in turn" influences individual-level attitudes and behavior. The second indirect influence occurs through leadership and supervision. In other words, organizational culture influences the types and styles of leadership and supervision. These leadership factors, in turn, influence organizational climate, which, once again, impacts individual-level attitudes and behaviors. In the following sections we discuss linkages between: (1) HR practices, organizational climate and normative contracts; (2) leadership/supervision and organizational climate and normative contracts; (3) organizational climate and normative contracts and individual attitudes/behavior; and (4) individual attitudes/behavior and organizational productivity/effectiveness. Table 22.3 summarizes some of the primary points behind HR practices and leadership/supervison as leverage points of influencing climate and normative contracts.

HR practices, organizational climate and normative contracts

One of the primary means by which culture affects individuals is through its influence on the types of policies, practices, and procedures within the organization. A number of authors have maintained that management practices, including HR systems and

TABLE 22.3   Culture leverage points

HR Practices
Must facilitate a supportive context by providing:

- Clearly defined goals
- Transparent work methods
- Motivating rewards
- Supportive management

Leadership/Supervision
*Must communicate the climate and establish expectations for employees regarding
the organization (Lewin, 1938; Scott & Bruce, 1994) by providing:*

- Determination and distribution of rewards
- Networking connections
- Access to resources and information
- Career advice
- Work assignments and training opportunities
- Emotional support

Adapted from Eisenberg, Fasolo, and David-LaMastro (1990) and Wayne, Shore, and Liden (1997).

managerial/leadership style, can be considered key mechanisms through which the organization can transmit to employees important values and beliefs (Kopelman et al., 1990;
Schneider et al., 1998; Tesluk et al., 1997). Concurrently, researchers in the strategic HR
area have discussed the importance of aligning organizational culture with HR policies,
practices, programs, and processes (Schuler, 1992; Ulrich & LaFasto, 1995). Given that a
number of studies have demonstrated that a firm's HR practices can impact organization
performance (Arthur, 1992; Huselid, 1995; MacDuffie, 1995), attention is now being
focused on the underlying mechanisms. We believe that individual performance is part
of the equation; however, the specific processes are yet to be well understood. According to our view, and consistent with similar arguments presented by others (e.g., Ferris
et al., 1998; Kopelman et al., 1990; Ostroff & Bowen, 2000), the connection between
macro-organizational factors (e.g., organizational culture) and micro-level attitudes and
behaviors occurs at the intersection between HR systems, organizational climate and
normative contracts.

Climate refers to members' shared perceptions of the types of behaviors and actions
that are rewarded and supported by the organization's policies, practices, and procedures
(Schneider, 1990). Therefore, climate is directly influenced by HR practices (e.g., Pfluger,
1988). From a broad perspective, Kopelman et al. (1990) have argued that climate
perceptions can be considered in terms of the following central core of five dimensions
that cut across different types of work environments and strategic foci:

- *Goal emphasis*—the extent to which management makes known the types of outcomes
  and standards that employees are expected to accomplish.
- *Means emphasis*—the extent to which management makes known the methods and
  procedures that employees are expected to use in performing their jobs.
- *Reward orientation*—the extent to which various organizational rewards are perceived
  to be allocated on the basis of job performance.
- *Task support*—the extent to which employees perceive that they are being supplied
  with the materials, equipment, services, and resources necessary to perform their jobs.

- *Socioemotional support*—the extent to which employees perceive that their personal welfare is protected by a kind, considerate, and generally humane management.

Conceptualizing climate in terms of these dimensions provides a clear connection between HR practices and the aspects of the work environment that need to be present for effective individual performance. A supportive context for facilitating performance is one where goals are clearly defined, work methods are made known, rewards are established that motivate effort, equipment, materials, supplies, etc., are made available so that work is accomplished efficiently, and management is supportive and fair. A strong organizational climate, whether it be for innovation (Scott & Bruce, 1994), service (Schneider, 1990), safety (Hofmann & Stetzer, 1996, 1998; Zohar, 2000) or some other organizational imperative, is one where each of these dimensions is made salient through a consistent and mutually reinforcing set of HR practices and management systems.

If climate functions as the perceptual medium through which HR and management systems influence individual attitudes and behaviors toward a particular strategic goal, normative contracts function as a complementary set of collective perceptions by capturing the nature of the exchange relationship between employees and the organization (Ostroff & Bowen, 2000). In addition to signaling the types of behavior that are expected and rewarded (climate), HR practices also communicate the organization's commitments to its employees and its expectations of what employees should provide to the organization in return. These commitments and expectations that define the collective set of exchange agreements or *normative contracts* represent the beliefs that employees have regarding the promises that have been made, accepted, and relied on between themselves and their employer (Rousseau, 1985).

Normative contracts are typically one of two types: either transactional or relational, depending on the HR practices that shape them (Ostroff & Bowen, 2000). HR practices that articulate well-specified behaviors and responses in exchange for explicit rewards, and/or are of a limited term in duration, form transactional contracts. Contingent reward systems, outsourcing arrangements, use of temporary workers, and work organization in the form of tightly defined jobs with clearly specified rules, responsibilities, and reward structures are examples of HR systems that foster transactional contracts. In contrast, relational contracts are more abstract in that they specify more long-term and open-ended arrangements that defined performance expectations in more general terms in the form of loyalty, dedication, and engagement in extra-role behaviors (Rousseau, 1995). HR practices that signal to employees the organization's intention to foster relational contracts include providing training, opportunities for career advancement and promotion, assurances of job security, flexible and family-friendly work arrangements, and forms of compensation that tie the employee to the organization's performance (Guzzo & Noonan, 1994; Ostroff & Bowen, 2000).

Leadership/supervision, organizational climate and normative contracts

Managers and supervisors function as mechanisms for communicating the climate and establishing expectations for employees about the relationship they have with the organization, because of their prominent and influential roles and close psychological proximity to the focal individual (Lewin, 1938; Scott & Bruce, 1994). Because supervisors are the most salient representatives of management's actions and the organization's policies and procedures, employees tend to generalize their perceptions of the supervisors to the organization at large (Kozlowski & Doherty, 1989). Also, according to social information processing (SIP) theory, individuals' attitudes and perceptions are likely to be influenced by the opinions and information provided by others in the work setting (Salancik & Pfeffer, 1978). Moreover, SIP theory predicts that other people's preferences will affect attitudes only if the values of others are seen as relevant. Because supervisors form one of the most important and frequently used sources that employees have for obtaining job-relevant information, and since they occupy a position of authority, supervisors' opinions are also likely to be seen as highly relevant and therefore influential in shaping how employees view their work environment. Consistent with this line of reasoning, Kozlowski and Doherty (1989) found that employees whose relationship with their supervisor (LMX) was characterized by higher levels of trust, communication and respect had more positive perceptions of the organization's climate.

Leadership and supervision also can impact the nature of the exchange relationship that employees share with the organization (Rousseau, 1995). Supervisors can influence perceptions of organizational support by determining and distributing rewards, introducing subordinates to key individuals in other parts of the organization, providing access to resources and information, as well as offering career advice, work assignment, training opportunities, and emotional support (Eisenberger et al., 1990; Wayne et al., 1997). Thus, leaders who develop high-quality working relationships with their subordinates signal to employees a relational approach built on providing respect, opportunities for development, and promises of future rewards in exchange for dedication and hard work. In contrast, a more transactional-contingent reward leadership style where the supervisor relies primarily on the use of specified rewards in exchange for effort and performance is more likely to lead to the development of a transactional contract between the employee and the organization.

Organizational climate/normative contracts and individual attitudes/affective states and behavior

Research investigating organizational climate and normative contracts has found that they are related to individual attitudes, affective states, and behavior. Within the climate domain, for example, research has shown that individuals' perceptions of climate affect their satisfaction and performance (e.g., Lawler, Hall, & Oldham, 1974; Pritchard & Karasick, 1973). Other studies have focused on particular types of climates and found relationships with more targeted attitudinal and behavioral outcomes. Examples include relationships between climate for safety and safe working procedures, accident interpretation, and accidents/injuries (Hofmann & Stetzer, 1996; 1998; Zohar, 2000), climate for innovation and innovative behavior in a R&D settings (Scott & Bruce, 1994), climate for high-involvement and participation in involvement activities (Tesluk, Vance, & Mathieu, 1999) and climate for innovation and updating and pursuing developmental and skills-updating activities (Kozlowski & Hults, 1987).

Research has also investigated employee reactions to either the breach or fulfillment of normative contracts. For example, the work of Robinson, Rousseau, and colleagues (Robinson, 1996; Robinson & Morrison, 2000; Robinson & Rousseau, 1994; Rousseau, 1995) has demonstrated that perceived breach of the psychological contract leads to

reduced trust, job satisfaction, intentions to remain, and in-role and extra-role performance. On the opposite side of the coin, Tsui, Pearce, Porter, and Tripoli (1997) found that
when employers pursue normative contracts that signify a mutual investment approach
by providing employees with significant training, career development opportunities, and
job security in exchange for dedication and commitment, employees displayed high
performance, commitment, citizenship, and trust.

The final link: the relationship between salient individual-level behavior and organizational productivity/effectiveness

The notion that employee attitudes, motivation, and behavior are related to organizational
effectiveness is a tacit assumption that underlies the position that culture can facilitate
organizational success. It is almost axiomatic to state that satisfaction does not lead to
performance. However, lower task performance is only one of many possible responses
to dissatisfaction (Ostroff & Bowen, 2000). Dissatisfied employees are more likely to file
grievances, engage in sabotage, ask for a transfers, be absent, and fail to pass on important
information (Locke, 1984). In contrast, satisfied employees tend to put more effort into
their work, engage in a greater number of citizenship behaviors, demonstrate more
consistent attendance, and make more suggestions on how to improve work procedures.

Making the connection between employee behaviors and organizational productivity
is more challenging. As Ostroff and Bowen (2000) note, organizational productivity is
most likely based on the interaction among different types of positive employee behaviors rather than the simple sum of individual and work unit performance due to
interactions and interdependencies in work processes. In addition, the effects of individual contributions are likely to be difficult to detect unless they are viewed in the
aggregate. For instance, many citizenship behaviors contribute in very subtle and minor
ways (e.g., helping coworkers when they need some assistance). It is only when viewed
across many employees over an extended period of time that the net benefit of these
individual contributions has any type of significant impact on organizational functioning
(Kopelman et al., 1990; Ostroff, 1992).

A Final Word about the Model

It is important to emphasize that the pathways linking culture to individuals are not unidirectional. HR practices, for instance, are not just manifestations of the organization's
culture. They are also important mechanisms for attempting to change culture (Ulrich &
LaFasto, 1995). For this reason, organizations looking to attempt dramatic turnarounds
often start with staffing at the senior executive level in order to bring in new ideas and
insights that will help create a new culture. These changes in personnel at the senior
level also send a message to those remaining about what it means to be successful.
Similarly, leadership and supervisory styles serve to either reinforce or cause members
to question the basic assumptions and values that define the culture (Schein, 1990).
Normative contracts are also not only a function of culture, but once people hold common beliefs about what they owe their employer and what they are owed in turn, these
mutually held expectations become part of the organization's social norms. As Rousseau
(1995) notes, in effect the normative contract becomes part of the organization's culture.
Finally, following Schneider's (1987) attraction–selection–attrition (ASA) model, it is

the aggregate personal characteristics and behaviors of those who retain membership in the organization that shapes, and to a great degree even defines, the culture.

IS THERE SUCH A THING AS THE "RIGHT" CULTURE?

Having discussed both the direct and mediated pathways through which we believe culture influences individual attitudes, affect, and behavior, we now turn our attention to identifying specific dimensions of culture that facilitate individual effectiveness. In other words, the question we now turn to is not so much how does culture influence performance, but rather what types of cultures are likely to best facilitate performance. We think that there are certain types of cultural traits that appear to be important for generating the types of attitudes and behaviors that lead to effective individual performance across many different types of organizational settings. However, because of the lack of systematic research attempting to connect culture with individual level outcomes, we instead have to base this assertion on the body of research relating culture to *organizational* effectiveness. Although a wide variety of different cultural characteristics have been suggested as important for facilitating attitudes, motivation, and behaviors that foster effectiveness, we focus on four broadly defined types of cultural traits that consistently appear in the literature as being important for organizational effectiveness. In defining these traits we rely on the labels provided by Denison and Mishra (1995); however, each of these four traits has been described using different terminology. These four traits are: involvement/participation, consistency, adaptability, and mission/vision. Some fundamental strategies for promoting these cultural traits are provided in Table 22.4.

A cultural trait that has been linked to both current and future firm financial performance (Denison, 1984) and sales growth (Denison & Mishra, 1995) is involvement and participation. This is supported with a growing body of research demonstrating that high-involvement workplace systems that promote employee development, participation in decision making through empowerment practices and teams, and work redesign strategies that enrich work and broaden jobs and roles positively impact effectiveness (Arthur, 1992; Lawler, 1992; MacDuffie, 1995). Values that emphasize involvement and participation create a sense of ownership and responsibility that generates commitment and motivation. Employees have also been found to prefer working in companies that

TABLE 22.4 Strategies to promote cultural traits associated with organizational effectiveness (Denison & Mishra, 1995)

- Promote *involvement and participation* by enriching work, broadening jobs and roles, and providing employee input into decision making (Arthur, 1992; Lawler, 1992; MacDuffie, 1995).

- Contribute to *consistency* by ensuring that values are internalized through establishment, communication, and reinforcement of routines and procedures (Wilkins & Ouchi, 1983; Weick, 1987).

- Encourage *adaptability* by emphasizing understanding changing needs of key constituencies (e.g., customers, employees, stockholders) (Calori & Sarnin, 1991; Denison & Mishra, 1995; Kotter & Heskett, 1992).

- Contribute to *mission* by establishing clear goals and ensuring a shared understanding of long-term objectives that motivate effort (Latham & Locke, 1991; Hackman & Oldham, 1980; Locke, Kirkpatrick, Wheeler, Schneider, Niles, Goldstein, Welsh, & Chah, 1998).

have strong values emphasizing teamwork and respect for people and, as a result, are less likely to voluntarily leave (Sheridan, 1992). Values that support and reinforce employees' involvement and participation also build employees' capability to work autonomously by developing flexible work orientations (Parker et al., 1997).

Another cultural trait that has been linked to organizational profitability and other indicators of effectiveness is *consistency*, or the degree of normative integration (Denison & Mishra, 1995; Truskie, 1999). Effective organizations tend to have a clearly defined set of behaviors, systems, and meanings that members agree on and understand. Another way to view consistency is to consider it as an indicator of culture "strength" (Calori & Sarnin, 1991; Denison, 1984; Saffold, 1988). Consistency may be particularly important in conditions of high uncertainty and environmental complexity because internalized values can better facilitate coordination and integration (Wilkins & Ouchi, 1983; Weick, 1987). In other words, consistency functions as an implicit control system that members of the organization rely on when presented with ambiguous or ill-defined situations. This type of implicit control system is particularly important in performance environments that require a great deal of close coordination across individual, groups, and units, such as on aircraft carriers and nuclear power plant control rooms (Weick, 1987).

Adaptability is another cultural trait that has been found to be associated with organizational effectiveness (Calori & Sarnin, 1991; Denison & Mishra, 1995; Kotter & Heskett, 1992). It refers to the organization's ability to effectively adapt to external environmental conditions by balancing an emphasis on the importance of trying new ideas and understanding the needs and wants of clients and customers, with the maintenance of core values and character of the organization as these changes are made (Denison & Mishra, 1995). Cultures that emphasize adaptability can support a strategic orientation of more aggressive environmental scanning (Lei et al., 1997) and may encourage front-line employees to be more open (and less cynical) toward how they view and react to new initiatives and changes (cf. Reichers, Wanous, & Austin, 1996). It is important to note that there is tension between the culture traits of adaptability and consistency in that cultures that emphasize consistency are resistant to change because of the singular mind-set that resists alternative viewpoints. We elaborate further on this and other tensions between the different culture traits later on.

A final cultural trait that has been associated with organizational effectiveness in the literature is *mission*, or the extent to which members of the organization have an understanding of the long-term vision of the organization (Denison & Mishra, 1995; Truskie, 1999). Although mission refers to long-term objectives that are defined at the organizational level, vision is based on fundamental values that have personal meaning (Locke et al., 1998). Organizations that have a strong sense of mission make clear to members the reason for the company's existence, its purpose, and its roadmap for the future in terms of major goals and objectives (Collins & Porras, 1996). Infusing a strong sense of purpose and vision defines an overall course of action for those in the organization and thus supports setting appropriate performance expectations and goals that are aligned with the organization (cf. Latham & Locke, 1991). Mission can also contribute to the development of a sense of purpose and meaning that serves to enrich work in ways that motivate effort (Hackman & Oldham, 1980; Locke et al., 1998).

It is important to note that involvement and consistency focus on the internal integration of the organization (Denison & Mishra, 1995)—how the organization operates internally with respect to the roles, status, systems, and norms that determine patterns of interaction among individuals, groups, and units within the organization. In contrast, adaptability and mission are more critical in determining how the organization is linked to its environment, the other fundamental set of questions that are answered by culture (Schein, 1990). Another contrast presented in the four traits is that involvement and adaptability describe traits that relate to an organization's capability to change and be flexible, both internally (involvement) and externally (adaptability). Alternatively, consistency and mission focus on the organization's capability to maintain stability and direction, again, internally (consistency) and externally (mission). Thus, Denison and Mishra's (1995) model of cultural traits can be summarized according to two contrasts that all organizations face: one between internal integration and external adaptation and the other between change and stability.

These contrasts highlight a critical aspect of the different cultural dimensions, which are not mutually exclusive, but rather are mutually complementary. In other words, in order to be effective organizations must balance these different cultural dimensions (Baxley, 1996; Kotter & Heskett, 1992). Organizations that focus too much on developing one of these specific dimensions while ignoring its complementary dimension may be implicitly encouraging counter-productive behaviors. For instance, an involvement culture may foster behaviors that facilitate teamwork and helping-oriented citizenship behaviors, but focusing on involvement and simultaneously ignoring consistency may result in lack of direction and accountability as decisions and responsibility become increasingly diffused (Truskie, 1999). Thus, it is the countervailing forces of involvement and participation, and a strong normative system of regulation (i.e., consistency), that provide an implicit mechanism for guiding decisions and behavior in a highly autonomous and empowered setting.

The four cultural dimensions presented above, based on Denison and Mishra's (1995) work, can be placed into a broader framework of organizational performance. The framework is based on the work of Quinn (1988) and his colleagues (Quinn & Rohrbaugh, 1983), who have conducted research encompassing a large number of different performance criteria and developed a fourfold competing-values model. Similar to Denison and Mishra, two value dimensions form the heart of the four approaches to organizational performance. The first dimension is along an internal versus external organizational focus. An internal focus stresses the development and well-being of employees, while the external focus emphasizes the organization's ability to succeed and successfully accomplish tasks. The second dimension contrasts stability and control with flexibility and change, where stability and control focus on order and direction and flexibility and change emphasize innovation and adaptation. Quinn and colleagues also make a distinction between the organizational performance criteria (or the ends) and the processes (or the means) that the organization primarily relies upon to maximize those criteria.

Figure 22.2 is a modified version of this framework, as presented by Ostroff and Bowen (2000) who relied on the framework to make associations between HR practices and organizational performance. We present their version in an attempt to draw connections between organizational culture, HR practices, and organizational effectiveness. The boxes in the figure represent organizational performance criteria, the ovals indicate the individual-level behaviors that are especially critical in the achievement of those ends. We have added in italics the cultural traits from Denison and Mishra (1995) that correspond with each of the four different performance approaches. Note that the

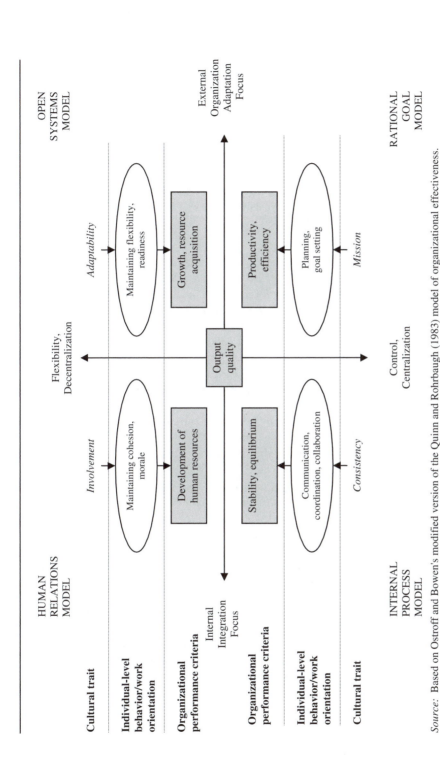

Source: Based on Ostroff and Bowen's modified version of the Quinn and Rohrbaugh (1983) model of organizational effectiveness.

FIGURE 22.2 Model of competing-values approach to organizational effectiveness

performance criteria of output quality corresponds to all performance approaches and is therefore located in the center.

Ostroff and Bowen (2000) use this framework on organizational performance to highlight the types of organizational factors that facilitate the types of work orientations and behaviors that employees need to demonstrate in order to best achieve certain performance objectives. In their words:

> "Growth and resource-acquisition outcomes require flexibility and adaptability from employees. Production and efficiency outcomes primarily require monitoring and control of employee behaviors. Stability and equilibrium outcomes require identification with and commitment to the organization, as well as monitoring and controlling of employee behaviors. For the development of human resource outcomes, relevant employee attributes include knowledge and skill development, satisfaction, intrinsic motivation, and citizenship." (p. 244)

The point that must be emphasized here is that an emphasis on certain organizational outcomes requires employees to be engaged in specific sets of work behaviors and adapt unique orientations to their work. Ostroff and Bowen focus on the different HR practices as the organizational factors of interest. We also include cultural values, thereby linking culture, HR practices, individual attitudes and behaviors, and organizational outcomes as presented in the model in Figure 22.1 that depicts the linkages between culture and individual-level outcomes.

There is evidence that the most effective organizations are those that are able to achieve a balance among the organizational factors that support different performance outcomes (Ostroff & Schmitt, 1993; Truskie, 1999). This balance, however, does not imply that certain cultural dimensions will not be more relevant to certain types of business strategies and environmental conditions (Calori & Sarnin, 1991). Specific business strategies require employees to engage their work with specific types of attitudes, work orientations, and behaviors (Miles & Snow, 1984; Schuler & Jackson, 1987). For instance, companies using an innovative–prospector strategy emphasize developing new and innovative products and service and being the first to introduce them into the markets. The effectiveness criteria for these firms, according to the framework in Figure 22.2, include adaptation to the environment, resource acquisition, growth, customer service, and increasing market share (Ostroff & Bowen, 2000). In order to accomplish these objectives, companies with this strategy need to have employees who think creatively, are innovative, and are flexible and adaptable. Organizations whose cultures emphasize adaptability are likely to facilitate these types of orientations and behaviors from their employees, particularly, if those cultural values are supported and reinforced by HR practices and leadership systems that are consistent with an adaptability focus (Ostroff & Bowen, 2000; Tesluk et al., 1997). Although clearly an adaptability focus would be beneficial in this situation, the competing values framework suggests that there are other complementary cultural dimensions that will need to be present in order to keep this adaptability focus "in-check". In other words, an adaptability focus that runs amok might lead to the constant development of new products to satisfy customer whims and, in the process, departure from the core competencies of the organization. In other words, it seems that an adaptability focus would need to be counter-balanced by a certain level of mission focus so that the innovation that does occur is consistent with the core competencies of the organization (i.e., the long-term vision of the organization).

In environments that are uncertain, complex, and dynamic, a more flexible and flatter organizational design is required to better enable rapid decision making and proactive responses to meet changing conditions (Galbraith, 1977). For example, Gordon and DiTomaso (1992) found that companies that faced this type of environment and placed greater emphasis on "action orientation", "initiative", and "organizational reach" tended to be more successful. These types of cultural values encourage flexibility, adaptability, and proactivity on the part of employees. In contrast, successful firms in more stable industries, emphasized "reliability", "integration", and "performance clarity", which encouraged employees to closely coordinate their work, make incremental and continuous improvements to work processes, and focus on improving efficiency.

In summary, consistent with models of organizational effectiveness that recognize that performance is multi-dimensional and that there are often trade-offs among effectiveness criteria, we have suggested that four sets of cultural traits appear to be particularly important for facilitating individual performance. While the most successful high-performance organizational cultures involve balancing competing values, effectiveness may be better served by emphasizing certain traits that are aligned with the specific business strategy and environmental conditions because these factors require particular sets of employee attitudes and behaviors. However, to a certain degree, moderation has to be emphasized as well. The other dimensions, even if they are not strongly emphasized, must still be present for effective functioning. While this seems to make sense theoretically, research needs to be conducted into investigating whether different organizational cultures that appear to be related to organizational performance are effective because they elicit and support specific sets of individual level attitudes, affect, and behaviors.

CONCLUSION

Our objective in this chapter has been to provide a framework for understanding the linkages that connect organizational culture to individual-level outcomes. As we have attempted to demonstrate, the associations between culture and worker outcomes can be complex and can take both direct and indirect pathways. In addition, the explication of these pathways requires an integrative approach drawing on both macro and micro organizational theory and research. If we are to make further progress in understanding the multiple mechanisms that appear to link culture to individual level outcomes, future empirical work is going to need to more integrative as well. Indeed, we believe that understanding these associations will require integrating the role of a variety of interrelated features of the organizational environment including, leadership, strategy, HR practices, climate, and normative contracts. Conducting this type of research will certainly not be easy, but it will allow us to answer some of the following important questions:

- Is it possible to be prescriptive when it comes to specifying a "high-performance" organizational culture—or, are the cultures that are most effective those that (a) are difficult to imitate (Barney, 1986) and/or (b) uniquely fit to an organization's strategy (Calori & Sarnin, 1991; Lei et al., 1997; Schwartz & Davis, 1981)? What does this imply in terms of individual-level performance in different organizational settings and contexts?
- Besides understanding the importance of having the "right" organizational culture, what is the importance of having a "strong" culture?

- If culture is an important consideration in individual performance, how do the influences occur (i.e., what are the *processes*)?
- Is changing an organization's culture a viable means to facilitate changes in individual-level behavior and work performance? If so, how is that process best accomplished and under what sorts of conditions can organizations expect this process to be more/less difficult?

Taking a meso approach that bridges culture and other organizational-level factors and connecting them to peoples' attitudes, affect, and behavior will provide a more complete understanding of employee performance and effectiveness at work and help address these and other questions. Ultimately, we believe that it will also help to develop greater integration of approaches that have been driven from either predominantly macro or micro perspectives to develop a more powerful means for researching organizational effectiveness.

REFERENCES

Allen, N. J., & Meyer, J. P. (1990). Organization socialization tactics: A longitudinal analysis of links to newcomers' commitment and role orientation. *Academy of Management Journal, 33*, 847–858.

Arthur, J. B. (1992). The link between business strategy and industrial relations systems in American steel minimills. *Industrial and Labor Relations Review, 45*, 488–506.

Ashforth, B. E., & Saks, A. M. (1996). Socialization tactics: Longitudinal effects on newcomer adjustment. *Academy of Management Journal, 39*, 149–178.

Baker, E. L. (1980). Managing organizational culture. *Management Review, 69*, 8–13.

Baker, H. E., III (1992). Employee socialization strategies and the presence of union representation. *Labor Studies Journal, 17*, 5–17.

Barley, S. R., Meyer, C. W., & Gash, D. C. (1988). Culture of cultures: Academics, practitioners and the pragmatics of normative control. *Administrative Science Quarterly, 33*, 24–60.

Barney, J. B. (1986). Organizational culture: Can it be a source of sustained competitive advantage? *Academy of Management Review, 11*, 656–665.

Baxley, D. J. (1996). *IBM I/T transportation consortium best practices benchmark.* A report by IBM Inc.

Bowen, D. E., Ledford, G. E., & Nathan, B. R. (1991). Hiring for the organization, not the job. *Academy of Management Executive, 5*, 35–51.

Bretz, R. D., & Judge, T. A. (1993). Person–organization fit and the theory of work adjustment: Implications for satisfaction, tenure, and career success. *Journal of Vocational Behavior, 44*, 32–54.

Cable, D. M., & Judge, T. A. (1996). Person–organization fit, job choice decisions, and organizational entry. *Organizational Behavior and Human Decision Processes, 67*, 294–311.

Calori, R., & Sarnin, P. (1991). Corporate culture and economic performance. *Organization Studies, 12*, 49–74.

Cappelli, P. (1999). *The new deal at work.* Boston: Harvard Business School Press.

Cappelli, P., & Sherer, P. D. (1991). The missing role of context in OB: The need for a meso-level approach. In B. M. Staw & L. Cummings (Eds.), *Research in organizational behavior* (vol. 14, pp. 55–110). Greenwich, CT: JAI Press

Chao, G. T., O'Leary-Kelly, A. M., Wolf, S., Klein, H. J., & Gardner, P. D. (1994). Organizational socialization: Its content and consequences. *Journal of Applied Psychology, 79*, 730–743.

Chatman, J. A. (1989). Improving interactional organizational research: A model of person–organization fit. *Academy of Management Review, 14*, 333–349.

Chatman, J. A. (1991). Matching people and organizations: Selection and socialization in public accounting firms. *Administrative Science Quarterly, 36*, 459–484.

Chatman, J. A., & Barsdale, S. G. (1995). Personality, organizational culture, and cooperation: Evidence from a business simulation. *Administrative Science Quarterly*, **40**, 423–444.

Chatman, J. A., & Jehn, K. A. (1994). Assessing the relationship between industry characteristics and organizational culture: How different can you be? *Academy of Management Journal*, **37**, 522–553.

Collins, J. C., & Porras, J. I. (1996). Building your company's vision. *Harvard Business Review*, *September–October*, 65–77.

Cooke, R. A., & Lafferty, J. C. (1986). *Level V: Organizational culture inventory* (Form III). Plymouth, MI: Human Synergistics.

Cooke, R. A., & Rousseau, D. A. (1988). Behavioral norms and expectations: A quantitative approach to the assessment of organizational culture. *Group and Organization Studies*, **13**, 245–273.

Cooke, R. A., & Szumal, J. L. (1993). Measuring normative beliefs and shared behavioral expectations in organizations: The reliability and validity of the organizational culture inventory. *Psychological Reports*, **72**, 1299–1330.

Deal, T., & Kennedy, A. (1982). *Corporate cultures*. Reading, MA: Addison-Wesley.

Denison, D. R. (1984). Brining corporate culture to the bottom line. *Organizational Dynamics*, **13**, 4–22.

Denison, D. R. (1990). *Corporate culture and organizational effectiveness*. New York: Wiley.

Denison, D. R., & Mishra, A. K. (1995). Toward a theory of organizational culture and effectiveness. *Organization Science*, **6**, 204–223.

Eisenberger, R., Fasolo, P., & Davis-LaMastro, V. (1990). Perceived organizational support and employee diligence, commitment, and innovation. *Journal of Applied Psychology*, **75**, 51–59.

Feldman, D. C. (1976). A contingency theory of socialization. *Administrative Science Quarterly*, **21**, 433–452.

Ferris, G. R., Arthur, M. M., Berkson, H. M., Kaplan, D. M., Harrell-Cook, G., & Frink, D. D. (1998). Toward a social context theory of the human resource management–organization effectiveness relationship. *Human Resource Management Review*, **8**, 235–264.

Galbraith, J. (1977). *Organization design*. Reading, MA: Addison-Wesley.

Goffee, R., & Jones, G. (1998). *The character of the corporation: How your company's culture can make or break your business*. New York: Harper Business.

Gordon, G. G. (1991). Industry determinants of organizational culture. *Academy of Management Review*, **16**, 396–415.

Gordon, G. G., & DiTomaso, N. (1992). Predicting organizational performance from organizational culture. *Journal of Management Studies*, **29** (6), 783–798.

Guzzo, R. A., & Noonan, K. A. (1994). Human resource practices as communications of the psychological contract. *Human Resource Management*, **33**, 447–462.

Hackman, J. R. (1992). Group influences on individuals in organizations. In M. D. Dunnette & L. M. Hough (Eds.), *Handbook of industrial and organizational psychology* (2nd edn., pp. 199–267). Palo Alto, CA: Consulting Psychologists Press.

Hackman, J. R., & Oldham, G. R. (1980). *Work redesign*. Reading, MA: Addison-Wesley.

Hattrup, K., & Jackson, S. E. (1996). Learning about individual differences by taking situations seriously. In K. R. Murphy (Ed.), *Individual differences and behavior in organizations* (pp. 507–547). San Francisco: Jossey-Bass.

Hofmann, D. A., & Stetzer, A (1996). A cross-level investigation of the factors influencing unsafe behaviors and accidents. *Personnel Psychology*, **49**, 307–339.

Hofmann, D. A., & Stetzer, A. (1998). The role of safety climate and communication in accident interpretation: Implications for learning from negative events. *Academy of Management Journal*, **41**, 644–657.

House, R., Rousseau, D. M., & Thomas-Hunt, M. (1995). The meso paradigm: A framework for the integration of micro and macro organizational behavior. *Research in Organizational Behavior*, **17**, 41–114.

Howard, A. (1995). A framework for work change. In A. Howard (Ed.), *The changing nature of work* (pp. 3–44). San Francisco: Jossey-Bass.

Huselid, M. A. (1995). The impact of human resource management practices on turnover, productivity, and corporate financial performance. *Academy of Management Journal*, **38**, 400–422.

James, L. R., & Jones, A. P. (1976). Organizational structure: A review of structural dimensions and their conceptual relationship with individual attitudes and behavior. *Organizational Behavior and Human Performance*, **16**, 74–113.

Jones, G. R. (1986). Socialization tactics, self-efficacy, and newcomers' adjustments to organizations. *Academy of Management Journal*, **29**, 262–279.

Judge, T. A., & Cable, D. M. (1997). Applicant personality, organizational culture, and organization attraction. *Personnel Psychology*, **50**, 359–394.

Juechter, W., & Fisher, C. (1998). Corporate culture. *Training and Development*, **52** (5), 63–68.

Katz, D., & Kahn, R. (1978). *The social psychology of organizations*. New York: Wiley.

Kilman, R. H., Saxton, M. J., Serpa, R., & Associates (Eds.) (1985). *Gaining control of corporate culture*. San Francisco: Jossey-Bass.

Klein, K. J., Dansereau, F., & Hall, R. J. (1994). Levels issues in theory development, data collection, and analysis. *Academy of Management Review*, **19**, 195–229.

Klein, H. J., & Weaver, N. A. (2000). The effectiveness of an organizational-level orientation training program in the socialization of new hires. *Personnel Psychology*, **53**, 47–66.

Klein, A. S., Masi, R. J., & Weidner, C. K. (1995). Organizational culture, distribution and amount of control and perceptions of quality. *Group and Organization Management*, **20**, 122–148.

Kohn, M. L., & Schooler, C. (1982). Job conditions and personality: A longitudinal assessment of their reciprocal effects. *American Journal of Sociology*, **87**, 1257–1286.

Kopelman, R. E., Brief, A. P., & Guzzo, R. A. (1990). The role of climate and culture in productivity. In B. Schneider (Ed.), *Organizational climate and culture* (pp. 282–318). San Francisco: Jossey-Bass.

Kotter, K., & Heskett, J. (1992). *Culture and performance*. New York: Free Press.

Kozlowski, S., & Doherty, M. (1989). Integration of climate and leadership: Examination of a neglected topic. *Journal of Applied Psychology*, **74**, 546–553.

Kozlowski, S., & Hults, B. M. (1987). An exploration of climates for technical updating and performance. *Personnel Psychology*, **40**, 539–563.

Kozlowski, S. W. J., & Klein, K. J. (2000). A multilevel approach to theory and research in organizations: Contextual, temporal and emergent properties. In K. J. Klein & S. W. J. Kozlowski (Eds.), *Multilevel theory, Research, and methods in organizations: Foundations, extentions and New directions* (pp. 3–90). San Francisco: Jossey-Bass.

Latham, G. P., & Locke, E. A. (1991). Self-regulation through goal setting. *Organizational Behavior and Human Decision Processes*, **50**, 212–247.

Lawler, E. E., Hall, D. T., & Oldham, G. R. (1974). Organizational climate: Relationship to organizational structure, process and performance. *Organizational Behavior and Human Performance*, **11**, 139–155.

Lawler, E. E., III (1992). *The ultimate advantage: Creating the high-involvement organization*. San Francisco: Jossey-Bass.

Lawler, E. E., III (1994). From job-based to competency-based organizations. *Journal of Organizational Behavior*, **15**, 3–15.

Lei, D., Slocum, J. W., Jr., & Slater, R. W. (1997). Global strategy and reward systems: The key roles of management development and corporate culture. *Organizational Dynamics*, **19** (2), 27–41.

Lewin, K. (1938). *The conceptual representation of the measurement of psychological forces*. Durham, NC: Duke University Press.

Locke, E. A. (1976). The nature and causes of job satisfaction. In M. D. Dunnette (Ed.), *Handbook of industrial and organizational psychology* (pp. 1297–1349). Chicago: Rand McNally.

Locke, E. A. (1984). Job satisfaction. In M. Gruneberg & T. Wall (Eds.), *Social psychology and organizational behavior* (pp. 93–117). New York: Wiley.

Locke, E. A., Kirkpatrick, S., Wheeler, J. K., Schneider, J., Niles, K., Goldstein, H., Welsh, K., & Chah, D. (1998). *The essence of leadership: The four keys to leading successfully*. New York: Lexington Books.

Louis, M. R. (1980). Surprise and sensemaking : What new-comers experience in entering unfamiliar organizational settings. *Administrative Science Quarterly*, **25**, 226–251.

Marcoulides, G. A., & Heck, R. H. (1993). Organizational culture and performance: Proposing and testing a model. *Organization Science*, **4**, 209–225.

MacDuffie, J. P. (1995). Human resource bundles and manufacturing performance: Organizational logic and flexible production systems in the work auto industry. *Industrial and Labor Relations Review*, **48**, 199–221.

Meglino, B. M., Ravlin, E. C., & Adkins, C. L. (1989). A work values approach to corporate culture: A field test of the value congruence process and its relationship to individual outcomes. *Journal of Applied Psychology*, **74**, 424–432.

Miles, R. E., & Snow, C. C. (1984). Designing strategic human resource systems. *Organizational Dynamics*, **13**, 36–52.

Murphy, P. R., & Jackson, S. E. (1999). Managing work role performance: Challenges for twenty-first-century organizations and their employees. In D. R. Ilgen & E. D. Pulakos (Eds.), *The changing nature of performance: Implications for staffing, motivation, and development* (pp. 325–365). San Francisco: Jossey-Bass.

Nemeth, C. J., & Staw, B. M. (1989). The tradeoffs of social control and innovation in groups and organizations. In L. Berkowitz (Ed.), *Advances in experimental social psychology* (vol. 22, pp. 175–210). San Diego: Academic Press.

O'Reilly, C., Chatman, J., & Caldwell, D. F. (1991). People and organizational culture: A profile comparison approach to assessing person–organization fit. *Academy of Management Journal*, **34**, 487–516.

Ostroff, C. (1992). The relationship between satisfaction, attitudes, and performance: An organizational-level analysis. *Journal of Applied Psychology*, **77**, 963–974.

Ostroff, C., & Bowen, D. E. (2000). Moving HR to a higher level: HR practices and organizational effectiveness. In K. J. Klein & S. W. J. Kozlowski (Eds.), *Mulitlevel theory, research, and methods in organizations: Foundations, extensions, and new directions*. San Francisco: Jossey-Bass.

Ostroff, C., & Schmitt, N. (1993). Configurations of organizational effectiveness and efficiency. *Academy of Management Journal*, **36**, 1345–1361.

Ostroff, C., & Rothausen, T. J. (1997). The moderating effect of tenure in person–organization fit: A field study of education organizations. *Journal of Occupational and Organizational Psychology*, **70**, 173–188.

Ouchi, W. G. (1981). *Theory Z*. Reading, MA: Addison-Wesley.

Parker, S. K., Wall, T. D., & Jackson, P. R. (1997). "That's not my job": Developing flexible employee work orientations. *Academy of Management Journal*, **40**, 899–929.

Peters, T. J., & Waterman, R. H. (1982). *In search of excellence*. New York: Harper.

Petty, M. M., Beadles, N. A., Lowrey, C. M., Chapman, D. F., & Connell, D. W. (1995). Relationships between organizational culture and organizational performance. *Psychological Reports*, **76**, 483–492.

Pfluger, O. (1988). The effect of two interventions on specific dimension of organizational climate. Unpublished doctoral dissertation. *Dissertation Abstracts International*, **50** (028), 775.

Posner, B. Z. (1992). Person–organization values congruence: No support for individual differences as moderating influence. *Human Relations*, **45**, 351–361.

Pritchard, R. D., & Karasick, B. W. (1973). The effects of organizational climate on managerial job performance and job satisfaction. *Organizational Behavior and Human Performance*, **9**, 126–146.

Quinn, R. E. (1988). *Beyond rational management*. San Francisco: Jossey-Bass.

Quinn, R. E., & Rohrbaugh, J. (1983). A spatial model of effectiveness criteria: Towards a competing-values approach to organizational analysis. *Management Science*, **29**, 363–377.

Reichers, A. E., Wanous, J. P., & Austin, J. T. (1996). Understanding and managing cynicism about organizational change. *Academy of Management Executive*, **11**, 48–59.

Robinson, S. L. (1996). Trust and breach of the psychological contract. *Administrative Science Quarterly*, **41**, 574–599.

Robinson, S. L., & Morrison, E. W. (2000). The development of psychological contract breach and violation: A longitudinal study. *Journal of Organizational Behavior*, **21**, 525–546.

Robinson, S. L., & Rousseau, D. M. (1994). Violating the psychological contract: Not the exception but the norm. *Journal of Organizational Behavior*, **15**, 245–259.

Rokeach, M. (1973). *The nature of human values*. New York: Free Press.

Rousseau, D. M. (1985). Issues of level in organizational research: Multi-level and cross-level perspectives. In L. L. Cummings & B. Staw (Eds.), *Research in organizational behavior* (vol. 7, pp. 1–37). Greenwich, CT: JAI Press.

Rousseau, D. M. (1990). Normative beliefs in fund-raising organizations: Linking culture to organizational performance and individual responses. *Group and Organization Studies*, **15**, 448–460.

Rousseau, D. M. (1995). *Psychological contracts in organizations: Understanding written and unwritten agreements*. Newbury Park, CA: Sage.

Saffold, G. S. (1988). Culture traits, strength, and organizational performance: Moving beyond a strong culture. *Academy of Management Review*, **13**, 546–558.

Salancik, G. R., & Pfeffer, J. (1978). A social information processing approach to job attitudes and task design. *Administrative Science Quarterly*, **23**, 224–253.

Schein, E. H. (1968). Organizational socialization and the profession of management. *Industrial Management Review*, **9**, 1–16.

Schein, E. H. (1971). The individual, the organization, and the career: A conceptual scheme. *Journal of Applied Behavioral Science*, **7**, 401–426.

Schein, E. H. (1985). *Organizational culture and leadership*. San Francisco: Jossey-Bass.

Schein, E. H. (1990). Organizational culture. *American Psychologist*, **45**, 109–119.

Schein, E. H. (1996). Culture: The missing concept in organization studies. *Administrative Science Quarterly*, **41**, 229–240.

Schein, E. H. (1999). *The corporate culture survival guide*. San Francisco: Jossey-Bass.

Schneider, B. (1987). The people make the place. *Personnel Psychology*, **40**, 437–453.

Schneider, B. (1990). The climate for service: An application of the climate construct. In B. Schneider (Ed.), *Organizational culture and climate* (pp. 383–412). San Francisco: Jossey-Bass.

Schneider, B., Gunnarson, S. K., & Niles-Jolly, K. (1994). Creating the climate and culture of success. *Organizational Dynamics*, **23**, 17–29.

Schneider, B., & Rentsch, J. (1987). Managing climates and cultures: A future perspective. In J. Hage (Ed.), *Futures of organizations* (pp. 181–200). Lexington, MA: Lexington Books.

Schneider, B., Smith, D. B., Taylor, S., & Fleenor, J. (1998). Personality and organizations: A test of the homogeneity of personality hypothesis. *Journal of Applied Psychology*, **83**, 462–470.

Schuler, R. S. (1992). Strategic human resource management: Linking people with the needs of the business. *Organizational Dynamics*, **22**, 19–32.

Schuler, R. S., & Jackson, S. E. (1987). Linking competitive strategy and human resource management practices. *Academy of Management Executive*, **3**, 207–219.

Schwartz, H., & Davis, S. M. (1981). Matching corporate culture and business strategy. *Organizational Dynamics*, **33** (Summer), 30–48.

Scott, S. G., & Bruce, R. A. (1994). Determinants of innovative behavior: A path model of innovation in the workplace. *Academy of Management Journal*, **37**, 580–607.

Siehl, C., & Martin, J. (1990). Organizational culture: A key to financial performance? In B. Schneider (Ed.), *Organizational culture and climate* (pp. 241–281). San Francisco: Jossey-Bass.

Sheridan, J. E. (1992). Organizational culture and employee retention. *Academy of Management Journal*, **35**, 1036–1056.

Stein, N. (2000). Winning the war to keep top talent. *Fortune, May 29*, 132–138.

Tesluk, P. E., Farr, J. L., & Klein, S. R. (1997). Influences of organizational culture and climate on individual creativity. *Journal of Creative Behavior*, **31**, 27–41.

Tesluk, P. E., Vance, R. J., & Mathieu, J. E. (1999). Examining employee involvement in the context of participative work environments. *Group and Organization Management*, **24**, 271–299.

Truskie, S. D. (1999). *Leadership in high-performance organizational cultures*. Westport, CT: Quorum Books.

Tsui, A. S., Pearce, J. L., Porter, L. W., & Tripoli, A. M. (1997). Alternative approaches to the employee–organization relationship: Does investment in employees pay off? *Academy of Management Journal*, **40**, 1089–1121.

Ulrich, D. O., & LaFasto, F. (1995). Organizational culture and human resource management. In G. R. Ferris, S. D. Rosen, & D. T. Barnum (Eds.), *Handbook of human resource management* (pp. 317–336), Cambridge, MA: Blackwell Business.

Van Maanen, J. (1975). Police socialization: A longitudinal examination of job attitudes in an urban police department. *Administrative Science Quarterly*, **20**, 207–228.

Van Maanen, J., & Schein, E. H. (1979). Toward a theory of organizational socialization. In B. M. Staw & L. L. Cummings (Eds.), *Research in organizational behavior* (vol. 1, pp. 204–264). Greenwich, CT: JAI Press.

Vandenberghe, C. (1999). Organizational culture, person–culture fit, and turnover: A replication in the health care industry. *Journal of Organizational Behavior*, **20**, 175–184.

Wageman, R. (1995). Interdependence and group effectiveness. *Administrative Science Quarterly*, **40**, 145–180.

Wayne, S. J., Shore, L. M., & Liden, R. C. (1997). Perceived organizational support and leader–member exchange: A social exchange perspective. *Academy of Management Journal*, **40**, 82–111.

Weick, K. E. (1979). The social psychology of organizing. Reading, MA: Addison-Wesley.

Weick, K. E. (1987). Organizational culture as a source of high reliability. *California Management Review*, **29**, 112–127.

Weiss, H. M. (1977). Subordinate imitation of supervisor behavior: The role of modeling in organizational socialization. *Organizational Behavior and Human Performance*, **19**, 89–105.

Wilkins, A. L., & Ouchi, W. G. (1983). Efficient cultures: Exploring the relationship between culture and organizational performance. *Administrative Science Quarterly*, **28**, 468–481.

Zohar, D. (2000). A group-level model of safety climate: Testing the effect of group climate on microaccidents in manufacturing jobs. *Journal of Applied Psychology*, **85**, 587–596.

Organizational Culture: A Case Study

Jaap J. van Muijen
LTP, Amsterdam, The Netherlands

SUMMARY

This chapter presents a case study about changing the organizational culture. The case study concerned a merger of 14 organizations into one. The culture within the organization was measured by using the FOCUS-questionnaire based on the competing values model. There were large cultural differences between several parts of the organization. The overall consequence was a strong focus on internal affairs, which could threatened the performance of the organization in a severe way. The organization was in need of a clear vision and strategy in order to create a unified whole. The process of formulating the desired strategy for the organization and the consequences for the culture and leadership style are described. Furthermore, there is a reflection on the pitfalls and challenges during the process of establishing a solid unified culture. In particular, the chapter describes the role of psychological contract violation during such process.

INTRODUCTION

This chapter presents a case study in an agriculture cooperation in the Netherlands. The organization, Boer, has more than a thousand employees and a turnover of more than $100 million. As consultants, we were asked to do research into organizational culture, as the organization was recently formed through a merger of 14 different units. The directors were interested in finding if there were large cultural differences between the former separate parties and how this could cause problems in the new organization.

Psychological Management of Individual Performance. Edited by Sabine Sonnentag.
© 2002 John Wiley & Sons, Ltd.

Furthermore, Boer was reflecting on an appropriate strategy in the near future. We will describe the results of a quantitative and qualitative study on organizational culture in Boer (present situation) and the process of forming a strategy (desired situation) and in which way the organization is moving to the desired state.

However, first of all we will consider the scientific debate on whether culture can be measured by quantitative methods. This will be followed by a description of the competing values model on which the questionnaire used in this study is based.

ORGANIZATIONAL CULTURE: HOW IS IT MEASURED?

Since the 1980s there has been an ongoing scientific debate between culture researchers on whether culture can be measured using quantitative methods. Some are pertinently opposed to this idea (Schwartz & Davis, 1981; Trice & Beyer, 1993), while others see no profound objections (Den Hartog et al., 1999; Denison & Mishra, 1995; Hofstede, 1980; 1991; House et al., 1999). This debate is related to the origins of the culture concept.

Traditionally, anthropologists studied culture as a scientific topic. However, the interest in organizational culture during the 1980s and 1990s stems from such different sources as anthropology, sociology, and psychology (Brown, 1995). In studying culture anthropologists and sociologists emphasize the importance of rituals, stories, and symbols in daily life. Ethnography which is, briefly, the study of the social impact of symbols in a culture over a long period of time (Cohen, 1974) is a commonly used method of research. "The key to understanding culture lies in a portrayal and analysis of how members of the culture structure the meanings of their world" (Barley, 1983, p. 395). In the case of organizational culture, the organization should be understood and interpreted by analyzing artifacts, behavioral patterns and other visible characteristics, and their symbolic implications. "The organizational analyst focuses on how organization members interpret their experiences, how these interpretations influence their behaviors, and, how they arrive at shared interpretations, meanings, and knowledge" (Van Muijen, 1998, p. 117). In other words, one is interested in the evolution of social systems over time.

Psychologists also influenced the concept of organizational culture, especially from work on organizational climate during the 1970s. In general, climate refers to "a set of conditions that exist and have an impact on individual's behavior" (Denison, 1990, p. 24). Most studies on organizational climate have used quantitative methods. In such research, individual organizational members are asked to describe the climate by filling in a standard questionnaire regarding several conditions or systems within the organization. The main interest of climate researchers is on the impact of these conditions or systems on groups and individuals (Ekvall, 1987; Rentsch, 1990; Schneider, 1975).

We argued elsewhere (Van Muijen et al., 1999) that there are no scientific constraints in the use of quantitative methods in a study of organizational culture. In fact quantitative and qualitative methods lead to differences in interpretation rather than differences in the phenomenon, that is organizational culture (see Denison, 1996). If one is interested in scanning national or organizational culture, it might be better to use questionnaires, and, in contrast, for a more comprehensive view of meaning one might be better to use qualitative methods. In our study we used both methods.

In our view organizational culture is about shared values, shared behavioral norms and behavioral patterns within an organization, which govern the ways people interact with each other and invest energy in their jobs and the organization at large.

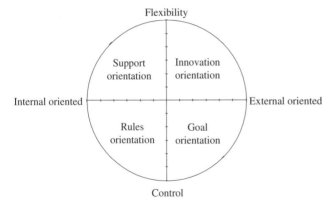

FIGURE 23.1 The competing values model of organizational culture

THE COMPETING VALUES MODEL OF ORGANIZATIONAL CULTURE

Our approach in measuring organizational culture is based on the competing values model (Quinn, 1988). This model consists of two dimensions with contrasting poles (see Figure 23.1). The first dimension represents the organization's point of view. The focus can either be directed internally, which makes the organization itself, its processes or its people, the central issue, or externally, which makes the relation of the organization with its environment the central issue. The contrasting poles of flexibility and control form the second dimension. Combining these two dimensions, four organizational culture orientations are obtained (Quinn, 1988). Organizations can score high on none, one or any combination of the orientations. The four orientations are the support, the innovative, the rules, and the goal orientation (Van Muijen & Koopman, 1994; Van Muijen, 1998).

Central to the *support* orientation are concepts like participation, cooperation, people based, mutual trust, team spirit, and individual growth. Communication is often verbal and informal. Employees are encouraged to express ideas about their work and feeling about each other. Decision making often runs through informal contacts. Commitment of the individual employee is emphasized. The *innovative* orientation is characterized by concepts like searching for new information in the environment, creativity, openness to change, anticipation, and experimentation. Control from above is neither possible nor required and management expects commitment and involvement of employees. The *rules* orientation emphasizes respect for authority, rationality of procedures, and division of work. The structure is hierarchical and communication is often written and top-down. Power is based on formal authority. The *goal* orientation emphasizes concepts like rationality, performance indicators, accomplishment, accountability, and contingent reward.

The competing values model is circumplex. In other words, the circle (Figure 23.1) can be read from left to right and vice versa. Values of behavioral patterns of each orientation share some characteristics with values or behavioral patterns of the adjoining orientation. For example, the support orientation and the innovative orientation share an emphasis on flexibility and cooperation between colleagues. The innovative orientation and the goal orientation have in common an external focus. There is tension between the values of the diametrical orientations. Stability and control (the rules orientation) are opposed to creativity and change (the innovative orientation). Team spirit and cooperation (the support orientation) contrast with contingent reward and accountability (the goal orientation).

BOER

Boer is an agriculture cooperation in the Netherlands. It was formed in the 1990s through a merger of 14 organizations. There are more than a thousand employees and there is a turnover of more than 100 million US dollars. Boer has a dominant market position in the Netherlands and did some international acquisitions. Their major problem is a shrinking market in the Netherlands, because of several national and EC regulations. Furthermore, there are new players in the field who penetrate the market. The structure of Boer located in the Netherlands is as follows: there is a corporate head office (CHO), a research center (R&D), a databank center (Data) and three divisions, North, East and South. The first three are situated in one large building; the three divisions are located in separate buildings throughout the Netherlands. The directors of Boer were interested to discover if there were cultural differences between the headquarters and the three divisions.

METHOD

We used the FOCUS questionnaire for measuring organizational culture. This instrument is based on the competing values model (Quinn, 1988) and measures the four cultural orientations. The instrument consists of two parts: a descriptive and a value-characteristic part (Van Muijen et al., 1999). The items of the descriptive part measure directly observable behaviors, procedures, and policies within the organization (for example, how many persons with personal problems are helped in this organization?). The items of the value-characteristic part measure the perception of some typically characteristics of the organization (for example, how typical is risk taking in this organization?).

In this study only the descriptive part was used. The respondents were asked to describe on a 6-point scale how often a certain event occurred ("never" to "always") or for how many people in the organization the event was true ("nobody" to "everyone"). Concerning the content of the items and the psychometric data of the scales we refer to Van Muijen et al. (1999).

Rousseau (1988) clarifies the importance of the instruction level of a questionnaire in climate research. The instruction level of a questionnaire directs a respondent to the appropriate frame of reference. In general, it is necessary to specify the unit of analysis on which the individual is asked to focus (e.g., department, organization, or job) and to construct items on that level of analysis (Van Muijen, 1998). In our case we were interested in organizational culture, so the items were formulated on the organizational level, that is Boer, and the instruction level concerning Boer. The instruction level was as follows: "On the following pages short statements are presented which might be typical for your organization. Please, think about your organization as a whole when answering. The statement should capture your opinion about the whole organization, not only about the department or unit in which you work daily." A corresponding item was "How often are work activities predictable at Boer?". If the formulation of the item was "How often are your work activities predictable?", the item would not be constructed on the organizational level, but on the, inappropriate, individual level.

Management installed a task force for this study. The task group was responsible for the study and the way employees would be informed about the results. The task force consisted of eight persons: three managers from R&D, two HRM specialists, two managers from the divisions, and the director of communication and internal affairs. We suggested that the task force should send the questionnaire to all the employees and, in this way, management would accentuate the message that each worker was important to the organization and that the organization was interested in everyone's opinion.

PROCEDURE

All employees received, at their home address, the FOCUS questionnaire, a letter from Boer, a letter from the researchers, and a prestamped envelope. The employees were requested to send the questionnaire back after completion to LTP, the consultancy firm. The researchers could be contacted by telephone at various prearranged times to answers questions.

To get a more comprehensive picture of the organization we interviewed several key figures in the organization. Furthermore, there were several work session with organizational members where we discussed the results of the quantitative survey.

THE RESULTS

Here we will present the results from the quantitative study and from the interviews and working sessions. After a merger it is usual for many people to be dissatisfied. In fact, most people show resistance against any forced change and this was also the case within Boer. The merger process has led to the following consequences:

- 14 organizations have merged into 1;
- the organization has gone from regional to national governance,
- the organization has moved from a stable situation to a dynamic situation.

Most people were more satisfied with the old situation. They described their situation before the merger, in contrast with the present situation, as warm, friendly and well organized. However, the data of the questionnaire show some remarkable differences between the various parts of Boer.

First of all, we compared the results of Boer with the mean scores of the reference group 'industry'. A lot of companies in this reference group showed up as Boer R&D activities and produced standard products. Therefore, we transformed the 6-point scale to a 9-point scale with 5 as standardized mean. Figure 23.2 shows a comparison of Boer with one of the reference groups.

Boer was characterized by a relatively high score on support orientation and lower scores on innovation, rules and goal orientation.

There were significant differences between the several divisions of Boer. Figures 23.3–23.6 show the differences between CHO, R&D, Data, and the three divisions on the four cultural orientations. In general, the divisions were more characterized by the control side of the cultural model than CHO, R&D, and Data. On the other hand, CHO, R&D and Data were more characterized by the flexibility side of the model. The divisions were more goal and rule oriented and the central parts more support and innovation

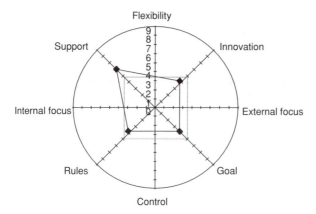

FIGURE 23.2 The results of Boer in comparison with reference group 'industry'

oriented. The differences on the support and innovation orientations suggested that the loss of warmth and respect (some of the results of the interviews) were mainly felt in the divisions and not at CHO, R&D and Data. This assumption was confirmed during several sessions with respondents. Before the merger, there were large differences between the 14 organizations in terms of productivity, client-orientation, power distance between management and workers, and scale. In the divisions the impact of the merger was more profound than for the R&D and Data. The people in the divisions had now to work closely together with former competitors within the same organization which in one division, resulted in a struggle for power. After the merger many people were angry and felt hurt, which led to the following vicious circle:

> wounded pride led to subtle opposition to the new managers or, in some cases, to counteraction; and this led to tensions and dissatisfaction for all involved, resulting in wounded pride for some others; and so on. The overall consequence was a strong focus on internal affairs, which could threatened the production process and the productivity rate.

Support orientation

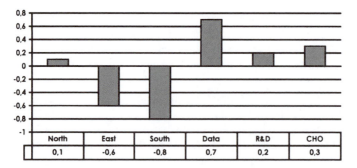

	North	East	South	Data	R&D	CHO
	0,1	-0,6	-0,8	0,7	0,2	0,3

FIGURE 23.3 The differences between the 6 units of Boer on support (North, South and East are the divisions; Data = databank center; R& D = research and development; CHO = corporate head office)

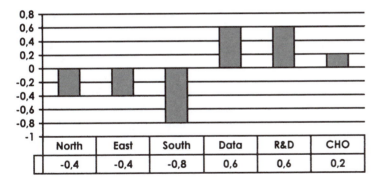

FIGURE 23.4 The differences between the 6 units of Boer on innovation

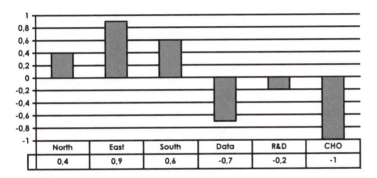

FIGURE 23.5 The differences between the 6 units of Boer on rules

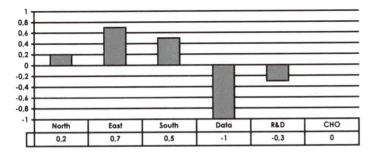

FIGURE 23.6 The differences between the 6 units of Boer on goals

Another effect of the results was that the divisions started a discussion about Data, R&D and CHO. They suggested that these parts were too flexible, that they should be more goal and rules oriented and, in particular, should become more effective and more oriented toward cost control.

In conclusion, the results of the survey and interviews and work sessions led to the conclusions that differences between the regional divisions and R&D, Data and CHO could be a potential danger for the organization. The problems in one division could escalate and need some interventions. This, in relationship with the dominant market position of Boer, could easily lead to an internal focus on political processes. The organization needed a clear and united vision, strategy and governance model for all parts of the organization.

PREFERRED SITUATION

Strategy, culture, and structure form a famous triangle. Strategy describes a preferred situation for the organization; culture describes desired shared behavior; and structure is the means of realizing it all.

There are three archetypes in the field of strategy or governance models: operational excellence, product leadership, and customer intimacy. Each type implies a certain structure and culture. Figure 23.7 shows the relationship between these governance models and organizational culture.

Operational Excellence is characterized by an emphasis on the production processes. The focus is on the bottom-line, and the ratio price quality is the central issue. The aim is to deliver a good product at a low price. The attention is fully fixed on optimizing the product processes; better results with fewer people. The environment of the organization is stable and simple that is, the environment has hardly any influence on the production process and the client is only interested in high-quality standard products. The market of such an organization is well developed and the organization has a large share of that market. Large-scale production is relevant because of the price quality ratio. In terms of structure, the accent is on well-oiled processes which are in detail predetermined. The

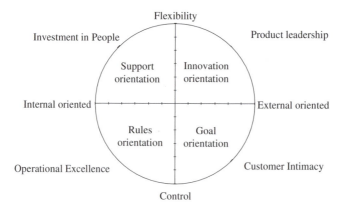

FIGURE 23.7 The competing values model of organizational culture, 3 strategies and investment in people

structure prevents potential disruptions in the production processes and the matching culture pays a great deal of attention to the hygiene of the production processes. The emphasis is on rules orientation. Individual performance is prescribed and individual performance indicators are anchored within the production process.

In case there is strong rules culture people accept that they have to follow the procedures and regulations. They understand the rational of the procedures and regulations, like employees of a nuclear plant.

Because of all the procedures and regulations, the organization has a formalized and rigid structure and members are expected to conform. The environment is well-structured, stable and orderly. In such organizations transactional leaders (Bass, 1985) are favored. Transactional leaders "approach followers with an eye to exchange one thing for another" (Burns, 1978, p. 4). Followers are rewarded for compliance with the leaders demands. House, Woycke and Fodor (1988) note that the general notion in theories about transactional leadership is that when the job and the environment of the follower fail to provide the necessary motivation, direction and satisfaction, the leader, through his or her behavior, will be effective by compensating for the deficiencies. The leader clarifies the performance criteria-in other words, what he or she expects from subordinates, and what they receive in return. The manager is expected to be dependable and reliable.

As an example, consider an assurance company. The several actions in the back office are prescribed completely. In the case of a claim for compensation the first response should be within 24 hours and a proposal should be handled within 36 hours. Another example of operational excellence is McDonald's, where timetables regulate the behavior of employees and the whole production process is designed behind a desk. Employees know how they should behave and what they can expect from the company. The manager monitors the individual performance, knows what is going on in the unit, and ensures that the employees comply with the rules and procedures. The manager is also expected to maintain the structure and flow of the system, which includes several forms of work facilitation such as scheduling, organizing and crisis handling.

Another archetype is **Product Leadership**. Here the focus is on innovation. In such an organization, a lot of money is allocated to research and development. Because the organization is aware that only a few new products will be successful, specialists are developing many different products. The market of such an organization is unpredictable. Today's success could be tomorrow's failure and it is very difficult to decipher the market demands in the near future. A product leadership organization is technology driven and the employees are highly educated. The environment has a strong influence on the processes within the organization. In terms of the culture model there is an emphasis on flexibility, creativity and innovation (the innovative orientation). The structure is loosely coupled. Knowledge management is a coordinating mechanism and employees work most of the times in changing project teams. People are intrinsically motivated and management primarily controls the quality of the project plans and do not prescribe the behavior of the employees.

Bass (1985) suggests that transformational or inspirational leadership is favored within organizations where goals and structure are flexible, members are highly educated and innovative and the climate is warm and trusting. Transformational leadership goes beyond the cost–benefit exchange of transactional leadership by motivating and inspiring employees to perform beyond contract. Transformational leaders broaden and elevate the interests of followers, generate awareness and acceptance among followers of the purposes and mission of the group, and motivate followers to go beyond their self-interests for the good of the group (Yammarino & Bass, 1990). They also state that "the transformational leader articulates a realistic vision of the future that can be shared, stimulates subordinates intellectually, and pays attention to the differences among subordinate" (p. 151). Conger and Kanungo (1988) postulate that inspirational leaders affects both organizational outcomes (such as high-value congruence, low internal conflict) and individual outcomes (such as high commitment to organizational goals and high performance).

In other words, in an organization characterized by product leadership the manager is expected to facilitate adaptation and change. He or she "pays attention to the changing environment, identifies important trends, conceptualizes and projects needed changes, and tolerates uncertainty and risk" (Quinn, et al., 1990, p. 18.). Furthermore, they state "that managers in an innovative culture are expected to be creative, clever dreamers who see the future, envision innovation, package them in inviting ways, and convince others that they are necessary and desirable" (p. 18).

This kind of leadership behavior enhances individual performance by inspiring individuals to realize the individual or departmental goals. This is in contrast to transactional leadership where the leader monitors if the individual employee will do what the leader expects.

Examples of product leadership organizations are Motorola, 3M and Solvay Pharmaceuticals. The mobile telephone market is very capricious and there is severe competition and acquisition. The present mobile telephone has utilities, like voice action, email and Internet possibilities, which did not exist two years ago. Furthermore, we simply do not know tomorrow's applications of a mobile telephone.

The third archetype is **Customer Intimacy**. The focus is on qualitatively high and tailor-made services or products. Instead of the bottom-line, there is an emphasis on the top-line, and the prices of such services and products are relatively high. The market is relatively young and there are many opportunities for market development. There is hard competition and the clients require high-quality products and services. The organization is aware of the needs of clients even before the clients are aware that they have these needs. Employees of such an organization go beyond contract. They walk the extra mile to realize their individual goals and performance indicators. Behavior is controlled by these goals and the organizational culture is characterized by elements of goal orientation. This type of structure encourages entrepreneurship, as the units are relatively small. The span of control is also small and employees are therefore responsible for realizing their goals, in the process of which they make their own decisions.

Here the desired leadership style is a hybrid between transactional and transformational. While individual employees are held responsible for realizing their individual performance indicators management inspires them to work in a certain way and in a certain direction. Control is focused on the results of individual employees and not on performance.

Consultancy firms, law firms and specialist shops are examples of an organization that emphasizes customer intimacy. The 4 Seasons hotels are highly customers focused. If a guest is unexpectedly invited to a 'black tie' party he can phone the reception and ask them to arrange something. One of the reception staff will visit several dress shops and return with a number of tuxedos. The guest will try the tuxedos, choose one and the price will be added to his hotel bill.

Customer Intimacy demands a structure that supports entrepreneurship. Taking initiatives, being decisive and being customer focused are examples of desired behavior within the organization. Where many employees exhibit this behavior, one could say that the organization has goal-oriented culture. The manager motivates employees by setting goals and defining roles and tasks. He or she is task oriented and work focused, has a lot of energy, and is personally driven to accomplish the goals and accept responsibility.

Pfeffer (1998) shows that organizations that support, encourage, and build the skills of their people outperform all competitors. Investment in people is not a governance model like operational excellence, customer intimacy and product leadership. Investment in people is about the conviction that people make the difference. People are the fuel that drives an organization to good results or excellent performance. Where people are motivated by certainty and stability (rules culture and operational excellence), or by creativity, innovation and experimentation (innovation culture and product innovation), or by performance-driven, profit and entrepreneurship (goal culture and customer intimacy) elements, such as training and development, individual consideration, trust and participation (support culture and investment in people) are important for better performance.

BOER AND THE PREFERRED SITUATION

Boer's strategy emphasized an increase in volume, especially abroad, and enabled them to become more market-oriented instead of product-oriented. What were the consequences of this strategy for the various divisions of Boer, and was there one governance model for the whole organization? Such a governance model could be translated into desired-shared behavior (organizational culture).

Boer has a large market share in the Netherlands and produces product with a small profit margin. The organization wants to penetrate international markets on the basis of a very good quality price ratio. Therefore Boer decided to implement operational excellence throughout the whole organization. The emphasis was put on cost reduction, process control and planning. Even Research & Development implemented these principles while maintaining their present level of product innovation and customer-orientation. Adjusting the various production processes increased the organization's profit and all members became cost conscious.

In terms of the culture model the organization became more rules oriented and goal oriented. It became rules oriented through the action of optimizing the production processes and improving its focus on cost control; and it became goal oriented through the shift from product orientation to market orientation. The cultural model shown in Figure 23.2 demonstrates that Boer, in comparison with other industrial organizations, had relative low scores on rules and goal orientations. So Boer had to do a firm job.

Boer did several things at the same time. First of all, they redesigned the various processes and monitored them by the implementation of performance indicators situated within the processes. The next step was to start an education program for all managers as many researchers (e.g., Bass, 1988; Den Hartog et al., 1999; Schein, 1992; Trice & Beyer, 1993) have found that there is a strong relationship between leadership and organizational culture. During the process of changing an organization's culture, the role model behavior

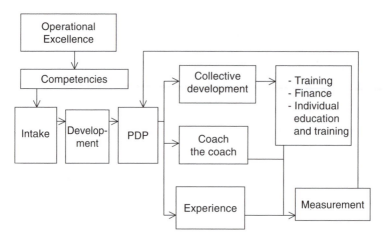

FIGURE 23.8 The management development process to get to the preferred situation

of management has been found to be crucial. Therefore, operational excellence was translated into competency profiles for the different layers of management. Over the course of several workshops the managers themselves formulated these profiles within the framework of operational excellence. For example, the management competency profile for team leaders is cooperation, cost consciousness, planning, coaching, customer orientation, result driven, monitoring, leadership, and decisiveness.

All the managers were assessed on these competency profiles. Personality tests and assessment center were used to describe their strengths and weaknesses. Each manager makes a Personal Development Plan (PDP). The primary objective of the PDP was to ensure any development actions were clearly aligned to the business goals. This focus was essential to enhance personal effectiveness, but personal development ought to be in line with organizational development. A secondary objective was to help participants to consider the long-term development strategies were required to support career aspirations.

On basis of the results of the development centers and on basis of the emphasis on cost reductions there were some collective and individual training programs. They followed financial courses at a business school and a training on effective management (see Figure 23.8).

Within two years after the training sessions there will be a 360-degree measurement to determine whether the behavior of management can change in the desired direction. It was not only the process structure and competency profiles that conformed to the preferred situation, but also HRM instruments, such as the appraisal systems. At this moment (summer 2000), Boer is changing into the preferred situation of operational excellence with an emphasis on the rules and support orientations.

IN CONCLUSION: PITFALLS AND CHALLENGES

Several pitfalls can occur during the process of establishing a solid unified culture. First of all, employees could experience a *psychological contract* violation. Psychological contract is about the individual perception of the employee concerning his or her (emotional) ability to deal with the organization. It reflects "individual beliefs in a reciprocal obligation between the individual and the organization" (Rousseau, 1989, p. 123). These obligations are implicit and are formed in the mind of individual. The organization can only manage the expectations of these obligations; for example, an employee who is *expected* to become a manager, because he or she had worked very hard and performed very well.

During a merger or acquisition the psychological contract is often violated. There is a new situation; there are new managers; and old implicit obligations are no longer valid. Such damage to the psychological contract "is likely to result in reduced commitment to the organization" (Guest, 1998, p. 655). The pitfall of damaging psychological contract could be avoided by making the implicit expectations explicit, by discussing the validity of these expectations in the new situation and by establishing a new psychological contract. Other pitfalls that can occur when changing a culture are:

- There is a lack of urgency.
- Management does not want to change.
- There is no unity within the board.
- There is no-win situation for many of the employees.
- There is negative talk of the old situation.
- The operation of the business is so urgent that employees cannot alter their habits.
- Management pays too much attention to opponents.

Where there is a lack of urgency employees do not understand why things should be changed. Why should they change their behavior? In their opinion business is going well. Sometimes the board is divided and this is becomes known to organization members. Owing to the lack of unity, they know that they can continue their daily practices. This can be a very subtle process. In one case a board member (director of a business unit) said to his management: the board is of the opinion that, from tomorrow, we should do things in such and such a way. Each of the managers knew that the director disagreed with the board's decision and that they had freedom to ignore it.

Another pitfall is that, in the eyes of employees, the desired cultural change can only have negative effects. There is nothing in it for them personally.

In changing a culture it is better to state the attractive parts of doing things differently rather than emphasize the errors of yesterday. Showing respect to the old culture and explaining why it is now necessary to change the way things are done will result in less resistance.

In some cases management may have been discussing a new strategy for several months without involving the rest of the organization. When management decides to implement the new strategy, which may have severe consequences for the existing culture, they are not surprised to find that people object to changing their behavior. It is not that they do not want to change, but the day-to-day running of the business is so urgent that they just continue in the same old way. The pitfall here is that management may stress the employees' unwillingness to change without praising their efforts under the present system.

The last pitfall is that management can pay too much attention to opponents of the proposed change, and by doing this they make the objections to the change process valid.

So what should management do in changing culture?

- Establish a sense of urgency.
- Create unity within the board.

- Create a win situation for many employees; explain why the proposed changes are good for the individual employee.
- Pay attention to employees who do not oppose the proposed changes, but are hesitant.
- Establish a new psychological contract.

In the case of the Boer, there was a sense of urgency. There is shrinking market in the Netherlands; there was a focus on internal affairs instead of a focus on the (international); market and there was a need for one governance model. The board was unified and spoke with one tongue and all manager received the opportunity to develop themselves in the desired direction. The communication between the board, managers and employees was intensive and frequent. The emphasis lay on the positive effects of the new governance model and the corresponding behavior. Last but not least, one of the HRM action was to facilitate managers in establishing a new psychological contract between Boer and the individual employees.

REFERENCES

Barley, S. R. (1983). Semiotics and the study of occupational and organizational cultures. *Administrative Science Quarterly*, **28**, 393–413.

Bass, B. M. (1985). *Leadership and performance beyond expectations*. New York: Free Press.

Bass, B. M. (1988). Evolving perspectives on charismatic leadership. In J. A. Conger & R. N. Kanungo (Eds.). *Charismatic leadership: the elusive factor in organizational effectiveness*. San Francisco: Jossey-Bass.

Brown, A. (1995). *Organsational culture*. London: Pitman.

Burns, J. M. (1978). *Leadership*. New York: Harper & Row.

Cohen, A. (1974). *Two-dimensional man: an essay on the anthropology of power and symbolism in complex society*. Berkeley: Univ. of California Press.

Conger, J. A., & Kanungo, R. N. (1998). The empowerment process: Integrating theory and practice. The Academy of Management Review, **13**, 471–482.

Den Hartog, D. N, R. J. House and other Globe country investigators (1999). Culture specific and cross-culturally generralizable implicit leadership theories: are attributes of charismatic/ transformational leadership universally endorsed? *The Leadership Quarterly* (in press).

Denison, D. R. (1990). *Corporate culture and organizational effectiveness*. New York: Wiley.

Denison, D. R. (1996). What is the difference between organizational culture and organizational climate? A native's point of view on a decade of paraigm wars. *The Academy of Management Review*, **3**, 619–654.

Denison, D. R., & Mishra, A. (1995). Toward a theory of organizational culture and effectiveness. *Organziational Science*, **6**, 204–223.

Ekvall, G. (1987). The climate metaphor in organizational theory. In B. M. Bass & P. J. D. Drenth. *Advances in organizational psychology*. Beverly Hills: Sage.

Guest, D. E. (1998). Is the psychological contract worth taking seriously? *Journal of Organizational behavior*, **19**, 649–664.

Hofstede, G. (1984). *Culture's consequences*. London: Sage.

Hofstede, G (1991). *Cultures and organizations*. London: McGraw-Hill.

House, R. J., Woycke, J., & Fodor, E. M. (1988). Charismatic and noncharismatic leaders: differences in behavior and effectiveness. In J. A. Conger & R. N. Kanungo (eds.), *Charismatic leadership: the elusive factor in organizational effectiveness*. San Francisco: Jossey-Bass.

House, R. J., Hanges, P. J., Ruiz-Quintanilla, S. A., Dorfman, P. W., Javidan, M., Dickson, M., & 170 co-authors (1999). Cultural influences on leadership and organziations: project GLOBE. In W. Mobley, M. J. Gessner, & V. Arnold (Eds.), *Advances in global leadership (pp. 171–233)*. Stamford, CN: Jai Press.

Hofstede, G. (1991). *Cultures and organizations*. London: McGraw-Hill.

Pfeffer, J. (1998). *The human equation*. Boston, Mass.: Harvard Business School Press.

Quinn, R. E. (1988). *Beyond rational management*. San Francisci: Jossey-Bass.

Quinn, R. E., Faerman, S. R., Thompson, M. P., & McGrath, M. R. (1990). *Becoming a master manager*. New York: John Wiley & Sons.

Rentsch, J. R. (1990). Climate and culture: Interaction andqualitative differences in organizational meanings. *Journal of Applied Psychology*, **75**, 668–681.

Rousseau, D. M. (1989). Psychological and implied contracts in organizations. *Employee Rights and Responsibilities Journal*, **2**, 121–139.

Rousseau, D. M. (1990). Assessing organizational culture: the case for multiple methods. In: Schneider, B. *Organziational climate and culture*. San Francisco: Jossey-Bass.

Schein, E. H. (1992). *Organizational culture and leadership*. London: Jossey-Bass.

Schneider, B. (1975). Organizational climate: an essay. *Personnel Psychology*, **28**, 447–479.

Schwartz, H. & Davis, S. (1981). Matching corporate culture and business strategy. *Organizational Dynamics*, **10**, 30–38.

Trice, H. M. & Beyer, J. M. (1993). *The culture of work organizations*. Englewood Cliffs, NJ: Prentice Hall.

Van Muijen, J. J. (1998), Organizational culture. Drenth, P. J. D., Hk. Thierry & Ch. De Wolff (Eds.) *Handbook of work and organizational psychology (second edition)*. Hove: Psychology Press.

Van Muijen, J. J. & Koopman, P. L. (1994). The influence of national culture on organizational culture: a comparative study between 10 countries. *The European Work and Organizational Psychologist*, **4**, 367–380.

Van Muijen, J. J., Koopman, P. L., De Witte, K., De Cock, G., Susanj, Z., Lemoine, C., Bourantas, D., Papalexandris, N., Branyiczki, I., Spaltro, E., Jesuino, J., GonzalvesDas Neves, J., Pitariu, H., Konrad, E., Peiro, J., Gonzalez-Roma, V., & Turnipseed, D. (1999). Organizational culture: the FOCUS-questionnaire. *The European Journal of Work and Organizational Psychology*, **4**, 551–570.

Author Index

Subject Index

Ability
  cognitive, 8–11, 38, 43
  general mental, 8, 16, 28–34, 39–40, 42–3,
    45, 61, 168, 171, 173
  meta-cognitive, 251
  as moderator in goal setting, 203–4, 209,
    216–17
  within potential analysis, 158, 167
  as predictor of performance, 6–7, 27–45,
    53, 168
  psychomotor, 7
  relationship with self-efficacy, 214
  spatial, 28
  and training success, 168
  and upper limit for performance, 78
  verbal, 28
Ability measure, 41–2
Absenteeism, 34, 72, 202, 303, 332, 426
Accountability, 169, 473–4
Acculturation, 450
Achievement orientation, 214
Action orientation, 463
Action plan, 186–7
Action process, 74
Action (regulation) theory, 13–14, 74, 79,
    96, 412
Adam Opel AG, *see* Opel
Adaptability, 458–63
Adaptation, 462, 446, 448, 460–1, 480
Adaptive behavior, 86
Adjustment
  emotional, 41
Advance organizer, 255
Advanced manufacturing technology, 81
Affective state, 448, 450
Agency theory, 335–6
Agreeableness, 35–6, 39–41, 332
Agriculture, 471, 474
Air traffic control, 32–3, 217
Altruism, 7, 17, 436
Ambiguity, 427, 435, *see also* Role ambiguity
Anger, 426
Anthropology, 472
Anxiety, 41, 412, 415, 426–7, 429, 433,
    435, 451
Appraisal, 115–31, 137–54, 169–70, 204–5,
    239, 384, 335, 339–40

accuracy, 117–18, 128, 169–70
attitudes towards appraisal , 119
cognitive processes, 117
criteria, 141–2, 145, 146–7
dimensions, 141–2, 148, 161, 356–7
definition, 116, 138
history, 116
non-performance issues, 121–2
performance appraisal versus potential
    analysis, 160–1
process, 356
purpose, 119, 138–140, 161–2
relationship between appraiser and
    appraisee, 127–9
Appraisal and reward system, 354–364
Appraisal dialogue, 143, 148
Appraisal interview, 118, 122, 130, 171, 271,
    284, 286
Appraisal system, 138–149, 387, 482
  development, 141
  and goal setting, 139, 144
  impact, 141
  introduction, 140–4
  quality assurance, 146
Appraisee, 122–7
Appraiser, 119–122, 126, 153
Artefact, 445–6, 472
Assembly worker, 33
Assessment center, 55, 61–2, 64, 66, 170–3,
    190, 271, 482
Assignment, 297, 314, 315–17
Assumptions (within organizational culture),
    445–50, 452
Assurance company, 479
AT&T, 194
Attachment, 451–2
Attendance, 457
Attention, 215, 221
Attitude, 38, 447–8, 462
Attraction-selection-attrition (ASA),
    453, 457
Attribution, 340
Attributional style, 122, 125, 127
Authority, 473
Automatic processing, 7
Automatization, 251, 254
Automobile manufacturing, 377, 392

Feedback
  within assessment center, 64–65
  attidude towards feedback, 145
  crediblity of source, 126
  control theory perspective, 350–3
  from customer, 272
  in enriched jobs, 203, 214
  within goal setting, 203–4, 206–7, 210,
      218, 242–4, 330, 356–8, 367
  informativeness, 364–8
  from the job, 11, 72
  multi-source, 116, 122, *see also* 360-degree
      feedback
  negative, 219, 255, 414
  normative, 210
  outcome, 235, 353
  participant feedback within training, 287
  within performance appraisal, 125–6, 139,
      145–6, 150–154, 194, 340, 384–5
  positive, 14, 255
  within potential analysis, 125–6, 139,
      145–6, 150–154, 194–6
  responses to feedback, 124
  self-related, 414
  task-related, 14, 71, 414
  360-degree feedback, 66, 116, 124, 126,
      130, 150–4, 194–6, 384 482, *see also*
      multi-source feedback
  within training, 252, 254–5, 257–8, 278–9,
      281
Feedback attitude, 126
Feedback dialogue, 139, 142
Feedback intervention, 14, 77, 229–247, 329,
    413–14
Feedback meeting, 356, 361
Feedback process, 353
Feedback processing, 13–15, 406, 411, 413
Feedback report, 234, 237–8, 240–2,
    244–5
Feedback seeking, 14, 125–6, 209, 217, 301,
    413–14, 417, 419
Feeling, 318–19
Financial data, 272
Financial problems, 410
Financial service firm, 319
Five Factor Model (FFM), 34–5, 39–40, 43
Flexibility, 463, 479
Flexible work orientation, 459
Flow, 318, 320–1
FOCUS questionnaire, 474–5
4 Seasons hotel, 480
Free rider, 341
Freedom cycle, 318–19
Friendship, 296, 303
Frustration, 408, 415
Fuji Photo Film B.V., 195–6

Gain sharing system, 341–2
General Electrics (GE), 194, 442
General factor, 43
General Motors (GM), 392–4, 401
Germany, 53, 172
Global competition, 442
Global market, 17
Globalization, 17, 180, 183, 250, 304
GM University, 401
Goal, 74, 202–222, 351–2, 383, 385
  definition, 204–5, 412
  distal, 210, 217–18, 222
  group/team, 205, 383
  learning, 206–7, 209, 217–18, 222
  multiple, 215, 315
  organizational, 295, 385, 442
  outcome, 206, 209, 218, 222
  performance, 207, 218
  personal, 207, 213, 218
  proximal, 210, 217–18, 222
  and rewards, 330–1
  self-set, 204–7, 209, 212–14, 330–1
  specific difficult, 14, 203–5, 208–9
  strategic, 52, 110, 142, 162, 166, 394, 455
Goal acceptance, 235–6, 243, 245, 352–3
Goal attainability, 364–8, 412
Goal attainment, 413
Goal clarity, 432
Goal commitment, 203–4, 206, 208, 210–11,
      213, 217, 219–20, 222, 235–6,
      331, 413
Goal development, 13
Goal difficulty, 205–8, 210–12, 219–20, 222
Goal emphasis, 454
Goal hierarchies, 351
Goal orientation
  learning goal orientation, 124, 207, 214,
      217, 221
  performance goal orientation, 124, 214, 221
  within organizational culture, 473–5, 477,
      480–1
Goal priority, 208
Goal pursuit, 406, 412
Goal setting, 14–15, 202–222, 229–247, 318,
    330–1
  acceptance, 232
  implementation, 229–237, 247
  participation, 208
  and performance appraisal, 139, 144
  and well-being, 412, 426, 436, 438
Goal system, 392
Governance model, 478, 481, 484
Grievance, 457
Group, 212, 222, 96–8, 100, 338, *see also*
    Team
  autonomous, 73, 83

Index compiled by Sabine Sonnentag